Anatolia, II

Anatolia

Land, Men, and Gods in
Asia Minor

Volume II
The Rise of the Church

STEPHEN MITCHELL

CLARENDON PRESS · OXFORD

OXFORD
UNIVERSITY PRESS

Great Clarendon Street, Oxford OX2 6DP

Oxford University Press is a department of the University of Oxford
It furthers the University's objective of excellence in research, scholarship,
and education by publishing worldwide in

Oxford New York

Athens Auckland Bangkok Bogotá Buenos Aires Calcutta
Cape Town Chennai Dar es Salaam Delhi Florence Hong Kong Istanbul
Karachi Kuala Lumpur Madrid Melbourne Mexico City Mumbai
Nairobi Paris São Paulo Singapore Taipei Tokyo Toronto Warsaw

and associated companies in Berlin Ibadan

Oxford is a registered trade mark of Oxford University Press
in the UK and in certain other countries

Published in the United States
by Oxford University Press Inc., New York

ISBN 0-19-815030-X

Printed in Great Britain
on acid-free paper by
Bookcraft (Bath) Short Run Books
Midsomer Norton

Preface

IN his *Mission und Ausbreitung des Christentums*, still the most authoritative investigation of the spread of Christianity in the early centuries, Adolf Harnack called Asia Minor quite simply 'das christliche Land'. No other part of the Roman world has produced so much information about Christian communities before the time of Constantine, and the quantity of Christian material from Asia Minor in late Antiquity—documentary, literary, and archaeological—is overwhelming. The copious and infinitely variegated evidence from inscriptions for pagan cults make it possible to view the emergence of Christian beliefs against a background that can be sharply defined. Indeed the devout and ascetic character of pagan Anatolian piety helps to explain why both Judaism and Christianity made such a decisive appeal to the people of Anatolia from an early date. However, no doubt because the documentation is so various and abundant, the spread of Christianity in Anatolia and its historical importance both in and beyond Asia Minor has been neglected in comparison, for instance, with the evidence from North Africa.

This volume has been conceived and written as part of a wider study of Anatolia in Antiquity. Nevertheless, not all those interested in the emergence and spread of Christian beliefs will be inclined to extend their reading to cover the history of Celtic settlements and the impact of Roman rule in Anatolia, and the volume can, I believe, stand on its own. However, the numerous cross-references to matters discussed in earlier chapters emphasize that the historical exposition in Volume II presupposes the picture of Anatolian society which has been reconstructed in Volume I. In particular the discussion in Chapter 11 of village communities, where

religion was always a controlling factor in the lives of the inhabitants, complements the discussion of pagans, Jews, and Christians in pre-Constantinian Asia Minor which forms Chapter 16 here.

The thesis central to this history of Anatolian Christianity is that Christian beliefs and the organization of the Church guided the historical and social evolution of Asia Minor in late Antiquity as decisively as the exercise of Roman imperial power had shaped it between the first and third centuries AD. Two relationships dominated the history of Asia Minor at all periods: that of the people to the land, and that of men to the gods. The beliefs and practices of the Christian communities of Anatolia were those of a population which lived on and from the land. If it achieves nothing else the historical material assembled in this study should suffice to scotch a widely held view of early Christianity, that it was a religion whose followers were mainly drawn from the poorer classes of the cities of the Roman world. Even at the height of the Roman Empire it is unlikely that more than 20 per cent of its inhabitants lived in cities. By late Antiquity many of these cities themselves had sunk to the status of villages and were barely distinguishable from other rural communities. The rise of Christianity, until it dominated and swamped the pagan cults of the Roman Empire, would be inexplicable if it had had no appeal for the rural inhabitants of the ancient world. The evidence from Asia Minor offers a more reliable perspective over a historical landscape where thousands of rural communities converted *en masse* to Christianity during the third and fourth centuries. It thus reveals conditions which were essential to the ultimate triumph of the Church.

Contents

Contents to Volume I   *page* ix
List of Figures   xi
List of Maps   xii
Abbreviations   xiii

III   The Rise of the Church   1

15   Christian Origins   3

16   Pagans, Jews, and Christians from the First to the Third Century   11
        I   Pagan Worship   11
        II   The Indigenous Cults of Anatolia   19
        III Jews   31
        IV   Christians   37
        V   One God in Heaven   43

17   From Pagan to Christian: Social and Civic Transformations in the
     Fourth Century   53
        I   Gregory the Wonder-Worker and the Age of Conversion   53
        II   Dominant Christian Groups before Constantine   57
        III   Persecution, Martyrdom, and the Importance of Saints   64
        IV   Rural Christianity in the Fourth Century: Cappadocia   66
        V   Cities, Bishops, and Imperial Authorities   73
        VI   Pagan Culture in Fourth-Century Ancyra   84
        VII   Julian   88
        VIII Christians in Fourth-Century Ancyra   91
        IX   The Novatian Church in Asia Minor   96
        X   The Epigraphy of the Anatolian Heresies   100

18   The Rise of Monasticism from the Fourth to the Sixth Century   109
        I   The Origins of Anatolian Monasticism   109
        II   The Spread and Impact of Monastic Christianity   114
        III Social Change in the Fifth and Sixth Centuries   119

19   Central Anatolia at the End of Antiquity: The Life of Saint Theodore
     of Sykeon   122
        I   The World of Theodore of Sykeon   122
        II   The Making of a Holy Man   134
        III Exorcism and Cure: The Saint in Action   139
        IV   Possession and Christian Belief   144

Appendix 1.   Provincial Boundaries in Asia Minor, 25 BC–AD 235   151
Appendix 2.   Provincial Boundaries in Asia Minor, AD 235–535   158

General Index 165
Index of Personal Names 174
Index of Non-Christian Cults 185
Index of Places and Peoples 188

Contents to Volume I

Contents to Volume II   *page* ix
List of Maps   xi
List of Figures   xii
Abbreviations   xiii

   1 Introduction   1

I   The Celts in Anatolia   11

   2 The Galatians in the Hellenistic World   13
      I   Invasion   13
      II Settlement in Central Anatolia   19
      III The Galatians, Pergamum, and Rome   21

   3 The Allies of Rome   27
      I   Tribal Organization and Political Structure   27
      II Rome in Asia Minor, 133–63 BC   29
      III The Settlement of Pompey   31
      IV Galatia during the Civil Wars   34

   4 Ethnography and Settlement of the Anatolian Celts   42
      I   Tribes and Leaders   42
      II Warfare   44
      III Clients and Slaves   46
      IV Religion   47
      V   Language   50
      VI The Settlement of Galatia   51

II   The Impact of Roman Rule   59

   5 *In formam provinciae redacta*: Annexation and the Framework of
      Roman Administration   61

   6 The Pacification of the Taurus   70

   7 City Foundations and Urban Growth   80
      I   The Graeco-Roman City   80
      II Central Anatolia before Augustus   81
      III Augustan City Foundations   86
      IV City Foundations from Tiberius to Hadrian: The North   91
      V   City Foundations from Tiberius to Hadrian: The South   94
      VI Cappadocia: The Exception   97

8   The Imperial Cult   100

9   The Euphrates Frontier and the Impact of the Roman Armies:
    Garrisons, Roads, and Recruitment   118
    I   Garrisons   118
    II   Roads and the Impact of Military Traffic   124
    III Legionary Recruitment   136

10 Estates and the Land   143
    I   The Physical Setting   143
    II   The Pattern of Settlement   148
    III Estates in Galatia   149
    IV   Estates in Phrygia, Bithynia, and Lydia   158
    V   Estate Administration   162

11 Rural Anatolia   165
    I   Two Views from the City   165
    II   Ethnic Diversity   170
    III Villages and Rural Communities   176
    IV   Villagers in Consort: The Organization of Large Villages   181
    V   The Rule of the Gods: Authority, Order, and Morality in Village
         Life   187
    VI   Worlds Apart   195

12 The Development of the Cities   198
    I   Changing Characteristics of City Life   198
    II   Administration and the Civic Community   199
    III Civic Patriotism and Benefactions   206
    IV   Public Buildings   211
    V   Agonistic Festivals   217
    VI   Central Anatolia: An Exception?   225

13 Crisis and Continuity in the Third Century   227
    I   Introduction   227
    II   Militarization   228
    III Brigandage and Insurrection   234
    IV   Goths and Sassanians: The External Threat   235
    V   The Resilience of the Countryside   239

14 Tax, Grain, and the Economy   241
    I   Reconstructing the Ancient Economy   241
    II   City and Country: The Economic Relationship   243
    III Central Anatolia under Grain and the Problem of Transport   245
    IV   Supplies for Troops   250
    V   Grain Supply and Living Standards in Cities and Villages   253
    VII Local Coinage and Money Taxes   255
    VII Economic Growth and Urbanization   257

General Index   261

List of Figures

1 The sanctuary of Mēn Askaēnos, Pisidian Antioch   *page* 15
2 List of subscriptions by members of the *Xenoi Tekmoreioi*   15
3 Dedication to Zeus Andreas from upper Tembris valley   15
4 Temple of Zeus at Aezani   17
5 Crypt of temple of Zeus at Aezani   17
6 Dedication to Zeus Thallos   21
7 Dedication to Zeus Abozenos   21
8 Statuette of the Meter Tymenene   21
9 Dedication to Zeus Petarenos   21
10 Dedication to Hecate   21
11 A priest consecrated to Zeus   27
12 Dedication to the 'God Kings'   27
13 Dedication to Artemis   27
14 Dedication to Hosion and Dikaion   27
15 Inscription for the synagogue of Iulia Severa at Acmonia   34
16 Dedication to Theos Hypsistos and 'Sacred Refuge'   34
17 Hebrew/Greek bilingual inscription from Acmonia   34
18 Epitaph of Eutyches, Cadi   61
19 'Christians for Christians' inscription, upper Tembris valley   61
20 Epitaph for Euphemus, Phrygian Pentapolis   61
21 Epitaph of Acacius, upper Tembris valley   61
22 Rescript of Maximinus authorizing persecution of Christians in AD 312   101
23 Epitaph for the Novatian priest Abras   101
24 Judaizing Novatian epitaph of Eugenius   101

List of Maps

1 West and central Phrygia   *page* 42
2 East Phrygia, east Pisidia, and Lycaonia   52
3 Western Cappadocia   66
4 Novatian Christianity   94
5 The world of Theodore of Sykeon   135
6 Provincial boundaries from 25 BC to AD 235   156
7 Provincial boundaries in Anatolia in late Antiquity   162

Abbreviations

AASS	*Acta Sanctorum*
ABSA	*Annual of the British School at Athens*
AE	*L'Année épigraphique*
AEMÖ	*Archäologisch-epigraphische Mitteilungen aus Österreich*
AJA	*American Journal of Archaeology*
AJPhil	*American Journal of Philology*
Alt. v. Perg.	*Altertümer von Pergamon* (1895–)
Anc. Soc.	*Ancient Society*
ANRW	*Aufstieg und Niedergang der römischen Welt*
Anz. Wien	*Anzeiger der Akademie der Wissenschaften, Wien*
I(–VIII) Araş	*I(–VIII) Araştırma Sonuçları Toplantısı.* Reports of the Archaeological Research Symposia, published by the Turkish Directorate General of Antiquities, Ministry of Culture (Ankara, 1983–90)
Armies and Frontiers	S. Mitchell (ed.), *Armies and Frontiers in Roman and Byzantine Anatolia* (1983)
AS	*Anatolian Studies*
ASBuckler	W. M. Calder and J. Keil (eds.), *Anatolian Studies Presented to William Hepburn Buckler* (1939)
ASRamsay	W. H. Buckler and W. M. Calder (eds.), *Anatolian Studies Presented to Sir William Mitchell Ramsay* (1923)
Ath. Mitt.	*Mitteilungen des Deutschen Archäologischen Instituts, Abteilung Athen*
Aulock, *Lykaonien*	H. von Aulock, *Münzen und Städte Lykaoniens* (1976)
Aulock, *Pisidien*	H. von Aulock, *Münzen und Städte Pisidiens,* i (1977), and ii (1979)
Barnes, CE	T. D. Barnes, *Constantine and Eusebius* (1981)
BASP	*Bulletin of the American Society of Papyrologists*
BCH	*Bulletin de correspondance hellénique*
BJb	*Bonner Jahrbücher*
BJRL	*Bulletin of the John Rylands Library*
Blanchetierre	F. Blanchetierre, *Le Christianisme asiate au IIe et IIIe siècle* (1977)
BMC	*A Catalogue of the Greek Coins in the British Museum*
Bosch, *Ankara*	E. Bosch, *Quellen zur Geschichte der Stadt Ankara im Altertum* (1967)
Bull. ép.	*Bulletin épigraphique,* published in REG (1938–84 by J. and L. Robert, 1985– by various authors)
Byz. Zeitschr.	*Byzantinische Zeitschrift*
CIL	*Corpus Inscriptionum Latinarum*
CJust.	*Codex Iustinianus*
CMRDM	E. N. Lane, *Corpus Monumentorum Religionis Dei Menis,* i–iv (1971–8)
Coll. Wadd.	E. Babelon, *Inventaire sommaire de la Collection Waddington* (1898)
CR	*Classical Review*
CRAI	*Comptes rendus de l'Académie des Inscriptions et Belles-Lettres*
CSHB	*Corpus Scriptorum Historiae Byzantinae*
CTh	*Codex Theodosianus*
DACL	*Dictionnaire d'archéologie chrétienne et liturgique*
DOP	*Dumbarton Oaks Papers*

Eck, *Senatoren* — W. Eck, *Senatoren von Vespasian bis Hadrian* (1970)

Epigr. Anat. — *Epigraphica Anatolica*

Foss, *Ankara* — C. Foss, 'Late Antique and Byzantine Ankara', *DOP* 31 (1977), 29–87

French, *Pilgrim's Road* — D. H. French, *Roman Roads and Milestones of Asia Minor*, i. *The Pilgrim's Road* (1981)

Gibson, *'Christians'* — E. Gibson, *The 'Christians for Christians' Inscriptions of Phrygia* (1978)

GRBS — *Greek, Roman, and Byzantine Studies*

Halfmann, *Senatoren* — H. Halfmann, *Die Senatoren aus dem östlichen Teil des Imperium Romanum* (1979)

Harnack — A. Harnack, *Die Mission und Ausbreitung des Christentums* (1906)

Haspels, *Highlands* — C. H. E. Haspels, *The Highlands of Phrygia* (1971)

Histoire des conciles — C. Hefele and H. Leclercq, *Histoire des conciles d'après les documents originaux*, i–ii (1907–8)

Horsley, *New Docs.* — G. H. R. Horsley, *New Documents Illustrating Early Christianity*, i–v (1981–9)

HSCP — *Harvard Studies in Classical Philology*

I. Apamea — T. Corsten, *Die Inschriften von Apamea (Bithynia) und Pylai*, IGSK 32 (1987)

I. Didyma — A. Rehm, *Didyma II. Die Inschriften* (ed. R. Harder, 1958)

IG — *Inscriptiones Graecae*

IGR — R. Cagnat *et al.*, *Inscriptiones Graecae ad res Romanas pertinentes*, i, iii–iv (1906–27)

IGSK — *Inschriften griechischer Städte aus Kleinasien*

I. Hadr. — E. Schwertheim, *Die Inschriften von Hadrianoi und Hadrianeia*, IGSK 33 (1987)

I. Iznik — S. Şahin, *Katalog der antiken Inschriften des Museums von Iznik (Nikaia)*, i, ii. 1–2, IGSK 9, 10. 1–2 (1979–82)

I. Kios — T. Corsten, *Die Inschriften von Kios*, IGSK 29 (1985)

I. Klaudiupolis — F. Becker-Berthau, *Die Inschriften von Klaudiupolis*, IGSK 31 (1986)

I. Kyme — H. Engelmann, *Die Inschriften von Kyme*, IGSK 5 (1976)

ILS — H. Dessau, *Inscriptiones Latinae Selectae*

I. Pergamon — M. Fraenkel, *Die Inschriften von Pergamon*, i–ii (1890–5)

I. Pessinus — J. Strubbe, 'The Inscriptions', in J. Devreker and M. Waelkens, *Les Fouilles de Pessinonte*, i (1984), 214–44.

Ist. Mitt. — *Mitteilungen des Deutschen Archäologischen Instituts, Abteilung Istanbul*

JAC — *Jahrbuch für Antike und Christentum*

JdI — *Jahrbuch des Deutschen Archäologischen Instituts*

JHS — *Journal of Hellenic Studies*

JNG — *Jahrbuch für Numismatik und Geldgeschichte*

JÖAI — *Jahreshefte des Österreichischen Archäologischen Instituts*

J.öst.Byz. — *Jahrbuch der österreichischen Byzantinistik*

Jones, CERP[2] — A. H. M. Jones, *Cities of the Eastern Roman Provinces* (2nd edn., 1970)

Jones, LRE — A. H. M. Jones, *The Later Roman Empire. A Social, Economic, and Administrative Survey* (1964)

JRA — *Journal of Roman Archaeology*

JRS — *Journal of Roman Studies*

JSav. — *Journal des Savants*

JTS — *Journal of Theological Studies*

KP[1,2,3] — J. Keil and A. von Premerstein, *Erster (Zweiter, Dritter) Bericht über eine Reise in Lydien und der südlichen Äiolis*, Denkschrift der Akademie, Wien 53. 2 (1908), 54. 2 (1911), 57. 1 (1914)

Laum, *Stiftungen* — B. Laum, *Stiftungen in der griechischen und römischen Antike: Ein Beitrag zur antiken Kulturgeschichte* (1914)

Levick, *Roman Colonies* — B. M. Levick, *Roman Colonies in Southern Asia Minor* (1967)

Magie, RR — D. Magie, *Roman Rule in Asia Minor*, 2 vols. (1950)

MAMA — *Monumenta Asiae Minoris Antiqua*, 9 vols. (1929–88)

MEFRA — *Mélanges de l'École Française de Rome—Antiquité*

Mendel, *Cat. Mus. Imp.*	G. Mendel, *Catalogue des musées impériaux ottomans*, 3 vols. (1910–13)
Millar, *ERW*	Fergus Millar, *The Emperor in the Roman World* (1977)
Mon. Ant.	*Monumenti antichi*
OGIS	W. Dittenberger, *Orientis Graeci Inscriptiones Selectae*, 2 vols. (1903–5)
PG	*Patrologia Graeca*
PIR²	*Prosopographia Imperii Romani*, 2nd edn.
PL	*Patrologia Latina*
PLRE	A. H. M. Jones, J. R. Martindale, and J. Morris, *Prosopography of the Later Roman Empire*, 2 vols. (1971–88)
Price, *Rituals and Power*	S. R. F. Price, *Rituals and Power: The Roman Imperial Cult in Asia Minor* (1984)
RAC	*Reallexikon für Antike und Christentum*
Ramsay, *Galatians*	W. M. Ramsay, *A Historical Commentary on St. Paul's Epistle to the Galatians* (1899)
Ramsay, *CB*	W. M. Ramsay, *The Cities and Bishoprics of Phrygia*, i. 1 (1895), i. 2 (1897)
RE	*Paulys Real-Encyklopädie*
REA	*Revue des études anciennes*
RECAM ii	S. Mitchell *et al.*, *Regional Epigraphic Catalogues of Asia Minor*, ii: *The Inscriptions of North Galatia* (1982)
REG	*Revue des études grecques*
Rev. hist. eccl.	*Revue d'histoire ecclésiastique*
Rev. num.	*Revue numismatique*
Rev. phil.	*Revue de philologie*
Rh. Mus.	*Rheinisches Museum*
Riv. arch. cr.	*Rivista di archeologia cristiana*
Robert, *Documents*	L. Robert, *Documents d'Asie Mineure* (1989)
Robert, *Hellenica*	L. Robert, *Hellenica: Recueil d'épigraphie, de numismatique et d'antiquités grecques*, 13 vols. (1940–65)
Robert, *OMS*	L. Robert, *Opera Minora Selecta*, 7 vols. (1969–90)
Sb. Berl.	*Sitzungsberichte der Königlichen Preußischen Akademie der Wissenschaften zu Berlin*
Schürer²	E. Schürer, rev. G. Vermes and F. Millar, *The History of the Jewish People in the Age of Jesus Christ*, 3 vols. in 4 pts. (1974–86)
SEG	*Supplementum Epigraphicum Graecum*
SERP	W. M. Ramsay (ed.), *Studies in the History and Art of the Eastern Roman Provinces* (1906)
Sherk ii	R. K. Sherk, 'Roman Galatia: The Governors from 25 BC to AD 114', *ANRW* ii. 7. 2 (1980), 954–1052
Sherk iii	R. K. Sherk, 'A Chronology of the Governors of Galatia, AD 114–285', *AJPhil.* 100 (1979), 166–75
SIG³	W. Dittenberger, *Sylloge Inscriptionum Graecarum*, 4 vols. (3rd edn., 1915–24)
SP	J. G. C. Anderson and F. Cumont, *Studia Pontica*, i (1903), ii (1906), iii (1910)
Sterrett, *EJ*	J. R. S. Sterrett, *An Epigraphical Journey in Asia Minor*, Papers of the American School of Classical Studies at Athens, 2 (1883/4, publ. 1888)
Sterrett, *WE*	J. R. S. Sterrett, *The Wolfe Expedition to Asia Minor*, Papers of the American School of Classical Studies at Athens, 3 (1884/5, publ. 1888)
Swoboda, *Denkmäler*	H. Swoboda, J. Keil, and F. Knoll, *Denkmäler aus Lykaonien, Pamphylien und Isaurien* (1935)
Syme, *RP*	R. Syme, *Roman Papers*, 7 vols. (1979–91)
TAM	*Tituli Asiae Minoris*
TAPA	*Transactions of the American Philological Association*
Tenth Congress	*Proceedings of the Tenth International Congress of Classical Archaeology*, Ankara and Izmir 1973 (1978)

TIB	*Tabula Imperii Byzantini*, 2: F. Hild and M. Restle, *Kappadokien* (1981); 4: K. Belke and M. Restle, *Galatien und Lykaonien* (1984)
YCS	*Yale Classical Studies*
ZfN	*Zeitschrift für Numismatik*
ZPE	*Zeitschrift für Papyrologie und Epigraphik*
ZNW	*Zeitschrift für die neutestamentliche Wissenschaft*

III

The Rise of the Church

καὶ μὴν εἰ ἔστιν ἐκ τῶν φαινομένων Θεοῦ παρουσίαν τεκμήρασθαι μᾶλλον δ' ἄν τις ἐν τῷ
ἔθνει τῶν Καππαδόκων τοῦ Θεοῦ διαιτᾶσθαι νομίσειεν ἤπερ ἐν οἷς ἔξω τόποις

Gregory of Nyssa, *Ep.* 2. 9

15 Christian Origins

The story of Christianity in Anatolia begins at the beginning. The Acts of the Apostles place the evangelization of the south Galatian communities of Pisidian Antioch, Iconium, Lystra, and Derbe at the centre of St Paul's first missionary journey outside Syria and Palestine.[1] More still, there is good reason to think that the Epistle to the Galatians was written soon after this journey, and thus becomes, quite simply, the earliest surviving document of the Christian church. These two sources together offer an unhoped-for, if elusive, glimpse into the Jewish, pagan, and nascent Christian communities of central Asia Minor in the middle of the first century AD. The information which they provide is hard to interpret, both because it is so isolated and because there is so much room for argument about the sources from which it comes, but it is a privilege to have so much with which to work.

The books of the New Testament have been overwhelmed by their interpreters. Paul's epistles have had a thousand meanings for their readers; by one reckoning almost every single year of the last century and this has seen a new commentary on Galatians alone.[2] But with rare exceptions there has been little effort to place Galatians, or even the relevant parts of Acts in their precise historical context.[3] The very nature of the books of the New Testament, and the legitimate arguments that will necessarily persist concerning their value as a historical source, clearly make them documents which can only be used with great caution; but hypercriticism has certainly led to a needless accretion of doubt on some basic issues. A prime case is the problem concerning the identification of the recipients of Galatians, a needlessly vexed crux of New Testament historical exposition.

The letter is addressed ταῖς ἐκκλησίαις τῆς Γαλατίας,[4] and the recipients are later apostrophized as ὦ ἀνόητοι Γαλάται,[5] the foolish Galatians. Should the churches be identified with those of the south Galatian cities of Antioch, Iconium, Lystra, and Derbe; the cities of Celtic north Galatia, Ancyra, Pessinus and Tavium; or, as a compromise, those of the whole province? There is virtually nothing to be said for the north Galatian theory. There is no evidence in Acts or in any non-testamentary source that Paul ever evangelized the region of Ancyra and Pessinus, in person, by letter, or by any other means. In so far as the gospel was taken here in the early years of the Church, the evangelist was surely Peter, who addressed the Jews of Pontus, Galatia, Cappadocia, Asia, and Bithynia in his first epistle.[6] Acts does record that Paul passed through a region described as τὴν Φρυγίαν καὶ Γαλατικὴν χώραν after leaving Derbe and Lystra, and that this was a stage in a journey that led through Mysia to the Troad.[7] The same passage shows that Paul and his companions were prevented by the Holy Spirit from preaching in Asia or passing through Bithynia. It is hardly conceivable that the Γαλατικὴ χώρα mentioned here is the region of north Galatia, which lay some 200 kilometres as the crow flies northeast of any natural route between Lystra and the region of Mysia. On the contrary, the phrase is naturally understood as denoting the country of Phrygia Paroreius, on either side of Sultan Dağ, an area that was ethnically Phrygian, but which lay partly in the province of Galatia and partly in Asia.[8] Even if it is

---

[1] Acts 13–14.
[2] P. Bonnard, *L'Épître de Saint Paul aux Galates* (2nd edn. 1972), 17: 'Dès le début du XIXe siècle rares sont les années qui ne voient paraître un commentaire ou une étude sur l'épître aux Galates.'
[3] This criticism cannot be levelled at the famous commentary of Bishop Lightfoot; at W. M. Ramsay's *Historical Commentary on the Epistle to the Galatians* (1899), which is polemical but far surer in judgement than much that he wrote; or at the series of articles by F. F. Bruce, published in *BJRL* 51 (1969), 292–309; 52 (1970), 243–66; 53 (1971), 253–71; 54 (1972), 250–67; and 55 (1973), 264–84. C. J. Hemer, *The Book of Acts in the Setting of Hellenistic History* (1989), 244–307 is very level-headed and substantially in agreement with Bruce.

[4] Gal. 1: 2; cf. 1 Cor. 16: 1.
[5] Gal. 3: 1.
[6] 1 Peter 1: 1.
[7] Acts 16: 6.
[8] Cf. Strabo, 12. 8. 14, 577; for further discussion, see above all, Ramsay, *Saint Paul the Traveller and Roman Citizen* (1895). Sir Ronald Syme observed in an unpublished lecture on St Paul, that he regarded this geographical interpretation of Acts 16: 6

taken to refer to Celtic Galatia, there is no hint that Paul stopped to preach there. A later passage in Acts, describing Paul's third journey, states that from Syrian Antioch he crossed, in turn, τὴν Γαλατικὴν χώραν καὶ Φρυγίαν, strengthening the faith of all his disciples, before coming down to Ephesus.[9] Again there is no reason to look beyond the natural geographical interpretation of this journey, from Syria through the Cilician Gates on to the plateau, across Lycaonia to the communities of Derbe, Lystra, Iconium, and Pisidian Antioch, and thence through the rest of Phrygia Paroreius to Apamea, and down the Maeander valley to the west coast. The region around Derbe, Lystra, Iconium, and Antioch was all part of the province of Galatia in the mid-first century AD, and the expression Γαλατικὴ χώρα, both here and in the earlier passage, naturally refers to it.[10] Although official terminology often distinguished several component parts of the province soon after the period of Paul's journey,[11] the compendious itemization of the many ethnic regions within the province of Galatia occurs commonly only on Flavio-Trajanic inscriptions. The earliest example comes with the description of Calpurnius Asprenas as *leg. pro pr. provinciae Galateae Paphlagoniae Pamphyliae Pisidiae* in AD 68–70;[12] the latest inscriptions of this type are of the late Trajanic period, or the first years of Hadrian.[13] By contrast, in the mid-first century it was normal to refer to the whole province, quite simply, as Galatia.[14] Thus, in AD 50 it was as natural to refer to the churches of Antioch, Iconium, Lystra, and Derbe as churches of Galatia, as it was to call that of Corinth a church of Achaea.[15]

No weight can be placed on the fact that Paul upbraids the recipients of the letter as foolish Galatians. It is true that this would not be a natural or formal mode of address to the inhabitants of cities which had few, if any, genuine Celtic inhabitants, but that is precisely the point. It is part of Paul's reproach that he equates them with the barbarous people who had given their name to the province, and who themselves had a

quite independent reputation for simple-mindedness.[16] The epistle, therefore, was certainly addressed to the Galatian churches which Paul had evangelized in the south of the province, and can be taken in conjunction with the account of that evangelization in Acts, not treated as an inexplicable anomaly in the Pauline corpus, that is as a letter addressed to a community with whom he had no other attested dealings.

The problems of relative and absolute chronology have also given rise to much debate. Indeed the supposed difference between Luke's description of Paul's early journeys to Jerusalem in Acts, and Paul's own account in Galatians has posed some of the most acute problems of New Testament analysis, and led to radical dismissals of either or both as reliable sources of historical information. This is too pessimistic. Paul visited the communities of south Galatia three times, during each of his major missionary journeys.[17] The earliest of these led not only to the first substantial effort to spread the gospel outside its Semitic homeland, but also involved widespread preaching to non-Jewish communities. It thus provoked discussion and controversy over one of the major issues with which Acts is concerned, the relationship of Christianity to Judaism, and the treatment of gentile converts. Paul and Barnabas returned from Asia Minor to be confronted by the violent opposition of Christians from Judaea, who argued that God's salvation could not be brought to those who had not been circumcised according to the law of Moses.[18] Paul and Barnabas, together with others, were accordingly sent to Jerusalem to discuss the issue with the apostles and elders of the church, at what has become known as the Apostolic Council.[19] This was Paul's third visit to Jerusalem since his conversion on the road to Damasacus. The first had taken place after Paul had begun to preach the Christian message in the synagogue at Damascus,[20] the second occurred a considerable period later, when,

---

and the correctness of the 'South Galatian' theory as 'evidential'.

[9] Acts 18: 22–3; 19: 1.

[10] All had been part of the province of Galatia since its creation; cf. App. 1 at nn. 12–24.

[11] This is clear from the titles of the Galatian governors discussed below, App. 1 at nn. 2–11.

[12] AE (1952), 232.

[13] ILS 1039, 1038; cf. OGIS no. 538 (undated).

[14] Eutropius 7. 10: 'Galatia ... provincia facta est ... eam M. Lollius pro praetore administravit' (late 20s BC); ILS 9499, for Rutilius Gallicus *legato provinciae Galaticae* (Neronian); IGR iii. 263 for L. Pupius Praesens ἐπίτροπος ... Γαλατικῆς ἐπαρχείας (AD 53/4). These examples are deliberately picked from the Julio-Claudian period.

[15] 1 Cor. 1: 1.

[16] The earliest witness is Callimachus, *Hymn to Delos* (4), 184, Γαλατῆσι ... ἄφρονι φύλῳ; Valerius Maximus, 2. 6. 10 remarks of the people of Massilia, who had learned to believe in the immortality of the soul from their Celtic neighbours, 'dicerem stultos, nisi idem bracati sensissent quod palliatus Pythagoras credidit'; Lucian, *Alex.* 27, described the Roman consular commander Severianus as ὁ ἠλίθιος ἐκεῖνος Κέλτος for putting too much trust in one of Glycon's false oracles. M. Sedatius Severianus apparently came from Poitiers and to date is the only known Roman senator of the Antonine period who came from Gallia Comata; see G. Nicolini, *Gallia* 37 (1979), 40 fig. 27 and G. Ch. Picard, *MEFRA* 93 (1981), 883–95 (AE (1981), 640).

[17] Acts 13: 13–14: 25; 16: 1–6; 18: 23. The visits to Antioch, Iconium, and Lystra are confirmed by the independent evidence of 2 Tim. 3: 11.

[18] Acts 15: 1–2.

[19] Acts 15: 2.

[20] Acts 9: 26.

after a sojourn in Cilicia and his native Tarsus, he and Barnabas had taken a collection raised in Syrian Antioch to the elders at Jerusalem, on the occasion of a prediction of worldwide famine, subsequently identified with a famine that occurred under Claudius.[21] An autobiographical passage at the beginning of Galatians accounts for two journeys to Jerusalem, one of which took place three years after Paul's conversion, the other fourteen years later, in the company of Barnabas and Titus.[22] During this second visit Paul discussed the issue of preaching to the gentiles and the crucial question of circumcision in private with prominent members of the Jerusalem church, and returned to Antioch with an agreement that he should continue to preach to the gentiles, leaving the mission to the Jews in the hands of the Jerusalem apostolic group—James the Just, Peter, and John.[23] Paul's description of this private meeting bears no relationship to the account of the full public Apostolic Council, which treated the same issues on the occasion of Paul's third visit to Jerusalem, and which would certainly have been discussed in Galatians, had it already taken place. The inference for the chronology of Galatians is clear. The letter must have been written after Paul's second visit to Jerusalem, and after his first journey to Galatia, but before the Apostolic Council and his subsequent return to the Galatian churches. Otherwise it should have referred to three journeys, and to the discussion and decision of the Council, which was highly relevant to the situation in Galatia.[24]

This conclusion is supported by Paul's astonishment expressed in the letter, that the Galatians had turned so quickly away from him and followed a different gospel.[25] The remark is perfectly consistent with the view that the gentile converts in the Galatian churches had been persuaded to subscribe to the Judaizing form of Christianity, which required adherents to be circumcised and to hold to Jewish law, in the relatively short period between the first journey and the Apostolic Council. This was a period of extreme ferment between the two parties in the church, and Christians from Judaea had come to Syrian Antioch to contest the Pauline view of gentile evangelization.[26] There is nothing implausible in the suggestion that their energy and zeal had extended to sending emissaries to woo back the Galatians from the Pauline view, or to instructing Jewish converts in Galatia to ensure that their

gentile associates were duly circumcised.[27] Galatians therefore, much the most polemical letter in the Pauline corpus with its urgent arguments that Christians need not be strict adherents of the Jewish law, can be seen as a document produced in the controversy which preceded the Apostolic Council, and which was resolved by the decision to lay no further burdens upon newly converted Christians than these essentials: to abstain from meat that had been offered to idols, from blood, from anything that had been strangled, and from fornication.[28] It thereby becomes, by a margin of several years, the earliest document of the Christian church.[29]

The absolute chronology of Paul's missions has also been much discussed, and in the absence of new evidence to anchor events narrated in Acts to fixed dates established by external criteria, many questions of detail will remain unresolved. Most commentators would agree in placing the first missionary journey somewhere between AD 45 and 49, the second between 50 and 53, and the third between 53 and 58.[30] The clearest fixed point is Paul's confrontation with Iunius Gallio, proconsul of Achaea, who is known to have been in office while the emperor Claudius carried the designation *imperator XXVI*, that is in the first half of 52.[31] The second journey through south Galatia occurred before this. Paul's second journey to Jerusalem, according to Acts, occurred at the time when a worldwide famine had been predicted, which in fact occurred under Claudius, and was roughly contemporary with the death of Herod Agrippa I.[32] These indications can be used to fix this journey to Jerusalem in or soon after AD 44,[33] and this in turn suggests that the first missionary journey took place not long afterwards, perhaps in 46 or 47.

The Galatian mission of the first journey was conspicuously the most important of Paul's three visits to central Asia Minor. The motive for it is barely

---

[21] Acts 11: 27–30.
[22] Gal. 1: 18; 2: 1.
[23] Gal. 2: 2–10.
[24] For this view see F. F. Bruce, *Commentary on Acts* (1954), 298–300, citing the earlier literature at 300 n. 10.
[25] Gal. 1: 6.
[26] Acts 15: 1.
[27] When Paul returned to Galatia after the Apostolic Council and reached Derbe, he took the trouble to have Timothy, the son of a Jewish mother and a gentile father, circumcised, διὰ τοὺς Ἰουδαίους τοὺς ὄντας ἐν τοῖς ἐκείνοις τόποις (Acts 16: 1–4). It is not excluded that these Jews were zealous evangelists from Jerusalem, whom Paul would be anxious not to offend, even if he did not at all concede the rightness of their position on the circumcision of Christians.
[28] Acts 15: 28–9. These regulations should be seen in the light of the complicated rules which governed the incorporation of 'godfearers', *theosebeis*, into Jewish communities. See J. Reynolds and R. Tannenbaum, *Jews and Godfearers at Aphrodisias* (1987), 61.
[29] So also F. F. Bruce, *BJRL* 54 (1972), 250–67.
[30] Hemer, *The Book of Acts*, 251 ff.
[31] *SIG*³ 801; cf. E. Groag, *Die römischen Reichsbeamten von Achaia bis auf Diokletian* (1939), 32–5; Acts 18: 12.
[32] Acts 11: 28–12.
[33] Schürer², i. 452–4, 457 n. 8.

explained by Paul himself, and not at all, explicitly at least, in Acts. Paul himself told the Galatians that he had first come to them as an invalid; precisely, in fact, on account of his affliction: οἴδατε δὲ ὅτι δι' ἀσθέ-νειαν τῆς σαρκὸς εὐηγγελισάμην ὑμῖν τὸ πρότερον, καὶ τὸν πειρασμόν μου τον ἐν τῇ σαρκί μου οὐκ ἐξουθενήσατε οὐδὲ ἐξεπτύσατε.[34] This affliction might be the same ill-ness to which Paul attached the famous description 'the thorn in the flesh' in his second letter to the Corinthians. If that is rightly interpreted as malaria, Paul's move from the low-lying country of Pamphylia to the plateau would have been salutary and prudent.[35] But the conjecture, even if correct, does not explain the selection of Pisidian Antioch (the first city Paul visited) as the springboard for the Galatian mission. There were plenty of other highland cities which could have served as salubrious resorts. The decision to go to Antioch was clearly occasioned by other considerations.

The clue lies in the immediately preceding episode of the first missionary journey. His travels had taken him by sea from Syrian Antioch to Salamis in Cyprus, and from there he had made his way across the island to the centre of provincial administration, Paphos. At Paphos, in the presence of the Roman proconsul Sergius Paulus, he temporarily struck blind a member of the governor's retinue, the pagan sorcerer Elymas bar-Jesus. Sergius Paulus was impressed enough by this display of divine power to become a believer.[36] The ultimate commitment to Christianity of this Roman senator may be questioned, especially as his patronage of Elymas the magician might suggest that he had some penchant for exotic mystical experiences, but the encounter would not have been a trivial one, least of all for Paul himself embarking on a world-wide mission. The association between the two bore immediate fruit, and it provides the clue to explain Paul's next move from Cyprus. He left the island and sailed to Perge; instead of pausing to seek converts in the thriving communities of Pamphylia, he travelled directly up-country, to Pisidian Antioch.[37] The adventurousness, or controversial nature of the journey may be hinted at by the fact that one of Paul's companions, John Mark, left the group in Perge to return to Jerusalem, leaving only Paul and Barnabas to venture north into the mountains; later the two were to fall out over their former colleague's show of weakness.[38] The author

of Acts, however, failed to spell out the real incentive that carried the mission inland from the coast: Sergius Paullus, Paul's most recent and most distinguished convert, was a native of Pisidian Antioch.

The family of the Sergii Paulli has become known through a series of inscriptions, found at Rome and in Asia Minor. A list of curators of the river Tiber, who set up a cippus on its bank ex auctoritate Ti. Claudi Caesaris Aug. Germanici, includes the name L. Sergius Paullus, who is thus shown to have been a senator of Claudian date.[39] He was to become consul: a dedica-tion was erected in Rome by the cultores domus divinae Aug. to an unknown emperor, on Augustus' birthday, 23 September, in the consulship of L. Nonius Torquatus Asprenas and L. Sergius Paullus. This should almost certainly date to the early years of Vespasian's principate, most probably to AD 70. Sergius Paullus, consul suffectus in this year, may confidently be identified with the Claudian senator.[40] Documents relating to other members of his family indicate a very close connection with Pisidian Antioch. The consul's son, L. Sergius L. f. Paullus filius, is shown by an inscription found at Antioch to have been IIIIvir viarum curandarum, trib. mil. leg. VI Ferratae, and quaestor, the early stages in a senatorial career whose sequel is unknown to us.[41] The younger senator's sister, Sergia L. f. Paulla, married C. Caristanius Fronto, one of the leading figures in the colony, who was adlected into the senate by Vespasian, and whose career led to a suffect consulship in AD 90.[42] Caristanius' senatorial career may have been helped by the marriage he made. His father-in-law, the elder L. Sergius Paullus, achieved the consulship in the first years of Vespasian's rule, a late reward for long senatorial service and also, it is reasonable to assume, for timely support offered to the Flavian cause during the civil war of 69. Caristanius Fronto was adlected inter tribunicios at precisely this period, perhaps even

---

[34] Gal. 4: 13–14.
[35] 2 Cor. 12: 7; Ramsay, Galatians, 422–8.
[36] Acts 13: 4–12.
[37] Acts 13: 13. The Augustan highway, the via Sebaste, led directly north from the Pamphylian coast, most probably from Perge, to the colony of Comana, and thence directly to the caput viae, Pisidian Antioch. See Vol. I, Ch. 6 n. 4.
[38] Acts 15: 36–40.

[39] CIL vi. 31545 (ILS 6926). Sergius Paullus stands third out of five, but these lists do not preserve the order of seniority; cf. CIL vi. 31544.
[40] CIL vi. 253; J. Devreker, Epigraphica, 38 (1976), 184; Gnomon (1980), 354; and above all Groag, RE iiA (1923), 1717–18. Groag leaves open the possibility that the consul might be L. Sergius L. f. Paullus filius, but the latter's career should have run parallel to that of C. Caristanius Fronto, cos. suff. in AD 90, who married his sister.
[41] The text was published by W. M. Ramsay, The Bearing of Recent Discovery on the New Testament (1915), 151, and discussed by Groag, RE iiA, 1718.
[42] Halfmann, Senatoren, 109 no. 13; there are drawings of this inscription, which can now be seen (badly worn) in Yalvaç Museum, in Ramsay, The Bearing of Recent Discovery, 154, and G. L. Cheeseman, JRS 3 (1913), 262, who provided the first and still fundamental discussion of this Antioch family.

in the year when Sergius Paullus was consul,[43] and the adhesion of the two families may not have been insignificant in helping to swing the communities of Asia Minor behind the Flavian effort at a crucial time in Vespasian's bid for power. Another member of the Sergian family, perhaps of the next generation, was Sergia L. f. Paullina, wife of one of the suffect consuls of AD 112, and the owner of an important property in central Anatolia, which the family had probably first acquired in the early Julio-Claudian period.[44] The accumulation of evidence leaves little room for doubt that although the Sergii Paulli, like the Caristanii, were ultimately of Italian origin, they were native to Pisidian Antioch.

The proconsul of Cyprus at the time of St Paul's visit should be identified with the curator of the banks of the Tiber under Claudius, L. Sergius Paullus, the only senator attested from this generation of the family. The argument that the post was held by a putative brother, Quintus, cannot be sustained. It rests on the belief that a fragmentary inscription from Chytri in Cyprus, which apparently contains regulations for the cult of a goddess, can be dated to the reign of Claudius and contains the name of a proconsul called Q. Serg . . . , to be expanded to Q. Sergius Paullus.[45] In fact the inscription cannot support this interpretation. The traces on the stone exclude the restoration of Claudius' name; other possibilities include Gaius, if this particular stone escaped erasure following his *damnatio memoriae*,[46] or an Antonine emperor of the second or third century. Moreover it does not appear likely that the name in the following line can be restored as Sergius; a form beginning Sera . . . , Serd . . . , or Serl . . . , can be more readily accommodated with what can still be seen. Finally, it is uncertain whether a governor's name should be restored at all at this point in the text. The stone must be dismissed from consideration.[47]

The importance of the link between Paul and the proconsul of Cyprus, his most prominent convert, is surely symbolized by the fact that precisely from this moment the former adopted the Roman *cognomen* Paulus, to supplant the name he had borne hitherto, Saul (Σαουλ, Σαουηλ). Some have asserted that Paul since his early years may have used the Roman Paul as a more familiar and acceptable form than Saul, but the claim does not stand up in face of two facts: Paul is

not a common Roman name, and there is no record that Saul assumed it until the immediate aftermath of the meeting with Sergius Paullus at Paphos. Just as Herod the Great honoured his friendship with Marcus Agrippa by giving the name Agrippa to his eldest son, who was to become ruler of Judaea at the time of Paul's conversion, so Saul reflected by his choice of name the gratitude and sense of achievement he must have felt at his first major conversion.[48]

The bearing of this enquiry on Acts and on Paul's missionary journey is simply this: the move from Paphos to Pisidian Antioch was determined in large measure by the fact that Antioch was Sergius Paullus' *patria*. We can hardly avoid the conclusion that the proconsul himself had suggested to Paul that he make it his next port of call, no doubt providing him with letters of introduction to aid his passage and his stay.

The argument still leaves unanswered the question why Paul should have heeded the advice and taken advantage of the assistance offered to him. To answer this it is necessary to move further into the realms of speculation, but the history of Antioch itself provides an excellent starting point for further reflection. The city had been refounded by Augustus and had emerged as the principal Roman colony in the Greek East, deliberately modelled, in some respects, on the imperial capital itself.[49] Under Tiberius, and probably without interruption throughout the reigns of Gaius and Claudius, a large building programme had translated aspirations into reality, and endowed the colony with an imperial temple, porticos, squares, and a triumphal arch which dominated its central area.[50] It was a place of some consequence as the second city in Galatia, but the Italian settlers there gave it an importance which Ancyra the capital lacked, and that importance was highlighted by the emergence, even at the beginning of Claudius' principate, of a senatorial family, among the first attested from the Greek-speaking part of the empire, and the first which is known to have produced a consul.[51] It would not have been difficult to persuade Paul of its significance as a major centre in the eastern Roman world, and that perception will have coincided with and reinforced his own view of his missionary strategy. The temporal success of the Christian mission depended not only on its ability to win converts, but above all to win converts of substance. Paul had made

[43] Halfmann, loc. cit., places the adlection in AD 73/4, but 70 is also possible.

[44] See above, Ch. 10 § III at nn. 68–77 for full discussion.

[45] *IGR* iii. 935; *SEG* xx. 302; E. Gabba, *Iscrizioni greche e latine per lo studio della Bibbia* (1958), 71 no. xxi.

[46] T. B. Mitford, *ANRW* ii. 7. 2 (1980), 1300 n. 54; Halfmann, *Senatoren*, 101 no. 4; against, S. Mitchell, *JRS* 71 (1981), 192.

[47] With the kind permission of Mr Maxwell Anderson I re-examined the stone in the Metropolitan Museum, New York, in 1984.

[48] H. Dessau, 'Der Name des Apostels Paulus', *Hermes*, 44 (1910), 347–68; cf. Mitford, *ANRW* ii. 7. 2, 1381 with n. 519. For Herod Agrippa, born c.10 BC, two years after the death of M. Agrippa, see Schürer², i. 442 n. 1.

[49] Levick, *Roman Colonies*, 76–8.

[50] See above, Vol. I, Ch. 8 at n. 42, and below at n. 75.

[51] Halfmann, *Senatoren*, 101 (missing the consulship); see his pp. 29–67 for the background.

it his business to seek out the proconsul of Cyprus, the most important man in the province; his journeys were not directed at insignificant cities, but at places of real, or supposed importance: Roman colonies like Alexandria Troas, Philippi, and Corinth, or major provincial centres like Thessalonica, Beroea, Athens, and Ephesus. Paul was as ambitious for his evangelical career as any sophist or orator who aimed to display his skills and win admirers in the major centres of power and learning. The ultimate goal, for both, would have been Rome itself.

Paul was not to achieve that final aim for several years, and then not with the success for which he may have hoped, but the Epistle to the Romans, probably his first surviving letter to be written after Galatians,[52] leaves no question that the Roman community was the principal and ultimate target of his preaching.[53] Antioch, the *simulacrum* of Rome in the East, providentially offered itself as a substitute.

If Antioch could pass as a new Rome, the people whom Paul encountered there and in the other cities of south Galatia, cannot be so easily defined as new Romans. The person of Sergius Paullus himself— Italian in origin, Asiatic in domicile, from a family who had freedmen active in Rome and estates in central Anatolia, who was commemorated by inscriptions set up in Latin and in Greek, and who combined the public functions of a Roman magistrate with a demonstrable receptiveness to the persuasion of a new eastern cult—points to some of the complexities of probing the character of Paul's earliest congregations.

The first Christian addresses in Antioch, and also in Iconium, were delivered in the synagogue to the Jewish community.[54] To the Jews Paul spoke of the coming of Christ as a fulfilment of the prophecies of the Old Testament,[55] but the message was heard with less than total enthusiasm by this first audience. Infected no doubt by the controversy which already engulfed the question of the Christian evangelizing of gentile communities, and alarmed at the threat to the integrity of their own posed by Paul, after some weeks they turned against the missionaries and had them driven from the city. For support they turned to high-born ladies who were Jewish sympathizers, and to the leading persons in the colony: τὰς σεβομένας γυναῖκας καὶ τὰς εὐσχήμονας καὶ τοὺς πρώτους τῆς πόλεως.[56] The expression αἱ σεβόμεναι γυναῖκες, clearly to be distinguished from Ἰουδαῖοι in the full sense, is illuminated by other passages in Acts which distinguish

Judaizers from Jews. Paul's first audience consisted of Jews (ἄνδρες Ἰσραηλῖται) and those who feared God, (οἱ φοβούμενοι τὸν Θεόν), and at the conclusion of the meeting, his first converts included πολλοὶ τῶν Ἰουδαίων καὶ τῶν σεβομένων προσηλύτων.[57] The same distinction is made at Athens, and is implicit in the description of the congregation in the synagogue at Iconium, which contained both Ἰουδαῖοι and Ἕλληνες.[58] Individual σεβόμενοι, or Jewish sympathizers recur on other occasions in the narrative of Paul's mission, and inscriptions from throughout the Diaspora, but above all from Asia Minor, which describe them as Θεοσεβεῖς, confirm that they were a regular feature of Jewish communities.[59]

The point is of importance for understanding the character of Paul's audience at Antioch in particular. It is perfectly clear from the epigraphical evidence that the leading citizens of the colony, to whom the Jews turned for help against Paul, were Roman citizens from families of Italian origin, established in the community only since its foundation by Augustus. While the example of Paul himself demonstrates that there was no incompatibility between being a Jew in the full sense and a Roman citizen, it is highly unlikely that many of these colonial families were fully Jewish. The sympathizers (σεβόμενοι) surely comprised not only a substantial proportion of the congregation, but included its most influential members, at least in the community at large.

Unfortunately no inscription known from Antioch can be shown to relate to this group,[60] but the situ-

---

[52] See W. S. Kümmel, *Einleitung in das Neue Testament* (13th edn. 1964), 222–3.

[53] Cf. Rom. 1: 13–15.

[54] Acts 13: 15–43; 14: 1.

[55] Acts 13: 16–41.

[56] Acts 13: 50.

[57] Acts 13: 16; 43. It is a moot point whether the references to proselytes in this second passage introduce a further distinction and indicate a third category of proselytes between the native Jews and the Jewish sympathizers, for which there is a large body of evidence outside the Gospels (see J. Juster, *Les Juifs dans l'Empire romain*, i (1914), 254–74, now confirmed for the later Roman period by the new inscription from Aphrodisias (n. 28)), or whether, as I am inclined to think, the proselytes envisaged by the author of Acts are simply to be identified with the Jewish sympathizers to whom the rest of the citations in the narrative refer. For a survey of the whole problem of proselytes and Jewish sympathizers, and reference to the recent literature, see Schürer[2], iii. 1. 150–76.

[58] Acts 14: 1 (Iconium); 17: 17 (Athens).

[59] Acts 16: 14; 18. 7. For inscriptions which mention *theosebeis* see L. Robert, *Nouvelles inscriptions de Sardes* (1964), 41–5; H. Hommel, 'Juden und Christen in kaiserzeitlichem Milet', *Ist. Mitt.* 25 (1975), 167–95; and Reynolds and Tannenbaum, *Jews and Godfearers at Aphrodisias*, esp. 48–66. The latter offer a full discussion and an interpretation with which I agree.

[60] A verse inscription from Apollonia in Phrygia Paroreius mentions a woman of Antioch called Debbora, who is said to have been 'born of renowned parents', to have married a man from Sillyum in Pamphylia, and who presumably settled in Apollonia (*MAMA* iv. 202; the proposed restoration of W. Peek, *Griechische Versinschriften aus Kleinasien* (1980), 53–4

ation is well illustrated by a telling document from the Phrygian city of Acmonia, inscribed probably within two decades of Paul's first journey.[61] The text refers to the building of a synagogue by Iulia Severa, a gentile woman from one of the city's leading families; related, in fact, to a Galatian dynasty which could trace its line back to the tetrarchs and kings of the Hellenistic period.[62] She had close connections with the Turronii, an emigrant Italian family, one of whose members, P. Turronius Cladus, is named on the same inscription as *archisynagogus*, while another, Turronius Rapo, was priest of the imperial cult, and appears alongside her on coins issued by the city.[63] This is the familiar milieu of aristocratic civic life of early imperial Asia Minor, with the striking modification that the Jewish synagogue, and some at least of its leading supporters, were completely assimilated within it. The synagogue had been endowed by Iulia Severa, a gentile, just as any other temple might be; closely related persons associated with her held and advertised positions, on the one hand in the synagogue, on the other in the hierarchy of emperor worship. Moreover, Iulia Severa herself had married into another Italian emigrant family, the Servenii; and her son, L. Servenius Cornutus, became a senator in the Julio-Claudian period, only a few years later than L. Sergius Paullus.[64]

If the Acmonian parallel is aptly invoked, we can argue that the synagogue at Antioch could well have been closely integrated into the framework of non-Jewish public life. Paul need not have been approaching the margins of colonial society, but aiming at its centre, for it would not have been unnatural for

important families, perhaps even pre-eminently that of the Sergii Paulli, to have taken an active interest in Jewish worship.

The Jews of Antioch were envious of the success of Paul's mission in attracting crowds of gentiles to pay heed to Christianity, and anxious for the effect that these conversions might have on the identity and nature of their own community. For gentiles themselves, other problems were inherent in conversion, briefly evoked in an important passage of Galatians: 'Formerly, when you did not acknowledge God, you were the slaves of beings which in their nature are no gods. But now that you do acknowledge God, or rather now that he has acknowledged you, how can you turn back to the mean and beggarly spirits of the elements? Why do you propose to enter their service all over again? You keep special days and months and seasons and years. You make me fear that all the pains I spent on you may prove to be labour lost.'[65]

The public religious life of Antioch was dominated by two deities, or at least two objects of worship, Mēn Askaēnos, the *patrios theos* of the colony,[66] and the person of the Roman emperor and his family. Mēn Askaēnos surveyed the plain of Antioch from two temples, one situated on the hill called Karakuyu, an hour's climb above the city, the other about fifteen miles away, in the north-west part of its territory, at the modern village of Sağır.[67] While the latter became the centre of a cult organization called the *Xenoi Tekmoreioi*, which during the third century attracted members from far afield in Pisidia and Phrygia,[68] the temple on Karakuyu made the more immediate impression on the life of Antioch itself. Devotees made their way up the steep pathway from the city, and left numberless dedications, inscribed or uninscribed, on the rocks beside the road or on the walls of the

---

no. 39 (*SEG* xxx (1980), 1507 and 1903) is based on old copies of the inscription, which were superseded by the text in *MAMA*, and is seriously defective). W. M. Ramsay, *The Cities of Saint Paul* (1907), 255 ff., followed by Juster, *Juifs*, 192 n. 7, took Debbora to be a Jewess of Pisidian Antioch. If that were correct, the nexus linking families of Pamphylia and Phrygia Paroreius would be reminiscent of the connections between the senatorial families of Perge, Attaleia, Pisidian Antioch, and Apollonia, which have a central role to play in the history of the Anatolian aristocracy in the first century AD (Mitchell, *JRS* 64 (1974), 27 ff.; Halfmann, *Senatoren*, 54). But it is notoriously difficult to be certain about the origin of persons with the ethnic Ἀντιοχεύς or Ἀντιόχισσα. The Semitic name Debbora appears incongruous in the context of Romanized Pisidian Antioch, and it is preferable to treat her as a native of Syrian Antioch. Several persons with Semitic names from Syrian Antioch occur at Athens: *IG* ii² 8137[60] (Βαρναῖος); 8321[61] (Μαθθαία); 8232[62] (Μάρθα); 8233-4 (Μαρίων), discussed by L. Robert, *Études déliennes*, *BCH suppl.* 1 (1973), 444-6. Reluctantly, therefore, the evidence of the Apollonia inscription should be set aside.

[61] *MAMA* vi. 262.
[62] *JRS* 64 (1974), 38.
[63] *MAMA* vi. 265; Halfmann, *Senatoren*, 102 no. 5a.
[64] Halfmann, *Senatoren*, 102 no. 5. For the Jewish community at Acmonia see below, Ch. 16 § III n. 194.

[65] Gal. 4: 8–11 (in the translation of the New English Bible): ἀλλὰ τότε μὲν οὐκ εἰδότες Θεὸν ἐδουλεύσατε τοῖς μὴ φύσει οὖσι θεοῖς· νῦν δὲ γνόντες Θεόν, μᾶλλον δὲ γνωσθέντες ὑπὸ Θεοῦ, πῶς ἐπιστρέφετε πάλιν ἐπὶ τὰ ἀσθενῆ καὶ πτωχὰ στοιχεῖα, οἷς πάλιν ἄνωθεν δουλεύειν θέλετε; ἡμέρας παρατηρεῖσθε, καὶ μῆνας καὶ καιροὺς καὶ ἐνιαυτούς. φοβοῦμαι ὑμᾶς, μὴ πως εἰκῆ κεκοπίακα εἰς ὑμᾶς.
[66] For the epithet, see *CMRDM* i nos. 164–74, 177, 270, 288, 290; iv nos. 83, 107, 127.
[67] Strabo, 12. 3. 31, 559: τὸ τοῦ Ἀσκαίου τὸ πρὸς Ἀντιοχείᾳ τῇ πρὸς Πισιδίᾳ καὶ τὸ ἐν τῇ χώρᾳ τῶν Ἀντιοχέων. The first of these was evidently the Hellenistic temple and sanctuary on Karakuyu, for which see Mitchell and Waelkens, *Pisidian Antioch*, forthcoming. The latter was located by Ramsay at Sağır on the strength of the discovery of the inscriptions for the *Xenoi Tekmoreioi* there. This identification is not completely certain, but the connection between the sanctuaries at Sağır and at Karakuyu is established by the fact that these are the only places where devotees performed the ritual described by the verb τεκμορεύειν.
[68] See W. Ruge's scrupulous critical summary of the discoveries of Ramsay, Calder, and others in *RE* vA (1934), 158–69.

temenos;[69] leading citizens held the priesthood of Mēn, combined with that of Demeter,[70] and the cult, like others, had its own festal days on which athletic contests were held, and a treasury.[71] Before the foundation of the colony most of the land in the plain below appears to have belonged to the temple, and many of its inhabitants were sacred slaves;[72] the hieratic organization had been dissolved when the Roman province was founded, but the names of those who inscribed dedications to the god show that the Roman settlers readily adopted the cult as their own.[73]

The new settlers naturally brought some of the cults of Rome itself with them, notably that of Iuppiter Optimus Maximus;[74] but this, and all else in the city itself, was overshadowed by the monuments set up to honour and worship the colony's founder Augustus and members of his family. The imperial temple, in its semi-circular portico, was begun soon after the accession of Tiberius, and was probably still under construction under Gaius and in the first years of Claudius' reign. It was hardly complete when Paul arrived at the colony. A triumphal arch celebrating Augustus' Pisidian victories, and decorated with a copy of the *Res Gestae*, was completed in AD 50 between Paul's first and second visit, and linked the temple area with a paved colonnaded street called the *Tiberia Platea*. The whole complex overwhelmingly dominated the centre of the site, and could be seen from miles away across the plain of Antioch.[75] There is no doubt that the imperial temple and the associated buildings provided the main focus for the public and religious life of the colony, whose principal citizens filled the priest-

hoods of Augustus himself, Vespasian, and Iulia Augusta, to name only those for whom records have survived.[76]

One cannot avoid the impression that the obstacle which stood in the way of the progress of Christianity, and the force which would have drawn new adherents back to conformity with the prevailing paganism, was the public worship of the emperors. The packed calendar of the ruler cult dragooned the citizens of Antioch into observing the days, months, seasons, and years which it laid down for special recognition and celebration. Its sacrifices were the chief source of meat which the Apostolic Council had forbidden Christians to touch. In the urban setting of Pisidian Antioch where spectacular and enticing public festivals imposed conformity and a rhythm of observance on a compact population, where Christians could not (if they wanted to) conceal their beliefs and activities from their fellows, it was not a change of heart that might win a Christian convert back to paganism, but the overwhelming pressure to conform imposed by the institutions of his city and the activities of his neighbours.

To comment on the meagre evidence for the evangelization of Antioch in Acts, and in the Epistle to the Galatians inevitably involves speculation that may be misdirected, and can, in any case, only provide very sparse clues as to the realities of social and religious life there in the mid-first century AD. It may help, however, to draw attention to the conditions which Christianity would have to fulfil before it could become a universal and dominant religion in the empire. Firstly, it would have to supplant the pagan institutions which regulated men's lives. Secondly, it had to take the place of a pattern of pagan religious observance which was both a response to and an integral part of daily life, public and private. The simple actions of prayer and sacrifice, at the lowest level, offered men an assurance that the world and society was in good order. Nothing less than a revolution could alter that. Paul's mission, in fact, stands isolated in the history of Christianity in central Asia Minor, finding no sequel until the pre-conditions for such a revolution could begin to make themselves felt.

[69] *CMRDM* i nos. 160–294 and iv nos. 1–161 for the inscriptions, and iii. 55–66 for an attempt at interpretation.

[70] *CMRDM* i nos. 164–74; iv no. 52. The suggestion advanced by Anderson, *JRS* 3 (1913), 267 ff. that these texts belong to the early 4th cent. AD is based on erroneous arguments and suppositions. They mostly belong to the mid-2nd cent., see Mitchell, *Pisidian Antioch*, ch. 1 (forthcoming).

[71] *CIL* iii. 295 = 6829; *CMRDM* i no. 178. A statue set up in honour of C. Albucius Firmus, aedile and IIvir, who had left money in his will 'ad certamen gymnicum quotannis faciendum diebus festis Lunae'. For the treasury see *CIL* iii. 6839 and 6840, *curator arcae sanctuariae*.

[72] Strabo 12. 8. 14, 577.

[73] *CMRDM* i and iv *passim* for examples.

[74] *CIL* iii. 6838; for other cults see *IGR* iii. 299 (Dionysus); *SEG* vi. 563 and *CIL* iii. 6820 (Asclepius).

[75] See above, Vol. I, Ch. 8 at n. 42.

[76] *CIL* iii. 6846; *JRS* 2 (1912), 102 no. 34; *JRS* 54 (1964), 99; cf. Levick, *RE* suppl. xi (1968), 53.

16 Pagans, Jews, and Christians from the First to the Third Century

1. *Pagan Worship*

Not every city visited by Paul was an Antioch. Expelled from there and from Iconium, he and Barnabas continued along the Roman *via Sebaste* to Lystra, also a Roman colony on a modest scale, but with a large native element in the population. The inhabitants, impressed by the miraculous cure of a lame man, hailed the visitors in their native Lycaonian language as manifest gods, Zeus and Hermes, and the priest of Zeus, whose temple lay in front of the city, was scarcely restrained from sacrificing oxen to them.[1] Paul and Barnabas responded with a speech that was designed to appeal to people whose culture and religious beliefs had little urban sophistication, and who were pagans, not Jews or Jewish sympathizers. God had never been absent from their lives in former times, but had allowed men to go their own way. His benevolence was shown by his care for a rural population: 'he sends you rain from heaven and crops in their seasons, filling your hearts with nourishment and good cheer.'[2]

The gods of pagan Anatolia were not abstract and remote. At Lystra they could walk among their people and make themselves seen or heard. After centuries of Christian or Christianizing thought, entangled in attempts to articulate the ineffable, the problems of understanding paganism do not lie in penetrating its mysteries but in perceiving the obvious, the gods made manifest.[3]

The pagan gods left their traces everywhere. In the case of Apollo, for example: in a village in north-west Galatia the passer-by was invited to look on the tomb of a priest of far-shooting Apollo, who had taken the same name as his god and lived a blameless life with his wife and children.[4] In the upper Tembris valley in north Phrygia the same Apollo, through the oracular shrine at Claros, told his devotees to set up an altar which looked towards the rays of the all-seeing sun, and to offer a monthly sacrifice which would ensure their safety and prosperity.[5] The Perminundeis of southern Pisidia established their rural shrine to Apollo at a rocky outcrop which looked due west across the flat fields of the valley bottom towards the hills that marked the edge of their territory and the setting sun. Cuttings in the rock show the position of a central altar, while niches were carved in the rock face at the rear and on either side, inscribed with the prayers of devotees. These included not only the indigenous people but Roman settlers from the nearby colony of Comama.[6] At Iconium in south Galatia Clarian Apollo

---

[1] For temples and sanctuaries πρὸ πόλεως see J. and L. Robert, *Fouilles d'Amyzon* (1983), 171–5.

[2] Acts 14: 8–18, esp. 11–13: οἵ τε ὄχλοι ἰδόντες ὃ ἐποίησεν Παῦλος ἐπῆραν τὴν φωνὴν Λυκαονιστὶ λέγοντες· οἱ θεοὶ ὁμοιωθέντες ἀνθρώποις κατέβησαν πρὸς ἡμᾶς. ἐκάλουν τε τὸν Βαρναβᾶν Δία, τὸν δὲ Παῦλον Ἑρμῆν, ἐπειδὴ αὐτὸς ἦν ὁ ἡγούμενος τοῦ λόγον. ὅ τε ἱερεὺς τοῦ Διὸς τοῦ ὄντος πρὸ τῆς πόλεως ταύρους καὶ στέμματα ἐπὶ τοὺς πυλῶνας ἐνέγκας σὺν τοῖς ὄχλοις ἤθελεν θύειν.

[3] This chapter was overtaken in the composition by R. Lane Fox's magnificent *Pagans and Christians* (1986), which says much more than I have to say on the subject, and says it much better then I am able to do. This account presents more detail in a local context, as befits a regional study. However, I have had to pass much more rapidly over some of the broader historical issues raised by this material. I differ from him in laying more stress on the observable similarities between paganism, Judaism, and Christianity and less on their doctrinal differences. The evidence of rural religious practice in Anatolia has far more to say about the former than the latter. Examples and illustrations have been chosen *exempli gratia* from an enormous bulk of material. One of the only attempts to analyse the cults of a region as a whole, and relate them to the history of settlement there, is J. Keil, 'Die Kulte Lydiens', *ASRamsay*, 239–66, although this has been overtaken by the publication of much new material (cf. *CR* 40 (1990), 430 for a brief survey of the current state of Lydian epigraphy). I have drawn in particular on texts published or republished in the various volumes of *MAMA*, and by Robert, *Hellenica*, iii (1948) and x (1955); *BCH* 107 (1983), 511–99 = *Documents*, 355–440; and by T. Drew Bear, *GRBS* 17 (1976), 247–68; *Nouvelles inscriptions de Phrygie* (1978); and (with C. Naour), 'Divinités de Phrygie', *ANRW* ii. 18. 3 (1990), 1907–2044.

[4] *RECAM* ii. 74a, Obruk Minetler.

[5] A. Souter, *CR* 11 (1897), 31–2; A. Petrie, in *SERP* 128.

[6] W. Ruge, *RE* xviii. 2 (1937), 872 cites the literature. The most useful description is by A. H. Smith, *JHS* 8 (1887), 228–9; see further L. Robert, *BCH* 107 (1983), 576–7, 599 = *Documents*, 420–1, 443. The shrine, by the modern village of Kızılcaağaç, is within easy reach of the modern highway running north from Antalya. A very similar sanctuary has been identified near Tymandus in Phrygia Paroreius, *MAMA* iv. p. xiii with pl. 7.

again intervened to tell the whole city, which was threatened by danger perhaps from local brigands, to set up statues for Heracles and Thesmos (Divine Justice), on either side of Ares the war god.[7] And at Ancyra the governor of Galatia, during the resurgence of persecution under the emperor Maximinus, offered a prominent local Christian the priesthood of Apollo if he denounced his faith; for through that office he would control the appointments of other priests, make representations to provincial officials, conduct embassies to emperors, and acquire wealth, glory, and fame in his native city.[8] Men served the gods, took their names from them, looked to them for prosperity and security both individually and collectively, and through the gods could rise to power and influence among their fellows.

The surviving evidence for pagan cults in central Asia Minor, as in most of the ancient world, has little time for mysteries or elaborate explanation. It simply exists, in abundance, in the form of temples and sanctuaries, statues and reliefs which show the gods and their attributes, or in the shape of documents to pagan piety, the vows and prayers of worshippers which, in the cities and the countryside alike, form the largest single class of inscriptions apart from gravestones. They are testimony to the divine power and presence which was felt and acknowledged by all.

Contact between men and gods was often disarmingly matter-of-fact. A priestess of Demeter Thesmophorus at Miletus asked Apollo at Didyma why the gods had appeared more often than ever before during her term of service, taking the form of girls, boys, and adults of both sexes. The god's answer implied that immortals spent much time among mortals, where they descried men's opinions and also judged the honours paid to them.[9] A god, accordingly, could be plain for all to see, like the river Eurymedon at Tymbriada in Pisidia churning through the gorge of the upper Aksu valley beside the rock-cut sanctuary where his statue stood;[10] or the Dioscuri at Fassiler, 'forever undefeated', on a rock relief south of Lake Beyşehir, warrior champions of a warlike people even in the time of the *pax*

Romana;[11] or they could come in a privileged vision to an individual.[12] The gods could make dramatic interventions, saving a child from a predatory wolf,[13] or reassuring ones in aiding recovery from an illness or securing the safe issue of a journey.[14] However, most votive texts do not make explicit the occasion of the vow. Men prayed to the gods because they were there. It was always prudent to acknowledge demonstrations of the gods' power, for to neglect them was to invite their anger. This is surely the chief reason why so many inscribed monuments were dedicated to them. Men were obliged to make a public demonstration of their respect and honour for the gods. If there was an overriding motive that caused men to pray, it was not gratitude for services rendered, but awe and fear of what the gods might do if their cult was overlooked.[15]

The gods were believed to speak directly to mortals, usually ordering them to set up a monument or to perform a pious action.[16] Tertullian was clear that the most important way they communicated with men was by dreams, and dedications obligingly confirm this.[17] Apollo, in particular, spoke through oracles. The great oracular shrines of Claros and Didyma are well known but they were matched on a humble scale all over Asia Minor.[18] Off the Lycian coast at Sura the god's

---

[11] Swoboda, *Denkmäler*, no. 16; cf. L. Robert, *RCH* 107 (1983), 574–5 = *Documents*, 418–9.

[12] See above all the religious experience of Aelius Aristides; the best introduction is A.-J. Festugière, *Personal Religion among the Greeks* (1954), 85–104.

[13] See, in general, R. MacMullen, *Paganism in the Roman Empire* (1981), 51.

[14] e.g. *MAMA* iv. 328 for Apollo Propylaios at Eumeneia, on recovery from chest pains. For reliefs depicting parts of the body cured after affliction, or for which help was sought, see Robert, *Hellenica*, x. 163 and MacMullen, *Paganism in the Roman Empire*, 34 with nn. 81–3.

[15] Here, like Lane Fox, I part company with MacMullen (*Paganism in the Roman Empire*, 49–53) who argues that the commonest reason for praying to the gods was to secure one's well-being, physical or otherwise. But see also the observations of G. Fowden, *JRS* 78 (1988), 176–7 insisting on the importance of the gods also as 'listeners' and 'saviours'. It will not do to deploy these various viewpoints against one another in order to establish a true picture. Men prayed to the gods because they were there.

[16] The normal formulas were κατὰ κέλευσιν, κατ᾽ ἐπιταγήν, and the like.

[17] Tertullian, *De anima* 47. 2 ('it is to dreams that the majority of mankind owe their knowledge of God'); MacMullen, *Paganism in the Roman Empire*, 60–1.

[18] Lane Fox, *Pagans and Christians*, 168–261 is the most important recent discussion, building on the work of Robert; H. W. Parke, *The Oracles of Apollo in Asia Minor* (1985), 171–202 contains a very incomplete account of oracles outside Didyma and Claros. See also H. C. Fontenrose, *Didyma: Apollo's Oracle, Cult and Companions* (1988), who is disinclined to include in his collection of authentic Didyma oracles many of the important theological texts which have been convincingly ascribed to the sanctuary.

[7] R. Heberdey and A. Wilhelm, *Reisen in Kilikien* (1896), 161 no. 267; commentary by L. Robert, *Documents de l'Asie Mineure méridionale* (1966), 96–100, cf. *Hellenica*, xi/xii. 546 n. 1 and *Bull. ép.* (1961), 716.

[8] *Life of Saint Theodotus*, 26, cf. *AS* 32 (1982), 109.

[9] A. Rehm, *I. Didyma*, no. 496; Robert, *Hellenica*, xi/xii. 544–6; Lane Fox, *Pagans and Christians*, 102–4.

[10] D. Kaya and S. Mitchell, *AS* 35 (1985), 39–55. For ἐπιφάνης see literature cited by Robert, *Hellenica*, vi. 51 n. 6; esp. F. Steinleitner, *Die Beicht . . . in der Antike* (1913), 15–21; H. Pfister, *RE* suppl. iv (1924), 277–323; E. Pax, 'Epiphanie', *RAC* 5 (1962), 832–909.

message was made known through the movement of fish in the water.[19] In almost every city of the south-west, through Lycia and Pisidia, a dice oracle stood in the civic centre to be used for routine consultation by men and women of all ranks and conditions.[20] Other oracular techniques competed in the same region, like the acrostic oracle of Apollo in remote country west of Pisidian Adada, a native sanctuary;[21] or the impeccably Hellenic shrine of Apollo excavated at Çavdarlı in Phrygia, on the territory of Prymnessus, where one dedicant set up a statue for Phoebus as witness to many oracles that he had received, and another erected a statuette on behalf of his wife and children in response to Apollo's prophecy.[22] In the forests of Mysian Olympus, east of Hadriani, an oracular shrine was busy throughout the imperial period. The prestige of the prophets was such that their names were used to date local inscriptions, and a village poet, Gauros of Torea, in addition to other compositions describing an imperial victory and the battles of the gods themselves, made a collection of the prophets' 'reliable predictions'.[23]

To the east, in the central Anatolian plateau, oracles are less conspicuous. Local facilities must have existed, but perhaps their relative scarcity gives a reason for the popularity of Glycon, the new Asclepius at Abonu-teichus in Paphlagonia, whose consultants came from Phrygia, Bithynia, Galatia—some speaking Celtic— and beyond.[24] The popularity of oracles needs no explaining. Alexander, Glycon's minder at Abonu-teichus, no less than Apollo at Claros, battened on the hopes and fears of men who craved to know what

the future held for them, or who sought guidance in difficult decisions. We may recall that the writer of the most famous modern anthropological study of oracles and magical soothsaying found no better means to take decisions and regulate the pattern of his own life than to adopt the oracular practices of the native people that he was studying. Nor are these practices the preserve of 'primitives'; many of the inhabitants of the Indian subcontinent, whose great and sophisticated poly-theistic culture offers the only viable comparison in the contemporary world to the paganism of Graeco-Roman Antiquity, turn at all moments of decision to the astrologer.[25]

Shrines or temples of the gods were ubiquitous. In the cities that had been founded the length and breadth of the empire the first buildings to be erected apart from their defensive walls were the temples of the gods who were to guide their future. So wrote Libanius in the late fourth century,[26] and the same had been true at the time when the city was first emerging as a form of communal life in archaic Greece.[27] Every city of the East worshipped an array of gods in shrines large and small. None of the central Anatolian sites has been excavated or surveyed with sufficient attention to reveal a true picture of the material remains of these sanctuaries, but it is possible to observe a sample in mountainous Pisidia, where the picture is consistent. At Adada there were four, perhaps five prostyle temples dominating the northward extension of the Roman city; at Cremna at least five temples have been noted, one peripteral the others prostyle, dating to the middle and later years of the second century AD; at Sagalassus the late Hellenistic Doric temple, perhaps dedicated to the native god Kakasbos, was eclipsed by massive temple-building in the first and second centuries AD, for Apollo Clarios, Dionysus, and for the emperor Antoninus Pius. There was still room within the city walls for a rock sanctuary in the Pisidian style, with holes cut in the cliff to hold votive monuments. At Termessus the first building on the approach to the city was a temple of Hadrian, and temples of late Hellenistic and Roman date, dedicated to Zeus and Artemis, clustered around the city centre close to the city's council chamber.[28]

Inscriptions and coins show that the city sites of the plateau were adorned in the same way. At Ancyra the

[19] W. Ruge, *RE* viiA (1931), 960 s.v. Sura 3.

[20] For a good discussion see C. Naour, *Tyriaion en Cabalide* (1980), 22–36 no. 5. A corpus of these oracles is being prepared by J. Nollé, see *Antike Welt*, 18 (1987), 41–9.

[21] Sterrett, *WE* no. 437 (Kaibel no. 1040); see Nollé, *Antike Welt*, 18 (1987), 47–9 with pl. 10–12; for the site, see N. Mersisch, *J.öst.Byz.* 36 (1986), 196–8.

[22] Unpublished texts in Afyon Museum, from the 1964 excavation by M. Akok.

[23] E. Schwertheim, *I. Hadr.* nos. 12, 19, 23, 25–6, 29, 30, 32–5. For Gauros the poet see no. 24, reading ἄ[θ]λους in l. 3. The letter forms exclude a date in the late 1st cent. BC, and rule out the possibility that the νίκην Καίσαρος was Augustus' victory at Actium.

[24] Lucian, *Alex.* 51. For the spread of the cult see L. Robert, *A travers l'Asie Mineure* (1980), 395–9; *CRAI* (1981), 513 ff.; Lane Fox, *Pagans and Christians*, 241–50; W. Ameling, *Epigr. Anat.* 6 (1985), 34–6. Glycon the oracular snake is portrayed on coins of Abonuteichus itself, Cius, Gangra, and Nicomedia. There are statues or statuettes from Tomis in lower Moesia, Byzantium (unpublished), Dorylaeum (unpublished), and Athens; and relevant inscriptions from Dacia, Thrace, and Bithynian Claudiopolis. Not all snakes need have depicted Glycon. A long and tightly coiled snake, identified as Asclepius, was worshipped at Mysian Hadriani in the second century AD; see *I. Hadr.* nos. 14, 15a, and 15b.

[25] E. Evans-Pritchard, *Witchcraft, Oracles and Magic among the Azande* (1937).

[26] Libanius, *Or.* 30 (*Pro Templis*), 5.

[27] A. M. Snodgrass, *Archaeology and the Origins of the Greek City State* (Cambridge Inaugural Lecture, 1978).

[28] For Termessus, see K. Lanckoroński, *Städte Pamphyliens und Pisidiens*, ii (1902). Lanckoroński's descriptions of the other Pisidian cities have been brought up to date by observations made in a current survey of Pisidia which began in 1982.

civic centre was dominated by the temple and *temenos* of Roma and Augustus, standing on a low hill. There are dedications or other inscribed references to the worship of Asclepius and Hygieia, the Dioscuri, Demeter, Mēn, Isis, Sarapis and the Egyptian deities that shared his temple, Tyche, the Muses, Zeus of Tavium, and a local pair known as the King and Queen, perhaps Mēn and the Mother Goddess.[29] The literary evidence mentions cults or priesthoods of Zeus, Artemis, Athena, and Apollo,[30] and there were fountains named after the demi-gods Midas and Maron.[31] Coin types enable us to add the names of Aphrodite, Dionysus, Hecate, Helios, Heracles, Hermes, Leto, and Nemesis.[32] The variety was perhaps even greater than elsewhere, for Ancyra was a cosmopolitan city where no single god seems to have been overwhelmingly prominent.[33]

At Pessinus excavations have uncovered the peripteral imperial temple. The inscriptions give pride of place to the cult of Attis and Cybele, the Great Mother, who appears in several guises, although her temple, built by the Attalids, has yet to be found.[34] Other inscriptions honour Zeus and Helios,[35] and coins give a list as long as Ancyra's: Aphrodite, Apollo, Artemis, Asclepius, Athena, Demeter, Dionysus, Eros, Harpocrates, Heracles, Hermes, Hygieia, Isis, Mēn, Nemesis, Nike, Poseidon, Sarapis, and Tyche, as well as the river gods

Gallus and Sagaris.[36] This is no place to review and list the cults of all the cities of central Asia Minor. Given the incompleteness of the surviving evidence such a catalogue would in any case give only an illusion of comprehensiveness, and further accumulation of detail would not alter the obvious conclusion, that the cults of Greek cities, even the newly-founded ones of the Roman empire, were as numerous as they were various. The evidence also underlines the familiar truth that the gods of paganism were famously tolerant of one another.

One would find dedications or offerings to a range of deities not only in a single city, but in any given sanctuary. At Didyma there was a circle of altars in the sanctuary of Apollo, set up for his immortal colleagues. Two oracles of the early third century prescribed that an altar of Fortune and an altar of Kore should be added to the group with appropriate ceremony and ritual.[37] In the sanctuary of Zeus at Panamara in Caria, better documented than any other pagan sanctuary of Asia Minor, the inscriptions refer not only to the principal temple of Zeus Panamaros, but to temples of Hera, Zeus Karios and Hera, a chapel and altar of Sarapis, and an altar of Artemis.[38] Multiple invocations were common on a single monument, for instance the relief set up as a dedication to the gods of the Motelleis, a small community in the territory of Phrygian Hierapolis, which depicts a bust of Zeus presiding over a group made up from Artemis, Mēn, and a rider god with a double axe, probably Apollo.[39]

[29] See Bosch, *Ankara*, nos. 178–80, 280, 184–5, 262, 188, 186, 287, 335, 211–12; *AS* 27 (1977), 89–90 nos. 91–2 (*SEG* xxvii. 851–2).
[30] Pausanias, I. 4. 5; *Life of Saint Theodotus*, 14, 26.
[31] See *AS* 32 (1982), 105.
[32] Head, *HN*² 747; M. Arslan, 'The Coinage of Ancyra in the Roman Period', in C. S. Lightfoot (ed.), *Recent Turkish Coin Hoards and Numismatic Studies* (1991), 3–42.
[33] But note the reference to πάτριοι θεοί in *IGR* iii. 156.
[34] See below, n. 70.
[35] Strubbe, *I. Pessinus*, nos. 53 (Waelkens, *Türsteine*, no. 753) and 126.

[36] Devreker, *Fouilles de Pessinonte*, i (1984), 24.
[37] *I. Didyma*, ii. 504; cf. L. Robert, *CRAI* (1968), 583–4. W. Günther, *Ist. Mitt.* 20 (1971), 97 ff.; Lane Fox, *Pagans and Christians*, 216–17.
[38] H. Oppermann, *Zeus Panamaros* (1924); A. Laumonier, *Les cultes indigènes en Carie* (1958). For the buildings see *BCH* (1887), 389 no. 5; (1891), 209, 151; (1904), 41, 16; (1927), 80–2.
[39] L. Robert, *JSav.* (1983), 45–52 (*SEG* xxxiv (1984), 1298).

Fig. 1. The outer wall of the sanctuary of Mēn Askaēnos at Pisidian Antioch. The votives take the form of *aediculae* carved on the blocks of the wall, with or without an inscription. The usual symbol of a crescent moon is sometimes replaced by a stylized ox-head or a wreath. For the inscriptions, see M. E. Hardie, *JHS* 42 (1912) and Lane, *CMRDM* i and iv.

Fig. 2. One of the earliest of the lengthy inscriptions from Sağır, on the territory of Pisidian Antioch, which listed subscriptions made by members of the religious association called the *Xenoi Tekmoreioi*, perhaps AD 215–30. On the left of the stone are the names, patronymics, and village ethnics of the subscribers; on the right their subscriptions ranging from the largest, 900, to the smallest, 300 *denarii*. Scrupulous accounting, inscribed records, the large number of individual cash contributions, and the huge geographical range of the villages represented emphasize the exceptional nature of this cult organization. W. M. Ramsay, *SERP* 333–7 no. 15.

Fig. 3. The sculptor Epitynchanos set up this stele as a votive to Zeus Andreas around AD 220. The bust of all-seeing Helios is in the gable; on the shaft there is a bust of Zeus himself above a garland which is hung between two ox-heads. The sanctuary where the stele was dedicated has been located near Appia in the upper Tembris valley. Now in Kütahya Museum; T. Drew Bear, *GRBS* 17 (1976), 252 no. 9; L. Robert, *BCH* 107 (1983), 543. For Epitynchanos, see M. Waelkens, in S. D. Campbell (ed.), *The Malcove Collection* (Univ. of Toronto, 1985), 19–20 no. 16.

1

2

3

Aspects of Anatolian paganism

A relief from Dorylaeum, gives an overlapping view of the Phrygian pantheon, showing the gods in three ranks: Zeus and his eagle flanked by busts of the Sun and the Moon occupied the pediment; a central band across the stele showed the Phrygian gods of justice, *Hosion kai Dikaion* (Holy and Just) with a female bust to the right depicting their female counterpart *Hosia* and a rider god, again perhaps Apollo, to the left. At the bottom of the stone Heracles with his club and Hermes stood alongside the peasant's plough and oxen.[40]

If the multiplicity of cults was generally more restricted in the countryside, it was not due to any intolerance, but to the relative cultural poverty of the inhabitants whose intellectual and religious horizons did not extend as far as those of the more cosmopolitan townsfolk. Indigenous, scarcely Hellenized deities such as Angdistis, Papas, Ma, or Sabazios occur more frequently in the countryside than in cities, while imports such as Sarapis and Isis, or less familiar Hellenic figures such as Dionysus, were relatively unusual.[41] Here too, however, the gods were everywhere. In the same speech that extolled urban temples, Libanius said that sanctuaries were the soul of the countryside; their creation had served as the prelude to the establishment of rural settlements; it was they who realized the hopes of the peasants for the well-being of men, women, and children; for their oxen; for the sowing; and for the harvest.[42] The pagan orator of the 380s echoed precisely the sentiments of the Christian missionary of AD 50.

Archaeology has virtually nothing to say about rural shrines in Anatolia, for none has been excavated.[43] Only in mountainous districts, such as Pisidia and Isauria, where shrines were often cut from the rock, can we form some impression of their physical appearance. Here the rock face of a cliff, or around a cave entrance, would be shaped as a shrine, with a place for an altar, votive niches, or perhaps a statue.[44] It is surely mistaken to argue that such architecture was characteristic of native or indigenous rural cults, and contrasted with the shrines of Greek or other imported gods, who warranted free-standing buildings.[45] The

distinction is due to geology and topography, not to culture. In the plains of central Anatolia built shrines would have housed the native deities, and votive monuments took the form of free-standing stelae, not niches carved in the rock face. On occasion the architecture of the shrines was Hellenized, since fragments of temple architecture are not unusual, but to build a *naos* was a sign that a community was wealthier and culturally more sophisticated than its neighbours.[46] A sacred enclosure, often with a stand of trees forming an *alsos*, fitted with altars and votive stelae, was perhaps the normal rural pattern.[47]

Many cults were obviously regional, with an appeal that went beyond the city in whose territory they lay. One of the most conspicuous is the organization called the *Xenoi Tekmoreioi*, whose centre was located at or near the village of Sağır to the north-west of Pisidian Antioch on the slopes of Sultan Dağ. The symbol called the *tekmor*, which offered a focus to their beliefs, remains an enigma,[48] but an important series of third-century inscriptions shows that the association worshipped Artemis in particular. The members came principally from the communities of northern Pisidia and southern Phrygia: from cities south and east of Lake Beyşehir like Malos[49] and Adada; from the territories of Antioch and Apollonia between which the cult centre lay; and from cities whose territories lay north of Sultan Dağ—Synnada, Metropolis, Prymnessus, Lysias,[50] and Philomelium.[51] The fol-

---

[40] Robert, *OMS* ii. 1355–60 (*Rev. phil.* (1939), 202–7), with many parallels. He published another comparable relief from Dorylaeum in *Hellenica*, x. 104–7. For the gods of Justice in Phrygia, see below, at nn. 124–33.

[41] For Dionysus see T. Drew Bear, *ANRW* ii. 18. 3, 1944–7.

[42] *Or.* 30. 9–10.

[43] Cf. T. Drew Bear, *GRBS* 17 (1976), 251, 254, and elsewhere on the desirability of such excavations. The rural sanctuaries of central Turkey have been ruthlessly plundered by illegal excavators in the last twenty years.

[44] Robert, *BCH* 107 (1983), 569–73 = *Documents*, 413–17 cites and illustrates some characteristic examples.

[45] *Contra* Robert, *BCH* 107 (1983), 569.

[46] Rural *naoi* seem relatively rare, and often reveal the patronage or interest of city dwellers or men of substance such as the freedmen who administered imperial and private estates. Compare the temples built on the *choria Considiana* for the imperial cult and for Mēn on the estate of the Sergii near Vetissus (above, Vol. I, Ch. 10 § III nn. 71 and 94). None of the other rural sanctuaries of the imperial cult discussed by Price, *Rituals and Power*, 83–6 seems to have contained a temple. In Lydia the temple at Dareiukōme, *TAM* v. 2. 1335–6, should be taken as an indication that this village had acquired some of the characteristics of a small town (see above, Vol. I, Ch. 11 § IV). *TAM* v. 2. 1352 attests a rural temple of the Mētēr Plastene, but it had been built by a city dignitary from Magnesia ad Sipylum. Of course, modest country or village temples are attested from time to time, as for instance for Asclepius at a village in the territory of Amorium, see Drew Bear, *GRBS* 17 (1976), 257 no. 13.

[47] The sacred grove or *alsos* was characteristic. See Drew Bear, *ANRW* ii. 18. 3, 1915–39 on Phrygian cults of Zeus and Apollo Alsenos. Note L. Robert's evocation of the sanctuary of Asclepius at Pergamum, before it was transformed by the great Hadrianic building programme, *BCH* 108 (1984), 481 = *Documents*, 469.

[48] Despite Ramsay, *SERP* 346–9 'a pledge of loyalty to the state in its contest with the Christians'!

[49] For the site near Sarıidris, north of Tymbriada, see N. Mersisch, *J.öst.Byz.* 35 (1985), 49–54.

[50] C. Habicht, *JRS* 65 (1975), 86–7 places Lysias between the Phrygian Pentapolis and Synnada.

[51] For the geography of the Tekmoreian lists see Ramsay, *SERP*

Fig. 4. The Ionic peripteros of the Hadrianic temple of Zeus, which was the centrepiece of Aezani's second-century AD building programme.

Fig. 5. The crypt beneath the cella of the temple which probably housed the cult of the Mother of the Gods. See R. Naumann, *Der Zeustempel zu Aezanoi* (1979); *MAMA* ix, pp. xxxiii–xxxiv; L. Robert, *BCH* 105 (1981), 331–60.

The Temple of Zeus at Aezani

lowers of the cult continued to contribute substantial sums of cash to pay for statues and other fittings in the sanctuary through the dark days of the mid-third century.

Sanctuaries on a smaller scale frequently served not one village but several in the same district. One example is the sanctuary on the territory of Appia in the upper Tembris valley, which has produced a splendid series of dedications to Zeus Ampelites (Zeus of the vine). The votive reliefs, which depict the live-stock of the peasant population, show that the god was thought to have wider powers than the name indicates. They were erected by villagers from throughout the area: Aragua, Gordus, Mossyna, Passita, Trikomia, and others.[52] Another comparable sanctuary was the shrine of Zeus Bussurigius in the territory of Ancyra close to the river Halys. A series of inscribed stelae, which date to the period between AD 220 and 250, refers to suppliants from the villages of the Klossamenoi, Ikotarion, Dallopoze, and Malos of the Kalmizene.[53]

Flourishing rural cults were readily adapted and introduced into the newly-founded cities of the Roman period. Sometimes the effect on the cult could be dramatic. The most successful local shrine of the Mother of the Gods in the southern part of the central plateau belonged to the Mētēr Theōn Zizimmene, located at Sizma on the territory of Laodicea Catace-caumene but close to Iconium. Her inscriptions have been found at Iconium, in various villages of the territory of Laodicea, and in the central plateau region towards Ancyra.[54] A dedication from Sizma itself links her to Angdistis, Apollo Sozon, and Helios,[55] and

another inscription associates her with Apollo.[56] Iconium adopted the Mētēr Zizimmene as a patron goddess, where she was Hellenized and doubtless worshipped in an imposing civic temple. A resplendent bilingual text calls her Minerva or Athena and sets her alongside Iuppiter Optimus Maximus and the Tyche of the city or of the emperors.[57] Her native identity as a mother goddess faded into the background and she was assimilated into both the Greek and the Roman pantheons, as Minerva and Athena.

A similar route may have brought the Phrygian goddess of justice, familiar in rural contexts through-out central Anatolia from Dorylaeum to Lydia and to the borders of Pisidia (see below, § 11 at nn. 124–33), into the city of Prymnessus, where the chief deity was Dikaiosyne. She was depicted on coins bearing the scales and holding two ears of corn, or was simply symbolized by the scales alone. A victorious competitor in a festival might hear his triumphs proclaimed by her altar in the city centre.[58] The ears of corn show that the Prymnessians believed that the goddess watched over their crops and guaranteed their harvests, the basic source of their livelihood, but her name shows clearly that her roots lay in rural sanctuaries where Hosion and Dikaion, Hosia, and the other Phrygian gods of justice presided over the dealings of peasant villagers.[59]

Native gods were transformed as the tastes and education of people changed. The most vivid example of the way in which the creation of cities acted as a catalyst, by absorbing native cults and decking them out in Graeco-Roman dress, comes from Aezani. Near the city lay the Steunos cave overlooking the river Penkalas, which was reputed to be the birthplace of Zeus. The famous legend of Zeus' birth, according to which the Corybantes clashed their weapons to drown the cries of the baby and preserve him from the mur-derous intentions of his father Cronos, found a home here far distant from its traditional location on Mount Ida in Crete. The cave near Aezani duly became a

---

361–70, to be read with W. Ruge, *RE* va. 158–69. New texts and identifications have been promised by Drew Bear, *Nouvelles inscriptions de Phrygie*, ix–x, cf. *GRBS* 17 (1976), 263 n. 62.

[52] L. Robert, *BCH* 107 (1983), 529–42 = *Documents*, 373–87; Drew Bear, *ANRW* ii. 18. 3, 1964–5.

[53] *RECAM* ii. 203–6, cf. 201, 209a. Emigrants took the worship of Zeus Bussurigius, and the presumably related cult of Zeus Bussumarus, as well as other cults from NW Galatia, Paphlagonia, and Bithynia to Dacia (A. Popa and I. Berciu, *Tenth Congress*, 953–6; Robert, *A Travers l'Asie Mineure*, 221–3, 397). Although the cult centres of the *Xenoi Tekmoreioi* and in north-east Galatia were devoted to Artemis and Zeus respectively, both appear to have incorporated features of the cult of a mother goddess, for both, like the cult of the Mētēr Zizimmene, have produced inscriptions for *archigalli*, priests who are particularly characteristic of the worship of Cybele at Pessinus. For *archigalli* at Pessinus, see Devreker, *Fouilles de Pessinonte*, i. 20 (cf. J. Carcopino, *Aspects mystiques de la Rome païenne* (1942), 76 ff.). At Sağır, Ramsay, *SERP* 343 no. 22; for Zeus Bussurigius, see *RECAM* ii. 206; also *archigalli* for Mētēr Zizimmene, J. G. C. Anderson, *JHS* 19 (1899), 280 no. 163.

[54] *Historia*, 28 (1979), 425 n. 109.

[55] W. M. Ramsay, *CR* 19 (1905), 368 no. 1; *AJA* 31 (1927), 28–9 (*SEG* vi. 392).

[56] Ramsay, *JHS* 38 (1918), 138; *AJA* 31 (1927), 27.

[57] The best text by Ramsay, *JHS* 38 (1918), 170 ff. (cf. *Historia*, 28 (1979), 425 n. 108). Price, *Rituals and Power*, 97 well notes that the native goddess has been assimilated to Minerva/Athena and adopted as a major public cult of the city. Compare the integration of Zeus Megistos into the public cults of Iconium from the countryside, below at nn. 88–9.

[58] Dikaiosyne at Prymnessus, J. Nollé. *BJb.* 189 (1989), 658–9. Note the verse inscription *JRS* 2 (1912), 259–60 no. 2 (*SEG* vi. 175): στέψε πάτρη ξυνπᾶσα Δικῆς ὑπ' ἀρείονι βωμῷ.

[59] Nollé seems to be over-sophisticated in arguing that by combining the functions of a goddess of the harvest with those of a goddess of justice, she embodied 'redistributive justice'. Rather, she thereby had the two attributes that enabled her to look after the moral as well as the physical needs of Prymnessus' citizens. But see also Robert, *Documents de l'Asie Mineure méridionale*, 25–9.

major centre of cult, and excavations have produced a mass of terracotta votive offerings as well as niches in the rock surrounding the cave mouth and two sacrifical pits or *bothroi*, which were in use from the first century BC to the mid-second century AD. Aezani meanwhile had emerged as an important city, and the crucial stage in its development came in the second quarter of the second century when an enormous temple complex was built also on the banks of the Penkalas, downstream from the cave. The temple itself, dedicated to Zeus, contained a subterranean vaulted chamber equal in size to the cella itself, which served part of the cult. It is an obvious inference that the underground chamber corresponds to the rock-cut cave of the rural sanctuary. Here, symbolically, was the home of the Mother of Zeus, the god's birthplace. The cella above became the proper and fitting home of Zeus himself, the chief god of Aezani. An unassuming rural cult thus grew to be the most impressive sanctuary of northern Phrygia. Even so, Hellenization, or urbanization, could never be complete in such an environment and imperial Aezani preserved examples of indigenous *hiera* alongside its magnificent Ionic temple: a coin of Domitian depicts the eagle of Zeus perched on a high column in what was evidently an open-air sanctuary. The sacred groves or rock monuments of the pre-Hellenic tradition were not swiftly erased by the sophistication of urban architecture.[60] We may be sure that the rural inhabitants of central Asia Minor preserved their own local traditions and culture intact in the face of the tide of Greek and Roman influence.

II. The Indigenous Cults of Anatolia

It is a hazardous business to attempt to classify the cults of Asia Minor. Interpretation has wavered between two traditions. One approach has been to aggregate the numerous separate cults for distinct local deities into protean unities, a sky god, an earth mother, or a prototypical warrior. However, it is palpably anachronistic to foist on the numerous separate communities of Asia Minor the notion that the gods they worshipped, which were all scrupulously distinguished not only by name but by their distribution patterns and by the attributes of each cult, could be reduced to a handful of divine beings which performed similar functions or fulfilled similar psychological needs. Viewed from the perspective of monotheistic Christianity we may be perplexed by the diversity of pagan cults; but for an inhabitant of Roman Asia Minor, the ubiquity and diversity of the pagan gods, which is implied by the bewildering mass of the surviving evidence, was a far simpler notion to grasp than the omnipresence of a single God.

The other approach has been to distinguish the cults from one another with ever-increasing precision, and thus reconstruct as accurately as possible the religious environment of each separate community. However, excessive atomization makes it impossible to draw any wider conclusions from the evidence, or to make comparisons between one cult and another. It is surely possible to argue for a close relationship between different local cults of Zeus, warrior gods, or whatever group may be under consideration, and discern some common religious pattern behind the kaleidoscopic evidence. Ancient authors themselves were prepared to do this, not merely during the later Roman empire, when sophisticated theories of syncretism were developed by philosophically-minded writers, but in a more artless way at an earlier date. Strabo said of the Phrygian tribe called the Berecyntians, the Trojans living around Mount Ida, and the Phrygians in general, that they were orgiastic worshippers of the goddess Rhea, calling her by various names—the Mother of the Gods, Angdistis, the Great Phrygian Goddess, Cybebe or Cybele—or simply designating her after the place where she was worshipped, such as Ida, Dindyma, Sipylus, or Pessinus.[61] Faced with the same problem as a modern commentator, Strabo rationalized the perplexing variety of cults into a manageable scheme. It may be hard to find agreement about what scheme precisely one should adopt, but some such procedure can hardly be avoided.

Four groups of cults give the best impression of the religious atmosphere of ancient Anatolia, namely those for Zeus, for the various Mother Goddesses, for Mēn, and for the several champions of divine justice and vengeance. These groups of cults share a broadly similar distribution pattern across Asia Minor. The heartland, where all are repeatedly found, was Phrygia, continental western Anatolia *par excellence*, but they also occurred in most of Lydia, Mysia, Bithynia, Galatia, Lycaonia, and northern Pisidia. There is no evidence that any of these cults was introduced to Anatolia from elsewhere, and it is an economical and convincing hypothesis that they make up the central core of the religious culture of the indigenous Anatolian population, whose traditions naturally reach far back into the prehistoric period.

As Strabo indicates, Mother Goddesses in central Anatolia were often simply styled Mētēr Theōn,[62]

---

[60] See Robert, *BCH* 105 (1981), 331–60 = *Documents*, 241–70; *MAMA* ix, pp. xxxiii–xxxv; for the coins depicting a column with an eagle, an altar, and a tree issued under Commodus and Gallienus, see *Bull. ép.* (1982), 398 and 399, p. 406.

[61] Strabo, 10. 3. 12, 469, cf. 15, 470.

[62] e.g. *MAMA* i. 1 (Laodicea Catacecaumene), 408; vii. 363, set up by the people of Vetissus. In northern Lydia, see *TAM*

or were distinguished by a local toponym: for instance Imruragene, Silandene, Quadatrene, Andeirene, Plitandene in Galatia; Plastene, Sipylene, Aliene, or Tarsene in Lydia.[63] The multiplicity is splendidly illustrated by an inscription of Iconium which appealed to the indigenous goddess Angdistis, whose cult spread throughout Phrygia and northern Pisidia from the mountain Angdissis, which stood south of the city of Docimeium and provided its polychrome marble quarries,[64] to the Great Mother Boethene, to the Mother of the Gods, to Apollo, and to Artemis; all were hailed collectively as the saviour gods and goddesses.[65] The list includes three female Phrygian goddesses, two explicitly labelled as Mētēr.

In the literary tradition the most famous Anatolian cult of a Mother Goddess was that of Cybele, or the Mother of Mount Dindymus, located at Pessinus. In the Hellenistic period the shrine had wielded political as well as religious influence and attracted attention from the Attalids and the Galatians, as well as from local worshippers. Its most holy cult object, a black stone, was transferred to Rome in 204 BC.[66] The best-known visitor to the sanctuary was the emperor Julian, who made a detour to Pessinus during his march against the Persians in AD 362. It was here that he

addressed a letter to Callixeine, making her high priestess of the Great Mother of the Phrygians to add to the priesthood of the most holy Demeter, which she already held.[67] From Syrian Antioch, after his impressions had been sharpened by what he had seen of Christian philanthropy in regions such as Cappadocia which had already largely abandoned paganism, he wrote again to Arsacius, the high priest of Galatia, instructing him to compete in good works with his Christian rivals, and above all to worship the Mother Goddess at Pessinus, whose inhabitants were chided for their indifference towards her.[68]

The indifference which Julian detected at Pessinus may not have been entirely due to the recession of paganism in the fourth century. Despite the antiquity and international reputation of the cult of Cybele, its best days were over even by the time of Augustus. Strabo observes that the powers of the temple state and its priests were much diminished in his time,[69] and the epigraphy of the imperial period does not suggest that the cult was then widely disseminated or attracted pilgrims from far afield. Her worshippers all seem to have been local.[70] Despite the fact that Cybele appears

---

v. 1. 77, 351?; v. 2. 955, 962–3, 996, 1172 (all Thyateira), 1353 (Plastene, Magnesia), 1375 (Sipylene).

[63] Galatia: *MAMA* i. 2b, 2c; *Rev. phil.* (1912), no. 47; *JRS* 14 (1924), no. 3; *RECAM* ii. 74a; Lydia: *TAM* v. 1. 202, 460 (Tarsene), 257–8 (Aliane); v. 2. 1353–4 (Plastene), 1357, 1375 (Sipylene).

[64] For Angdistis see Robert, *A travers l'Asie Mineure*, 236–40.

[65] *MAMA* viii. 297.

[66] See Magie, *RR* ii. 770.

[67] Julian, *Ep.* 81 (Bidez-Cumont); Ammianus, xxii. 9. 5. The visit to Pessinus is discussed by Devreker, *Fouilles de Pessinonte*, i. 26. See below, Ch. 17 § VII at nn. 332–3.

[68] *Ep.* 84, cited by Sozomen, *HE* 5. 16; Greg. Naz., *Or.* 4. 40. Julian was to compose a hymn to the Mother Goddess, *Or.* 5.

[69] Strabo, 12. 5. 3, 567.

[70] On coins and three inscriptions she is called the *Mētēr Theōn* sometimes with the adjective *megalē* (*IGR* iii nos. 225, 230; P. Lambrechts and R. Bogaert, *Hommages à Marcel Renard II*, Coll. Latomus, 102 (1969), 405–14. For the coins see Devreker, *Fouilles de Pessinonte*, i. 173–4 nos. 1–10). Other

---

Fig. 6. Zeus Thallos. The relief shows four saddled donkeys, with the remains of a fifth above them, which Nannas perhaps rented for transport (0.255 × 0.29). The inscription reads [N]αννας Γορδιοκωμήτης Δὶ Θάλλ[ῳ ε]ὐξάμενος ἀνέθηκε. The stone which is now in Afyon Museum (Inv. E. 1985) was brought from Akça Köy in the upper Tembris valley, and the stele is rigorously comparable with other votives for Zeus Thallos and for Zeus Ampelites, who had a sanctuary near the same village. See L. Robert, *BCH* 107 (1983), 526–42.

Fig. 7. Zeus Abozenos. The lower half of a limestone stele (0.25 × 0.20) depicting a leg, which had presumably healed after injury. The inscription reads [K]αρικὸς Ῥούφου ὑπὲρ ἑαυτοῦ σωτηρίας Δὶι Ἀβοζηνῷ εὐχήν. The stone is in Afyon Museum (Inv. E. 1982) but was brought from Aslanlı Köy NW of Emirdağ, which lay between Nacolea and Amorium. Other dedications for this god have been published from Nacolea and from Tavşanlı north of Aezani, see T. Drew Bear, *ANRW* ii. 18. 3, 2022–6.

Fig. 8. The Mētēr Tymenene. White marble statuette of a goddess wearing a polos, with phiale and tympanum, seated between two lions (0.28 × 0.13). Μητρὶ Τυμενηνῇ εὐχήν. From Eyüpler near Pisidian Antioch, now in Yalvaç Museum (Inv. no. 323). F. Naumann, *Die Ikonographie der Kybele in der phrygischen und griechischen Kunst* (1983); *SEG* xxxv (1985), 1403. The goddess is also reported on an unpublished inscription from Ilgın: see L. Zgusta, *Kleinasiatische Ortsnamen* (1986), 640: 1384-1.

Fig. 9. Zeus Petarenos. Crudely carved limestone stele dedicated by a mother on behalf of her child. The cloaked and veiled figure is presumably the dedicator. Κρατήσα ὑπὲρ παιδίου Δὶι Πεταρηνῷ εὐχήν. Kütahya Museum. Many dedications to Zeus Petarenos can be traced to a sanctuary of Zeus Alsenos near Çoğu on the territory of Amorium. See Drew Bear, *ANRW* ii. 18. 3, 1916 n. 20 and 1920 n. 24.

Fig. 10. Hecate. Limestone stele (0.19 × 0.115), depicting a male figure, wearing a heavy shepherd's cloak, presumably Auxanon. In Afyon Museum (Inv. E. 1746) but said to be from Kütahya. [Ἄ]μια ὑπὲρ Αὐξάνοντος Ἑκάτῃ εὐχήν. For Hecate in Lydia and Phrygia, see Robert, *Hellenica*, x. 113–17.

6

7

8

9

10

Central Anatolian votive dedications

frequently on the city coinages of Asia Minor,[71] there is remarkably little evidence that the Pessinuntine cult of Mētēr Dindymene travelled. A dedication has been found in the Cillanian plain north of Lake Beyşehir.[72] Elsewhere she was overtaken by other Mother Goddesses. It would be a mistake to attribute the decline of the sanctuary to waning devotion. The power of the Mother Goddess was as strong as it had always been; only Pessinus itself had been eclipsed. While it had once been an imposing cult centre, boasting almost the only marble temple of Hellenistic central Anatolia, it was now simply one among dozens of Roman provincial cities.

A first-century-AD inscription found in central Lydia north of Sardis carries a dedication to the Lydian Mother of the Gods. The Mētēr is more widely attested in Lydia than any other native deity except Zeus, but the ethnic neatly makes the point that this autochthonous Mother of the Lydians was to be distinguished from the much-better-known Phrygian Mother of the Gods, the Mother *par excellence*, whose cult spread to the west coast of Asia Minor, to the Black Sea, to Rome, and beyond.[73] The ubiquity and importance of these Phrygian cults underlines that this region more than any other preserved the cultural traditions of Anatolia.[74]

The most widely worshipped god in central Asia Minor was certainly Zeus. It is an over-simplification to see him as the consort of the Mother Goddess, the god of the sky corresponding to the goddess of the earth. The simple equation of the two as consorts for one another is not supported by epigraphic evidence or by the iconography of Anatolian votive steles, and is of course flatly at odds with the legend that the Mother of the Gods was Zeus' parent.[75]

Shrines of Zeus were ubiquitous. In Pontus the most important centre was the sanctuary of Zeus Stratios, sited on the summit of Büyük Evliya Dağ east of Amaseia, a famous native shrine where Mithridates had offered sacrifice.[76] Newly discovered inscriptions show that the various regions into which Pontus was divided made official dedications there, confirming that the cult was significant for the whole region.[77] The title suggests that he was worshipped as a god of war, and it is interesting to note an inscription for Zeus Stratios Megistos, which was set up in the Lycaonian plain south of Lake Tatta by a Roman *beneficiarius*, an appropriate gesture by an official whose responsibilities included keeping the peace on the roads.[78]

In all cultures mountains have been especially associated with divinity; fear and awe are natural human emotions in the presence of mountains and gods alike. An epiphany of the Mountain Mother led a Pisidian slave to erect a dedication in the wild territory of Tymbriada,[79] and rural gendarmerie cut rock inscriptions for her at the remote end of their 'beat' in a mountain cave of the Pisidian Taurus on the territory of Ariassos or Sia.[80] Northern central Anatolia was cut off from the Black Sea by the towering massif of Mount Olgassys, Ilgaz Dağ, whose bare peaks thrust out from a black forest of pine trees, 'exceedingly lofty and hard to cross'. The Paphlagonians maintained sanctuaries all over the mountain.[81] The people of Gangra located the fall of Tantalus here and called the

---

coins have the legend ΘΕΑ ΙΛΕΑ, ibid., no. 11. One inscription is dedicated to the Μητρὶ θεῶν Σατυρηναίᾳ ἐπηκόῳ, *AEMÖ* 7 (1883), 166 no. 37 (*I. Pessinus*, no. 27; cf. H. Graillot, *Le Culte de Cybèle* (1912), 354). She was also known as the Μήτηρ Μάγνη, *I. Pessinus*, no. 146, clear evidence of reciprocal influence from Rome after the cult had been adopted in Italy as that of the *Magna Mater*. Her consort Attis is much less prominent. His head appears on the reverse of autonomous issues of Pessinus but never without accompanying symbols of the goddess. He was the object of a dedication by the *phyle Sebaste*, *I. Pessinus*, no. 25. It seems implausible that the figure of Attis, who was relatively inconspicuous in the pagan worship of Anatolia, should have been assimilated into the Christian St Michael, whose cult is so widespread in these regions, as is argued by C. Mango, Δέλτιον τῆς Χριστιανικῆς Ἀρχαιολογικῆς Ἑταιρείας Περιοδὸς Δ', τομός ΙΒ' (1984, publ. 1986), 39–62.

[71] For Cybele in central Asia Minor, distinguished from other goddesses, see Drew Bear, *ANRW* ii. 18. 3, 1944 n. 122.

[72] *MAMA* viii. 363. For other Phrygian cults in this region note Angdistis at Viran köy north of Anaboura, *MAMA* viii. 396. There are dedications to the θεᾷ Μητρί by the demos of the Pedieis near Beyşehir, and to a Μήτηρ Οὐετνα or Οὐεγνα between Lake Beyşehir and Lake Suğla (A. S. Hall, *AS* 18 (1968), 67 no. 7 and 75 no. 19), which should also probably be seen as examples of Phrygian culture penetrating into this Pisidian territory.

[73] L. Robert, *BCH* 106 (1982), 359–61 = *Documents*, 321–3.

[74] For the Mother Goddess as virtually a defining characteristic of indigenous Anatolian culture, see (*exempli gratia*!), W. M. Ramsay, *Luke the Physician*, 131.

[75] See above, n. 60.

[76] F. Cumont, *SP* ii. 171–84; *RE* ivA (1931), 258–61.

[77] See above, Vol. I, Ch. 7 §IV n. 123.

[78] Copied by M. H. Ballance. Compare the remarks of T. B. Mitford jun. on inscriptions set up by *beneficiarii* in Pontus for the god Pylon, who seems to have been a guardian of gates, *Byzantion*, 36 (1966), 480–4. For cults of *beneficiarii* see A. von Domaszewski, *Westdeutsche Zeitschrift*, 21 (1907), 158–211 at 206–11, cited by Robert, *Hellenica*, x. 175 n. 1. The account has been superseded by the sensational new finds of dedications by *beneficiarii* at Oberbürken in Germania Superior, which are published by E. Schallmeyer *et al.*, *Der römische Weihbezirk von Osterbürken I: Corpus der griechischen und lateinischen Beneficiarier-inschriften des römischen Reichs* (1990), nos. 147–75.

[79] Sterrett, *WE* 400.

[80] Robert, *BCH* (1928), 407–9 (*OMS* ii. 878–90); *Ét. anat.*, 105. See S. Şahin, *Epigr. Anat.* 17 (1991), 126–32 for another group of similar dedications from the Karain cave.

[81] Strabo, 12. 3. 40, 562: ἔστι δ' ὁ Ὀλγασσυς ὄρος σφόδρα ὑψηλὸν καὶ δύσβατον· καὶ ἱερὰ τοῦ ὄρους τούτου πανταχοῦ καθιδρυμένα ἔχουσιν οἱ Παφλαγόνες.

mountain, and their city, the hearth of the gods, *hestia theōn*, and from this derived their claim to be the most ancient city of Paphlagonia.[82] An inscription from Ilgaz reveals precisely one of these many sanctuaries, a dedication to the Great Gods of stoas and an adjoining banqueting hall with kitchens on either side, the usual buildings for a thriving temple complex.[83]

Zeus' most important Galatian shrine was at Tavium whose sanctuary, which is mentioned by Strabo, may have rivalled those of the neighbouring Pontic temple states.[84] The god is portrayed on coins of Tavium seated on an elaborate high-backed throne, holding a sceptre and a thunderbolt and usually accompanied by an eagle. The throne is sometimes depicted with two columns supporting an arch which itself was adorned with three statues.[85] Although Zeus Tavianos does not appear in any of the modest collection of inscriptions from Tavium itself, the cult was exported to Ancyra and by Galatian emigrants to Dacia.[86] At Ancyra there must have been a substantial secondary sanctuary, for the twelfth and last of the city tribes took his name, probably in or soon after the reign of Hadrian.[87]

A *hieron* of Zeus Megistos stood at Iconium where he appears on the early autonomous civic coinage, and he may also have given his name to one of the four city tribes.[88] The cult clearly had its origin in the country-side and Zeus Megistos may have been imported to Iconium, like the Mother Goddess of Zizma, from a specific shrine. One candidate has been located on the imperial estates around Lagina, modern Ilgın.[89] Three of the dedications belonging to this sanctuary were set up by imperial freedmen or slaves, persons of sufficient substance to endow a native sanctuary with substantial buildings.[90] Wealthy local people would have played a key role in the dissemination and promotion of specific local cults. It is interesting that a native of Lagina offered a dedication to Zeus Megistos in another group of imperial estates on the east side of the central plateau at the village of Pillitokōme, doubtless recalling the sanctuary of his native place,[91] and it is possible

that other dedications in Pillitokōme and elsewhere in the central plateau were inspired by the same *hieron*.[92] However, there was also an important temple for Zeus Megistos at Perta in northern Lycaonia,[93] and it is likely that so prominent a god was worshipped in several rural shrines. The reliefs from the Lagina sanctuary show his bust with ears of corn and bunches of grapes, leaving no doubt that this Zeus was above all a protector of crops; in the same areas he is explicitly called *Epikarpios* or *Eukarpios*.[94] At Laodicea Catacecaumene there is a Zeus Phatnios, Zeus of the stable, also shown holding ears of corn and a cluster of grapes, set up by the same imperial slave who had offered a dedication to Zeus Megistos. The allusion to the stable may reflect the fact that Laodicea lay on the courier route across Asia Minor, and the imperial domains here had special responsibilites for keeping mounts in good condition.[95] Zeus Keraunios and Zeus 'sender of thunder and lightning' were also worshipped at Laodicea.[96] The epithets recall the cult of Zeus Bronton, who was most widely worshipped in the territories of Dorylaeum and Nacolea, but whose cult extended westwards across the whole of northern Phrygia, and east into north Galatia and into the central plateau.[97]

Like the Mother Goddess Zeus naturally often took his name from a locality. In north-west Galatia, for instance, there is a large group of dedications scattered across several villages to Zeus Narenos;[98] another cult of wide repute belonged to Zeus Sarnendenos, attested in the same area of Galatia, in the eastern part of

[82] Robert, *Noms indigènes*, 449–52, 656–9; *A travers l'Asie Mineure*, 201–19.
[83] I. Kaygusuz, *Epigr. Anat.* 1 (1983), 51–60, with *Bull. ép.* (1984), 480.
[84] Strabo, 12. 5. 2, 567.
[85] *BMC Galatia*, 27 no. 17 (Caracalla).
[86] Bosch, *Ankara*, nos. 211 and 212; Popa and Berciu, *Tenth Congress*, 956–60, with texts from Apulum (*CIL* iii. 1088; *Studii si comunicari*, iv. 101–2), and Apulum (*CIL* iii. 860).
[87] See *AS* 27 (1977), 80.
[88] Sterrett, *EJ* nos. 227–8, cf. *JHS* 22 (1902), 122 no. 52 (Zeus alone); Aulock, *Lykaonien*, 76 ff. nos. 204–44. See *Historia*, 28 (1979), 425.
[89] Drew Bear, *ANRW* ii. 18. 3, 1970–3.
[90] *MAMA* vii. 1. 107, 135; 130 also presumably relates to the same sanctuary.
[91] J. G. C. Anderson, *JHS* 19 (1899), 129 no. 48.
[92] *MAMA* vii. 432, 521 (Pillitokōme); *JHS* 19 (1899), 132–3 nos. 160 (Herkenli), 161 (Eski-il, SE of Pillitokōme). Also *MAMA* i. 373 from Sengen, which lies between Laodicea and Pillitokōme, a dedication made ὅτι ἐνιαυτοῦ καλοῦ ἱερεὺς ἐγένετο, priest in a prosperous year; cf. Robert, *Hellenica* xi/xii. 546–55 on the term καλλιέτης, discussing this text.
[93] *MAMA* viii. 259, but for the full text see above, Vol. I, Ch. 7 § v n. 179. There was also a cult of Zeus Akoueos at Perta, according to an unpublished inscription found by M. H. Ballance.
[94] *MAMA* vii. 476 (Kötü Uşak) and 453 (Bulduk).
[95] *MAMA* i. 7, cf. Robert, *Hellenica*, x. 108–9, and 33–7 for Zeus Enaulios (Zeus of the stall) in Thrace. The iconography is identical to *MAMA* i. 5 and to the Zeus Megistos of the sanctuary near Ilgın (cf. *ANRW* ii. 18. 3, 1972–3). For the courier route, see above, Vol. I, Ch. 9 § II at nn. 78–86.
[96] *MAMA* vii. 7a; *Ath. Mitt.* 13 (1888), 235 no. 1: Μηνόδωρος ἀρχιερεὺς Διὶ Βροντῶντι καὶ Ἀστράπτοντι εὐχήν.
[97] For Zeus Bronton, see Cox and Cameron, *MAMA* v. pp. xxxviii ff. especially in the region of Dorylaeum and Nacolea, and Drew Bear, *ANRW* ii. 18. 3, 1992–2113, who cites with approval A. Körte, *Ath. Mitt.* 25 (1900), 410, describing the distribution of Zeus Bronton inscriptions: 'ist zugleich das Gebiet, in dem sich das phrygische Volkstamm am meistens und kräftigsten erhalten hat'; in Galatia see *RECAM* ii. 13, 74a, 77.
[98] *RECAM* ii. 11, 12, 42, 53, 67, 80, 86.

the territory of Bithynian Nicaea, and, like Zeus of Tavium, in Dacia.[99] Such cults clearly served to bind together several communities within the same region. This is shown quite explicitly by another dedication found in the same part of Galatia to Zeus 'of the seven villages'. The communities, in this case, seem to have made up the imperial estate known as the *choria Considiana*.[100]

Zeus was often associated with other deities, and one case is worth particular notice. South-west of Iconium he was regularly linked with Hermes. An inscription from Homonadensian territory near Lake Suğla recorded the dedication of a statue to Hermes Megistos and a sundial to Zeus Helios,[101] and the two gods were linked in a dedication from Isaura.[102] At Kavak on the territory of Lystra a relief shows Hermes accompanied by the eagle of Zeus,[103] and at Lystra itself a stone showing Hermes and a second god with unidentifiable attributes was dedicated to Hermes with one or two other gods, possibly Earth (*Gē*) and Zeus *Epēkoos*.[104] The pair are found elsewhere in Asia Minor, notably in the upper Tembris valley and at Dorylaeum in Phrygia,[105] but the concentration of evidence in the region of Lystra is highly suggestive and confirms the historical precision of the famous episode in Acts, where Barnabas and Paul were hailed as Zeus and his messenger. It is also worth recalling that in the Epistle to the Galatians Paul himself wrote that he had been received as though he were the messenger (*angelos*) of God, a phrase which surely recalled this incident.[106]

The third deity whose worship was virtually ubiquitous in central Asia Minor was Mēn.[107] On coins or reliefs he was usually depicted wearing a Phrygian cap and cloak, with a crescent moon behind his shoulders, carrying a pine cone and often a cock. In many instances he can be recognized by the crescent moon alone. His cult centres were spread over much of Anatolia. In Pontus there was a famous shrine of Mēn Pharnakou at Cabeira,[108] and there were notable sanctuaries in central Lydia where he was the principal deity.[109] There, often in combination with Anaeitis or Artemis Anaeitis, his sanctuaries were the main focus of authority in villages, and the gods' judgements directly governed the lives of the inhabitants (see above, Vol. I, Ch. 11 § v).

In central Anatolia his most important home was the temple of Mēn Askaēnos at Pisidian Antioch, where he was hailed as the chief god of the colony, *patrios theos*. According to Strabo there were two *hiera*, one close to the city and one in the territory.[110] The latter may be identical with the headquarters of the *Xenoi Tekmoreioi* at Sağır, while the former is certainly the sanctuary on the hill called Karakuyu about four kilometres south-east of the city site. It comprises two temples which were built around the middle of the second century BC, the larger set in a monumental *temenos* with porticoes along all four sides, up to twenty *oikoi* or houses designed to accommodate worshippers' banquets, and a small stadium where games were held at festival time. The larger temple, of Mēn himself, was an Ionic building built to a Hermogenian design, and the surrounding *temenos* was covered, inside and out, with votive dedications to the god, both inscribed and anonymous.[111] So dominant was the influence of Mēn at his own sanctuary that apart from the second smaller

[99] *RECAM* ii. 76, where the reading should be emended from Saruendenos to Sarnendenos, the form confirmed by the inscription from Göynük in the territory of Nicaea, S. Şahin, *I. Iznik*, ii. 1. 1128. For the cult in Dacia see Robert, *A travers l'Asie Mineure*, 222. See too *RE* xa. 358 and xv. 1474 (Schwabl).

[100] *RECAM* ii. 37.

[101] W. M. Calder, *CR* 24 (1910), 117 no. 2; cf. *CR* 1924, 29 no. 1, A. Deissmann, *Light from the Ancient East* (Eng. trans. of 4th edn. 1927), 281 fig. 53. There was a priest of Zeus at nearby Akkisse, ibid. no. 1, cf. Hall, *AS* 21 (1971), 161.

[102] Swoboda, *Denkmäler*, no. 146: Διὶ Βροντῶντι καὶ Ἑρμεῖ Κέλερ Χρυσάνθος ἱερεύς.

[103] S. Reinach, *Rev. arch.* (1926) ii. 281; Robert, *Hellenica*, xiii. 29.

[104] *MAMA* viii. 1, with commentary indicating the uncertainties of the restoration.

[105] Robert, *BCH* 107 (1983), 539 with n. 24, a bust of Zeus with Hermes at his right shoulder from the upper Tembris valley (early 3rd cent. AD); *OMS* ii. 1357–60, citing F. Cumont, *Catal. sculpt. inscr. antiques de Bruxelles* (1913), no. 53 and G. Rodenwaldt, *JdI* 34 (1919), 77 ff., for a relief from Dorylaeum featuring Zeus and Hermes among other gods, and citing other examples from the area, notably Mendel, *Cat. Mus. Imp.* iii. 48 ff. no. 843 from Inönü.

[106] Gal. 4: 14. See further L. Malten, *Hermes*, 75 (1940), 168–76, and A. S. Hollis, *Commentary on Ovid Metamorphoses VIII* (1970), 108–12 who both follow Calder in locating the story of Philemon and Baucis at Lake Trogitis (Suğla Göl); L.

Robert, *JSav.* (1961), 149–50 = *OMS* vii. 54–5, showed that the story belongs in Lydia near Mount Sipylus; Lane Fox, *Pagans and Christians*, 99–100.

[107] The sources, barring omissions, have all been collected by E. N. Lane, *CMRDM* i–iv: see now his essay 'Men: A Neglected Cult of Roman Asia Minor' (*sic!*), *ANRW* ii. 18. 3, 2161–74. There are useful critical observations by Horsley, *New Docs.* iii. 20–31.

[108] Strabo, 12. 3. 31, 556.

[109] See *TAM* v. 1, index; Keil, 'Die Kulte Lydiens', *ASRamsay*, 255–7.

[110] Strabo, 12. 8. 14, 577; cf. 12. 3. 31, 556. See above, Ch. 15 nn. 67–8. Compare the two shrines of Zeus Stratios at Amaseia, Cumont, *SP* ii. 145–6, 176–7.

[111] See Mitchell, in S. Mitchell and M. Waelkens, *Pisidian Antioch: The Site and its Monuments*, ch. 3, for a full description. For the psychology of anonymous dedications, note Robert, *CRAI* (1982), 132 = *OMS* v. 776, and *BCH* 107 (1983), 572 = *Documents*, 416. Both Christians and pagans knew that their names were known to God in any case, and sometimes state the fact in their inscriptions; L. Robert, *Le sanctuaire de Sinuri*, i. 103 no. 78 with n. 1; *Bull*

temple on the site, whose dedication is not known, the many inscriptions refer to remarkably few other deities: Luna, the Latin moon goddess whose appearance in a Roman colony alongside the Anatolian moon god is inevitable,[112] the Nymphs, and Zeus imported from another Roman colony, Heliopolis in Syria.[113] The cult of Mēn Askaēnos travelled abroad. Dedications have been found at Laodicea Catacecaumene, Apollonia, Anaboura in the Cillanian plain, Appola in Phrygia, Sebaste, Eumeneia, and Aphrodisias.[114] Types of Mēn Askaēnos also feature on the coinage of Pappa Tiberiopolis, Antioch's eastern neighbour, which enjoyed ties of *homonoia* with the colony.[115]

Mēn appeared in many other local guises. The epigraphy of the central plateau contains references to Mēn Andronēnos,[116] Mēn Gaineanos,[117] and, from the west side of the Axylon, to Mēn Selmeanos.[118] A temple of Mēn was built by one of the freedmen in charge of the estate of the Sergii Paulli.[119] An interesting relief found near Konya carries a dedication to *theos Ouindieinos*, the god of Vindia, set up by a citizen of Asian Hadrianoupolis. The stone shows Mēn with his typical cap and crescent, but the epithet is reminiscent of the Celtic place name Vindia, located by the Antonine itinerary between Ancyra and Pessinus precisely at the site of the old Phrygian capital of Gordium.[120] It seems legitimate to infer that Mēn, the god of Vindia, had previously been a god of Gordium, and this takes his worship back to old Phrygian times.

He was thus worshipped in local *hiera* throughout the region. His cult, like that of the Mother Goddess, extended beyond ethnic Phrygia into the highlands of Pisidia and across the Lycaonian plain. In the desolate steppe country where south-east Phrygia and Lycaonia merge west of Lake Tatta he was invoked as both god of the heaven and god of the underworld to protect graves from disturbance.[121] In Pisidia a relief of Mēn

was found at Bostandere on the site of Vasada;[122] he also occurs on coins and an inscription of Tymbriada.[123]

The most unusual and distinctive gods of the Phrygians were 'Holy and Just', *Hosion kai Dikaion*, who were at home across the whole of Phrygia and beyond, being found also in Lydia to the west and Galatia to the east. The cult was particularly widespread in the villages and the countryside, the authentic Phrygian environment, where divine justice was closer to hand than any that might be sought from officials or from the courts, and where gods ruled villages in a real sense (see above, Vol. I, Ch. 11 § v). A funerary inscription found in the Haymana district recalls how a woman had deposited two silver bracelets and some wool with a third party for safe keeping before she died. The husband who buried her concluded the epitaph by invoking Holy and Just and the all-seeing Sun to take vengeance on behalf of the deceased and her surviving children if the objects were not returned.[124] Holy and Just were naturally fully at home in the parts of Galatia where much of the population derived from Phrygian stock. In the wooded hilly country of the middle Tembris basin, immediately next to the territory of Phrygian Dorylaeum, *Hosion kai Dikaion* occur on two inscriptions, once with Apollo, the Hellenic god of divine justice, who often accompanied them.[125] Apollo was also found in company with a female goddess *Hosia* and with Holy and Just on reliefs from Dorylaeum;[126] and the same group was united in a verse text from Philomelium.[127] The pair was worshipped above all across the communities of northern and central Phrygia, from Nacolea and the Phrygian highlands, throughout the territory of Cotiaeum and the upper Tembris valley, to Aezani and Tiberiopolis.[128] The only precisely located sanctuary of

ép. (1964), 533; (1970), 383; (1971), 408; P. Herrmann, on *TAM* v. 1. 644.

[112] See Lane, *CMRDM* ii. 57–8 for the interpretation of the formula LVS as *Lunae votum solvit*.
[113] See Lane, *CMRDM* iv. 109 (*SEG* xxxi (1981), 1233) for Zeus of Heliopolis; 136 (*SEG* xxxi. 1258) for the Nymphs.
[114] *CMRDM* i nos. 130, 131, 105, 987, 101, 113. For Laodicea Catacecaumene see *MAMA* vii. 4.
[115] *BMC Lydia* etc., 233 nos. 1–2. For *homonoia* see Sterrett, *EJ* no. 97 with Levick, *Roman Colonies*, 129 n. 1.
[116] *RECAM* ii. 230.
[117] *RECAM* ii. 393.
[118] Anderson, *JHS* 19 (1899), 299 nos. 220–1; *MAMA* vii. 243–5; *CMRDM* i nos. 107–9.
[119] *MAMA* vii. 486, cf. 311.
[120] *JRS* 14 (1924), no. 1. Vindia or Vinda features in *Itin. Ant.* 201. 5, 202. 8 and Ptolemy, 5. 4. 7. Its location at the earlier Gordium was established by David French. See above, Vol. I, Ch. 4 § VI n. 114.
[121] *CMRDM* i nos. 143–51, 154–6, and unpublished texts copied by M. H. Ballance.

[122] Hall, *AS* 18 (1968), 87 no. 48, pl. xxiv *a* and *b*.
[123] *AS* 35 (1985), 53–4 no. 4.
[124] *RECAM* ii. 242; for a Phrygian inscription which attests the intervention of Holy and Just in a case of perjury, see T. Drew Bear, *GRBS* 17 (1976), 262 ff. no. 17, with commentary. See, in general, L. Robert, *BCH* 107 (1983), 515–3 = *Documents*, 359–67.
[125] *RECAM* ii. 44, 45.
[126] *MAMA* v. 11, a dedication to Hosios Dikaios. The relief on the front shows a radiate bust (presumably Helios) above a boss which is decorated with a cross. Presumably, like the boss with a cross in the pediment of a stele dedicated to Papas Zeus Sōtēr from Nacolea (*MAMA* v. p. 154 R. 19) this should not be taken as a Christian symbol. On the back of the stele is a female figure holding scales in one hand, to be identified as Hosia. *MAMA* v. 183 is a dedication to Hosion and Dikaion, Hosia, and Apollo. See also the reliefs from Dorylaeum, above, n. 40.
[127] W. M. Calder, *Rev. phil.* (1922), 130 no. 20.
[128] See Drew Bear, *Nouvelles inscriptions de Phrygie*, ch. 3 nos. 3–8 (territory of Nacolea); *MAMA* ix. 63, 64 and P64 (Aezanitis).

the pair lies at a village south of Cotiaeum. The cache of relief dedications depicts an identical couple, face-on to the viewer, one carrying the scales of justice, and the other the staff of authority.[129] A little further to the south their female counterpart, 'blessed Hosia' joins them in a dedication.[130] An unpublished inscription from the borderland between Pisidia and Phrygia invoked a leading god, perhaps Hypsistos rather than Heracles, Hosion Dikaion 'new-born child of Heracles', and a new figure, *Chrysea Parthenos*, 'golden maiden', whose name embodies the concepts of a strict sexual morality and hopes for copious abundance which were integral to Phrygian peasant consciousness.[131] Dikaiosyne, the goddess of Prymnessus, takes a natural place in this series (see above, at n. 58). A common concern for justice, vengeance, righteousness, and fair dealings between men, as well as the penetrating light of the sun which exposed all wrongdoing to view, linked together a group of indigenous or Hellenized divinities, who commonly occurred together in Phrygia. A characteristic cluster is found at Laodicea Cata-cecaumene, where there are dedications to the god Sōzōn *epēkoos*, who gives ear to all, to Apollo illustrated by a relief of Apollo, a wolf, and a radiate bust of Helios, to the 'Divine and Just God', and to the 'Divine God'.[132] Holy and Just, and a female counter-

part Hosia and Dikaia, were equally at home in central Lydia, especially in Maeonia, whose god-ruled villages mirrored exactly the pious sensibilities of Phrygian communities.[133]

The Phrygians were not renowned warriors in the ancient tradition; the mountain tribesmen of Pisidia and Isauria were. It seems no coincidence, then, that the gods of justice give way to mounted and armed warrior gods in the highland country of the south and south-west. These were variously identified with Apollo, Ares, Pluto, and Poseidon, when they were not left unhellenized, most famously as the rider god Kakasbos; the diversity of names underlines the thesis that they should not be assimilated into one another and treated as a single 'être protéiforme'.[134] Apollo Sōzōn or Sōzōn, whose monuments are above all typical of Pisidia and Pamphylia, was also found in central Anatolia around Iconium and in Phrygia, a warning that armed and mounted gods have a place there too, if not in such profusion as in the real high-land country.[135] Another fine relief from Iconium was dedicated to Poseidon, and shows the god on horseback galloping towards the left holding a trident in his left hand.[136] Poseidon was widely worshipped in south-west Asia Minor, and was evidently identified with the Greek god in his role as earthshaker, in a zone where earthquakes are common, not as god of the sea. There are reliefs from Tefenni in north-west Pisidia, Gebren, and from the country between lakes Beyşehir

---

[129] See Drew Bear, *Actes du VIIᵉ Congrès int. d'épigr. grecque et latine 1977* (1978), 359; M. Ricl, *Epigr. Anat.* 18 (1991), 24–36; A. R. R. Sheppard, *Talanta*, 12/13 (1980/1), 77–101 (*SEG* xxxi (1981), 1130). See Fig. 14.

[130] *MAMA* x. 158.

[131] Mentioned by Robert, *Hellenica*, x. 107; there are doubts about the initial dedication to Heracles, expressed in *Anadolu*, 3 (1958), 121 (= *OMS* i. 420) n. 68. Perhaps not Ἡρακλεῖ but simply Ὑψίστῳ, although the term on its own is not common (Schürer, *Sb. Berl.* (1897), 211 citing six texts from Athens and one from Carian Stratonicaea; see below, § v n. 262).

[132] *MAMA* i. 8, 9, 9a, 9b.

[133] For Holy and Just in Lydia see *TAM* v. 1. 247 (AD 257/8), 246, 248–9; 337–41; 450a, 586, 598. In the last two cases the god's power was invoked to remedy sight defects.

[134] Robert, *Hellenica*, iii. 56 ff.

[135] *JHS* 38 (1918), 138; *CR* 19 (1905), 368; Robinson, *AJA* (1927), 27. For Phrygia, see Drew Bear, *GRBS* 17 (1976), 251 no. 6 and esp. *ANRW* ii. 18. 3, 1933–9 for a series of reliefs depicting a mounted Apollo Alsenos carrying a double axe.

[136] *JRS* 14 (1924), 29 no. 8; and an unpublished example, *Bull. ép.* (1956), 319 p. 175.

Fig. 11. Stele of a priest, 'honoured by Zeus', who was 'consecrated' at his death. From the upper Tembris valley; now in Ankara Kale depot. At top, a wreath (cut away). In upper panel, bust of the priest with a bird carrying a wreath in its beak to the left and a naked figure of Hermes with purse and kerykeion to the right. The bird represented the dead man's soul, escorted by Hermes to the other world. In the main panel, bust of Zeus with two trees (perhaps representing the grove (*alsos*) at his sanctuary), two portable amphorae, and a large two-handled jar with three unidentified objects. Below, an ox. [Ἀλ]έξανδρος Μητ[ροφίλ]ον τὸν ἱερέα [τιμηθέντα] ὑπὸ Διὸς καθ[ιέρωσεν]. W. H. Buckler, W. M. Calder, and C. W. M. Cox, *JRS* 15 (1925), 154 no. 140 and E. Pfuhl and H. Möbius, *Die ostgriechischen Grabreliefs*, ii (1979), 511 no. 2120.

Fig. 12. The 'God Kings'. Small limestone altar with pyramidal top (0.62 × 0.18). On shaft a cloaked rider god, carrying a spear. Αὐρ. . . . ρμος Ιμενος . . . MY. θεοῖς βασιλεῦσ[ι] εὐχή. Yalvaç Museum (Inv. no. 310). Compare the dedications to mounted 'theoi athanatoi' from the same region, L. Robert, *BCH* 107 (1983), 583–7.

Fig. 13. Artemis of Ephesus. A crude representation from an unknown Phrygian sanctuary of Ephesian Artemis holding two unidentifiable beasts. [. .]ρκία Ἀρτεμ[ίδι] εὐχήν (0.165 × 0.145). Afyon Museum.

Fig. 14. Hosion and Dikaion. This limestone stele from the sanctuary at Yayla Baba Köy, south of Kütahya, shows two 'neuter' figures, one holding the scales of justice, the other a staff, ... ὑπὲρ τῶν εἰδίων Ὁσίῳ Δικαίῳ εὐχήν. Kütahya Museum. Virtually all the other steles recovered from this sanctuary had been deliberately broken, perhaps by Christians, in Antiquity.

11

12

13

14

Religious reliefs from central Asia Minor

and Suğla.[137] Another mounted god of north Isauria was identified with Pluto,[138] and the cult of Pluto also occurs at Lystra, Iconium, and Perta.[139] A well-studied series of reliefs whose distribution extends across south Pisidia from Termessus to the Cibyratis, and eventually to the coast at Telmessus, depicts two rider gods on either side of a female figure; the gods are commonly identified as the Dioscuri, and the goddess once by name as Artemis, at other times by the symbol of the crescent moon as Selene.[140]

The Pisidians and the other native peoples of south-west Anatolia equated their warrior gods with Ares more frequently than with any other Greek deity. At Zekeriye in eastern Pisidia there is a series of rock reliefs dedicated to him;[141] the cult occurs at Isaura Palaia (Bozkır),[142] at Isinda, and at Amblada, where coins hailed the emperor Geta as the 'new Ares'.[143] Between Bubon and Balbura in the Cibyratis a sanctuary of 'the greatest god Ares' straddled the frontier between the two cities and marked the site of a rural market which doubtless functioned on his festival days; this is only one of several attestations in this region north of Oenoanda.[144] The distinction between the native deity and the Roman or Greek war god was doubtless blurred; the dedication erected by a Roman soldier from one of the praetorian cohorts to Ares Enyalios in the country west of Lake Eğridir surely reflects both the Graeco-Roman and the indigenous tradition.[145] One relief more than any other emphasizes the military character of the native Ares, an altar erected by a village in the north part of the territory of Sagalassus at the behest of Ares Kiddeudas. On the front, with the dedication, it shows a corn stalk and a bunch of grapes; on the rear is a bull's head; to the left is a wreath, but to the right there is a splendid Pisidian panoply with full length cuirass, crested helmet in the shape of a griffin's head, a short broad-bladed sword with an eagle's head forming the pommel, and a belt lying across a round shield and two spears. The image, alongside the tokens of agricultural prosperity, is a striking and disturbing one to find in the full flowering of the Roman peace.[146]

Outside Pisidia one city in particular worshipped a native Ares, or rather Ares and the Areioi, Savatra in northern Lycaonia. Among several dedications to these gods,[147] one inscription honours a leading figure of Savatra as high priest of the imperial cult and priest of the *patrioi theoi* Ares and the Areioi.[148] One of the monuments dedicated by a soldier, L. Cattius Cornelianus, shows the god as a broad-shouldered bearded figure, a grizzled veteran of war. It comes as no surprise that the inscriptions of this small Lycaonian city mention several soldiers in Roman service.[149]

These pages have offered a selection, designed merely to evoke the native cults of central and south-western Anatolia. The distribution pattern which shows Zeus, Mother Goddesses, Mēn, and the Justice deities predominating in Phrygia and the surrounding regions, in contrast to the rider and warrior gods of northern Lycia, Pisidia, Isauria, and the Cibyratis to the south, corresponds to the distinction between the settled agricultural uplands of west-central Anatolia and the true highlands of the western Taurus mountains. In the Greek cities the old Hellenic gods were worshipped too, as would be natural, and native gods were Hellenized to suit their new surroundings. Even in the countryside the very fact that they were identified by names taken from the Greek pantheon and received dedications inscribed in Greek shows a certain modification of native cultural attitudes. Occasionally in the countryside Greek culture made palpable progress, as at the oracular shrine of Apollo at Çavdarlı, where the reliefs and sculptures, all products of the Docimian ateliers and carved from the white marble of these nearby quarries,[150] have a polish and sophistication that is far removed from the crude native reliefs typical of most country areas. Such sophisticated shrines no doubt reflect the progress made even by country dwellers to acquire Greek culture, as is also shown by the spread of literacy and the fashion for

[137] Tefenni: Robert, *Hellenica*, iii. 64 n. 2; Gebren: G. E. Bean, *Belleten*, 18 (1954), 469 ff. no. 17 (*Bull. ép.* (1956), 319), cf. *Hellenica*, vii. 56 n. 3; Suğla basin: Swoboda, *Denkmäler*, no. 111 (with a relief of a galloping horseman). There is an unpublished Poseidon relief in Isparta Museum.

[138] *JRS* 14 (1924), 68 no. 96; cf. Robert, *Hellenica*, iii. 64 n. 3.

[139] *MAMA* viii. 4 and 260, cf. *Hellenica*, xiii. 26–9; *JHS* 22 (1902), 119 no. 45, set up for Pluto by an *archiereus* of Tiberius Caesar Augustus (Nero?).

[140] L. Robert, *BCH* 107 (1983), 553–79 = *Documents*, 397–423.

[141] *Hellenica*, iii. 63 n. 4 for the reliefs, originally published by F. Sarre, *AEMÖ* 19 (1896), 48–51 and Swoboda, *Denkmäler*, 45–6.

[142] Swoboda, *Denkmäler*, no. 135.

[143] G. F. Hill, *ASRamsay*, 220 ff. no. 14; Swoboda, *Denkmäler*, no. 76.

[144] F. Schindler, *Die Inschriften von Bubon*, no. 4, interpreted by Robert, *BCH* 107 (1983), 579; for Oenoanda see *Hellenica*, iii. 63 n. 2.

[145] *SEG* vi. 597; Robert, *Hellenica*, x. 75–7.

[146] Robert, *BCH* 107 (1983), 580–3.

[147] Robert, *Hellenica*, x. 72 = Callander, in *SERP* 158 no. 1; G. F. Hill, *ASRamsay*, 221; *MAMA* viii. 227. There is some confusion about these texts, observed by Robert, *Hellenica*, xiii. 44.

[148] H. S. Cronin, *JHS* 22 (1902), 371 no. 144.

[149] *JHS* 22 (1902), 372 n. 145, for T. Servaeus and his son L. Servaeus Sabinus. There were Savatrans in the *cohors I Cyrenaica Augusta* stationed at Ancyra, Bosch, *Ankara*, no. 113. See above, Vol. I, Ch. 9 §1 n. 29.

[150] See M. Waelkens, *AJA* 89 (1985), 652 n. 87; *III Araş.* 194–5.

verse epitaphs. It is no coincidence that reliefs from the Çavdarlı shrine show Apollo in the company of the Muses.[151] However, to judge at least from the story of Paul and Barnabas, who were greeted in Lycaonian—not Greek—for all that they were taken for Greek gods, the transformation was superficial. The indigenous inhabitants of central Anatolia preserved their own indigenous cults, little affected by outside influence, until the late Roman empire.

There was, nevertheless, ample room for imports. Roman settlers brought Iuppiter Optimus Maximus to Pisidian Antioch, their most important colony,[152] to Iconium, the double community where the Roman Iuppiter acted as patron for the colonists as Minerva Zizimmene presided over the native population,[153] and to Olbasa where the colonists created games known as the *Capitolina*, recalling the Capitoline triad.[154] Individual Romans could also bring the famous civic cult with them, as is shown by a base for the three Capitoline deities, Iuppiter, Hera, and Minerva, which was set up on the territory of Bithynian Nicaea by a Roman settler whose family also had strong connections at Rome itself.[155] The role of Roman or Italian settlers was also highly significant in the introduction of the imperial cult into newly annexed provinces (see above, Vol. I, Ch. 8).

The cults of the Roman colonies, however, show more clearly than anything else that the new Roman influence did anything but cancel out existing native culture. The act of adopting the gods of the country is dramatically illustrated by the *devotio* of Publius Servilius, the Latin inscription set up on the spot after he had captured Isaura Palaia in 67 BC, in which he offered vows to whichever gods or goddesses had protected the enemy city.[156] Even at Pisidian Antioch the chief god, for Roman immigrants and natives alike, was always the Anatolian Mēn, and the villages around abounded with dedications to local gods, above all the distinctive local series distributed east and west of Sultan Dağ in the territories of Philomelium and Antioch, which honoured the 'Immortal Gods' and depict one or more mounted figures brandishing swords.[157]

Before the Romans came to Anatolia the Galatians had taken over native cults, notably by insinuating themselves into the priestly hierarchy of Pessinus, although they retained important features of their own politico-religious organization at least in the pre-Roman age.[158] From the East, Semitic settlers imported Astarte from northern Syria not only into adjoining Cilicia but north of the Taurus to Tyana, whose chief temple was dedicated to her, and to the old Assyrian merchant colony of Anisa.[159] Persian religious groups were widespread and proved defiantly tenacious, even against the Christian onslaught of the fourth century. Indeed the distribution of Persian cults across the landscape of Asia Minor is by far the best guide to the main concentrations of Persian settlement in these, their richest satrapies. The temples in Lydia, above all at Sardis, Hypaepa, and in the Hyrcanian plain remained dominant local landmarks throughout the imperial period. From the archaic period until the fourth century AD the priesthood of Artemis at Ephesus was held by a Persian family.[160] In central Asia Minor Persians were thinly spread, but they were certainly responsible for introducing Mithras, who is attested on the territory of the Phrygian cities of Amorium and Synaus, and at Pessinus and Aspona, south-east of Ancyra, in Galatia.[161] The last find-spot lies close to the border of Cappadocia where Persian cults and Persian nomenclature are a distinguishing characteristic, especially of the aristocracy. Mithras again occurs at Tyana, Caesareia, and, in the Hellenistic period, at Ariaramneia, where a Graeco-Aramaic bilingual text shows a regional official called a *stratēgos* conducting a Mazdaean ceremony for the god.[162] Demonstrably in

[151] L. Robert, *BCH* 106 (1982), 373–8; 107 (1983), 545 = *Documents*, 335–40, 389.

[152] *ILS* 7200, and note the Roman *flamines* and *sacerdotes* at Antioch, Levick, *Roman Colonies*, 88.

[153] *Historia* 28 (1979), 411 ff., see above, n. 57.

[154] *IGR* iii. 411–14; L. Robert, *CRAI* (1978), 275.

[155] L. Robert, loc. cit. on G. Mendel, *BCH* (1900), 389 no. 44 and G. Moretti, *IGUR* ii. 837.

[156] A. S. Hall, *Akten des VI Int. Kongr. Gr. und Lat. Epigraphik* (1973), 570; *AE* (1977), 816: 'Serveilius C. f. imperator / hostibus victeis, Isaura Vetere / capta, captiveis venum dateis, / se deus seive deast, / quoius in / tutela oppidum vetus Isaura / fuit, [...] votum solvit.'

[157] L. Robert, *BCH* 107 (1983), 583–7 = *Documents*, 427–31, citing a series of texts from Eyüpler in the territory of Antioch (*JRS* 2 (1912), 231), and three which probably all come from Philomelium or its territory: *JRS* 14 (1924), 25–6 no. 2; *JHS* 10 (1890), 161 no. 7; and *BCH* (1983), 586. Other unpublished inscriptions from the Antioch region in the museum of Yalvaç identify spear-carrying mounted gods as the *theoi basileioi* (see Fig. 12).

[158] See Vol. I, Ch. 4 § IV.

[159] L. Robert, *Rev. phil.* (1939), 210–1 (*OMS* ii. 1363–4); *Noms indigènes*, 499–503; see above, Vol. I, Ch. 7 § II n. 31.

[160] Robert, *CRAI* (1975), 306–30 = *OMS* v. 485–509; *Rev. num.* 18 (1976), 25–48 = *OMS* vi. 137–60; *CRAI* (1978), 271–6 = *OMS* v. 733–42; *BCH* 107 (1983), 503–9 = *Documents*, 347–53; *Fouilles d'Amyzon*, 115–17.

[161] See *ANRW* ii. 7. 2, 1065–6; M. J. Vermaseren, *Corpus Inscriptionum et Monumentorum Religionis Mithriacae*, i (1966), nos. 22, 23 for Amorium and Synaus. Devreker, *Fouilles de Pessinonte*, i. 24; *RECAM* ii. 404. Note the evidence for a Persian settlement on the E. side of Mount Dindymus, *RECAM* ii. 121 and J. Strubbe, *Mnemosyne*, 34 (1981), 121–4.

[162] Vermaseren no. 18 (Tyana); 17 (Caesareia = *CIL* iii. 6772 = 12135); 19 (Ariaramneia, see H. Grégoire, *CRAI* (1908), 445).

the last case, and in all the others except perhaps for the Caesareia dedication which was made by a Roman official, these dedications to Mithras were offered by an Iranian or Iranizing population, and should not be seen as products of the later popularization of the cult, which came from soldiers in the Roman armies.[163] Iranian cults lingered. In the fourth century when Christianity was prevalent among the majority of Cappadocians, one of the few pagan groups mentioned in the copious writings of the Cappadocian church fathers were the Magusaioi, a sect scattered throughout the country, which was supposedly descended from Babylonian settlers. These enduring pagans, who did not mix with the rest of the province's inhabitants, passed on their creed by word of mouth from father to son, and worshipped fire as a god, thereby demonstrating their Zoroastrian affiliations.[164]

It is tempting to interpret this vast diversity of cult, which reflected fundamental ethnic as well as religious differences, as evidence for the incoherence of ancient paganism, but this would be misconceived. An inscription found in the foothills of Ekecek Dağ, which rises over 2,000 metres above sea level north of Cappadocian Archelais, reveals a local woman, Flavia Prima, who dedicated three of her dependants, a man and two women, to be sacred slaves of the greatest goddess Anaeitis Barzochara, Anaeitis of the high mountain peak. The title is Persian and the text manifestly derives from a Persian mountain-top *hieron*, doubtless a modest version of the type most splendidly represented by the royal Commagenian sanctuary on Nemrud Dağ.[165] The dedication of sacred slaves at first calls to mind the sanctuaries of Iranian Aneitis in Pontus and at Acilisene in Armenia,[166] but this was not a practice peculiar to Iranian or east Anatolian cults. Parallels quoted at random for the Cappadocian inscription come from shrines for Pluto and Kore in Pisidia and for Artemis in Macedonia. Sacred slaves and great temple territories were certainly typical of Pontus and Cappadocia, witnessed by the sanctuaries of Zeus at Venasa, Ma at Pontic Comana, and Mēn Pharnakou at Cabeira, but they were also to be found in Phrygian Pessinus and Aezani, and at the impeccably Hellenized cult of Mēn Askaēnos at Pisidian Antioch.[167]

A traveller in the eastern part of the Roman empire would find cults that were new to him in every community through which he passed; occasionally he would encounter bizarre cult practices, like the fire-walking priests of Artemis Perasia at Cilician Hierapolis, or unusual oracles, none more original than the talking snake of Abonuteichus.[168] But he would always feel comfortable with the similarities, a pattern of worship based on the sacrifice of animals, the burning of offerings, and the dedication of stone monuments. Public rituals would be accompanied by food, drink, and good cheer. In the cities there would be fine stone temples which typically embodied the finest and most lavish public architecture,[169] served by a hierarchy of priests and *neokoroi*, who were not a class apart from their fellow citizens but prominent members of the community for whom the priesthoods were, among other things, simply another form of public honour. In the countryside the cults were also served by priests, but they too fitted unobtrusively into the fabric of society, often making their way in life, like many of the Christian presbyters that followed them, as peasants or artisans.

In the second century AD the oracle of Apollo at Claros in Ionia prescribed religious advice to suppliants who came from a great swathe of the eastern empire. The god couched his counsel in similar terms for men from Thrace, Caria, Lycaonia, or eastern Pontus. The influence of Claros also spread far to the west. Nothing confirms the universality of paganism better than four virtually identical Latin dedications 'to the gods and goddesses' erected at the instigation of Clarian Apollo at a fort on Hadrian's Wall, in Sardinia, in North Africa, and in Dalmatia.[170] The outlines of paganism were well defined and consistent from one city or region to another. The traveller felt at home with other men's gods as with his own. Pagan religious practice stretched beyond Graeco-Roman culture and bound together the experience of almost all the inhabitants of the ancient world. The virtually limitless tolerance which the pagan gods showed to newcomers made the system almost infinitely flexible. As Hellenized culture and literacy slowly embraced the native populations of Anatolia, it had no difficulty in acknowledging the

---

[163] There may be a reference to a Mithraic soldier at Amaseia in Pontus, *SP* ii. 132 no. 108 = Vermaseren no. 15, but the adjective εὐσεβής may indicate a Christian or a Jew.

[164] Basil, *Ep.* 258; see below, Ch. 17 § IV at nn. 147–8.

[165] *Bull. ép.* (1968), 538; (1970), 668.

[166] Strabo, 11. 14. 16, 532–3; 12. 3. 37, 559. For another possible temple of Anaeitis, E. of the Euphrates, see S. Mitchell, *Aşvan Kale* (1980), 46.

[167] The parallels from Pisidia and Macedonia were evoked, *exempli gratia*, by Robert, *Bull. ép.* (1968), 538. For the Pontic and Cappadocian temple states see above, Vol. I, Ch. 7 § II at nn. 11–12; for Pessinus, see Devreker, *Fouilles de*

Pessinonte, i. 14–15 and, at length, B. Virgilio, *Il 'tempio-stato' di Pessinunte fra Pergamo e Roma nel II–I secolo a. C.* (1981); Aezani, *MAMA* ix. pp. xxxvi–xliii; Antioch, Mitchell and Waelkens, *Pisidian Antioch*, chs. 1 and 3.

[168] L. Robert and A. Dupont-Sommer, *La Déesse de Hierapolis Castabala* (1961).

[169] Note the observation of W. Burkert, *Greek Religion* (Eng. trans. 1985), 88, quoting Karl Schefold, that Greek culture was a temple culture 'for it was in the building of temples, not of palaces, amphitheatres, or baths, that Greek architecture and art found its fulfilment'.

[170] See Lane Fox, *Pagans and Christians*, 178, 194–5.

religious beliefs and practices of Asia Minor's indigenous inhabitants as part of one and the same religious system.

III. *Jews*

The narrative of Acts opens a window onto the redoubtable Jewish groups of the dispersion in the eastern Roman provinces. At Antioch, Iconium, and later in Ephesus Jews at first listened and then swiftly objected to Paul's teaching. With the connivance of the city authorities they evicted him by force from the two Galatian cities, and followed him to Lystra where, although there was no local synagogue, they incited the mob to stone him. Jews from Ephesus were in due course to denounce Paul and his companions to the authorities in Jerusalem, setting in motion the events that eventually brought him to face trial in Rome.[171] The same story was repeated with variations in Macedonia at Philippi, where the Jews persuaded the magistrates to imprison the missionaries; at Thessalonica, where Paul's host was accused of treasonous behaviour; at Beroea; and at Corinth where he himself was arraigned by the Jews before the proconsul Gallio.[172] Luke, therefore, consistently portrayed the Jews as a section of the population which was readily distinguishable from the pagan majority; their social and religious organization was based on local synagogues; they were sufficiently respectable and respected in their cities to be able to influence decisions by local pagan magistrates; and they were tolerated, if with some exasperation, by Roman governors; above all, after initial toleration of Paul as one of their own kind, they proved implacably hostile to his Christian teaching.

It is important to note the internal divisions of those who attended the synagogues. The evidence from Antioch has already been surveyed (above, Ch. 15). There the *laos*, under the presidency of *archisynagogoi*, consisted, in the words of Paul's address, of the Israelites or children of the race of Abraham, and 'those who feared God'.[173] When Paul spoke at the second Sabbath many of the Jews and devout proselytes were persuaded by his message, but in the third week the Jews, full of jealousy, abused Paul's followers. When Paul and Barnabas tried to defend themselves the Jews turned to aristocratic women sympathizers, also described as devout (*sebomenai*), and to the leading men of the city to have the missionaries evicted. At Iconium the congregation consisted of Jews and Greeks (Acts 14: 1). At Philippi, where in place of a built

synagogue there was still only a designated place of prayer (*proseuche*),[174] another 'devout woman' (*sebomene*) of the congregation, the purple-seller Lydia from Thyateira, joined the ranks of the converted (Acts 16: 13–14). At Thessalonica Paul's address in the synagogue persuaded a large number of devout Hellenes and several of the leading women of the city, and there were similar converts at Beroea, namely many Jews as well as several Greek noblewomen and some men.[175] At Athens the synagogue contained both the Jews and the devout (*sebomenoi*, Acts 17: 17) and at Corinth there were again Jews and Hellenes (Acts 18: 4). One of the Corinthian congregation Titius Iustus, whose names suggest that he was one of the Roman colonists, is singled out, like Lydia of Thyateira, as one who revered God.[176] The overall picture is confirmed by the description of Paul's followers at Ephesus, who came from all over Asia, to form an audience of Jews and Hellenes (Acts 19: 17).

The terminology which Luke used for two of these groups is uncomplicated. Full Jews, of the race of Abraham, were called *Ioudaioi* or, in one case, *Israelitai*. One passage alone refers to proselytes, the technical term for one who was not a born Jew but a full, circumcised convert.[177] The others were variously styled Hellenes, *sebomenoi* or *sebomenai*, or (more fully) *hoi sebomenoi ton theon*, those who revered God, and *hoi phoboumenoi ton theon*, those who

---

171 Acts 13: 50; 14: 2; 21: 27.
172 Acts 16: 19–24; 17: 1–9, 10–15; 18: 12–17.
173 Acts 13: 16.

174 For the term see Schürer[2], ii. 425–6; 439–40, and note on *RECAM* ii. 209b.
175 Acts 17: 5: τῶν τε σεβομένων Ἑλλήνων πόλυ πλῆθος γυναικῶν τε τῶν πρώτων οὐκ ὀλίγαι. 17: 12: πολλοὶ μὲν οὖν ἐξ αὐτῶν (i.e. Ἰουδαῖοι) ἐπίστευσαν, καὶ τῶν Ἑλληνίδων γυναικῶν τῶν εὐσχημόνων καὶ ἀνδρῶν οὐκ ὀλίγοι.
176 Acts 18: 7; Iustus was a name often used by Jews or their sympathizers, see Robert, *Hellenica*, xi/xii. 259–62 and Drew Bear, *Nouvelles inscriptions de Phrygie*, 86, for it translated the Hebrew Zadok. Iustus' house stood beside the synagogue. Perhaps, like the Polycharmus of the famous inscription from Stobi in Macedonia, he had donated part of his own property for use as a synagogue (see M. Hengel, *ZNW* 57 (1966), 145–83, Schürer[2], iii. 1. 67). Compare the generosity of another Gentile sympathizer of Roman extraction, Iulia Severa of Acmonia, who provided a synagogue described as τὸν κατασκευασθέντα οἶκον (above, Ch. 15 n. 61). Note also the Jewish inscription from Cyme or Phocaea in Aeolis (*IGR* iv. 1327; *I. Kyme*, 45), Τατιον Στράτωνος τοῦ Ἐνπέδωνος τὸν οἶκον καὶ τὸν περίβολον τοῖς ὑπαίθροις κατασκευάσασα ἐκ τῶν ἰδίων ἐχαρίσατο τοῖς Ἰουδαίοις. The phrasing suggests that Tation herself was not Jewish. For architectural discussion see L. Robert, *Rev. phil.* (1958), 41, 46 (*OMS* v. 181 and 186).
177 Schürer[2], iii. 1. 150–76, and now J. Reynolds and R. Tannenbaum, *Jews and Godfearers at Aphrodisias* (1987), 45. The full commentary of Reynolds and Tannenbaum looks set to be only a prelude to further study of this text. For a hint at some problems, see M. Goodman, *JRS* 78 (1988), 261–2, and H. Botermann, *Zeitschrift der Savigny-Stiftung für Rechtsgeschichte* (1989), 606 ff.

feared God.[178] Despite the variations of wording it seems overwhelmingly clear that these groups should all be classed together as a third category within the community, Jewish sympathizers who had not taken the full step of converting to the Jewish law and becoming proselytes. It is also clear from Acts that Paul's converts were most frequently drawn from their ranks. The conversion of a full Jew was less common and a matter for special remark.

The *sebomenoi* of Acts should also certainly be equated with the 'God-reverers' or *theosebeis* who are attested on inscriptions in many cities of the eastern empire, in Rome itself, and in Italy.[179] Their status and significance is illuminated above all by the newly-discovered Jewish inscription from Aphrodisias, dated tentatively to the third century AD, which appears to record a list of benefactors who contributed funds for the building of a 'soup-kitchen' for the needy in their city. If the editors have correctly interpreted a difficult text, this inscription first named eighteen members of an inner circle of 'students of the law who especially praise God', made up of thirteen full Jews, three proselytes, and two *theosebeis*. On a separate column there were the names of a further seventy-four Jews and sixty-three *theosebeis* drawn from the community at large; thus the text as a whole offers ninety Jews (including proselytes) against sixty-five 'God-reverers'. Although this only represents a sample of the community at Aphrodisias, it indicates dramatically the numerical importance of the *theosebeis*. The evidence of Acts implies that they were a significant element in every synagogue that Paul visited; the inscription from Aphrodisias, although we should be wary of generalizing too readily from it,[180] shows how numerous they could be in any one place. Acts shows that this class often included prominent citizens in positions of power locally. Aphrodisias confirms this, for the first nine *theosebeis* of the longer list were all members of the city council. It is also worth remarking that Acts underlines the importance of influential female *theosebeis*. This class surely also existed at Aphrodisias, but remains undetected since the inscription lists only male donors.

An important part of the Jewish community in central Anatolia probably derived from 2,000 cleruchs from Babylon, who were sent by Antiochus III at the end of the third century BC to fortresses and the most critical points of Lydia and Phrygia, where they were expected to keep a watch over his rebellious subjects. The king wrote to his regent Zeuxis in Asia and requested that each settler be given land on which to cultivate crops and vines, and a plot for building a house. The Jewish settlers were to retain their own laws and remain immune from levies on their produce for a decade.[181] One of the critical positions in Asia was certainly the chief Lydian city of Sardis which had sided with the rebel Achaeus from 220 BC and served as his headquarters until it fell to a prolonged siege in 214. In the following year Zeuxis organized a synoecism and the rebuilding of the city; Antiochus' Jewish cleruchs were undoubtedly among the new inhabitants.[182] Three documents recorded by Josephus reveal the continued importance of the community in the first century BC. In 50/49 BC L. Antonius, the proquaestor of Asia, wrote to the Sardians with the instruction that the Jews of the city, including Roman citizens, should be allowed to use their own court to settle disputes. A city decree followed which allowed the Jews to practise their religion without obstacle, to live according to their own customs, and to adjudicate their own disputes; the city *agoranomoi* were even to make sure that they could obtain suitable types of food for their own use. Lastly, under Augustus around 12 BC, C. Norbanus Flaccus the proconsul of Asia, in accordance with imperial instructions, told the people of Sardis not to prevent the Jews from sending money for religious purposes to Jerusalem.[183] The archaeological evidence strikingly confirms this tradition; the largest synagogue yet found in Asia Minor has been one of the principal discoveries of recent excavations at Sardis. It stood on the north side of the main east–west street of the Roman city, and was an integral part of a very large bath–gymnasium complex, adjoining the palaestra. There could be no more telling architectural illustration of the integration of a privileged and respected Jewish community into a Graeco-Roman city.[184] The Jews were valued citizens of Sardis, and

---

[178] Note also the centurion Cornelius of Acts 10: 22, who was φοβούμενος τὸν Θεόν.

[179] See above, Ch. 15 n. 59 for references. The latest discussion of the problem is by Reynolds and Tannenbaum, *Jews and Godfearers*, 53–4. For scepticism in the face of a growing consensus about the godfearers, see A. T. Kraabel, 'The disappearance of the "God-fearers"', *Numen*, 28 (1981), 113–26.

[180] Note that the unpublished epigraphic evidence from Sardis apparently contains references to some eighty Jews but only six *theosebeis*; see, with a more cautious discussion than the one offered here, Reynolds and Tannenbaum, *Jews and Godfearers*, 88.

[181] Josephus, *AJ* 12. 147–53, whose authenticity need not be questioned (see Schürer², iii. 1. 17 n. 32). For the political context of the decision, see now Ph. Gauthier, *Nouvelles inscriptions de Sardes*, ii (1989), esp. 39–45.

[182] Polybius, 7. 15–17; 8. 15–21; G. M. A. Hanfmann, *Sardis from Prehistoric to Roman Times* (1983), 117–18; 135; 260 n. 20; Gauthier, *Nouvelles Inscriptions de Sardes*, ii, 13–45.

[183] Josephus, *AJ* 14. 10. 17. 235; 24. 259–61; 16. 6. 6. 171, cf. 6. 3. 162. Dated soon after 12 BC by Schürer², iii. 1. 119 n. 3 and at *MAMA* ix. 13 n.

[184] See A. R. Seager and A. T. Kraabel, in Hanfmann, *Sardis from Prehistoric to Roman Times*, 168–90 for a fine survey

their inscriptions demonstrate their own attachment to the city by advertising their local citizenship. Some were also members of the *boulē*.[185] The god-fearing city councillors of Aphrodisias are here well matched.

This detailed and suggestive evidence from Sardis and Aphrodisias helps with the sparser clues about Jewish communities in other parts of Anatolia. By the mid-first century BC there were impressive concentrations of Jews in several Phrygian cities. In his defence of Lucius Valerius Flaccus, proconsul of Asia in 62 BC, Cicero answered charges that his client had directed to Rome gold which had been collected by Jews for the temple at Jerusalem.[186] Jewish funds had been confiscated in four cities, Phrygian Apamea, Laodicea on the Lycus, Adramyttium, and Pergamum. All four were assize centres of Roman Asia in the middle of the first century BC, and it is clear that Jewish gold was collected annually at these assize centres before being sent to Jerusalem.[187] The Roman authorities themselves had no part to play in the collection and dispatch of these dues, but they were well placed to keep an eye on what went on. The sums which Flaccus found at the various centres may serve as a rough guide to the size of the Jewish populations in the districts which depended on them. Apamea in Phrygia produced almost a hundred pounds of gold, by far the largest quantity. As a Seleucid city it was surely one of the strong-points where Antiochus' Jewish settlers had been settled, but its assize district also included several other cities whose inscriptions later show them to have had significant Jewish populations, including Eumeneia, Sebaste, and above all Phrygian Acmonia. Laodicea, the assize city for the Cibyratis as well as for the communities of the Lycus and middle Maeander valleys, collected twenty pounds of gold. There were Jews at Laodicea itself, at neighbouring Hierapolis, and of course, as is now known, at Aphrodisias. The other two assize centres together, Adramyttium and Pergamum, collected 'not much'. The observation is likely to be true to the facts and not a piece of Ciceronian evasion, since there is little evidence for Jewish settlers in their respective assize districts, which covered Aeolis, Mysia, and the Troad.[188]

In the mid-first century BC, therefore, some of the largest Jewish settlements were in the Phrygian cities which belonged to the assize district of Apamea. This is fully confirmed by inscriptions of the second and third centuries AD. These were long-established Jewish communities, whose likely origin lay with Seleucid military colonization. At Apamea itself an unambiguously Jewish gravestone shows that its owner adhered to the Law of Moses.[189] Another epitaph which ends with the imprecation that anyone who disturbed the tomb would have to reckon with 'the hand of God' may be Jewish or the work of a Christian who was heavily influenced by local Jews, as was much of the Christian community at neighbouring Eumeneia (see below).[190] The most telling evidence for the importance of the local Jewish community comes from coins struck between AD 200 and 250 which illustrated the story of Noah's Ark and the Flood.[191] While local pagans could have given currency to a myth which localized an apocalyptic flood in their city (as they did at Iconium, for instance),[192] only Jews would have

---

of the Sardis evidence and its implications; A. R. Seager, *AJA* 76 (1972), 425–35 discusses the history of the building, but see now H. Botermann, *ZNW* 81 (1990), who argues that the published record to date is consistent with the view that there was no synagogue in the gymnasium building before the 4th cent., the date of the Jewish mosaics and other direct evidence. If she is right, the picture of a Jewish synagogue cheek by jowl with a pagan bath-house in the Severan period must be jettisoned.

[185] L. Robert, *Nouvelles inscriptions de Sardes*, i (1964), 37–58.
[186] Cicero, *Flac.* 68–9: 'Apameae manifesto comprehensum ante pedes praetoris in foro expensum est auri pondus c paulo minus per Sex. Caesium, equitem Romanum, castissimum hominem atque integerrimum, Laodiceae xx pondo paulo amplius per hunc L. Peducaeum, iudicem nostrum, Adramytii per Cn. Domitium legatum, Pergami non multum.' For recent discussion, see A. J. Marshall, *Phoenix*, 29 (1975), 139–54, and especially W. Ameling, *Epigr. Anat.* 12 (1988), 11–14. There is no need to insert a figure for the amount of gold collected at Adramyttium, as suggested by many editors (Ameling, op. cit. 11 n. 13; for instance T. B. L. Webster in his 1931 edn. would supply c (100)); the expression *non multum* applies both to Adramyttium and to Pergamum. Note also Josephus, *AJ* 17. 162 ff., 167 ff., and 172 ff. for the *conventus* centres of Ephesus and Sardis acting as collecting centres for Jewish contributions.
[187] For the assize system in Asia see E. W. Gray, *Tenth Congress*, ii. 965–77; C. Habicht, *JRS* 65 (1975), 80–7. Ameling, *Epigr. Anat.* 12 (1988), 9–24 provides decisive arguments against Gray to show that the system was introduced to Asia before Sulla's settlement of 85 BC, most likely when the province was first organized by M' Aquillius in 129 BC, who may, however, simply have inherited and adapted Attalid practice. The status of Laodicea is controversial, but Cicero administered justice there in 51 BC on the way to Cilicia, and it appears to have operated as the centre of the *dioecesis Cibyratica* until the time of Augustus (Ameling, 18–24). For the suggestion that the sums collected at Apamea and Laodicea were gathered from the whole assize district, see also Ramsay, *CB* i. 2 (1897), 667.

[188] Schürer², iii. 1. 17–36 summarizes the Asia Minor evidence. See also Seager and Kraabel, in Hanfmann, *Sardis from Prehistoric to Roman Times*, 181–2. For Hierapolis, see C. Humann *et al.*, *Altertümer von Hierapolis* (1898), nos. 69, 212, and 342.
[189] Ramsay, *CB* i. 2 no. 399 bis: τὸν νόμον οἶδεν Ἐιουδέων.
[190] *MAMA* vi. 231 = *CB* i. 2. 535 no. 392.
[191] See Ramsay, *CB* i. 2. 668–72; Schürer², iii. 1 (1986), 28–30; H. Leclercq, *Dictionnaire de l'archéologie chrétienne et liturgique*, i. 2 (1907), 2500–23.
[192] Stephanus Byz, s.v. Ikonion (*FGrH* 800 F. 3); see the discussion of W. M. Calder, *Journal of the Manchester*

Fig. 15. Inscription from Acmonia in Phrygia, recording the construction of a synagogue with funds provided by Iulia Severa. Now in Afyon Museum (Inv. no. E. 1619). *MAMA* vi. 264.

Fig. 16. Altar dedicated to Theos Hypsistos and *Hagia Kataphyge* (Sacred Refuge) from Sibidunda in Pisidia. Θεῷ Ὑψίστῳ καὶ Ἀγείᾳ Καταφύγῃ Ἀρτίμας υἱὸς Ἀρτίμου Μομμίου καὶ Μαρκίας ὁ αὐτὸς κτίστης ἀνέστησεν καὶ τὸν θυματιστήρ(ι)ον κάλκεον ἐκ τῶν ἰδίων. G. E. Bean, *AS* 10 (1960), 70 no. 122; cf. L. Robert, *Bull. ép.* (1961), 750; (1965), 412.

Fig. 17. Greek/Hebrew bilingual inscription from Acmonia. Probably fourth century AD. *MAMA* vi. 334.

Jewish inscriptions

connected it with the story of Noah. As the Jews of Sardis and Aphrodisias had been incorporated into the social and political fabric of their cities, so a Jewish myth, which could be traced back to the origins of the race, had become blended with the foundation legends of the Greek city of Apamea.

The Jews of Acmonia were even more conspicuous. The synagogue built in the reign of Nero by Iulia Severa (see above, Ch. 15 at nn. 61–4) here provides a bridge between the evidence of Cicero in the *Pro Flacco* and a considerable dossier of dedications, epitaphs, and other epigraphic evidence which mainly dates to the third century.[193] Acmonia has produced the only Hebrew inscription found in the interior of Asia Minor outside Sardis,[194] and there was an entire Jewish quarter in the city close to one of the gates.[195] The Jewish epitaphs include dated gravestones from AD 233, 248/9, and 255/6, all belonging to prosperous families. Aurelius Frugianus, who protected his tomb with all 'the curses that are written in the Book of Deuteronomy' had been *agoranomos*, *sitonēs*, *paraphylax*, *stratēgos*, and had fulfilled all the civic offices and liturgies.[196] T. Fl. Alexander, who invoked the curses of blindness and bodily infirmity against disturbers of his family grave, had been eirenarch, *sitonēs* twice, *agoranomos*, chairman of the council, and *stratēgos*.[197] Other family heads called on the 'curse of the scythe', the 'iron besom', and the wrath of God to punish intruders.[198] Most curious is the quasi-legal document drawn up by Aurelius Aristeas, who had bought a small parcel of land from a Jewish neighbour, Marcus son of Mathias, and bequeathed it to the neighbourhood of the Protopyleitai along with a set of garden tools, on condition that they cultivate roses, which every year, in the Roman fashion, should be scattered on the grave of his wife. Delinquents

would have to face 'the Justice of God'.[199] Acmonia's population included an important group of Roman settlers; many of these, as at Pisidian Antioch may have been attracted to Judaism, and their own practices reciprocally influenced the local Jews.[200]

Jews occured in smaller numbers elsewhere in Phrygia. In the mid-third century at Eumeneia, where the settlement may originally have been an offshoot of the Apamean or the Acmonian group, the Jews were closely linked with the Christian population and in some cases it is hard to distinguish the epitaphs of the two groups (see below). Judaizing practices, notably the worship of angels, were to be found in the earliest evidence for Christianity in southern Phrygia, especially in St Paul's admonition against angel worship in the Epistle to the Colossians. The later fruits of this close relationship between Anatolian Jews and the Christian communities living alongside them are clear in the Judaizing strain of Novatian Christianity which is attested above all in Phrygia in the late fourth and fifth centuries (see below, at nn. 268–71, and Ch. 17 §§ IX and X). Relations between Christians and Jews that were too close for orthodox and disciplinarian bishops also seem to have been normal at Laodicea on the Lycus, where church canons of the mid-fourth century were at pains to put a stop to this fraternization.[201]

The Jews were not confined to cities. The conventional picture of diaspora Jews as a distinct urban minority group, which earned a living from crafts and trade, has never carried much conviction. Inhabitants of the cities of Phrygia or Galatia in general earned a living from the land and the Jews were no exception. Epitaphs from the Phrygian upper Tembris valley include the Jewish names Mathias and Elōn, and a group of unpublished texts and reliefs both there and at Docimeium where Jews also worked in the marble quarries, feature the menorah and other Jewish symbols.[202] They serve as a reminder that Antiochus III's settlers were first and foremost farmers.

In Galatia and on the central plateau the epigraphic evidence for Jewish settlement is thinner. Except for the synagogues of Antioch and Iconium mentioned in Acts, to which may be added the account of Timothy of

---

Egyptian and Oriental Society (1924), and A. S. Hollis, *Comm. on Ovid Metamorphoses VIII*, 108–12.

[193] *MAMA* vi. 334, a bilingual text. The Sardis inscriptions remain unpublished.

[194] Robert, *Hellenica*, x. 247–56, xi/xii. 409–12, and *JSav.* (1975), 158–60 = *OMS* vii. 190–2 are the principal studies. See too A. R. R. Sheppard, *AS* 29 (1979), 169–80 and the bibliography on the Jews of Acmonia in Waelkens, *Türsteine*, 162.

[195] See below, n. 199.

[196] *MAMA* vi. 335; Robert, *Hellenica*, x. 249–50, of AD 248–9.

[197] Chamonard, *BCH* (1893), 263 no. 48, AD 233.

[198] ἀρᾶς δρεπάνου, *CB* i. 2, 562 no. 463 and 565 no. 466 = *MAMA* vi. 316; ἡ ὀργὴ Θεοῦ, *CB* i. 2. 615 no. 526 = *MAMA* vi. 325, AD 255/6 (note Robert, *Hellenica*, xi/xii. 407 on divine anger in Jewish and pagan epitaphs); σᾶρον σιδαρόν, *CB* i. 2, 654 no. 569 = *SEG* vi. 171 and *Ath. Mitt.* 25 (1900), 467 = *SEG* vi. 172. Note also in a Judaizing Christian inscription of Eumeneia, λήψεται παρὰ τοῦ ἀθανάτου Θεοῦ μάστειγα αἰώνιον, *CB* i. 2. 520 no. 361.

[199] *CB* i. 2. 562 nos. 455–7 = Laum, *Stiftungen*, ii no. 174, dated between AD 215 and 295.

[200] Robert, *JSav.* (1975), 158–60 = *OMS* vii. 190–2.

[201] For the canons of Laodicea see Hefele and Leclercq, *Histoire des Conciles*, i. 2 (1907), 989–1028, esp. canon 35 (angelolatry), 37 (sharing festivals with Jews and heretics), 38 (celebration of the Jewish Passover).

[202] Waelkens, *Türsteine*, nos. 230, 270, and 258. See Robert, *Hellenica*, xi/xii. 411. The other texts and reliefs are included in *MAMA* x. 27, 28, and 62. For Docimeium see Drew Bear, *II Araş.*, 111–12; and *Anatolia Antiqua*, 1 (1987), 102 n. 141, where he also reports evidence for Jewish workers in a marble quarry south of Amorium.

Derbe, son of a Jewish mother and a gentile father, whom Paul had circumcised (Acts 16: 1–5), there is hardly a trace of Jewish presence in the cities before the late empire. Iconium preserved a version of the legend of the Flood, although the account which survives seems to have been detached from its Jewish origins, and a late inscription begins with an invocation to 'God of the Men of Israel.' It continues, however, with the epitaph of a deacon, 'the wise Paulus', and appears to come from a heretical Judaizing Christian sect, for which there is other local evidence.[203] In north Galatia Theodotus of Ancyra is alleged to have converted both Jews and pagans in the early fourth century,[204] and there is evidence for a number of rural groups. A third-century dedication found at Malos in north-east Galatia to the great and highest God of the heavens, to his holy angels and to his adored place of worship (proseuche) was certainly a Jewish not a pagan text.[205] A village near Tavium had a cemetery in late Antiquity which contained both Jewish and Christian graves, further evidence for the close relations that existed between these groups in parts of rural Asia Minor, and a Tavian dedication to the 'highest God' by a trades-man may perhaps be treated as Jewish rather than pagan.[206] Best of all is the evidence from the village of Holanta on the east slope of Mount Dindymus in the territory of Germa, where there is an inscription with the unambiguous Jewish names Esther and Jacob, and another text evoking the power of the Jewish God.[207] Modern Holanta preserves the name of the ancient Goeleon, and the seventh-century *Life of Saint Theodore of Sykeon* reveals that Jews from this village were among the spectators at the saint's greatest miracle of exorcism, which he performed on the occasion of the annual synod held at the nearby bishopric of Germia.[208] Jews appear nowhere else in this long and detailed saint's Life, and so the narrative confirms the evidence of the inscriptions with par-ticularly telling effect.[209]

The position of the Jews in the eastern Roman em-pire was juridically privileged.[210] Since Julius Caesar's time successive Roman rulers and administrators had issued directives, which recognized their religious and social practices, the Jewish law, and attempted to guarantee their integrity against pagan interference. Despite the interminable conflicts which led to suc-cessive insurrections and civil war in Palestine, cul-minating in the great revolts of AD 66–73 and 135, the diaspora population was tolerated and escaped reprisals. Furthermore, while pagans and Jews often came into conflict, it is equally clear that they fre-quently enjoyed a peaceful and fruitful coexistence. Even at the level of cult this appears to have been true. At Didyma, Apollo's oracles praised the law of the Jews.[211] At Smyrna in AD 250 pagan worshippers of Dionysus and Jews at the festival of *Purim* stood beside one another to jeer at the impending martyrdom of the Christian Pionius.[212] The influence of Jewish beliefs and cultic organization on the monotheistic strands of paganism in the third century AD, is palpable, above all in the cults of Theos Hypsistos (see below, § v). The prosperous Jewish minorities in Phrygia, at Sardis, and at Aphrodisias had a significant and valued part to play in local life. It is here, surely, that the *theosebeis* were so significant. They were not obliged by strict adherence to the letter of Mosaic law to shun the pagan overtones of public life. As Hellenes themselves they inherited a tradition of participation in civic life, to which they had added a large measure of sympathy for Jewish cult. The beneficiaries were not only the cities, but the rest of the Jewish community, who thereby acquired a means of integrating themselves into the pagan world. It is beyond question that Sardis, Aphrodisias, Acmonia, and Apamea would have been lesser places without their participating Jewish popu-lation. Not only the Roman authorities but Hellenized local communities provided a stamp of approval.

The affinities between Jews and pagans may have run even deeper in the Asian countryside of Phrygia and Lydia. The Phrygians maintained a strict and dis-ciplined moral code within traditional village society. Much of their lives was literally ruled by the gods, especially the gods of justice and vengeance, Hosion and Dikaion, Apollo, Helios, Nemesis, Hecate, and even by abstract divinities 'Justice' ($\Delta\iota\kappa\alpha\iota\sigma\sigma\acute{\upsilon}\nu\eta$)

[203] *CIG* 9270 discussed by Ramsay, *Luke the Physician*, 402–3, accepting Boeckh's emendation $\phi\upsilon\lambda\hat{\omega}\nu$ for $\phi\omega\tau\hat{\omega}\nu$. For the Hypsistarian Gourdos of Iconium, see below, n. 292.

[204] *Life of Saint Theodotus*, ch. 3.

[205] *RECAM* ii. 209b; and see A. R. R. Sheppard, *Talanta*, 12/13 (1980–1), 94 no. 11.

[206] *RECAM* ii. 509–12, but not 504–8 from the same cemetery which are Christian. For Theos Hypsistos at Tavium see *RECAM* ii. 418.

[207] *RECAM* ii. 133, 141.

[208] For this episode, see below, Ch. 19 § III.

[209] An inscription from Sarayönü (Laodicea Catacecaumene), which had previously been taken for a dedication to 'Orondian Jehovah' ($\Upsilon o\eta$ $\Ὀρονδίω$), has now been read as a simple gravestone, *SEG* xxxiv (1984), 1375.

[210] T. Rajak, *JRS* 74 (1984), 107–23 demonstrates that there was no universal order conveying these privileges, but that they were the result of successive *ad hoc* responses by Roman authorities.

[211] *Theosophy of Tübingen*, no. 44 classes the Egyptian Hermes, Moses, and Apollonius of Tyana together as having status equal to the gods.

[212] *Life of Pionius* (ed. Musurillo), 3. 6, ἐγεμίσθη πᾶσα ἡ ἀγορὰ καὶ αἱ ὑπερῷαι στοαὶ Ἑλλήνων τε καὶ Ἰουδαίων καὶ γυναικῶν. ἐσχόλαζον γὰρ διὰ τὸ εἶναι μέγα Σάββατον.

and 'Moderation' ($\Sigma\omega\phi\rho\sigma\sigma\acute{\upsilon}\nu\eta$) (see above, Vol. I, Ch. 11 § v). When the gods' will was defied men suffered the discipline of summary and often violent punishment in the form of disease, destitution, or death. Those who escaped such drastic retribution begged for mercy and sang their lords' praises. The words that constantly recur on the confession inscriptions of Lydia are $\epsilon\dot{\upsilon}\lambda\sigma\gamma\acute{\iota}\alpha$ and the verb $\epsilon\dot{\upsilon}\lambda\sigma\gamma\epsilon\hat{\iota}\nu$. These precise concepts were also central to Jewish theology. The Jews and the indigenous peoples of Lydia and Phrygia both worshipped a wrathful god of Justice, to be appeased not only by adhering to divine law but by songs of praise. It is highly plausible that the use of the particular term $\epsilon\dot{\upsilon}\lambda\sigma\gamma\acute{\iota}\alpha$ became current in Lydia, at Sardis, and in Maeonia to the east, because of the influence of Jewish settlers in the region. The native population must soon have become aware that the Jewish community shared many of their values; they were happy enough also to share the vocabulary of their cult. In such an environment contemporaries may have been as hard pressed as modern scholars to ascertain whether a dedication to the highest god was the work of a pagan or a Jew.[213]

IV. *Christians*

According to Acts during Paul's prolonged stay at Ephesus the whole population of Asia, Jewish and Gentile, came to hear the word of the Lord (Acts 19: 8–10). By about AD 110 the younger Pliny reported that Christians were numerous in his province of Pontus and Bithynia, for persons of every age and class were being denounced and brought for trial, and the cult had spread beyond the towns to the villages and the countryside.[214] Luke may be suspected of exaggeration, and in any case his words presumably imply no more than that people from the whole province, not the entire population, heard the gospel at Ephesus which, as the seat of the provincial governor, attracted visitors on business from every quarter.[215] Pliny's testimony too is a unique and unparalleled claim that Christianity had established a major hold in northern Asia Minor by the early second century, although Lucian, in satirical vein, made Alexander of

Abonuteichus proclaim that Pontus in the middle of the century was overrun with atheists and Christians (*Alex.* 25). Other pagan writers of the period have observations to make about the Christians, but none yields helpful clues as to their number, distribution, or importance.[216]

Christian authors of course help to localize Christian communities. The letters of St Paul himself, those to the seven churches of Asia contained in the book of Revelation, and the mid-second-century letters of Ignatius of Antioch give an invaluable bird's-eye view of these groups and provide an inkling of their distinctive local character: Antioch and the other churches of south Galatia; Laodicea on the Lycus, Hierapolis, Colossae, Tralles, and Magnesia in the Maeander valley; Ephesus, Smyrna, and Pergamum, the three great rival cities in the west; Sardis, Thyateira, and Philadelphia in Lydia. The story of the martyrdom of Polycarp at Smyrna in the 150s provides evidence for another central Anatolian church, at Philomelium, for whom the account was written, and throws light on the Christian community of Smyrna itself, which had been led by its charismatic bishop for more than half a century, who had thus served as a crucial link between the apostolic age and the years of the high empire.[217] But although these texts provide the bare bones of early Christian geography, and invaluably evoke Christian ideals and values in the midst of a hostile pagan world, they too give no clue to Christian numbers and only few hints as to the impact that Christians might be making on non-Christian society.

In many areas the documentary evidence is no more helpful. There is only a handful of Christian inscriptions from Pontus and Bithynia which can be dated before the peace of the Church under Constantine: the epitaph of a carpenter born at Arados in Phoenicia who plied his trade at Nicomedia;[218] a group of probably third-century Christian epitaphs from Nicaea, identified as such by references to the tomb as a *koimeterion* (an exclusively Christian term) or by the formula that molesters of the grave would have to give

---

213 See L. Robert, *CRAI* (1978), 244–53 (= *OMS* v. 700–9), esp. 249 n. 47 on Phrygian *sophrosyne*. For possible Jewish influence in the use of the term $\epsilon\dot{\upsilon}\lambda\sigma\gamma\acute{\iota}\alpha$ in the Lydian confession inscriptions, see Robert, *Nouvelles inscriptions de Sardes*, i. 28–30; *Hellenica*, xi/xii. 392–6.
214 *Ep.* 10. 96. 9.
215 Cf. Pliny, *NH* 5. 120: 'verum Ephesum alterum lumen Asiae remotiores conveniunt Caesarienses, Metropolitae, Cilbiani inferiores et superiores, Mysomacedones, Mastaurenses, Briullitae, Hypaepeni, Dioshieritae'—all members of the Ephesian assize district. Of course Ephesus also attracted people from throughout the province and beyond.

216 See P. A. Brunt, 'Marcus Aurelius and the Christians', in C. Deroux (ed.), *Studies in Roman History and Latin Literature*, i (Coll. Latomus, 1979), 483–519.
217 There is little substantial to add to the great edn. and comm. on the works of Ignatius and Polycarp by J. B. Lightfoot, *The Apostolic Fathers: Ignatius and Polycarp*, i–iii (1889).
218 L. Robert, *BCH* 102 (1978), 413 ff. = *Documents*, 109 ff. *TAM* iv. 1. 352 may be Diocletianic; 360 is not Christian (for the sense of $\pi\iota\sigma\tau\acute{\sigma}\varsigma$ here see Robert, *Hellenica*, xiii. 36–7). 361 is probably a Novatian text of the 3rd or 4th cent. For further texts from Chalcedon and Nicomedia, mostly Christian although none before the 4th cent., see D. Feissel, *Travaux et Mémoires*, 10 (1987), 405–36.

account to God at the day of judgement;[219] the grave-stone of an Ephesian, C. Ofellius Iullus, found at Claudiopolis; and another gravestone from Claudiopolis for a member of the city nobility, Marcus Demetrianus, and his wife, who are described as 'most holy believers in God'.[220] They truly appear to have been 'aliens in a foreign land'.[221] In Pontus there are no early Christian texts from the region of Amastris, where Pliny appears to have first recognized the Christian problem, but three pre-Constantinian texts have been identified in or around Amisus further east.[222] It is striking that no epigraphic trace survives of the intensive evangelization of Neocaesareia and neighbouring areas of Pontus by Gregory the Wonder-Worker in the mid-third century, although some credit should be given to the largely legendary stories of his work there (see below, Ch. 17 §1). The same is true in Cappadocia to the south. Despite unimpeachable evidence for Christian communities at Caesareia and elsewhere by the early third century, this 'Land ohne Inschriften' has produced hardly a document to their presence, except for the epitaph at Caesareia of a Christian wagon-master from Phrygia, whose formulas link it not to the Cappadocian but to the Phrygian Christian tradition. Galatia, narrowly defined as the area settled by the Celtic tribes, has produced only a single Christian inscription which can be dated before the fourth century.[223] Palpably there is little hope of reconstructing the spread of Christianity in these parts of Anatolia from such scanty documentation.

In parts of west and south-west Asia Minor the prospects are no better. One very early Christian inscription, probably dating before 200 AD, comes from Cayster valley in southern Lydia, but it remains isolated.[224] Despite the fact that three of the 'Letters to the Seven Churches' were addressed to the Lydian cities of Sardis, Thyateira, and Philadelphia, Christian inscriptions in the area are extremely sparse. Three early texts have been found at Thyateira or in its territory, one from Sardis, none from Philadelphia.[225] The undoubted Christian communities of Ionia, particularly those of Ephesus and Smyrna, which are well attested in the written tradition, have left no epigraphic traces of the second and third centuries, and the harvest from Caria, Lycia, and Pisidia is likewise a complete blank. It is surely the case here that Christians, from prudence or simply in conformity with pagan habit, simply did not make any show of their religion on their tombstones.

In contrast there is abundant evidence for pre-Constantinian Christianity in the inscriptions of the inland regions of northern Isauria, Lycaonia, and above all of Phrygia, where the literary tradition is almost silent.[226] The contrast between the epigraphic sources of information about the spread of early Christianity in Phrygia and the literary testimonia for the cities of the western coastal area is extraordinary. The earliest Christian inscriptions of the central region date to the second half of the second century. Two dated texts (of AD 157/8 and 179/80) come from the territory of Cadi in the upper Hermus valley. The figures of the deceased are shown carrying a circular object with a cross cut on it (probably representing the bread of the Eucharist), and a bunch of grapes whose stalk in the later example ends in the distinctive T-shape of the cross.[227] Another far better-known Phrygian stone belongs to the next generation, the verse epitaph of bishop Abercius from Hierapolis in the

[219] A. M. Schneider, *Die römischen und byzantinischen Denkmäler von Iznik-Nicaea* (1944), nos. 59–61 (cf. *Bull. ep.* (1946/7), 189); *BCH* 24 (1900), 389 no. 45.

[220] F. K. Dörner, *Bericht über eine Reise in Bithynien* nos. 159–60 (= *I. Klaudioupolis*, nos. 44 and 174).

[221] 1 Pet. 2: 11; for Bithynian Christianity see also A. M. Schneider, *Reallexicon der Antike und Christentum*, ii. 410 ff.

[222] *SP* iii. 11 (Amisus), 15, 72.

[223] Caesareia: G. de Jerphanion, *BCH* 33 (1909), 67 no. 46; cf. Calder, *ASBuckler*, 25. Ancyra: apparently the only pre-Constantinian Christian inscription of the city is Bosch, *Ankara*, no. 325, a *heroon* set up by Aquilina, daughter of Archedemus, for her children Theotimus and Paulus (Timothy and Paul), as well as for herself and her husband Mommon (a Phrygian name, cf. Robert, *Hellenica*, x. 93 n. 0 and *RECAM* ii. 288 n.). As H. Leclercq, *Revue bénédictine*, 23 (1906), 95–6 observed, Paulus is a name found almost exclusively in Christian contexts, and the correct reading of his brother's name as Theotimus (rather than the earlier false reading Theoteikos) strengthens the argument that this was a Christian family. Further on N. Galatian Christianity, Ch. 17 § II n. 56.

[224] *KP³* no. 114, cf. Robert, *Hellenica*, xi/xii. 424 n. 5.

[225] Sardis: Buckler and Robinson, *Sardis*, vii. 2 no. 164 (with the Eumeneian formula which may indicate an emigrant from S. Phrygia); Thyateira: *TAM* v. 2. 1157 (εἰ δέ τις ἐναντίον ποιήσει τούτων τὸν κρίνοντα ζῶντας καὶ νέκρους Θεὸν κεχολωμένον ἔχοιτο καὶ τὴν ἰδίαν συνείδησιν: a copy of this imprecation was placed in the city archives!) and 1299 (see below Ch. 17 n. 423).

[226] Note Eusebius' evidence for non-Montanist Christians at Apamea and Eumeneia before the end of the 2nd cent., *HE* 5. 16. 22.

[227] W. M. Calder, *AS* 5 (1955), 33–5 no. 2 for the later text giving as the find-spot Çeltikçi near Gediz, which is confirmed by the notebook of I. W. Macpherson. In *MAMA* vii. p. xxxiv Calder suggested less precisely that the stone came from Aezani. For the earlier stone from Cadi which is now in Izmir, see Waelkens, *Türsteine*, 147 n. 367, and T. Lochmann, *Bulletin du Musée Hongrois des Beaux-Arts*, 74 (1991), 16 Fig. 5. The type of monument is related to gravestones found in NW Lydia in the upper Hermus valley close to Cadi, e.g. *TAM* v. 1. 36 from Bagis. Indeed the early Christian epitaph, *TAM* v. 1. 21 from the territory of Bagis may be a product of the Cadi workshops. For the discreet but not hidden crosses, cf. the cross inserted unobtrusively into the lettering of the epitaph of the Phoenician carpenter found at Nicomedia, Robert, *BCH* 102 (1978), 414 = *Documents*, 110.

Phrygian Pentapolis, who had travelled and preached in Rome and had journeyed east beyond Syria as far as Nisibis in Mesopotamia.[228] The verses claim that he encountered Christians everywhere, but this can be pressed no further than Luke's boast about Paul's congregation at Ephesus.

As these early Christian texts begin to appear more frequently, they enable us to locate Christian communities, not simply to identify individual Christians. The groups are often well defined by their distribution patterns and by distinctive funerary formulas. The isolated early gravestone from the region of Cadi is succeeded by a small cluster of second- or third-century epitaphs from Cadi, Synaus, and Ancyra Sidera, west of Aezani. One identifies a family explicitly as '*Chresiani*', while the others display the bread of the Eucharist as a plain upright cross in a disc.[229]

The eucharistic symbol also helps to identify a group of Christian epitaphs at Temenothyrae, a city which marked the western boundary of Phrygia with Lydia, and which lay within the same orbit as the north-west Phrygian cities of Cadi, Synaus, and Ancyra.[230] These inscriptions, which have been dated between the first decade and the second quarter of the third century, mention the distinctive clergy of the Montanist church, including female presbyters, an unambiguous mark of the so-called 'Phrygian heresy', which had been propagated, so its detractors said, by a renegade pagan eunuch and two dubious prophetesses.[231] It appears that the workshop which produced the grave steles of this Montanist community moved east to Acmonia after the middle of the third century, where the earliest dated Christian inscription of AD 278/9 is identified as the work of a sculptor called Phellinas of Temenothyrae. It is an economical conjecture that the Christians of Temenothyrae had been forced to move by local persecution. The fact that they were Montanists leaves open the possibility that their enemies were not pagans but members of an orthodox community.[232]

The group from Temenothyrae is the largest concentration of Montanist texts yet identified. The geography of early Montanism is still problematical. Neither the Mysian village 'Ardabau', where Montanus first began to prophesy, nor Pepuza, the 'new Jerusalem', which became the spiritual centre of the sect, can be confidently identified.[233] In fact Montanist inscriptions occur in many parts of western central Asia Minor between the third and the fifth centuries, broadly confirming the literary sources which repeatedly emphasize that their Anatolian strongholds were in Phrygia. In the third century there were Montanists at Dorylaeum, Cotiaeum, and in the Phrygian Highlands, as well as in the territory of Dionysopolis, the most likely location of Pepuza.[234] Further west in northern Lydia, Montanist epitaphs of the fifth or sixth century have been found in the territories of Philadelphia and Bagis, which use formulas and expressions that may be compared with those found on contemporary Phrygian texts from Sebaste and Hierapolis.[235] The presence of Montanists in Lydia is confirmed by a remark of the fourth-century bishop of Salamis, Epiphanius, that they took over the whole Christian Church at Thyateira between the later second and later third centuries.[236] Montanism had also spread eastwards into Galatia at an early date. Within a few years of the heresy making its first appearance around 170 they were a challenge to the orthodox congregation of Ancyra, and they persisted in numbers into the fourth century and probably beyond.[237] Some have argued that the ecstatic and prophetic character

---

[228] Most recently edited and discussed by W. Wischmeyer, *JbAC* (1980), 22–47.

[229] Discussed in the introd. to *MAMA* x; but see already Gibson, 'Christians', 101 no. 31, and 99 no. 30.

[230] E. Gibson, *GRBS* 16 (1975), 433–42; cf. Waelkens, *Türsteine*, nos. 366–7, 372–5, who dates the earliest of these stones to the first decades and the others to the second quarter of the 3rd cent. See also T. Drew Bear, *Chiron*, 9 (1979), 279–302.

[231] Eusebius, *HE* 5. 16. 6 ff.

[232] Gibson, 'Christians', no. 36 with three other early Christian texts from Acmonia and its territory; Waelkens, *Türsteine*, no. 392.

[233] A. Strobel, *Das heilige Land der Montanisten: Eine religionsgeschichtliche Untersuchung* (1980); cf. *JTS* 35 (1984), 224–6.

[234] For the Montanist inscription at Dorylaeum see H. Grégoire, *Byzantion*, 1 (1924), 708 (with fuller bibliography in Strobel, *Das heilige Land der Montanisten*, 93), a rare Christian text in a city that converted late (see below, Ch. 17 § 11 n. 52); for a possibly Montanist text from Cotiaeum, see the verse epitaph published by Calder, *JRS* 15 (1925), 142–4 no. 125; cf. *Bull. John Rylands Library* (1929), 18–20; Grégoire, *Byzantion*, 8 (1933), 60–1 (Ch. 17 § x at n. 419); for the Phrygian Highlands, see C. H. E. Haspels, *The Highlands of Phrygia* (1971), nos. 40 (below, n. 291) and 107. Territory of Dionysupolis, *MAMA* iv. 321 (?5th cent.); cf. Strobel, op. cit. 73 ff.

[235] Mendechora near Philadelphia: W. H. Buckler, *JHS* 37 (1917), 95; Grégoire, *Byzantion*, 2 (1925), 329–35, and 10 (1935), 247 ff.; Strobel, *Das heilige Land der Montanisten*, 87–9; Bagis: *TAM* v. 1. 46; Sebaste: Calder and Grégoire, *Bull. de l'Académie Royale de Belgique, Classe des Lettres*, 38 (1952), 163–83; Calder, *AS* 5 (1955), 37 no. 7; Strobel, op. cit. 89–90; Gibson, 'Christians', 137; Hierapolis: Grégoire, *Byzantion* 8 (1933), 69 ff.

[236] *Pan.* 51. 33.

[237] Eusebius, *HE* v. 16. 4; for the later history of Montanism at Ancyra, see *AS* 32 (1982), 103–4, and for other heresies below, Ch. 17 § VIII.

of Montanism had its origins in Phrygian pagan culture,[238] but the wide distribution and long persistence of the Montanists show that the intellectual and spiritual vitality of the heresy had little to do with its roots in Phrygian paganism, whatever the cultural origins of the sect may have been. As Tertullian, its most famous adherent, could explain, it offered a real doctrinal challenge to comfortable conformist thinking.[239]

On the territory of Appia in the upper Tembris valley more than twenty inscriptions are known to have been erected by 'Christians for Christians' between AD 248 and the middle of the fourth century. No unambiguous evidence supports the widely held view that they too were Montanists, although it is likely that they followed their own distinctive and possibly sectarian traditions within the Church at large.[240] The social and economic status of this community is unusually well defined for a rural population of the eastern part of the empire. They were prosperous peasants in a rich and fertile region. Their agricultural way of life was displayed explicitly on their gravestones, which were decorated with all the tools and equipment required for cereal-growing, animal husbandry and viticulture; and by the pagan dedications, mostly of the second and early third centuries, set up in local shrines of Zeus, of Mother Goddesses, and other deities, who here were pre-eminently concerned with the success of the harvest and the health of their livestock. Many of them worked on imperial or private estates where they doubtless had close dealings with imperial officials and landowners. A new study of the inscriptions from this region, which now exceed 600, appears to show that Christians outnumbered the rest of the population well before the end of the third century, and they formed a community that was as proud of its Christianity as of its rural prosperity and its aspirations to Greek culture.[241]

Christianity also flourished in the cities of southern Phrygia during the third century. The main centre was probably Phrygian Eumeneia, whose territory has produced a large number of epitaphs ending with the formulaic threat against violators of the tomb that they would have to 'reckon with God' (ἔσται αὐτῷ πρὸς τὸν Θεόν), the so-called Eumeneian formula.[242] Around twenty texts dating between AD 243 and 273, which include this formula or other clear signs of Christianity, have been recorded from Eumeneia and its villages, and from its neighbours Dionysupolis, Apamea, and Sebaste.[243] These represent only a frac-

[238] Strobel, *Das heilige Land der Montanisten*, esp. 222–30 for a survey of modern views on the origins of the heresy. His is the fullest case for the view that the roots of Montanism lay in Phrygian paganism. For the opposing view see W. Schepelern, *Der Montanismus und die phrygischen Kulte: Eine religionsgeschichtliche Untersuchung* (1929).

[239] For a penetrating discussion of Montanism, demonstrating how through its new revelations it offered a genuine and rigorist challenge to the existing Church, see Lane Fox, *Pagans and Christians*, 404–18; see also W. H. C. Frend, *Bull. John Rylands Library*, 70 (1988), 25–34 and *Rivista di storia e letteratura religiosa*, 30 (1984), 521–37 = *Archaeology and History in the Study of Early Christianity* (1988), Ch. 7.

[240] Gibson, 'Christians'. See S. Mitchell, *JTS* (1980), 201–4; T. Drew Bear, *REA* 82 (1980), 347–8; *Bull. ép.* (1979), 522. Apparently 23 stones are now known with the full formula. Gibson, 'Christians', 4 dates the series between 248 and the early 4th cent. I would place her nos. 25–30 a little later in the 4th cent. extending up to 350 at least.

[241] See J. G. C. Anderson, in *SERP* 183–227 for a fine sketch of the history of the upper Tembris valley. For local pagan monuments see now L. Robert, *BCH* 107 (1983), 526–44 = *Documents*, 370–88 and Drew Bear, *ANRW* ii. 18. 3, esp. 1952 ff. and 2038 ff. For the imperial estate see J. Strubbe, *Anc. Soc.* 6 (1975), 230–6 based above all on the great inscription from Aragua. For an important private estate, of the Sestullii, S. Mitchell, *AS* 29 (1979), 13–22 (see above, Vol. I, Ch. 10 §IV at nn. 143–4). M. Waelkens is preparing a corpus of the gravestones with special attention to the workshops which produced them. Many new texts will be published in *MAMA* x. The figures are suggested by M. Waelkens, while the local pride is well observed by Gibson, 'Christians', 143–4 and Drew Bear, *RÉA* 1980, 347–8.

[242] W. M. Calder, *ASBuckler*, 15–26; Robert, *Hellenica*, xi/xii. 423 ff.; D. Feissel, *BCH* 104 (1980), 459–70; W. M. Tabbernnee, in Horsley, *New Docs.* iii. 136–9.

[243] F. Blanchetierre, *Le Christianisme asiate aux IIe et IIIe siècles* (1977), 473, has a useful list of dated inscriptions from the 3rd cent. which is in need of some updating. Those with the 'Eumeneian fomula' appear to come from the territories of Apamea, Eumeneia, Dionysupolis, and Sebaste. Since the texts seem to relate to a relatively homogeneous community, and the boundaries between these city territories are still debatable, it is convenient to treat them as a single group. 242/3, Gibson, 'Christians', 116 no. 42 = Strobel, *Das heilige Land der Montanisten*, 118–20, without the Eumeneian formula (Üçkuyu); 243, Ramsay, *CB* i. 2. 321 (Apamea); 246 *AS* 5 (1955), 38 (Emircik, Eumeneia); it is interesting to note the lengthy form ἔσται αὐτῷ πρὸς τὸν Θεὸν καὶ νῦν καὶ τῷ παντὶ αἰῶνι καὶ μὴ τύχοιτο τῆς τοῦ Θεοῦ ἐπαγγελίας in this early text; 247/8, *MAMA* vi. 222 (Apamea, for a *pragmateutes* of Aelius Tryphon, three times Asiarch); 247/8, T. Drew Bear, *Nouvelles inscriptions de Phrygie* (1978), no. 48 (Eumeneia); 248/9, *JRS* 16 (1926), 69–70 no. 192 (Eumeneia); 250, *MAMA* vi. 226 (Apamea); c.250, Ramsay, *CB* i. 2, no. 373, when Castrius Constans was governor of Phrygia (Eumeneia); 253/4, *MAMA* iv. 353 (Kırbasan, Eumeneia); 253/4, *MAMA* iv. 354 (Sirikli, Eumeneia); 253/4, *CB* i. 2, no. 443 (Sebaste); 253/4, Ramsay, *CB* i. 2 no. 385 (Apamea); 255, *MAMA* iv. 355 (Sirikli, Eumeneia); 256/7, Ramsay, *CB* i. 2, 350 (Beyköy, Eumeneia/Apamea); 256/7, Ramsay, *CB* i. 2. 449 (Selçikler, Sebaste); 257/8, *MAMA* iv. 356 (Dumanlı, Dionysupolis?); 259, Ramsay, *CB* i. 2. 388 (Apamea); 260/1 (Ramsay, *CB* i. 2 no. 375 (Aydan); 260/1, Ramsay, *CB* i. 2. 652 (Kilter near Acmonia?); 263/4, Ramsay, *CB* i. 2 no. 365/6 (Eumeneia); 273/4, *MAMA* iv. 357 (Dumanlı, Dionysupolis?).

tion of the total number of third-century texts produced by this apparently homogeneous Christian community, which may, at Eumeneia at least, have outnumbered pagans before 300. Two bishops among them belong to the period between 250 and 300.[244] These Christians were well integrated into pagan society, for four Eumeneian texts and one from neighbouring Sebaste mention Christian councillors, one of whom, Aurelius Helix, was also a competing athlete, probably a wrestler.[245] They both influenced and were influenced by the local Jewish groups, for the Eumeneian formula, or one of its variations, was used on Jewish gravestones at Eumeneia itself and at Acmonia to the north; and two inscriptions from the same Eumeneian cemetery, including the famous epitaph of Gaius, a local legal official (*pragmatikos*), invoked the protective spirit or angel of a prominent member of the Jewish community, Rubes.[246] Here was a church in free contact with the local Jewish community, with which it had much in common, confidently holding its own in pagan surroundings.

Inscriptions show that one further tightly-knit Christian community emerged as a dominant group before the peace of the Church, in the valley of the Çarşamba river south-east of Lystra and south-west of Iconium. The clear profession of Christianity, by the use of visual symbolism or by the open mention of bishops and other clergy, show that similar toleration was to be found here as in south Phrygia (see below, Ch. 17 § II at nn. 39–44). There is no evidence to show that these Lycaonian or Isaurian Christians were descended from groups evangelized by Paul in south Galatia. The city sites of Derbe and Lystra themselves

have not produced any texts that can be assigned to this group; and Pauline tradition does not seem to have been strong in a community which was certainly sectarian, if not heretical.

The pre-Constantinian Christian community was also conspicuous in eastern Phrygia between Philomelium and Iconium, but particularly around Laodicea Catacecaumene. One third-century inscription can be assigned to the church at Philomelium, which had received the letter describing the martyrdom of Polycarp around AD 156.[247] The sectarian groups at Laodicea attracted the attention of persecuting Roman officials at the beginning of the fourth century, but were resilient enough to make rapid strides immediately thereafter. The history of these groups, however, belongs mainly to the fourth not to the third century (see below, Ch. 17 § II at n. 45 and § x).

The emergence of several Christian communities in central Anatolia, above all in Phrygia, reveals the same discrete cellular structure within Christianity as is implied by the letters of the apostolic and post-apostolic age. Each group made headway under different local conditions with more or less success. In so doing they forged different styles of belief and Christian practice. It is interesting that the Asian communities with which Paul himself had been involved, for instance the churches in south Galatia, and at Laodicea and Colossae, by no means always prospered.

There is virtually no evidence to show how the gospel had spread. It is tempting to suggest that geography had been a determining factor, and that Christianity had penetrated inland Anatolia by following the main lines of communication from the coasts: up the Maeander valley to Eumeneia, Apamea, and southern Phrygia; up the Hermus valley to Cadi, Temenothyrae, and thence to the upper Tembris valley. But Christianity was not a contagious disease passed step by step from one adjacent community to the next along the easiest lines of communication. Human agency was the key element; travel within and beyond Anatolia in the second century AD posed no serious problems; Christian missionaries, like Abercius bishop of Hierapolis, journeyed to the ends of the empire and beyond as part of their calling; the Phrygian churches had contacts in Gaul.[248] Letters were crucial not only in spreading the Christian message but in maintaining links between the

[244] For the bishops, see *JRS* 16 (1926), 56 no. 177 and 73 no. 200 with this dating against Ramsay's suggestion that they belong to the first half of the 3rd cent. Note also such overt signs of Christianity as the earliest epigraphic attestation of *ΙΧΘΥΣ* as a Christian code word, on a gravestone for a man of Antioch on the Maeander found at Apamea (*MAMA* vi. 224), and another epitaph for a shoemaker of Apamea, Aurelius Valens, which begins with the formula *ΖΩΕΠΑΡΧΧΡΕΙ*, apparently the first use of the Christogram, and perhaps to be expanded to read ζῶν ἐποίησε δοῦλος Χρίστου Χριστιανὸς Χριστιανοῖς (most recently, Gibson, 'Christians', 113 no. 40). M. Waelkens, *Actes du VIIᵉ Congrès int. d' épigr. grecque et latine 1977* (1978), 127 dates *MAMA* iv. 31 on stylistic grounds to the first quarter of the 3rd cent., making it the earliest attestation of the Eumeneian formula.

[245] The councillor from Sebaste, Ramsay, *CB* i. 2. 560 no. 451; from Eumeneia, ibid. nos. 359 and 371; *JRS* 16 (1926), 69 no. 194 and 80 no. 204. The last is Helix the wrestler, on whom see Robert, *Hellenica*, xi/xii. 423 ff. and Lane Fox, *Pagans and Christians*, 295, 302. The 3rd-cent. Christians of Phrygian Apollonia, attested to by the inscriptions *MAMA* iv. 201, 219–22, also included a family of the curial class (*MAMA* iv. 221).

[246] *JRS* 16 (1926), 61 no. 183; Robert, *Hellenica*, xi/xii, 429–35; Sheppard, *AS* 29 (1979), 175–7.

[247] *JHS* 4 (1883), 434–5 no. 43. Note also the group of Christian epitaphs of the 3rd or 4th cent. from the W. side of the central plateau, in the borderland between the provinces of Galatia and Asia, esp. in the territory of Amorium; references listed in Blanchetierre, *Le Christianisme asiate aux IIᵉ et IIIᵉ siècles*, 506–7 nos. 133–53.

[248] See Lane Fox, *Pagans and Christians*, 276–7; and 408 for Lyons.

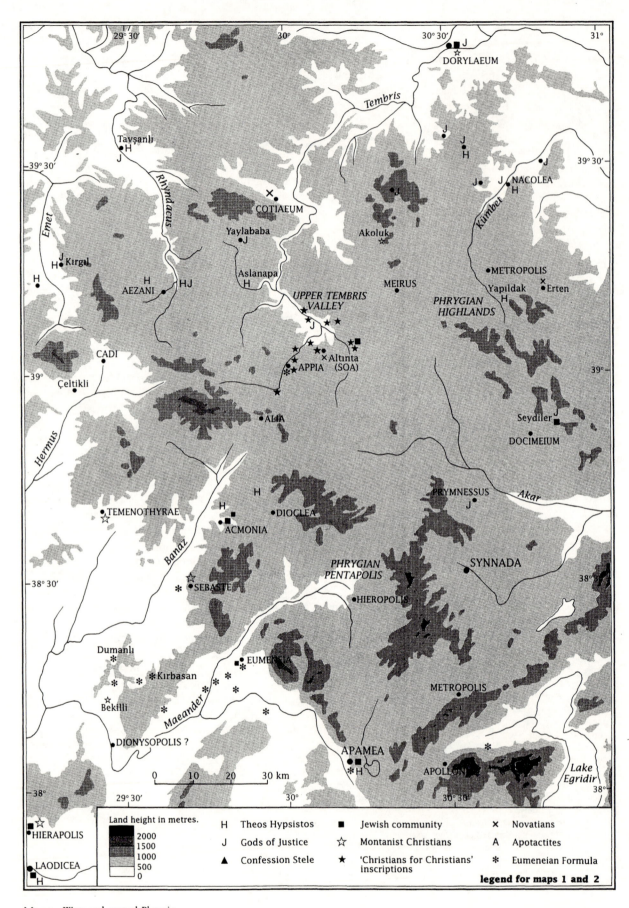

29° 30′ · 30° · 30° 30′ · 31°

Tembris

DORYLAEUM J

J
J
H

J   J NACOLEA
J   H

Tavşanlı
H
J

Rhyndaeus

COTIAEUM

Emet

Yaylababa
J

Akoluk

METROPOLIS

J Kırgıl
H

Aslanapa
H

MEIRUS

Yapıldak
× Erten
H

H

H   HJ
AEZANI

UPPER TEMBRIS
VALLEY

PHRYGIAN
HIGHLANDS

★
J ★ ★
★
★ ■
CADI

★ ★
★ ★ ×Altınta
✱★ APPIA (SOA)

Çeltikli

★

ALIA

Seydiler J ■
DOCIMEIUM

Hermus

H

H ■
ACMONIA

DIOCLEA

PRYMNESSUS
J

TEMENOTHYRAE ☆

PHRYGIAN
PENTAPOLIS

SYNNADA

Banaz

☆
✱ ●SEBASTE

HIEROPOLIS

Dumanlı
✱

✱Kırbasan
✱
✱ ★ EUMENIA
✱★★
✱ ✱ ✱
METROPOLIS
✱

Bekilli ☆
✱
Maeander

✱

DIONYSOPOLIS ?

APAMEA
✱ H
APOLLON

0   10   20   30 km

Lake
Egridir

✱

29° 30′ · 30° · 30° 30′

HIERAPOLIS ☆ ■
●

LAODICEA
■ H

Land height in metres.	H	Theos Hypsistos	■	Jewish community	×	Novatians
2000 1500 1000 500 0	J	Gods of Justice	☆	Montanist Christians	A	Apotactites
	▲	Confession Stele	★	'Christians for Christians' inscriptions	✱	Eumeneian Formula

legend for maps 1 and 2

Map 1. West and central Phrygia

churches, and a letter from afar could have as much effect as a visit from a neighbouring community.

Rather than attempt the fruitless and insoluble problem of identifying the agents who brought Christianity to central Anatolia, it seems more profitable to attempt to explain why the message which they brought found such ready listeners in Phrygia and the surrounding regions. Christian missionaries there encountered two flourishing religious traditions. The population of the country as a whole adhered to pagan beliefs which dominated and governed the lives of rural communities; they worshipped gods and goddesses who protected their crops and animals, but who also upheld the strict standards of justice and moral behaviour for which the Phrygians were famous. Judaism itself had taken root readily in this environment, and well-established diaspora communities integrated with their pagan neighbours and throve without discomfort. Jewish religious ideas commanded respect and may often have influenced the thinking and behaviour of the pagans around them. Some at least of the population may have been prepared for conversion by close acquaintance and sympathy with Judaism. Paul had had most success with Judaizing 'God-fearers'. It is absurd to imagine that large numbers of pagans in central Anatolia enjoyed the exposure to Judaism that would lead them to attend synagogues as *theosebeis*, but many more surely shared the religious outlook of such people. These were the families and communities which swelled the numbers of the churches of Phrygia, village by village, city by city, as the tide turned for Christianity during the middle years of the third century AD.

v. *One God in Heaven*

The most explicit formulations of religious thinking in late Antiquity came from the oracles of Apollo at Claros and Didyma, which between about 150 and 250 forged a new way of talking about the gods, precisely a new theology, which is central to the understanding of religious and intellectual developments of the late empire. The oracles of Didyma in particular suggest that there was a persistent effort to integrate the pantheon of paganism into a system governed by a single guiding principle or a supreme god. The origins of such thought go back at least as far as the fifth century BC, when the pre-Socratics had postulated a single guiding hand directing the kosmos,[249] and such ideas were commonly discussed by pagan thinkers of the first and second centuries AD. For instance Aelius Artistides said of Asclepius that his powers were great and numerous, or rather they were universal and not

such as man's experience could encompass. 'Those who founded the temple of Zeus Asclepius at Pergamum did it in no other sense but this. Zeus Asclepius is the one who does and distributes everything, who preserves what always exists and what comes into existence.'[250] The circular temple itself was modelled on the Pantheon at Rome, representing the whole heaven and earth in microcosm, under the protection and control of their guardian god.[251]

Much oracular theology of the late second and third centuries was collected by the pagan Porphyry in a work which was probably compiled in the 270s but is now lost, entitled *Philosophy to be Learned from Oracles*, and this in turn may have served as a source for several later collections of oracles made for different purposes. The most important of these to survive is a late fifth-century collection of oracular sayings known as the *Theosophy of Tübingen*, which formed the eighth book of a lengthy work of Christian polemic called *On True Belief*.[252] Several of these oracles may be quoted to give a flavour of their contents. *Theosophy* no. 15, with its emphasis on the primacy of fire among the elements, echoes the cosmological tradition of Heraclitus, which found much favour in the late empire, especially among worshippers of the 'Highest God', who treated fire as a holy thing: 'There is an undying burning flame above the heavens, creator of life, source of all things and origin of all things, which gives life to everything and, giving life, destroys everything.' *Theosophy* no. 43 is closer to the philosophical ideas of neo-Platonism:

Itself it is the lord of everything, born from itself, generated from itself, and it guides all things with an inexpressible skill, embracing heaven, spreading out the lands of the earth, driving the seas. It has mixed fire with water, earth with air, and land with fire; in turn it rings the changes on winter, summer, autumn, and spring, and it leads everything into the light and provides them with measured harmonies.

---

[249] W. Burkert, *Greek Religion* (Eng. trans. 1985), 305–37.

[250] Aelius Aristides, *Or.* 42. 4 (335, 4 Keil).

[251] C. Habicht, *Alt. von Perg.* viii. 3. 11–14.

[252] See G. Wolff, *Porphyrii de philosophia ex oraculis haurienda librorum reliquiae* (1856, repr. 1962); K. Buresch, *Klaros: Untersuchungen zum Orakelwesen des späteren Altertums, nebst einem Anhange, des Anecdoton Χρησμοὶ τῶν Ἑλληνικῶν θεῶν enthaltend* (1889); H. Erbse, *Fragmente griechischer Theosophien herausgegeben und quellenkritisch untersucht, Hamburger Arbeiten zur Altertumswissenschaft IV* (1941). The background to these texts is expounded in two of L. Robert's finest studies, 'Trois oracles de la Théosophie et un prophète d'Apollon', *CRAI* (1968), 568–99; 'Un oracle gravé à Oenoanda', *CRAI* (1971), 597–619 (now in *OMS* v. 584–639). They are the main focus of Lane Fox, *Pagans and Christians*, ch. 4. See too A. D. Nock, 'Oracles théologiques' (1928), repr. in his *Essays in Religion and the Ancient World*, i. 160–8.

It was clearly necessary for conventional worshippers to reconcile the abstract ideas of such a creed with the existence of the conventional Olympian gods, and another text in the *Theosophy* illustrates the process:

There is one god in the whole universe, who has set boundaries to the wheels of heavenly rotation with divine ordinances, who has distributed measures of equal weight to the hours and the moments, and has set bonds which link and balance the turnings of the heavens with one another, whom we call Zeus, from whom comes the living eternity, and Zeus bearer of all things, life-providing steward of breath, himself residing in himself, proceeding from the one into the one.

A further example is to be found on a famous inscription from the north Lycian city of Oenoanda. The first three lines of a 6-line hexameter verse inscribed on the city walls are identical with the last three lines of a 16-line text preserved in *Theosophy* no. 13. The same verses were also quoted by Lactantius as the beginning of a 21-line oracle from Claros.[253] These details raise problems which have yet to be resolved, but the inscribed section is enough to show the nature of the text:

Born of itself, without a mother, unshakeable, possessing no name, known by many names, dwelling in fire, this is god. We, his angels, are a small part of god. To those who ask this question about god, what his essential nature is, he has pronounced that *Aether* is god who sees all, on whom they should gaze and pray at dawn, looking towards the sunrise.[254]

Here then is another oracle which combines an explanation of the nature of the supreme god, redolent of the religious philosophy of the third century, with a rational explanation of the place of the traditional Olympians, Apollo among them, within this cosmological scheme, and practical instructions on the form of worship which should be offered. The Oenoanda text prescribed dawn prayer exactly at the point where the rays of the rising sun first struck the old Hellenistic city wall.[255] Beside the oracular inscription there is another more commonplace text, which reveals this remote but all-powerful divinity in the guise by which he was known to worshippers across Asia Minor and beyond, Theos Hypsistos, 'The Highest God', whose cult more than any other embodied the growing predilection to worship a remote and abstract deity in preference to the anthropomorphic figures of more conventional paganism.[256] In this case the worshipper made a dedicatory offering of a lamp, the humble earthly counterpart of the deity's divine fire. There is every reason to believe that the oracle and the dedication together identify one of the outdoor shrines of a 'Hypsistarian' sect, whose beliefs and practices overlapped substantially with contemporary Jewish and Christian practice (see below, at nn. 297–8).

One notion that these oracles should dispel at once is that there was any dichotomy in the middle and later empire between rational thinkers, who based their religious and philosophical ideas on the exercise of a logical critique, and devotees of the god or of the gods, who relied for their religious intuitions on a form of divine inspiration which was denied to others. The language and ideas of these oracles are in no way out of place in the philosophy of the period, even if they lack the elaborate argumentation that might be found in a philosophical treatise. There is no evidence for any conflict between those who adhered to intellectual reasoning and those who simply turned to the god for instruction. Porphyry's *Philosophy to be Learned from Oracles* shows that the boundaries of the rational and the irrational are not those which we would draw today.

How far does this material throw light on the religious preoccupations of the age as a whole? It might be argued that the obscure abstraction of the Didyma texts would appeal only to a small minority of the population, educated enough to respond to such subtleties; the common people, by contrast, would adhere

---

[253] For the inscription see Robert, *CRAI* (1971), 597–619; Lactantius *Div. Inst.* 1. 5. 7 is the only evidence that this was a Clarian oracle. The language is so close to several of the Didyma texts collected in the *Theosophy of Tübingen* that I wonder whether Lactantius has not made a mistake. The theological flavour is redolent of Didyma rather than Claros. Robin Lane Fox promises to publish a solution to the problems raised by the tradition. Further bibliography and discussion in Horsley, *New Docs.* ii. 39. This pagan theology is paralleled by the Chaldaean oracles, the religious philosophy of Numenius, and later of Iamblichus, all of which may have been familiar in the religious circles of Didyma and Claros. See F. W. Cremer, *Die Chaldäischen Orakel und Jamblich* de mysteriis (1969), 63 ff. and 145 ff., esp. on the divine hierarchy and on fire as the embodiment of divinity.

[254] G. Fowden, reviewing Lane Fox, in *JRS* 78 (1988), 178–9 argues vigorously that the Oenoanda oracle should be taken as the reply to a private enquiry and has nothing to do with an official public cult. The question posed to Apollo, 'Are you god, or another?', would have been 'a short fuse under the whole edifice of civic cult'. But this is to assume that civic cult was an artificial construct distinct from the beliefs and traditional practices of private citizens acting in their own right. There is no reason why civic cult should not have moved with the times as well. And if the question was risky, the answer was reassuring, leaving room for the whole pagan pantheon to be angelic servants of a supreme *Aether*.

[255] For the position of the inscription, see A. S. Hall, *ZPE* 32 (1978), 263–8.

[256] See Hall, loc. cit. Compare another dedication of λυχναψίαι, lamps, to Theos Hypsistos, from Sarıçam, a Lydian village N. of Magnesia ad Sipylum, *TAM* v. 2, 1400, and note that there is a dedication from Pergamum ['Ηλ]ίῳ θεῷ ὑψίστῳ, I. Pergamon, 330.

to the older and simpler anthropomorphic gods. This distinction seems plausible enough but is not borne out by the evidence. The countless delegations sent by civic magistrates to Claros from various parts of the eastern Mediterranean world spoke for the concerns of all their citizens not for an educated minority. Oracles concerning the nature of pagan theological belief, no less than those that prescribed or authorized particular cult practices, were addressed to a wide public.

It is possible to glean something of the range and nature of this developing pagan theology from the reliefs and dedications of Phrygia, Lydia, and other Anatolian contexts, although these naturally do not provide the explicit philosophical background of the Milesian or Clarian oracles. A group of early third-century religious acclamations illustrates the tendency both to exalt a divinity to hierarchical supremacy over the other gods, and to represent him as an abstract power or name, rather than as a tangible being. An unpublished text from Aezani, which is matched almost word for word by an inscription from the island of Thasos, calls on this 'one god' alongside his Phrygian familiars Holy and Just: 'One god in the heavens! great is the Holy! great is the Just!'[257] A very similar text from Ephesus runs 'Great is the name of the god! great is the Holy! great is the Good!' The stress on the name of God is a feature also of Jewish worship, and this text, although probably pagan, would not be out of place in a synagogue.[258] Another acclamation for the god Mēn from Saittai in Lydia, reads 'One god in heaven! Great is Mēn Ouranios! Great is the power of the immortal god!' The power of God, *Dynamis Theou*, easily reversible as *Theos Dynameōn*, the Lord of Hosts, is another aspect which received special emphasis from the Jews.[259] The use of the word one (*heis*) in such pagan inscriptions is not evidence for literal monotheism, but was designed to emphasize the unique character of the god acclaimed.[260]

However, when a man could be identified as a priest of the One and Only God and of Hosion and Dikaion, as on another Lydian inscription dated to AD 256/7, the space for other deities in his religious universe had surely been significantly reduced.[261]

Another characteristic group of dedications, which come from a sanctuary which stood close to the gymnasium of Carian Stratonicaea, was addressed to combinations such as 'highest Zeus and the divine', 'highest Zeus and the divine angel', 'highest Zeus and the good angel', 'highest Zeus and the divine heavenly angel' as well as to 'the highest god and the divine angel', 'the ruling divine and the highest', and to 'the angelic divinity'.[262] These texts draw a distinction between a highest god, identified in most but not all cases as Zeus, and the divine being or angel, who was worshipped separately as well as in consort with the highest god. The phraseology of these dedications is not without ambiguities, but the basic theological idea that they embody, that of a supreme being and his heavenly messenger, reflects in an unsophisticated form the religious philosophy of the later empire. Plotinus' Neoplatonic cosmology eventually settled for a tripartite division of the divine being between the three hypostases of Soul (*psyche*), Universal Intelligence (*nous*) and Absolute Unity (*to hen*) itself. In his view reality was generated by a process of emanation, which came not from Absolute Unity itself, far too remote to be touched in this way, but from the lower hypostases. In the second or third centuries Numenius of Apamea, whose work stands in a close relationship to theological oracles of the period, affirmed the existence of three gods or divine powers, also hierarchically arranged, namely the Father, the Creator, and the Creation, the last being identical to the Kosmos and accessible to men.[263] The less rarefied world of epigraphy offers an analogy, with 'the divine' standing in the same relationship to 'the highest god' as the lower hypostases stand to Absolute Unity, or the created Kosmos to the Father in Plotinus' and Numenius' systems. While the highest god or Zeus the highest were remote

---

[257] The Thasos text, *IG* xii. 8. 613. For a discussion of these acclamations, which are rare on stone, but much commoner on amulets, see Robert, *Hellenica* x. 85–7.

[258] Ephesus: *JÖAI* (1908), Beibl. 154–6. Compare a Jewish imprecation πρὸς τὸ ὄνομα τοῦ Θεοῦ, *CB* i. 2, 525 no. 369.

[259] KP² no. 211; *TAM* v. 1 75. For δύναμις Θεοῦ, the power of God, in Jewish or Judaizing texts, see *RECAM* ii. 141 (δύναμις Ὑψίστου); Sheppard, *AS* 29 (1979), 175–7 restores το[ῦ]το Δυνά[μεων] Θεός in ll. 49–50 of the epitaph of Gaius (see above, n. 246). Compare also an inscription from Samaria, reading Εἷς Θεὸς ὁ πάντων δεσπότης. Μεγάλη Κόρη ἡ ἀνείκητος, D. Flusser, *Israel Exploration Journal*, 25 (1975), 13–20 discussed by Horsley, *New Docs.* i. 105–7. Note that both Jews and pagans laid stress on the greatness of god; see Sterrett, *EJ* no. 138 (Antioch on the Maeander, Jewish), and Ramsay, *CB* i. 2, 700 no. 365 (Brouzos, pagan).

[260] The major study is by E. Peterson, *ΕΙΣ ΘΕΟΣ: Epigraphische, Formgeschichtliche und Religionsgeschichtliche Untersuchungen* (1926).

[261] *TAM* v. 1. 246.

[262] The texts are quoted by L. Robert, *Anadolu*, 3 (1958), 115 = *OMS* i. 414. The formulations Διὶ ὑψίστῳ καὶ Θείῳ (twice), Διὶ ὑψίστῳ καὶ θείῳ ἀγγέλῳ, and Θείῳ ἀγγελικῷ are quoted from Stratonicaea, and there is a dedication to Διὶ ὑψίστῳ καὶ θείῳ τῷ βασιλικῷ at Lagina, in the territory of Carian Stratonicaea. A new group from Stratonicaea has recently been published by E. Varınlıoğlu, *Epigr. Anat.* 12 (1988), 79 no. 6 (Διὶ ὑψίστῳ καὶ τῷ θείῳ), 85 no. 7 (Διὶ ὑψίστῳ καὶ θείῳ ἀγγέλῳ οὐρανίῳ), 86 no. 8 (θεῷ ὑψίστῳ καὶ θείῳ ἀγγέλῳ), 86 no. 9 (θεῷ βασιλεῖ καὶ ὑψίστῳ), 87 no. 10 (Δειὶ ὑψίστῳ κὲ Θείῳ), and 87 no. 11 (Διεὶ ὑψίστῳ καὶ Θίῳ).

[263] For Numenius see the edn. by E. des Places (Budé, 1973), pp. 10–14 and fr. 21. For Plotinus, J. M. Rist, *Plotinus: The Road to Reality* (1967), 21–37.

and distant from man's conception, their messengers were divinity made manifest—*angelikos* or *epiphanes*.

Divine angels had an important place in the pagan world of the second and third centuries. One of their functions is exactly illustrated by a Lydian inscription of AD 165, which shows the workings of divine justice in village society. Here the moon-god Mēn informed a thief who had stolen a garment from the local bath-house that by way of reparation he should pay the cost of the item and engrave a stele in honour of the god. The message was conveyed by an angel. An unpublished text from the same region confirms that the angel in question was indeed a divine being, not a human messenger.[264] It is easy to understand from this case how the Phrygian gods Holy and Just, who themselves intervened directly to regulate men's affairs, were in particular cast as angels. A stele found at the only securely located sanctuary of the cult, on the territory of Cotiaeum, was set up for them by the *philangelōn symbiōsis*, the 'association of the lovers of the angels'.[265] Another Lydian inscription, perhaps from the neighbourhood of Saittai, identified the god Holy and Just precisely as an angel.[266] In the inscriptions from Stratonicaea the subsidiary deity was described sometimes as *angelikos*, bringer of messages, and at others as *theios*, divine; it is reasonable to suppose that when the 'great Divine' appears in another Lydian inscription alongside the highest god, it fulfilled a similar role as a divine messenger.[267] Clearly the oracle found at Oenoanda, which ranked the lesser gods as angels, offered a view of the heavenly order which would have been instantly intelligible to the devotees of these rural Lydian shrines.

Belief in angels as divine messengers had a long history in central Anatolia, and was certainly en-couraged by Jewish practice. A Jewish dedication from north Galatia to 'the great God, highest and ruler of heaven, and to his holy angels' (τῷ μεγάλῳ Θεῷ ὑψίστῳ καὶ ἐπουρανίῳ καὶ τοῖς ἁγίοις αὐτοῦ ἀνγέλοις) might readily be taken for a pagan text were it not for the mention of the Jewish place of prayer, *proseuche*, which follows.[268] The worship of angels was the particular heresy of the earliest Christian community at Colossae, who were admonished for their error by Paul. Theodoret, commenting on Paul in the fifth century, remarked that the disease of angel worship survived until his own time in large parts of Pisidia and Phrygia.[269] A stone from the upper Tembris valley commemorates the fourth-century Christian Aquila, who was the servant of God and loved by his angels.[270] The early fourth-century gravestone of a Catharite presbyter from Laodicea Catacecaumene contains the ringing lines 'First I shall sing a hymn of praise for God, the one who sees all, second I shall sing a hymn for the first angel, Jesus Christ'. The identification of Christ as God's first angel, and the riddling use of the Semitic number 'Tisa Tisin', ninety-nine, to provide the isopsephic name of Christ, clearly mark the Jewish strain in this heretical Christian text. It is scarcely surprising that no saint was to be more widely worshipped in central Asia Minor than the archangel Michael.[271] Angels, who linked men with the gods in all three religious systems, helped to bind together the diverse strands of pagan, Jewish, and Christian belief in later Roman Anatolia.

Another intermediary was the prophet. Peasants living in the remoter reaches of inland Anatolia obviously had neither the means nor the opportunity to visit Claros or Didyma for guidance in matters theological or otherwise. In Phrygia, they had the chance to turn to individual prophets who are attested not in cities but in rural areas of north Phrygia and eastern Mysia.[272] The prophetic character of Phrygian Montanism can perhaps be linked to this local practice, although it was to assume a much deeper significance

[264] For angels, see A. R. R. Sheppard, *Talanta*, xii/xiii (1980/1), 77–101 collecting the epigraphic evidence and arguing that Jewish influence lies behind these pagan cults. Note too C. P. Jones, *Phoenix*, 36 (1982), 264–71 at 268. For the angel which carried Mēn's command see *TAM* v. 1. 159 with n.; cf. G. Petzl, *ZPE* 30 (1978), 257 n. 41.

[265] Sheppard, *Talanta* xii/xiii. 87–9 no. 8.

[266] Robert, *Anadolu*, 3 (1958), 120 (*OMS* i. 419); *TAM* v. 1. 185. The name of the god associated with the angel is missing from the stone, Ὑψίστῳ would probably fit the gap (above, n. 131).

[267] A dedication θεῷ ὑψίστῳ καὶ μεγάλῳ θε[ῷ], or better Θε[ίῳ] comes from Philadelphia in Lydia, Buckler, *JHS* 37 (1917), 93 no. 6 discussed by Robert, *Anadolu*, 3 (1958), 118 (*OMS* i. 417). A text from Borlu in Lydia (Robert, *Anadolu*, 3 (1958), 112 (*OMS* i. 411, *TAM* v. 1. 186) of AD 181 contains the dedication of a stele depicting the θεὰ Λαρμηνή to θεῷ ὑψίστῳ καὶ μεγάλῳ Θείῳ. Note also *TAM* v. 1. 609 from a village in the territory of Lydian Satala, dedicated θεῷ Θείῳ; 434 (of AD 194/5) where τὸ μέγα Θεῖον was invoked to protect the grave memorial; and 761 from Tutluca in the northern part of the territory of Iulia Gordus, where a certain Flaccus made a vow to Θείῳ, having escaped a plague, ἀργαλέην νοῦσον.

[268] See n. 205.

[269] Col. 2: 16, with Theodoret's commentary, *PG* 82. 614 and 619. Origen, *Contra Celsum*, 5. 4–5 condemned angel worship in Phrygia. See further Sheppard, *Talanta*, 11/12 (1980/1), 84 n. 39.

[270] Petrie, *SERP* 125 no. 7, cf. Sheppard, *Talanta*, 12/13 (1980/1), 90 n. 55.

[271] See below, Ch. 17 n. 406.

[272] For rural prophets see Robert, *Villes*², 91–2 and *Hellenica*, vi, 131–2 (Lydia, W. of the Hyrcanian plain); T. Wiegand, *Ath. Mitt.* (1904), 335 and *MAMA* ix. 60 (Mysia and the Myso-Phrygian border near Tiberiopolis); these texts can now be seen as part of a series found on the territory of Hadrianoi, *I. Hadr.* nos. 6, 12, 19, 23, 25–6, 29–30, 32–5; *JHS* 20 (1900), 75 no. 4, with Robert, *Ét. anat.* 99 n. 4 and *La Carie*, ii. 37 (Caria); Robert, *OMS* i. 411 ff. (Borlu in Lydia, the prophet from Saittae).

for Christian belief.[273] The common ground between paganism and Christianity again seems evident in the tombstone from Akoluk in the Phrygian highlands of the Christian, probably Montanist prophetess Nanas, who claimed to have gazed in awe on the face of the Lord. The text records her prayers and entreaties, and the hymns of praise which she sustained day and night. Her special status, as an inspired intermediary between man and god, is made clear by the expression *episkopē angelikos*, indicating her role as a messenger to the Christian community. Yet her prayers, hymns, prophecy, and angelic status were all familiar outside the Christian community. Compare this text with the famous inscription which commemorates the extraordinary Epitynchanos, one of the last standard-bearers of pagan polytheism in Phrygia, who had been honoured by Hecate, by Manes Daos Heliodromos Zeus, and by Apollo Archegetes giver of oracles, from whom he had received the true gift of prophecy. He and his family had probably been singled out as champions of the attempted pagan revival of Maximinus in 312. Epitynchanos, his parents, and his brothers all took the name Athanatos, immortal, and the title 'first high priest'. They were described as saviours of their country and givers of the law, and Epitynchanos himself claimed to have been initiated into the mysteries by the good high priestess of the people, Spatale, who had been honoured by the immortal gods within and beyond the community's boundaries since she had saved many from evil tortures.[274] Another inscription

says of Epitynchanos that he was versed in knowledge of the heavenly bodies, from which all human life derived; he knew the unerring oracles of the spirit, and spoke true prophecies to men, about what existed, about what would occur and about what had happened before. By his own virtue he had set out measures and limits of the Kosmos, but had now reached the darkness which is the lot of all men.[275] The last text breathes the same spirit as many of the theological oracles of Didyma; just as they could be quoted by Christians as harbingers of the True Belief, so Epitynchanos' theology and prophetic role was not vastly different from that of Phrygian Christian contemporaries.

Other features of the Christian epigraphy of the third century find close parallels in contemporary paganism. The all-seeing God of the Laodicean Catharite calls to mind a phrase from the most famous of all early Christian inscriptions, the epitaph of bishop Abercius, where God, the pure shepherd, is described as 'he whose eyes are great and see everything', an idea which can readily be traced in Christian writings of the second century.[276] Equally striking, however, is the parallel with the pagan Helios, whose all-seeing eye was the only guarantee of justice and vengeance for members of society unable to protect or revenge themselves by earthly means. A characteristic text from the territory of Chalcedon invoked πανεπόπτης Ἥλιος to witness any infringement of a boundary marker.[277] Helios, as we have seen, was frequently associated on inscriptions with Apollo, and with Holy and Just, both easily accommodated in the entourage of the supreme pagan deity.[278] A third-century Christian epitaph from Sebaste in Phrygia, with the Eumeneian formula that the disturber of the grave would have to settle up with God, ἔσται αὐτῷ πρὸς τὸν Θεόν, was decorated with the bust of the avenging Helios.[279] The confusion, or affinity, between the

---

[273] See Lane Fox, *Pagans and Christians*, 404–18.

[274] The epitaph of Nanas: Haspels, *Highlands*, 338 no. 106: προφήτισα / Νανας Ἑρμογένου / εὐχῆς καὶ λιτανίης / προσκυνητὸν ἄνακτα / ὕμνοις καὶ κολακίης / τὸν ἀθάνατον ἐδυσώπι, / εὐχομένη πανήμερον / παννύχιον Θεοῦ φόβον ἀπ' ἀρχῖς· / ἀγγελικὴν ἐπισκοπὴν / καὶ φώνην εἶχε μέγιστον / Νανας ηὐλλογημένη / ἧς κυμητήρ[ιον..] / κτλ. The inscription of Epitynchanos has been discussed and published on several occasions. See, in particular, Ramsay, *CB* i. 2, 566 nos. 467–9; F. Cumont, *Catalogue des sculptures et inscriptions des Musées Royaux* (Bruxelles) (1913), 158–63 no. 136; H. Grégoire, *Byzantion*, 8 (1933), 49 ff. The best explanation of how Spatale had brought an end to evil tortures is that she had persuaded Christians who were threatened with torture in Maximinus' persecution, to apostasize (although Robert, *BCH* 107 (1983), 584 n. 8 allows only a general sense, namely that by admitting devotees to the mysteries she delivered them from suffering). An earlier inscription of AD 249/50 may relate to members of the same family: Ἀγαθῇ Τύχῃ. Αὐρήλιοι Ἐπιτύγχανος καὶ Ἐπίνικος σὺν τῇ μητρὶ Τερτύλλῃ πατέρα Τελέσφορον ἀπείρωσαν. ἔτους τλδ' σὺν τῇ εἰερῷ εἰσ[π]είρῃ ἧς καὶ εἰροφάντης. λάτυπος Λούκιος (Ramsay, *REA* 3 (1901), 275, now S. G. Cole, *Epigr. Anat.* 17 (1991), 41–49 with the false provenance of Acmonia—she does not suggest any connection with the later text). If so, the religiosity of its members is palpable two generations before the 'Athanatoi'. Both texts come originally from the upper Tembris valley, see M. Waelkens, 'Privatdeifikation in Kleinasien und in der griechisch-römischen Welt', *Archéologie et religions de l'Anatolie ancienne: Mélanges en*

l'honneur du Prof. Paul Naster (1984), 285–6, who also discusses the significance of the 'consecration' of mortals, attested in both inscriptions.

[275] It is almost certain that the Epitynchanos who was high priest in 313/14 should be identified with Epitynchanos who is commemorated in this verse inscription from Doğarslan in the upper Tembris valley, A. Souter, *CR* 11 (1897), 136 ff. (ll. 9 ff.: τῆσδε μαθημοσύνης Ἐπιτύγχανον ἴδριν ἐόντα, / πνοίης δ' ἀ[π]λάνκτους εἰδότα μαντοσύνας, / θέσφατά τ' ἀνθρώποισιν ἀληθέα φημίζοντα / ὄντων, μελλόντων, ἐσσομένων πρότερο[ν], / ἄστεσι δ' ἐν πολλοῖσιν ἰθαγενέων λάχε τειμάς, / λείψας κὲ κούρους οὐδὲν ἀφαυροτέρους· / σ ῆ δ' ἀρετῇ κὲ μέτρα δαεὶς κὲ πείρατα κόσμου / εἰς ὄρφνην ἱκόμην πᾶσιν ὀφειλομένην.

[276] See A. Wilhelm. *Sb. Berl.* (1932), 830 = *Akademieschr.* ii. 374; note τὸν πανεπόπτην Θεόν, Polycarp, *Ep. ad Philippos* 7. Cf. Clement 55, 58 (64) with Lightfoot's n. on 55.

[277] D. Feissel, *Travaux et mémoires*, 10 (1987), 411–13 no. 12.

[278] See above, n. 132.

[279] LW no. 734, observed by Waelkens, in *Archéologie et religions de l'Anatolie ancienne*, 127. There is no need, however, to infer from the presence of Helios on this stone

sun-god and the God of Christianity, which has a part to play even in Constantine's conversion, seems natural enough in the religious melting pot of third-century Phrygia.

The wording of other Christian inscriptions from fourth-century Phrygia also approaches the ideas of the Didyma oracles concerning the supreme god. One begins with two lines which could be grafted onto some of the texts found in the *Theosophy of Tübingen* with no incongruity: 'No one is immortal except for the one God himself alone, he who gives birth to all things and assigns everything to everyone.'[280] If such affinities had not existed, the collection itself, which was designed to show how the truths of Christianity had been anticipated by pagan theology, could never have been compiled. Inscriptions from eastern Phrygia and Lycaonia regularly use the terms *hiereus* and *archiereus* to denote Christian priests. Late pagan texts also show traces of infection from Christian ideas. Ma, daughter of Pappas, an Isaurian priestess who paid for a temple roof to be retiled, was described as παρθένος κὲ κατὰ γένος ἱέρεια τῆς θεοῦ κὲ τῶν ἁγίων.[281] The resemblance to Christian phraseology is so striking that the editor was tempted to read Θε(οτόκ)ου for θεοῦ, making her not a priestess of the goddess and her holy attendants, but a priestess of the Virgin and the Saints.

The relationship between Christians and pagans, like that between pagans and Jews, was complex, and the difficulty of disentangling Christian, Jewish, and pagan strands from one another in the documentary evidence is a direct reflection of these complications. Constant enquiry and reflection, philosophical discussion, and the replies of oracles had taught men to think and theorize about their gods, modifying their beliefs and practices as fresh notions emerged and were adopted even by humble and uneducated groups. Pagans in a deeply religious society could not have ignored the injection of new ideas brought by Jews and Christians, especially when Christian and Jewish morality appeared to have so much in common with their own traditional standards of behaviour. It is inconceivable that their own brand of paganism should not have been affected by what they learned in the process.

It is difficult to be certain about men's affiliations in third century Anatolia, where the religions rubbed

shoulders.[282] The areas of overlap surely encouraged attempts to reconcile not only Christian with Jew, as surely occurred at Eumeneia, where Christians invoked the protection of a Jewish protective angel, but also Christian with pagan. When the proconsul of Asia of AD 250, Iulius Proculus Quintillianus, himself an initiate of the Eleusinian mysteries, examined the intransigent Smyrniot priest Pionius, he offered him the chance to sacrifice to Air, a suggestion that even a hard-line Christian might accept. Pionius, in no mood to compromise with the Jews of Smyrna, still less with an agent of the emperor Decius' anti-Christian policy, refused and went to his death.[283] Perhaps within the same generation Oenoanda had received its oracle commending the worship of *Aether*, the Upper Air. The vagueness of the oracle's phraseology, omitting to name any pagan god, has suggested to one observer the notion that it was a formula designed to suit both pagans and Christians, bringing them together in a form of worship that would be acceptable to both.[284]

Outwardly, at least, there was much in common between the paganism of late Roman Asia Minor and contemporary Judaism and Christianity. God was an awesome, remote, and abstract figure to be reached through the agency of divine intermediaries, such as angels, or human ones, such as prophets. The language which men chose to describe the supreme god of both pagans and Christians was sometimes indistinguishable, and had close affinities with language that was taken over and elaborated in the philosophy of the age. Fourth-century Christian doctrine and thought is shot through with philosophical, sometimes specifically Neoplatonic ideas, which were draped like a sophisticated cloak round the homely figure of New Testament Christianity. If the cosmological notions elaborated by philosophers and the intellectual devotees of the oracular shrines of Asia Minor could permeate down to the humblest levels of pagan society, it is surely to be expected that their Christian counterparts were similarly affected. If Clement or Origen could adapt Greek philosophy for theological purposes, the Phrygian peasant could make similar modifications to the ideas of contemporary paganism to shape his own brand of

that the Eumeneian formula, found in the inscription, was adopted by pagans.

[280] *SERP* 129 no. 11; cited below, Ch. 17 n. 440.
[281] For the terminology of pagan priesthoods on Christian texts in Lycaonia see *MAMA* i and vii indexes s.v. ἱερεύς and ἀρχιερεύς; cf. Ramsay, *Luke the Physician*, 388–9. For the inscription of Ma, see Radet and Paris, *BCH* 11 (1887), 63; Ramsay, *Pauline and Other Studies* (1906), 107–8, and *SERP* 348–50.
[282] See Robert, *Hellenica*, xi/xii. 438: 'il est difficile d'atteindre à la précision—et d'après une famille isolée—dans le monde religieux de cette Asie Mineure du IIIe siècle de notre ère où se coudoient les religions: chrétiens orthodoxes (des laxistes et les intégristes) et hérétiques de toutes les sectes, montanistes et gnostiques, juifs et judaïsants avec les doctrines d'une intensité très différente que peuvent exercer les doctrines ou les pratiques juives sur les païens et les chrétiens, païens syncrétisants et tenants de cultes qui sont alors travaillés par des mouvements rénovateurs, adorateurs du Saint et du Juste, de divinités solaires.'
[283] *Mart. Pionii*, 19.
[284] L. Robert, *CRAI* (1971), 618–19 = *OMS* v. 637–9.

Christianity. In Phrygia pagan, Christian, and Jew, living together in the same communities, in harmony more often than in conflict, found ways and devices to accommodate one another's beliefs.

One of the users of the oracle at Didyma was a member of the Milesian council, Ulpius Carpus. One of his enquiries, preserved in the *Theosophy*, had concerned the worship of Sarapis, but two inscriptions from Miletus show him to have been a prophet of the most holy and highest god, τοῦ ἁγιωτάτου καὶ ὑψίστου θεοῦ. The presence of so exalted a divinity in a Milesian context clearly fits happily with the theology of a remote and rarefied Zeus, which was developed in Didyma's oracles. It is interesting that his prophet and priest should not be a member of the highest rank in society; more significant still Ulpius Carpus, precisely in his prophetic capacity, was honoured by two associations of much humbler status, the *statio* of municipal gardeners, and the *stolos* ('fleet') of razor-fish spearers.[285] By honouring a priest of the highest and most holy god, these groups, making a bare living from selling shellfish or tending public gardens and surely representing the poorest fringe of the Milesian community, showed their devotion to the same cult.

The cults of Theos Hypsistos more than any others occupied the common ground shared by all three religious systems. The distribution of dedications, not only across Asia Minor but across the Greek-speaking parts of the later Roman empire, is well attested and has been much discussed. The term θεὸς ὕψιστος was used by Jews to describe their god as early as the Hellenistic period, but in the second and third centuries AD it appears with increasing frequency in pagan contexts, for instance in the inscriptions of Carian Stratonicaea where, on a minority of the surviving dedications, Theos Hypsistos supplanted Zeus Hypsistos. In many cases only the context of the discovery serves as a clue to the religion of the dedicator. A vow to Theos Hypsistos found at Yenice köy on the territory of Phrygian Acmonia has been identified as a Jewish or a Judaizing text on the grounds that the same site has produced an unquestionable Jewish epitaph, which ends with the threat that violators of the grave would have to settle with God the Highest and the sickle, ἔσται αὐτῷ πρὸς τὸν Θεὸν τὸν Ὕψιστον καὶ τὸ ἀρᾶς δρέπανον. A virtually identical dedication to Theos Hypsistos found in another village on Acmonia's territory, where no other Jewish evidence is to hand, is regarded as pagan.[286] Apparently pagan dedications to Theos Hypsistos have been noted in many of the villages and small cities of northern Lydia,

in the hinterland of Sardis.[287] It is not impossible that some impetus from the important Jewish community at Sardis may have helped the cult to spread. At Tavium in east Galatia, an isolated dedication to Theos Hypsistos may be connected with a group of Jewish epitaphs of late Antiquity although no obvious Jewish influence can be traced in identically worded dedications from elsewhere in Pontus and Cappadocia; the Jewish cult seems certain at two remote locations, at Malos in Galatia, and at Sibidunda in the Bozova, southern Pisidia, where the Highest God is associated with 'Sacred Refuge' (ἁγία καταφυγή), a concept derived from the Old Testament, and in particular the Psalms.[288] In the face of such examples it is prudent to be cautious about assuming that otherwise undistinctive dedications to Theos Hypsistos are necessarily pagan. The chance discovery of a Jewish text from the same site would alter the picture.

Texts discovered across northern Phrygia from Aezani to Nacolea have generally and plausibly been treated as pagan.[289] A group from the upper Tembris valley, including one of AD 256 and a very late example announcing the gift of columns and a propylon for a sanctuary of Theos Hypsistos in AD 308, are also more likely pagan than Jewish, although given the presence of Jewish families in the area, Jewish influence cannot be excluded.[290] Cross-fertilization with Christianity, however, is also in question. A remarkable inscription from the Yapıldak in the Phrygian Highlands, south of

248 no. 2, which is preceded by the formula Ἀγαθῇ Τύχῃ, comes from a village where Judaism is not previously attested and is taken for pagan (*SEG* xxvi. 1355 and 1356).

[287] *TAM* v. 1. 52, 186, 220, 266, 461a; v. 2. 897–900, 1258, and 1400; C. Naour, *Epigr. Anat.* 2 (1983), 116 no. 6; θέα ὑψίστη also in *TAM* v. 1. 359. Jewish influence might also be traced to Philadelphia where a synagogue is attested, (KP³ 32 no. 41) as well as mention of Theos Hypsistos (Keil, *ASRamsay*, 255). T. Drew Bear, *ANRW* ii. 18. 3, 2032–43, publishing new examples of the cult from Phrygia, usefully reviews most of the bibliography relevant to Theos Hypsistos in Asia Minor, and selectively beyond. The essential study remains the classic article by E. Schürer, 'Die Juden im bosporanischen Reich und die Genossenschaften der σεβόμενοι θεὸν ὕψιστον ebendaselbst', *Sb. Berl.* (1897), 200–25.

[288] *RECAM* ii. 418 and 209b, cf. n. 205 above; Pisidia: G. E. Bean, *AS* 10 (1960), 70 no. 122, with *Bull. ép.* (1961), 750 and 1965, 412, but note the clearly pagan dedication to Theos Hypsistos set up at nearby Andeda by a priest of Mēn Ouranios, *AS* 10 (1960), no. 115. Other Pisidian dedications to Theos Hypsistos, *Mon. Ant.* 23 (1914), 262 no. 174 (found between Isparta and Burdur), and *TAM* iii. 1. 32 (Termessus). For the cult on the Paphlagonian coast, at Tieium and Sinope, see Robert, *Ét. anat.* 287–8.

[289] Drew Bear, *Nouvelles inscriptions de Phrygie*, 41 no. 8; *MAMA* ix. 59; P67 (= Drew Bear, *ANRW* ii. 18. 3, 2039 no. 33); P68 (= Drew Bear, op. cit. 2041 no. 34).

[290] Drew Bear, *ANRW* ii. 18. 3, 2038 no. 32 and 2041 no. 35.

[285] L. Robert, *CRAI* (1969), 594–9 = *OMS* v. 610–15.
[286] T. Drew Bear, *GRBS* 17 (1976), 247 no. 1 and Robert, *Hellenica*, xi/xii. 399–400 from Yenice; *GRBS* 17 (1976),

Nacolea, refers to Zosimus, a man of good birth and of 'the most high people', who used inspired scriptures and Homeric verses to compile prophetic answers to enquiries, which were set down on a writing tablet. The inspired scriptures (πνευματικαὶ γραφαί) are most naturally to be taken as Christian, although the use of Homeric verse as a source of prophetic inspiration goes far beyond the conventional use of mythological topoi on Christian verse epitaphs, which is common in the area. It is tempting to make capital out of the phrase 'the highest people', λαοῦ ὑψιστοίο, to which Zosimus belonged, and see him as one of a devout group of worshippers of Theos Hypsistos, precisely Hypsistarians, whose beliefs and practices were not readily to be distinguished from those of some Christian communities.[291]

The Phrygian inscription recalls another enigmatic text which seems to hover between paganism and Christianity, the epitaph from Iconium of Gourdos, 'a good man, who sleeps here like a dove. He was among men priest of the highest god. Trokondas his successor and companion made this in his memory and adorned his tomb.'[292] Phrases here can be readily interchanged with the texts of fourth-century Christian epitaphs for Lycaonian presbyters and deacons. One report of the inscription suggests that it may originally have been flanked by crosses. Here, surely, was a Hypsistarian who had acquired so much from Christianity that conversion was only a step away, or a Christian with no compunction about identifying his God with the pagan or Jewish Theos Hypsistos. We may assume that this step had finally been taken by Neikatoris son of Xenophon, from Mysian Hadriani, who according to his epitaph, 'had gained greatest honour among all men, and brought joy to the holy people of the highest God, and charmed them with sacred songs and readings, and who sleeps now immaculate in Christ's place'.[293]

The gap was narrow indeed. The Highest God might, for some worshippers, be identified with Zeus, or acquire some of the attributes of Zeus' cult, as at Carian Stratonicaea, in the villages around Nicomedia, or at Tanais in the Crimean Bosporus, where the votive steles set up by the cult organizations of Theos Hypsistos displayed Zeus' eagle. However, devotion involved no blood sacrifice, only prayer as at Oenoanda. Virtually the only physical sign of the god's presence is the footprint on a dedication made to *theos hypsistos epēkoos* at Pisidian Termessus, a tangible indication that he paid heed to a worshipper's prayer. Otherwise no one attempted to depict so remote a power—no reliefs have been found that show the god in human form—so neither a Christian nor a Jew would be barred by a revulsion from pagan idols; homage done to the sun and to fire, sources of light and life, would cause offence only to a sensitive minority.[294]

The evidence of church fathers of the fourth century provides the final link in the chain that bound together pagans, Jews, and Christians of Asia Minor in the late empire, especially in their common focus on a highest god. Gregory of Nyssa in the *In Eunomium* contrasted the true piety of those who acknowledged the Christian God, father of all, unchanging, one and unique, with those who feigned another god beside the father. Let them be counted among the Jews and the so-called Hypsistiani, who acknowledged god as 'Hypsistos' or 'Pantokrator', but denied him the role of father.[295] The use of the term *pantokrator* was virtually confined to Jewish literature before it was adopted by the Church, while *hypsistos* was the common property of a much broader community whose beliefs inclined towards monotheism.[296] 'Hypsistiani', under the influence of Jewish theology, might well be another name for the groups which Epiphanius labelled Massaliani or Euphemitai. He described them as being purely Hellene, or pagan, acknowledging the existence of many gods but worshipping only one, calling him Pantokrator. Their form of cult involved prayer, without sacrifice, at dawn and sunset in open places of

[291] Haspels, *Highlands*, 313 no. 40 with Lane Fox, *Pagans and Christians*, 404. It is possible that the 'spiritual writings' were pagan, like, presumably the πνοία of Epitynchanos (above, n. 275), but *graphai* are more likely to be Christian.

[292] H. S. Cronin, *JHS* 22 (1902), 124 no. 58: Γούρδος ἀνὴρ ἀγαθὸς / ἐνθ' εὕδει ὥστε πέλεια / ἦεν ἐν ἀνθρώποις ἱερεὺς / θεοῦ ὑψίστου. / τῷ στήλην Τροκονδας / ὁ διάδοχος καὶ ὀπάων / τεῦξ' ἕνεκα μνήμης / καὶ κοσμήσας ἐπὶ τύμβῳ. See Ramsay, *Luke the Physician*, 389–90, who draws attention to another inscription (Sterrett, *EJ* no. 197) set up by Aur. Gourdos, a *presbyter*, for his *threptos*, whom he believes to have been the same person.

[293] R. Merkelbach, *Epigr. Anat.* 2 (1983), 142–3 (*SEG* xxxiii. 1069), with bibliography: [ὅ]ς τειμὴν πλείστην ἐκτή[σ]ατο πᾶσι βροτοῖσιν, / [εἰν ἁγί]ῳ τε λαῷ Θεοῦ ὑ[ψίσ]του ποίμνεια τέρπ[εν] / [καὶ] ψαλμοῖς τε ἁγίοις [κ]ἀναγνώσμασιν πάντας ἔθε[λγεν], / ἐν ἁγείῳ τε τόπῳ εὕδ[ει νῦν] Χριστοῦ ἄχραντο[ς].

[294] Schürer, *Sb. Berl.* (1897), 219–20. For Nicomedia see *TAM* iv. 1. 62 (Zeus Hypsistos with eagle), 80 (Theos Hypsistos

with eagle), and 81 (cf. *Bull. ép.* (1974), 579). The Termessus inscription is a dedication θεῷ ἐπηκόῳ ὑψίστῳ set up κατὰ κέλευσιν αὐτοῦ...σὺν τῷ ἐπόντι ἴχνει θεοῦ (the stone carried a bronze statue of a left foot); see Lanckoroński, *Städte Pamphyliens und Pisidiens*, ii (1892), 16 fig. 27; *TAM* iii. 1. 32; and K. Dunbabin, *JRA* 3 (1990), 88 and 95 with further bibliog.

[295] Greg. Nys. *In Eunomium*, 2 (*PG* 45. 482, 484): ὁ γὰρ ὁμολογῶν τὸν πατέρα πάντοτε καὶ ὡσαύτως ἔχειν, ἕνα καὶ μόνον ὄντα, τὸν τῆς εὐσεβείας κρατεύει λόγον.... εἰ δὲ ἄλλον τινα παρὰ τὸν πατέρα θεὸν ἀναπλάσσει, Ἰουδαίοις διαλεγέσθω ἢ τοῖς λεγομένοις Ὑψιστιανοῖς· ὧν αὕτη ἐστὶν πρὸς τοὺς Χριστιανοὺς διαφορὰ τὸ θεὸν μὲν αὐτοὺς ὁμολογεῖν αὐτὸν εἶναί τινα, ὃν ὀνομάζουσιν ὕψιστον ἢ παντοκράτορα· πατέρα δὲ αὐτὸν εἶναι μὴ παραδέχεσθαι.

[296] Schürer, *Sb. Berl.* (1897), 205.

worship known as *euketeria* or *proseuchai*, amid lamps and torches.[297] The description perfectly fits the place of prayer at Oenoanda, where worshippers will have assembled at dawn and dedicated lamps to Theos Hypsistos, precisely, according to the wording of the oracle itself, the god who 'dwelt in fire' (see above, at n. 256). Despite Epiphanius' view that these were purely pagan groups the use of the term Pantokrator indicates strong Jewish influence.[298]

Clearest of all these Christian observations is the description which Gregory of Nazianzus gave of his own father's early beliefs.

He was a branch sprung from a root not at all to be admired... (the cult was) a mixture of two elements sharply opposed to one another, Hellenic tolerance and adherence to the (Jewish) law. Shunning some parts of both it was made up from others. Its followers reject the idols and sacrifices of the former and worship fire and lamp-light; they revere the Sabbath and pay scrupulous heed not to touch certain foods, but have nothing to do with circumcision. To the humble

they are called Hypsistarians, and the Pantokrator is the only god they worship.[299]

This explicit testimony makes perfect sense of the growing number of inscriptions from Asia Minor which are so hard to classify as Jewish or pagan. Worshippers of Hypsistos might be all but Jews; equally, like Gourdos of Iconium or Zosimus of Phrygia, they might be all but Christians. No doubt Christian or Jewish rigorists would have abhorred the stance of their eclectic contemporaries who jumbled together elements of their faith in the worship of a highest god who still maintained links with the multiple but fading gods of the pagan universe. But the Hypsistarians had travelled almost the whole road towards monotheism, and stood on the brink of a new faith. The father of Gregory of Nazianzus, worshipper of Hypsistos, was converted to Christianity by a party of bishops passing through Cappadocia to attend the Council of Nicaea in 325. Within three years the elder Gregory was himself bishop of his small town, and busy preparing his community for the full experience of Cappadocian Orthodoxy.[300]

[297] Epiphanius, *Pan.* 80. 1–2: ἀλλ' ἐκεῖνοι μὲν ἐξ Ἑλλήνων ὡρμῶντο, οὔτε Ἰουδαϊσμῷ προσανέχοντες οὔτε Χριστιανοὶ ὑπάρχοντες οὔτε ἀπὸ Σαμαρειτῶν, ἀλλὰ μόνον Ἕλληνες ὄντες δῆθεν, καὶ θεοὺς μὲν λέγοντες, μηδενὶ μηδὲν προσκυνοῦντες, ἑνὶ δὲ μόνον δῆθεν τὸ σέβας νέμοντες καὶ καλοῦντες παντοκράτορα. For their prayers they used outdoor places of worship ὡς προσευχὰς καλούμενα καὶ εὐκτήρια, ἐν ἄλλοις δὲ τόποις φύσει καὶ ἐκκλησίας ὁμοίωμά τι ποιήσαντες, καθ' ἑσπέραν καὶ κατὰ τὴν ἕω μετὰ πολλῆς λυχναψίας καὶ φώτων συναθροιζόμενοι.

[298] Schürer, *Sb. Berl.* (1897), 221 connects the worship of fire with Persian influence. This is possible, especially in Cappadocia where Persian religious traditions were still strong in the 4th cent., but fire worship and the cult of Theos Hypsistos were also central to the Greek tradition, promulgated by oracles at Didyma and Claros, and it is probably otiose to seek further eastern influence.

[299] Greg. Naz. *Or.* 18. 5 (PG 35. 990 ff.): ἐκεῖνος τοίνυν... ῥίζης ἐγένετο βλάστημα οὐκ ἐπαινετῆς... ἐκ δυοῖν ἐναντιωτάτοιν συνκεκραμένης Ἑλληνικῆς τε πλάνης καὶ νομικῆς τερατείας. ὧν ἀμφοτέρων τὰ μέρη φυγὼν ἐκ μερῶν συνετέθη. τῆς μὲν γὰρ τὰ εἴδωλα καὶ τὰς θυσίας ἀποπεμπόμενος τιμῶσι τὸ πῦρ καὶ τὰ λύχνα· τῆς δὲ τὸ σάββατον αἰδούμενοι καὶ τῆς περὶ τὰ βρώματα ἔστιν ἃ μικρολογίαν τὴν περιτομὴν ἀτιμάζουσιν. Ὑψιστάριοι τοῖς ταπεινοῖς ὄνομα, καὶ ὁ Παντοκράτωρ δὴ μόνος αὐτοῖς σεβάσμιος. For Cappadocian Jewish communities, notably at Caesareia, see Schürer², iii. 1. 35. Note also Ramsay, *Luke the Physician*, 401–2 on Hypsistarians.

[300] See below, Ch. 17 § IV n. 86.

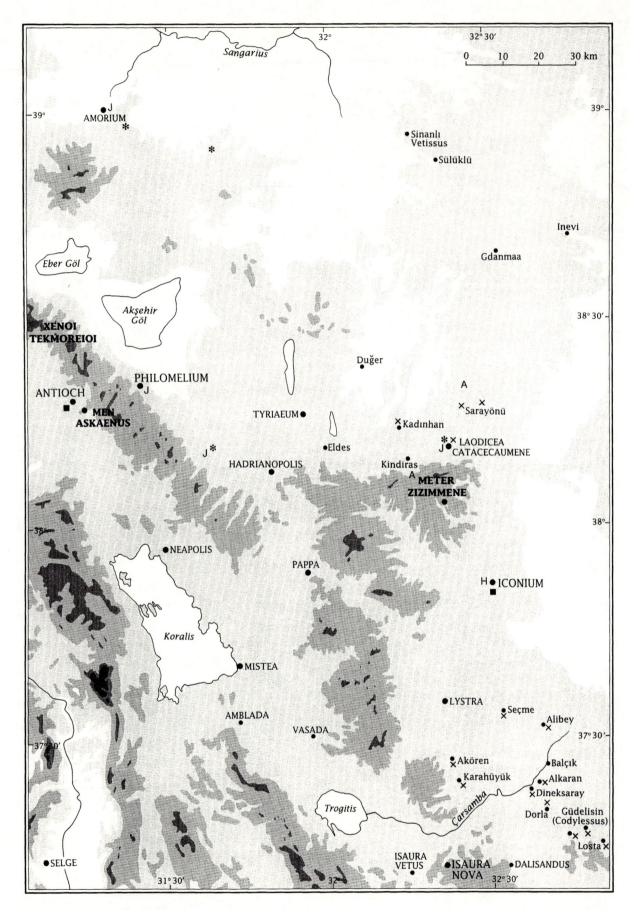

Map 2. East Phrygia, east Pisidia, and Lycaonia

Social and Civic Transformations in the Fourth Century

1. *Gregory the Wonder-Worker and the Age of Conversion*

Soon after AD 240 a young man, aged about 30, returned from the city of Caesareia in Palestine to his home, Neocaesareia in Pontus, where in his absence he had been consecrated bishop. Theodore, a member of a wealthy and well-educated pagan family, had originally travelled to Palestine as an escort for his sister, whose husband, a legal expert, had been sent to advise the governor of the province. Theodore's original purpose was to study law himself in the famous school at Berytus, but already since early adolescence he had inclined to Christianity.[1] At Berytus he had persisted in his studies, in particular the task of mastering the challenging Latin of legal texts and imperial pronouncements, and he intended, no doubt, to emulate his brother-in-law's successful career in imperial service. The subtleties and difficulties of Roman law won his admiration even while they threatened to subvert his traditional skills in Greek rhetoric.[2] But his Christian leanings proved stronger than either. Berytus lay close to Caesareia, the administrative centre of Palestine, which was also the home from about 235 to 245 of the greatest Christian theologian and teacher of the pre-Constantinian period, Origen. The young man spent eight years as his pupil, mastering the exegesis of biblical texts and absorbing the sophisticated philosophical theology with which Origen strengthened the Church's doctrines.[3] On his departure he delivered an address of thanks to his teacher which survives as the vividest portrait of Origen's inspirational instruction.[4] As testimony to the thoroughness of his conversion he took a new name, Gregorios, 'the reawakened one'.[5]

The lessons he had learned from Origen were soon put to practical use. When Gregory, a studied picture of humility, head bowed, alone, as though walking through a wilderness, returned to his bishopric, there were said to be only seventeen Christians in Neocaesareia. When he died thirty years later around AD 270, only seventeen pagans remained unconverted.[6] If the story is to be believed, Gregory evangelized the entire pagan population of a middle-ranking city of the eastern Roman empire in the course of a generation during the middle of the third century.

The problem, of course, is how much to believe. The account of Gregory's years with Origen comes from his own pen, the speech of thanks to his teacher, and it is guaranteed by unimpeachable background details—the career pattern of members of the local aristocracy which lead them to serve as professional advisers to provincial governors, the use of the imperial transport system to travel from Pontus to Palestine, the setting of the Roman law school itself in Berytus.[7] Indeed Gregory's own background as a member of the local aristocracy, and his advance from a rhetorical and legal training to a bishopric finds a close parallel in the career of his North African contemporary, Cyprian

---

[1] Greg. Thaum. *In Origenem*, 5. 64–72 (ed. H. Crouzel, *Remerciement à Origène*. Sources chrétiennes 148 (1969)).

[2] *In Origenem*, 1. 18–21, well discussed by J. Modrzejewski, 'Grégoire le thaumaturge et le droit romain', *Rev. hist. de droit français et étranger*, 49 (1971), 313–14. For fears that Latin, the language of law and administration, would undermine traditional Greek culture and education see the remarks of Libanius, discussed by J. H. W. G. Liebeschuetz, *Antioch: City and Imperial Administration in the Later Roman Empire* (1972), 242–5, and in general, W. H. Zilliacus, *Zum Kampf der Weltsprachen im oströmischen Reich* (1935). The broader issues are evoked by F. Millar, 'Culture grecque et culture latine: La Foi et la loi', in *Les Martyrs de Lyon (177)* (1978), 187–93.

[3] Eusebius, *HE* 6. 30 (five full years with Origen); *In Origenem*, 1. 7 (eight years in Palestine). See Crouzel, *Remerciement à Origène*, 20–2, 42–3.

[4] H. Crouzel, *Origène* (1984), 47–9.

[5] Eusebius, *HE* 6. 30.

[6] Greg. Nys. *Life of Gregory Thaumaturgus*, PG 46. 920a, 909b–c. The description of his entry into the city is consciously modelled on descriptions of imperial *adventus* in the 4th cent., for which the *locus classicus* is Amm. Marc. 16. 10. 13–4.

[7] For Gregory's use of the imperial post see *In Origenem*, 5. 76, ἐξαίφνης γοῦν . . . ἡμῖν ἐπέστη στρατιώτης φέρων ἐντόλην, παραπέμπειν μὲν καὶ διασώζεσθαι τὴν ἀδελφὴν ἡμῶν καταλαμβάνουσαν πλειόνων τῶν δημοσίων ὀχημάτων τῆς χρήσεως, καὶ σύμβολα πλείονος ἀριθμοῦ ἡμῶν μᾶλλον ἢ τῆς ἀδελφῆς μόνης ἕνεκα, a splendid illustration of the diploma system (*JRS* 66 (1976), 125–7).

of Carthage.[8] But the story of the conversion of Neocaesareia comes from a far more problematical source, the panegyrical Life of Gregory written over a century later around AD 380 by the Cappadocian Gregory of Nyssa.

The life of Gregory 'the Wonder-Worker' paints a portrait of a formidable community leader, certainly no member of an oppressed and struggling minority.[9] People came to him who were suffering or distressed, and he sent them away full of the Holy Spirit, inspired by his advice, teaching, and healing, all visible manifestations of the divine power. He comforted, reassured, advised, and above all consolidated a community which underwent not a revolution, and certainly no fundamental change in its social structure, but a reorientation, so that its members looked on the world not simply as good citizens of Neocaesareia but as Christians.[10] The impetus of conversion was sustained by demonstrations of miraculous power: demons were overthrown, giant boulders shifted, the river Lycus sent back in its course, and plague brought to an end.[11] Pagans who had crammed into the theatre for a festival got more than they bargained for when they clamorously begged Zeus for space; by the will of God, which had been invoked by Gregory's prayers, many died soon afterwards of disease.[12] No pagan or Jew could claim such impressive command of divine power.[13] Conventional authority was allied to miraculous deeds. During the brief persecution of Trajan Decius in 250, close to the beginning of his term, he advised the members of his congregation to leave the city and conceal themselves in the countryside rather than seek an ostentatious martyrdom, advice which he observed himself so that the church emerged all the stronger from the brief challenge.[14] Gregory's reputation led him to be called in by the neighbouring city of Comana, where he resolved a bitter dispute among the leading citizens, and his intervention led to the election of a new bishop.[15] His pre-eminence in his own city was such that not only sacred but temporal disputes were submitted to his arbitration, causing him to be seen as a new Solomon, the bringer of peace and justice

to the whole community.[16] Above all, he permanently changed the outward appearance and forms of public life in the city by building churches to replace pagan temples, and by supplanting the old festivals of the pagan year with a Christian calendar, which imposed a fresh rhythm to community and social life.[17] Priest and counsellor, judge, politician, and reformer—in Gregory all the threads were spun together that made for the formidable power and influence of a great bishop in a late Roman city.

The story of Gregory was told as an inspiration, not as a historical record. It circulated both in Gregory of Nyssa's Greek and in a derivative Syriac version to edify credulous hearers far beyond eastern Anatolia.[18] It can be regarded as a charter-myth for the founding of the church at Neocaesareia, as a fictitious exemplar for the dominant role of bishops in their late fourth-century sees, or as a parade of the power of Christian faith to work miracles. The truth behind the fable is now almost beyond recovery.[19] In writing his panegyric Gregory of Nyssa appears to have been ignorant of, or at least to have ignored his namesake's own writings, and he relied on local traditions about his deeds and achievements, occasionally supplemented by surviving material evidence such as the church which Gregory himself had built, or the creed which he had written out in his own hand and was still displayed there.[20] Not only was the content of the panegyric the

---

[8] For Cyprian see M. M. Sage, Cyprian (1975), 95–113.
[9] PG 46. 921b.
[10] PG 46. 921d–24a, which shows with perfect clarity that Gregory reinforced the social order rather than subverted it; cf. the summary of his achievement at 944a, πάντων κατά τε τὴν πόλιν καὶ τὴν περίοικον πρὸς τὴν εὐσεβῆ τοῦ δόγματος πίστιν μετατεθέντων. The reference to the destruction of pagan shrines which follows this must be an anachronism.
[11] PG 46. 913d–20a.
[12] PG 46. 956b–57a.
[13] PG 46. 940c–41c, 941c–44a.
[14] PG 46. 944d–48d.
[15] PG 46. 933b–40b.
[16] PG 46. 924d ff.
[17] PG 46. 924b–c for Gregory's church—the only building, according to Gregory of Nyssa, which had survived a recent earthquake; 944b for other churches; 935a–c for the cult of martyrs, through which Gregory established a new calendar: καὶ γὰρ δὴ καὶ τοῦτο τῆς μεγάλης αὐτοῦ σοφίας ἀπόδειξις ἦν, ὅτι πρὸς καινὸν βίον μεταρρυθμίζων πᾶσαν ἀθρόως τὴν κατ' αὐτοῦ γενεάν, οἷον τις ἡνίοχος ἐπιστὰς τῇ φύσει, καὶ τοῖς τῆς πίστεως καὶ θεογνωσίας χαλινοῖς ἀσφαλῶς αὐτοὺς ὑποζεύξαι, ἐνεδίδου τὸ μικρὸν τῷ ζυγῷ τῆς πίστεως δι' εὐφροσύνης ὑποσκιρτᾶν τὸ ὑπήκοον. The passage was rightly emphasized by Harnack ii. 758. See also below, nn. 76, 117–18.
[18] V. Ryssel, 'Eine syrische Lebensgeschichte des Gregorios Thaumaturgus', Schweizerische Theologische Zeitschrift 11 (1894), 228–54 published a Syriac life of Gregory, which concentrates heavily on the miraculous episodes, which he dated to the early 4th cent. P. Koetschau, Zeitschrift für wissenschaftliche Theologie, 21 (1898), 211–50 showed that this was derived from Gregory of Nyssa's version. R. MacMullen, Christianizing the Roman Empire (1984), 145 n. 1 favours it over the Greek version, but he missed Koetschau; cf. R. Lane Fox, Pagans and Christians (1986), 760.
[19] PG 46. 893–957, recently studied by R. van Dam, 'Hagiography and History: The Life of Gregory Thaumaturgus', Classical Antiquity, 1 (1982), 272–308 (seeing it as a charter myth), and Lane Fox, Pagans and Christians, 528–39 (sceptical of historical worth). See too H. Telfer, 'The Cultus of Gregory Thaumaturgus', Harvard Theological Review, 29 (1936), 225–344. There are three splendid pages by Harnack, ii. 757–9.
[20] Creed in PG 46. 912d–13a; a Latin version was added to Rufinus' Latin version of Eusebius' Church History, see E.

product of all the distortions and suppressions inherent in any partisan oral tradition, but, in a period of intense doctrinal skirmishing between warring factions of the Church, it was Gregory of Nyssa's avowed aim to claim authority for his own position in current theological controversy from the supposed views of the founding father, Gregory the Wonder-Worker. In the face of these obstacles to the truth, Gregory of Nyssa's claim, that the facts of his predecessor's life were so marvellous as to need no embroidery, should be treated as conventionally disingenuous.[21]

What condemns the work as an accurate record of mid-third-century Neocaesarea most decisively is not what it says but what it omits. Whatever strides Christianity made in Gregory's day it certainly did not supplant paganism entirely. The bronze coins of Neocaesareia and of the other cities of the region show that it clung proudly to its pagan traditions well beyond the middle of the third century. The commonest reverse types relate to games and festivals, the most public face of pagan cult, events which necessarily embraced whole communities not dwindling groups of worshippers. New contests founded in the 230s were still celebrated in the 260s when minting ceases. It is inconceivable that we should take the panegyric of Gregory literally, and accept that the non-Christian community had been reduced to seventeen, the size of a single pagan thiasos, by the time of Gregory's death only ten years later.[22]

Is there anything that remains credible? Miracles, which in this case occupy so much of the story, were an invariable ingredient of early Christian lives, and often modelled on the Gospels' accounts of Christ himself. According to one estimate they acted as the strongest persuasive force in winning unbelievers over to the faith—to see the power of God was to believe.[23] But miracles achieved most of their force and power to persuade through telling and retelling; they were rather a crucial part of a Christian literary tradition than of Christian reality. Many more people have been persuaded to accept the truth of Christianity by learning about Christ's miracles from the Gospels than

were converted by witnessing the miracles themselves. We rightly hesitate to accept the actuality of Gregory's supernatural deeds as we hesitate before the more extravagant miracles in other Christian stories. Even in a society which was accustomed to treating extraordinary or uncanny events as signs of divine power, direct experience of this power was surely exceptional.

Gregory, however, stands out from his Life not simply as a worker of miracles but as a leader and a wielder of power. Many, surely, will have joined the Church because its leaders could offer help and protection, or could threaten reprisals against men who defied them. Where the Christians were strong, there will have been sound reasons for pagans to join them. From the second century onwards, leadership in the Church was mainly the preserve of the local bishop. A third-century source, the *Didascalia Apostolorum*, shows the ways in which a bishop wielded his authority, by judging disputes, appointing clergy, collecting and distributing resources, and by the moral and social supervision of the whole community. He had no obvious counterpart in pagan or Jewish society.[24] The panegyric of Gregory well illustrates the precepts of the *Didascalia* and probably exemplifies a widespread phenomenon of third-century life in the eastern Roman empire. The strains and stresses to which the empire was subject during this period were manifested in one symptom above all, the collapse of local civic life. Between the 230s and the 280s the traditional pattern of élite behaviour in the Greek cities changed radically. The members of the local aristocracy, who had both directed and derived prestige from the political and public life of their cities, slipped from prominence. When they reappeared at the end of the century their ambitions and energies had been redirected from civic to imperial service.[25] The life of the cities would never

Schwarz and Th. Mommsen, *Eusebius: Die Kirchengeschichte*, ii. 2 (1908), 952–6. In general see M. van Esbroeck SJ, *Studia Patristica* 22 (1989), 155–66.

[21] *PG* 46. 918c, 921c. 912c insists on his strict orthodoxy and cites *ipsissima verba* of the Creed. Basil of Caesarea appealed to Gregory Thaumaturgus with the same purpose, *Epp.* 28, 204, but some things that he had written could cause embarrassment, *Ep.* 210. 5. One had to make allowance for loose formulations of doctrine before the hard lines of 4th-cent. controversy had been drawn up. Origen would be cited by both Arians and Orthodox in support of their positions.

[22] See Lane Fox, *Pagans and Christians*, 533–7.

[23] R. MacMullen, *Vigiliae Christianae*, 37 (1983), 174–92; *Christianizing the Roman Empire*, 17–42.

[24] Lane Fox, *Pagans and Christians*, 499–517, is outstanding (endorsed by T. D. Barnes, in *L'Église et l'Empire au IV\u1d49 siècle*, Entretiens Hardt (1987, pub. 1989), 300).

[25] For two excellent examples see Aurelius Plutarchus of Oxyrhynchus in Egypt, *POxy.* 1204, discussed by F. Millar, *JRS* 73 (1983), 91–2, and Bryonianus Lollianus of Side, discussed by J.-M. Carrié, *ZPE* 35 (1979), 213–24 whose remarks may be quoted, '(il) a pu échapper aux fonctions municipales de Sidé, et réserver sa fortune personelle pour une évergétisme librement consenti. Sa carrière publique est modeste... Pourtant, elle n'est pas incompatible avec une alliance matrimoniale dans une riche famille locale de rang senatoriale. Ces deux faits, réunis, montrent que la réussite sociale ne s'exprime plus dans l'exercice des fonctions municipales, fardeau financier de plus en plus lourd, mais dans celui des fonctions de l'état, même relativement subalternes. Les officiales avantagés par les privilèges afférent à leur condition, protégés des difficultés curiales par leurs immunités, assurés de faire entrer et progresser leur fils dans la carrière publique, représentent dès lors la classe montante de l'Empire restauré.'

be the same again. But the troubled years of the third century demanded leadership even if they did not always receive it; and it is tempting to suggest that in many cities the place of the local aristocracy was taken by energetic Christian bishops. Gregory the Wonder-Worker, had he lived in the second century, would certainly have played the role of a city magnate. With the collapse of organized civic politics, his opportunity for leadership was to be found within the Church. As the strength of this Christian leadership became plain, the number of converts would have increased dramatically. The culmination of this process was to come, in Anatolia at least, in the fourth century, when the bishops of Gregory of Nyssa's day, above all Basil of Caesareia, wielded temporal power on a grand scale. The panegyric of Gregory the Wonder-Worker, written in AD 380, naturally portrayed him in a role similar to that of the great political bishops of the late fourth century, but this should not obscure the fact that there was genuine political work for a bishop to do a century earlier, and it is unlikely that a self-confident Christian leader would have shirked so obvious an avenue to power.

One work survives from Gregory the Wonder-Worker's own œuvre which gives an authentic taste of his episcopal style, revealing him precisely as a judge and arbiter for the community of Pontic Christians. In the early 250s Gothic raiders had reached the southern shore of the Black Sea and twice invaded Pontic territory, most notably in the territory of Trapezus which they sacked (see above, Vol. I, Ch. 13 §IV at n. 59). Christian captives of the Goths had been forced to eat sacrificial meat; women had been raped. Gregory, in the first of eleven canons which were probably addressed to the bishop of Trapezus, exempted these victims from blame, except in the case of women whose former lewdness gave rise to suspicion that they had submitted willingly to their captors. Otherwise they might play a full part in the prayers of the Church. The remaining canons confronted more disturbing issues. Christians had apparently taken advantage of the barbarian raids to loot one another's property (canon 2), to keep spoils recovered from the Goths for themselves (canon 3), to claim property left abandoned as their own, sometimes in compensation for what they had lost, without attempting to return it to the rightful owner (canons 4 and 5). There were those who had forcibly detained escaped prisoners of the Goths and collaborated with the barbarians in showing them the local roads and pointing out the houses of their fellow countrymen, no doubt in hope of sharing the plunder (canons 6 and 7); others had raided their neighbours' unguarded homes and stolen their abandoned property, or expected rewards for returning it to them intact (canons 8–10). Gregory cited Genesis, Joshua, Deu-

teronomy, or Paul's Letter to the Ephesians, not the precepts of Roman law, to identify the crimes and to prescribe punishment. He sent Euphrosynos, an elder of his own church, to help deal with the problem of property unlawfully acquired, and recommended his fellow bishop to dispatch men into the countryside to deal with those who were forcibly detaining their fellow countrymen (canons 5 and 6). He is indignant that Christian men of Pontus should lower themselves to behaviour that identified them as barbarians. By behaving like the Boradi, the northern raiders, and the Goths, they became Boradi and Goths (canon 5). Innocence or guilt was a matter for the bishop to decide, although in one case future repentance was to be assessed by a synod of bishops sitting in judgement (canon 7). Punishment lay in physical exclusion by various degrees from the church. The worst offenders were shut out altogether from the church, and would have to rely on the prayers of the faithful for their redemption; lesser crimes warranted banishment to the narthex, where offenders could hear the mass but not participate; another group could stand inside the door at the back of the congregation among the catechumens preparing for baptism; mild offenders could stand among the faithful but were refused the sacrament; only the innocent, finally, could take part in the consecration of the mass (canon 11).[26]

Reading between the lines of this isolated letter, the only contemporary document to reveal Gregory at work, some assessment can be made of the condition of the Church in eastern Pontus. It was well established with numerous adherents. If not it would have made little sense to draw such fine distinctions between the various offences that had been committed in the Gothic raids, and to compile such an elaborate system of penalties. If canon 11 is an authentic part of the letter, the description of a typical church which it implies suggests that like the basilicas of the fourth century it already possessed an exterior courtyard beyond the gate, an antechamber or narthex, and the main part of the building large enough for the congregation to be segregated into the catechumens and the faithful.[27] The diocese as a whole was centrally organized, presumably from the city itself, since the bishop was encouraged to send his agents 'into the countryside' to detect offenders, and this in turn implies that Christians were

---

[26] See Lane Fox, *Pagans and Christians*, 539–45. Lane Fox argues for the authenticity of canon 11, which has been disputed. The main ground for suspicion is the implication that the Christians of Pontus in the 250s had erected regular public basilicas; these are completely absent from the archaeological record, see J. Vaes, *Anc. Soc.* 15–17 (1984–6), 305–443 at 341–52, although they were to be found at least by the end of the 3rd cent., see below, n. 82.

[27] See below, nn. 82–3.

to be found, as Pliny had found them a century and a half earlier, in the villages as well as in the towns. But the rugged and inaccessible countryside of eastern Pontus, hard against the north-eastern frontier of the Roman empire, was notoriously the home of wild and unruly men who even in the mid-second century AD refused to pay their taxes to Rome.[28] The provincial authorities would have been at one with Gregory in classing them as virtual barbarians, and might have felt less surprise than he that they took advantage of a genuine barbarian invasion to turn to banditry.

Gregory the Wonder-Worker lived through a period which for many counts as a crucial phase in the rise of the Church, the second and third quarters of the third century when the Christian community grew from being a marginalized group to a respectable minority if not a majority of the citizens of the Roman empire, at least in the eastern provinces.[29] That, of course, is precisely the implication of Gregory of Nyssa's appraisal of his hero's life and achievements. On close inspection the hard evidence for his ministry can sustain no firm conclusion, offering only a vivid but restricted glimpse of the bishop at work. Above all it leaves open the large question about the period when Christian numbers grew to the point where they could challenge or dominate their pagan peers. It is necessary to look elsewhere in Anatolia for firmer data.

II. *Dominant Christian Groups before Constantine*

A number of passages in Eusebius' *Church History*, of varying authority, suggest that certain communities were largely Christian at or soon after the outbreak of persecution in AD 303. For instance, virtually all the citizens of Edessa in northern Syria are said to have been Christians since the mission of Thaddaeus to King Abgar, while Christ himself still lived. The mission followed a famous, though apocryphal exchange of letters between Christ himself and the Edessan king Abgar V, copies of which, published in Syriac and in Greek, acquired a talismanic significance in and beyond Edessa.[30] There are reasonable grounds for believing that a later king, Abgar VIII, who ruled in the early third century, was also a convert along with a sizeable number of his fellow citizens. Edessa thereby became

the centre of Syrian Christianity, but a detailed analysis of the pagan and Christian evidence in this period shows that Eusebius' claim is greatly exaggerated. One point of detail in Edessa's history is worth stressing, her continued rivalry with neighbouring Carrhae (Harran), which remained a pagan stronghold. A visitor to the city in about 385 reported that scarcely a single Christian was to be found there.[31] The opposition of Christian and pagan in neighbouring cities was also a notable feature of the religious landscape in third-century Anatolia. Another important pocket of eastern Christianity became established in Armenia. Christians were reported in the royal entourage around the middle of the third century, and Eusebius states baldly that the Christianity of the population led the persecuting emperor Maximinus to attack them in AD 312.[32]

Another story from the Great Persecution which bears further examination, although it should not be taken literally, is the report that the entire population of a small Phrygian town, including its magistrates, was put to death in 303 for refusing to comply with the order to sacrifice.[33] The strength of Christianity in parts of Phrygia was so great that the report could be true in essence, if exaggerated, and attempts have been made to identify the town with Eumeneia, whose inscriptions suggest a strong Christian presence by the later third century and where Christians were certainly to be found in the governing class.[34] The persecution reached its climax under Maximinus between late 311 and 312. Eusebius tells us that he was stung to action especially when he noticed that a majority of the inhabitants of Nicomedia, the home of the imperial court itself, was already Christian, and that when he finally relented in 313 he did so because he realized that by then almost the whole world had been converted.[35] If the last observation has any value, it must relate to the condition of the Anatolian provinces which Maximinus had observed at close hand throughout 312.[36]

---

[28] Appian, *Periplous*, 11. 1–2: (of the Sanni) καὶ γὰρ μαχιμώτατοι εἰς τοῦτο ἔτι καὶ τοῖς Τραπεζουντίοις ἐχθρότατοι, καὶ χωρία ὀχυρὰ οἰκοῦσιν, καὶ ἔθνος ἀβασίλευτον, πάλαι μὲν γὰρ καὶ φόρου ὑποτελὲς Ῥωμαίοις, ὑπὸ δὲ τοῦ λῃστεύειν οὐκ ἀκριβοῦσιν τὴν φοράν. ἀλλὰ νῦν γε διδόντος θεοῦ ἀκριβώσουσιν, ἢ ἐξελοῦμεν αὐτούς. Thus the governor of Cappadocia to the emperor Hadrian! However, Pliny, *NH* 21. 77 tells us that they paid their tribute in wax!

[29] See below, nn. 60–1.

[30] *HE* 2. 1. 7, cf. Harnack ii. 678–82; J. B. Segal, *Edessa: The Blessed City* (1970), 62 ff.; Lane Fox, *Pagans and Christians*, 279–80.

[31] For pagan Harran see Procopius, *Bell. Pers.* 2. 13; Harnack, ii. 682–3. According to one observer in about 385 (*Peregrinatio Silviae* 20) 'in ipsa civitate extra paucos clericos et sanctos monachos, si qui tamen in civitate commorantur, penitus nullum Christianum inveni, sed totum gentes sunt.'

[32] *HE* 9. 8. 2; Harnack, ii. 750–4, 757–62.

[33] Eusebius, *HE* 8. 11. 1, cf. Lactantius, *Div. Inst.* 5. 11. Lucian of Antioch was quoted by Rufinus, *HE* 9. 6, for the belief that whole cities in Asia Minor at this date were Christian.

[34] Identified by Ramsay, *CB* i. 2 (1897), 502–5 as Eumeneia, doubted by Lane Fox, *Pagans and Christians*, 771 n. 4; Chastagnol *MEFRA* (1981), 381 suggests Orcistus, but there is no echo of the massacre in Constantine's rescript. For Eumeneian Christianity see above, Ch. 16 § IV at nn. 242–6.

[35] *HE* 9. 9a. 1, 5.

[36] *JRS* 78 (1988), 118–19.

Another item of evidence of similar quality to these stray remarks in Eusebius, but much more specifically located, comes from the rescript which Constantine sent in the late 320s to the small Phrygian town of Orcistus, and which granted their petition to be raised to the status of an independent city, partly on the grounds that all of its inhabitants were 'followers of the most holy religion'.[37] Although none of these claims can be taken literally, neither Constantine nor Eusebius would have made them if Christians had not been present in large numbers and perhaps formed a majority in the relevant communities.

Where early Christian inscriptions, usually gravestones, survive in bulk, there may be some chance of assessing the size and strength of the group in relation to the pagan population. The process, however, is fraught with difficulties which must be spelled out. Firstly, can we be sure that the surviving gravestones are a representative sample of those that were originally set up? Secondly, can we confidently distinguish Christian from non-Christian stones? Thirdly, can we date them accurately enough to be sure that we are comparing Christian and pagan numbers at the same period, and not at altogether different stages in the community's history? Since a positive answer to these questions is often impossible, it is only feasible to form a rough impression of the relative strength of Christian populations, which leaves room for much refinement and alteration. Even so, the effort is worth making.

The case of Eumeneia, where the gravestones suggest a large Christian population by the middle of the third century has already been cited and examined (Ch. 16 §IV at nn. 242–6). There is a good chance that Christians were in a majority in the population by 250, and two bishops are attested by third-century inscriptions. The Christian presence in southern Phrygia certainly extended well beyond the city, since gravestones protected by the so-called Eumeneian formula, the threat that anyone who interfered with the burial would have to reckon with God, are found outside the limits of the city's territory, in neighbouring Dionysupolis and Apamea, and in the dependent villages of Eumeneia as well as the town itself. Given that most of the inhabitants of Eumeneia presumably lived off the land as peasant farmers, it is worth emphasizing that the stereotype of the early Christians as an urban sect has little validity here.[38]

This is confirmed by evidence from elsewhere in central Anatolia. Another important series of Christian epitaphs comes from the borderland of Isauria and Lycaonia, in the valley of the Çarşamba river. The complete regional corpus has yet to be assembled, but from a representative sample of 120 inscriptions from this region,[39] fifty are explicitly and another ten probably Christian, while the remaining sixty give no indication of religious affiliation and may, for the most part, be pagan.[40] According to the original editors, the Christian texts range in date from the second quarter of the third to the end of the fourth century, and include the gravestones of no less than five bishops, all to be dated before Constantine or in the early fourth century.[41] Many of the texts come from a very homogeneous series of stones, which was produced

---

[37] MAMA vii. 305. i ll. 39–42, 'quibus omnibus quasi quidem cumulus accedit quod omnes ibidem sectatores sanctissimae religionis habitare dicantur.' Dated to 328–30 by A. Chastagnol, 'L'Inscription constantinienne d'Orcistus', MEFRA 93 (1981), 381–416.

[38] See above, Ch. 16 §IV. For Eumeneia's rural territory see T. Drew Bear, Nouvelles inscriptions de Phrygie, 53–5, 112–14.

[39] MAMA viii. 99–210, 303–10. This collection republishes most but not all of the texts copied in the region by earlier travellers, notably, Sterrett, WE nos. 18–55; A. M. Ramsay, JHS 24 (1904), 260–92, which is amplified in SERP, 3–62; W. M. Ramsay, JHS 25 (1905), 163–80; G. Radet and P. Paris, BCH 10 (1886), 500 ff. nos. 15–28; 11 (1887), 63–70; Buckler, Calder, and Cox, JRS 14 (1924), nos. 43–95. Ramsay above all brought attention to bear on this material and discussed it at length in an essay 'The Church of Lycaonia in the Fourth Century', in Luke the Physician (1908), 331–410. It is appropriate to quote Harnack's judgement of his achievement (766) 'Was sonst nur durch vereinte Kräfte und Mittel einer Akademie geleistet wird, hat hier ein Mann erarbeitet.' It is often necessary to go back to the earlier publications in view of the deficiencies of MAMA viii in commentary and illustration. The observations on the chronology of these monuments offered here are very provisional. Firm conclusions need to be based on a reinspection of the stones themselves, many of which are collected in Konya Museum.

[40] In the following lists I have italicized the numbers which I would date before 260. Christian: *100, 101–2, 116, 118–20, 121–8, 131, 132–3, 158–9, 160, 161–5, 166, 167, 168–9, 199, 200, 201–2, 203–5, 210, 303–7, 310.* Perhaps Christian: 117, 129, 130, 144, 152, 180, 182, 193, 196. Apparently pagan: 99, 103–10, 112–15, 134–9, 141–3, 145–51, 153–4, 155, 156–7, 170, 171–3, 175–9, 181, 186–7, 188–90, 192, 194–5, 197–8, 206–9, 308–9. Note also MAMA viii. 62–5 (from Seçme = Çeşme), 88–91 (Akören), and 98 (Karahüyük), which are all probably pre-Constantinian Christian texts.

[41] A. M. Ramsay, JHS 24 (1904), 261 ff. and SERP 7, and W. M. Ramsay, JHS 25 (1905), 163–70 suggest 240–400 for the main series of gravestones (cf. Harnack ii. 739 n. 1, 250–400). Buckler, Calder, and Cox, JRS 14 (1924), 50 ff. have little to say on dating. For the bishops see MAMA viii. 162 (= SERP 22 no. 7), ὁ μακάριος Παπᾶς (or παπᾶς); 161 (= SERP 35 no. 13), Μαμμας. These two texts might perhaps belong to the middle of the third century along with MAMA viii. 164, for a Ταβεις, ὁ τειμιώτατος διάκονος, which, pace Ramsay, need not be dated to a later Byzantine period; SERP 41 no. 18, for Ἰνδακω ἐπισκόπω δικέω ἀγαφητῷ, to be dated 210–40, perhaps the earliest bishop; SERP 30 no. 9, Σισαμοας, ὁ ἁγνότατος καὶ ἡδυεπὴς καὶ πάσης ἀρετῆς κεκοσμημένος (Ramsay's late 3rd-cent. date may be too late); MAMA viii. 163 (a developed epitaph of the 4th cent.).

by a workshop at or near the site of Dorla, usually depicting an arch between two triangular gables, all standing on a series of four pilasters. Two very simple examples of the type, which may belong late in the series, probably served as gravestones for victims of the Great Persecution between 303 and 313; one for Paul the martyr, the other for 'the suffering Demetrios'.[42] Both appear from the style of carving to postdate the gravestones of the bishops Papas and Mammas and of 'the most honourable deacon Tabeis'.[43] All these were decorated with simple crosses incised in circles, or other early Christian symbols.[44] By contrast, none of the stones was decorated with a Christogram or the chi-rho sign typical of fourth-century monuments. If anything, therefore, the suggested dates for the Christian inscriptions may be too late, and a high proportion probably belongs between 220 and 310. Detailed dating of individual stones in this sample is impossible, but they may perhaps be divided into two groups: one of eighty stones dating before about 260, characterized by simple second- to third-century grave formulae, usually ending in μνήμης χάριν, and omitting such obviously Christian features as christograms at the head of the inscription itself; the other of forty stones of the later third or fourth century. Within these groups the proportions of Christian to pagan texts are 26:54 and 35:5, counting all the likely Christian texts as certain, or 20:60 and 30:10 if we classify doubtful cases as pagan. Since a certain number of Christian texts may in any case be entirely concealed by traditional pagan formulas the higher Christian figures are more likely to be correct. In any case, it is evident that there was a substantial Christian minority in the population, perhaps approaching 33 per cent before 260, rising above 80 per cent in the fourth century. In 325 Isauria sent no less than thirteen bishops and four *chorepiscopi* to the Council of Nicaea. By the 370s Basil of Caesareia was manœuvring anxiously to ensure that the priests of these 'small towns and villages' were trusted appointees of the Orthodox Church, subject to the discipline of the bishop of Isaura (see below).

The inscriptions from the territory of Laodicea Catacecaumene and the central Anatolian plateau between Ancyra and Iconium, much of which formed imperial estates, tell a similar story. More than 1,200

texts have been found here, mostly dating to the second century AD or later. There is no clearly pagan text belonging to the fourth century; moreover from a sample of 178 fourth- or early fifth-century inscriptions from Laodicea itself only seven are not demonstrably Christian.[45] Laodicea has long been recognized as an important centre for heretical sects during the fourth century (see below, §x). These crude statistics make it clear that there was no room for pagans among them.

The cautious and vague claims that can be made for the Christianizing of Isauria and eastern Phrygia are overshadowed by more precise conclusions for another rural district well known for its imperial estates, the upper Tembris valley in northern Phrygia, which lay in the city territories of Cotiaeum and Appia. The preliminary conclusions of a current detailed study of its prolific sculpture workshops suggest that 80 per cent of those who used or appear on gravestones between 280 and 310 professed to be Christians.[46] Here, then, there is not only evidence that Christians formed an overwhelming majority, but that they had achieved that position before the end of the third century.

Early Christian writers have little to say about these distant areas of central Asia Minor, but the occasional allusion confirms that parts of Phrygia and Lycaonia were widely known as the home of substantial, and usually heretical Christian communities. In book 7 of his Church history Eusebius cited Dionysius of Alexandria on the question of rebaptizing repentant heretics. Dionysius acknowledged that the issue had been a source of strife in North Africa, and also 'in the populous churches and synods at Iconium and Synnada'.[47] At roughly the same period in the mid-third century Firmilian, bishop of Caesareia, wrote to Cyprian at Carthage on the same question of baptizing heretics. He pointed out that neither the 'Cataphrygae', who asserted the superiority of their false prophet Montanus over the teachings of Christ, nor any other heretical group could legitimately baptize. This point had been firmly established by a synod at Iconium where bishops had gathered from Galatia, Cilicia, and

---

[42] *MAMA* viii. 168. The adjective ἄθλιος used to describe Demetrios, who was buried by his father, should be connected with the more explicit ἀθλοφόρος, which was used exclusively for victims of persecution (cf. *AS* 32 (1982), 100–1).

[43] If *MAMA* viii. 168 is properly dated to the period 303–13 it provides a useful chronological peg for the whole series. It appears stylistically later than *MAMA* viii. 161–3.

[44] For this feature on early Christian gravestones from the territory of Phrygian Ancyra, Synaus, and Cadi, see *MAMA* x, xxxvi–xli.

[45] The great majority of inscriptions from this area are published in *MAMA* i, *MAMA* vii, *RECAM* ii, and J. G. C. Anderson, 'Explorations in Galatia cis Halym', *JHS* 19 (1899). The sample of inscriptions discussed here is *MAMA* i nos. 157–260 and *MAMA* vii. 64–104d. The only texts which are not explicitly Christian are *MAMA* i. 204, and vii. 68 and 87a.

[46] For the Tembris valley, see above, Ch. 16 §IV at nn. 240–1; *MAMA* x, xxvii–xxxii; J. Strubbe, *Anc. Soc.* 6 (1975), 229–50 (estates). For the figures I anticipate one of the conclusions of a detailed study of the Altıntaş workshops by M. Waelkens; see also *MAMA* x, introd.

[47] Eusebius, *HE* 7. 7. 5, μεμάθηκα καὶ τοῦτο μὴ νῦν ἐν Ἀφρικῇ μόνον τοῦτο παρεισήγαγον, ἀλλὰ καὶ περὶ πολλοῦ κατὰ τοὺς πρὸ ἡμῶν ἐπισκόπους ἐν ταῖς πολυανθρωποτάτοις ἐκκλησίαις καὶ τοῖς συνόδοις τῶν ἀδελφῶν, ἐν Ἰκονίῳ καὶ Συνάδοις καὶ παρὰ πολλοῖς, τοῦτο ἔδοξεν.

the other neighbouring regions.[48] He illustrated the dangers posed by heretics with the colourful story of a prophetess who had won a following in his own diocese around AD 235–8 during a persecution instigated by the governor of Cappadocia Licinius Serenianus. She had persuaded the credulous by her apparent ability to predict the occurrence of earthquakes, and seduced a rural priest and a deacon. This work of the devil had only been expunged by the intervention of an exorcist.[49] It may have been the need to strengthen the faith of the orthodox that led early third-century bishops at Laranda, Iconium, and Synnada to send skilled lay teachers to preach to the Christian community; the precedent was cited by Origen's defenders, when they attempted to ward off the criticism that he had engaged in theological argument with bishops at Caesareia before he himself was even a priest.[50] All the areas in question were notable strongholds of heretical Christian sects in the fourth century (see below). Apparently these communities were already thriving a century before.

It is clear from all these passages that the activities which took place at and around Iconium and Synnada were not confined to the cities. On the contrary, the main focus of concern was always the conduct of the country brethren. These can with confidence be identified with the Christian groups of the Çarşamba valley in Lycaonia and of the upper Tembris valley in Phrygia. Lycaonia and Isauria probably lay within the Roman assize district of Iconium, which was the natural administrative centre for the southern half of the central Anatolian plateau, as it had been when Cicero held court there in 50 BC. Synnada was certainly the equivalent assize centre for all the cities of north-east Phrygia, including specifically the small city of Appia which was in the heart of the Christian area.[51] Justice and discipline within the Church was administered precisely within the administrative framework of the Roman provinces.

The evidence reviewed here, relating to specific cities and country districts does not lead to the conclusion that all or most of central Asia Minor had abandoned paganism by the early fourth century. It is implicit in the panegyric of Gregory the Wonder-Worker that his missionary work took place within a single city territory. Christianity had evidently not made such startling progress elsewhere. This point is reinforced by the terms of Constantine's rescript to the people of Orcistus. There would be no sense in giving special favours to the whole population on the grounds that it was Christian if this was generally true of Orcistus' neighbours also. In fact, there is scarcely a single pre-Constantinian Christian inscription attested in the territory of neighbouring Nacolea, with which Orcistus was in dispute and to which it had been subordinate, or even in the large area around Dorylaeum.[52] Christian

---

[48] Cyprian, Ep. 75. 7. 5.

[49] Ibid. 75. 10 ff. For a similar story in Pontus around 260, see Hippolytus, Comm. in Danielem, pp. 232 ff. (ed. Bonwetsch), cited by Harnack, ii. 755 n. 1, where a prophet who placed more faith in his own dreams than in the Gospels persuaded people in a rural community to abandon their lands and sell their animals in anticipation of the imminent Day of Judgement.

[50] Eusebius, HE 6. 19. 18. One of these lay readers, a διδάσκαλος, may be identified on an inscription from the Çarşamba basin, MAMA viii. 210.

[51] The Acts of Paul and Thecla, 15, which were probably written in the late 2nd cent., imply that Iconium was then a conventus centre where the governor held court on the bēma (see W. Ameling, Epigr. Anat. 12 (1988), 233). Synnada was the administrative headquarters for imperial estates and quarries in eastern Phrygia as well as the centre of a conventus which extended N. to Dorylaeum and included Cotiaeum, and, explicitly, Appia (Pliny, NH 5. 105, cf. MAMA ix. p. lx).

[52] Well-remarked by Cox and Cameron, MAMA v. pp. xxxii–xxxiii 'only one pre-Constantinian monument has been found in this whole area, which is certainly Christian, a Montanist

---

Fig. 18. Gravestone of Eutyches from the territory of Cadi, AD 179/80. Now in Kütahya Museum. The deceased carries the bread of the Eucharist in his right hand and grapes in the left. The writing tablet below left signifies literacy; the pruning hook, whip, and dog his daily pursuits. W. M. Calder, AS 5 (1955), 33 no. 2.

Fig. 19. 'Christians for Christians' inscription of around AD 275. The Latin cross in a wreath and the overall decoration of the stone are typical of the main workshop in the upper Tembris valley which produced gravestones for Christians (and others) between the mid-third and the early fourth century. A whip, a writing tablet, carding comb, distaff, and spindle survive in the panel. W. M. Calder, AS 5 (1955), 35 no. 3; Gibson, 'Christians', 30 no. 13.

Fig. 20. Christian inscription from Çepni Köy, on the north side of the Phrygian Pentapolis. Two male and one veiled female figure below a wreath. The text combines a typical Phrygian warning against disturbing the tomb with the threat of God's judgement. Αὐρ. Νανα Μηνοφίλου κατεσκεύασεν τὸ μνημῖον τῷ υἱῷ Εὐφήμῳ ἐκ τῶν ἀπολειφθέντων ὑπὸ αὐτοῦ ὑπαρχόντων. ὃς ταύτῃ τῇ ἱστήῃ κακοεργέα χεῖρα προσοίσι, ἔστη αὐτῷ πρὸς τὸν Θεόν. Perhaps c. AD 250. W. M. Calder, AS 5 (1955), 36 no. 5.

Fig. 21. Verse epitaph of Acacius, from the upper Tembris valley, made by Aur. Athenodotus of Docimeium. Kütahya Museum. W. M. Calder, AS 5 (1955), 31 no. 1; Robert, Bull. ép. (1956), 293, fourth century.

18

19

20

21

Aspects of Phrygian Christianity

Orcistus had good grounds to hope that Constantine would give them a favourable ear; Nacolea was later to erect a dedication to Julian the Apostate (see below, n. 333). Precisely the same observation is valid for the city and territory of Aezani, adjoining the thoroughly Christian communities of the upper Tembris valley. Here, from a total of about 1,000 inscriptions that have been found in the city and on its territory, not more than a handful is Christian and none pre-dates Constantine.[53] Clearly the well-entrenched Phrygian cults of Zeus Bronton, Zeus Bennios, Mēn, Theos Hypsistos, Hosion and Dikaion, Papas and others, which belonged to the common religious culture of the cities of northern Phrygia,[54] and above all the resplendent and important cult of Zeus at Aezani itself (above, Ch. 16 §1 at n. 60) ensured a continuing adherence to pagan culture which had faltered elsewhere. The entrenched pagan character of Aezani is thrown into even sharper relief by the fact that there were strong early Christian communities not only to the east, but also in its western neighbours, Cadi, Synaus, and Phrygian Ancyra.[55] There is a similar, although less striking contrast between the north Galatian territories of Ancyra, Germa, and Pessinus, where pre-Constantinian Christian inscriptions are extremely unusual,[56] and the territory of Laodicea

and the imperial estates to the south. At Ancyra the resilience of paganism is manifest in the hostility of the crowd to the provocative speech which a local saint Theodotus made before the governor Theotecnus on the eve of his martyrdom in 312, and later in the largely pagan culture of the city aristocracy during the 350s and 360s.[57] At Pessinus, one may point to the lingering prestige of the famous temple of Cybele, which Julian was to make the foundation stone of his attempt to revive Anatolian paganism.[58]

If we stand back from the individual cities to inspect the emergence of Christianity on a regional scale, the same pattern can still be discerned. Inscriptions are the principal source of information for the history of two vast inland regions of Asia Minor, Lydia and Phrygia. In the former, from Thyateira to Tripolis, the number of Christian texts erected before 300 is negligible; in the latter they can be numbered in hundreds. The conclusion suggested by this crude survey of the evidence is clear: the Christianization of much of central Anatolia from the mid-third century onwards was intense, but patchy. Areas where virtually the entire population had been converted contrasted, sometimes starkly, with others where pagans still prevailed.

When and how had the early Christian communities in Anatolia been converted? Gregory's Life implies that Neocaesareia converted during the time of his ministry, a period of twenty or thirty years, thanks to his personal missionary zeal. Elsewhere we cannot identify the guiding spirits behind the conversion of communities, but it is almost possible to match this rate of change. There were surely few Christians in Eumeneia before 200, but they may have reached a majority by the third quarter of the century. In northern Isauria and Lycaonia progress from a small minority to a majority may have taken two generations between 220 and the end of the century. In the upper Tembris valley the detailed analysis of datable stones indicates that less than 20 per cent of the population was Christian in 230, more than 80 per cent by 300. Laodicea Catacecaumene may have converted later, perhaps waiting for the victory of Constantine before swerving to Christianity outright, but the enormous preponderance of Christian inscriptions in the fourth century suggests that almost no one was left behind in the transformation.

It is hard to find comparable data in other parts of the Roman world but the conclusions of a recent study of conversion in third and fourth century Egypt are

epitaph *Ath. Mitt.* 22 (1897), 352 n. 1 ... the inscriptions bear cogent witness to the vitality of paganism at Dorylaeum and Nacolea'. For early Christianity in the territory of Amorium, immediately east of Orcistus, see W. M. Calder, *MAMA* vii. pp. xxxviii–xxxix.

[53] See *MAMA* ix. p. xxvi, but note already, in anticipation, Cox and Cameron, *MAMA* v. p. xxxiii at n. 6 'no Christian monument of this epoch is known to us'. Note the conjecture that an inscription of AD 308/9, attesting construction of columns and a propylon at a sanctuary of Theos Hypsistos, might belong to one of the outlying villages of Aezani, E. of the city, T. Drew Bear, *ANRW* ii. 18. 3, 2041–3.

[54] Drew Bear, *ANRW* ii. 18. 3, 1913–14 on the Phrygian cults of Aezani and Dorylaeum, which have many points in common with one another.

[55] *MAMA* x, introd.

[56] There is only one inscription from Ancyra itself (see above, Ch. 16 §IV n. 223), although Montanism is reliably attested there in the late 2nd or early 3rd cent. (Eusebius, *HE* 5. 16. 4). For the emendation of an explicitly Christian name in a 2nd- or 3rd-cent. inscription, see *AS* 27 (1977), 78. J. Strubbe, *Mnemosyne*, 34 (1981), 115–19 collects the epigraphic evidence for Christianity at Pessinus. None need be dated before Constantine, although *I. Pessinus*, nos. 117, 120, 122, 125, and *SEG* xxxviii (1988), 1283 should not be later than about 350. All the Christian inscriptions of Germa/Germia, the latter a great centre of pilgrimage from the 5th cent., are relatively late, see *RECAM* ii. 130, 135–7, 142; Strubbe, *Mnemosyne*, 34 (1981), 107–14 (texts from the summit of Mt Dindymus); C. Mango, *J.öst.Byz.* 36 (1986), 126–31. Likewise there are no Christian inscriptions from the N. Galatian countryside which are likely to belong to the 3rd or early 4th cent., although early Christian texts do occur in the

adjacent area of the central plateau in the region of Haymana, *RECAM* ii. 269–71, 273–4, 287, 292, 316, 323, 328–9, 331, 333, 340, 347, 352–4, 360, 365, and 385.

[57] *AS* 32 (1982), 102; *Life of St Theodotus*, 20–1; below, § VI.

[58] See below, n. 332.

worth citing.[59] Here, an analysis of four papyri of 309, the 340s, *c*.350, and *c*.450 respectively, which contain lists of personal names and patronymics which can be classified as explicitly Christian, explicitly pagan, or indeterminate, appear to show an accelerating growth of Christian numbers to about 12 per cent of the total population in 280, followed by a spectacular increase to 78 per cent in 345, and a more gradual elimination of the residual pagan population thereafter. If these figures are projected onto a graph, the steepest increase of all takes place within a single generation, from around 17 per cent in 290 to 70 per cent in 325—figures, and a time span, that are at least roughly comparable to the supposed achievement of Gregory Thaumaturgus. The evidence from Egypt is not so precise that it allows the claim that most of these conversions took place before the peace of the Church; the victory of Constantine may have had a dramatic effect on people's allegiance, but at least the speed of change seems assured.

There has been much debate about the period at which the Roman empire, or at least its eastern provinces, became Christian. On one view the crucial time was the second half of the third century. Accordingly the persecutions carried out by Diocletian and his colleagues were doomed to failure as a desperate last resort against a movement that had already undermined the foundations of paganism, and Constantine's espousal of Christianity showed a timely awareness of the new social and religious order.[60] For others, the Church had made little headway, at least in the number of its converts, before the victory of Constantine. Even with the many privileges offered to Christians and to clergy during Constantine's reign, most of the empire remained obstinately pagan until the second half of the fourth century.[61]

The sample of evidence which Anatolia has to offer on both sides of the argument shows that the original question has been too crudely posed. The eastern Roman empire was not homogeneous, but consisted of thousands of separate communities each with its own distinct history and culture. Christianity did not take a uniform hold across the area, but emerged as the dominant religion at different times. After 313, when it became the 'official religion' of the empire and enjoyed a wide range of valuable privileges, the transformation from pagan to Christian accelerated and became virtually universal. But in the third century local religious and social patterns of behaviour played a key role. No wonder then that one city might become Christian, while its neighbour, perhaps deliberately, remained pagan. Inter-city rivalry was an ineradicable part of provincial life, and it was not unusual for it to acquire a religious dimension. It is unrealistic to envisage the whole empire, or even whole provinces, adopting Christianity under these conditions. In the greatest of all studies of the spread of Christianity in the Roman world, Asia Minor is described as 'das christliche Land', and the appropriate map shows an uninterrupted block of Christian communities from the Aegean to the Euphrates by the year 300.[62] There is no reason to quarrel with the judgement that Christianity made more headway in Asia Minor, above all in Phrygia, than anywhere else in the Roman world in the third century AD, but its progress was irregular and the map of Christian progress resembles an irregular patchwork quilt not a simple monochrome blanket.

However, the Anatolian evidence gives no comfort to those who would argue that the Christians had made little headway before the fourth century. In an unusually perceptive passage the Church historian Sozomen contrasted the differing history of Christianity in Syria and in Asia Minor. Monks, or 'philosophers' as he terms them, had been largely instrumental in the conversion of Coele and Upper Syria, apart from the city of Antioch, and this had taken place slowly (after the conversion of Constantine). The desert-dwelling monks and hermits of Syria were to be distinguished, however, from the monks of Asia Minor both in their habitat and in their influence. 'I suppose that Galatia, Cappadocia, and the neighbouring provinces contained many other ecclesiastical philosophers at that time, for these regions had zealously espoused the Christian doctrine at an earlier date.'[63] A modern survey of the epigraphic evidence confirms that paganism lingered

[59] R. S. Bagnall, *BASP* 1982, 105–24, and also *ZPE* 69 (1987), 243–50 against E. Wipscycka, *ZPE* 62 (1986), 173–81 and *Aegyptus*, 68 (1988), 117–65. Bagnall's figures are questioned by Lane Fox, *Pagans and Christians*, 589–91 and MacMullen, *Christianizing the Roman Empire*, 83. Other papyrus evidence for Christianity, usefully assembled and discussed by E. A. Judge and S. C. Pickering, *JAC* 20 (1977), 47–71 does not suggest so early a Christian majority as Bagnall's statistics, but the latter should reveal a more reliable picture than sporadic references to Christians which happen to survive in mainly official, non-Christian documents.

[60] From a mass of literature I pick, on the side of early conversion, Harnack, ii, *passim*, and Barnes, CE, 191–207.

[61] Jones, *LRE* i. 91 and 96; MacMullen, *Christianizing the Roman Empire*, 32, 82 ff.; Lane Fox, *Pagans and Christians*, 586 ff. Against the last two, see now Barnes, in *L'Église et l'Empire*, 306–10. Even if we accept low figures for the number of Christians in 300 (and global figures in themselves are misleading for they make no allowance for the differential advance of Christianity in different places) the increase in numbers in the middle and later third century was enormous.

Cf. Origen, *De Princ.* 4. 1. 1–2 contrasting the small numbers of Christians in 200 compared with the period 230–50.

[62] Harnack's map at the end of vol. ii of *Mission und Ausbreitung*. For criticism, see Blanchetierre, 313.

[63] Sozomen, *HE* 6. 34.

very late in many of the sanctuaries of Syria.[64] There is no need to mistrust the epigraphic evidence of Anatolia when it appears to confirm the essence of Sozomen's observation.

III. *Persecution, Martyrdom, and the Importance of Saints*

Diocletian's resolve in 303 to persecute the Christians inaugurated an important new phase in the history of the Church, which was to culminate in the victory of Constantine at the Milvian Bridge in 312, when he was the first emperor openly to espouse the Christian cause, and the 'Edict of Milan' of 313 whereby he and Licinius reversed all the preceding anti-Christian legislation and laid the foundations for a new regime in which the Church was to enjoy an unparalleled position of privilege within the empire. For contemporary Christian writers, especially Eusebius and Lactantius, this decade was crucial. The persecutions followed by the peace of the Church could be seen as an allegory of the crucifixion and the resurrection of Christ himself, and were accordingly interpreted as the decisive turning point in the history of early Christianity.[65] To ascribe such stress to any single event or series of events inevitably distorts the historical perspective, and in this case it disturbs the picture of an unbroken development in the power of the Church which is evident in many of the rural communities of Anatolia through the third and fourth centuries. Moreover the inspirational rhetoric with which the story of the persecutions was told often does more to conceal than to reveal the truth of what actually took place.

Many of the key events in the history of the Great Persecution took place on the soil of Asia Minor. Apollo's oracle at Didyma strengthened Diocletian's purpose; his first actions were directed against Christian slaves and freedmen attached to the imperial court at Nicomedia, where the large Christian presence in the city acted as an affront and a spur to the pagan emperors.[66] The most vigorous opponent of the Christians was the emperor Maximinus, who controlled Asia Minor and the Near East, namely the administrative dioceses of Asiana, Pontica, and Oriens, as sole ruler from 311 to 313. During the spring of 312 he made a wide sweep through western Anatolia, from Nicomedia to Sardis, Carian Stratonicaea, and perhaps Lycia, before reaching his southern capital at Syrian

Antioch. The purpose of this journey was to reinforce pagan centres by his presence.[67] The cities in the east had been encouraged to declare their hostility to Christians and to petition him for rewards for doing so. The bait which he dangled before them was probably exemption from the urban poll-tax, recently imposed on resentful subjects by a hard-pressed Diocletian.[68] The small towns of Arycanda in Lycia and Colbasa in Pisidia are known to have responded positively to his suggestions, and copies of his rescript to them, a standard document, have survived. His attempt to revive the old religion hinged on the appointment of high priests of important cults, supervised from provincial centres. At Carian Stratonicaea a certain Sempronius Arruncius became the first and only high priest of Zeus of Panamara at the time of the emperor's visit, and marked his term of office with lavish displays of munificence unmatched by any of the previous priests of this important regional cult.[69] In the upper Tembris valley Aurelius Epitynchanos also assumed the high-priesthood of a bevy of local cults, certainly as part of a direct challenge to the strong Christian presence in the region (cf. above, Ch. 16 § v at nn. 274–5). Ironically his gravestone of 314 is the latest surviving product of a workshop whose other clients were then all Christian.[70] At Ancyra in Galatia, the Christian hero of one of the vividest martyr-acts relating to the persecution of 312, refused an offer to become high priest of Apollo, a position which would have given him decisive influence in the city.[71] Provincial governors were chosen for their

---

[64] J. H. W. G. Liebeschuetz, 'Epigraphic evidence on the Christianisation of Syria', *Akten des XI Int. Limeskongresses 1976* (1977), 485–508.

[65] Peter Brown, 'The Saint as Exemplar in Late Antiquity', *Representations* (Univ. California Press), 1: 2 (1983), 1–25.

[66] *I. Didyma*, 306.

[67] *JRS* 78 (1988), 119.

[68] *JRS* (1988), 121–3, doubted by T. D. Barnes, *JRA* 2 (1989), 257, who argues again for the old view of Seeck that the urban poll-tax was remitted to all the eastern provinces as Maximinus advanced through Asia Minor in 311. This involves more radical emendation of the text of *CTh*. 13. 10. 2 than the change to the consular date proposed in *JRS* (1988), 123, and it seems more likely that when Maximinus remitted the tax (perhaps not just in the cities) in Bithynia in 311 (Lactantius, *De mort. pers.* 36) he did so as a special favour to the province which contained the imperial palace at Nicomedia. Barnes's objection, that blanket exemption from the urban poll-tax in 312 was not possible since it would also have extended to Christians, carries no weight, since by definition to qualify for this exemption cities would have had, at least notionally, to have expelled all Christians from their territory. Finally, Barnes offers no explanation of his own for the most puzzling feature of Maximinus' rescript, the invitation to the recipients to ask for and be granted a further favour. The essence of Maximinus' policy was re-enacted by Julian; see below, § VIII at nn. 370–1.

[69] Arycanda, *CIL* iii. 12132; Colbasa, *JRS* (1988), 108; Stratonicaea, *SIG*³ 900, discussed by Lane Fox, *Pagans and Christians*, 584–5.

[70] Ramsay, *CB* i. 2, 566–7 nos. 467–9, other refs. at *AS* 32 (1982), 110 n. 93.

[71] *AS* 32 (1982), 93–113.

known animosity towards the Christians. Theotecnus in Galatia, Valerius Diogenes in Pisidia, and perhaps Eusebius in Lycia all played an active part in persecution as agents of the imperial will.[72] For nearly a year and a half between November 311 and the spring of 313 the policies of Maximinus were dominated by his obsession to root out the Christians.

It still remains impossible to form a real picture of the impact of the persecution on the communities of Asia Minor. The stories of individual suffering, like the martyrdom of Theodotus at Ancyra, Lucian of Antioch at Nicomedia, or the sufferings of the heretic bishop Eugenius at Laodicea Catacecaumene, tell us little about what happened to the bulk of the Christian population. It is a fair guess that the great majority looked to survival rather than a showy martyr's death, and the safest refuge would have been the countryside. Although Maximinus made an attempt to weed Christians out of rural as well as urban settlements,[73] villages must generally have offered a secure haven from soldiers or other official agents of imperial policy. Like Gregory the Wonder-Worker and his congregation in 250, the grandparents of Basil of Caesareia took to the hills of Pontus, doubtless to their family estates, for seven years (perhaps from 305 to 312),[74] and the Montanist Christians of Ancyra could assemble without fear in the country village of Malos by the river Halys, and could even avoid notice in the suburbs, although they risked arrest at the centre of Ancyra.[75] Given the strength of rural Christianity in Asia Minor by the end of the third century, the failure of the persecutions may readily be understood.

Nevertheless, the years of persecution, and particularly the vigorous efforts of Maximinus did claim many new martyrs, and thereby gave Christianity a resource which it was to exploit to the full in the coming centuries. Martyred saints provided Christians with inspiring examples of virtue and constancy. They also gave the Church the means by which to supplant pagan religious institutions with their own. Festivals in honour of the new saints began to fill the ecclesiastical calendar; local martyrs readily took on the role previously filled by pagan gods as champions and protectors of their former homes. The cult of the saints helped to endow the newly converted world with a wholly Christian organization of space and time.[76]

The beliefs of the earliest Christian communities, that the end of the world was at hand and that the righteous dead would be raised, made it inevitable that their cemeteries became foci of cult and worship, just as it caused Christians, in contrast to most pagans, to indicate their religion by word or symbol on their grave monuments. The supply of martyrs resulting from systematic persecution intensified the drawing power of the *coemeteria* where their bodies were buried, and it is significant that some of the earliest imperial legislation against Christians specifically outlawed such meetings, and that efforts were made to withhold or retain the remains of martyrs in the hope of restricting their posthumous influence.[77] Conversely Christians themselves made every effort to secure the bodies of their martyred champions and thereby give fresh impetus to the local church.[78]

In rare cases the epitaphs of martyrs have survived, as of Paulus in the valley of the Çarşamba,[79] or Gennadius at Laodicea Catacecaumene, who invited his own death by defying one of the imperial letters which required him to renounce his faith.[80] In themselves they are hardly distinguishable from other contemporary tombstones, but in peaceful times it was a simple step to provide not mere tombs but monumental chapels for martyrs or other prominent churchmen, with the result that extra-mural *martyria* became, even more than before 303, the centres of early Christian worship. The development is clear at Laodicea from the simple tomb of Gennadius to the funerary memorial of a later bishop, Severus, erected before AD 345 to serve as a chapel.[81]

Although the archaeology of pre-Constantinian Christianity in Asia Minor has hardly been studied,

---

[72] Eusebius, *HE* 8. 14. 9; Theotecnus in the *Life of St Theodotus* (see last n.); Val. Diogenes, responsible for persecuting bishop Eugenius of Laodicea, *MAMA* i. 170; Eusebius of Lycia may have tried and put to death bishop Methodius of Olympus, *JRS* (1988), 119 n. 40.

[73] *JRS* (1988), 121. Maximinus hoped that civic authorities would expel Christians from towns and from the countryside. If all complied, there would be no refuge for Christians in a friendly neighbouring city, as there had been for Cappadocia's Christians in the persecution of 235–8: 'in hac autem perturbatione constitutis fidelibus et huc atque illuc persecutionis metu fugientibus et patrias suas relinquentibus atque in alias regionum partes transeuntibus (est enim transeundi facultas eo quod persecutio illa non per totum mundum sed localis fuisset)', Cyprian, *Ep.* 75. 10. 2.

[74] *PG* 36. 501a ff.

[75] *AS* 32 (1982), 108–9.

[76] H. Delehaye, *Les Origines du culte des martyrs* (1912).

[77] Meetings in cemeteries, Eusebius, *HE* 7. 11. 10 (in the persecution of Valerian and Gallienus); 9. 2. 1.

[78] *HE* 8. 6. 7; the archetype is *Mart. Polycarpi* 17–18; cf. Lactantius, *Inst. Div.* 5. 11; Ammianus Marcellinus 22. 11. 10 (at Alexandria the people burnt the bodies of Bishop George and his colleagues, 'id metuens ne collectis supremis aedes illis exstruerentur ut reliquis qui deviare a religione compulsi pertulere cruciabiles poenas, ad usque gloriosam mortem intemerata fide progressi et nunc martyres appelluntur)'.

[79] *MAMA* viii. 200, cf. 168; see above, n. 42.

[80] *MAMA* i. 157 with *JRS* (1988), 105 n. 4 *contra* A. Wilhelm, *Sb. Berlin* (1932), 370–2, 375–8 (= *Akademieschriften*, ii. 826–8, 831–4).

[81] *MAMA* i. 171 with Wilhelm, *Sb. Berl.* (1932) 382–8 (838–44).

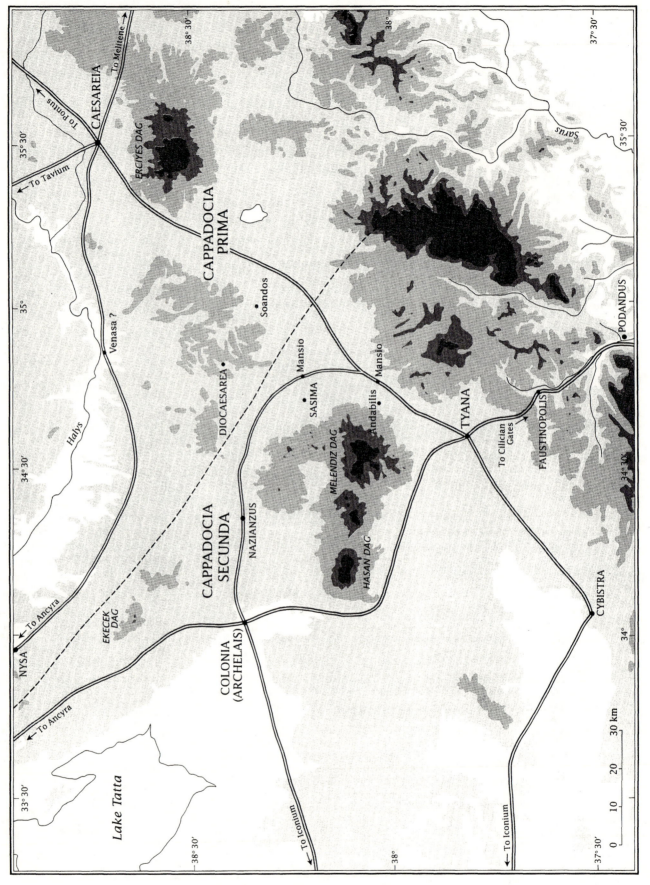

Map 3. Western Cappadocia

it is not difficult to envisage how this development might have taken shape in architectural terms. It was commonplace throughout the Roman period in Anatolia, especially in the southern and western coastal regions, to bury the members of wealthy families in *heroa*—built tombs which are often scarcely to be distinguished from temples and which could sometimes be numbered among the most lavish and imposing buildings of their cities. These evidently formed the locus for family cults. Christians who chose to bury prominent members of their community in chapels, which then became centres of worship, were behaving in a way that would have been readily intelligible to pagan contemporaries. In the primitive period of Christianity, worship was confined to private houses, and no public churches were erected. As the communities began to grow in size and confidence in the later third century, the pattern began to change. Public basilicas were built in the cities. Oxyrhynchus in Egypt had at least two before the time of Constantine, each large enough to give its name to the street where it stood. There were basilicas in several of the cities of North Africa before 300, and the exiguous written evidence suggests that this was also the case in Asia Minor, although none has been identified archaeologically. The church at Neocaesareia had allegedly been built by Gregory the Wonder-Worker; more famously the basilica at Nicomedia overlooked the imperial palace itself, and had been razed to the ground in the first act of Diocletian's persecution.[82]

But in many cities it may not have been easy to find a central site for a basilica large enough for the growing number of Christians. City agoras were already crowded with public buildings; there were sound practical reasons, therefore, for placing some of the earliest public churches in cemeteries where sites were readily available. Although certain prominent pagan shrines were apparently demolished in the middle years of the fourth century at the instigation of Constantius, in Anatolia Christian basilicas only appeared in city centres in the last quarter of the fourth and at the beginning of the fifth century. By this period the direction of persecution was reversed and focused on the remnant pagan communities. Imperial legislation, particularly between the 380s and the 420s, encouraged the demolition of pagan shrines. The consequences are

visible in almost every city of Asia Minor whose buildings have been studied: temples were systematically demolished or converted for Christian use. Christian worship by the end of the fourth century definitively occupied the centre of the civic stage.[83]

The city of Caesareia in Cappadocia furnishes a nice example of the processes at work. In 362 an attempt to demolish the temple of Fortune led the emperor Julian to punish the city by demoting it to the status of a village. The temples of Apollo and Zeus, we learn, were already in ruins. Meanwhile the Christians of Caesareia, certainly the great majority, worshipped in the extra-mural churches of local saints: St Mamas, St Eupsychius (allegedly martyred in Julian's time precisely for helping destroy the temples), St Damas, and St Gordius. In a sermon of the 370s Basil described the crowd which attended the annual festival of St Gordius, swarming like bees to his *martyrium* outside the city, and at such a festival he condemned the women of his congregation for drunken dancing in the chapels that stood in front of Caesareia. When at the end of his life Basil laid plans for a great new Christian foundation, comprising a hostel for travellers, a hospice for the poor, a monastery, and a church—no less he claimed than a miniature city itself—it too was to be sited in the suburbs.[84]

IV. *Rural Christianity in the Fourth Century: Cappadocia*

Cappadocia in the first three centuries AD was a region hardly noticed by literary sources and almost without inscriptions. It is thus virtually impossible to form an impression of the early progress of Christianity except to observe the presence of two important bishops of Cappadocian Caesareia in the early and middle years of the third century, Alexander and Firmilian.[85]

[82] Lactantius, *De mort. pers.* 12. 2. In general, on 3rd cent. basilicas, see Lane Fox, *Pagans and Christians*, 587; J. B. Ward-Perkins, 'Memoria, Martyr's Tomb, and Church', *JTS* 17 (1966), 24–5; 'Constantine and the Origins of the Christian Basilica', *PBSR* 22 (1954), 69–90; F. W. Deichmann, 'Entstehung der Christlichen Basilica und Entstehung des Kirchengebäudes', *Gesammelte Schriften* (1982), 35–46; further bibliography in J. Vaes, *Anc. Soc.* 15–17 (1984–6), 349 n. 116.

[83] *CTh.* 16. 10, *passim.* Several important texts which explicitly proscribed paganism are collected by P. R. Coleman-Norton, *Roman State and Christian Church*, ii (1966), notably nos. 184 (*CTh.* 16. 10. 7, AD 381), 242 (*CTh.* 16. 10. 12, AD 392), 340 (*CTh.* 16. 10. 20, AD 415), 424 (*CTh.* 16. 10. 25, AD 435), with discussion at p. 705 n. 3. See in general M. A. Huttman, *The Establishment of Christianity and the Proscription of Paganism* (1914). Recent discussion by G. Fowden, 'Bishops and Temples in the Eastern Empire', *JTS* 29 (1978), 53–78; F. W. Deichmann, *JdI* 54 (1939), 105–36, updated in *RAC* 2, 1228–41; J. M. Speiser, 'Le Christianization des sanctuaires païennes en Grèce', *Neue Forschungen in griechischen Heiligtümern* (1977), 309–20; J. Vaes. *Anc. Soc.* 15–17 (1984–6), 305–443.

[84] For Julian and Caesareia, see below, §VIII at nn. 367–9. Extra-mural churches: St Gordius, Basil, *Hom.* 18 (*PG* 31. 489b–c); St Mamas, Basil, *Hom.* 23 (*PG* 31. 592b); St Eupsychius and St Damas, see below n. 111; drunken dancing, Basil, *Hom. in ebriosos* (*PG* 31. 444).

[85] Harnack, ii. 743 ff.

There was a decisive advance in the first half of the fourth century. The father of the oldest of the three great fathers of the Cappadocian Church, Gregory of Nazianzus, who was born around AD 280, was a member of the pagan Hypsistarian sect until 325, when he was converted by a convoy of bishops travelling through his home town to the Council of Nicaea (above, Ch. 16 n. 300).[86] Within three years he became the first bishop of Nazianzus, at about the time that his second child, the famous Gregory, was born. It was by his efforts and with his funds that Nazianzus acquired a first public church by the time of his death in 374.[87] Spiritual development accompanied material progress. In the funeral oration delivered by his son he is said to have taken over a rustic and uncivilized church, accustomed to the crude doctrines of a former bishop, and moulded it into a civilized, theologically sophisticated, and above all Orthodox congregation.[88]

The brothers Basil bishop of Caesareia and Gregory bishop of Nyssa, who were born around 329 and 340 respectively, came from a family with a longer Christian tradition. Their grandparents on the paternal side, who came from Pontus, were already Christians by the time of the Great Persecution, and avoided the authorities for seven years by retreating to their Pontic estates; the grandfather may have suffered a martyr's death and died relatively young.[89] Their father Basil the elder was born around 280 and had a career as a Christian rhetor at Neocaesareia.[90] He married a well-born Cappadocian woman from Caesareia and they produced a devout family, not only the two famous bishops, but their elder sister, the saintly Macrina, a younger brother Peter, who became a priest at Pontic Sebaste, another brother Naucratius, to be killed in a hunting accident, and four other sisters.[91] Pontic estates, hunting, rhetoric, and the leisure for study helped to form the background of this large and influential family, which would doubtless have played a dominant role in the affairs of Pontus and Cappadocia in any age. The elder Gregory and the elder Basil were members of the first Christian generation to grow up under Constantine; they might even have been the personalities in Eusebius' mind, when he spoke of Cappadocians who were a match for anyone in their Christian education and learning.[92]

The voluminous writings of the great bishops of the next generation, Gregory of Nazianzus, Gregory of Nyssa, and Basil of Caesareia, provide an unparalleled mine of information about the Church during the second half of the fourth century. The cautious statements that can be hazarded about the character and extent of the Christian communities in third-century Phrygia or Lycaonia can be replaced by a more confident reconstruction of churches and congregations in fourth-century Cappadocia. Although there are good grounds for thinking that Cappadocia differed significantly from other regions of Asia Minor, and a clear contrast can be drawn with the situation in Galatia (below, § VI) and in Phrygia (§ IX), the unparalleled quantity of detail revealed by the writings of the Cappadocian fathers helps also to throw light on the social and religious development of other areas in the later fourth century. An important thread that runs through the history of Anatolian Christianity in the previous centuries is the paramount importance of the rural churches. The culmination of this process, and the winning of the countryside for Christianity, is to be learned from the Cappadocians.

The creation of shrines in the countryside is a notable feature of the fourth-century evidence as a whole. As early as 312, and at any rate by about 360 when the Life was written, Theodotus of Ancyra had attempted to collect the remains of a martyr (Victor) that had been scattered near the river Halys, in order to found a shrine at an otherwise unknown Galatian village. His later efforts to recover the bodies of seven Christian virgins from a local lake led to his own arrest and martyrdom at Ancyra, but his own relics were collected and carried to the village of Malos forty miles to the north-east, where remains of his church have survived.[93] An inscription commemorating the cult of St Lucian of Antioch, another victim of the persecution in Nicomedia in 312, has been found in north-west Cappadocia near Kırşehir, another witness to the same process, whereby martyr-cults acted as standard-bearers and carried Christianity to remote country districts.[94] Later in the century the Cappadocian fathers referred continually to rural shrines and country festivals, and were anxious to add to their number by

[86] Greg. Naz. Or. 18. 12, PG 35. 1000b.

[87] Greg. Naz., in Anth. Pal. 8. 15; T. A. Kopecek, Church History, 43 (1974), 293–303, repr. in J. Martin and B. Quint, Christentum und Antike Gesellschaft, Wege zur Forschung, 649 (1990), 300–19.

[88] Greg. Naz. Or. 18. 16, PG 35. 1004c–d.

[89] See above, n. 74. For the martyred grandfather see Greg. Nys. Life of Macrina 2, 20. 11.

[90] Greg. Naz. Or. in Basilium 13. 12 (PG 36. 509a–b); Basil, Ep. 210. 1.

[91] J. E. Pfister, Vig. Chr. 17 (1964), 108–13. NB three modern studies are particularly helpful for the non-ecclesiastical background to Basil's correspondence: B. Treucker, Politische und sozialgeschichtliche Studien zu den Basilius-Briefen (1961); R. Teja, Organizacion social e politica de Capadocia en el siglo IV, segun los padres capadocios (1974), which I reviewed ungenerously in JRS 66 (1976), 256–7; B. Gain, L'Église de Cappadoce au IVe siècle d'après la correspondance de Basile de Césarée (330–379) (1981).

[92] Eusebius, Life of Constantine, 4. 43.

[93] AS 32 (1982), 93–113.

[94] S. Eyice and J. Noret, Analecta Bollandiana, 91 (1973), 363–77.

acquiring new relics and building new churches. Before he became bishop of Caesareia in 370 Basil wrote to Arcadius, the bishop of an unknown Anatolian community, to congratulate him on his church-building, and says how ready he would be to emulate him if only he too could lay his hands on some martyr's remains.[95] A few years later he wrote to correspondents in Scythia north of the Danube (a region supposedly evangelized by Cappadocians who had been taken prisoner and transported there during the Gothic raids of the 250s and 260s) to make arrangements for the transfer back to Caesareia of the relics of Sabas, martyred as recently as 372. He concluded by remarking that if the persecutions still continued there, the Scythians would do well to send the remains of fresh martyrs back to their fatherland.[96] In the same spirit he deplored the struggles within the Church during his own day, for despite the righteousness of the Orthodox cause, victims of violence in these disputes could not be treated as martyrs, since they had died at the hands of fellow Christians.[97] Eastern Anatolia had its own remains to export also. Basil's single letter to Ambrose of Milan concerned the return of the remains of St Dionysius from Caesareia to his native city;[98] John Chrysostom reported the arrival of the relics of St Phocas at Antioch from Pontus,[99] and after his own death in exile at Pontic Comana, his body too was transported to Constantinople and made the object of a cult there.[100] The cult of the forty martyrs of Sebaste, Roman soldiers belonging to the local garrison who had perished for their faith under Licinius, owed much of its popularity to their numbers. The will that they were supposed to have made laid down that they should be buried together and their remains not scattered,[101] but by Basil's day they were to be found all over Cappadocia,[102] and Gregory of Nyssa buried his own father at a chapel where a portion of the relics were preserved, in a village near his family's estate in Pontus.[103]

The dispersal of these shrines is clear testimony to the strength of rural Christianity, and the gatherings which assembled around them provided the most important meeting places for a scattered population, offering important alternative arenas for economic activity and social intercourse to the towns and cities. There were places of worship throughout rural Paphlagonia,[104] and gatherings or synods at Attagaina in eastern Pontus, where characteristically Basil hoped to mediate between a young acquaintance Valerian and other persons with whom he was in dispute.[105] At Venasa, formerly one of the chief pagan centres of Cappadocia, crowds would come together from every direction at a festival 'in the usual manner',[106] and at Euchaita in Pontus the cult of the soldier St Theodore was celebrated at an annual gathering to which pilgrims flocked, coming and going along the highway, 'as numerous as ants'.[107] Theodore, like Theodotus of Ancyra, was buried not in the city where he had lived and died, but in the village of Euchaita on its territory.[108] Basil also speaks of a visit to an unnamed Cappadocian village at the time of its annual synod, and of a place, barely a village, called Pharmagoun in Armenia Minor, famous for the distinction of its martyrs and for the crowds that gathered for its yearly festival.[109] These synods attracted congregations from town and country, high clergy from far afield as well as the local laity.[110] Basil repeatedly sent out invitations to the festival of St Eupsychius and St Damas at Caesareia, and hoped that it would be an opportunity for him to present his country bishops (*chorepiscopi*) to the accountant of the imperial prefects (*numerarius*), so that he could plead for tax exemptions on their behalf.[111] This mingling of secular with sacred business was inevitable. A casual remark in Basil's *Homilia in Divites* portrays church festivals as market-places, where any one could take delight in a good bargain, and confirms that like the *panegyreis* which

[95] *Ep.* 49.
[96] *Epp.* 155, 164, 165. 155 was sent to Iunius Soranus, *dux Scythiae*, cf. *PLRE* i. 848, Iunius Soranus, 2.
[97] *Ep.* 164 and 257, contradicting the claim in *Ep.* 139 that victims of sectarian persecution were also martyrs.
[98] *Ep.* 197.
[99] *PG* L 799; Delehaye, *Les Origines du culte des martyres*, 55–6, and 169.
[100] Socrates, *HE* 7. 45; Theodoret, *HE* 5. 36.
[101] Delehaye, *Les Origines du culte des martyres*, 61 citing N. Bonwetsch, 'Das Testament der vierzig Märtyrer', *Studien zur Geschichte der Theologie und Kirche*, i (1897), 76.
[102] Basil, *Hom.* 19. 8, *PG* 31. 521b, οὗτοι εἰσιν οἱ τὴν καθ’ ἡμᾶς χώραν διαλαβόντες, οἱονεὶ πύργοι τινὲς συνεχεῖς ἀσφάλειαν ἐκ τῆς τῶν ἐναντίων καταδρομῆς παρερχόμενοι οὐχ ἑνὶ τόπῳ ἑαυτοὺς κατακλείσαντες ἀλλὰ πολλοῖς ἤδη ἐπιξενωθέντες χωρίοις, καὶ πολλὰς πατρίδας κατακοσμήσαντες.
[103] *PG* 46. 784b–c.

[104] Basil, *Epp.* 226 (region of Gangra), 251. Compare Firmus of Caesarea (c. AD 430; edn. in *Sources chrétiennes* 350 (1989)), *Ep.* 15 on a gathering to commemorate a saint at Ἀργοκνοῖς, an unknown place in Cappadocia.
[105] *Ep.* 278.
[106] *Ep.* 169.
[107] Greg. Nys., *PG* 46. 736c.
[108] For the cult of St Theodore at Euchaita, see H. Delehaye, *ASRamsay*, 129–34, and especially the important inscriptions of the 5th cent. published by C. Mango and I. Ševčenko, *Byz. Zeitschr.* 65 (1972), 379–93 nos. 1 and 2.
[109] *Ep.* 95.
[110] Basil, *Hom.* 23, *PG* 31. 592b (St Mamas); Greg. Nys., *PG* 46. 736c (St Theodore); Basil, *Ep.* 169.
[111] *Ep.* 142; note Basil's invitations to bishops (*Epp.* 100, 176, 252) to attend the gathering for St Eupsychius and St Damas at Caesareia. Eupsychius was a recent martyr, put to death by Julian for helping to demolish the temple of Fortune, Sozomen, *HE* 5. 11; cf. Greg. Naz. *Ep.* 57 (to Basil).

accompanied pagan festivals throughout the Hellenistic period and in the early Roman empire, these were important centres of commerce and barter.[112]

But the importance of these festivals as centres of cult remained paramount. Asterius, bishop of Amaseia a generation after Basil, described them as schoolrooms for men's souls, where a congregation could assemble to honour its saints and, by its piety, emulate the fortitude which the martyrs had shown.[113] Gregory of Nyssa stressed the importance of a martyr for the members of a community, who would consider themselves his kinsfolk.[114] The encomiastic sermons which fourth-century bishops delivered in honour of their country's saints did everything possible to strengthen these ties and to intensify Christian feeling by parading these inspiring examples before their congregations.[115]

With the new style of worship at these annual festivals, there came a new rhythm to the year, sometimes conforming to the old pagan calendar, but more often radically different. Martyrs were celebrated not on their birthdays, a pagan custom, but on the anniversary of their execution, the moment which marked their transition to a real life in the Kingdom of God.[116] The Church also found other reasons for declaring holy days, such as those most suitable for baptisms, and a part of a bishop's power lay in the fact that he would dictate these to his people.[117] 'Instead of the Pandia and Diasia and Dionysia and all your other festivals, feasts are celebrated for Peter, Paul, Thomas, Sergius, Marcellus, Leontius, Panteleemon, Antoninus, Maurice, and the rest of the martyrs, and sober gatherings are celebrated instead of the old processions,

bawdy behaviour, and bawdy language'.[118] Sermons of the day were directed to this end, denouncing old pagan customs such as the riotous and ineradicable festivities of New Year's Day, and extolling instead the new Christian calendar.[119] By the end of the fourth century the transformation may have been almost accomplished. At least Gregory of Nyssa, denouncing the practice of making pilgrimages to the Holy Land, which were fraught with corrupting influences for men out of sight of their family and their neighbours, could say that 'if it is really possible to infer God's presence from visible symbols, one might justly consider that he dwelt in Cappadocia rather than anywhere outside it. For how many altars are to be found there on which the name of our Lord is glorified? One could hardly count so many in all the rest of the world.'[120]

The most important clergy in the Anatolian countryside were the country bishops (*chorepiscopi*).[121] They are first mentioned in the canons of the church councils of Ancyra in 314 and of Neocaesareia, perhaps in 319, which attempted to limit their powers and status, in the first case by forbidding them to elect presbyters or deacons without reference to their city bishop, and in the second by explicitly subordinating them to these bishops.[122] Similar issues faced the Council of Antioch in 341, which reinforced the rule of Ancyra that *chorepiscopi* could not appoint clergy without the authority of a city bishop, and forbade them to sign

---

[112] *Hom. in Divites*, 80–1, *PG* 31. 281c. Note also *PG* 31. 1020b–d, deploring the excessive commercial activity at martyrs' festivals. For *panegyreis* in general see now J. de Liegt and P. W. Neeve, *Athenaeum* 66 (1988), 391–416. Despite their arguments that the prime purpose of a *panegyris* was not commercial, they collect an impressive body of evidence which suggests that economic activity was of great importance (pp. 403 ff.).

[113] Asterius, *Hom. 3 in avaritiam*, *PG* 40. 193 ff.

[114] Greg. Nys., *PG* 46. 443a.

[115] Asterius delivered sermons for St Phocas of Sinope, St Euphemia, and St Stephen; Gregory of Nazianzus for the Maccabees (assimilated into Christian martyrology), St Cyprian, and St Athanasius; Gregory of Nyssa for his sister St Macrina, St Gregory Thaumaturgus, St Theodore, and the Forty Martyrs of Sebaste; Basil for St Mamas, St Gordius, and the Forty Martyrs (three times); both Gregorys delivered encomia for Basil himself.

[116] Delehaye, *Les Origines du culte des martyrs*, 24 ff.

[117] Greg. Nys. *De baptismo*, *PG* 46. 516c; ἰδοὺ τοίνυν ὁ τῶν ὅλων ἀγαθὸς οἰκονόμος, ὁ τοὺς ἐνιαυτοὺς ἀνακυκλῶν καὶ κυβερνῶν τὴν τῶν χρόνων περίοδον, ἤγαγεν ἡμέραν σωτήριον, καθ' ἣν σύνηθες ἡμῖν καλεῖν εἰς υἱοθεσίαν τοὺς ξένους, εἰς χάριτος μετουσίαν τοὺς πενομένους, εἰς κάθαρσιν ἁμαρτιῶν τοὺς ἐρρυπωμένους τοῖς πλημμελήμασιν.

[118] Theodoret, *Graec. affect. curat.* 8 fin., ed. Schulze iv. 923 ff. The whole passage runs, τὰ μὲν γὰρ ἐκείνων διελύθη τεμένη, ὡς μηδὲ σχημάτων διαμεῖναι τὸ εἶδος, μηδὲ τῶν βωμῶν τὸν τύπον τοὺς νῦν ἀνθρώπους ἐπίστασθαι· αἱ δὲ τούτων ὗλαι καθωσιώθησαν τοῖς τῶν μαρτύρων σηκοῖς. τοὺς γὰρ οἰκείους νέκρους ὁ δεσπότης ἀντεισῆξε τοῖς ὑμετέροις θεοῖς· καὶ τοὺς μὲν φρούδους ἀπέφηνε, τούτοις δὲ τὰ ἐκείνων ἀπένειμε γέρα. ἀντὶ γὰρ δὴ τῶν Πανδίων καὶ Διασίων καὶ Διονυσίων καὶ τῶν ἄλλων ὑμῶν ἑορτῶν Πέτρου καὶ Παύλου καὶ Θωμᾶ καὶ Σεργίου καὶ Μαρκέλλου καὶ Λεοντίου καὶ Παντελεήμονος καὶ Ἀντωνίνου καὶ Μαυρικίου καὶ τῶν ἄλλων μαρτύρων ἐπιτελοῦνται δημοθοινίαι, καὶ ἀντὶ τῆς πάλαι πομπείας καὶ αἰσχρουργίας καὶ αἰσχρορρημοσύνης σώφρονες ἑορτάζονται πανήγυρεις, οὐ μεθὴν ἔχουσι καὶ κῶμον καὶ γέλωτα, ἀλλ' ὑμνους θείους καὶ ἱερῶν λογίων ἀκρόασιν καὶ προσευχὴν ἀξιεπαίνοις κοσμουμένην δακρύοις. For the solemnity of Christian festivals at this period, cf. Basil, *Ep.* 243. 2.

[119] Asterius, *Hom.* 4, *PG* 40. 216 ff., cf. *Hom.* 12, *PG* 40. 338d–40a and *Hom.* 8, *PG* 40. 264b; Greg. Nys. *Ep.* 14; in general *Dict. d'arch. chrét. et de liturgie*, i. 1717–28, esp. 1719–21.

[120] Greg. Nys. *Ep.* 2. 9 (Pasquali): καὶ μὴν εἰ ἔστιν ἐκ τῶν φαινομένων Θεοῦ παρουσίαν τεκμήρασθαι, μᾶλλον ἄν τις ἐν τῷ ἔθνει τῶν Καππαδοκῶν τοῦ Θεοῦ διαιτᾶσθαι νομίσειεν ἤπερ ἐν οἷς ἔξω τόποις.

[121] H. Leclercq, *DACL* iii. 1 (1948), 1423–52 s.v. choréveques, with full bibliography, and 'La législation conciliaire relative aux choréveques', in Hefele and Leclercq, *Histoire des conciles*, 2. 2 (1908), 1197–237; Gain, *L'Église*, 94–5.

[122] 13th Canon of Ancyra (*Histoire des conciles*, 1. 1 (1907), 314); 14th Canon of Neocaesareia (ibid. 314).

canonical letters which transferred clerics from one diocese to another.[123] A synod held at Phrygian Laodicea towards the end of the fourth century abolished the post altogether, and substituted the new clerical position of *periodeutes*, a type of itinerant priest, in their place.[124] *Chorepiscopi*, however, continue to be attested from the fifth to the eighth centuries, and the ruling evidently fell into desuetude.

Chorepiscopi were to be found throughout central and eastern Asia Minor. Gregory of Nazianzus goes so far as to say that there were fifty serving under Basil of Caesareia, perhaps an exaggeration,[125] but we know for certain that two Cappadocian country bishops attended the Council of Neocaesareia, to be succeeded by five at the Council of Nicaea in 325, when they were accompanied by five colleagues from Isauria, two from Bithynia, and two from Cilicia.[126] Two more are attested by inscriptions from north Galatia, and Sozomen has a record of a bishop operating in several villages of Galatia in the early fifth century. In the rural communities of Phrygia where Montanist and Novatian Christianity were dominant, village bishops were the norm.[127]

The problem confronted in the successive canons of the Church councils was one of authority, that of the city bishop over his rural subordinates, and as such it is evidence not only for the need for discipline within a diocese in an age of intense sectarianism, but also for the resurgent strength of rural communities and their leaders at a time when the cities were faltering under pressure. These issues emerge clearly in the letters of Basil, which give the best picture of the role of the country bishops and at the same time illustrate the insurmountable difficulties of exercising ecclesiastical discipline. One letter, addressed to an accountant of the state treasury, shows a *chorepiscopus* operating within a rural district called a *symmoria*; one of his duties was to see to the maintenance of the destitute, and Basil asked that a modest property set aside for the

poor should continue to be exempt from levies.[128] In this and in another similar case Basil wrote on behalf of his subordinates, but these were responsible for dealing directly with the officials themselves. Elsewhere he threatened *chorepiscopi* with excommunication if they accepted bribes from candidates for election to the clergy,[129] and set out careful rules for the admission of church servants (*hyperetai*), since many unsuitable persons had been let in by country bishops. In future the *hyperetai* should be sought out by local priests and deacons, who would present a list to the *chorepiscopi*; these in turn were required to collect the votes of the local congregation and send a memorandum with the chosen names for the bishop to approve. Only at the end of this process might they be admitted to the clergy.[130] The issue was of urgent practical importance, since there had been a mass of applications to the clergy by unsuitable persons who wanted to avoid conscription into the army.[131] Bribery and corruption was naturally not unknown in the elections of *chorepiscopi* themselves to the rural districts.[132]

A similar concern to control the affairs of churches in remote rural areas, something that was also often beyond the powers of the imperial authorities, lay behind the complicated intrigue between Basil and Amphilochius of Iconium to appoint bishops or other church leaders (*proistamenoi*)[133] in Isauria. Basil agreed that the old custom of dividing the episcopal burden of Isauria between many bishops was a valuable one, but he shied away from the popular elections prescribed by the canons of Nicaea, since this would lead to the appointment of unworthy men who would inevitably have a bad influence on the laity.[134] These sees, described as 'small towns' or 'small villages' (*mikropoliteiai*, *mikrokōmiai*) and their bishops correspond without doubt to the rural communities and modest bishops known from the epigraphy of the Çarşamba basin south-west of Iconium (see above, § 11 at nn. 39–44). Basil's favoured solution was to appoint a *prostates* at Isaura who could then co-opt fellow clergy. If this failed, they could simply allocate

[123] 8th and 10th Canons of Antioch (*Histoire des conciles*, 1. 2 (1907), 716–17).

[124] 57th Canon of Laodicea (ibid. 1024). The purpose of the change was quite explicitly to assert the authority of the bishops over rural clergy. For full references and bibliography on these councils, see M. Geerard, *Clavis Patrum Graecorum IV. Concilia* (1980). A περιοδεύτης appears in one of the inscriptions of the Çarşamba valley, *MAMA* viii. 303.

[125] *De vita sua* (ed. Jungck, 1974), 447–8 with comm.

[126] For the list of bishops who attended the Nicene Council see H. Gelzer, H. Hilgenfeld, and O. Cuntz, *Patrum Nicaenorum Nomina* (1898).

[127] *RECAM* ii. 237 (Bağıcı, near the Salt Lake); J. H. Mordtmann, *Marmora Ancyrana* (1974), 22 no. 11, which acclaims a country bishop and his clergy, including a deacon, for their labour in building (presumably) a church. See also Sozomen, 8. 1.

[128] *Ep.* 142.
[129] *Ep.* 53.
[130] *Ep.* 54.
[131] See below, nn. 176 and 193.
[132] *Ep.* 290.
[133] *Ep.* 190. For *proistamenoi* in the early Church, see P. J. Fedwick, 'The Function of the *Proestos* in the Earliest Church Koinonia', *Recherches de théologie ancienne et médiévale*, 48 (1981), 5–13. It seems that Basil may have used the term in order to avoid calling these appointees *episcopi*. For a possible example in this area see W. M. Ramsay, *JHS* 25 (1905), 172 no. 45. The term also occurs in a number of inscriptions of the upper Tembris valley, where it is used to denote office-holders in the local church, Gibson, 'Christians', 91, and below, nn. 439, 444, 445, and 451.
[134] See below, § v at nn. 201–9.

proistamenoi to the lesser communities, and only then allow an election to the main bishopric at Isaura, so that the incumbent would not interfere with their selection of subordinates. The main obstacles to this plan were seen as the ambitions of many local people to hold high Church office, and their reluctance to accept appointments, or elections, made by outside bishops. If this plan also failed, because the Isaurians insisted on electing their own people, then Basil and Amphilochius would have to make every effort to limit the damage by controlling all future appointments. Not all the details of the letter can be fully explained, but taken as a whole it is a striking example of strenuous, but evidently unsuccessful efforts by Church leaders to control an area whose history of dissent from authority extended far beyond ecclesiastical matters. Amphilochius faced similar problems in another outlying area dependent on Iconium, eastern Pisidia; to circumvent an obscure problem involving a dissident priest and his successor there, Basil recommended that a village which had hitherto been subordinate to the town of Mistea be transferred to the jurisdiction of neighbouring Vasada, thus cutting through various complicated obstacles which beset the case.[135] Gerrymandering was evidently quite acceptable so long as the cause was just—and Orthodox. Firm and if need be unscrupulous action was the watchword of Basil's political creed.

The great rural expanses of Cappadocia and Pontus posed a constant challenge to the Church's authority. Paradoxically, and perhaps because it was as hard for the imperial authorities as it was for bishops to exercise control in rural areas, villages seem to have retained more powers of self-government than many of the cities. When a peasant from his home village of Annisa in Pontus assaulted Basil, and broke into his house, Basil appealed to the governor of Cappadocia for help, asking him to authorize the local *pagarch* to arrest the man and have him locked up.[136] The episode shows that the provincial governor had to rely on local officials to enforce the law, and these must have retained some autonomy. The Church, which jealously guarded its juridical privileges in its own affairs and often extended them to other cases, naturally had a large role to play in reinforcing *Volksjustiz* at a village level. In one instance a man had been arrested at a country fair for stealing cheap clothing which had been collected for the poor; the case was handled exclusively by the ecclesiastical authorities, although Basil wrote to a secretary (*commentariensis*) of the local military

commander (*comes*) to keep him informed. He offered to hand the man over, but expressed a clear preference that the matter be handled by the Church, which could inflict its own punishment.[137] In another instance a man twice ignored a summons to face judgement which had been served on him by village magistrates. When he ignored a third demand issued in the name of the Church, he was excommunicated and excluded from dealings with his fellow-villagers.[138] The Church likewise could give point to local feeling by excommunicating an abductor.[139] The Church thus took every opportunity to establish itself as the principal source of authority in social as well as religious matters. Divine justice had a long pedigree in Anatolian villages (see above, Vol. I, Ch. 11 § v).

Local priests themselves, of course, might flout the discipline of their bishops. This is illustrated by the case of a clergyman living with an, admittedly elderly, unmarried woman, who was instructed by Basil to send her to a monastery;[140] and more vividly by the episode of the eccentric deacon Glycerius of Venasa, who had surrounded himself with a troupe of unmarried women, turned the local church upside down by flouting the orders of the presbyter and the local *chorepiscopus*, filled the whole community[141] with riot and commotion, taken to the hills, and finally returned to disrupt a local festival. The most convincing interpretation of this strange event is that Glycerius had become the leader of an ascetic group inspired by the early monastic teaching of Eustathius of Sebaste.[142] Such mavericks were not unprecedented in Cappadocian history (see above, § 11 at n. 49). The issue which they raised was ever present, the problem of imposing discipline on the vast expanses of the Anatolian countryside, without resorting to force on a scale which was beyond the means even of the imperial government, let alone the Church, to command.

There were some areas which even Basil's energy never touched. His correspondence rarely alludes to paganism. In one letter he expressed the wish that a widow would follow her son's example and become Christian;[143] in another he held out similar hopes for the pagan father of a Christian son,[144] and the canons which he drew up for Amphilochius of Iconium included the rule that the unbelief of a husband should

---

[135] *Ep.* 188 Canon 10; cf. Ramsay, *ABSA* 9 (1892), 266 ff. K. Holl, *Amphilochius von Ikonion* (1904), 20 n. 1; W. Ruge, *RE* (1932), 1767 s.v. Mindana, and 2129 s.v. Mistea.

[136] *Ep.* 3. For a *pagarch* at Laodicea Catacecaumene, see *Ath. Mitt.* 13 (1888), 238 no. 11 with *JRS* (1988), 113 n. 22.

[137] *Ep.* 286.

[138] *Ep.* 288.

[139] *Ep.* 270. See below, Ch. 18 § 1 n. 34.

[140] *Ep.* 55. The priest had ignored an earlier request by the *chorepiscopus* to send the woman away.

[141] Which is called a *polis*.

[142] *Ep.* 169; cf. Ramsay, *HGAM* 292–3; *The Church in the Roman Empire*² (1893), 443–64.

[143] *Ep.* 10.

[144] *Ep.* 276.

be no grounds for a wife to leave him.[145] Perhaps the addressees of the first two letters were educated people who clung to their traditional pagan beliefs even in a heavily Christian environment, as they did in greater numbers in Syrian Antioch or the larger cities of western Asia Minor.[146]

One pagan group stands apart from the rest, the Magusaioi, a race, as Basil said, which was to be found all over the country and had originally been colonists from Babylon. In answer to a request from the antiquarian bishop of Salamis, Epiphanius, he outlined some of their customs: they had no sacred books but transmitted the substance of their beliefs by word of mouth from father to son; they abhorred animal sacrifice, worshipped fire as a god, and contracted unholy marriages. Basil had enquired into the origin of their people and learned that they claimed descent from a certain Zarnuas.[147] Half a century earlier Eusebius, drawing on the work of the Syriac Christian Bardesanes of Edessa, had also described their incestuous habits and oral traditions, and observed that their settlements were to be found in Media, Egypt, Phrygia, and Galatia.[148] Unquestionably these were remnants of the Persian population which had colonized widely not only in Cappadocia, although this was a major stronghold, but also over the rest of Anatolia. They left their mark in cults of Ahura-Mazda, Anaeitis, and Mithras, and in their nomenclature.[149] The Persian settlement of Anatolia, and Persian cultural influence, marked the countryside not the cities.[150] They can be detected in the central plateau on the eastern skirts of Sultan Dağ at Laodicea Catacecaumene, in the plain of Neapolis near Lake Beyşehir, in the fertile valleys east of Mount Dindymus in Galatia, and scattered elsewhere in Phrygia, Pisidia, and Caria.[151] It is a remarkable tribute to the tenacity with which they clung to their traditional culture, that the Magusaioi in the late fourth century could still resist the deep inroads which Christianity had made on the rural populations. The Koran still attests their presence, although not specifically in Anatolia, in the seventh century. However,

the very terms in which Basil describes them suggests that they could be regarded as eccentric exceptions to the general rule.

For the most part, the east Anatolian countryside was Christian, and at least notionally controlled by the city bishops. When Gregory of Nazianzus pronounced his laudatory assessment of Basil's achievement, he stressed that he had paid as much attention to the Church in the countryside as in the cities.[152] The detailed evidence of Basil's letters fully bears out the judgement, but makes it clear that, although the issue of control had been firmly grasped, no easy solutions lay to hand.

v. *Cities, Bishops, and Imperial Authorities*

For over a hundred years after the middle of the third century reliable information about civic life in central and eastern Anatolia virtually ceases. It is difficult not to interpret this as a sign of declining vitality, but the argument essentially has to be made from silence. By the later fourth century equivocal hints give way to a mass of detailed testimony from the Church fathers. Basil, the two Gregorys, and their less prolific contemporaries, Amphilochius of Iconium and Asterius of Amaseia, were all bishops of central or east Anatolian cities who, like Ambrose and Augustine in the West, created by their actions and writings a mould from which Orthodox eastern Christianity was cast. Social and civic structures were part of the material which underwent this transformation.

Despite the importance of rural clergy in fourth-century Cappadocia, the organization of the Church revolved around the cities, still the essential units into which the provinces were divided. It is evident that the physical structure of the eastern empire had survived essentially intact since the 'golden age' of the second century. Then, a Chinese ambassador, sent to establish contact with the Roman empire, had been told by Parthian informants in Mesopotamia that it consisted of 400 cities, many subject provinces, post-stations and milestones.[153] The cities, with their magnificent public buildings, and the all-embracing network of paved roads were the most tangible physical features of the Roman landscape. Both cities and roads survived into the fourth century since both had a purpose to fulfil.

Caesareia was a famous and glorious city, dwarfing its Cappadocian neighbours.[154] There are passing references to its streets, colonnaded on either side, to the public baths and gymnasia, to the agora, theatres,

---

[145] *Ep.* 188 Canon 9.

[146] For Antioch, see Liebeschuetz, *Antioch*, 224 ff.

[147] *Ep.* 258. Epiphanius, *Panarion adv. haer.* 3. 2. 12 (*PG* 42. 804c–d) briefly alludes to them.

[148] For Bardesanes (Bardaisan) see *RE* iii (1897), 8–9 (Jülicher), Lane Fox, *Pagans and Christians*, 278–9.

[149] For Persians in Asia Minor see above all L. Robert, *CRAI* (1975), 306–30 (*OMS* v. 485–509); *Rev. num.* 18 (1976), 26–48 (*OMS* vi. 137–60), and other studies cited above, Ch. 16 § II n. 160. Iranian names were particularly common in Cappadocia, see Robert, *Noms indigènes*, index s.v. Perses.

[150] J. and L. Robert, *Fouilles d'Amyzon*, i (1983), 105 ff.

[151] S. Mitchell, *ANRW* ii. 7. 2, 1065–6; J. Strubbe, *Mnemosyne*, 34 (1981), 122–6 for Pessinus and the region of Mount Dindymus.

[152] Greg. Naz. *Or.* 43, *PG* 36. 580c (Basil's philanthropy).

[153] Quoted by D. L. Kennedy, *The Roman Frontier in North East Jordan* (1982), 137–8.

[154] Greg. Naz. *Or.* 43, *PG* 36. 512a.

and town houses two or three stories high.[155] The surviving encomia praise it as a centre of learning. It had already become a home of sophists in the second century but its reputation had been enhanced since Basil's father had founded a school of rhetoric there.[156] The chief city of Galatia, Ancyra, also retained a whole set of public buildings from the Roman period, now supplemented by various ecclesiastical foundations, and it too could boast of a well-educated and cultured aristocracy.[157] There were baths and a gymnasium at Sebaste in eastern Pontus, which was also the subject of an encomium, which stressed that it preserved all the characteristics of a great city,[158] and at Amaseia the theatre and the agora still survived even if a young Christian soldier, Theodore, had burnt down the temple of the Mother of the Gods in the time of Diocletian.[159]

The roads of Cappadocia, Pontus, and Armenia Minor were maintained through the fourth century. The great southern artery from Caesareia to Melitene had been extensively rebuilt under the Severans. Milestones imply continued care and attention especially during the Tetrarchy and under Constantine. The northern highway, which ran through Paphlagonia to Neocaesareia, Nicopolis, and the legionary fortress at Satala, was fully operational in the last quarter of the fourth century. A milestone of 367–75 has been reported twenty-four miles east of Nicopolis, implying that this remote stretch was still fully commissioned.[160] The letters of the Church fathers reveal an excellent and reliable system of communications. The only serious impediment to travel which they mention was the severe winter weather of Cappadocia, which could bury a house up to its eaves in snow for two months at a time.[161] For the rest of the year, despite the huge distances involved, travel, at least within Asia Minor, was almost a matter of routine. Basil regarded the 100-kilometre journey along the northern military highway between Nicopolis and Neocaesareia, as a short one,[162] and there is no hint that he had difficulty in finding couriers to take letters anywhere in Cap-

padocia, Pontus, Galatia, or to Constantinople.[163] Indeed he twice speaks of the rapidity with which letters defaming him had spread in these areas.[164] Gregory of Nazianzus' famous description of the road station at Sasima, to which he had virtually been banished by Basil in 372 to fill the vacant bishopric, gives a vivid, if prejudiced glimpse of the traffic that passed through such places:

It is a staging post in the middle of the highway that crosses Cappadocia, where the road divides into three; waterless, barren, with no real freedom, a benighted place like a poor village. Everywhere there is dust, the din of carts, groaning and wailing, men of the transport service, the clank of wheel and chains. As for the people, they are all foreigners and travelling folk.[165]

Problems did occur with more distant destinations, such as Edessa in Syria, Colonia in Armenia Minor, Alexandria in Egypt, or Thrace, to which one of Basil's most important correspondents, Eusebius of Samosata, had been exiled.[166] But the difficulty was usually to find a willing and trustworthy courier.[167] Except in the last case, where the roads were filled with deserters and bandits in the wake of the Gothic invasions of AD 377, Basil was never troubled for the security of travellers. The roads, with their regular staging posts designed for the use of the increasingly numerous mobile armies and official parties, offered a familiar point of reference for the whole population, and Basil, addressing his congregation, could compare a man's passage through life with travel along a road with its post-houses, or could refer to an incomplete sermon as a journey which had not accomplished the full number of stages that marked its route.[168]

Security of travel may have been in part due to the deployment of garrisons not only along the empire's frontiers but also, increasingly, in the interior. Already by the mid-third century the ideal of a Roman empire

[155] Ibid. 5; Sozomen, *HE* 5. 4; Basil, *Hom. 6 in divites*, PG 31. 272b.

[156] Basil, *Hom.* 18, PG 31. 492c–d, 502c for shops and houses.

[157] Foss, 'Ankara', 60–1.

[158] Basil, PG 31. 508f; Greg. Nys., PG 46. 749f.

[159] Greg. Nys., PG 46. 744a.

[160] See T. B. Mitford, *ANRW* ii. 7. 2 (1980), 1210 n. 130.

[161] Basil, *Epp.* 48, 27, 198 (no travel after a severe winter from Caesareia to Samosata before Easter), 213 (difficult for a man in poor health to reach Mesopotamia in winter), and 156 (the Armenian mountains impassable in winter). For the winter climate of Cappadocia and Galatia, see the remark of Sozomen, *HE* 6. 34, who said that it rendered a hermit's life impossible there. Also John Chrysostom, *Epp.* 127, 134, 135.

[162] *Ep.* 126.

[163] For the whole subject see D. Gorce, *Les Voyages, l'hospitalité et le port des lettres dans le monde chrétien des IVe et Ve siècles* (1924). Gain, *L'Église*, 1–39 puts too much stress on the difficulties.

[164] *Epp.* 223 and 234.

[165] Greg. Naz. *De vita sua* (ed. 1974), 439–45. Compare John Chrysostom, PG 47. 458 for another detailed evocation of *stathmoi* along the imperial roads.

[166] *Epp.* 267, 195, 139, 198.

[167] Basil generally relied on government officials (*Epp.* 71, 115, 198) or clergy. The public post (*demosios dromos*) is little mentioned. The letter of Julian to Basil, *Ep.* 29, which is probably not authentic, invited him to use it. *Ep.* 306 is a request to the *praeses* of Armenia Minor for a permit to allow use of the service from Sebaste to Alexandria. Discussion in B. Treucker, *Politische und sozialgeschichtliche Studien zu den Basilius-Briefen* (1974), 97–100; Gorce, *Les Voyages*, 41–63; and Gain, *L'Église*, 17–18.

[168] *Ep.* 268 for deserters. The metaphor was used by Basil, *Hom.* 20, PG 31. 544b, and *Hom. in Iulittam*, PG 31. 241c.

whose inhabitants never set eyes on the soldiers who protected them, had been fatally compromised. Complaints from civilian communities in quiet areas against the rapacity of undisciplined gangs of soldiers were as familiar a story in the fourth century as they had been in the third. Soldiers were permanently deployed in many provincial cities. There were garrisons at Comana Pontica, Sebastopolis, and Sebaste,[169] and a permanent military entourage for the vicar of Pontica, whose headquarters were probably at Ancyra.[170] Inscriptions of the fourth century show soldiers stationed in east Phrygia or Lycaonia at Laodicea Catacecaumene, Tyriaion, Philomelium, Iconium, and Kana,[171] in Phrygia at Dorylaeum, Nacolea and Sebaste,[172] and in Galatia at Iuliopolis, Germa, and Tavium,[173] all cities where no permanent military presence is attested between the first and third centuries.

The recruiting officer was a familiar figure, for the security of the empire could not be guaranteed without conscription any more than it had been in the first or second centuries,[174] and press-gangs sometimes came into violent conflict with villagers.[175] Men attempted to join the clergy to avoid the draft.[176] The uneasy relations between soldiers and civilians naturally surfaced in the sermons of the time. Basil in one sermon evoked for his congregation the spectacle of the drunken soldier, who becomes a laughing-stock for small boys in the city's agora and has to be carried home unable to walk.[177] Better still, in his treatise on virginity he produced a metaphor which provides as vivid a picture as any in ancient literature of the impact of billeting on a civilian population. He says

A girl should avoid taking pleasure in sensual sights and sounds, for these are the first steps in the corruption of her virginity; one thing leads to another just as when a soldier comes into a city with his battalion, and prowls round looking for a place to lodge. Sometimes he is forcibly locked out by the master of the house, but once he is through the door he is well on the way to the inner chambers. He leaves his helmet or some piece of his armour inside and you think that he has left to join his companions. But the weapon that he has put down gives him reason to come in again, and in no time at all he is back bringing his companions into the house as well, all treating the place as if it was their own.[178]

While the agents of imperial authority in the form of governors, other officials, and soldiers were prominent—at least along the main roads and in the cities—the institutions of the cities themselves were in decline. In the second and early third centuries there had been an active political life, when members of the local aristocracy dominated the civic arena, holding important priesthoods and magistracies, staging shows and games at their own expense to enhance their prestige, erecting public buildings, providing distributions of cash and goods to their fellow citizens, and representing their cities' interests to Roman governors and emperors. The characteristics of this competitive and open-handed behaviour are writ large in the history of almost every eastern city, and the civic generosity, the euergetism, which it fostered can almost be described as the fuel on which civic life ran, a guarantee of continued prosperity. By the later fourth century the same cities present a very different picture. At least in central and eastern Anatolia, the only remaining position of eminence was to be a member of the city council, the 'political class',[179] and that was

---

169 Comana: Greg. Nys. *de Baptismo*, PG 46. 420; Sebastopolis: Greg. Nys. *Vita Macrinae* (ed. P. Maraval, *Sources chrétiennes* 1971), 36, and the garrison was still there in the 6th cent. when Justinian, *Nov.* 28 indicates that the place should be reckoned among the garrison posts not the cities. Sebaste: Greg. Nys., PG 46. 757d, Basil, *Ep.* 306.

170 Foss, 'Ankara', 33–4 n. 19.

171 Laodicea: *MAMA* i. 167–69b, 218, 306 (at Atlandı), indicating four *lanciarii*, an *ordinarius e campiductoribus*, a *signifer*, and a *draconarius*; Tyriaion: a *comes*, *MAMA* vii. 109b; Kana: a *scholarius*, *MAMA* viii. 225; Iconium: an *excubitor*, *MAMA* viii. 323, and an *actuarius lanciariorum*, *CIG* 4004; Philomelium: a *comes tou theiou consistoriou*, Drew Bear *et al.*, A. Pullinger, *An Early Traveller in Syria and Asia Minor* (1985), 64–6.

172 Nacolea: a *ducenarius e num. Io. Sen. Cor.* of AD 356 (T. Drew Bear, *HSCP* 81 (1977), 257–74); Dorylaeum: a *senator* (Drew Bear, *Glotta*, 50 (1972) 220), and a *comes scholae gentilium iuniorum* (Drew Bear and Eck, *Chiron*, 6 (1976), 305–7 no. 12 of the 5th or 6th cent.); Sebaste: a military gravestone of 390 (M. Speidel, *Roman Army Studies*, i (1984), 381–9; M. H. Ballance will publish a new reading of this text from his own copy).

173 A *comes* on the territory of Iuliopolis, *RECAM* ii. 159; a *primicerius* on the territory of Germa, *RECAM* ii. 121a; a *flavialis* and an *apo primiceriorum* at Tavium, *RECAM* ii. 450 and 499.

174 P. A. Brunt, *Roman Imperial Themes* (1990), 188–214, 511–12 (earlier, *Scripta Classica Israelica*, i (1974), 90–115). For conscription to the 4th- and 5th-cent. forces, see now J. H. W. G. Liebeschuetz, *Barbarians and Bishops* (1990), ch. 1.

175 Greg. Nys. *Hom. in XL mart.*, PG 46. 784b–c: ἐν δὴ ταύτῃ, κατὰ τὸν συνήθη Ῥωμαίοις νόμον, καταλόγου στρατιωτῶν διάγοντος, εἴς τις τῶν ὁπλιτῶν ἐπὶ τὴν κώμην τὴν προλεχθεῖσαν ἀφίκετο, πρὸς φυλακὴν τοῦ χωρίου παρὰ τοῦ ταξιάρχου δοθείς· ἵνα τῶν συστρατιωτῶν ἑαυτοῦ τὰς ὁρμὰς καὶ τὰς ὕβρεις ἀνείργῃ, ἃς εἰώθασιν ἐπάγειν τοῖς ἀγροίκοις ὑπὸ θράσους οἱ ὁπλιτεύοντες. For earlier evidence of the press-gang, see above, Vol. I, Ch. 9 § III at nn. 194–201.

176 Basil, *Ep.* 54; cf. *Ep.* 200 for a young recruiting officer who took a letter for Basil from Caesareia to Iconium.

177 Basil, *Hom. in ebriosos*, PG 41. 457.

178 Basil, *De virginitate* 15, PG 30 700d–701a. I am grateful to Fergus Millar for bringing this splendid passage to my attention.

179 Basil, *Ep.* 183 shows that the word *politeuomenoi* was used to denote members of the council. See *RECAM* ii. 476 n. for other uses and bibliography.

seen as a burden not a privilege.[180] The duties of a councillor could be summed up in three phrases, 'to make a contribution towards the council' (which surely means to fulfil civic liturgies), to collect taxes, and to organize grain supplies for the imperial armies.[181] The last task was perhaps an exceptional commitment, and men were conscious that when the emperor fought a war it imposed enormous additional burdens on the population, and especially on the curial class from which the councillors were drawn.[182] But the various forms of routine taxation, the 'many-headed hydra', exerted a constant pressure on councillors, whose position was defined precisely in terms of their responsibility to maintain the flow of income from taxation to the state.[183]

Apart from specialized local forms of taxation, such as that imposed on breeding-mares for which Cappadocia was famous,[184] or the levy on iron extracted from mines in the Taurus mountains, which was probably diverted directly to the imperial arms factory at Caesareia,[185] households were assessed for their contribution in terms of the number of persons which they contained, and on the property attached to them, as they had been at least since the time of Diocletian.[186] The assessment, or *apographe*, was carried out by local censors, or by officials called *exisotai*, whose title suggests that they were notionally charged with the fair distribution of the tax burden.[187] The responsibility for both tasks fell principally on local nominees who were designated by treasury officials,[188] and although the posts might offer opportunities to reward one's friends and to penalize one's enemies, and Gregory of Nazianzus delivered a homily to warn an *exisotes* against avarice,[189] the task of both the censor and the *exisotes* was seen as a burden, partly, no doubt, because the job required much time and effort and was hardly likely to enhance the office-

holder's local popularity, but principally because the official was held responsible for collecting a fixed sum which he would have to contribute himself if he failed to collect it from others. Basil had occasion to remark that being an *exisotes* impeded a man from carrying out his proper obligations to his city; and at another time he had to urge a reluctant friend to take the post of censor in the small Pontic town of Ibora, so that the office was not run like a slave-market.[190]

A very substantial proportion of Basil's correspondence consists of letters written to officials ranging in rank from the praetorian prefect of the East, through officials of the treasury in Constantinople, to provincial governors and censors, asking for remittance of taxes due from individuals or communities. In one specific instance he wrote on behalf of the local landowners to a treasury official to ask for prorogation of the tax in gold which was raised to pay for clothing for the troops. The reason that he alleges for the delay is that many of the councillors were scattered about the countryside, no doubt on their estates, and that it was difficult physically to collect the money.[191] The episode hints clearly at one route taken by councillors to avoid their duties, flight from the cities to the remoteness of the countryside, which was immeasurably harder for the authorities to control. Another means of escape from financial burdens was to seek specific exemption, if not from taxes, at least from local civic liturgies. The point has been well made that a fundamental characteristic of the administration of the Roman empire and of the emperor's role in it was the tension between the formulation of general rules and the grant of particular exemptions. This enabled the empire to operate within a set of universal laws and principles, while it fostered the growth of what has been called a beneficial ideology.[192] For a would-be councillor in the fourth century there were exemptions if he became an imperial official himself, if he joined the army, or if he became a member of the clergy. But obtaining such exemptions naturally created tensions at a local level, for it deprived already hard-pressed communities of potential supporters. So we find Basil not only asking that an *exisotes* be exempted from service so that he could better serve his city, but also attempting to dissuade a correspondent from becoming a soldier and thus abandoning the tradition, long-established in his family, of service to the city.[193]

A study of the council of Syrian Antioch in the fourth century, which was far larger than any city in

---

[180] See *Ep.* 75 on the plight of the council of Caesareia at the time of the division of Cappadocia, and *Ep.* 237 on the attempt by Demosthenes vicar of Pontica to have the clergy of Caesareia and Sebaste enrolled in the council, while rewarding the followers of the Arian Eustathius 'with the greatest honours'.

[181] *Ep.* 84: οὐ γὰρ δήπου τὸ παιδίον εἰς βουλευτὰς συντελέσει, ἢ ἐκλέξει τὰς εἰσφοράς, ἢ στρατιώταις χορηγήσει τὸ σιτηρέσιον, ἀλλ᾽ ἀνάγκη πάλιν τοῦ ἀθλίου γέροντος τὴν πολιὰν καταισχύνεσθαι.

[182] Cf. Liebeschuetz, *Barbarians and Bishops*, 163, 165–6, and *Rh. Mus.* 104 (1961), 242–56.

[183] See above, nn. 25, 181; compared to a hydra by Basil, *Ep.* 285.

[184] *Ep.* 303.

[185] *Ep.* 110.

[186] Cf. *Ep.* 37, which implies that a larger number of slaves in a household would give grounds for a higher tax rating.

[187] See *Epp.* 36, 98, 198, 281.

[188] *Ep.* 281 shows *exisosis* to have been a burdensome liturgy.

[189] Greg. Naz. *Or.* 19, PG 35. 1044–64.

[190] Basil, *Ep.* 299.

[191] *Ep.* 87.

[192] Fergus Millar, 'Empire and City, Augustus to Julian: Obligations, Excuses and Status', *JRS* 73 (1983) 76–96 at 77.

[193] *Epp.* 281 and 116.

central Asia Minor, charts a similar picture of decline in the face of increasing demands, and concludes that while the councils continued to some degree to pay for civic services, and to perform as tax-collectors for the government, the function that they most conspicuously failed to fulfil was to lead the community.[194] This was even truer of Cappadocia. There is no trace in any of the fourth-century evidence of a council discussing a political issue, acting as a court of law, or taking a political initiative, even in the banal and familiar guise of sending an embassy to the emperor or to other authorities in the imperial capital.[195] The powerlessness and vulnerability of what should have been the strongest political body in the province is vividly illustrated by the famous episode in 372 when the emperor Valens divided Cappadocia into two provinces, and gave instructions that a large proportion of the *bouleutai* of Caesareia be forcibly transferred to the small town of Podandus in the new province, to ensure that it had its appropriate quota of liturgists.[196] Basil exercised himself strenuously, but without immediate success, to reduce the impact of the decision.[197]

As the power of the traditional political class decreased, that of the Church and the bishops grew. The point is made by another famous story which arose from imperial interference with Cappadocia's affairs at about the same date. Late in 371 or early in 372 the emperor Valens, accompanied by his praetorian prefect Modestus, travelled across Asia Minor and stopped at Caesareia in order to force Basil to abandon support for Orthodoxy and endorse the Arian creed. Furious and frustrated at the end of a long and unsuccessful interview, Modestus said that no one to that day had ever addressed him with such brazen outspokenness. 'Perhaps', replied Basil, 'he had never met a bishop.'[198] While secular political debate was virtually unknown outside the immediate confines of the imperial court, and the great cities of the empire—Rome, Alexandria, Constantinople, and Antioch—ecclesiastical politics flourished in every city. The literature of these ecclesiastical disputes is overwhelmingly theological in form, and the issues as they are presented in sermons, tracts, polemical treatises, and private correspondence concerned questions of doctrine and the interpretation of Scripture. There is no need to doubt the sincerity with which the conflicting views were presented or their importance to the protagonists of the arguments, but the torrent of words cannot disguise the fact these were also disputes about power. Heresies and doctrinal disputes were nothing new in the history of the Church; indeed before Constantine it is possible to argue that the Church consisted entirely of conflicting heresies, with no Orthodoxy to set against them; but from the moment that the Church could claim the membership of the majority of the inhabitants of the empire, and had acquired privileges for its members, as well as wealth and property for itself on a large scale, the arguments ceased to be merely doctrinal but affected access to wealth and power. No one appreciated the fact better than Gregory of Nazianzus when he was dispatched to the dusty road-station of Sasima.

It was a no man's land between two rival bishops. A division of our native province gave occasion for the outbreak of a frightful brawl. The pretext was souls, but in fact it was desire for control, control, I hesitate to say it, of taxes and contributions which have the whole world in miserable confusion.[199]

The winners of such arguments, especially as judged by the emperors, gained control of the full resources of the Church and all the temporal power at its command. When Constantine endorsed the Nicene Creed, or Valens inclined to favour the Arians, the consequences could be devastating for the parts of the Christian community which found themselves out of step.

Some ecclesiastical politics was carried out on a grand scale: the confrontation between Basil and his Orthodox supporters with Valens; the attempt, in the wider context of the Arian controversy, to mobilize bishops in the western empire and the Pope at Rome to support the Orthodox cause.[200] But the most palpable effects of these disputes were felt locally. The key position was that of the bishop, and elections to the bishopric were often a matter of intense controversy. Since the third century, at least, clear principles had to be observed in choosing a candidate, which did not however lead to a fixed and universally observed procedure. Essentially a bishop had to be chosen by a vote of his congregation (*suffragium populi*), but could only be ordained by his fellow bishops (*episcoporum*

---

[194] Liebeschuetz, *Antioch: City and Imperial Administration in the Later Roman Empire*, 103.

[195] Councils, as a body, received letters from Basil (*Ep.* 97 to Tyana; 182 to Samosata; 102 to Satala; 228 to Colonia in Armenia Minor; 230 to Nicopolis) and orders from emperors (*Ep.* 75, Caesareia's councillors instructed to go to Podandus). There is no evidence for local magistrates. The *archons* referred to at this period were always provincial governors.

[196] Basil, *Epp.* 74–6; Greg. Naz. *Or.* 43, *PG* 36. 572a.

[197] See R. van Dam, 'Emperors, Bishops, and Friends in Late Antique Cappadocia', *JTS* 37 (1986), 53–76, and T. A. Kopeček, 'Curial Displacements and Flight in Later Fourth-Century Cappadocia', *Historia*, 23 (1974), 320–6 for discussion of this event.

[198] Greg. Nys. *In Eunomium*, 1. 59–66; cf. *Encomium in Bas.* 14, *PG* 46. 804; Greg. Naz. *Or.* 43, *PG* 36. 572a.

[199] Greg. Naz. *De vita sua*, 467–72; *Ep.* 48 (the meagre revenues of Sasima came from its suckling pigs and chickens!); cf. *Or.* 43. 58, *PG* 36. 569c for this war between bishops, and van Dam, *JTS* 37 (1986), 64–7.

[200] Basil, *Ep.* 70.

iudicium).[201] An election that adhered to these principles ought to enjoy both local and wider support, and the method found approval in the canons of the Council of Nicaea. For all that, the practice was not so clear-cut. Popular elections were not a widespread form of political expression in the later Roman empire, and could certainly be arranged so as to represent the wishes of an influential local minority more often than the will of the whole populace. There were communities that had no suitable local candidates, and many cases of bishops being appointed who had no previous connection with their new see. Disagreement could often be predicted between the existing bishops of a province, who were required to give their approval to a nomination. Electoral controversy therefore was the rule rather than the exception. Basil had failed controversially to become bishop of Caesareia in 361; when he took the place of his old rival Eusebius, after the latter's death in 370, there was further disturbance in the Cappadocian church hierarchy.[202] His letters show him anxiously concerned that the vacant sees of Ancyra and Neocaesareia did not fall to unsuitable candidates,[203] and he writes in anguish of the election of an Arian to the bishopric of Tarsus.[204] The intricate controversy over the election of bishops to Armenia Minor shows that in the absence of firmly defined procedures it was often a case of victory for the strongest pressure group. Terentius, a military commander in the region, had been ordered by Valens to supply it with bishops.[205] Meanwhile one of the cities, Satala, had asked Basil to send a candidate;[206] while a rival of Basil, Anthimos, had managed to secure the election of one his own supporters Faustus to an Armenian see without canvassing a single vote.[207] The role of the count Terentius in Armenia Minor shows that the imperial authorities were not above intervening in these matters, and the hand of the emperor Valens can be detected behind the machinations of Demosthenes, vicar of Pontica, to place Arian sympathizers in the minor Cappadocian sees of Nyssa, Doara, and Parnassus.[208] In the face of this highhanded approach Basil similarly matched men with vacancies, with scant regard for electoral niceties or, in the case of the appointment of Gregory of Nazianzus to Sasima, for the wishes of the candidate himself. Gregory of Nyssa wrote to the clergy of Nicomedia urging them to elect a bishop without regard for birth, wealth, or rank; Gregory of Nazianzus, perhaps disillusioned by personal experience, suggested that the main voice in determining the choice ought to be given to members of the clergy and to monks; at Ancyra in the mid-fourth century the disputes surrounding episcopal appointments probably went far to discredit the Church in the eyes of local pagans, and particularly in the judgement of the emperor Julian.[209]

At their worst, the bitter theological controversies of the fourth century involved persecution as vindictive as anything that the pagans had inflicted on the Christians before Constantine. Orthodox bishops in a time of Arian dominance could be driven out of their cities and condemned to die in the wilderness.[210] The views of a bishop would infect those of his congregation, which naturally tended to follow its leader.[211] In a letter to his uncle Gregory, Basil attempted to secure a reconciliation between them, hoping that this would lead to peace in the Church and bring tranquillity to whole cities and other communites which were affected by their dispute.[212] At the end of a long letter to Demosthenes the vicar of Pontica Basil reminded him of the fact that, in the course of schisms, many common people could be harmed;[213] and during an admittedly highly rhetorical appeal to the western churches, he painted a picture of whole congregations being forced out of their churches into the wilderness by the Arians, and condemned to endure the extremes of winter cold and summer heat without a shelter to protect them.[214]

Theological controversy thus had serious material consequences not simply for the protagonists but for the Christian public that stood behind them. Two points in particular may be stressed to show how such dispute changed the political climate of the time. Firstly, there was widespread and open participation in matters which were both theologically and politically important, something that had hardly been possible in the Roman empire since the time of Augustus. Secondly, the battles were not always won by the emperor or the emperor's supporters. The Church offered a serious and recognized alternative source of power to the court. When Basil confronted Valens in defence of the Orthodox creed, Gregory of Nyssa compared his demeanour to that of John the Baptist before Herod.

[201] On episcopal elections in general, see Jones, *LRE* 915–20; R. Gryson, *Rev. hist. eccl.* 68 (1973), 353–404 (3rd cent.) and 74 (1979), 301–45 (4th cent., esp. 336–41 on Cappadocia and eastern Anatolia); elections in Cappadocia, Gain, *L'Église*, 81–6.
[202] *Ep.* 59, cf. *Ep.* 47 and van Dam, *JTS* 37 (1986), 64.
[203] *Epp.* 28 and 34.
[204] *Epp.* 99, 102, 103, 120–2, 128.
[205] *Ep.* 99.
[206] *Ep.* 102.
[207] *Epp.* 120, 122.
[208] *Epp.* 237–40.
[209] Greg. Nys. *Ep.* 17; Greg. Naz. *Or.* 18. 35, *PG* 35. 1032b; for Ancyra see below, § VIII.
[210] Basil, *Ep.* 242.
[211] *Ep.* 66.
[212] *Ep.* 59.
[213] *Ep.* 225.
[214] *Ep.* 243.

This was the very embodiment of the courage and frank talk of a Christian speaking out in front of a tyrant.[215]

A bishop's power was most commonly made plain in local dealings, for instance in the control which he exercised over lesser clergy or in his administration of Church law. The importance of controlling the clergy is illustrated by Basil's relationship with his country bishops, but it recurs in other contexts. Exemptions from taxation and from liturgies were an important but generally undesirable incentive to men to join the priesthood. The emperors were inevitably driven to limit the number of exempted clerics in any one community,[216] and the problem confronted Basil, who petitioned the praetorian prefect Modestus for the Church's right to administer the exemptions without outside interference, since otherwise persons who argued from outdated census lists might claim prolonged immunities for themselves and their families and leave no place for *bona fide* priests.[217] The episode shows the Church attempting to demarcate territory where its authority would be free from interference. It displayed similar tenacity in securing and extending its powers of jurisdiction. The code of ecclesiastical law was set out in canons issued both by individual bishops and, more authoritatively, by episcopal synods. These extended far beyond matters of religious observance, individual morality, or discipline within the clergy, as is already clear from the canonical Letter of Gregory the Wonder-Worker (see above, §1).

The power of Church law is most evident in a letter which Basil sent to Athanasius, bishop of Alexandria, who had recently excommunicated a tyrannical governor of Libya, himself a native of Cappadocia. Basil agreed to mobilize the consensus of Caesareia's citizens against him, informing his household, friends, and strangers by a published proclamation and by letters that they were to withhold fire and water and were to have no converse with the man, in the hope that this universal condemnation would sufficiently punish him for his abuse of power.[218] It is no surprise that Basil did everything in his power to persuade a friend not to hand over delinquent slaves to the secular machinery of justice, which was controlled by provincial governors and other officials,[219] but to punish them according to Church canons. The issue emerges more starkly

still from a letter written to the clergy of Colonia in Armenia Minor, which advised them in strong terms not to resort to the governor's court to establish the legality of their own candidate for the bishopric, for in that case they would give a powerful lever to laymen whose most earnest prayer was for the downfall of the Church.[220] Many cases, such as that of the thief at the church fair (see above, n. 137) stood on the borderline between sacred and secular justice. Basil's report on that affair, while granting that the governing authorities had every right to intervene, shows his anxious concern that they should refrain. The political priority and the interest of the Church in reserving juridical power to itself and allowing as few matters as possible to be referred to the provincial governors precisely mirrored the concern of Greek cities in the early empire that they exercise their own limited autonomy in a responsible way, and give provincial governors no reason to intrude into their business.[221]

The Church in the fourth century, moreover, could also argue with the conviction that it had more right than any other body to administer justice. The Church's law was God's law, and the canons issued by the various synods based their decisions on scriptural precedent. Imperial decisions might be backed by force but they lacked such moral authority. As Basil said in passing of a political opponent, Demosthenes the vicar of Pontica, the more the churches slip into weakness, the more man's love of power grows strong.[222]

The clash not so much of Church with secular law, although this was at issue, as of ecclesiastical and imperial authority lies behind the single most colourful episode in the politics of fourth-century Cappadocia. A woman of good family, recently widowed, fled for asylum to the church at Caesareia, to escape the violence of an assessor on the governor's staff who wished to marry her. Basil, whose own canons provided a woman with precisely this protection, defended her, was arrested in his own bedroom, and taken before the tribunal of the vicar of Pontica, where he was stripped and flogged. As word of this reached the inhabitants of the city they swarmed angrily from every side to defend their bishop, led by the workers in the imperial armaments factory and the weaving mill. Men and women alike, equipped with the weapons they were making, torches, stones, and the shuttles from the factory's looms, took the tribunal by storm, and only Basil's own pleas saved the vicar from their fury.[223]

---

[215] Greg. Nys. *Encomium in Bas.* 14, *PG* 46. 804; *In Eunomium*, 1. 59–66 (*PG* 45. 288–96b): note the phrase ἀρετὴν καὶ παρρησίαν Χριστιανοῦ πρὸς δυναστείαν φονῶσαν.

[216] *CTh.* 16. 2. *passim* for constitutions throughout the 4th cent.; Eusebius, *HE* 10. 7; in general Jones, *LRE* 745–6 and 912 with nn.

[217] *Ep.* 104; cf Greg. Naz. *Ep.* 67.

[218] *Ep.* 61.

[219] *Epp.* 86–7; the only courts in the cities were those of provincial governors or diocesan *vicarii*.

[220] *Ep.* 227.

[221] The *locus classicus* is Acts 19: 35–40 (the *grammateus* of the people at Ephesus anxious that the uproar caused by Paul does not come to the attention of the proconsul). See above, Vol. I, Ch. 12 § II at nn. 23–4.

[222] *Ep.* 239.

[223] Greg. Naz. *Or.* 43, *PG* 36. 568a–69c.

The episode sets in high relief the tension between Church and state, and demonstrates with perfect clarity one of the chief sources of the Church's strength, the loyalty of a congregation to its bishop. A local leader whose roots in the community were as deep as Basil's could easily weather the arbitrary behaviour of imperial officials.

A still clearer index of ecclesiastical, or specifically episcopal power, was the part played by the Church in interceding with imperial authorities, whether locally or at Constantinople, on behalf of individuals or of whole communities. The correspondence of Basil illustrates in considerable detail the potential which a church leader had for establishing himself as the natural and supreme patron of his community. Only three letters, all addressed to governors of Cappadocia, directly concerned Basil's personal affairs. They asked, respectively, for intervention on Basil's behalf with an obstructive local *pagarch*, for support against critics of his church-building programme, and for the delay of a court-hearing which affected some of his property.[224] The largest group of this correspondence, already briefly discussed, consists of pleas for remission from taxation or from liturgical service, addressed to officials whose rank ranged from locally nominated censors to the praetorian prefect or to high officials of the imperial treasury.

Modestus, praetorian prefect of the Orient from 369 to 377, received requests on behalf of the iron miners of the Taurus mountains, and of Helladius, a *curialis* of Caesareia, that he be relieved of the post of *exisotes*.[225] Successive governors of Cappadocia were sent similar appeals, on behalf of a friend of Basil to give a tax rebate on a property called Capralis;[226] on behalf of an old man whose 4-year-old grandson was being burdened with liturgies which would naturally revert to the grandfather, who had already received exemption from them;[227] on behalf of a priest called Dorotheus, to restore grain which had illegally been taken away as a tax payment;[228] and on behalf of the hard-pressed citizens of Ariaratheia, in particular a group of Basil's relatives who owned property there.[229] There were petitions to the *comes privatorum*, the official in charge of imperial estates, to remit the tax on breeding-mares, which had been unjustly levied;[230] to an unidentified treasury official concerning the gold levy;[231] to minor local officers on behalf of a man whose tax liability had remained unadjusted while he himself had sunk into poverty;[232] and on behalf of a country bishop, to ask that revenue could be diverted to maintain the poor.[233] Individual censors, themselves presumably local liturgists,[234] were also asked to show favour to individuals or, in one case, to monks who by renouncing their worldly wealth could not be liable to taxation.[235]

The volume and nature of these requests is significant for three reasons in particular. Firstly, they show that the imposition of taxation was by far the most conspicuous way in which the state intervened in the lives of the inhabitants of the province, and the one that caused the greatest hardship. Secondly, it was an essential and universally understood feature of the system that the demands, which might be inordinately heavy, could be tempered from time to time by concessions administered at various levels, by persons whose rank ranged from the humble position of local censor to the lofty eminence of the praetorian prefect. Thirdly, the dynamics of the system required the intervention of influential patrons on a regular basis, who would act as spokesmen for the taxpayers to the officials. This would naturally reinforce the authority of the patron.

There were other important issues beside taxation, and in these cases Basil commonly addressed either natives of Cappadocia or Caesareia who had achieved high imperial office—like Sophronius the *magister officiorum*, Aburgius praetorian prefect of the Orient from 378, or Martinianus prefect of the city of Rome in the same year[236]—or influential persons whom he knew to be sympathetic to the cause in question. Sophronius was his most important connection at Constantinople, and was asked to intercede in the case of the disputed will of Caesarius, brother of Gregory of Nazianzus;[237] to speak up for all the citizens of Cappadocia against the division of their province in

---

224   *Epp.* 3, 94, and 137.
225   *Ep.* 110 for the ironworkers, cf. van Dam, *JTS* 37 (1986), 65 n. 59; *Epp.* 280–1; cf. *Ep.* 111 on behalf of an anonymous friend.
226   *Ep.* 308.
227   *Ep.* 84.
228   *Epp.* 86–7.
229   *Ep.* 310; the addressee is not in fact named in the surviving text.
230   *Ep.* 303.
231   *Ep.* 88.
232   *Ep.* 309.
233   *Ep.* 142.
234   Cf. *Ep.* 299.
235   *Ep.* 83, on behalf of a friend for a tax rebate on property in Chamanene; *Epp.* 312–13; 284–5 on behalf of the monks. Note also *Ep.* 144 to a *tracteutes eparchon* on behalf of an unspecified petitioner, and *Ep.* 85, unaddressed, on behalf of all Christians, that they might not be made to swear oaths in connection with tax arrears to tax-gatherers. (Compare the Phrygian reluctance to make statements on oath, above, Vol. I, Ch. 11 § v n. 230). In general, the greed and inhumanity of tax-collectors was a topos in the sermons of the Cappadocian fathers, see Greg. Nys., *PG* 46. 505b–c, 888c, 44. 1233d–36a; Greg. Naz., *PG* 35. 864d–65a, 1060b–61a.
236   For the personalities, see *PLRE* i Sophronius 3, Domitius Modestus 2, Aburgius.
237   *Ep.* 32.

372;[238] to defend Helias, a recent governor of Cappadocia, who had been dismissed from office;[239] to support Basil's fellow bishop and closest ally, Eusebius of Samosata, when he was threatened with exile for his Orthodox views;[240] and to add his name and authority to a petition which Basil had addressed directly to the emperors.[241] Aburgius was also asked to help in the first two and last of these causes, and to speak for another former Cappadocian governor, Maximus, who faced charges of embezzlement.[242] Martinianus, whose known career was confined to the western part of the empire, received only a single letter, on the major issue of the division of the province.[243] The other letters to prominent individuals concerned the politics of the Church. Victor, *magister equitum* for the East from 363 to 378, was asked to use his influence as a prominent Orthodox Christian at a synod of bishops held in Constantinople in 373.[244] His companion in arms Flavius Arinthaeus, *magister peditum* at the same period, received a further letter concerning Eusebius of Samosata.[245]

The volume of traffic led to an elaborate protocol of petitions, of which Basil was acutely conscious. It might be rash to ask for a small favour, if it used up credit which was better expended in more important causes.[246] Even while still a priest he had to apologize to an unnamed addressee for the number of letters which his position in the Church obliged him to send, and to hope that a particular request would not be overlooked.[247] He would not approach the praetorian prefect of the East directly in a case which affected only an individual, preferring instead to write to one of his staff.[248]

Unless Basil's correspondence is grossly unrepresentative, it is legitimate to conclude that the petitioning letter was the single most important medium of political expression in the later empire and, at least from the viewpoint of the empire's provincial subjects, the most fruitful way of securing action on their behalf. Where (as in Caesareia) the bishop took a larger role than anyone else in channelling these petitions to the authorities, the consequences for his own political role are obvious. He became the most important figure in the community, not simply as God's minister on earth, but as its natural leader in secular business.

What were the consequences for civic life of this shift from lay persons to churchmen? It was perfectly possible, of course, for bishops to act as cynical power-brokers without letting the teachings of their religion impinge at all on their political actions.[249] Basil himself, as his intrigues with Amphilochius of Iconium show, was as liable to this charge as anyone. But at the same time it is clear that there were substantial changes in the ethos of local politics, in particular the perspective which the powerful adopted in their relationship with the poor and less-privileged members of the community, and it is reasonable in turn to link these changes with the fact that civic leadership lay to such a large degree with the Church.

It was no novelty in the ancient world for the wealthy to redistribute their goods to other members of the community. Indeed in societies which offered very limited opportunities for the investment of profits or surplus income, redistribution in some form can be seen not simply as a social but as an economic necessity.[250] But, barring exceptions, the great part of this redistributive spending in the Graeco-Roman world was not organized primarily to help the needy, although these often benefited incidentally, but to reflect well on the donor and increase his prestige. The motive that led a benefactor to make gifts to his fellow citizens, to erect public buildings which would serve the whole community, or to help finance the institutions of his city, was *philotimia*, the love of honour, which accrued in proportion to the lavishness with which he was prepared to contribute to these well-defined areas of public life. The ideology of this public generosity, or euergetism, was not disinterested and charitable but political and self-serving. The point is well illustrated by the many inscriptions from Greek cities which draw distinctions between the various classes of recipients of such generosity. Always, when distinctions are drawn, the high-status members of a community received more than the low-status members, sometimes in proportions that are as high as fifty to one. Since a key motive was to enhance a donor's reputation, publicity was also an essential element. Almost without exception the thousands of inscriptions of the first three centuries AD set up to honour city notables in the empire drew attention to the honorands'

[238] *Ep.* 76.
[239] *Ep.* 96.
[240] *Ep.* 177.
[241] *Ep.* 180.
[242] *Epp.* 33, 75, 147, and 178.
[243] *Ep.* 74.
[244] *Epp.* 152–3.
[245] *Ep.* 179.
[246] *Ep.* 110.
[247] *Ep.* 37.
[248] *Epp.* 107, and 109.

[249] Compare T. D. Barnes's assessment of Athanasius of Alexandria, 'Athanasius wielded political power by means very reminiscent of a modern American gangster or big city boss' ('The Career of Athanasius', *Studia Patristica*, 21 (1989), 390–401 at 397); for the bishops of Ancyra, see below, § VIII.
[250] Cf. E. Patlagéan, *Pauvreté économique et pauvreté sociale à Byzance: 4ᵉ–7ᵉ siècles* (1977), 184.

benefactions, usually as demonstrated in one of the ways briefly outlined above.

The Christian ethic, by contrast, was based on ideals of humility and charity, and its essential content is well summed-up by the story of Dives and Lazarus in Luke, indicating that the man who kept his worldly wealth to himself would suffer in the afterlife, and the verse of Matthew, that when performing a charitable action one should not trumpet the fact before you so as to gain higher esteem from other men, for the true and only reward for such action awaits the Christian in heaven.[251] At a philosophical level the contrast between the two ideologies was worked out in some detail by Lactantius in his discussion of parts of Cicero's *De Officiis*, but it perhaps emerges more forcefully in an anecdote told by the pagan historian Ammianus Marcellinus about Lampadius, the Christian prefect of the city of Rome in 365:

When this man during his praetorship gave magnificent games and very abundant largesse, and yet could not endure the taunts of the common people continually shouting that a mass of gifts should be given to persons unworthy to receive them, to show his generosity and his contempt for them he summoned some of the destitute from the Vatican, and presented them with valuable gifts.[252]

When his political generosity was abused he turned to Christian charity.

There was a duality of political purpose in the Rome of the mid-fourth century which befitted a city where the battle between Christianity and paganism still hung in the balance. There would have been similar ambiguities in Cappadocia, but only at a much earlier date. The introduction of a Christian ethic into aristocratic behaviour in the later third and fourth century deserves wider study; for the moment a brief sketch and some suggestive passages must suffice. One of the most explicit occurs in the Funerary Oration delivered by Gregory of Nazianzus for Basil, in which he recalled the bishop's grandparents hiding on their Pontic estate during the persecution of Maximinus in 312, where they had done so much that was remembered now— giving sustenance to beggars, hospitality to strangers, purging the soul by continence, and distributing their property by consecrating it to the Church. These practices, Gregory adds, were not then much in fashion, although now they are commonplace and held in high honour in consequence of those early examples.[253] The change in behaviour that had taken place during the

earlier part of the century was clearly visible to an observer in 380.

The shift, however, was a subtle one and the contemporary evidence is not always clear-cut. One of the best-known fourth-century inscriptions of Asia Minor was carved on the sarcophagus of Eugenius, heretic bishop of Laodicea Catacecaumene, who had himself endured persecution in 312 before his ordination. The text commemorated him in terms which are entirely familiar from an earlier age. He had conducted the episcopate for twenty-five full years with great distinction, and had constructed the whole church from its foundations, along with all the adornment round it, that is to say the colonnades, the quadrangle, the wall-painting and mosaics, the fountain, and a monumental gateway, all finished once and for all in sculpted stone. Then, on the verge of leaving his mortal life, he had made a sarcophagus and a funerary mound, on which all the above details had been engraved as an ornament to his church and to his family.[254] There is no self-effacing modesty here, and the last words spelled out the message of the inscription as a whole; it proclaimed the fame not of Eugenius and his city, as an earlier pagan text might have done, but of Eugenius and his church. It is not hard to find other inscriptions of the fourth or even the early fifth century from Anatolian cities which honour prominent citizens for their benefactions and their civic generosity, and which imply that the civic patriotism of earlier centuries was far from dead.[255] Indeed, in suitable contexts Basil and Gregory of Nazianzus themselves use language which shows that their own public behaviour could be similarly motivated.[256] On the other hand texts from the same period, or even a little earlier, praise their subjects explicitly because they had cared for the needy, for widows, and for orphans.[257] In an age of

---

[251] Luke 16: 19–31; Matt. 6: 2, cf. 25: 40.
[252] Lactantius, *Inst. Div.* 6. 10–12, discussed by J. W. H. G. Liebeschuetz, *Continuity and Change in Roman Religion* (1978), 273; Ammianus Marcellinus, 27. 3. 5.
[253] Greg. Naz. *Or.* 43, *PG* 36. 504d–505a; cf. Greg. Nys. *Vita Macrinae*, 15.
[254] *MAMA* i. 170; W. M. Ramsay, *Luke the Physician*, 346 well compares the inscription with Eusebius, *HE* 10. 4, which describes how Paulinus, bishop of Tyre, built and dedicated a new church after the ending of the persecutions. For pride in the appearance of a church, see Greg. Nys. 46. 756c. See also W. Wischmeyer, 'M. Iulius Eugenius. Eine Fallstudie zum Thema Christen und Gesellschaft im 3. und 4. Jhdt.', *ZNW* 81 (1990), 225–46.
[255] e.g. *MAMA* i. 220 (Laodicea Catacecaumene); *AS* 27 (1977), 91–2 no. 36 with the reading corrected in *Bull. ép.* (1978), 494 (Ancyra).
[256] See T. A. Kopeček, 'The Cappadocian Fathers and Civic Patriotism', *Church History*, 43 (1974), 293–303, repr. in J. Martin and B. Quint, *Christentum und antike Gesellschaft. Wege der Forschung*, 649 (1990), 306–19 citing esp. Greg. Naz. *Or.* 17 and 18, and *Epp.* 141–2, and Basil, *Ep.* 94. Note the language of Firmus of Caesarea, *Ep.* 17, referring to the activities of a *vicarius*, ἀνανέωσις οἰκοδομημάτων . . . ὡς εὐεργέτας δευτέρους, οἰκίστας ὀνομάζοντες.
[257] *MAMA* viii. 121 (from the Çarşamba valley), with Ramsay, *Luke the Physician*, 352 n. 2.

cultural transition these variations are the reverse of surprising.

It was at a time when the memory of civic euergetism was still strong that Basil wrote a splendid passage in his homily on Luke's verse that the rich man who hoarded his wealth was no better than a pauper in the sight of God:

If you honour wealth because of the honour that it brings to you, think how much more it will profit your reputation to be called the father of ten thousand children, reared by your charity, than to have ten thousand gold pieces stored in the treasury. You will leave the money there, whether you want to or not, but you will take your honour, earned by your good deeds, before the Lord, when the whole people, standing round you in the presence of the Universal Judge, calls you its nurturer, its benefactor, and by all the names which it gives to philanthropy. Look at the men who spend their fortunes on the theatre, on pancratiasts, on actors, and on men fighting wild beasts, men whose very sight one abhors, simply to obtain a fleeting honour, or the cheers and applause of the people. Are you going to be mean in your own spending, when you can excel their glory by so much? God will be the one to receive you, the angels will sing your praises.... Come then, give out your wealth in a dozen ways, and become honoured and famous for your spending on the poor.[258]

The language of civic euergetism, including many of its characteristic technical terms, has been transposed and rephrased to tell a Christian message.

The ideology of Christian charity as a civic virtue found its clearest expression in the actions and words of the bishops of the later fourth century. The proper use of wealth offered a recurring theme for sermons on loving the poor, on riches, on usury, and on the relief of famine.[259] The role of the Church was to instruct men in their moral duty. Gregory of Nyssa described charity as a river that ran through the whole world and found its outlet in Paradise.[260] Basil used a similar metaphor: 'As a great river flows by a thousand channels through fertile country, so let your wealth run through many conduits to the houses of the poor. Wells that are drawn from flow better; left unused they

go foul. Money left standing is worthless; moving and changing hands it helps the community and gives increase.'[261] The wealth of a single household could save whole communities, provided that it was not stopped by a mean and uncharitable spirit which, like a stone jammed in an outlet, prevents the stream from flowing.[262] Gregory of Nyssa's descriptions of the homeless poor, huddled under colonnades in the main streets or in the empty corners of the agora,[263] disfigured by disease, without arms or legs, reduced to little more than animals,[264] have no parallel in pagan classical literature. They illustrate the sharpened sense of the gulf between rich and poor, which for a Christian father was the overriding division in society, replacing the elaborate gradations of rank and status that stratified the civic bodies of the early empire.[265]

In a time of famine it was no longer sufficient to condemn the rich for hoarding their grain in the hope of getting a higher price as the famine intensified; Basil brought the starving poor together, and fed them from his own stores.[266] Later, as bishop, he began to build a great hospice outside Caesareia. 'Step a little outside the city', said Gregory Nazianzus, 'and look at this whole new city which has become a treasury of piety, a common storehouse for the rich, into which all their surplus wealth, and their basic provisions, have been put at Basil's injunction.'[267] The institution, the *Basileion*, a new palace for the Christian world, served as a model for institutionalized Byzantine charity. The dedication of land or resources to endow hospices, at least on a smaller scale, became widespread during the third quarter of the fourth century. The dispensing of charity became a chief duty of those clergy closest to the poor, the *chorepiscopi*.[268] Ironically the best, or at least the best-known, witness to the impact of this

[258] Basil, *Hom. in Luc.* XII.8, PG 31. 265d, discussed by Robert, *Hellenica*, xi/xii (1960), 569–76; cf. Asterius, *Hom.* 2, PG 40. 188c–d, 189a and in particular Greg. Nys. *De paup. amand.* 1 (ed. van Heck), 10, 13 ff. (PG 46. 461); ὡς γὰρ οἱ ἀγωνοθέται τῆς ματαιότητος ὑπὸ σάλπιγγι τὴν ἑαυτῶν φιλοτιμίαν σημαίνοντες πᾶσι τοῖς τῆς παλαίστρας τὴν τοῦ πλούτου διανομὴν ἐπαγγέλλοντες, οὕτως ἡ εὐποιία ἅπαντας πρὸς ἑαυτὴν καλεῖ τοὺς ἐν δυσκολίαις καὶ περιστάσεσιν, οὐ πληγῶν τιμὰς τοῖς προσιοῦσιν, ἀλλὰ συμφορῶν θεραπείας μερίζουσα.

[259] Notably Greg. Nys. two sermons on loving the poor, Greg. Naz. on the same theme; Basil, *Hom. VI in divites.* For the importance of the theme, see P. R. L. Brown, *The Body and Society* (1988), 303–4.

[260] Greg. Nys. *De baptismo*, PG 46. 420c.

[261] Basil, *Hom. in Luc.* XII.8, cited by B. Gordon, 'Scarcity and the Fathers', *Studia Patristica*, 22 (1989), 108–20.

[262] Greg. Nys. *De paup. amand.* 1. 13. 3–4, PG 46. 464d, οὕτως καὶ μιᾶς οἰκίας εὐπορία δήμους πενήτων ἐξαρκεῖ διασώσασθαι, μόνον ἐὰν μὴ γνώμη φειδωλὸς καὶ ἀκοινώνητος, ὡς λίθος ἐμπεσοῦσα τῇ διεξόδῳ τὴν ἐπιρρόην ἀνακρούσηται; cf. Basil, *Hom. VI in divites*, PG 31. 272b.

[263] Greg. Nys. *De paup. amand.* 1. 6. 17 f. (PG 46. 457b).

[264] Greg. Nys. *De paup. amand.* 1. 16. 1–5; 2. 24. 13 f. (PG 46. 468, 476b–77a, 484d–85a).

[265] Cf. Patlagéan, *Pauvreté économique et pauvreté sociale à Byzance*, 156–235.

[266] Greg. Naz. *Or.* 43, PG 36, esp. 577c; cf. Basil, *Ep.* 319 for the principle, πάσης τῆς παρὰ τῶν Χριστιανῶν ὀφειλομένης τοῖς ξένοις παραμυθίας.

[267] Basil's buildings, Sozomen, *HE* 6. 34; other sources and discussion in Gain, *L'Église*, 287–9. Add Firmus of Caesarea, *Ep.* 43 (first pub. 1989), which refers to the indigents who lived in the 'Basilias', and implies that the tax-evasion of landowners was one of the causes that brought them there.

[268] See above, n. 128.

active promotion of the Christian ethic of charity was the emperor Julian the Apostate. He resolved to establish *xenodocheia* throughout all the cities of Galatia, endowed with grain and wine from imperial estates, so that strangers might enjoy other than Christian hospitality (see below, § VIII at n. 347). His effort found no resonance in other pagan initiatives. The tide towards Christianity had long since turned.

As a young priest, Basil wrote to the people of Neocaesareia and joined the mourning at the death of their bishop Musonius:

Now withered in the bloom of your beauty; your church is dumb; your assemblies are full of mournful faces; your sacred synod craves its leader; your holy utterances wait for an expounder; your young men have lost a father, your elders a brother; your nobles have lost their leader, your people their champion, and your poor their nurturer.[269]

It is hard to find a better epitaph for Basil himself.

VI. *Pagan Culture in Fourth-Century Ancyra*

In AD 347 a young man from an obscure Black Sea town took his chance before the Roman emperor.[270] Constantius, emperor in the East since the death of Constantine in 337, was marching at the head of an army from Syrian Antioch across Asia Minor to Constantinople. He arrived at Ancyra, a city increasingly familiar with such imperial progresses along the main military artery of the eastern empire, and stopped to listen to an address from the youthful orator Themistius in praise of the supreme virtue of kings—philanthropy. The opening paragraphs brilliantly evoked the size of the empire, the number of Constantius' subjects, the regiments of foot-soldiers, all at peace, the troops of cavalry, the lavishness of their equipment, the unbreakable wall of their shields, and the dragon standards of fine-woven cloth that billowed in the breeze at the top of gilded poles. These sentences deftly move from evoking the abstraction of imperial power to the material scene which actually confronted the speaker, but for him, a philosopher, what counted was none of this but the soul of the monarch.[271] This was where the emperor's true virtue resided, and the most important virtue was not courage, justice, self-control, or resolution, but the love of men, for this alone was a quality aptly predicated of god as well as man. The rhetoric and the theme were conventional, although not uninteresting for that, but one circumstance peculiar to the age in which it was delivered gave the speech particular piquancy. The speaker was a pagan intellectual, the faithful and self-conscious heir to a long tradition in classical philosophy and rhetoric; the emperor, like Constantine before him, was an avowed and sometimes militant Christian.[272] This vignette, from the mid-point of the fourth century, demands that questions be asked about the issue which it so gracefully disguises, the coexistence, co-operation, or conflict between pagan and Christian at the highest levels of society.

The audience at Ancyra would have appreciated the display put on for them by Themistius, for outside the four main centres of intellectual activity in the Greek world—Athens, Antioch, Alexandria, and Constantinople—there was no better place for a sophistic orator to display his prowess. Certainly, three centuries earlier, St Paul had castigated the converts from his first missionary journey as 'witless Galatians', but like their distant kinsmen from Gaul and even Britain in the western empire,[273] the Hellenized Celtic inhabitants of the Anatolian plateau had worked hard to dispel this judgement. In the 140s AD C. Iulius Severus, the leading citizen of Ancyra, of Celtic descent but himself a high-ranking Roman senator, was regarded by the most famous rhetor of the day, Aelius Aristides, as a connoisseur of public speaking.[274] He and many of his fellow citizens had mounted a band-wagon of educational advance, or cultural pretension, and its progress was rapid. During the second century there were inscriptions from Ancyra for several philosophers and for a philologist.[275] Epideictic oratory, Themistius'

[269] Basil, *Ep.* 28. It is revealing for his approach that Gain, *L'Église*, 49 n. 2 chooses a different passage from this same letter as his point of departure for analysing Basil's own role as a bishop, concentrating on doctrine and the question of the faith of the Church. He devotes only six pages of his study to 'les relations de l'Église aux pouvoirs publics'.

[270] Themistius, *Or.* 1. Themistius was perhaps from Abonuteichus; his family estates were in Paphlagonia. Ancyra would have been familiar to him before this occasion; he might even have studied there. For the date of the speech, see Barnes, *L'Église et l'empire*, 304 n. 8 against the *communis opinio* for 350. The options are set out by G. Dagron, 'L'Empire romain d'Orient au IVᵉ siècle et les traditions politiques de l'hellénisme: Le Témoignage de Thémistios', *Travaux et mémoires*, 3 (1968), 20. The description of Constantius' escort may well be compared with Ammianus Marcellinus 16. 10. 4 ff.

[271] The speech is riddled with allusions and quotations from Aristotle, Xenophon, but above all Plato, as is made clear in the edition by R. Schenkl and G. Downey (1965).

[272] See esp. Barnes, *L'Église et l'empire*, 322–35 for Constantius' militant Christianity in the tradition of Constantine.

[273] The *locus classicus* is Tacitus, *Agric.* 21, on which see the commentary of Ogilvie and Richmond; R. Syme, *Tacitus*, ii. 614–15 for Gaul.

[274] Aelius Aristides, *Sacred Tales*, 4. 27 (26. 432K).

[275] Bosch, *Ankara*, no. 161, C. Aelius Flavianus Sulpicius; *AS* 27 (1977), 91 no. 34 (*SEG* xxvii. 889). For philosophers in Greek inscriptions see M. N. Tod, *JHS* 77 (1957), 132–41; L. Robert, *Bull. ép.* (1958), 84; *Hellenica*, xi/xii. 108 n. 1; C. Habicht, *Alt. v. Perg.* viii. 3 (1969), 162–4. The philologist, Bosch, *Ankara*, no. 73, Ti. Cl. Gentianus.

speciality, enjoyed an increasing vogue in the high empire, whose unlikely cultural heroes were the sophists, wealthy and ostentatious practitioners known to us from inscriptions and literature, but above all from the *Lives of the Sophists*, written in the first half of the third century by Philostratus.[276] These men often moved in lofty political circles, and Ancyra produced some typical examples. Sempronius Aquila was a Roman *eques* who had served as an imperial secretary, *ab epistulis Graecis*, sometime in the late second century. His daughter, Sempronia Romana, married a senator, who died young on the eve of attaining the rank of praetor.[277] The father should perhaps be identified with the Galatian sophist Aquila, a pupil of Chrestus of Byzantium who had himself been taught by the famous Herodes Atticus.[278] The family's known descendants included a third-century rhetor, Aquila Romanus, part of whose treatise on rhetoric has survived,[279] and the emperor M. Antonius Gordianus Sempronius Romanus Africanus, to whom Philostratus dedicated his *Lives of the Sophists*.[280] Another Ancyran who received a sophistic training was Aelius Lycinus, who joined his fellow students in erecting a monument at Ephesus for his instructor Soterus.[281] P. Aelius Sempronius Lycinus (the second family name hints at a link with Sempronius Aquila and his kin) went on to an equestrian career including financial procuratorships in Gaul, Dacia, Alexandria, and Syria under Septimius Severus and Caracalla, and he erected a dedication to the *numen* of Caracalla when the emperor passed through Ancyra in 215.[282] Either his brother or his son, P. Aelius Sempronius Metrophanes, was a Roman senator.[283]

Ancyra, then, was one of the cities of the Greek East to supply the accomplished and cultured administrators who established a vital niche for themselves in the government of the empire in the second and third centuries. It was also a city where the arts were valued. Two sisters—prudent ladies according to their epitaph—were buried in a tomb dedicated to the Muses,[284] and a legionary veteran in the third century erected a gravestone for his 13-year-old son, who had been born in the camps, which described him as adorned with every grace, with knowledge, and with culture.[285] Two Ancyran citizens brought back their brother's body from Alexandria to give it burial. It seems likely that the last had been studying in Egypt, perhaps in the famous Museum or in its medical school. It is not difficult to find other examples where young students from Anatolian cities who had died abroad were brought back by their families for burial.[286] Certain city aristocrats made it their business to promote their compatriots' education. One, a second-century descendant of the Galatian tetrarchs, was noted for his culture, fine speech, and sober moderation;[287] another in the time of Hadrian had 'adorned the metropolis with his culture and fine speech'.[288] While not to be reckoned with Athens, Alexandria, Smyrna, or Pergamum, Ancyra occupied a respectable place in the second division as a cultural as well as an administrative centre.

Moreover, it was not isolated. The outlying parts of central Anatolia show surprising evidence for intellectual pursuits. Philosophers are found in small cities like Amblada in east Pisidia,[289] and Tavium in east Galatia,[290] and there were philologists at Savatra and Perta in northern Lycaonia.[291] A student from Savatra duly turns up in the inscriptions of Ephesus,[292] just as a law student from the small Phrygian city of Tiberiopolis made his way to Smyrna for training,

[276] G. W. Bowersock, *Greek Sophists in the Roman Empire* (1965); E. L. Bowie, 'The Importance of Sophists', *YCS* xxvii (1982), 46 ff.; G. Anderson, *Philostratus: Biography and Belles Letters in the Third Century AD* (1987).

[277] Bosch, *Ankara*, no. 203. He also appears at Isaura, *AE* (1937), 257.

[278] Philostratus, *VS* 591K; cf. A. R. Birley, *Britain and Rome: Essays pres. to E. Birley* (1966), 58–60; T. D. Barnes, *Latomus*, 27 (1968), 581 ff.; Bowersock, *Sophists*, 20 n. 2.

[279] For Aquila Romanus see *PIR*[2] i. 192: A no. 983. C. Holm, *Rhetores Latini Minores* (1863), 23–37.

[280] Either Gordian I or II; see Anderson, *Philostratus*, 297–8. For Gordian's origins, almost certainly ultimately in Cappadocia, see R. Syme, *Emperors and Biography* (1971), 167. The first known Cappadocian senator was Ti. Cl. Gordianus from Tyana, *AE* (1954), 138, the second was M. Antonius Gordianus, perhaps the emperor's father; see Syme, *Chiron*, 10 (1980), 430 = *RP* iii. 1318.

[281] J. Keil, *JÖAI* 40 (1953), 15–18 = *GIBM* iii. 2, 195 no. 548.

[282] Bosch, *Ankara*, nos. 226–7 with Pflaum, *CP* ii (1960), 70–1 no. 267; Bosch, *Ankara*, no. 259.

[283] Bosch, *Ankara*, nos. 228–9.

[284] Bosch, *Ankara*, no. 335.

[285] *AS* 27 (1977), 84 no. 18 (*SEG* xxvii. 863).

[286] *AS* 27 (1977), 81 no. 12; the suggestion that he was a student not a businessman comes from Prof. C. P. Jones, who cites as parallels the cases *IGR* iii. 374 for a youth who had studied medicine and died in Alexandria and was brought home for burial at Pisidian Adada, and Bean and Mitford, *Inscriptions from Rough Cilicia 1964–68*, D. Ak. Wien, 102 (1970), no. 49 for a young lawyer brought back to Cilicia from Egyptian Thebes. See Robert, *Hellenica*, xiii. 45–54.

[287] Bosch, *Ankara*, no. 100, Ti. Cl. Bocchus.

[288] Bosch, *Ankara*, no. 117, Latinius Alexander.

[289] A. S. Hall, *AS* 18 (1968) no. 22; note in passing that the emperor Constantius banished Aetius the Arian to Amblada. Philostorgius, *HE* 5. 2, writing in the 5th cent. observed, ἐκεῖ κακῶς ἀπορρῆξαι τὸν βίον, διὰ τὸ βάρβαρον καὶ μισάνθρωπον τῶν ἐνοικούντων (αὐχμοῦ δὲ καὶ λοίμου τὴν χώραν ἔχοντος ἀνυποίστου).

[290] *RECAM* ii. 417, a man from the Museum at Alexandria; 519.

[291] *MAMA* viii. 241, 203; Philologos was also used as a proper name at Iconium, *MAMA* viii. 298.

[292] Robert, *Hellenica*, xiii. 43.

where he died.[293] A survey of the nomenclature of central Anatolia has revealed a surprising number of names that reflect cultural interests,[294] which were perhaps fostered by village schoolteachers.[295] Some of this interest may be reflected in the increasing vogue for verse epitaphs which can be charted in the villages of Phrygia, Galatia, and Lycaonia, and which reached its peak during the third and fourth centuries (see below, § x at n. 434).

Cappadocia at first appears even less promising ground for cultural advance. Except in the west, at Caesareia and Tyana, it could hardly offer a Hellenized urban centre (see above, Vol. I, Ch. 7 § II at n. 65), and much of the province may have been administered as a series of vast rural estates or ranches. But these cities too produced philosophers or sophists; the semi-legendary Apollonius of Tyana;[296] Pausanias of Caesareia, another pupil of Herodes Atticus;[297] and his fellow-citizen M. Acilius Diodotus.[298] The latter's family, most probably the philosopher in person, had gained Roman citizenship through the mediation of a Roman noble, M. Acilius Glabrio, who had seen service in Cappadocia as a military tribune. The same Aelius Aristides who had noted Iulius Severus as a connoisseur of rhetoric labelled Acilius Glabrio 'the sophist'.[299] The interests of this 'eccentric patrician' mirrored those of his Cappadocian client. The nexus of culture and power that joined the provincial aristocracy to the Roman governing class is clear to see again.[300]

We can chart the development of this intellectual activity across the divide that separates the empire of the first three centuries from the new empire of Diocletian and Constantine. By the fourth century three major centres of intellectual activity occupied the limelight; Athens endured, but it was now matched by two new foci at Syrian Antioch and at Constantinople. Cultural ambitions kept step with political power as these two cities assumed their positions as the major imperial centres of the fourth century. The intellectual pretensions of each are best exemplified by the surviving works of the professional orators who presided over their schools of rhetoric and taught a generation of pupils: Himerius at Athens, Libanius at Antioch, and the mature Themistius at Constantinople. All three paid striking tribute to the learning and culture of the cities of central Anatolia, above all of Ancyra.[301]

To judge from his surviving work Himerius, pagan partner to the Christian Prohaeresius at Athens, offered a sickly style of quasi-poetic oratory, which claimed inspiration from the Muses, Dionysus, and other by now somewhat muddied springs of classical inspiration, to pupils from all parts of the eastern empire.[302] This was an élitist culture:

Let us shut out the trivial sport of the wrestling ground, and open up the workshop of the Muses; shun the packed theatre, but give ear to a greater theatre... This is the summons to everyone, but above all to you, young men, who have come freshly formed to us, whom Mount Argaeus has sent, from the mountain in whose shadow my own family sprouts from golden shoots, and those whom the cities and peoples of Galatia have dispatched as their first colony in search of learning.[303]

Himerius himself was from Prusa, the Bithynian city at the foot of Mysian Olympus; Argaeus was the mountain that dominated Cappadocian Caesareia,[304] and Himerius' most famous pupils were precisely the two fathers of the Cappadocian church, Basil and Gregory of Nazianzus.[305]

Between the 350s and the 380s Themistius founded his own school of rhetoric in Constantinople, and his speeches helped to frame a practical ideology for the emperors of the time, whom he flattered and sought to guide.[306] In a speech of 377/8 in defence of his philosophical teaching he appealed as witnesses to students from Syrian Antioch, and to his numerous pupils from the cities of Greek Galatia, modest though they were. For the inhabitants of this region were quick-witted, receptive, and readier to learn than excessively cultured Greeks (ἀγὰν Ἕλληνες). 'They cling', he said, 'to the hem of a philosopher's cloak like iron filings to a magnet.' Many were in his audience that day, preparing themselves for careers as legal advisers to governors. They were the people to ask if Themistius was truly a philosopher.[307]

---

[293] MAMA x. 529.
[294] Robert, Hellenica, xiii. 43; note RECAM ii. 47, Μαθητική.
[295] MAMA vii. 406 (Vetissus); Ath. Mitt. 25 (1900), 441 no. 69.
[296] See E. L. Bowie, ANRW ii. 16. 2 (1978), 1652–99; Anderson, Philostratus, 121–239.
[297] Philostratus, VS 593 K.
[298] VS 617; Habicht, Alt. v. Perg. viii. 3 no. 35.
[299] Sacred Tales, 4. 100.
[300] R. Syme, 'An Eccentric Patrician', Chiron, 10 (1980), 427–48 = RP iii. 1316–36.

[301] For Ancyra in the mid-4th cent. I have drawn heavily on C. Foss's two excellent studies, 'Late Antique and Byzantine Ankara', DOP 31 (1977), 29–87; and 'Ankyra', Reallexicon für Antike und Christentum (1985), 448–65.
[302] H. Schenkl, RE viii (1913), 1622–35.
[303] Or. 49 (ed. Colonna, 1951).
[304] For a full collection of sources concerning Argaeus, see P. Weiss, JNG 35 (1985), 21–48.
[305] Socrates, HE 4. 26; Sozomen, HE 6. 17.
[306] Ed. Dindorf (complete) 1832; and G. Downey and A. F. Norman (completing the edn. of R. Schenkl), Teubner, 3 vols. 1965, 1970, 1974. For his career see W. Stegemann, RE v. 2 (1934), 1442–80. There is an exhaustive discussion of the political content of his speeches by Dagron, Travaux et mémoires, 3 (1968), 1–242.
[307] Or. 23. 299a–b.

But the most detailed and explicit testimony comes from the vast correspondence of Libanius, whose letters form the strands of an immense web of contacts and influence which he spun from his base in Syrian Antioch between the 350s and 390s.[308] The influence was quite simply that of a professor, exercised on behalf of and through his former pupils. Ancyra had a central place in his affections. Soon after Themistius had delivered his youthful address to Constantius, between 348 and 353, Libanius had twice stayed in the city for a period of weeks or months as the guest of a local councillor, Agesilaus. He taught both his sons, one of whom as leader of the city council was to lead the delegation that congratulated the emperor Jovian on his accession in 363,[309] while the other served as a lawyer on the staff of the provincial governor, presumably of Galatia.[310] He had many opportunities to profess his feelings for the city and for his friends among its inhabitants. In 365 in writing to the councillors he apologized for the unusual sending of a collective letter, but excused his behaviour by referring to their collective cultural and literary aspirations: 'You have a passion for every type of learning; you are masters of culture yourselves and delightedly listen to experts... You have been praised by the words of orators and poets. More than any cities that we know, your praises will be sung until you are indeed the friends of the Muses.'[311] In another letter written to a native of the city, Bosporius, he remarked that there was nothing surprising about an Ancyran turning to the liberal arts, for the city bred noble natures. When a man of Ancyra chose to learn the art of medicine, instead of enjoying his leisure at ease, that was only to be expected.[312]

The children of Agesilaus belong to a bevy of Ancyran pupils of Libanius, who came from a group of interrelated curial families. A typical letter was addressed to Arion, the son of a philosopher called Agathius, who had made a teaching career at Ancyra:

I am delighted to see your sons; one has come to study, the other is escorting him to his studies (at Antioch). I think that the whole thing is splendid in every way, but for you it is now also a matter of necessity, as long as you think it right to maintain the reputation which your family has inherited from

the wisdom of Agathius, and indeed sacrilegious to destroy it. I myself will use all my enthusiasm and all my eloquence both for the sake of Ancyra, to which I owe many thanks, and for the sake of you and the boys' uncle.[313]

The relations between Libanius and Ancyra are evident in the ten Ancyran pupils known to us by name, and in correspondence written on their behalf to four Galatian governors between 359 and 364, as well as to a fifth in 392, who was himself one of Libanius' former pupils.[314] The letters from this group which best illuminate the society and conditions of the Galatian metropolis are those that concern Maximus, perhaps Ancyra's richest citizen in the middle of the fourth century, and his son Hyperechius, who had been Libanius' student, almost in fact a perpetual student between the early 340s and the late 350s.[315] In 361 and 362 Libanius wrote to newly appointed provincial governors commending them to pay their respects to Maximus, who had retired after a military career to his estate near the city, where he cultivated suitably aristocratic interests in agriculture and hunting.[316] Both letters are part of the huge and pathetic dossier that was written to further the career of Hyperechius. Libanius himself saw more clearly than most of his contemporaries that the well-being of the empire coincided with the continued vitality of the curial class, whose liturgies sustained the corporate activity of the cities.[317] Avoidance, evasion, and exemption from liturgies were the monotonous theme of a councillor's life and dominated local politics as no other issue. His own advice to Hyperechius had been to aim at a post as legal adviser to the provincial governors,[318] and he urged him to resist his father's suggestion that he seek entry to the senate at Constantinople, which would exempt him from his local duties, since such a step would undermine his local reputation and his influence in the city.[319] Notwithstanding, Hyperechius pressed

[308] P. Petit, *Les Étudiants de Libanius* (1957).
[309] *Ep.* 1444.
[310] O. Seeck, *Die Briefe von Libanius zeitlich geordnet* (1906), 50–2.
[311] *Ep.* 1517.
[312] *Ep.* 756. Note that Ancyra's mid-4th-cent. bishop Basil had also had a medical training, below, § VIII n. 353. We are in the same world as that of C. Calpurnius Collega Macedon of Pisidian Antioch, a pagan intellectual and probably also a doctor; see C. P. Jones, *Phoenix*, 36 (1982), 264–71, esp. 265 n. 9 where he collects other examples of the combination of philosophy and medicine in the 4th cent.
[313] *Ep.* 728.
[314] See Foss, 'Ankara', 43 and 47, citing *Epp.* 267, 1359, and 1419 to Ecdicius; *Ep.* 298 (cf. 308) to Acacius; *Ep.* 779 to Maximus; *Ep.* 1267 to Leontius; *Ep.* 1049 to Adelphius.
[315] For Hyperechius see *PLRE* i, s.v.; Seeck, *Die Briefe*, 182–3; and the excellent analysis by Foss, 'Ankara', 43–4, which I follow.
[316] *Epp.* 298 and 779.
[317] In general see R. Pack, *Curiales in the Correspondence of Libanius*, TAPA 82 (1951), 176–92, repr. in G. Fatouros and T. Krischer, *Libanios. Wege der Forschung*, 621 (1983), 185–205.
[318] *Ep.* 267: ὃν ἐβουλόμην μὲν ἕνα τῶν παρά σοι συνηγόρων εἶναι καὶ πολλάκις γε πρὸς τὸν Ὑπερέχιον ἐπήνεσα τούς τε περὶ ταῦτα πόνους τό τε ἀπὸ τῶν πόνων ὄνομα.
[319] *Ep.* 731: σὺ μὲν γὰρ τῶν τε ἡμετέρων μεμνήμενος λόγων καὶ τὸ πρᾶγμα ἐξετάζων ὀρθῶς οἷος εἶ τῇ πατρίδι λειτουργεῖν, ἐξ οὗ δόξα τε καὶ δύναμις γένοιτ' ἂν καὶ πρό γε τὸ τὰ δίκαια πρὸς τὴν οἰκείαν ποιεῖν· ὁ δὲ σὲ πέμπει ῥίψαντα τὰ ὄντα εἰς τὴν θάλατταν. εἰ γὰρ μήτε ἐκεῖ μέγα τι παρὰ τὴν δαπάνην ἕξεις οἴκοι τε οὐκ ἰσχύσεις ἑτέρωθι δαπανώμενος, πῶς οὐκ ἀπολεῖταί σοι τὰ χρήματα;

on in search of higher things, and Libanius obliged him with a series of recommendations to the four successive provincial governors of 359–64, to the tax-assessor for the neighbouring province of Bithynia, and to the praetorian prefect of the East, Modestus.[320] The constant rebuttals, and promises of posts that were never fulfilled, made Hyperechius a figure of fun; his fellows called him a half-way soldier,[321] until he finally obtained a minor post in charge of supplies to the Imperial Guard at Constantinople. The catering corps in the fourth century was rated no higher than it is today. Hyperechius' job, in the acid words of a contemporary historian, was to provide supplies to the mess, that is to be a servant of the belly and the gullet. The failed career had a squalid ending. Hyperechius was implicated in the rebellion of Procopius, who challenged the emperor Valens in 365 and led a force, doubtless of dissident Galatians, to face the imperial army at Dadastana in eastern Bithynia. His own men calculated the odds better than he had done, arrested him, and handed him over in chains to the enemy.[322]

Some pupils failed; others prospered. The fact remains that learning thrived and was esteemed. Eusebius had commented admiringly on the culture and rhetorical skills of Cappadocians in the 330s (see above, n. 92). The pagan writer of the *Expositio Totius Mundi* in the 350s, perhaps a native of Palestine, offered a broader assessment of all the central Anatolian cities:

Above Syria lies Cappadocia, which also is the home of noble gentlemen; then come Pontus and Paphlagonia, the home of wealthy and extremely distinguished men, similar to the Cappadocians and Galatians, who are good in every way, and also in culture.... If you want to assess the vigour and intelligence of their menfolk, look in the imperial courts of East and West, and you will find men of Pontus and Paphlagonia, Cappadocia and Galatia, more than from any other city or province.[323]

In their political significance the cities of central Anatolia, stretched out along the highway between Constantinople and Antioch, now outweighed the famous names of Ephesus, Smyrna, Sardis, and Pergamum. In cultural achievement the pendulum had swung their way too.

VII. *Julian*

The careers and personalities of Himerius, Themistius, and Libanius, as well as the culture which they promoted, can all be illustrated by a much more famous name, Julian the Apostate. Himerius had spoken of the young Julian as standing above his contemporaries like a bull at the head of a herd of cattle, bounding in the meadows of the Muses, tossing his head like a young race horse, as if possessed with divine enthusiasm.[324] In 355 Julian went to Athens, where he would have been one of Himerius' audience. On the face of it they should have been well matched, for Himerius, a native of Prusa in Bithynia, had married the daughter of a *dadouchos*, one of the oldest priesthoods attached to the mysteries of Eleusis, one of the last homes of militant paganism in the empire.[325] Like Himerius, Julian himself was initiated into this antique cult.[326]

In fact he had little time for the debilitating gush of his teacher's style, and took more readily to the sober tone of Themistius, inspired by the philosophers rather than the poets. Probably at the time of his accession in 361 he wrote a long letter, which appears to be a reply to a speech made in his honour by Themistius, and declared his inadequacies in face of the vast administrative task that confronted him.[327] The tone of this reply was modest, tolerant, and respectful. Themistius' practical philosophy must have appealed to a serious and intellectually gifted emperor, but there were deep temperamental differences here too. Themistius was an adept of conciliation and compromise. At a later date he was even to plead with the Arian emperor Valens to cease persecuting his Orthodox subjects.[328] If Sozomen's summary of the argument is correct it was a masterpiece of misunderstanding. Valens ought not to wonder at the discussion of ecclesiastical doctrines, for it was more moderate and less divisive than dissent among pagans, whose opinions about God are multifarious. It was not surprising that dogmatic differences

---

[320] Foss, 'Ankara', 43 n. 61.

[321] Libanius, *Ep.* 308, ἥμισυ στρατιώτου.

[322] Ammianus Marcellinus, 26. 8. 5.

[323] *Exp. Tot. Mundi* 44 (ed. J. Rougé, *Sources chrétiennes*, no. 124, 1966).

[324] Himerius, *Or.* 48 (Colonna), written between 351 and 354 according to Schankl, *RE* viii, 1463. See J. Bidez, *La Vie de l'empereur Julien* (1930), 95.

[325] Bidez, *La Vie de l'empereur Julien*, 114 with 373 n. 4 for refs.

[326] Eunapius, *VS* 475–6; Bidez, *La Vie de l'empereur Julien*, 115–7. Priestly office at Eleusis was natural for a wealthy committed pagan; compare the case of Quintillianus, the governor of Asia who condemned Pionius to death at Smyrna in 250, who was an honorary Eumolpid and *hierokeryx* at the Eleusinian mysteries, Lane Fox, *Pagans and Christians*, 491, and above, Ch. 16 § v n. 283.

[327] Julian, *Letter to Themistius*, 253–67; a work by Themistius addressed to an emperor survives in an Arabic translation of a Syriac version of the original Greek, G. Bowersock, *Julian the Apostate* (1978), 31 n. 23; now edited by I. Shahid and A. F. Norman, *Themistius*, iii (1974), 75–119, who prefer to regard the addressee as Theodosius between 382 and 388, rather than Julian. For relations between Themistius and Julian see Dagron, *Travaux et mémoires*, 3 (1968), 218–35.

[328] Socrates, *HE* 4. 32; Sozomen, *HE* 6. 36; unfortunately [Themistius], *Or.* 12, purporting to be the actual speech, is fake; see *Themistius*, iii. 137–44, and further discussion in Dagron, loc. cit.

led to further contention and discussion. After all it probably pleased God not to be so easily recognized, and that there was a divergence of opinions about Him. Since an accurate knowledge of Him was unobtainable, each man would fear Him the more. In a vain attempt to summarize His vast power, one could only conclude how good and great He was. Another speech survives showing Themistius pleading with Valens to preserve pagan temples.[329] Religious compromise was not to be Julian's favoured strategy.

The fame of the young Libanius also acted as a magnet for Julian. In the late 340s Constantius had forbidden him to attend the orator's lectures at Nicomedia, and Julian had relied on transcripts, copied by a fellow student. Years later, from Gaul, he was to send copies of speeches to Antioch for Libanius' appraisal. Libanius himself, in return, wrote voluminously on the culture, politics, and personality of the last pagan emperor.[330]

In the early 340s Julian and his brother Gallus had passed seven years of political seclusion at Macellum, 'The Market', a fortified villa on the slopes of Mount Argaeus outside Cappadocian Caesareia.[331] Here he had an opportunity to witness at close quarters the spectacle of a city rapidly converting to Christianity. He was to return to Caesareia with a vengeance in the summer of 362 as he crossed Anatolia on the journey to Antioch, and thence on campaign to Persia, where he met his death. The journey included the climactic stages of his attempt to undermine Christianity's hold on the empire and to restore the vitality of paganism.

He made one deviation, as far as we know, from the well-worn military route across Anatolia, to visit Pessinus with its venerable sanctuary of the Mother of the Gods, from which the sacred stone of Cybele had been transported to Rome itself five centuries before. Incubating at the sanctuary he wrote a prose hymn for the goddess in the course of a single night, a substantial contribution to the fourth-century corpus of pagan theology, which attempted to dignify the old rituals of the 'mother and spouse of mighty Zeus' with elaborate Neoplatonic theory, thus assimilating her myths and religious characteristics into a coherent pagan universe. He also promoted the local priestess of Demeter, Callixeine, to become high priestess of the Mother of

the Gods herself.[332] Later in Antioch, replying to a petition from the people of Pessinus, he promised to help them if they would only show more zeal for their goddess. Otherwise they would feel his displeasure. If they expected favours from Julian they should one and all address their prayers to the Mother of the Gods.[333] The disappointment evident in the letter makes it clear that, despite his efforts, Christianity's hold was too strong to be easily dislodged.

Julian advanced to Ancyra and spent the second half of June 362 holding court there.[334] Ammianus' account of his stay focuses on his judicial role—the emperor's most familiar function—as he dealt justly but severely with petitions, complaints, and charges laid before him. He shared Libanius' concern that councillors should fulfil their liturgies and gave no latitude to pleas for exemption.[335] He also issued three laws, collected in the Theodosian Code. One concerned the public post, which was growing ever more important with the centralization of administration in the later empire.[336] The others had a closer bearing on his interest in paganism, and can be linked precisely with his experiences in the congenial surroundings of aristocratic pagan Ancyra.

The first forbade provincial governors from undertaking new building projects until those started by their predecessors were complete—unless they were new pagan temples.[337] As the willingness or spending power of local nobles had declined, governors were now virtually the only initiators of new public building in provincial cities, and construction became a central feature of what was otherwise an unglamorous official

[329] *Or.* 5; For Julian's own exasperation at Christian infighting, see *Ep.* 114 (Bidez) to the people of Bostra; below, § VIII n. 364.

[330] Bowersock, *Julian the Apostate*, 28; P. Petit, 'L'Empereur Julien vu par le sophiste Libanios', in *L'Empereur Julien de l'histoire à la légende* (1978), 67–87. Libanius' speeches concerning Julian have been collected and translated by A. F. Norman for vol. i of the Loeb *Libanios*.

[331] For the stay at Macellum, see Bidez, *La Vie de l'empereur Julien*, 22–6.

[332] Julian, *Or.* 8 (5) (Bidez, 1963); *Ep.* 81.

[333] *Ep.* 84, 431d–32a. Greg. Naz. *Or.* 5. 40 apparently suggests that the people of Pessinus had written to Julian to ask for help in repairing Christian outrages. This seems unlikely, for Julian would surely not have hesitated to assist pagans making such a request. More likely they had asked for some other favour, perhaps for tax relief, but risked rebuttal because of their lukewarm support for the cult. At the time of his visit to Pessinus the citizens of neighbouring Nacolea erected a dedication to him (latest text by T. Drew Bear and M. Christol, *Tyche*, 1 (1986), 53–4), and according to one circumstantial story three Christian martyrs were put to death in the little highland city of Meirus (Socrates, *HE* 3. 15 and Sozomen, *HE* 5. 11; for Meirus, see *Bull. ép.* (1972), 461). It is probably no coincidence that Julian was honoured in Nacolea which remained pagan while its neighbour Orcistus had been Christian at least since the 320s (see above, n. 37). Further on Julian's visit to Pessinus, above, Ch. 16 § II nn. 67–8.

[334] For the dates see Foss, 'Ankara', 39 n. 40.

[335] Ammianus Marcellinus, 22. 9. 8–12.

[336] *CTh.* 8. 5. 13. For the *cursus publicus* in the late empire see E. J. Holmberg, *Zur Geschichte des Cursus publicus* (1933), and Gorce, 41–63, who splendidly illustrates the use and abuse of the system by clerics.

[337] *CTh.* 15. 1. 3.

duty, celebrated in this period by an efflorescence of verse epigrams set up to honour such occasions.[338] The *praes* of Galatia at the time of Julian's visit, who doubtless served as a model of the type of governor that Julian wished to encourage, and to control, was the pagan Maximus, not to be confused with his namesake, the local aristocrat. During his term of office, perhaps from 362 to 364, Ancyra was transformed, according to Libanius, so that the great and beautiful city of Midas, its Phrygian founder, could now better be called the city of Maximus. He earned the title of founder by erecting fountain-houses and nymphaea. Moreover he had enhanced its reputation as an intellectual centre by offering rewards for teachers and by establishing contests in rhetoric in which they could compete.[339] Libanius' rhetoric needs careful handling here, for Maximus need not have built more than a single fountain-house to earn such praise,[340] but the references to the encouragement of teachers and to the competition for rhetors are by no means conventional. The proposals naturally fit well with Ancyra's reputation as an intellectual centre, but above all they harmonize with the political thrust of Julian's own policies, which surely provided the crucial stimulus for Maximus to take his unusual initiative. In the letter that stands at the centre of his own campaign against the Christians, Julian had barred Christians from taking positions as teachers.[341] Now, precisely in Ancyra, he issued a third law, that masters and teachers must excel first in character, then in eloquence. He would have wished to assess candidates in person, but since this was impossible the responsibility would fall on local councils; would-be teachers must obtain a decree of approval from the decurions, with the consent and agreement of the best citizens.[342] Beyond question Julian expected the assessment of character (*mores*) to be governed by the criterion of religion.[343]

He must have felt confident that the largely pagan senators of Ancyra, shortly to receive Libanius' letter commending them for their discernment of poetry and philosophy, would deliver judgements in accordance with his own opinions.

The law of 362 reveals a long-term strategy to eradicate Christian influence, not by the blunt instrument of direct persecution, which had been a spectacular failure even in more favourable conditions half a century earlier, but by denying Christian preachers a platform from which to spread their new moral teaching. Julian saw more clearly even than his Christian predecessors Constantine and Constantius, that the strength of the Christian message lay in the spoken and written word, not in their liturgical practices.[344]

The battle plan for restoring paganism also aimed to provide an alternative to the Christian programme. A key element in paganism's decline had been the demise of the institutions which supported it. The failure of local city councils was simply one symptom of the collapse of the whole system of liturgies and benefactions which had underwritten the costs of temple-construction, public worship, sacrifices, festivals, and games. As funds had dried up the priesthoods had withered away and become marginalized. In the second century the priests and *neocori* of public cults were members of the civic élites, and to hold a religious office was one way to adorn a public career. By the fourth century many sources depict priests as ill-kempt fanatics, who could no more maintain the physical fabric of pagan worship than they could command the respect of their communities. Julian, like the most zealous of his anti-Christian forerunners, Maximinus in 312, planned to revive the pagan hierarchy and himself appointed incumbents to take over local cults, like Callixeine in Pessinus, as well as high priests to supervise the pagan religious institutions of an entire province.[345] In Galatia his new high priest was Arsacius, and when Julian reached Antioch he sent him a letter which spelled out a programme for positive pagan revival. Pagans themselves, he argued, were to blame for the failure of 'Hellenism', they should not be content with the evidence that the gods themselves had provided of their own power, by favouring Julian's elevation to the throne, but should try to reinforce their position. Christians had achieved success through three conspicuous qualities—the charity which they offered to strangers, the attention which they paid to the burial of the dead, and their impressively serious conduct in

[338] Robert, *Hellenica*, iv (1948); C. Roueché, *Aphrodisias in Late Antiquity* (1989), p. xxi, and *passim*.

[339] *Ep.* 1230.

[340] Foss, 'Ankara', 46 takes the expression οἰκοδομίαις, νυμφαίαις, κρήναις as literal plurals. There is no archaeological trace of his work (cf. Foss, 'Ankara', 62–5). It is tempting to see a connection with the inscription Bosch, *Ankara*, no. 306 which lists the building projects of an unknown benefactor of the city, including an aqueduct and a well or fountain (ἐπιμεληθεὶς καὶ τοῦ δημοσίου φρουρίου καὶ τοῦ ὑδραγωγίου καὶ τοῦ ὑδρίου τοῦ [. . .]) but there is nothing else in the text to help establish a link with the governor Maximus.

[341] *Ep.* 61 (Bidez) 422a–24a; trans. in Coleman-Norton, *Roman State and Christian Church*, i. 277–80 no. 116. See the other sources collected by Bidez and F. Cumont, *Iuliani Epistulae, Leges, Poemata* (1922), 69–75.

[342] *CTh.* 13. 3. 5; abrogated on 4 Jan. 364, *CTh.* 13. 3. 6.

[343] Compare the attacks on the *mores* of the Christians in the propagandistic imperial letters and edicts of the Great Persecution of the early 4th cent., cf. *JRS* 78 (1988), 113.

[344] Cf. Bowersock, *Julian the Apostate*, 79–93.

[345] For Maximinus, see *JRS* 78 (1988), 105–24. For Julian's programme, see W. Koch, *Rev. belge de philologie et d'histoire* 6 (1927), 123 ff.; 7 (1928), 49 ff.; 511 ff.; 1363 ff.

life.[346] The high priest himself and all his fellow priests must meet this challenge. If they allowed members of their own household to neglect pagan cults and embrace Christianity they should be expelled from office. A priest should set high standards of behaviour, avoiding the theatre, drinking-houses, and involvement in dishonest or shameful occupations. Each city should establish hospices for strangers to enjoy pagan hospitality. In Galatia these were to be provisioned with 30,000 *modii* of corn and 60,000 measures of wine from the emperor's own estates. A fifth of this was for the poor who aided the priests in their work, while the rest was to be given to strangers and beggars. It was shameful that Jews and Christians, by their charitable institutions, could keep their poor off the streets, while pagans remained destitute. Wealthy pagans must be urged to support such schemes, and villages should reserve the first-fruits of their harvests for the gods, and thence for the poor.[347]

Soon afterwards Julian developed the theme further in a letter to the high priest of Asia, Theodorus. The arguments to Arsacius, especially concerning the discipline and moral example to be shown by pagan clergy, were repeated with greater emphasis. Pagans should promote philanthropic activity and maintain the temples and sacred places. Their own conduct in life should be dignified and sober; indecency and profanity should be avoided, even in speech. They should pray, in public, twice or three times daily. Julian defined elaborate rules of priestly conduct which precisely mirrored the code laid down by a Christian bishop for his clergy. The letter shows signs of hasty composition. It had surely been compiled on the basis of observations made recently as the emperor passed through deeply Christian Cappadocia, and it was fuelled by personal conviction. Punishment for delinquents was scarcely feasible, and there were no significant inducements to compliance beyond the passion of the emperor's own rhetoric.[348]

Julian's former fellow student, Gregory of Nazianzus, and the later historians of the Church saw the truth at once. Julian was doing no more than copy Christian practice in his doomed attempt to win back support for the old religion.[349] The very contents of Julian's programme condemned it to failure. It offered nothing

that current Christian practice did not provide. It did not even attempt to build on existing pagan beliefs, by appealing to civic patriotism, or the cultural heritage of Greece which was preserved by traditional religion. The model of good pagan practice which Julian recommended was an intellectual construct, not something that distilled the best of existing pagan values. Even in material terms, the proposals were built on air. While charity and good works were already increasingly supported by the Church and Christian communities, Julian's schemes to help the poor would have to be supported by a pagan governing class which was already unequal to the tasks which it faced.

For all that, Ancyra, of all the stopping-points on Julian's journey in 362, was the one Anatolian city where such a programme had a chance of success. The local aristocracy was still steeped in a pagan intellectual culture and had been educated to adopt a cultural and political outlook that will have seemed reassuringly like Julian's own. The company of men like the two Maximi, local landowner and provincial governor, may have deluded Julian into forming hopes which far outreached anything that could be achieved by anti-Christian legislation. He may also have found encouragement in the deep divisions of the Christian community of the city.

VIII. *Christians in Fourth-Century Ancyra*

The state of Christianity at Ancyra at the time of Julian's visit contained more than a hint that the Church's fortress was vulnerable. The city had had an important role to play in the turbulent ecclesiastical history of the early fourth century, but not always an inspiring one. After the peace of the Church had been confirmed by the so-called 'Edict of Milan' of July 313, a general synod met at Ancyra in 314, principally to discuss matters arising from Christian behaviour, and especially Christian lapses under the pressure of the Great Persecution.[350] A decade later the city was intended by Constantine to be the seat of the synod that resolved the Arian controversy and the dispute over the date of Easter. Circumstances led him to transfer the meeting to Nicaea. Had they not prevailed, Christians thereafter would have endorsed an Ancyran, not a Nicene creed.[351]

Literary sources recount the history of fourth-century Christianity largely through the doings of bishops, and Ancyra was dominated by two important rival personalities, Marcellus and Basil. Marcellus had

[346] Julian, *Ep.* 84 (Bidez), 429d; ἡ περὶ τοὺς ξένους φιλανθρωπία καὶ ἡ περὶ τὰς ταφὰς τῶν νεκρῶν προμήθεια καὶ ἡ πεπλασμένη σεμνότης τοῦ βίου.

[347] See also Sozomen, *HE* 5. 16. E. Kislinger, 'Kaiser Julian und die (christlichen) Xenodocheia', *Festschrift H. Hunger* (1984), 171–84.

[348] *Ep.* 89. Bidez argues that the lengthy 'Letter to a priest' inserted in the MSS of Julian's address to Themistius was part of this letter to Theodorus, Budé edn. pp. 102–5.

[349] Greg. Naz. *Or.* 4. 111; Sozomen, *HE* 5. 16.

[350] C. Hefele and H. Leclercq, *Histoire des conciles*, i. 1 (1907), 298–334.

[351] Preserved in a Syriac translation of Athanasius, H. G. Opitz, *Athanasius Werke*, iii. 1 (1934) no. 20; Foss, 'Ankara', 36–7; *Clavis Patrum Graecorum*, 5 no. 8511.

been bishop as early as 314, represented the city at Nicaea, and remained unopposed until 336, when he was deposed in favour of Basil. He regained the see soon afterwards and stayed in control until he was again supplanted by his old rival in 350. Basil's second term lasted until 360, when he too was removed. The two stood on either side of the divide in the Church that arose from the struggle between the Arians, who drew a sharp distinction between the persons of God and Christ, and were accordingly considered by their opponents either to have denied the divinity of Christ or to have created two gods, and the Orthodox signatories of the Nicene creed, who endorsed the doctrine of the *Homoousion*, the consubstantiality of God and Christ. Marcellus the Orthodox bishop, according to Eusebius a doughty opponent of the many heretics who beset Ancyra, had signed the doctrines of Nicaea, but his views on the unity of the Divinity were so old-fashioned and extreme that he lapsed into a heresy of his own, akin to the Sabellianism of the later third century, which virtually denied a divine identity to Christ by identifying his nature with that of God the Father. Marcellus was deposed for these unorthodox doctrines by decisions of the synods of Tyre in 335 and Constantinople in 336, but his followers acquired a name of their own, Ancyro-Galatians, and their influence persisted until the 370s, when they were vigorously attacked by Basil of Caesareia.[352]

Basil of Ancyra, who replaced Marcellus, earned a place in Jerome's *De viris illustribus*, according to which he had been trained as a doctor. The observations of a practitioner may lie behind some of the startlingly frank passages of one of his two surviving theological works, the *De virginitate*.[353] He appears to have been a popular figure as well a free-thinking intellectual, for when Marcellus briefly regained his see

in 337, there were riots at Ancyra, graphically described in a letter sent by the eastern bishops assembled at Serdica in 343 to their colleagues in Africa:

Houses were burned down and all manner of fighting broke out. Priests were dragged naked to the forum by the bishop himself...he profaned the sacred Host of the Lord by hanging it openly and in public from the necks of the priests, and with horrendous barbarity tore the vestments from holy virgins, dedicated to God and Christ, and displayed them naked to the public in the forum, in the middle of the city.[354]

Marcellus, who relied on the support of western bishops and the emperor Constans, was deposed and exiled again after the latter's death in 346 by the Arian Constantius, perhaps precisely in 347 when Constantius passed through the Ancyra for the first time, or on his return in 350. Basil, after being restored to the see, tried to steer a middle path between Arians and Orthodox, and is credited with helping to forge the doctrine of the *Homoioousion*, that the Son was of like substance with the Father. In 358 he founded a new church at Ancyra on the occasion of a synod held there, which aimed to resolve the conflict between Arians and Orthodox by promoting the new homoioousian doctrine. Strong-arm tactics were used against rivals. An Arian priest from Antioch, hurrying to communicate with the emperor, was arrested and sent into exile in the Phrygian city of Midaeion, and provincial governors were pressured into banishing clerical rivals to Heracleia Pontica and the Montanist stronghold of Pepuza.[355] The tide, however, was moving in favour of the Arians, and Basil's compromising theology combined with heavy-handed politics won him no friends in 360 at the synod of Constantinople, when he was deposed by the emperor Constantius. His enemies were able to bring a pot-pourri of charges against him, including those of handing over clergy to the civil authorities for punishment and of personally arresting an Alexandrian priest who was making his way through Ancyra to Constantius' court.[356] However, it seems that his main offence was to affront the emperor himself with the charge that the more extreme Arian doctrines which he favoured went

[352] Marcellus bishop in 314, see C. H. Turner *et al.*, *Ecclesiae Occidentalis Monumenta Iuris Antiquissima*, 2. 30, 50, 51; Eusebius, *In Marcellum*, 1. 1. 1 shows him to have been a vigorous champion of Orthodoxy, and persecutor of heretics; for his deposition in 336 see T. D. Barnes, *Constantine and Eusebius* (1981), 240–2, 264–5; Basil of Caesareia denounced his doctrines especially in *Epp.* 69, 125 and 263; for the Ancyro-Galatae see Socrates, *HE* 2. 19. His career and other sources outlined in Foss, 'Ankara', 37.

[353] Jerome, *De vir. ill.* 89, *PL* 23. 732; for his treatise on virginity, see P. R. L. Brown, *The Body and Society* (1988), 267–9.

[354] See Socrates, *HE* 2. 20 and 23, where the abuses which occurred at Basil's deposition are mentioned, ἡ πρόφασιν λοιδορίας παρέσχε τοῖς τὰ ἐναντία φρονοῦσιν; *Corpus Scriptorum Ecclesiasticorum Latinorum* 65. 55 = *PL* 10. 658 ff. (collected by Hilary of Poitiers) is a letter sent to the African church mentioning the riots. Note Athanasius, *Apol. contra Arianos* 33, *PG* 25. 301–4, quoting from a letter from the bishop of Rome Julius, which described abuses that had taken place in Ancyra, when men were put into jail and bishops and presbyters prevented from attending synods.

[355] For Basil's career see R. Janin, *Dictionnaire d'histoire et de géographie ecclésiastiques*, vi (1932), 1104–6. For the council of 358 see Sozomen, *HE* 4. 13–14, and Philostorgius, *HE* 4. 8–9.

[356] Socrates, *HE* 2. 42; Philostorgius, *HE* 5. 1; Theodoret, *HE* 2. 20; Sozomen, *HE* 4. 24: Ἰδίᾳ δὲ ἐγκλήματα ἐπέφερον, Βασιλείῳ μὲν ὡς Διογένην πρεσβύτερον ἕνα τῆς Ἀλεξανδρείας τὴν Ἀγκύραν διοδεύοντα, χάρτας τε ἀφεῖλε καὶ ἐτύπτησε, καὶ κληρικοὺς ἐκ τῆς Ἀντιοχείας καὶ παρὰ τὸν Εὐφράτην ποταμόν, Κιλικίας τε καὶ Γαλάτας καὶ Ἀσιανοὺς ὑπερορίοις φυγαῖς καὶ ἄλλαις τιμωρίαις ζημιοῦν ἀκρίτως τοῖς ἄρχουσιν ἐπέταττες· ὡς καὶ σιδηρῶν αὐτοὺς πειραθῆναι δεσμῶν, καὶ τὰ ὄντα προσαπολύειν τοῖς ἀπάγουσι στρατιώταις ἵνα μὴ ὑβρίζωνται.

against the Apostolic Decrees. Constantius' riposte was to blame Basil for 'disturbances in the churches', a likely allusion to the charges of his enemies, and send him into exile.[357] An attempt to secure reinstatement under Jovian in 363 proved unavailing.[358]

The main church community at Ancyra, therefore, had been rent by dispute throughout the generation before Julian's visit; leadership had oscillated between the old-fashioned and entrenched conservatism of Marcellus, and the innovative improvisation of Basil. As elsewhere the theological disputes had spread to the population at large and led to violence, perhaps even bloodshed in the streets of the city. Basil had meddled too much with secular politics, and it was not encouraging that both rival bishops had been variously promoted or exiled at the behest of emperors, not as a result of episcopal elections. An outside observer, looking for signs of weakness, might readily have concluded that this particular Christian church was too fond of politics for its faith to command respect.

There is more besides. Ancyra was also a noted centre for heretical groups, which lay beyond the main lines of the Orthodox–Arian dispute. When Eusebius described Marcellus as an enemy of heresy he may have had more in mind than his opposition to Arianism. The earliest Christian community attested in the city, before the end of the second century, was Montanist; and there is good reason to believe that the Life of St Theodotus, probably written in the 360s to commemorate a martyrdom of 312, was also the product of a Montanist community. It implies the existence of at least two Montanist churches in the city itself, as well as one at the village of Malos overlooking the river Halys. The same Life tells us that there was also a group of Apotactites in Ancyra, an early quasi-monastic schismatic community best known from Egypt but attested elsewhere in Anatolia, who claimed that some of the victims of the persecution belonged to their group.[359] A doubtless apocryphal martyr act,

attached to the visit of Julian to the city, tells the story of an Encratite, Busiris.[360] The most widespread heretical group of fourth-century Asia Minor were the Novatians, with a distribution that covered much of Bithynia and Phrygia (see below, § IX); it is no surprise that they should have had followers at Ancyra. Their church was closed down in the reign of Arcadius at the end of the fifth century by the Orthodox bishop Leontius, but their origins must go back to the fourth if not to the third century.[361] At the beginning of the fifth century, in his Commentary on St Paul's Epistle, Jerome seized on the famous reference to the foolish Galatians to castigate the Ancyrans for the heresies that flourished in their city.

You can understand the address if you look at Ancyra, now torn apart by schismatic groups, depraved by a plethora of dogmas. To say nothing of the Cataphrygians (i.e. Montanists), Ophitae, Borboritae, and Manichees, which are already familiar descriptions of human ruin, who ever heard of the Passalorhyncitae, the Ascodrobi, the Artotyritae, and others which are more like monsters than names, in any other part of the Roman world?[362]

An imperial constitution directed against the sect of Tascodrungitai was sent to the vicar of Pontica, whose headquarters were in the city. The sect was also named by Epiphanius and Theodoret and should certainly be identified with the otherwise unique Ascodrobi of the manuscripts of Jerome. Epiphanius further explained that Passalorhyncitae, those who placed their finger on their nose in the course of the liturgy, was another name for Tascodrungitai, a word which bore the same meaning in the native Galatian or Phrygian dialect. Jerome could not resist using both names, the Greek hardly less barbarous than the term it translated, for full rhetorical effect. These obscure heretics belong in Ancyra, and nowhere else. In an address delivered in Constantinople attacking heresies of all descriptions, but especially targeting the Montanists, Gregory of Nazianzus placed the madness of the Phrygians alongside the senseless Galatians, whose impieties were known by a wealth of different names. Unlike Jerome he refrained from listing them.[363] This is an impressive

[357] Theodoret, *HE* 2. 23 (ed. Parmentier, *GCS*, 1954); 'Basil (of Ancyra), relying on his former intimacy, ventured boldly to object to the emperor that he was attacking the apostolic decrees; but Constantius took this ill, and told Basil to hold his tongue, for to you, said he, the disturbance of the churches is due.'

[358] Janin, *Dictionnaire d'histoire et de géographie ecclésiastiques*, vi. 1106.

[359] *AS* 32 (1982), 93–113; for Apotactites at Laodicea Catacecaumene, see below, § x nn. 413–15; Apotactites in Egypt appear to have adopted an independent monkish stance within communities, but had not withdrawn entirely into hermit-like seclusion (E. A. Judge and S. C. Pickering, *JAC* 20 (1977), 471). Epiphanius, *Panarion*, 60. 1. 1 says that they were to be found in Phrygia, Pamphylia, and Cilicia. Julian, *Or*. 7 (Bidez), 224b, likened them to the Cynics. They seem to anticipate the role which Basil of Caesareia envisaged for his model monastic communities.

[360] Sozomen, *HE* 5. 11 ὃν τῆς αἱρέσεως ὄντα τότε τῶν καλουμένων Ἐγκρατιτῶν, συλλαβὼν ὁ τοῦ ἔθνους ἄρχων, ὡς νεανευσάμενον κατὰ τῶν Ἑλληνιστῶν αἰκίζεσθαι ἠβούλετο.

[361] Sozomen, 8. 1; for the Novatians see below, § IX at n. 396.

[362] *Comm. in ep. ad Galatas*, 2. 3, *PL* 10. 382 with comm.

[363] *CTh*. 16. 5. 10, (20 June 383); they are also mentioned in the all-embracing constitution of 20 May 428, *CTh*. 16. 5. 65; Epiphanius, *Panarion*, 48. 4. 3; Theodoret; Timotheus Constantinopolitanus; Antiochus Monachus ('gente Galata ex vico Medosaga vicesimo ab Ancyra lapide') are cited in the commentary to *PL* 10. 382. The Artotyritae are also found in *Panarion*, 49. 2. 6. Is there any connection with the *panis divinus* of Ancyra mentioned in *Exp. Tot. Mundi*, 44? See

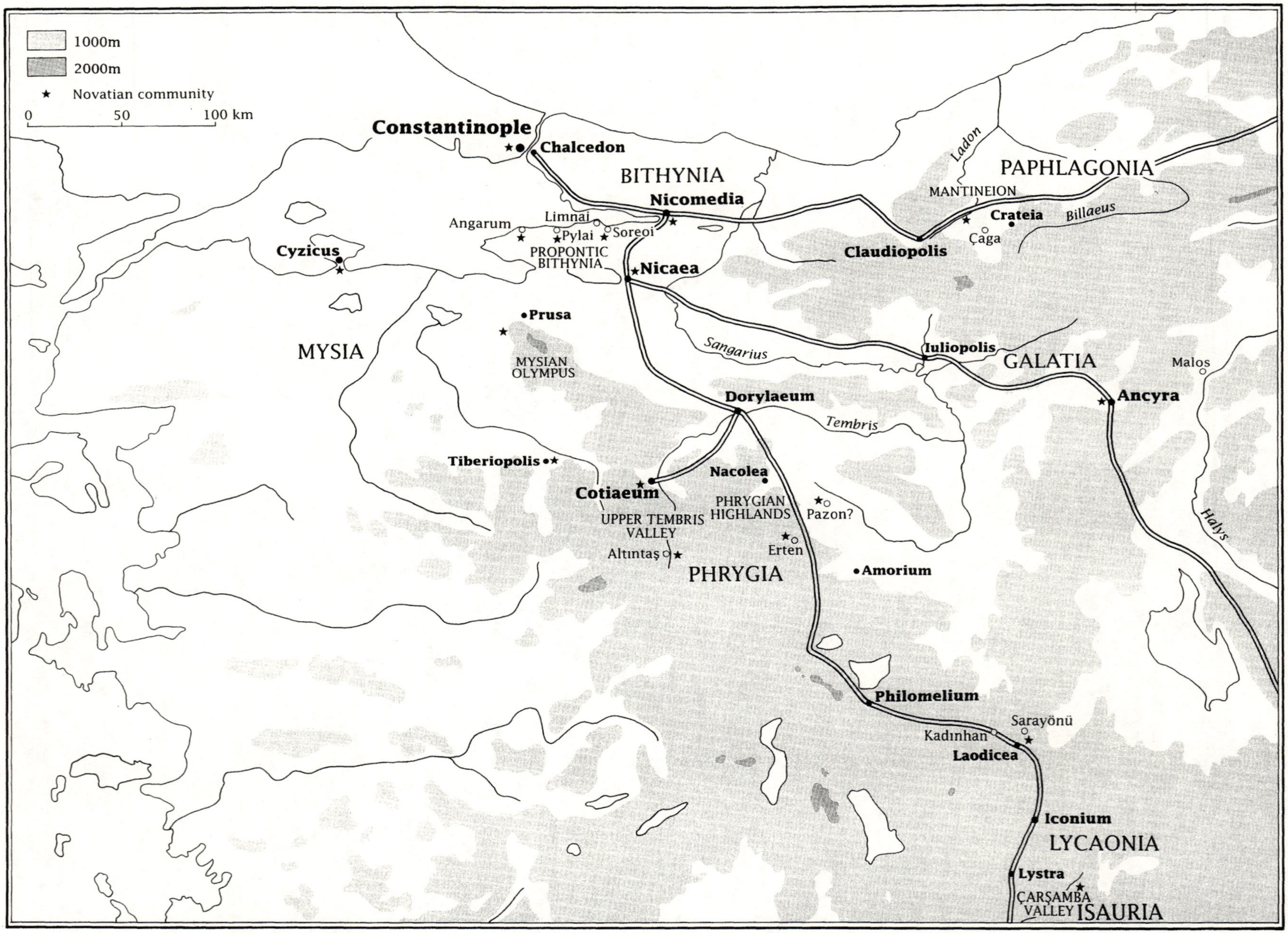

Map 4. Novatian Christianity

dossier. Ancyra, like Laodicea Catacecaumene at the other side of the central plateau, was one of the heretic capitals of Asia Minor.

None of this was lost on Julian. From Antioch he wrote to the people of Bostra in Arabia:

I thought that the leaders of the Galileans would have greater regard for me than for my predecessor Constantius. For during his reign many of them had been sent into exile, persecuted, or imprisoned; at Samosata, at Cyzicus, in Paphlagonia, in Bithynia, in Galatia, and in many other provinces villages were indiscriminately ravaged or destroyed, while in my time the opposite has happened. Exiles have been recalled and confiscated goods restored.[364]

The claim was disingenuous, for Julian himself was believed by both Christian and pagan historians to have made a deliberate attempt to set Christian groups at odds with one another by recalling those who had been exiled for religious dissent.[365] However, he and other pagans could congratulate themselves on their good sense in avoiding such behaviour. The strong pagan intellectual group at Ancyra may have owed its standing at least in part to the disarray of its Christian contemporaries. In the 360s Galatia was a land of divided religious loyalties. Julian did well to seize the chance to advance the pagan cause there as nowhere else. Unfortunately for his policy, such disarray among the Christians was far from typical of the rest of Anatolia.

He left Ancyra and entered less promising terrain in Cappadocia, his old place of exile. Julian's correspondence includes a letter to Aristoxenus, a pagan philosopher of Tyana.[366] The gist of his reaction to his surroundings comes in two sentences: 'Show us a genuine Hellene among the Cappadocians. So far, I have only seen people who refuse to sacrifice, or a small number who are willing to do so but do not know how.' He himself makes no reference to the metropolis Caesareia; the story of what happened there emerges first from a speech of Libanius, in which he counselled his fellow Antiochenes not to provoke Julian's anger in the famous contest of wills between them. They should keep in mind the example of Caesareia, a prosperous and famous place which had been abruptly struck off the register of cities when its insolence exceeded its power.[367] The details were provided by Sozomen in the mid-fifth century.[368] Caesareia had been reduced to a village and stripped of its imperial name on account of its zealous attachment to Christianity. The temples of Apollo and Zeus had long since been pulled down, and a temple of Fortune was demolished in Julian's own reign. The vigorous assault on pagan temples during the 350s was not unparalleled elsewhere in the East, for Christians everywhere may have taken their cue from the militant anti-pagan pronouncements of Constantius, a true heir to his father Constantine in this and other matters.[369] Indeed, Julian's own mission to restore pagan worship certainly acquired a sharper urgency in the face of the physical demolition of its old centres. At Caesareia Christians and pagans were punished alike, the former for their uncompromising militancy, the latter for allowing matters to reach such a state. Church possessions were confiscated, clergy forcibly enlisted into the provincial governor's bodyguard, supposedly the most onerous and least privileged branch of military service. Christians were to be registered in a census and made liable for the poll-tax from which city-dwellers were normally exempt.[370] The punishments hark back to the policies of Maximinus in 312, when Christian soldiers in governors' bodyguards were refused leave to resign their posts and compelled to join in pagan rites, and exemption from urban capitation was offered as an inducement to cities to expel their Christian communities.[371] Finally the Christians of Caesareia were threatened with annihilation if the temples were not speedily rebuilt. It is difficult to know how much of Sozomen's later account should be accepted as accurate. Julian's measures would have been hard to enforce, without strong local support or direct military intervention. Soldiers were more urgently needed for the emperor's planned Persian campaign than for local anti-Christian reprisals, and the Christian population of Caeareia evidently outweighed the remaining pagans in both numbers and weight of influence. When the emperor himself died within a year, there was no one to enforce his policy. The militant and universal Christianity of Cappadocia in the last third of the fourth century shows that Julian's appraisal of the crisis of paganism at Caesareia was absolutely accurate; the city was now Christian. Galatia had offered him a scintilla of hope; Cappadocia had extinguished it. His attempted solution was futile; there was nothing to be done.

Greg. Naz. *Or.* 22. 12: ἡ εἰσέτι καὶ νῦν *Φρυγῶν μανία* τελούντων τε καὶ τελουμένων μικροῦ τοῖς παλαιοῖς παραπλήσια (a reference to Montanism), καὶ ἡ *Γαλατῶν ἄνοια* πλουτούντων ἐν πολλοῖς τῆς ἀσεβείας ὀνόμασιν.

[364] Julian, *Ep.* 114 (Bidez).
[365] Ammianus Marcellinus, 22. 5. 3–4; Sozomen, *HE* 5. 5; Coleman-Norton, *Roman State and Christian Church*, i. 273–4 no. 112.
[366] *Ep.* 78 (Bidez).
[367] Libanius, *Or.* 16. 14.

[368] Sozomen, *HE* 5. 4.
[369] Barnes, *L'Église et l'empire*, 325–35.
[370] Cf. Barnes, *The New Empire of Diocletian and Constantine*, 232.
[371] See above, § III n. 68.

IX. *The Novatian Church in Asia Minor*

At the close of the Council of Nicaea in 325 the emperor Constantine interviewed Acesius, leader of the most prominent schismatic sect of the early fourth century, the Novatians. Since the Novatians had always celebrated Easter at the time agreed by the Council, and were happy with the Orthodox Creed proposed by the assembled bishops, Constantine wished to know why they had separated from the rest of the Church. Acesius referred back to the persecution of Trajan Decius in AD 250, after which the Church had swiftly readmitted communicants who had apostasized. Novatianus, a priest in Rome, had demurred, adhering to the stern rule which declared that it was impossible for persons who had committed a mortal sin after baptism to be readmitted to the sacraments; repentance might indeed bring absolution, but no priest could grant remission, only God. Acesius and his followers concurred. 'Then', replied the emperor, 'take a ladder, Acesius, and climb alone into heaven.'[372] Thus the Church historian Socrates made his first mention of a sect who continued to occupy a significant place in fourth- and fifth-century Church history. The episode reveals with clarity the origins and the ambiguous status of a group whose ideals and conduct were too rigorous for the body of the Orthodox Church to accept, but whose doctrines and beliefs were essentially identical to theirs. The bishops at Nicaea accorded Novatianism a uniquely privileged status among non-Orthodox Christians. The eighth canon of the Council made it possible for a Novatian priest to be admitted to the Orthodox clergy simply by abjuring his rigorist stance; even as a Novatian his clerical rank was recognized, and the standing of Novatian bishops was acknowledged in sees where there was no Orthodox incumbent.

Despite the apparently narrow division which separated them from the main Church, the Novatians remained distinct, and the origin of their schism was never forgotten. More than a century after Trajan Decius, when the time of the persecutions was only a memory, they continued to define their position just as Acesius had to Constantine. The Church should not admit to the holy sacraments those who had sacrificed. They left the pardoning of offences to God, who alone had the power to forgive all sin.[373] This emblematic pronouncement was itself irrelevant to contemporary conditions, but it symbolized a rigorist stance and a measure of moral discipline which they deemed to be lacking in the rest of the Church.

Socrates' interest in the Novatians is providential, for over the seven books of the Ecclesiastical History, much of it faithfully reproduced by Sozomen, he recalled several salient episodes in the sect's history from Constantine to Theodosius, which allow us to assign it a distinct place in Church history, above all in the story of Christianity in rural Anatolia. Much of the material which he supplies concerns the sect in Constantinople. We learn that the congregation was large enough to fill four churches, one of which was dismantled under threat from the Arian bishop Macedonius late in Constantius' reign, and re-erected in Sykai across the Golden Horn, although it was later to be rebuilt on the old site, supposedly at the behest of Julian. The closeness of the Novatian and Orthodox communities emerges from another observation concerning these years; when the Arians closed Orthodox homoousian churches, the congregations resorted to the Novatian communion.[374] The episcopal succession in the capital can be reconstructed through most of the fourth and early fifth centuries, as well as the episcopal style and personality of several of the bishops.[375] The norm among the clergy was an austere simplicity of life—the bishops might go barefoot, wore only a single garment, and fasted rigorously.[376] The exception who proves the rule was the maverick Sisinnius, bishop from 395 to 407, whose fondness for luxurious food, twice-daily baths and ostentatious white robes, allied to a sharp and clever tongue, contrasted unfavourably with the severe demeanour of his Orthodox counterpart, John Chrysostom, and helped to provoke a serious schism in the movement.[377] When other members of the com-

[372] Socrates, 1. 10; Sozomen, 1. 22; Gelasius, *HE* 2. 30. Here, as elsewhere, Socrates insists that he had obtained the information from private Novatian sources. In the letter preserved by Eusebius, *VC* 3. 64–5, Constantine had outlawed the Novatians along with other heretics by forbidding them to meet and confiscating their churches. The decision, also implied in *CTh*. 16. 5. 1 of 1 September 326, was rescinded in a letter of 26 September 326 to the praetorian prefect, *CTh*. 16. 5. 2; see Millar, *ERW* 598.

[373] Socrates, 4. 28.

[374] Socrates, 2. 38; Sozomen, 4. 20; Theodosius I allowed the Novatians to retain their church in Constantinople, Socrates 5. 20.

[375] There is a useful summary of the main outlines of Novatian history by E. Amann, *Dictionnaire de théologie catholique*, 11 (1931), 816–49, and a thoughtful study of the role of the church in the 4th and early 5th cents. by T. Gregory, 'Novatianism. A Rigorist Sect in the Christian Roman Empire', *Byzantine Studies*, 2 (1975), 1–18, on which I have drawn freely. For Novatian theology, see H. J. Vogt, *Coetus Sanctorum: Der Kirchenbegriff Novatus und die Geschichte seiner Sonderkirche* (1968).

[376] Bishop Agelius wore simple dress and went barefoot, Socrates, 4. 9; for his simple piety see 5. 10 and Sozomen, 7. 12. In the 5th cent. Bishop Paul ate no meat, took little oil or wine, and generally adopted a monkish demeanour, Socrates, 7. 17.

[377] Socrates, 6. 22; Sozomen, 8. 1. For Sabbatius' schism, see Socrates, 7. 5.

munity a few years later showed signs of apostasizing towards Orthodoxy, stricter brethren stood in their way, reminding them of the 'ancient precept' which kept them apart.[378] Theologically the movement was unsophisticated. When their bishop Agelius was invited by the emperor Theodosius to contribute to a debate with the now discredited Arians and thus show the inferiority of the Arian creed, Agelius refused and sent his clever priest, the future bishop Sisinnius, in his place.[379] The asceticism of the movement extended to the laity, which was expected to adhere to the same puritanical regime as the clergy. In particular, remarriage was forbidden.[380]

The real strength of the Novatians clearly lay outside Constantinople in the hinterland of Asia Minor.[381] Socrates indicates that they were particularly strong in Paphlagonia, Phrygia, Bithynia, and Galatia. When the Arian Macedonius launched his vigorous assault on the Novatians, picking them out as the most vulnerable wing of those who endorsed the Nicene Creed, the most dramatic confrontation came not at Constantinople but in rural Paphlagonia. The emperor Constantius was persuaded to make four troops of soldiers available to attack the recalcitrant Novatians of Mantineion. Animated by desperation and religious fervour, and armed with scythes and axes, the victims resisted stoutly; at the end of a bloody battle many of the heretics, but also most of the soldiers had been killed. The rustic church evidently prevailed.[382] The district of Mantineion has been securely located in the deep wooded valleys east of modern Bolu, (ancient Claudiopolis) in whose territory it lay. The territory of Claudiopolis can show as long a Christian tradition as any part of north-west Asia Minor, beginning with the funerary inscription of an early third-century civic *archon* and *agonothetes* whose first lines declare him and his family to be 'most holy and believers in God', and extending to a redoubtable monastic tradition in the middle Byzantine period.[383] The Novatians of

Mantineion take their place in the middle of this sequence. Although they lived in uncompromisingly rural territory, as much a home for shepherds and foresters as for agricultural peasants, it is important to note that they were not remote and isolated. Their villages lay astride the route of the northern highway that led from Constantinople to the north-east frontier, much traversed by soldiers and officials, and ease of access may have made it simpler to persuade Constantius to release troops for this unorthodox operation. Another point deserves greater emphasis: both Socrates and Sozomen stressed the fact that a very large number of the Paphlagonians were of the Novatian persuasion, especially those around Mantineion.[384] The Council of Nicaea had acknowledged that there were areas where the Orthodox had no bishops. Here, palpably, was one of them.

In a later passage of prime importance, Socrates explains why the sect had such a strong appeal in Paphlagonia and Phrygia: the natural puritanism of the conservative country people offered the perfect climate for a rigorist church, which saw itself as a true heir to the simple piety of apostolic times.[385] The sources for Novatian history repeatedly emphasized the Phrygian connection. Philostorgius, doubtless drawing a false inference from the heavy preponderance of Phrygian Novatians in his own day, even implausibly suggested that the founder of the sect, Novatianus himself, was a Phrygian who had risen in the Christian community of Rome.[386] The latest Novatian bishop known to Socrates, Marcion, was summoned to his post in Constantinople from Phrygian Tiberiopolis in 458.[387] The literary evidence is fully borne out by the distribution of Novatian inscriptions (see below, § x).

Another area of Novatian strength was in Bithynia, especially on the southern shores of the Propontis. Nicomedia and Nicaea, along with Phrygian Cotiaeum and Constantinople, made up the four senior Novatian bishoprics.[388] Cyzicus, in neighbouring Mysia, had a

---

[378] For the ἀρχεῖον παράγγελμα see Socrates, 2. 38. But for their allegiance to this, the Novatians might have been completely united with the Orthodox community. Sozomen, 4. 20 comments that they would have been united, εἰ μὴ βασκανία ὀλίγων οἶμαι τὴν τοῦ πλήθους προθυμίαν ἔβλαψεν, ἀρχαῖον εἶναι λόγον ἰσχυριζομένων παραιτεῖσθαι τοῦτο ποιεῖν.

[379] Socrates, 5. 10; Sozomen, 7. 12.

[380] Epiphanius, *Panarion*, 59. 6.

[381] Gregory, *Byzantine Studies*, 2 (1975), 1–18.

[382] Socrates, 2. 38, citing the eye-witness authority of an aged Paphlagonian peasant; Sozomen, 4. 21.

[383] See L. Robert, *A travers l'Asie Mineure*, 132–46, esp. 138 ff. making full use of the hagiographic evidence and the Christian texts and remains found in the eastern parts of the territory of Claudiopolis by F. Dörner, *Bericht über eine Reise in Bithynien* (1952), 59–67. Note the early text 59 no. 159, τοῖς ἁγνοτάτοις καὶ Θεῷ πιστεύσασιν Μάρκῳ Δημητριανῷ τῷ α'

ἄρξαντι καὶ πάντα πολειτευσαμένῳ, ἀγωνοθετήσαντι ἐπιτείμως (now *I. Klaudiupolis*, no. 44); 160 no. 60 (*I. Klaudiupolis*, no. 174) may not be much later.

[384] See C. Mango, *Analecta Bollandiana*, 100 (1982), 401–9, who stresses the importance of the location of Mantineion on this main military route. In this respect it may be compared with the monastic complex founded by St Theodore at Sykeon; see below, Ch. 19 § 1 at nn. 29–31.

[385] Socrates 4. 28; see above, Vol. I, Ch. 11 § v at n. 220. In general on Novatian values see Vogt, *Coetus Sanctorum*, stressing Novatian puritanism, and Gregory, placing the emphasis on primitivism, and an attempt to impose the discipline and practical values of the early Church.

[386] Philostorgius, *HE* 8. 15 (ed. Bidez, *GCS* 21).

[387] Socrates, 7. 46.

[388] For Nicaea, Nicomedia, and Cotiaeum as the main Novatian sees outside Constantinople, see Socrates, 4. 28, οὓς δὴ κυρίους

Novatian church which was first destroyed and later rebuilt by Eleusis, the Arian bishop of the city.[389] Socrates also tells how Eutychianus, a Novatian holy man who led a solitary life on the slopes of Mysian Olympus, came to Constantinople in the time of Constantine to intercede with the emperor for the life of a prisoner suspected of treason. The intercession was successful and Eutychianus stayed in the capital with his younger associate Auxanon and Alexander, a Paphlagonian, where they led a monastic life a generation before the introduction of organized monasticism to the capital.[390]

The presence of most Novatians in Constantinople, however, is more simply explained. A majority surely came to the city as part of the stream of migrants to the capital, which swelled to a flood during times of famine and shortage during the fourth century. Socrates highlighted one episode in particular which perfectly illustrates the process. It was widely believed that when Valens' praetorian prefect Modestus drowned eighty members of the Orthodox clergy in a boat off the gulf of Astacus, God punished the Arians by sending so great a famine to Phrygia that a large proportion of the population abandoned the countryside and came to Constantinople, 'for Constantinople, notwithstanding the vast population it supplies, yet always abounds with the necessities of life, all manner of provisions being imported by sea from various regions, and the Euxine, which lies near it, furnishes it with wheat to any extent it may require.' The story acquires even more point if many of the Phrygians were also Novatians, whose church the Arians strove to extinguish.[391] Epiphanius made the same point about the Montanists of the fourth century. Although they were

really at home in Cappadocia, Galatia, Cilicia, and above all Phrygia, from which they derived their name of Cataphrygae, and although persecution after the Council of Nicaea had driven many to take refuge in the remote interior of Phrygia, more Montanists were to be found in Constantinople than anywhere else.[392]

The most compelling evidence for seeing the Novatians as a largely rural sect whose heartlands lay between Phrygia and the Propontis comes from Socrates' and Sozomen's accounts of the schism of the late fourth century which arose from a dispute over the date of Easter. A group of Phrygian Novatians, intent on distinguishing themselves from the Orthodox Church, began to celebrate Easter at the same time as the Jewish Passover, in line with the practice of the Judaizing Quartodecimani and the Montanists, who were also notably strong in the region. There had been a strong Jewish strain in some of the Phrygian Christian groups in the third century. Jewish influence did not diminish.[393] The change was agreed by a group of obscure bishops meeting at a village called Pazon near the sources of the river Sangarius, perhaps on the territory of Phrygian Amorium.[394] Significantly, Agelius of Constantinople and the senior bishops of Nicomedia and Cotiaeum were absent. A second council met later at Angarum, a port town near Helenopolis, which has been located on the south side of the gulf of Izmit,[395] to resolve the dispute. An improbable compromise was reached between the schismatics, mostly poor people from Phrygia and Galatia (there was a Novatian church at Ancyra, see above, n. 361), led by a former Jew Sabbatius, and the main church authorities: Easter could be celebrated at any date the local church decided, on condition that Sabbatius renounced any personal ambition to become

---

καὶ κολοφῶνας, ὡς εἰπεῖν, οἱ Ναυατιανοὶ νομίζουσι τῶν περὶ τὴν οἰκείαν αἵρεσιν καὶ τὰς αὐτῶν Ἐκκλησίας πραττομένων; the ἐκκλησία τῶν Εὐσεβῶν at Nicaea was probably Novatian (I. Iznik, i. 577; cf. Horsley, New Docs. iv. 259 no. 127; Bull. ép. (1980), 517); Socrates, 7. 27 reveals that the bishop of Nicaea, Asclepiades, had served for 50 years; cf. 7. 12 for his successor Ablabius. TAM iv. 1. 361 from Nicomedia, referring to Μαρᾶς ὑποβολεὺς τῆς ἁγίας τοῦ Θεοῦ ἐκκλησίας should also be Novatian, by analogy with comparable expressions on the inscriptions of Laodicea Catacecaumene (below, § x at n. 406).

[389] The church was later rebuilt at the behest of Julian in his attempt to divide the Christian communities, Socrates, 3. 11.

[390] Socrates, 1. 13 and 2. 38, who had heard the story from Auxanon, an aged Novatian presbyter, while he was a young man. Note a ἡγούμενος μωνῆς τῶν Καθαρᾶ among the inscriptions of Bursa Museum (Dörner, Bithynien, no. 29, Robert, Rev. phil. (1943), 178; now I. Kios, no. 117 and I. Iznik, i no. 802), presumably a head of the important Monastery of the Cathari near Yalova (Foss, DOP 41 (1987), 191, citing R. Janin, Les Églises et monastères des grands centres byzantins (1975), 158–60). See also below, Ch. 18 § II at n. 58.

[391] Socrates, 4. 16.

[392] Panarion, 48. 14. 2, ἔστι γὰρ καὶ τὸ γένος ἐν τῇ Καππαδοκίᾳ καὶ Γαλατίᾳ καὶ ἐν τῇ προειρημένη Φρυγίᾳ, ὅθεν κατὰ Φρύγας ἡ αἵρεσις καλεῖται, ἀλλὰ καὶ ἐν Κιλικίᾳ καὶ ἐν Κωνσταντινουπόλει τὸ πλεῖστον.

[393] Socrates, 4. 28, 5. 21–2; Sozomen, 7. 18. For the Quartodecimani, see Panarion, 50. 1. 1. For the Jewish element at an earlier date see above, Ch. 16 § III at nn. 201–9. Judaizing practices were later characteristic of the middle Byzantine heretical group known as the Athinganoi, who were strong in Phrygia and Lycaonia, but especially around Amorium; see the literature cited by K. Belke and N. Mersisch, TIB 7: Phrygien und Pisidien (1990), 130–1, and esp. J. Starr, 'An Eastern Christian Sect: The Athinganoi', Harvard Theological Review, 29 (1936), 93–106.

[394] Socrates, 4. 28; Sozomen, 6. 24. Pazon is not identified by any other source. Note Sozomen, 7. 19 on country bishops in Arabia, Cyprus, and among the Novatians and Montanists of Phrygia, where they acted as priests in villages. For Montanist bishops of modest standing, see below, nn. 425 and 428.

[395] Socrates, 5. 21, Sozomen, 7. 14; for Angarum, see Foss, DOP 41 (1987), 191.

a bishop.[396] The location of the two synods in Phrygia and Bithynia rather than in Constantinople, and the ability of the dissident rural group to wrest so crucial a concession from the authorities, show clearly where the balance of power lay. It comes as no surprise that Sabbatius and his 'protopaschists', as they were called, subsequently challenged the main stream of the church in Constantinople, then led by the lax Sisinnius, on their home ground. Sabbatius organized night-time meetings in the city at a place called Xerolophus, which continued until a panic-stricken riot in mysterious circumstances ended in the death of seventy of his followers.[397] A few years later Sabbatius renounced his oath and mounted a direct challenge to Sisinnius' successor, Chrysanthus, for the bishopric of Constantinople.[398] As far as we know the attempt failed and Sabbatius' followers appear to have drifted back to join the main body of the Novatian community.

Many of the strands of this story come together in the brief and surprisingly unsensational Life of Saint Autonomus, written during the reign of Justin between 518 and 527. Autonomus, whose church and monastery occupied a commanding site at Soreoi, modern Tepeköy, overlooking the southern shore of the gulf of Izmit, had come to Asia Minor from Italy. He converted his host, Cornelius, ordained him deacon of a chapel of St Michael, and undertook a journey to Isauria and Lycaonia, as a 'herald of piety'. His return to Soreoi coincided with the persecution of Diocletian, and so, after promoting Cornelius to the priesthood, he undertook a second journey to Mantineion and Claudiopolis, 'cities by the Black Sea', where he successfully repeated his mission. Cornelius was promoted to the rank of bishop before Autonomus undertook a final missionary journey to Asia. His martyrdom came not as a result of Roman persecution, but at the hands of a pagan mob, who stormed the church at Soreoi and struck down Autonomus as he celebrated mass at the altar, a reprisal attack against the Christians who had destroyed their temple at nearby Limnai.[399] The geographical details of the Life and a number of other puzzling features of the narrative are perfectly explained if we treat Autonomus not as an Orthodox but

as a Novatian Christian. His chapel lay in the heart of Novatian country along the Propontis. One of the largest Novatian establishments of the sixth century, the monastery of the Cathari founded in 571, lay about thirty kilometres to the west near the spa town of Yalova, and the site of Angarum, the location of the second Novatian synod, was also adjacent at the modern village of Engere.[400] More decisively, the three missionary journeys led Autonomus to areas where Novatianism is known to have been dominant. Mantineion and Claudiopolis have already emerged as a notable centre; the parts of Asia visited on the third journey were surely the upland regions of Phrygia; while Isauria and especially Lycaonia, not recognized in the literary sources, have produced the heaviest concentration of Novatian inscriptions. It may be going too far to see the Life of St Autonomus as a historical record of how Novatianism was brought from Italy and spread to its Anatolian strongholds, but it is entirely convincing as a charter myth, which offered an explanation of the origin and the observable geographical spread of the church in the early sixth century.

On the ground things may not have been so clear-cut and simple. Socrates' description of the split over the date of Easter and the decision to allow the two branches of the Church to celebrate the most important festival of the Christian year at different times reveal not only an internal division between the puritans of the countryside and the laxer community of the capital, but also show that strong directional authority was lacking. The ascetic disciplines which the Novatians imposed on themselves were not matched by organizational discipline within the community. Unlike their Orthodox rustic confrères in Cappadocia, the Christian villagers of Paphlagonia, Phrygia, Lycaonia, and Isauria had no Basil to supervise them. Basil indeed, as his letters to Amphilochius of Iconium show, was aware of the need to bring these remote churches under central control, but he was equally conscious of the limits of his authority over the small churches and petty bishorics of Isauria. Amphilochius, as Orthodox metropolitan of Iconium, found these difficult heretical groups on his doorstep, and wrote to Basil for practical advice. The replies came in two lengthy letters, whose

[396] Socrates, 5. 21–2 and Sozomen, 7. 15, mentioning Sabbatius' Galatian and Phrygian followers, and Socrates, 5. 22, contrasting the Novatians in Phrygia who repudiated second marriages, with those in Constantinople who neither accepted nor rejected the practice. Sozomen 7. 18 provides more detail concerning the Judaizing practices.

[397] Socrates, 7. 5. Two imperial constitutions bracket the Sabbatiani with the Novatians, *CTh.* 16. 5. 59 (9 April 423) and 65 (30 May 428); but a decision of 21 March 413, *CTh.* 16. 6. 6 = *CJust.* 1. 6. 2, explicitly denied privileges to the protopaschists.

[398] Socrates, 7. 12.

[399] *PG* 115. 692–7.

[400] See C. Foss, 'St. Autonomus and his Church in Bithynia', *DOP* 41 (1987), 187–98, which I follow, except to the point of believing in the strict historicity of Autonomus' mission to Asia Minor. There may be truthful elements, but the three journeys into Anatolia so neatly explain the spread of Novatianism to exactly the areas where the church is known to have been strong subsequently, that they have the ring of a *post eventum* explanation. This does little to diminish the value of the Life as a source for Novatian history.

canons deal both with general issues and particular cases.

Basil reaffirmed the by now well-established position of the Orthodox Church in drawing a clear distinction between genuinely heretical groups, including the Manichees, Valentinians, Marcionites, and Montanists (whom he calls the Pepuzeni), who disagreed with the Orthodox over actual matters of faith, and mere schismatics, including the Cathari (a name adopted for themselves by the Novatians), Encratites, and 'Hydroparastatae' who condemned the drinking of wine and used water for the communion. Heretics such as the Montanists, who gave their own prophets Montanus and Priscilla the title of Paraclete, had blasphemed the Holy Spirit, a sin which admitted no forgiveness. By contrast, the schismatic groups could be taken back into the Church if members were rebaptized. Indeed Basil hesitated to condemn even their own forms of baptism, for fear that genuine Christian souls might thus be lost, and he admitted to Amphilochius that he had recognized the episcopal status of two Encratites, Izois and Saturninus, in accordance with the prescript of the eighth canon of the Council of Nicaea.[401] In his second canonical letter to Amphilochius he distinguished three schismatic sects—the Encratites, the Saccophori, and the Apotactitai—from the Novatians, who had been accorded special treatment in earlier canons. This distinction was maintained in a group of imperial decisions made by Theodosius between 381 and 383, which allowed privileges to the Novatians which were not available to the Encratites and other groups.[402] The latter should not be treated with the same leniency since their practices, which included the abomination of marriage, the refusal of wine, and the belief that even Christ shared in mortal pollution, were akin to those of the heretical Marcionites. Even so, they were eligible for admission to the Church after baptism.[403]

x. The Epigraphy of the Anatolian Heresies[404]

The exploration of the mountains and fertile valleys of central Phrygia and of the steppic countryside north and south of Iconium, in east Phrygia, Lycaonia and northern Isauria, has been a triumphant success for epigraphers, who have converted a 'land without history' into one of the few areas where serious study of a rural segment of the eastern Roman empire is both possible and rewarding. It is tempting to give pride of place among the discoveries to the lengthy series of third- and fourth-century Christian inscriptions found in the upper Tembris valley, in the valley of the Çarşamba south-west of Iconium, at Laodicea Catacecaumene and its surrounding villages, and in the largely imperial estates of the southern part of the central plateau.

The material from Laodicea includes an impressive series of documents from fourth-century heretical churches which leave no serious doubt that these were the communities which taxed the theological and administrative skills of Basil in his letters of guidance to Amphilochius. Epiphanius' account of the Encratites began with the observations that they were numerous in Pisidia and so-called 'Burnt Phrygia', and that there were many heresies to be found there.[405] Phrygia Cecaumene can only be Laodicea Catacecaumene, and virtually every group in Epiphanius' and Basil's lists is well represented.

The Novatians or Cathari of Laodicea Catacecaumene head the catalogue. There are gravestones for Abras, a presbyter (MAMA i. 172), and Tieos, a deacon (ASRamsay 75 no. 3) of 'God's holy church of the Novatians', as well as for Marcus, a presbyter (MAMA i. 227), and for Melanippe, a nun (askētria) of 'the holy church of God' (MAMA i. 174), probably members of the same community. Three epitaphs, erected for Eugenius, a presbyter, Doudousa wife of Imen (MAMA vii. 92), and for Diomedes (ASRamsay 82–3 no. 7), refer to the community as 'the holy church of God of the Cathari', or the 'holy Catharite church of God'. The pearl among these texts is Eugenius' epitaph with its grand peroration declaring the twin foundations of his faith and his own reputation:

Firstly I shall sing a hymn for God, who oversees everything; secondly I shall sing a hymn for the first angel, who is Jesus

---

[401] Ep. 188. Izois clearly bears an indigenous Isaurian or Lycaonian name, although no close parallel appears in L. Zgusta, Die Kleinasiatischen Personennamen (1964).

[402] Ep. 199. CTh. 16. 5. 7 (10 Jan. 381), against the Manichees, Encratites, Apotactitae, Hydroparastatae, and Saccophori; CTh. 16. 5. 9 (31 March 382), against Manichees, Encratites, Saccophori, and Hydroparastatae; CTh. 16. 5. 11 (25 July 383), against the Manichees, Encratites, Apotactites, Saccophori, and Hydroparastatae. It is impossible to believe that Basil's letters of 374/5, which might have been passed to the emperor Theodosius by Amphilochius and Nectarius the bishop of Constantinople (K. Holl, Amphilochius von Ikonion, 36–7), had no influence on these decisions.

[403] Ep. 199 canon 47. Note that Basil himself had travelled among the churches of Pisidia and was acquainted with these sects at first hand, Ep. 216.

[404] The title is taken directly from W. M. Calder's key article in ASRamsay, 59–91, to be read with the contemporary paper 'Philadelphia and Montanism', BJRL 7 (1922), 309–54; such updating as it requires is largely furnished by his own subsequent discoveries; note in particular BJRL 13 (1929), 254–71.

[405] Panarion, 47. 1. 1–2, πληθύνουσι δὲ οὗτοι καὶ εἰς δεῦρο ἔν τε τῇ Πισιδίᾳ καὶ ἐν τῇ Φρυγίᾳ τῇ κεκαυμένῃ οὕτω καλουμένῃ.... πολλαὶ γὰρ αἱρέσεις ἐν τῷ χώρῳ εἰσὶ δὲ καὶ ἐν μέρεσι τῆς Ἀσίας καὶ ἐν τῇ Ἰσαύρων καὶ Παμφύλων καὶ Κιλικῶν γῇ καὶ ἐν Γαλατίᾳ.

Fig. 22. Part of Maximinus' rescript of 6 April 312, outlawing Christians, sent to Colbasa in Pisidia. S. Mitchell, *JRS* 78 (1988), 105–24.

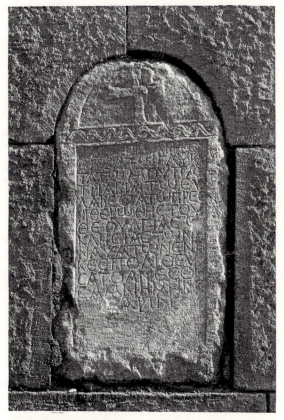

Fig. 23. Gravestone of Abras, priest of God's holy church of the Novatians. Kadınhan, near Laodicea Catacecaumene; fourth century AD. *MAMA* i. 172.

Fig. 24. Metrical epitaph for the Novatian priest Eugenius from Sarayönü, near Laodicea Catacecaumene; fourth century AD. See Ch. 17 § x n. 406.

Persecution and schism

102 THE RISE OF THE CHURCH

Christ. Great is the remembrance on earth for the dead Eugenius. Eugenius, you died young; all men under the sun knew you, the East and the West, the South and the North, in your prosperity, your wealth, your nobility and your stout heart. While alive you gave stout support for the poor, and were outstanding among all in the village. Phrygia and Asia, the East and the West (mourn) you.[406]

It is interesting to note that the puritanical streak in Novatianism was not strong enough to suppress Eugenius' natural pride in his own wealth and status. There was ample room for stricter attitudes.

Another inscription carries the verse epitaph of Severus, 'interpreter of the wisdom of Christ, the wise man and doughty sufferer for the Heavenly Father, overall bishop of cities and leader of the folk who wear sackcloth'. Severus' predecessor had been Eugenius, 'the worthy driver of a spiritual flock', and on the most likely interpretation of the inscription, arranged for both of them to be buried in the same memorial chapel.[407] Eugenius should probably, but not certainly, be identified with the M. Iulius Eugenius, married to a Roman senator's daughter, who had emerged from the persecution of Maximinus to found a church at Laodicea, which was commemorated in an elaborate inscription on his own sarcophagus (see above, § v at n. 254).[408] These circumstances pose a problem. It is remarkable that Severus should identify himself as a member of the Saccophori, which was clearly one of the obscurer sects of the district, for Eugenius' epitaph proclaims that he was one of the most prominent citizens of Laodicea, and the church which he built was a source of pride and admiration in the whole community. It is more natural to see both bishops as leaders of the most important Christian community at Laodicea and its neighbourhood, than of a minor sectarian group. There may be a solution to the dilemma. The logic of the verse inscription demands that Severus had stepped down from his post as bishop to make way for Eugenius, when he himself would have assumed the monkish pose of a cleric in retirement. If the description of his official position is punctuated so as to reveal two posts not one, πόλεων πανεπίσκοπον, ἡγητῆρα [λ]αοῦ σακκοφόρου, this interpretation is con-

firmed and the result allows us to see Severus and Eugenius as bishops of the main church at Laodicea. Severus had successively been overall bishop of the Church, and then leader of the community wearing sackcloth. This suggests that the Saccophori were an early monastic group, although one that kept close contact with its mother church. Imperial constitutions and Basil in his second canonical letter to Amphilochius distinguished the Saccophori from the Novatians and the other schismatic groups. In Basil's earlier letter their place was taken by a group called the Hydroparastatae, and although the two sects were distinguished in imperial decisions of the 420s, they were identified with one another by Timothy the presbyter writing in the early sixth century.[409] From this it seems safe to conclude that the Saccophori and Hydroparastatae were very closely related if not identical groups, distinguished by their use of water not wine in the sacraments. If this interpretation of Severus' inscription is right, membership may have been dominated by clergy who had retired from active participation in the community into an early form of monastic retirement. They were not the only such grouping in fourth-century Laodicea (see below).

This implies that Severus was originally a member of the Novatian Church, for Basil's letters placed the Saccophori and Hydroparastatae in the same category as the Novatians. We know that simple dress, perhaps indeed sackcloth, was adopted by some Novatian bishops even in Constantinople.[410] The adoption of water not wine for the sacrament represented an austerer form of discipline than that adopted by the rest of the Church; commitment to a monkish life might readily be accompanied by the symbolic renunciation of wine in the Mass. The dividing line between clergy and laity in Novatian Christianity was much less clear than in Orthodox communities; it would be no surprise if its real holy men, like Severus, chose to mark themselves off by this additional discipline.

If so, it is also not surprising that they should have encountered competition from other 'over-achieving'[411] members of the community. The chief challenge to the Novatians among the other schismatic groups surely came from the Encratites, whose name, proudly advertised on fourth-century inscriptions, proclaimed greater moral discipline and self-control than that of their

[406] ASRamsay, 76 no. 4; D. M. Robinson, TAPA 57 (1926), 209 no. 20a, with the corrections of A. Wilhelm, Sb. Berl. (1932), 373 (= Akademieschr. ii. 829), and the brilliant interpretation of l. 2 by H. Grégoire, Byzantion, 2 (1925), 449 ff. Robert, Hellenica, xi/xii. 434 n. 2 observes the Jewish features (isopsephism; Christ identified as an angel). The Semitic name Μαριάμη/Μαριόμη is found at Laodicea Catacecaumene, MAMA vii. 98, 580; cf. Robert, Hellenica, xi/xii. 592 n. 3.
[407] MAMA i. 171; Calder, JRS 10 (1920), 42–59, whose interpretation is endorsed by Wilhelm, Sb. Berl. (1932), 382–7 (838–43), and supported by his improved restoration of ll. 7–8, against Grégoire, Byzantion, 1 (1924), 699.
[408] Calder, loc. cit.; MAMA i, 170.

[409] See above, nn. 401–3; Tim. presb., PG 86. 379; Calder, ASRamsay, 72–3. The interpretation of the Saccophori as a distinct monastic community is supported by the fact that Epiphanius, Ep. ad Acacium et Paulum (ed. Oehler 2. 1. 4), mentions them alongside the Apostolici or Apotactici, who were clearly monks.
[410] See above, n. 376.
[411] The term is Lane Fox's, Pagans and Christians, 336–40.

weaker contemporaries. A simple grave epitaph reveals a brother and sister serving as priest and deaconess of the 'Encratite persuasion' (*MAMA* vii. 69a and b); C. Iulius Patricius buried his aunt Orestina, 'who had displayed her self-control' (ἐγκρατευσαμένη, *MAMA* i. 175); a certain Athanasius had lived a holy life and 'shown sober self-control' (ἐνκρατίαν σεμνήν, *MAMA* i. 233); Meirus son of Aentinus, 'of the Encrati' erected a family tombstone, and ended with a warning to those who might disturb his tomb which revealed the most conspicuous divergence from the mainstream Novatian community: 'if any of the wine-drinkers throws (another body) on top, he shall reckon with God and Jesus Christ.' Epiphanius expounded at length on the follies of this and other groups whose abstention from wine led them to substitute water for wine at the Eucharist.[412] The distinction between the Encratites and the Saccophori or Hydroparastatae was that these total abstainers were members of the community at large, laymen as well as clergy. None of these texts speaks of a separate church of the Encratites. The explanation may be that they regarded themselves as part of the Novatian Church, but, through their stricter observance, truer heirs to the apostolic tradition. There is no evidence that they formed their own ecclesiastical organization, or baptized their own members, although they will have celebrated the liturgy, for preference, among their own kind and not with their less rigorous contemporaries, and thus presumably constructed or designated their own separate places of worship.

If the Encratites in some sense sought to outdo the Novatians, the Apotactites (or Apotactici as they were known to Epiphanius) may have been rivals of the Saccophori. In Egypt the word itself, indicating that they were 'off the register', had evidently been coined to distinguish them from genuine hermits or anchorites, who had retreated altogether into the desert. The papyrus evidence for Apotactites seems to confirm that they lived monastic lives within and not outside the lay community.[413] The two relevant inscriptions from Laodicea, however, indicate that they kept their distance from the villages and towns. One reveals an entourage of celibate male clergy: Anicetus, priest of the Apotactites, who was buried by his unrelated heirs, the brothers Eugraphius and Diophantus, both priests (*MAMA* i. 173). The second is another tombstone erected by Gaius and his fellow priests of an Apotactite

monastery, for their colleague Primus (or Pribeis), having due regard for his instructions and the admirable way in which he had conducted his life.[414] The key to both inscriptions is that they were found in remote villages, respectively north and west-south-west of Laodicea, which have produced no other epigraphic finds. These monks sought genuine isolation.[415]

The overwhelming majority of Christian gravestones from Laodicea and the surrounding countryside, including an extraordinarily high percentage for members of the clergy, make no mention of the church to which the families belonged. One text, found thirty kilometres north-west of Laodicea at Düger in the central plateau, stands out as an exception, the tomb of Germanus, 'priest of the holy church of the Orthodox' (*MAMA* i. 290). Should we regard all the other ecclesiastically anonymous texts as Orthodox too, and restrict the schismatic community only to those that declared their allegiance on their gravestones, or were the silent majority also Novatian or Encratite? The answer is surely that the Orthodox were as rare as the solitary gravestone of Germanus suggests they were. The texts for Eugenius and Severus reveal powerful and respected bishops, not marginalized leaders of a dwindling rump. Indeed unless we assume that Novatians, if not Encratites, formed the bulk of the Christian population, it is impossible to make sense of Basil's and Amphilochius' problems, of Epiphanius' claims about the numerical strength of schismatic groups in central Asia Minor, and of Socrates' narrative as a whole. Laodicea may safely be regarded as a southern equivalent to Mantineion. It lay on a route favoured by couriers but little used by military traffic.[416] No imperial troops made their way into Lycaonia to repress these groups at the behest of an Arian bishop.

In contrast to the rich cocktail of heretical texts from Laodicea Catacecaumene, only two of the many Christian inscriptions of north Phrygia directly allude to a schismatic or heretical sect. One comes from Erten in the Phrygian Highlands, the grave of Alexander, reader in God's holy church of the Novatians.[417] The

---

[412] *MAMA* vii. 96 with commentary in *BJRL* (1929), 265 and *Byz. Zeitschr.* 30 (1929–30), 645. Waelkens, *Türsteine*, no. 666 and *Actes du VIIᵉ congrès int. d' épigr. grecque et latine* (1978), 127–8 dates the inscription about a century earlier than Calder, to the later 3rd cent. Note Busiris, the Encratite monk at Ancyra who was (moderately) persecuted at the time of Julian's visit, Sozomen, 5. 11.

[413] See above, n. 359.

[414] *MAMA* vii. 88, discussed at *BJRL* (1929), 266. Some of the restorations are vulnerable.

[415] Another group of monks is perhaps revealed by the gravestone of three presbyters at Tyriaion, mentioned by Ramsay, *Luke the Physician*, 395. It is unlikely that they were martyrs of the Great Persecution, as Ramsay suggests.

[416] Calder, *ASRamsay*, 60–1 concludes that there were many more heretics and schismatics than the inscriptions directly reveal. See above, Vol. I, Ch. 10 § v n. 208 for the *tabellarii* of this area, evidently following a route which ran from Byzantium to Dorylaeum, Laodicea, Iconium, and then through the Cilician Gates or through the pass down to Seleuceia on the Calycadnus. See above, Vol. I, Ch. 9 § 11 at nn. 78–86.

[417] Haspels, *Highlands*, no. 50, with comments on p. 217.

other is the gravestone of Aurelius Trophimus, son of Eutyches, and his family, inscribed in ambitious verses on the four sides of a funerary altar, which ranges, typically for such texts, through a gamut of Homeric tags and pagan mythological allusions to end with an epitaph for one of the granddaughters, Ammia. She had received baptism from the hands of a priest, the just reward for her virginity, as a holy virgin, devout in her faith, possessing the everlasting light, and remaining one of the holy Novatians.[418] It is worth comparing this text with a much grander verse inscription from nearby Cotiaeum which probably also belongs to the mid-fourth century. Domnus, 'famous among the living and outstanding among mortal men, leader of the council and of the whole city, friend of the destitute', had received a burial befitting his piety. He, like Ammia, had remained unmarried, 'loved by the immortals', and his chaste virtue had been rewarded with baptism.[419] Both Ammia and Domnus had apparently chosen to devote their lives to the Church into which they had been baptized; her piety, in a modest rural community, had been devotional, while he, clearly drawing on the resources of a rich city family, had thrown himself into charitable work. He too might well have been a Novatian. The sect was strong in the city and soon to become militant in its own defence. In 368 the bishop of Cotiaeum was one of the pillars of the Novatian community at large.[420] In the fifth century, according to John Malalas, four candidates were sent from Constantinople to occupy the Orthodox see; all were put to death by the local inhabitants.[421] It is surely legitimate to infer that Cotiaeum was largely a Novatian city in the fourth century.

We cannot be quite so confident about the neighbouring upper Tembris valley, most of which lay in the territory of Cotiaeum's southern neighbour Appia. It is an open question whether the Novatian Ammia of Kurd köy and her family were part of a minority or a majority Christian community. The question is complicated by the famous series of inscriptions found in this area which carry the tag 'Christians for Christians'. It has often been argued that this group of texts should be assigned to the Montanists, since the brazen proclamation of faith before the peace of the Church matches the uncompromising message of Montanus' preaching perfectly, but would not be expected from a

non-heretical community.[422] A powerful supporting argument rests on a third-century text found on the territory of Lydian Thyateira, put up by a Christian husband for his Christian wife, Χρειστιανός ... Χρειστιανῇ.[423] According to Epiphanius the whole Christian community of Thyateira had adopted the Montanist heresy around AD 170 and adhered to it for ninety-three years.[424] If the inscription (one of only three pre-Constantinian Christian texts from the area) is indeed Montanist, then so may be those of the Tembris valley, which employ exactly the same formula.

However, the case is far from complete. None of the Tembris valley texts set up by 'Christians for Christians' contains any of the more reliable distinguishing marks of Montanism—the distinctive clerical ranks of patriarchs and coenoni, who ranked above their modest bishops,[425] the ordination of women as presbyters,[426] or the designation of living members of the church as 'saints', hagioi.[427] At Temenothyrae to the south-west there was an unambiguous group of third-century Montanists, with characteristically modest bishops, hardly superior to presbyters, and female presbyters.[428] The Montanist belief that the Holy Spirit was still in their midst, accessible to inspired prophecy, led them repeatedly to refer to the pneuma, or spiritual inspiration of the sect. One inscription from Dorylaeum (again almost the only early Christian text from the region) carries the heading Π Π, which may be expanded to read Πνευματικοὶ Πνευματικοῖς, 'the spiritual for the spiritual', and ascribed with confidence to the Montanists.[429] The term pneumatikos is not found in the Tembris valley group, and it has been suggested that the Dorylaeum inscription was phrased in deliberate contrast to the blander formula 'Christians for Christians'.[430]

[418] Buckler, Calder, and Cox, JRS 17 (1927), 49–58, reinterpreted by Grégoire, Byzantion, 8 (1933), 61–5.

[419] Buckler, Calder, and Cox, JRS 15 (1925), 142 no. 125. There is no compelling reason to follow Grégoire, Byzantion, 8 (1933), 60–1 and interpret ll. 5–6 as a reference to the Montanist baptism of the dead.

[420] Socrates, 4. 28; 5. 21.

[421] John Malalas (CSHB), p. 362.

[422] The view argued above all by Calder. For a survey of the controversy see Gibson, 'Christians', 125–44, and A. Strobel, Das heilige Land der Montanisten (1980), 104–12, both of whom incline against Calder's view.

[423] TAM 5. 2. 1299.

[424] Panarion, 51. 33. 3–4; the Montanist domination ran from 170 to 263/4, see Herrmann, in TAM 5. 2, p. 310.

[425] Jerome, Ep. 41. 3, with Grégoire, Byzantion, 2 (1925), 329–35 and 8 (1933), 69–76; Gibson, 'Christians', 136–7; Strobel, Das heilige Land der Montanisten, 267–74.

[426] Epiphanius, Panarion, 59. 2.

[427] Robert, Hellenica, xi/xii. 428 n. 1; a new example from Lydia, TAM 5. 1. 46 with Herrmann's note.

[428] E. Gibson, GRBS 16 (1975), 433–42; Gibson, 'Christians', 136–7, republished with more precise dating by Waelkens, Türsteine, nos. 366–7, 372–5; see above, Ch. 16 §IV n. 231.

[429] Grégoire, Byzantion 1 (1924), 708; Strobel, Das heilige Land der Montanisten, 93–4. The text reads Π. Π. Λουπικῖνος Μουντάνη συνβίῳ Χρειστιανῇ πνευματικῇ μνήμης χάριν.

[430] W. Schepelern, Der Montanismus und die Phrygischen Kulte (1929), 80–2.

The arguments against Montanism in the upper Tembris villages carry much weight; the balance of probability lies decisively with the view that the 'Christians for Christians' texts are either Orthodox or schismatic. The sturdy Christian peasantry of the region appears reassuringly conformist and unthreatening when set against some of the more extravagant Christianity from neighbouring areas. A vein of ecstatic, inspired Christianity, probably to be identified with the New Prophecy of Montanus, occurs in the Phrygian Highlands, east of the upper Tembris. Here are the gravestones of Nanas, the Christian prophetess, and Zosimus, Christian or Hypsistarian, who used texts from Scripture and verses from Homer to produce his own brand of prophetic wisdom (see above, Ch. 16 § v at nn. 274 and 291).[431]

It is tempting to invoke the literary evidence and the parallel of Laodicea Catacecaumene and identify the Tembris valley 'Christians for Christians' group as Novatian. That would cause no discomfort, except for the fact that the series includes a dated inscription of 248, three years before Novatius' schism occurred.[432] Not all rustic Asian Christianity should be treated as an indistinguishable unity. Regional diversity prevailed even within these heartlands of nonconformity. There were divergences from the Novatians of Lycaonia. The extreme rigorist sects have not been attested in north Phrygia, and although the funerary inscriptions reveal much common ground in the beliefs and behaviour of the two groups, there is a case for arguing that the Tembris valley people had more time for worldly values than the Laodicean group, perhaps reflecting a higher level of material prosperity.

The best guide to the character and beliefs of the Phrygian Christians are their longer verse texts. The earlier and simpler inscriptions contain little beyond the 'Christians for Christians' tag to distinguish them from contemporary pagan epitaphs. The stones were cut by masons who also worked for pagans; the decoration, apart from the motif of a Latin cross in a wreath decorating the pediment, was conventional, and alluded directly to the agricultural life of these prosperous villagers; there is no hint that family structure, or the affective relations between kin differed from those of pagan neighbours.[433] Matters changed in the fourth century when there was an increasing preference for lengthier verse texts, corresponding to the fashion for verse elogia among the governing class (see above, n. 338). The written word increasingly dominated the monument, squeezing decoration to

the margins although rarely replacing it altogether. The spread of literacy and rudimentary culture lay in the background to this development. Just as Ancyra had enjoyed a cultural renaissance in the mid-fourth century, built on foundations laid in the early imperial period, so the villages of Phrygia came into their own in the late empire. The stylus and writing tablet had been a common motif on the Tembris valley gravestones since the beginning of the third century;[434] one fourth-century epitaph contained the explicit boast that it had been compiled by the owner of the tomb himself, who 'prepared the memorial with his own intelligence and wrote the text'.[435] Another addressed the reader as 'sharer in culture, read this tombstone, and learn why my memorial is carved here in writing'.[436] Like other texts, the verses that followed combined individual features in prose with an interweaving of metrical or semi-metrical tags. Rather than see a sculptural workshop equipped with a repertoire of stock phrases, it seems preferable to suppose that many of these epitaphs were genuinely composed by the peasant families themselves, relying of course on a repetitive repertoire of poetic expressions.[437]

Thus the virtues that occur in the texts should genuinely reflect what individuals aspired to. Religion of course took pride of place, especially where clergy were concerned. 'Stand, stranger, and read this inscription. Here is the tomb of a bishop, a famous man, Heortasius by name, dear to men, an honoured eunuch, who always performed liturgies for God and served his people and the honoured church.'[438] The

---

[431] Haspels, *Highlands*, nos. 107 (Nanas) and 40, on which see above, Ch. 16 § v at n. 274. See also her nos. 36–8.

[432] Gibson, 'Christians', 56 no. 22.

[433] For the iconography, see provisionally M. Waelkens, *Anc. Soc.* 8 (1977), 277–315.

[434] *MAMA* v. 41 n., and Waelkens, *Türsteine*, index s.v. *stilus*.

[435] Gibson, 'Christians', 70 no. 27 ll. 13–15.

[436] A. Petrie, *SERP* 124 no. 6, Παιδείας μέτοχος κὲ ἀνάγνωθι τοῦτο τὸ σῆμα / τίνος χάριν μνήμης γράμμασιν ἐντετύπωτη. Compare the epitaph of Gaius from Eumeneia (above, Ch. 16 § IV no. 246), who says of himself, γράμμασι δ' ἠσκήθην ἐκπονέσας μετρίοις, *JRS* 16 (1926), re-edited by A. R. R. Sheppard, *AS* 29 (1979), 178–9, who mistranslates this line; it does not mean 'I worked hard and gained a modicum of learning' but 'I worked and practised the skill of writing in verse'. Gaius went on to say that he had put this skill at the disposal of his friends. His epitaph is markedly superior to most of the compositions of the upper Tembris valley.

[437] Gibson, 'Christians', 85–97 *contra* at 94. T. Drew Bear, *REA* 80 (1982), 348 suggests that the use of 'age-rounding' in these texts indicates that the population was largely illiterate and could not have read the elaborate metrical epitaphs they commissioned. This flies in the face of the explicit claims of the texts themselves. The use of round figures (especially τριάκοντα and ἑξήκοντα) in place of more precise figures is largely due to metrical convenience. Despite R. D. Duncan-Jones, *Chiron*, 7 (1977), 333–53 there is no likelihood that the use of age-rounding corresponds very closely with illiteracy. See further W. Harris, *Ancient Literacy* (1989), 271–2.

[438] C. W. M. Cox, *ASBuckler*, 63–6: τίμιος εὐνοῦχος ἀεὶ Θεὸν λιτανεύων. στέμμα τε λιτουργῶν καὶ ἐκλησίαν πολύτιμον. As with the

tombstone of Aquila reads, 'minister of God, longed for by the angels, champion of the people, who administered justice according to the law';[439] another epitaph began with the ringing acclamation, 'No one is immortal except for the one God himself, creator of all things, and distributor of all things to all men.'[440] Others tended to stress a person's achievements and status as much as his or her religious devotion. The self-declared poet already cited was a 'Lover of Christ, prominent in his mansion and among the people';[441] Theodora was 'acclaimed in all the neighbourhood for her beauty, greatness, and especially for her innate good sense';[442] 'Cornas(?), renowned for his good name among men, who longed for God, lies buried widely honoured, having left the world';[443] 'here lies a mortal, honoured and longed for by all, Trophimus son of Anterus, who according to the assessment and opinion of everyone excelled in his fatherland in wisdom, judgement, and especially knowledge';[444] Domnus was a 'great soldier, conspicuous for his courage among all men, who had toiled for such great achievements'; one son, Cyrillus, followed a gentler path as 'lover of all the arts, a most distinguished great man'; other sons were 'Christian priests, leaders of the people, administering justice under the law'.[445] Not all these virtues were explicitly Christian. These men proudly advertised their virtues and their status in society, and the reputation they enjoyed among their contemporaries. None more so than Aurelius Menandrus who set up his family grave, 'which would endure as long as the waters rise in flood and the tall trees bloom, and the rivers glide by and the sea swells'; here lay his son Proculus, 'longed for by all, but most excellent in his life; the Earth-Shaker himself had killed him, trident in hand, on the banks of the

Tembrogius.'[446] As nowhere else in Christian Anatolia these epitaphs were incongruously sprinkled with allusions to pagan mythology; no dogmatic beliefs prevented them from advertising their culture. There was no attempt to hide wealth or secular power with Christian moralizing. Family, *patris*, and Christian beliefs were yoked together into an unshakeable unity. This view of the world would have been instantly familiar to their pagan forebears.

There were, however, clear exceptions to the pattern. One is the lament for the Novatian Ammia, for whom Christian baptism was the deserved reward for her virginity. Although the text provides no warrant for the belief that her wishes conflicted with those of her parents, her virtues and her devotion stand out in plain contrast to those of the rest of the family.[447] Another remarkable text is the beautifully carved and personalized monument for Acacius (Fig. 21). Here, on a stele made by a master mason, unadorned except by a knotted wreath, is the epitaph which Acacius drafted himself,

a serious man, truly honoured by God, who in this world was honoured in every way in his *patris*. He had lived for thirty years as a widower; his only child of his single marriage, Lucilla, had been betrothed to a cousin so that the couple might look after Acacius in his old age, but the marriage had been a failure, and she had died within eighteen months. As for Acacius himself, what offence had he ever given to anyone, old, young, or of his own generation? Now, with great honours he would be escorted wherever God bid him go, be it to Hades or to Paradise. You receive your rewards from immortal God himself. I care not, I have left the wicked world; God preserves the seal of baptism which he gave me as a child. A mortal I have fallen into the immortal bosom of Abraham; a slave to God I dwell in Paradise.[448]

Transparently these lines recall the passionately felt personal theology of a dignified, sad figure, bereft of the only family he had allowed himself in a life of sexual restraint. The most apposite comment on the loneliness of this *mounogamos* is the burgeoning family tree of a contemporary, the 'great soldier' Domnus.[449] The approbation of his fellows, vaunted by so many of his contemporaries in their epitaphs, was here replaced by the hope, verging almost but not quite to confident belief, that he was loved by God. Acacius, like Ammia, dwelt in the city of God, not in his robustly earthy Phrygian *patris*.

---

eunuch of Laodicea (*MAMA* vii. 467), Cox is disinclined to take the term literally.

439 A. Petrie, *SERP* 125 no. 7, λιτουργὸν Θεοῦ, ἀγγέλοις τε ποθητόν, λαοῦ προστάμενον, νόμῳ τὰ δίκεα φρονῶντα.

440 Petrie, *SERP* 129 no. 11, οὐδὶς ἀθάνατος, εἰ μὴ μόνον Ἷς Θεὸς αὐτός, ὁ πάντων γενέτης κὲ πᾶσι τὰ πάντα μερίζων.

441 Τὸν φιλοχρήστοραν αὐθις ἐνὶ μεγάροισι φανέντα.

442 Petrie, *SERP* 120 no. 1, Ἐνθάδε γῆ κατέχει Θεοδώραν τὴν περί[βωτον], / καὶ κάλλι καὶ μεγέθι καὶ ἐμφροσύνῃ δὲ μάλιστα.

443 Buckler, Calder, and Cox, *JRS* 14 (1924), 34 no. 250, Κορ[νᾶ]ς (?) ἐπωνυμίης κεκλημένος ἐν μερόπεσσι, / ὃς ἐπόθησε Θεὸν λιπὼν τὸν κόσμον ἅπαντα, / πολὺ τίμιος ἐνθάδε κῖται.

444 A. Körte, *Ath. Mitt.* 25 (1900), 410 no. 20, ἔνθα βροτὸς κατάκιτη ὁ τίμιος καὶ πᾶσι ποθητός, / ὃς σοφίῃ καὶ γνώμῃ καὶ ἐπιστήμῃ δὲ μάλιστα / πατρίδος προστάμενος βούλῃ τε καὶ γνώμῃ.

445 Gibson, 'Christians' 80 no. 20, ἐνθάδε γῆ κατέχι Δόμνον μέγαν ἰστρατιώτην, / τὸν πάσης ἀρετῆς κὲ ἐν ἀνθρώποισι φανέντα, / ὃν τὰ τοσαῦτα καμόντα κὲ ἐνδοξότατον μέγαν ἰστρατιώτην... Κύριλλον τέκνον ἴχον, πάνμουσον μέγαν ἄνδρα... Δόμνου ἱοὶ Χρηστιανοὶ πρεσβύτεροι λαοῦ προεστάμενοι νόμῳ δίκεα φρονοῦντες, ἄνδρες ἀριστῆς μεγαλήτορες.

446 Petrie, *SERP* 126 no. 8, πᾶσι ποθητὸν ἐόντα καὶ ἐν βιότῳ πανάριστον... αὐτὸς δ' Ἐννοσίγαιος ἔχων ἐν χείρεσσι τρίαιναν / κτεῖνέ με τὸν μέλεον Τευβρογίου παρὰ ῥεῖθρα.

447 See above, n. 418.

448 W. M. Calder, *AS* 5 (1955), 31 no. 1; Calder's word division and punctuation need correction (cf. *SEG* xxx (1980), 1484).

449 See n. 445; the family tree displayed by G. Mendel, *BCH* 33 (1909), 429. But note Petrie, *SERP* 124 no. 6 for a sole daughter, Philopatra, surviving to look after her widowed mother.

In the rigorist territory of Laodicea Catacecaumene theology and Christian morality intruded more conspicuously into the lives of ordinary families. Orthodox trinitarian doctrine found its way into the formulas cursing those who interfered with tombs,[450] and Christ's name was much more prominent. In blunt iambic lines, Hesychius, priest of the Holy Trinity, wise, true and faithful servant of Christ Jesus, threatened any one who interfered with the grave he had set up with just punishment rendered to the Living Judge (*MAMA* i. 162). Bishop Severus was 'interpreter of the wisdom of Christ' (*MAMA* i. 171). The pious Photinus, who had made charitable distributions and benefactions, was confident that Christ would settle the souls of his family in heaven (*MAMA* i. 220a). Paulus, deacon of all-blessed Christ, erected the tomb of his dear brother Helladius, to last until the sounding trumpet brusquely roused mortals to face the judgements of God (*MAMA* i. 226). The priest Anicetus, noble worshipper of God, was described by his children as obedient and meek, mild in his own manner, lover of God, lover of God's laws, companion of Christ, and elected by God (*MAMA* i. 237). Nestorius, a presbyter, shone like a star in the churches of God, because he possessed the glory of his apostle Christ the King (*MAMA* i. 238).

Monogamy, and better still virginity, were a matter for pride. Nicephorus laid to rest his 'virgin mother' and brothers, soon to be taken up into heaven by the Great King. The mother had eschewed remarriage (*MAMA* i. 176). A mother and child were buried alongside the former's virgin sister, revealingly called Sophronie (*MAMA* i. 364), a match for the aristocratic and ecclesiastical family of Aelius Eugenius, whose wife was Iulia Herennia Pansemnion, 'all-restraint' (*MAMA* i. 280). Piety is the leitmotiv of the verse epitaph elaborated with the very hands of the parents of noble and renowned Diomedes, 'who brought grief to his *patris* and especially to his parents, and left behind him much lamentation since he was dearly beloved, holy, not ready for marriage, and loved by Christ; God had snatched him away before the evils of the world deceived his wits, and placed him, immortal and unageing, in Paradise' (*MAMA* vii. 560). A priest, to avoid the temptations of the wicked world, made, or declared himself a eunuch (*MAMA* vii. 167).

The pervasive Christian ideals of this society were matched by the extraordinary abundance of clergy revealed by the inscriptions. It is worth turning back to the two sample collections of Christian inscriptions from the valley of the Çarşamba and the territory of Laodicea used to assess the density of the Christian population, to establish the point and to make the contrast with the more secular community of the upper Tembris. The 'Christians for Christians' inscriptions name or imply one certain bishop, three presbyters, and four 'leaders of the people', who may be the village bishops of this sectarian community.[451] The sixty probable or certain Christian texts from the Çarşamba valley list five bishops, seven presbyters, five deacons, perhaps two martyrs, and a *periodeutes*.[452] In the 178 fourth-century texts from Laodicea and its villages, the clerical tally is two bishops, fifty presbyters, thirteen deacons or deaconesses, four sub-deacons, three nuns, two monks, and a reader.[453] The figures speak for themselves.

The Christianity of fourth-century Phrygia and Lycaonia presents an artless individuality quite different from the dragooned Orthodoxy of Basil's Cappadocia, or the violent doctrinal disputes that surfaced in mid-century Ancyra. During the fourth century neither Arians nor Orthodox had the means to break into these heretical groups and win them over to the mainstream of metropolitan dogma. Basil wrote a letter to Amphilochius asking him to send a reliable man to Lycia, to find out who was of Orthodox faith there. He held out some hope for the region since a traveller had informed him that they were often at odds with the opinions of the people of Asia. The latter, surely the inhabitants of up-country Phrygia, were beyond reach, and Basil could only utter his gratitude to God if any of the inhabitants of this region were clear of the heretic's pest.[454]

Lycaonia, eastern Phrygia, and Bithynia cut a swathe across the Anatolian peninsula quite as large as Cappadocia and Galatia, and their densely packed villages were certainly more heavily populated than the regions further east. The inhabitants had reached a level of literacy, culture, and self-confidence rare in rural communities in the ancient world. They produced no father of the Church comparable to Basil or the two Gregorys, whose theology could influence the Church at large or the thought of future generations. But the part they played in establishing a pattern to the

450 *MAMA* i. 160 and 168.

451 Gibson, '*Christians*', no. 28 l. 16, and no. 30 l. 16. Perhaps another 4th-cent. presbyter in Anderson, *SERP* 219 no. 18, for Αὐρ. Στεφανῳ . . . πρεσβυτάτῳ ἐννόμῳ οὐρανίου βασιλῆος. It is likely that the λαοῦ προστάμενοι (*vel. sim.*) of Gibson, '*Christians*', no. 29, Petrie, *SERP* 126 no. 7, and *Ath. Mitt.* 25 (1900), 410 no. 20, the first of whom are also called οἱ πρεσβύτεροι were also clerics, possibly village bishops typical of the central Anatolian heretic churches (above, nn. 133 and 394). The bishop was the 'honoured eunuch' Heortasius (n. 438).

452 *MAMA* viii. 160, 161, 162, and above, n. 41 (bishops); 119, 121, 163, 183, 184, 204, 303, 305 (presbyters); 131, 164 (deacons); 168, 200 (martyrs); 303 (*periodeutes*).

453 Figures taken from *MAMA* i. 157–260 and vii. 64–104d.

454 Basil, *Ep.* 218.

Christian empire in Asia Minor, and in pointing the way towards the evolution of Christian society in the fifth and sixth centuries, was no less significant. In the final analysis there was one fundamental and overriding link that joined Basil's Cappadocia with Novatian Lycaonia or Phrygia. Long before the end of the fourth century these largely rural areas of central Anatolia were utterly dominated by the Church. Village headmen, great landowners, and the pagan gods gave way entirely to bishops, priests, and deacons. The social as well as the moral triumph of Christianity was here complete.

18   The Rise of Monasticism from the Fourth to the Sixth Century

I. *The Origins of Anatolian Monasticism*

Around AD 420 Palladius of Ancyra compiled his *Lausiac History*, a collection of biographical sketches of eastern monks and other ascetics, who now occupied so large a place on the ecclesiastical stage. Most of these edifying portraits depicted the heroic achievements of Christian holy men in the Egyptian wastes, or in the desert penumbra around the cities of Palestine and Syria. A handful, not altogether in the same style, concerned his native region.

There was the octogenarian priest Philoromus, child of a citizen by a slave woman, who had openly defied Julian, thereby incurring tortures which were modest indeed compared to the self-imposed discipline which followed—eighteen years of seclusion, wearing chains, and abstinence from wheaten bread and all cooked foods—all designed to strengthen his defences against the temptations of lust and greed. Thereafter he spent forty years in the same monastery, earning his keep as a copyist, evidently of sacred books, and donated his earnings to the support of cripples. He made four pilgrimages in his life, all on foot and at his own expense, to the shrine of St Peter at Rome, to the tomb of St Mark at Alexandria, and twice to the Holy Places in Jerusalem. Never had his faith in God wavered, even in his private thoughts.[1]

Another chapter described the wealthy couple Verus and Bosporia, who devoted the revenues from their estates to the poor, leaving nothing for four male children and only dowries for two daughters. They distributed all their harvest surplus in the churches of Ancyra and of the surrounding villages, and opened their granaries in times of famine, thus winning over many of Galatia's numerous heretics to Orthodoxy. They themselves adopted simple dress and spent most of their lives in the country, avoiding the tumult and temptations of the city.[2]

A third story featured Magna, leader of a community of more than 2,000 virgins, including many distinguished women who had adopted the ascetic life. She had been widowed young after an unwanted marriage, and donated her remaining private wealth to hostels, hospices for the poor, and for the entertainment of journeying bishops, who duly held her in high esteem. Appropriately she was the dedicatee of a work on *aktemosyne*, the renunciation of possessions, written by Palladius' contemporary, Nilus of Ancyra.[3]

The last Galatian story was devoted to an unnamed monk, formerly a soldier, who had been a member of the bishop's retinue for twenty years. At night he would go round the prison and the hospital, to champion the oppressed, resolve disputes, and supply food and clothing. As in all the great cities, the porches of the churches were crowded with the sick and with homeless pregnant women. Food and succour for the destitute counted for more than pious learning. Books given by admirers were sold at once, for how might he persuade a disciple that he had learned the lesson of practical Christian charity unless he sold the book for money which made that charity possible?[4]

One can derive historical significance from these little biographies without necessarily accepting their literal accuracy. The stories presumably reflected conditions prevalent in Palladius' day and palpably resume and amplify some of the themes which had played a prominent part in the history of the previous century. The energy which the ascetic Philoromus channelled into copying books is a reminder that Christianity, the religion of the Book, and the enormous dissemination of ecclesiastical literature in the fourth century depended on small armies of devoted scribes.[5] The landed gentleman Verus is easily recognizable as a

---

[1] Palladius, *Lausiac History*, ii (ed. C. Butler, 1904), ch. 45. For this and the other stories fom Palladius, see Foss, 'Ankara', 51–5, and for summary references to monasteries at Ancyra, Foss, *RAC Suppl.* s.v. Ankyra (1985), 463–4.

[2] *Lausiac History*, ch. 66.

[3] Ibid. ch. 68; Nilus' work is in *PG* 79. 968–1060.

[4] Ibid. ch. 69.

[5] See H. C. Teitler, *Notarii and Exceptores: An Enquiry into the Role and Significance of Shorthand Writers in the Imperial and Ecclesiastical Bureaucracy of the Roman Empire* (1985). More briefly, H. Hunger, *Schreiben und Lesen in Byzanz: Die byzantinische Buchkultur* (1989), 89–94 with further references.

successor to the reluctant *curiales* of Ancyra or Caesareia in the fourth century, although his retreat from the city to the country doubtless derived from sound Christian principles. His wife was surely a descendant of Bosporius, one of Libanius' best-known Ancyran correspondents.[6] Their decision to disinherit male heirs simply perpetuated the family's withdrawal from active participation in the life of the city. This shift from an active pagan citizenry in the 360s to an entirely different social and religious culture in the 420s was surely widespread. Magna led a community which had given practical form to the theoretical esteem with which Christianity regarded celibacy. A girl who refused marriage could not always find a place for herself within a traditional family structure after she reached sexual maturity, and she could not live on her own. Sometimes devout families would proudly cherish their virgin daughters, but a new type of society had developed to accommodate the majority of these new Christian idealists.[7] It was natural, moreover, that such communities should concentrate on forms of practical Christian action, above all the dispensation of charity. The sermons of the Cappadocian fathers had drawn attention to the duty of all Christians to attend to poverty and suffering. When this was plain for all to see at the doors of the church, many doubtless came forward not merely to give alms but to take an active part in helping the destitute.

It is important to observe the range of behaviour encouraged by the new moral order. Asceticism and self-denial could take many legitimate forms. Philoromus, striving for holiness through extremes of physical hardship and mental resolve, lived in a reclusive isolation which would have been abhorrent to the practical ex-soldier, turned monk. Neither enjoyed the comfortable existence of their social superiors, Verus and Bosporia, who clearly suffered little from the decision to withdraw from active city life. Charitable support of rural communities may have ensured their place in society as effectively as more traditional means of distributing surplus wealth.[8] Magna, a member of the same aristocratic class, had forfeited none of her family status, when she followed a path well-trodden by Christian widows for centuries, and devoted her financial and other resources to the Church. Freed from the toils of family life, and public responsibilities, the upper classes provided ample officer material for the army which the Church could mobilize against poverty.

Three of the stories emphasize that there was no conflict between the lives of these champions of asceticism and the local church leaders. Philoromus was held in the highest regard by 'blessed Basil', probably a reference to Basil of Caesareia himself, not to Basil of Ancyra who had stepped down as bishop before Philoromus' ascetic career was launched (above, Ch. 17 § VIII). Magna, herself a deacon, was revered by the bishops whom she received in her hospices when their journeys took them through Ancyra, and the anonymous monk was a faithful companion of Ancyra's bishop throughout his life. There is other evidence that ascetics and established clergy lived together harmoniously in the early fifth century. Palladius himself was bishop first of Helenopolis in Bithynia and later of the small Galatian city of Aspona.[9] Nilus of Ancyra, perhaps a monk himself, wrote a short work in praise of Albianus, evidently a young aristocrat who chose to become a hermit in the Egyptian desert. His first step in this direction was to join a monastery situated on the mountain opposite the city which was led by a certain Leontius. Sozomen identifies the latter as one of the leading ascetic figures of Galatia, later to become the bishop of Ancyra who shut the Novatians out of their church.[10] These examples, however, cannot disguise the fact that conflict between monks and the established Church was endemic, and as conspicuous in Asia Minor as in other parts of the Greek East.

Eastern monasticism began in Egypt with the solitary eremitic tradition founded by Antony, and the communal, cenobitic tradition founded by Pachomius. From Egypt both practices spread to Libya, Palestine, Syria, and Arabia,[11] which could all claim to be the habitats, *par excellence*, of the eastern ascetic tradition.[12] In fact a valuable distinction can be drawn between the monks of Egypt, who lived in the true desert, remote from secular communities, and those of

---

[6] Cf. Foss, 'Ankara', 52.

[7] Peter Brown, *The Body and Society: Men, Women, and Sexual Renunciation in Early Christianity* (1988), 263–70 for the options.

[8] See E. Patlagéan, *Pauvreté économique et pauvreté sociale à Byzance* (1977), 181–96.

[9] See the introduction to Butler's edition of the *Lausiac History*. According to the preface Palladius wrote the work as bishop of Aspona, after 412 and perhaps in 417.

[10] Nilus, *PG* 79. 696–712. For Nilus' letters, many of which are demonstrably not authentic, see A. Cameron, *GRBS* 17 (1976), 181–96. Leontius was identified as one of the key figures in early Anatolian monasticism by Sozomen, *HE* 6. 34. 7 (εὐδοκιμώτατος δὲ ὢν ἐπυθόμην τότε ἐγένοντο ἐνθάδε μοναχοὶ Λεόντιος ὁ τὴν ἐν Ἀγκύρᾳ ὕστερον ἐπιτροπεύσας καὶ Πραπίδιος (later in charge of the Basileias at Caesareia), and as persecutor of the Novatians at *HE* 8. 1.

[11] Three lengthy excursuses by Sozomen provide the framework for our knowledge of the spread of eastern monasticism, *HE* 1. 12–14; 3. 14; 6. 28–34. See esp. 1. 13. 11.

[12] For overall surveys see S. Schwinietz, *Das Morgenländische Mönchtum*, i–iii (1904–38); H. Leclercq, 'Cénobitisme', *Dictionnaire d'archéologie chrétienne et liturgique*, ii. 2 (1910), 3047–3248; and P. Wirth (ed.) *Reallexicon der Byzantinistik* (1968), s.v. Abendland und Byzanz: Mönchtum, 641–735 (unfinished). Both of the latter have very full bibliographies.

Syria who occupied the semi-desert fringes of cultivated land and accordingly played a much more conspicuous part in society at large.[13] No one better explained the fundamental reason why monasteries were situated in remote areas than John Chrysostom, when he expressed the hope that the monasteries themselves would one day become useless, since life in the cities would be so well-ordered that no one needed to take refuge in the desert. Unfortunately, in reality, everything was upside-down; the cities, with their tribunals of justice and their law codes, were full of wrongdoing and injustice, while solitude produced in abundance the fruits of philosophical contemplation.[14]

Sozomen acutely observed the geographical and climatic factors which determined the pattern of monasticism and pointed out that monks in Asia Minor were to be found in cities and villages, since severe winters prevented them from living in the real wilderness.[15] This is an oversimplification. Some of the main concentrations of monastic settlement in Anatolia were to be found in remoter parts of the countryside; and individual monasteries and even occasionally an isolated hermit were scattered across rural areas. The pattern of monastic settlement in this respect is closer to the Syrian model than Sozomen allows. However, it is clear that monasteries were also to be found in cities, such as Ancyra, and above all at Constantinople, where they had a significant effect on political and social life at least until the middle of the fifth century.[16]

For all monks life as part of secular society, even as members of the clergy, was incompatible with the pursuit of true holiness and blocked the path to God. From its beginnings Christianity had followers for whom the practices of ordinary believers were compromised by the allowances which had to be made for normal social behaviour. The split between rigorists, who aimed at an other-worldly standard of holiness and piety, and more moderate realists was one of the principal legacies of Judaism to Christianity. The choice offered by these contrasting attitudes to the relationship between religious belief and social behaviour led to rancorous dispute, and also to competition. In the hierarchy of the established Church compromise

had usually prevailed, most obviously when the pressure of official persecution forced normal Christians to flee or to offer sacrifice rather than profess their beliefs and take the dire consequences. The mechanism of penitence, administered by clergy, provided the means by which sinners could be absolved from these acts of pardonable weakness.

It galled those who stood firm in such crises, that their own steadfastness earned them no higher standing. For most of the Christian community only those who actually died for their faith were recognized as *hagioi*, saints. Heretical groups, however, tended to emerge or were strengthened in the aftermath of persecution, especially the Novatians; the Montanists too put much store by intransigence in the face of persecution and even recognized some of their own living members as saints. The crisis brought about by the persecution of Trajan Decius in 250 acted like a catalyst on the Church at large, separating rigorists from moderates as no issue had done before. It served as a symbol of this division for centuries after pagan persecution of Christians was extinct (see above, Ch. 17 § IX at n. 373).

In Asia Minor the strenuous pursuit of holiness through self-denial and self-control in food, drink, dress, and sexual continence was already a defining characteristic of several heretical groups; Novatians, Encratites, Saccophori and others, competed not only with post-Nicene Orthodoxy but with one another in their claims to be the truest guardians of Christian faith and tradition. It is not surprising that the earliest epigraphic evidence for genuine monasticism comes from the Apotactites of Laodicea Catacecaumene, who went beyond the austerity even of the Novatians, signed out of normal society, and, it seems, chose to live in remote rural monasteries (see above, Ch. 17 § X n. 415). Another Novatian, Eutychianus, was living a hermit's life on the slopes of Mysian Mount Olympus before the death of Constantine, and introduced a form of monastic life to Constantinople by the 340s, more than thirty years before the practice became widespread there.[17]

Christian groups in Asia Minor, therefore, were as ready to embrace asceticism and to adopt it as a practical way of life as their brothers in Egypt, Palestine, and Syria.[18] Sozomen identified the true founder of Anatolian monasticism as Eustathius, later bishop of Sebaste in the province of Armenia from around 355 to his death in 380. Under his guidance celibate communities, which had been formed in Armenia, Paphlagonia, and Pontus, followed strict rules of diet and dress, the outward symbols of their rigorous social

---

[13] Peter Brown, *JRS* 61 (1971), 80–101 = *Society and the Holy in Late Antiquity* (1982), 109–14.

[14] John Chrysostom, *Adversus oppugnatores vitae monasticae*, PG 47. 328–9, cf. 48. 992.

[15] *HE* 6. 34. 7–9 καὶ Γαλάτας δὲ καὶ Καππαδόκας καὶ τοὺς ἐκκλησιαστικοὺς φιλοσόφους οἷα γε πάλαι τὸ δόγμα σπουδαίως πρεσβεύοντας. κατὰ συνοικίας δὲ ἐν πόλεσιν ἢ κώμαις οἱ πλείονες ᾤκουν. οὔτε γὰρ παραδόσει τῶν προγεγενημένων εἰθίσθησαν, οὔτε ὑπὸ χαλεπότητος χειμῶνος φύσει τοῦ τῇδε χώρου ἑκάστοτε συμβαίνοντας δυνατὸν ἴσως κατεφαίνετο ἐν ἐρημίαις διατρίβειν.

[16] I follow the exposition of G. Dagron, 'Les Moines et la ville: Le Monachisme à Constantinople jusqu'au Concile de Chalcédoine', *Travaux et mémoires*, 4 (1970), 229–76.

[17] Sozomen, *HE* 1. 14. 9.

[18] See Leclercq, 'Cénobitisme', *DACL* ii. 2. 3144 ff.

and ethical standards.[19] Eustathian practices seem to have been established by 340 and were immediately identified as a challenge to the episcopal church, for they were largely condemned in a council attended by thirteen bishops, including Eusebius of Nicomedia, Basil of Ancyra, and Prohaeresius of Sinope, which met at Gangra in the early 340s, perhaps in 343.[20] The rulings of this synod, which were known to Sozomen, reveal the basis of the opposition to Eustathius and his followers. It was alleged that they denounced the institution of marriage, persuaded many wives to leave their husbands, refused to pray in married households, and held married clergy in contempt. Slaves who defected from their masters were welcomed into their new communities. Even the apparently natural distinctions of sex were considered to be inconsequential, and women in the movement cut their hair short and wore men's dress.[21] They declared their own fasts on Sundays, abhorred the eating of meat, and celebrated the mass in their own conventicles, apart from the rest of the community. The bishops at Gangra prefaced the canons with a synodical letter addressed to the bishops of Armenia, Eustathius' power-base, which condemned Eustathius himself as well as his more extreme followers for these practices. However, the appeal of self-denying asceticism was a powerful one, and well-grounded in much of Christ's own teaching, and the bishops were also obliged to conclude their proceedings by acknowledging that asceticism in accordance with Holy Scripture was welcome in the Church; only excesses which set ascetic purists above their fellow believers were deplorable.[22] The strength of the Church lay above all in the allegiance of the common man, and the canons of the Council of Gangra implicitly defended the faith and practices of ordinary believers. Eustathius' followers formed a Christian élite; it is revealing that some of them had deplored the most popular and spectacular demonstrations of popular Christian belief, the martyrs' festivals.[23]

Despite the decisions of the Council, Eustathius' influence was not diminished. He himself was elected bishop of Sebaste in about 355, and the example of his new communities surely inspired the most famous and influential of all the early monastic experiments in Asia Minor, that of the family of Basil of Caesareia, and especially of his sister Macrina. As we know from the life written by her brother, Gregory of Nyssa, Macrina had chosen a life of celibate piety at the age of twelve, when the man to whom she was betrothed died. Emmelia, her mother, claimed to have had a vision of St Thecla as she gave birth to Macrina, and the latter took Thecla as her secret name, pinning her allegiance on this archetype of virginal piety.[24] Thereafter she became the spiritual and practical leader of a great household, persuading her mother to follow her example. The menfolk complied too. One brother, Naucratius, led the life of a hermit in a corner of the family's property at Annesoi, which lay in the territory of Pontic Neocaesareia, until he was drowned by flood waters when fishing in the river Iris which bordered the estate.[25] Peter the youngest sibling became head of a celibate male community, which matched the group of holy women led by Macrina.[26]

Basil himself might easily have lost contact with the family during his years of education at Caesareia, Constantinople, and Athens, but he acknowledged that Macrina's practical asceticism had a greater appeal than conventional philosophical study.[27] It seems certain that Macrina had reforged the family and its dependants into a monastic community in the early 350s, certainly before Basil's return to Asia Minor from Athens in 357, and she must have been influenced

---

[19] Sozomen, HE 3. 14. 31, καὶ τῆς ἐν ταύτῃ σπουδαίας ἀγωγῆς, ἐδεσμάτων τε ὧν χρὴ μετέχειν καὶ ἀπέχεσθαι, καὶ ἐσθῆτος ᾗ δεῖ κεχρῆσθαι, καὶ ἠθῶν καὶ πολιτείας ἀκριβοὺς εἰσηγητὴν γενόμενον. See J. Gribomont, 'Le Monachisme au IVᵉ siècle en Asie Mineure de Gangres au Messalianisme', Texte und Untersuchungen, 65 = Studia Patristica, ii (1957), 400–15; 'Le Monasticisme au sein de l'Église en Syrie et en Cappadoce', Studia Monastica, 7 (1965), 7–24.

[20] For the Council of Gangra see C. Hefele and H. Leclercq, Histoire des conciles, i. 2 (1907), 1029–45; Sozomen, HE 3. 14. 31 summarizes the conclusions of the Council and implies a date shortly before 341. A Syriac MS (Synodicon Orientale, 278 n. 4) places it in the consulship of Placidus and Romulus, AD 343 (R. S. Bagnall et al., Consuls of the Later Roman Empire (1987), 220–1). Leclercq, Histoire des conciles, i. 2. 1029–30 n. 1 argues for a date around this time and suggests identifications for several of the thirteen bishops, who are unfortunately listed without reference to their dioceses. T. D. Barnes, JTS 40 (1989), 120–4 suggests a date around 355, which fits better with Eustathius' career.

[21] The annulling of the difference between the sexes (see canons 13 and 17) was apparently a particularity of the extreme Eustathians; see discussion by Ruth Albrecht, Das Leben der heiligen Makrina vor dem Hintergrund der Thekla-Traditionen (1986), 174–89; Peter Brown, The Body and Society, 288; Dagron, Travaux et mémoires, 4 (1970), 251.

[22] See the epilogue to the Synod of Gangra (text at Hefele and Leclercq, Histoire des conciles, i. 2. 1042–3), ταῦτα δὲ γράφομεν, οὐκ ἐκκόπτοντες τοὺς ἐν τῇ Ἐκκλησίᾳ τοῦ Θεοῦ κατὰ τὰς γραφὰς ἀσκεῖσθαι βουλομένους, ἀλλὰ τοὺς λαμβάνοντας τὴν ὑπόθεσιν τῆς ἀσκήσεως εἰς ὑπερηφανίαν, κατὰ τῶν ἀφελέστερον βιούντων ἐπαιρομένους τε καὶ παρὰ τὰς γραφὰς καὶ τοὺς ἐκκλησιαστικοὺς κανόνας καινισμοὺς εἰσάγοντας.

[23] Canon 20.

[24] Gregory of Nyssa, Vita Macrinae (excellent edn. and comm. by P. Maraval, Sources chrétiennes, 1971), 2. 10. On the Life of Macrina, see A. Momigliano, The Craft of the Ancient Historian: Essays in honour of Chester G. Starr (1985), 443–58 = Ottavo contributo alla storia degli studi classici e del mondo antico (1987), 333–47.

[25] Life of Macrina, 8.

[26] Ibid. 12.

[27] Cf. Ep. 223 and Greg. Nys. Ep. 19; Brown, The Body and Society, 277–8.

by the example of her neighbour Eustathius. Strong arguments have been mustered to suggest that Basil's first surviving letter, written in 357 to 'Eustathius the philosopher', was indeed addressed to the bishop of Sebaste. Basil had sought him on his return from Athens and pursued him doggedly but unavailingly through the monastic heartlands of Syria and Egypt, where Eustathius must have been travelling, before returning to Caesareia where he was halted by illness.[28] Within a year he had been baptized and had withdrawn to Macrina's retreat, where he spent most of the following decade, apart from visits to Caesareia, where he was ordained as a reader of the church in 360 and a priest in 362.[29] Several letters written in the 360s explained his preference for Annesoi over an offer to join Gregory of Nazianzus at Arianzus in western Cappadocia, and elaborated the blessings of a contemplative life and an ascetic regime which rested almost entirely on the guidance of the New Testament.[30] Years later in 375, after their friendship had been dramatically ruptured by theological differences, he recalled how in the 360s Eustathius had often visited the community at Annesoi and showed no sign of the heretical theology of his later years.[31] The household at Annesoi may have been, in essence, a Eustathian monastery. Many of the Rules for monastic life which Basil later formulated as bishop of Caesareia, surely drew on the practices he had shared with Macrina, and both may have taken them from Eustathius. Sozomen later observed that many people in his day believed that Eustathius was the true author of Basil's Rules.[32]

Such ascesis, however, bred intense competition. Just as the Encratites of Laodicea Catacecaumene claimed to out-perform Novatians, the Canons of Gangra hint that some of Eustathius' followers preached and practised extremes which he himself did not countenance. Epiphanius tells the full story of Aerius, who had been a rival of Eustathius for the see of Sebaste, before he was appointed by him to take charge of the Poor-House in the city. Aerius disagreed with his bishop about the proper use of the church's wealth, and argued that all of it should be given to the poor. The split between the two became insupportable and Aerius left the city, taking a band of men and women from the neighbouring cities and villages into the mountains and forests of eastern Pontus. Like the hermits of Egypt Aerius not only believed in dispensing entirely with worldly wealth, but also sought holiness in complete isolation from the secular world.[33] The story may be compared with the account of the deacon of Venasa, Glycerius, which is to be found in three letters formerly attributed to Basil but now thought to be the work of Gregory Nazianzus.[34] Glycerius had led a band of *parthenoi* off into the hills, and then brought them back to interrupt a public festival, to general dismay. The letters written by Gregory allowed room for Glycerius to mend his ways. He is treated as though he were an over-zealous extremist, not an irredeemable heretic. Perhaps he is best seen as a follower of Eustathius, disrupting the too-secular celebration of a popular festival, and offering the women who had followed him a glimpse of a life of piety untrammelled by the demands of family and the community. His story and that of Aerius highlight the potential for conflict, and in rare cases the outright incompatibility between ascetic ideals and a church facing the realities of maintaining its dominance in society at large. In Egypt and Syria physical separation reduced the chances of outright conflict; in Asia Minor the juxtaposition of monastery and city or village increased the risks.

It is against this background that Basil forged the final versions of his Rules, which laid the foundation for all future eastern monasticism. Celibate communities, modelled on Macrina's household at Annesoi and devoted to prayer and to productive labour, were founded or sanctioned in villages, on estates, or in the cities. They thus served both God and the community. Monks and nuns distributed their surplus produce to the poor and manned the hospices and other charitable institutions that increasingly filled the Anatolian landscape. Simple dress, a sparse diet, conspicuous devotion, and celibacy separated their communities from secular society; it was appropriate that the clergy, in part at least, should be drawn from their ranks; but Basil's monks, subjected to the firmest discipline he could devise, were subordinated to the authority of the

28 J. Gribomont, 'Eustathe le philosophe et les voyages du jeune Basile de Césarée', *Rev. hist. eccl.* 54 (1959), 115–24. For a careful and detailed study of Macrina and the tradition of female asceticism in Asia Minor see Ruth Albrecht, *Das Leben der heiligen Makrina vor dem Hintergrund der Thekla-Traditionen: Studien zu den Ursprüngen des weiblichen Mönchtums im 4. Jhdt. in Kleinasien* (1986), with a remarkable bibliography. She establishes clearly (p. 93) that Macrina's monastic household pre-dated Basil's return from Athens.

29 For the chronology I follow P. J. Fedwick, *The Church and the Charisma of Leadership in Basil of Caesarea* (1979), app. A, 133–55.

30 Basil, *Epp.* 8 and 22; see also Greg. Naz. *Epp.* 1–6 to Basil, disputing Basil's choice of Annesoi with much good humour.

31 Basil, *Ep.* 223.

32 Sozomen, *HE* 3. 14. 31. P. Maraval, in his edition of the Life of Macrina, 51 n. 2 collects the epigraphic evidence for ascetics in Pontus: *SP* iii nos. 134, 194, 197, 202, 248d; three of the texts concern female communities.

33 Epiphanius, *Pan.* 75. 1–3.

34 [Basil], *Epp.* 169–71 interpreted by Albrecht, *Das Leben der heiligen Makrina*, 186–7, who also cites the bibliography for attributing these letters to Gregory of Nazianzus.

bishops; they had to remain part of society, not outside it, an adornment not a threat to a united church.[35]

II. *The Spread and Impact of Monastic Christianity*

The dearth of source material for Anatolian history in the fifth and early sixth centuries makes it almost impossible to assess the extent to which the creation of monasteries changed the face of Anatolian Christian society. The appeal of celibate asceticism is so alien to most modern experience that it is tempting to play down the evidence, mostly from supposedly partisan Church historians or other Christian writers, and to reduce monasticism to proportions which would make sense in the modern world. This is unjustified; evidence that cannot otherwise be impugned should not be jettisoned too readily.

Palladius gives the only relevant figures, the 2,000 *parthenoi* of Ancyra led by Magna. By way of comparison, sources of varying reliability suggest that the larger monastic groups in Egypt could be numbered in thousands: Pachomius' original community, formed from several smaller houses and a large central foundation, is said to have grown from 3,000 before 346 to 7,000 by the early fifth century. Nitria and Scetis reputedly contained 5,000 and 3,500 hermits respectively. Palladius himself gives figures for his own times of 2,000 monks in Alexandria, and 1,200 in or near Antinoopolis, where there were also twelve convents for women. Even higher, but highly suspect figures for Oxyrhynchus (10,000 nuns, 20,000 monks) and the Arsinoite (10,000 monks) are listed in Rufinus' *Historia Monachorum*. Larger communities in Egypt, Palestine, and Mesopotamia held between 600 and 1,000 inmates.[36] In addition to large numbers who inhabited the most important monastic centres, smaller foundations were very widely distributed. Basil framed a rule in his *Regulae fusius tractatae* to discourage the formation of two monasteries in a single village.[37] The impact which monks are said to have made on contemporary society, especially in Syria, is only intelligible if their numbers were large. In a famous passage of his *Pro Templis* Libanius inveighed against the monks around Syrian Antioch as destroyers of pagan buildings, comparing them to black-clad carrion birds.[38] In contrast Sozomen held monks largely responsible for the conversion of Syria's pagans, many of whom had

clung to their beliefs long after Asia Minor had become thoroughly Christian They have been described accordingly as the 'shock troops' of Christianity.[39] None of these observations makes sense unless monks were both numerous and conspicuously active.

In Asia Minor the greatest concentration of monasteries was inevitably in and around Constantinople. The first communities were founded around 380 by Isaac, a refugee from Syria, by his closest associate Dalmatius, and by Hypatius from Phrygia, whose Life is one of the best sources for monasticism in the capital.[40] It is plausibly argued that they followed the Eustathian tradition; certainly the Eustathian tendency to abolish the distinction between the sexes, which was condemned by the Synod of Gangra, was perpetuated by Messalian monastic groups in fifth-century Constantinople.[41] The number of ascetic communities grew rapidly and can be estimated from the number of monastic signatories to various petitions at major Church councils. In 448 twenty-three abbots and archimandrites endorsed the deposition of Eytyches; in 518 fifty-three signed the decision of the Synod that brought an end to the Acacian schism; and in 536 seventy-three participated in the council directed by Menas. By the mid-fifth century the total monastic population has been put between 10,000 and 15,000, and this appears to have risen again by the time of Justinian.[42] The influx of immigrants to the city will have done much to accelerate this growth,[43] although it is interesting to note that in the sixth century the only communities specially created for Anatolian immigrants were two monasteries of the Lycaonians, in contrast to numerous foundations for monks who had originated in the other eastern provinces between Thrace and Egypt.[44]

The relationship between the monks and the episcopal church at Constantinople was notoriously tense. The pagan historian Zosimus, describing events around 400, recorded remarkable scenes of hostility between the bishop, John Chrysostom, and the monks who had struck up an allegiance with the poorer people of the

[39] Sozomen, *HE* 6. 34.

[40] See Dagron, *Travaux et mémoires*, 4 (1970), 229–76. A French trans. and comm. on the life of Hypatius, A. J. Festugière, *Les Moines d'Orient*, ii; edns. by G. Karo *et al.* (Teubner, 1895), and by G. Bartellinck, *Sources chrétiennes*, 177 (1971).

[41] Dagron, *Travaux et mémoires*, 4 (1970), 251.

[42] Dagron cites the figures and gives an overall estimate of numbers at p. 253. See also for the council of Menas in 536, R. Janin, *Les Églises et les monastères des grands centres byzantins* (1975), 422 indicating 68 monks representing the institutions of Constantinople and 39 from Chalcedon (different figures in Jones, *LRE* 931).

[43] See above, Ch. 17 § IX at nn. 391–2.

[44] R. Janin, 'Les monastères nationaux et provinciaux à Byzance', *Echos d'Orient*, 32 (1933), 229–38 at 231.

[35] Basil's monastic works are to be found in *PG* 31: *Asketikon*, 870–87; *Regulae fusius tractatae*, 890–1051; *Regulae brevius tractatae*, 1051–1306; *Poenae in monachos delinquentes*, 1306–20; *Constitutiones Monasticae*, 1321–1428. See D. Amand, *L'Ascèse monastique de S. Basile* (1948).

[36] See Jones, *LRE* 930–1 for these figures.

[37] Basil, *PG* 31. 1004.

[38] Libanius, *Pro Templis*, 8–14.

city, and his highly coloured account was reflected in more muted tones by ecclesiastical sources.[45] The clash between ascetic celibate communities and the bishops who were nominally in charge of all the Church's affairs, which can be traced back to the beginning of the monastic movement in rural Asia Minor, was here reproduced on a large scale in the capital. Predictably, several of the canons of the Council of Chalcedon, held in 451, had to confront the same basic issues as the Synod of Gangra, and laid down further rules for the subordination of monasteries and individual ascetics to bishops.[46] It has been suggested that the bishops at Constantinople may have been vulnerable to such challenges to their authority because they themselves were often provincial priests transferred to the capital. Moreover the capital itself, during its formative years between 330 and 450, peopled largely by newcomers from the provinces, was in many respects a provincial city writ large.[47] If these suppositions have any truth it also suggests that conflict between monks and bishops would have been as much a feature of ecclesiastical politics in the provinces as in Constantinople. Certainly the Life of Thecla, produced at Seleuceia in the later fifth century, contains graphic illustrations of the antagonism.[48]

It is extremely difficult to form more than a rough impression of the number and distribution of monasteries in Asia Minor, especially in the central regions of Anatolia. There are serious problems in interpreting the evidence, most of which derives from obscure and often unreliable sources. The literature and inscriptions of late Antiquity allude unambiguously only to a small proportion of the monasteries which were actually founded during that period. When written documentation, as often, dates from the Middle Byzantine period or later, it is often impossible to be certain about the period when the community was founded. Archaeological evidence brings its own problems, not only in dating but in identifying a given structure unambiguously as part of a monastic complex.

The only systematic geographical survey of Anatolian monasteries concentrates on limited regions, mostly around the coast: Mount Latmos or Latros in Caria above the city of Heracleia ad Latmum, the city of Trapezus and its hinterland in north east Pontus, but above all north-west Anatolia including Cyzicus, Mysian Mount Olympus, and the territories of Nicaea, Nicomedia, and Chalcedon.[49] It is noteworthy that the monasteries of late Antiquity in these areas rarely predated AD 440, and there appears to have been a rapid growth in the late fifth and sixth centuries. The areas close to the capital were especially favoured. The Asiatic coast of the Bosporus was lined with more than a dozen identifiable monasteries, and thirty-nine monastic leaders from Chalcedon signed the petition to the Council of 518.[50] Ease of access to Constantinople may also have been a reason why Nicomedia, and the southern shores of the Sea of Marmara around Pylai, the modern spa of Yalova, were particularly favoured for monastic settlements.[51] On the other hand, the slopes of Mount Olympus, between the cities of Prusa and Hadrianoi, corresponded much better to a classic monastic habitat—a thinly populated mountain area, famous in Antiquity only for its bandits.[52] The communities of the eighth and ninth centuries here are well documented in the detailed lives of St Ioannicius and St Peter of Atroa, and most of the monastic settlements appear to date to the iconoclastic period, but isolated indications suggest that hermits at least lived here in late Antiquity.[53]

Indirect evidence suggests that there were several monasteries in the district of Mantineion in western Paphlagonia, the Novatian stronghold of the fourth century (see above, Ch. 17 §IX at nn. 382–4). There are literary references to hermits and monks in the ninth and tenth centuries, but Christian architectural remains of the fourth to sixth centuries are plentiful in the area and the earliest monasteries probably came into existence during this period.[54] The chief source of

[45] Zosimus, 5. 23, discussed by Dagron, *Travaux et mémoires*, 4 (1970), 261 ff. For a discussion leading to similar conclusions about the relationship between John Chrysostom and the monks of Constantinople, see J. W. H. G. Liebeschuetz, *Barbarians and Bishops: Army, Church, and State in the Age of Arcadius and Chrysostom* (1990), 208–16.

[46] Canons of the Council of Chalcedon (Hefele and Leclercq, *Histoire des conciles*, ii. 2 (1908), 767–828) nos. 4, 8, 18, 23, 24, discussed briefly by Dagron, *Travaux et mémoires*, 4 (1970), 272–5 and at length by H. Bacht, 'Die Rolle des orientalischen Mönchtums in den Kirchenpolitischen Auseinandersetzungen vor Chalkedon (431–519)', in A. Grillmeier and H. Bacht (eds.), *Das Konzil von Chalkedon*, 2 (1953), 193–314, and by L. Veding, ibid. 569–76.

[47] Dagron, *Travaux et mémoires*, 4 (1970), 275–6.

[48] Dagron, *Vie et miracles de Ste Thècle*, chs. 12, 46.

[49] R. Janin, *Les Églises et les monastères des grands centres byzantins* (= *Géographie ecclésiatique de l'empire byzantin*, 2). Much information on the Christian antiquities of Asia Minor is assembled by V. Schultze, *Altchristliche Städte und Landschaften*, ii, *Kleinasien* (1922).

[50] Ibid. 5–29 (Asiatic shore of the Bosporus) and 30–60 (territory of Chalcedon).

[51] Ibid. 77–104. For the Byzantine geography of the gulf of Izmit, see L. Robert, 'Les Voyages d'Antiphilos de Byzance', *JSav.* (1979), 257–95 = *OMS* vii. 427–64.

[52] Janin, *Les Églises et les monastères*, 127–91; R. Menthon, *Une Terre de légende: Olympe de Bithynie* (1935); see above, Vol. I, Ch. 11 §1 at nn. 7–14.

[53] Janin, *Les Églises et les monastères*, 126–7. See V. Laurent, *La Vie merveilleuse de Saint Pierre D'Atroa* (d. 837), *Subs. Hag.* 29 (1956); Life of Ioannicius, *Acta Sanctorum*, ii. 1 (1894), 332–83.

[54] Robert, *A travers l'Asie Mineure*, 132–46.

information for Galatia is the Life of St Theodore of Sykeon, which indicates the existence of late sixth-century monastic establishments not only at Sykeon itself, but also in a number of the surrounding villages and at isolated points elsewhere in the province.[55] There is an extraordinarily large concentration of Christian epitaphs of the fourth to the sixth century in the territory of Tavium in east Galatia, but apart from a stone found in Ancyra which mentions a Tavian *ptocheion* or Poor-House, there is no indication for monasteries as such.[56]

Cappadocia is more readily associated with churches and early monasteries than any other part of Asia Minor, thanks to the abundant and spectacular remains at Göreme, in the Peristremma valley, and elsewhere in the western part of the province, in the triangle between Kayseri, Aksaray, and Niğde. It seems inconceivable that many of these did not trace their origin back to the age of Basil and Gregory of Nazianzus, who were active precisely in this region, but the claim is very hard to prove. Most of the surviving buildings and settlements, including many likely monasteries, have been dated between the ninth and the thirteenth centuries. Basil's letters referred from time to time to individual monks and to female ascetic groups, notably to the *kanonikai*, while Gregory of Nazianzus explicitly mentioned monasteries at Pasa near the road station of Andabilis (Andaval), and at Sannabolae, south of Heracleia (modern Ereğli).[57] An interesting passage of John of Ephesus, writing in the late sixth century, described how seventy Novatian monks were transferred from Gordasun, which lay close to Tyana, to the large Novatian establishment of the Cathari by the Sea of Marmara.[58] About fifteen likely or possible monastic sites of this period have been identified from archaeological remains alone; these, of course, only amount to a fraction of the original number.[59]

Lycaonia also apparently contained many purely ecclesiastical settlements. Apart from isolated monasteries attested at random in literary sources or by archaeological remains, there were two notable centres. One was Karacadağ, the volcanic massif which stands

out from the bleak steppe south of the Salt Lake.[60] The other was situated on Karadağ, north of Laranda, at the settlement of Madenşehir, or, as it is more eloquently named, Binbir Kilise, the thousand and one churches.[61] Here forty-eight separate churches or chapels have been recorded, most dating to late Antiquity, and the earliest perhaps an Arian foundation of the second half of the fourth century.[62] Both sites perfectly illustrate John Chrysostom's idealized conception of the monastery as a haven of tranquillity in an otherwise deserted land, remote from the toils of the city. It is striking, nevertheless, that the bishop of Barata, the minor city which lay in the immediate neighbourhood of Binbir Kilise, headed the list of Isaurian representatives at the Council of Nicaea in 325. The importance of the area as an ecclesiastical centre may have preceded the foundation of monasteries.[63]

In addition to the foundations which can be strictly defined as monasteries, and which were often relatively small, the fourth and fifth centuries also saw the creation and growth of large complexes of churches and associated buildings which, like the 'Basileias' outside Caesareia, had the appearance almost of small towns in themselves. These major Christian centres, which attracted crowds of pilgrims from the whole of Anatolia and beyond at major festivals, should not be confused with monasteries, which belonged to a different and much more exclusive tradition; they nevertheless contained communities of monks and nuns, as well as housing temporary visitors, and thus formed major centres of asceticism. Perhaps more importantly they, like the smaller monastic foundations, were places whose importance derived exclusively from their intrinsic sanctity and holiness, not because they were already centres of economic or political power. They acted as foci for a charismatic divine power, which was a new phenomenon, and were largely independent of the authority of metropolitans and city bishops.

The best-studied Anatolian centre of the fourth to sixth centuries is the complex of churches, monasteries, and other buildings which grew up near Seleuceia on the Calycadnus around the *martyrium* of St Thecla, the aristocratic girl of Iconium converted by St Paul. Her life and martyr's death were commemorated in the largely apocryphal *Acts of Paul and Thecla*, written in the later second century, and offered a major inspira-

---

[55] See below, Ch. 19 §1 at nn. 51–2.

[56] AS 27 (1977), 99 no. 41.

[57] Greg. Naz. *Epp.* 163 and 238. Basil, *Ep.* 52 to the *kanonikai*, cf. *Epp.* 173 and 46 (to a lapsed *parthenos*); letters to monks (who are never addressed as *monachoi* by Basil), *Epp.* 44 and 45 (to lapsed ascetics), 295.

[58] See F. Hild and M. Restle, *TIB* ii s.v. citing John of Ephesus, 34, 82; F. Drexl, *Byz. Zeitschr.* 40 (1940), 445.

[59] *TIB* ii, index s.v. Kloster; the individual entries in the gazeteer naturally register many uncertainties over date and identification. I have not seen A. M. Lebides, *Αἱ ἐν μονολίθοις μοναὶ τῆς Καππαδοκίας καὶ Λυκαονίας* (Constantinople, 1899).

[60] K. Belke, *TIB* iv s.v. Dağören, Hyde, Thebasa.

[61] *TIB* iv s.v. Barata, Boratinon Oros. See above all, W. M. Ramsay and Gertrude Bell, *The Thousand and One Churches* (1909).

[62] G. Laminger-Pascher, *Anz. Wien*, 117 (1980), 179–84; the interpretation of a text which is hard to read and much restored appears precarious (*SEG* xxx (1980), 1542).

[63] *TIB* iv. 139.

tion to female ascetics in the later empire.[64] At the heart of the site stood a great basilical church, probably built around AD 375, set in a sanctuary which was defended by its own fortifications against Isaurian raids. Huge cisterns, built to supply monks and clergy as well as the numerous pilgrims, reinforced the impression that the walled sanctuary and the extensive extra-mural buildings made up a city in their own right, outshining neighbouring Seleuceia, the metropolis of the province of Isauria, which lay less than five kilometres away. In the fifth century the sanctuary of St Thecla benefited from the imperial patronage of Zeno the Isaurian, who endowed the greatest Christian centre of his own homeland with a new church, built soon after 476, whose unusual design drew on a local Isaurian tradition but also acted as an inspiration for sixth century architects in Constantinople.[65]

The nearest equivalent in central Anatolia was the little-studied church, or cathedral, of St Michael at Germia in western Galatia. The Life of Theodore of Sykeon provides the best evidence that Germia was also a great pilgrimage centre, famous for preserving a fragment of the tunic in which Christ's body had been wrapped, mentioned by Gregory of Tours, and visited by the emperor Justinian shortly before his death.[66] A late source, a collection of Miracles of St Michael compiled by Pantoleon in the later ninth century, states that Studius, the consul of AD 454 responsible for building the church of St John Studius in Constantinople and a church of St Michael at Phrygian Nacolea, also constructed the church dedicated to St Michael at Germia. This should be identified with the five-aisled basilica, over fifty metres long and twenty-seven metres wide, whose remains still survive. Certain architectural details, in particular the presence of a central tower with a pyramidal roof, are in fact also to be found in Zeno's roughly contemporary church in the Sanctuary of St Thecla, and confirm that, despite clear evidence of rebuilding under Justinian, the original phase of the Galatian church also belongs to the later fifth century. Pantoleon also referred to hospices for the old and for

visitors, and there are visible traces of other buildings as well as many inscriptions of the fifth and sixth centuries at the site. Germia had its own bishop, who, as was appropriate for the spiritual leader of a major pilgrimage centre, was not subject to the metropolitan of Galatia, but answered directly to the patriarch of Constantinople. Like the shrine of St Thecla, the church of St Michael at Germia offered a powerful fusion of the traditions of monastic asceticism and of the popular religious festival, which generated a tremendous appeal to inhabitants of the early Byzantine world.[67]

In fourth- and fifth-century Syria the monks had been key figures in the conversion of the rural population to Christianity, as much by violence and intimidation as by demonstrations of exemplary sanctity. If they played a similar role in Asia Minor it was on a very restricted scale. It is possible to compile an impressive dossier of evidence for the survival of strongly held pagan beliefs in the early Byzantine world. Communities and individuals from all walks of society were to be found sacrificing, practising theurgy, and celebrating traditional festivals in the old pagan temples, in defiance of imperial legislation, which began with Constantine and was reiterated with special emphasis by Theodosius, and which outlawed such practices.[68] However, the relevance of this to Anatolia is restricted. If the evidence for the conversion of central Asia Minor between Phrygia and Pontus presented above is correctly interpreted, it seems unlikely that that paganism still posed a major threat to the Church even by the mid-fourth, still less by the sixth century.

Evidence for non-Christian belief and practice can still be observed but its interpretation needs care. It is important to distinguish between those who maintained their pagan convictions as part of a coherent intellectual religious outlook, and others who preserved unsystematic, superstitious beliefs in pagan powers, usually narrowly localized at old shrines or associated with natural features of the environment. The latter appear frequently in the hagiographical literature, for it was characteristic of Byzantine saints that they demonstrated their power by miraculously mastering pagan forces.[69] Typically such stories were told of

---

[64] For Thecla see Albrecht, *Das Leben der heilige Makrina*; the *Acts of Paul and Thecla* in *Acta Apostolorum Apocrypha* (1959), 235–72; the late 5th- or early 6th-cent. Life of St Thecla, ed. with comm. by G. Dagron, *Vie et miracles de Sainte Thècle*, Subs. Hag. 62 (1978).

[65] See E. Herzfeld and S. Guyer, *MAMA* ii. 4–46. For recent discussion see H. Hellenkemper, *Reallexicon für byzantinischen Kunst*, 4 (1984), 228–35 (dating the main basilica around 375), and *Wallraf-Richartz-Jahrbuch*, 47 (1986), 63–90 on the church built by Zeno, proposing a pyramidal roof in place of a cupola over the nave; this is also a feature of the E. Church at Alahan and the largest church at Dağpazarı (cf. S. Hill, 'Early Church Planning in Isauria', in J.-M. Hornus (ed.), *Architecture of the Eastern Churches* (1981), 27–37).

[66] See Belke, *TIB* iv. 166–8, and below, Ch. 19 § 1 n. 48.

[67] For Pantoleon see C. Mango, Δέλτιον τῆς Χριστιανικῆς ἀρχαιολογικῆς ἑταιρείας, 4: 12 (1984 pub. 1986), 45–54; for the architecture see *J.öst.Byz.* 36 (1986), 117–32.

[68] K. W. Harl, 'Sacrifice and Pagan Belief in Fifth and Sixth Century Byzantium', *Past and Present*, 128 (1990), 7–27; M. Whitby, 'John of Ephesus and the Pagans: Pagan Survivals in the Sixth Century', in M. Salamon (ed.), *Paganism in the Later Roman Empire and in Byzantium* (Cracow, 1991), 111–31.

[69] F. R. Trombley, 'Paganism in the Greek World at the end of Antiquity: The Case of Rural Anatolia and Greece', *Harvard Theological Review*, 78. 3–4 (1985), 327–52 wrongly assumes that superstitious fears about surviving pagan spirits

events that took place in the countryside, and the writers may assume a tone of urban sophistication in presenting a picture of this primitive, uneducated, and supposedly pagan rural environment. For instance, the *Life of Hypatius* says of fifth-century Phrygia that there were then no more than one or two monks in the country, and hardly any churches, a picture which conforms to the stereotype of the pagan countryside contrasted with the Christian city, but which is completely at variance with the fact that much of the Phrygian countryside had been Christian since the third century AD.[70] Even if all such accounts are taken at face value as truly reflecting what Christian saints and holy men were thought to have achieved, they provide no evidence that any coherent system of pagan belief and practice still existed. The fate of the oracular temple of Apollo at Claros provides the clearest warning against taking residual superstitions as a sign of the resilience of genuine pagan belief. Unlike most important temples there was no attempt to convert it to a church; the colossal statues of Apollo and Artemis were left in the heap of ruins above the underground vault and spring which was the source of the oracle's inspiration. The superstitious awe surrounding this pagan haunt was so strong that no Christian church could be constructed on the same spot.[71] However, it is nonsense to take this as evidence for the survival of paganism. The fears of supernatural powers associated with an old pagan haunt reveal something about the nature of Christian, not pagan belief.

More serious attention needs to be given to the pagan beliefs of educated intellectuals. These were naturally to be found in the cities of the empire, above all in the cultural centres. Only one example stands out in the interior of Asia Minor, Aphrodisias in Caria, where paganism flourished in the fifth and early sixth centuries, and was focused on an important philosophical school which had close links with Alexandria.[72] Its members certainly included some of the wealthiest and most cultivated members of the community. They met in a large converted house adjoining the early imperial Sebasteion (whose use in late Antiquity is unclear), and decorated the niches of the main hall with some of the finest sculptures that have survived from the period, depicting philosophers past and present.[73] Hostility between pagans and Christians at Aphrodisias is predictably attested both in the epigraphic and the archaeological record. The Temple of Aphrodite seems not to have been converted for Christian use before the mid-fifth century, later than the transformation of pagan temples in other cities; the decision to make the very substantial structural changes that were necessary may have been taken when the emperor Theodosius II visited the city in AD 443, or even later.[74]

There is one indication that monks played a part in eradicating paganism from sixth-century Anatolia, namely the account of the mission of John, the Monophysite Syrian monk, who was appointed bishop of Ephesus by Justinian in 535 and charged with the task of converting non-believers in Asia. The details of the tradition are confused but in essence John claimed to have converted 80,000 pagans in Asia, Caria, Lydia, and Phrygia, and to have constructed ninety-six churches and twelve monasteries in the thirty years up to Justinian's death in 565.[75] He recorded in more detail the elimination of an important cult centre and temple at Daeira near Tralles in Caria, whose older inhabitants recalled an earlier age when it had had 1,500 smaller shrines under its supervision.[76] The name Daeira has a convincing Anatolian appearance, and neither its existence nor the presence of a pagan sanctuary need be questioned, but it appears in no earlier source and can hardly have been a major regional cult centre, as the narrative implies. The only parallel for such a centre controlling a large pagan diocese of minor shrines are the ephemeral province-centred organizations established by Maximinus in 312 and Julian in 363.[77] John in this instance was at least guilty of serious exaggeration, and his other reports need cautious handling. A recent analysis suggests that we should treat the figure of 80,000 converts as equivalent to the inhabitants of around 100 villages, which fits admirably with the figure of ninety-six churches built at the same time. However, the reported number of converts is clearly no more than an im-

---

imply the survival of pagan belief. Perhaps the best examples are the dangerous demons exorcized by Theodore of Sykeon, which were thought to haunt old pagan graves (see below, Ch. 19 §§ III and IV). See esp. Festugière's note on the *Life of Theodore of Sykeon*, ch. 16.

[70] *Life of Hypatius*, 88; but see above, Ch. 16 § IV.

[71] J. and L. Robert, *Claros I. Décrets hellénistiques* (1989), 2.

[72] See C. Rouché, *Aphrodisias in Late Antiquity* (1989), index s.v. paganism, esp. 85–93. The agenda for studying the whole subject has been brilliantly laid down by G. W. Bowersock, *Hellenism in Late Antiquity* (1990).

[73] R. R. R. Smith, 'Late Roman Philosopher Portraits from Aphrodisias', *JRS* 80 (1990), 127–55.

[74] Rouché, *Aphrodisias in Late Antiquity*, 153–4 argues for a date between the mid-5th and early 6th cent., and points to the possibility of 443 as a starting point. R. Cormack, 'The Temple as Cathedral', in Rouché and K. Erim, *Aphrodisias Papers: Recent Work on Architecture and Sculpture* (1990), 75–88 at 84, concurs.

[75] The main texts are in John of Ephesus, *Historia ecclesiastica* (*Corpus Scriptorum Christiani Orientis*, 105–6), 2. 45 (activity in Asia, Caria, Lydia, and Phrygia); 3. 36 (Daeira); *Lives of the Eastern Saints, Patrologia Orientalis*, 17 (1923), 1–307; 18 (1924), 511–698; 19 (1926), 152–285; 18, 681 provides the figures for the converted, churches, and monasteries.

[76] *Hist. eccl.* 3. 36.

[77] See above, Ch. 17 § III at nn. 69–70, § VII at nn. 345–7.

pressionistic estimate from a source that had every reason to exaggerate. There is also no reason to believe that all the churches were new foundations in villages where none had existed hitherto. Even if the figures are accurate the achievement that they represent should be kept in perspective. John's efforts were spread across four provinces, in an average of twenty-five villages per province. It was not unusual for there to be twenty-five villages in the territory of a small Anatolian city. Even if the evidence can be trusted, therefore, it is compatible with the notion that there were small but resilient pockets of pagans in western Anatolia in the sixth century, but not with the view that pagans made up a significant minority of the rural population at large.[78] It remains broadly true, therefore, that monks in Asia Minor played an insignificant part in the conversion of the population from paganism.

III. *Social Change in the Fifth and Sixth Centuries*

The main historical significance of the rise of the monastic movement is to be found not in its contribution to the eradication of paganism but in the impact which ascetic ideas and practices made on the Christian world. It seems likely that the influence of this new outlook was profound, and closely linked to major transformations in social organization and even in family structure. The nature of the evidence dictates that, for Anatolia at least, it is easier to argue for the importance of this influence as a hypothesis, than to demonstrate its impact with specific examples. Strictly secular developments in political and economic organization, above all in the nature of city life in the fifth and sixth centuries, also made a radical contribution to social change. Detailed analysis of these critical developments, which in any case can only be studied when substantial archaeological remains of a city have survived, lies beyond the scope of this sketch.[79]

Almost any attempt to write the history of Anatolia after the fourth century yields unsatisfactory results. Apart from the detailed reconstruction of events in the Constantinople, and the disembodied chronicling of external wars and internal revolts, the sources seem to allow only isolated, if occasionally vivid glimpses of episodes unrelated to one another. Some sense can be made of these by formulating broad hypotheses about social trends, above all those related to the spread of a Christian ethic. The viewpoint of Christian writers makes it possible to study the history of poverty in a way that is inconceivable for classical times, as the

material division between rich and poor asserted itself as the main factor that distinguished classes in the early Byzantine world.[80] Asceticism and continence profoundly changed both the expectations of individuals for themselves and the structure of society based on the family. Since attitudes to sexual differences and sexual behaviour were fundamental to this new Christian morality, the differentiated study of women becomes a more fruitful task, and can be pursued in a way that is also not possible for earlier periods. Historians can begin to pay attention to the half of society which they normally neglect.[81] Narrower themes, such as the rise of the charismatic Christian holy man, have also been enormously helpful in structuring an approach to the *disiecta membra* of the history of late Antiquity.[82]

However, those very *disiecta membra* may tell their own story about the period. The evidence, both written and archaeological, seems inarticulate because the society from which it comes was losing its classical coherence. Two structures had defined the organization of the Graeco-Roman world since its inception, the city with its political organization, and the household based on kinship structure. Both showed signs of serious disintegration in this period.

Changing perceptions of the family and of the household are illustrated by the tombstones of the period. Up to the end of the fourth century grave inscriptions in Anatolia, and in most of the rest of the ancient world, presented the dead in the context of their household or in their relationship to a wider range of kin. Children buried their parents or parents their children; siblings might put up an inscription for a brother or sister; more distant family relations were often invoked in elaborate family memorials; graves themselves were regarded as houses of the dead, perpetuating the life of the family on earth.[83] In the early Byzantine period family tombs, and even the inscriptions which identified close kin as responsible for the burial, gave way to much simpler monuments naming the deceased, and a formula indicating that the deceased was not dead, but lay in repose awaiting resurrection to eternal life; he or she was described in relationship not to kinsfolk but to God. Out of ninety-six Christian epitaphs from Tavium and its territory, thirty-seven simply identified the deceased as 'slave of God', while a further sixteen

[78] F. R. Trombley, *HTR* 78. 3–4 (1985), 327–52 usefully discusses the evidence from John of Ephesus, although I disagree with his conclusions.

[79] S. J. B. Barnish, 'The Transformation of Classical Cities', *JRA* 2 (1989), 385–400 reviews the recent literature and gives a sense of the difficulty of the interpretative problems.

[80] Patlagéan, *Pauvreté*.

[81] Brown, *The Body and Society*. See also the review-article by Averil Cameron, 'Redrawing the Map: Early Christian Territory after Foucault', *JRS* 76 (1986), 266–71.

[82] Peter Brown, 'The Rise and Function of the Holy Man in Late Antiquity', *JRS* 61 (1971), 80–101 = *Society and the Holy in Late Antiquity* (1982), 103–52.

[83] See M. Waelkens, 'Hausähnliche Gräber in Anatolien', *Palast und Hütte* (1982), 421–45.

added a mention of clerical or official rank. Filiation was certainly indicated in only five cases. Just as monks and hermits cut themselves off from their families and households, so, in this modest Anatolian city, ordinary people, in the sleep of death, the moment when they were closer to God than ever before, cut themselves off from their kin and awaited the call to judgement and resurrection as slaves of His mercy. Burial was no longer a means to perpetuate a man's existence as part of an earthly family; elaborate family tombs accordingly give way to simple burials, clustered around the church. This rule applied not simply to extra-mural *martyria*, but increasingly to churches within the settlement itself. Even in the early Byzantine period extramural graves were no longer *de rigueur*, and the traditional distinction between a city for the living and a separate cemetery for the dead, which had helped to define the ancient concept of a city, was broken down by the new ideas about the meaning of burial, and the urge to find a place for a grave as close as possible to a sanctified site.[84]

There were other, more drastic changes in the nature of the urban communities. The cities of the Graeco-Roman period were instantly identified, if not actually defined by their public buildings (see above, Vol. I, Ch. 7 §1 and Ch. 12 §1). The organization of public space around temples, civic meeting places, and places of entertainment, was the clue to Roman city planning. Without its gymnasium and theatre, stoas lined with shops, council chamber and civic offices, sanctuaries and altars designed for public ceremonial and pagan worship, a would-be city had only a hollow claim to civic status. The development of cities in late Antiquity has been endlessly discussed, and no consensus has emerged. It cannot be disputed that larger provincial cities, and in particular the centres of provincial government, retained many of their public buildings and showed considerable evidence of economic and cultural activity. The most conspicuous examples in Anatolia away from the west coast are Ancyra in Galatia,[85] and Aphrodisias, chief city of the province of Phrygia and Caria.[86] However, the initiative in maintaining and promoting such cities as flourishing urban centres in the fourth century lay almost exclusively with imperial officials, notably provincial governors, the *vicarii* of the eastern dioceses, or the praetorian prefects.[87] From the early sixth century wealthy local men were from time to time given the title 'father of the city', *pater tēs poleōs*, and appeared to take credit for new construction or restoration of old buildings, but the phenomenon was in general restricted to the larger cities.[88]

The other side of the coin was displayed by smaller cities which did not qualify for attention as seats of government or for other special reasons. Some simply faded from view after the fourth century; others underwent radical change, which can usually only be appreciated when the site is available for detailed archaeological investigation. The key development was the systematic devaluation of a city's public buildings, apart from churches and related religious structures. Other civic buildings were demolished or allowed to collapse and the domestic areas of the city encroached on to and covered the old squares and colonnades.[89] Clearly recognizable classical cities simply became towns, or centres of population, whose size alone distinguished them from larger villages.

These physical changes had significant implications for the inhabitants. The old cities still continued to fulfil, at least to some degree, their former role for the surrounding territory as markets where rural produce could be sold or exchanged, and centres for the production and manufacture of more specialized goods. The fullest evidence for the shops, workshops, and providers of services in any ancient city comes from the third- to fifth-century cemeteries of Corycus on the coast of Rugged Cilicia,[90] and the use of a man's profession to distinguish him from his fellows is more frequent on the inscriptions of the early Byzantine than the Roman imperial period.[91] But this was balanced by the corresponding decline in evidence for political activity, well illustrated by the disappearance of the curial class as an effective force in the cities. Very few inscriptions between the fourth and sixth century indicated that a man held civic office. The cities had ceased to operate as fora for public activity. Consequently the former civic ruling class, drawn above all from the local landowning aristocracy, turned more

[84] The Tavium inscriptions (*RECAM* ii. 423–528) are a drastic example of a phenomenon that can be illustrated in several other central Anatolian cities; in western Asia Minor, where the classical tradition was more deeply embedded, the tendency is less marked. For the changed topography of early Christian cemeteries see Peter Brown, *The Cult of the Saints* (1981), *passim*; and G. Dagron, 'Le Christianisme dans la ville byzantine', *DOP* 31 (1977), 11–19.

[85] C. Foss, 'Ankara'.

[86] Rouché, *Aphrodisias in Late Antiquity*.

[87] See above all Robert, *Hellenica*, iv.

[88] Rouché, *GRBS* 20 (1979), 173–85; D. Feissel and G. Dagron, *Inscriptions de Cilicie* (1987), 215–20.

[89] Peter Brown, *The Making of Late Antiquity* (1978), 105–6.

[90] J. Keil and A. Wilhelm, *MAMA* iii. 200–788; valuable discussion by Patlagéan, *Pauvreté*, 158–69, and note also Feissel, *Inscriptions de Cilicie*, 221–5. Compare now the smaller collection of funerary inscriptions indicating professions from Tyre, J. P. Rey-Coquais. *Inscriptions . . . de Tyr*, i, *Inscriptions de la nécropole* (BMB 29) (1977) (SEG xxvii (1977), 995).

[91] Rouché, *Aphrodisias in Late Antiquity*, 213.

and more to their rural estates where their power bases lay. Here they could be, effectively, a law unto themselves. Evidence from the reign of Justinian illustrates the lawless power of landowners in two of the least urbanized provinces of central Asia Minor. A major task of the governor of Cappadocia was to control the landowners who commanded small private forces in the form of gangs of armed peasants.[92] Precisely similar developments clearly took place in Paphlagonia, where an inscription contains the edict of an imperial official, passed on to the population by the bishop of Hadrianopolis in Honorias, which aimed to abolish posses of *xylokaballoi*, mounted club-bearers, who had carried out acts of terror and brigandage evidently in the interests of powerful local landowners.[93]

The inscription from Paphlagonia implies that the local bishop was the only competent local authority with whom the imperial government could communicate. It confirms, in this one instance at least, that by the mid-sixth century local government, in so far as it existed at all, was in the hands of the Church. The organization of the Church, with its metropolitans and bishops, had been built up during the third and fourth century on the back of the civic organization of the provinces. It was logical that ecclesiastical authority should coincide with the underlying power-structure of the Roman empire. But as the latter disintegrated, it began to cut the ground from under the bishops' feet. In areas where the cities had lost their importance, a bishop might find his own role reduced to leading, or rather supporting a predominantly poor community, which had relinquished all political initiative to rural landowners or to the central government. The Church, with tenacious conservatism, clung to the old structure of city-based bishops beyond the end of Antiquity, in many areas until the eleventh and twelfth century. By that date, and often centuries earlier, many of their sees simply did not exist as centres of population.

In the history of the early Church, the great age of episcopal power was the fourth and early fifth centuries, when the tradition, and sometimes the reality of classical civic life provided Church leaders, who were based in the cities, with a firm platform from which to make their authority felt. In the centuries that followed Christian leadership was usurped by figures unconnected with the former urban centres, hermits, monks, but above all by holy men. As power, defined narrowly in political or economic terms, slipped from the hands of urban leaders to rural property-owners, so the monks, hermits, and holy men of the countryside slowly usurped the authority of city-based clergy. The invested power of bishops was outshone by the charismatic power of spiritual ascetics who needed no secular political platform from which to project their influence on the world at large.[94]

---

[92] Justinian, *Novella*, 31.

[93] D. Feissel and I. Kaygusuz, 'Un mandement impériale du VIᵉ siècle dans une inscription d'Hadrianupolis d'Honoriade', *Travaux et mémoires*, 9 (1985), 397–419 (*SEG* xxxv (1985), 1360).

[94] A similar interpretation, linking the rise of the monastic tradition to the decline and demise of the classical city, is suggested by Peter Brown in P. Veyne (ed.), *Histoire de la vie privée*, i (1985), 278–83. There, as in these pages on Asia Minor, the thesis needs further detailed examination. An interesting study by D. Savramis, *Zur Soziologie des byzantinischen Mönchtums* (1962), offers a clear, if schematic analysis, in which it is argued that the monasteries, by acquiring a large proportion of the available land between the 7th and 9th cents., brought an end to the livelihood of small farmers; further, their tax-free status deprived cities and the imperial government of revenue.

19   Central Anatolia at the End of Antiquity

The Life of Saint Theodore of Sykeon

1. *The World of Theodore of Sykeon*

The historian of central Anatolia has to wait until the final centuries of Antiquity before encountering a written account which even begins to offer something of the full flavour of life in this rural provincial milieu. The importance and value of the Life of St Theodore of Sykeon, completed around the middle of the seventh century, but describing events and conditions between the reigns of Justinian and the accession of Heraclius, has been often noted,[1] and a recent edition, with translation and commentary, which prints many hitherto unpublished chapters of the Life, makes it readily accessible.[2]

It is completely characteristic of the Life that much of its chronology remains obscure, or recoverable only by intricate reconstruction. The stages of Theodore's life are precisely datable only at the moments when they intersect with great events on a larger stage, usually the accession of emperors, or campaigns against rebels or foreign enemies, which are attested by other sources. Theodore was born under Justinian (AD 527–65; 3. 10–11), and at the age of 12 barely survived an attack of bubonic plague (8. 1–2). If this

was the first and greatest epidemic of the disease in the sixth century, which reached its height in AD 542, then Theodore must have been born in about 530,[3] but the plague is known to have recurred in 555, 558, and 560–1, and Theodore's illness might have happened at any of these times also.[4] His mother Maria, aunt Despoinia, and grandmother Elpidia are said to have run a *pandocheion* (3. 5–6) at Sykeon, on the Pilgrim's Road near Iuliopolis in north-west Galatia, where they served both as hosts and as prostitutes for passing travellers—Theodore's alleged father was an imperial official Cosmas, who had slept with Maria on a journey taking certain imperial orders to the East (3. 10 ff.)—but they had later upgraded the place from a bawdy house to a respectable inn (6. 1–7). The family was evidently not poor. They owned slaves (7. 16–17) and received high-ranking visitors (12. 4); Theodore himself as a child wore a quantity of gold jewellery (12. 10–16; cf. 5. 8–9); his mother later married a leading citizen of Ancyra, the *protector* David (25. 6); and on the death of his grandmother Theodore was able first to build a large church of St Michael, with chapels of John the Baptist and the Virgin Mary, and later to reconstruct a church of St George as a large, three-aisled basilica, with accompanying chapels of St Plato and St Antiochus, from the family money remaining to him.[5] The suggestion that Theodore's immediate family had been prostitutes may be little more than a slander or a hagiographical motif.

---

[1] See E. Dawes and N. Baynes, introd. to their trans. (*Three Byzantine Saints* (1948), 87): 'We have chosen this biography for translation since it gives us the best picture known to us of life in Asia Minor in the Byzantine period before the Arab invasions of the Empire.' Foss, 'Ankara', 56–60 takes it as the basis for his account of Ancyra in the later 6th and early 7th cents., and there is a useful analysis, with a very different focus from the one offered here, by R. Cormack, *Writing in Gold: Byzantine Society and its Icons* (1985), 9–49. The Life is also extensively used by Peter Brown, 'The Rise and Function of the Holy Man in Late Antiquity', *JRS* 61 (1971), 80–101 (*Society and the Holy in Late Antiquity* (1982), 103–52), and by E. Patlagéan, *Pauvreté sociale et pauvreté économique à Byzance* (1977), for which see the index s.v. Théodore.

[2] A. J. Festugière, *La Vie de Théodore de Sykéon I–II, Subs. Hag.* 48 (1970). Citations hereafter are by the chapter and line numbers of Festugière's edn. Previously the only accessible text of the Life was published by Th. Ioannu, Μνημεῖα ἁγιολογικά (1884), 361–495, which served as the basis for Dawes and Baynes' abridged translation. This edn. was based on MSS which omitted the important concluding chapters of the Life, from 149–70.

[3] So Foss, 'Ankara', 56 with n. 118.

[4] The evidence is discussed by J. Teall, 'Barbarians in Justinian's Armies', *Speculum*, 40 (1965), 294 ff., esp. 305; Patlagéan, *Pauvreté*, 87–8. Foss's chronology implies that chapters 24–54 of the Life cover a period of about 34 years up to the accession of Maurice in 582. This seems rather long but is not impossible. If Theodore had had the plague between 555 and 561, that period would be reduced to between 15 and 20 years.

[5] 40. 13–23 for the church of St Michael, which became the main monastic centre; 55. 8–14 for the church of St George, built soon after 582. The Life specifies that Theodore gave τὰ ὑπολειφθέντα αὐτῷ γενικὰ χρήματα for the building. Note too that his aunt had left her possessions to Theodore (25. 12–13), and that his grandmother had also given him everything which she owned when she became *hegoumene* of the female monastery of St Christopher (25. 25–43). Perhaps the truth about

In his youth he renounced his worldly goods (12. 10–16) and spent two years as a recluse in a cave (19. 23), before emerging to be promoted through all the lower ranks of the clergy to the priesthood at the age of 18 (23. 1–2). Soon after the accession of the emperor Maurice in 582, which he had predicted to the future emperor in person (54), he became bishop of Anastasiopolis (58), and held the post until he resigned, in an atmosphere of controversy, in his 11th year of office (78. 28), probably in the early to mid-590s. During these years he had three times made the pilgrimage to the Holy Land (24; 50; 62). After resigning his bishopric he made a first visit to Constantinople, during the patriarchate of Cyriacus (AD 596–606), but before the death of Maurice in 602, who gave asylum status to his monastery and made it directly dependent on the patriarch, not on the local bishop (82. 11–15). He subsequently predicted Maurice's own death (119), and encountered Domnitziolus, the nephew of the emperor Phocas, who was travelling east to take command of the army (120. 2 ff.), and who thereafter became Theodore's most influential friend and an important patron of his monastery (120. 46–54). He visited Constantinople for a second time during the patriarchate of Thomas (133. 2) and was present at his death in the early months of 610 (135). After his return to Sykeon he witnessed first the passage of the *comes* Bonosus to suppress a serious Jewish uprising at Syrian Antioch in 610,[6] and then, in the same year but after the death of Phocas and the accession of Heraclius, the appearance of ambassadors attempting to defuse the otherwise unattested revolt of Phocas' brother Comentiolus against the new regime.[7] Theodore went to Constantinople for the third and last time in 611, at the same time as Heraclius' expedition to confront the Persians in Caesareia (154. 1–9), but he stayed long enough as the guest of the patriarch Sergius to see the emperor on his return, and bless his infant son Constantine (155. 1–8). In 613 Heraclius again passed through Sykeon, *en route* for the East (166), in time for a last, brief encounter with Theodore before the latter's death on 22 April 613 (170. 24–31).

Theodore's biographer George, who was to become *hegoumenos* of the monastery at Sykeon,[8] was not yet 18 when the saint died (165. 19–20), and would have been born about AD 595. His birth to parents who had hitherto been childless was owed, they thought, to the saint's blessing, and they sent him to the monastery while he was still a young child in about 601/2 (170. 1–9), and he had been twelve years in the monastery by 613 (170. 15). He had been taught to read and write by the old *hegoumenos* Philumenus,[9] and had begun to make his first notes about Theodore while the saint was still alive (165. 15 ff.). He did not, however, begin to write the Life in earnest until after Theodore's death (22. 8), and certainly did not complete the work before the death of Heraclius in 641 (166. 33–5). For the later events of Theodore's life he could rely on his own memory as an eyewitness (22. 1–5; 165; 170. 14–16, cf. 123. 5; 126. 11–12); for the earlier period he drew on what the saint himself had said (22. 5–8) and what others could recall (22. 2–3; 170. 16–20). The value of the different sources of information is clearly reflected in the discrepancy in length between the account of the first seventy-two years of Theodore's life, up to the death of Maurice in 602, which fill 119 chapters, or ninety-six printed pages of the text, and the eleven years to 613, which make up fifty generally longer chapters, or sixty-five printed pages of text, a much fuller account of the final years which George was present to witness.

Sykeon was a village that lay on the great road across Asia Minor running from Constantinople to Ancyra, and then to Syrian Antioch, the spinal cord of Byzantine Anatolia.[10] This road, the 'public highway of the imperial post',[11] which is simply referred to as 'the highway' in a number of passages,[12] dominated

---

Theodore's background is hinted at in the epitaph of another Maria of the 5th or 6th cent., discovered at Archelais in Cappadocia: ἐνθάδε κατάκιτε ἡ τῆς εὐλαβοῦς κὲ μακαρίας μνήμης διάκονος Μαρία, ἥτις κατὰ τὸ ῥητὸν τοῦ ἀποστόλου ἐτεκνοτρόφεσεν, ἐξενοδόχησεν, ἁγίων πόδας ἔνιψε, θλιβομένοις τὸ ἄρτον αὐτῆς διένεμε. μνήσθητι αὐτῆ, Κύριε, ὅταν ἔρχη ἐν τῆ βασιλίᾳ σου (*SEG* xxvii (1977), 948a = Horsley, *New Docs.* ii. 193 no. 190).

6 142. 1 ff. For the Jewish revolt see Theophanes, I. 296. 16–25 (de Boor).

7 152; cf. W. Kaegi, 'New Evidence on the Early Reign of Heraclius', *Byz. Zeitschr.* 66 (1973), 308–30; D. Barker, 'Theodore of Sykeon and the Historians', *Studies in Church History*, 13: *The Orthodox Churches and the West* (1976), 83–96.

8 22. 8–13 implies that he wrote the Life as *hegoumenos* for the edification of the young acolytes. His predecessors had been Philumenos, appointed at the inauguration of the church of St Michael (41), who died at an advanced age between 607 and 610 (130), and Ioannes, who was certainly *hegoumenos* in 613 (168. 1–2, 54). Both men had been associated with Theodore from very early days; Philumenos was his second, and Ioannes his third disciple and associate (26. 12 ff.; 45–7).

9 26. 10 ff.; 170. 10–13. Compare the case of Theodore himself, who learned his letters at the age of 8 (5. 18).

10 See above, Ch. 9 §11 n. 72. The course of the road between Nicomedia and Syrian Antioch, and evidence for physical remains along it, the surviving milestones, and many topographical identifications are discussed by French, *Pilgrim's Road*.

11 3. 5–6, ἡ δημοσία στράτα τοῦ βασιλικοῦ δρόμου, trans. Dawes and Baynes (cf. 120. 46).

12 125. 1–4 ἡ δημοσία στράτα; 56. 8, 20; 74. 29; 112. 6; cf. 67. 1 which refers to the road in the neighbourhood of Kinna south of Ancyra (to be located at Karahamzılı, cf. *RECAM* ii. 21–2).

the life of the community there. The *pandocheion* at Sykeon was evidently typical of many such places. The Life mentions two others at the seventh and tenth milestones on the road south of Nicomedia (160). The fact that none of these is indicated on the various itineraries that describe the road, indicates that facilities for entertaining travellers were considerably more varied than the regular sequence of official *mansiones* and *mutationes* which those describe. At Sykeon there was also clearly a relay for the official transport system, and when Domitziolus and his retinue were travelling east in 610 they punished a leading man of Ancyra for failing to supply fresh horses for their needs at the place.[13] It is possible that the camels which Theodore encountered near Nicomedia made an important contribution to the transport of goods along the route.[14] Couriers could make the journey from Sykeon to Constantinople in two days.[15] Other official traffic was certainly heavy. Like its neighbour Iuliopolis in the early second century,[16] Sykeon witnessed the passage of an emperor (166), a whole range of military and administrative officials,[17] and soldiers, whose

presence, as always, could lead to disturbance and upheaval.[18] It is clear that the monastery founded by Theodore itself offered hospitality to travellers (104. 3–4), as was also true of another monastery which lay close to the highway in southern Galatia (64. 2).

The negative consequences of occupying a site along the great highway are evident from the stories of the oppressive behaviour of soldiers and officials, but it is also clear that the monastery's prosperity was closely linked to its favoured location. The principal benefactors of Theodore's churches were important men who had encountered him on their journeys from Constantinople to the East: Maurice, who, in response to an embassy and letter from Theodore, was to make an annual gift of 600 *modii* of grain to the monastery after his accession (54. 30–2), and later granted asylum rights (82. 11–18; cf. 148. 12–13; 149. 49 ff.); and Domnitziolus whose regular visits led him to make important gifts in the form of precious objects, building materials, and alms for the poor (120. 46–54; cf. 128. 1–2). Theodore's own personal success and fame clearly owed much to the publicity which such travellers could give him in Constantinople, where his first visits were at the invitation of the emperor or the patriarch, and where he cultivated an aristocratic as well as a popular clientele.[19]

---

[13] 148. 27–34. Compare also the description of Tautaendia, where there was a bridge over the Sangarius, a *pandocheion* (106. 10–13, 37), and horses in stables (109. 20). These features suggest that the place lay on a major highway, perhaps the road from Dorylaeum to Ancyra, in which case it is tempting to identify it with Vindia, formerly Gordium, which could have provided the last part of the name. Cf. above, Vol. I, Ch. 4 § VI n. 114, and *TIB* iv. 232 s.v.

[14] 160. 24–48; compare the *camelarius* mentioned on an inscription of Ancyra, *AS* 27 (1977), 97–8 no. 39 with the commentary there; see also Basil, *Ep.* 158, written to the brother of a camel-master, and *Hom. in divites*, *PG* 31. 285a referring to herds of camels, τῶν μὲν ἀχθοφόρων, τῶν δὲ νομάδων. Basil's *Hexameron*, 8. 1 (*PG* 29. 165c) shows that camels were familiar in 4th-cent. Cappadocia.

[15] 152. 2–6. News of the assassination of Phocas in Constantinople on 5 Oct. 610 reached Sykeon on the 7th; cf. W. Kaegi, *Byz. Zeitschr.* 66 (1973), 310. The distance is about 330 km. (206 mls.). Allegedly word of Theodore's own death reached the capital in a single day, εἴτε θεόθεν εἴτε ἐκ ταχυδρομίας (169. 25–6). For couriers in Asia Minor in the Roman period, see L. Robert, *Rev. phil.* 13 (1939), 207–11 (*OMS* ii. 1560–4) and above, Vol. I, Ch. 9 § II at nn. 78–86. The equivalent in the Ottoman empire were the Tatar couriers who, by using relays of horses, would travel between 100 and 150 mls. in a day. For two 19th-cent. accounts of this form of travel, see the Rev. Vere Munro, *A Summer Ramble in Syria with a Tartar Trip from Aleppo to Stamboul*, ii (1835), and James Baillie Fraser, *A Winter's Journey (Tatar) from Constantinople to Tehran* (1838), the latter evoked by L. Robert, *A travers l'Asie Mineure*, 70–1; see also his index s.v. Tatar.

[16] Pliny, *Ep.* 10. 76–7; above, Vol. I, Ch. 9 § II n. 111.

[17] Cosmas, a *magistrianus* (3. 10 ff.); Maurice, *chartularius* and *comes* before his elevation (54. 1 ff.); Phocas, an *a secretis* (121); Domnitziolus (120. 2 ff., 37 ff., 46 ff.; 148. 27–34); Bonosus, the *comes* (142. 1 ff.); Marcianus, a *logothetes* from Constantinople (148. 38–43); Priscus, who succeeded Comentiolus in command of the army (153. 11–24).

[18] 19. 14–20 for soldiers suspected of abducting the young Theodore; 147. 42–5 implies that στρατιωτῶν πάροδος ἢ τινων ἀρχόντων ἢ ἀξιωμάτων was a regular source of disturbance. See also 125. 1–4 for the heavy guard of *scribones* and soldiers who accompanied a soldier suspected of treason back to Constantinople.

[19] During Theodore's first visit, although he had been invited by the emperor and the patriarch, and had been lionized at court (82. 9–10), he stayed at a lodging house (*metatum*, 83. 4; 93. 34) and most of the people whom he encountered were comparatively humble: a woman of unidentified status (83), the female servant of a leading nobleman (μεγιστάν, 84), a crippled widow (85), the son of a shopkeeper (86), a shipowner (87), a wrestler (88), an innkeeper (91), three slaves (92. 94), three unidentified persons (93), an 8-year-old girl in a monastery (95), and another woman (96). The exceptions to this pattern were the childless daughter of the deacon and *castrensis* of the patriarch, Sergius, surely the future patriarch Sergius (93. 23 ff.), a *silentarius* from among the leading men of the city (89), and, at the end of the stay, the infant child of the emperor Maurice (97). His two later visits appear to have been briefer and fewer contacts are recorded, but these were generally of higher status. During the second he cured the emperor Phocas himself (133), and blessed the childless wife of Domnitziolus (140). His status at this time was much enhanced, as is made clear by his plain-spoken dealings with emperor and patriarch and by his authoritative pronouncement to assembled clerics, that communicants should not take baths immediately after Mass (137). During the third visit he played something of a celebrity's role, receiving the crowds which thronged to him. His two recorded cures were of the son of an unidentified man and of the patrician Nicetas, *comes* of the divine *excubitus* (154).

Both the position of Sykeon and Theodore's growing reputation will explain the appearance of many outsiders at his monastery. There were private individuals seeking cures, including a landowner from Heraclea Pontica (44. 1–2); a man from Ancyra and his mute son (61); a shipowner from the *emporium* of Kalleon in the Propontis;[20] and the two senatorial ladies from leading Ephesian families, who came in litters, attended by a large retinue, to seek cures for their children (110). Then there were officials of the imperial government, including an *a secretis* of the emperor (121), the patrician Photius, later to be exarch of Rome (127. 1–2), and the *strator* Theodorus, from Pylai in Bithynia, who acted as Theodore's host on his second visit to the capital, when he travelled overland for the first part of his journey and then completed it by ship from Pylai to Constantinople.[21] Finally there were clerics from the East, like the priest from one of the cities of Armenia Minor subordinate to Sebasteia (122. 1–2), Dometianus bishop of Melitene (169. 14–15), or, most distinctive of all, the centenarian African hermit Antiochus, returning to the East from Constantinople, where he had acted as an ambassador to the emperor Maurice to plead for help for his city, which had been ravaged by barbarians (73. 1–11).

It is important also to see Sykeon in its local context. The village[22] lay on the east bank of the river Siberis, which was spanned by a bridge.[23] There are further details in Procopius who records that Justinian had built a bridge, together with a jetty on the east and a church on the west bank, which was intended as a refuge for travellers during the winter season, over the Siberis in Galatia at a place called Sykeai, ten miles east of Iuliopolis.[24] The bridge was for long identified with a structure which could be seen until recent years on the Aladağ Çay,[25] but it has now been demonstrated that the site at that crossing should be identified not with Sykeon but with Iuliopolis, where Justinian also, it so happens, took measures to prevent the circuit wall

from being undermined by the flow of the river.[26] In consequence the Aladağ Çay should be identified not with the Siberis but with the Bithynian river Scopas, while the Siberis was clearly the modern Girmir Çay, whose course lies several miles further east.[27] No significant remains of a bridge, church, or other buildings have been noted at the spot where the Roman road crossed the Girmir Çay, some ten kilometres south-south-west of Beypazarı, but there has been little detailed investigation, and it is evident that not only stone-robbing but also flash floods could have removed all traces of any bridge that may once have been there.[28]

During Theodore's early years, apart from the church on the west bank of the Siberis mentioned by Procopius, the nucleus of a small ecclesiastical or monastic community already existed at Sykeon. There was a church of the Paphlagonian saint Gemellus close to the road and to the inn (10. 2; 142. 5–6; cf. 25. 13), another of John the Baptist (8. 3–5) and somewhere above these, on the nearby rocky hillside, there was a modest *martyrium* of St George.[29] It was presumably at or near this spot that Theodore built his new, much larger church of St George, with attendant chapels of St Plato and St Antiochus on either side, and of Saints Sergius and Bacchus above it.[30] To the right of these buildings Theodore had already constructed another church dedicated to the archangel Michael, on a site where a smaller chapel had already existed (35. 17), flanked by chapels of John the Baptist and the Virgin Mary (40. 13–23). This was to serve as the regular place of lodging for visitors (70. 4; cf. 103. 7). Below the rocky hill another monastery was built by Theodore

---

[20] 123. 1–2 calls it an *emporium* of the Pontus, but in 158. 12 the ἐμπόριον Κάλλεον is identified as lying near the church of St Autonomus, which was on the S. shore of the Propontis (above, Ch. 17 § IX at n. 399). For Pontic *emporia* see Robert, *A travers l'Asie Mineure*, 71–6.

[21] 129. 131–2; for the topography see L. Robert, *Bull. ép.* (1974), 574; 'Un Voyage d'Antiphilos de Byzance', *JSav.* (1979), 269 ff. (*OMS* vii. 439 ff.).

[22] χωρίον: 3. 1; 45. 17; 167. 40.

[23] 121. 27–8 implies that a traveller from the monastery would cross the river as he headed towards Constantinople.

[24] Procopius, *Aed.* 5. 4. 1–4.

[25] J. G. C. Anderson, 'Explorations in Galatia cis Halym', *JHS* 19 (1899), 65–7 with a plan, which is also reproduced by M. H. Ballance, *Reallexicon zur byzantinischen Kunst*, ii (1971), 613–14 Abb. 3. There is a photograph by I. W. Macpherson, *AS* 4 (1954), pl. XI. 1 opp. p. 114.

[26] Procopius, *Aed.* 5. 4. 5–6.

[27] French, *Pilgrim's Road*, 33–47.

[28] For flash floods which completely removed all traces of a bridge near Nicaea, see Procopius, *Aed.* 5. 3. 4–5. These were a regular occurrence on both the Scopas and the Siberis; see below, at nn. 66–9, and the discussion in M. Hendy, *Studies in the Byzantine Monetary Economy* (1985), 61–6. Anderson, *JHS* 19 (1899), 65 noted an ancient site at Mal Tepe, about seven kilometres up the Siberis from the point where it was crossed by the Roman road, and observed 'numerous chambers cut in the rocks which form the left bank of the stream' (cf. the good map in French, *Pilgrim's Road*, harıta 1 (p. 130)). These would, in fact, have been close to the supposed site of Sykeon, and the steep rocky slopes might be the ὄρος close to the village where the saint lived for two years, and where there were several chapels. A visit to the area in 1990 revealed a small Bronze-Age settlement at the river-crossing and a Galatian fortress on a prominent hill close to the village of Tahırler to the east, but no remains of late Antiquity.

[29] 7. 2; ἐπὶ τὸ παρακείμενον πετρῶδες ὄρος; cf. 167. 75, which refers to many εὐκτήρια on the λόφος.

[30] 55. 11–15; for St Plato cf. 60. 5–6; 102. 15–16; St Antiochus, 126. 1–3; St Sergius and St Bacchus, 152. 5.

dedicated to the Virgin Mary,[31] and described as a winter church of St Kerykos (169. 90), a church of the Orthodox (5. 3–4), which should probably be identified with one of those already discussed, and a church (13. 5–6) and female monastery of St Christopher, lying a little to the east, but close to Sykeon (25. 37–8; 124. 5; 167. 44–5). These details show that there was already a substantial group of churches and chapels at the place before the ascendancy of Theodore, but that their number and size was much increased during his lifetime, above all by the successive construction of major churches of St Michael, St George, and the Virgin Mary between perhaps AD 560 and 600. By 610 the monastic population exceeded fifty persons (142. 40–2). It is important to recognize that the reputation of Theodore as a holy man was solidly reinforced by these institutional provisions. He was no isolated hermit, but the central figure, the archimandrite (64. 23) of a wealthy and populous monastic community.

Sykeon lay about half way between two bishoprics situated on the Pilgrim's Road: Iuliopolis, at this date generally called Heliopolis,[32] which the Life describes as being fifteen Roman miles (22 km.) from the church of St George (13. 19–20), and which by modern measurements lay eleven and a half miles (17 km.) along the Roman road west of the crossing of the Siberis,[33] and Anastasiopolis, twelve miles (18 km.) to the east, in whose territory or enoria Sykeon lay.[34] The system of dividing the province between civic territories clearly persisted and there are other references to the klima or enoria of Heliopolis (79. 23, 25) and to the klima of Mnizos (37. 2). The province was also, it

seems, divided into sections called merē, whose relationship to the enoriai is not clear. When Theodore returned from his third pilgrimage to the Holy Land, he entered the districts of Galatia (τὰ μέρη τῆς Γαλατίας) in the neighbourhood of the city of Kinna (64. 1), and a section of north-west Galatia which included the valley of the upper Siberis, and which was at least partly within the territory of Mnizos, was called the Protomeria.[35]

In north-west Galatia as a whole the principal form of settlement was the village (χωρίον).[36] The Life names twenty-four such settlements which can be located in the territories of Iuliopolis, Anastasiopolis and Mnizos alone, as well as a number of others further afield. One or two, such as Balgatia, located six miles (9 km.) from Sykeon (4. 2) and probably to be identified with Valcaton, a way-station depicted on the Peutinger Map twelve miles (18 km.) west of Iuliopolis,[37] and Arania, which lay five miles (7.5 km.) east of Sykeon (122. 25; cf. 72. 2) were certainly on the main road, but the majority evidently lay in the hinterland. Even so detailed a source of information as the Life provides a very incomplete picture of the topography. It is salutary to recall that the Turkish census of 1950 lists seventy-two villages in the kaza of Beypazarı (the modern town nearest to Anastasiopolis),

[31] 119. 4–6; note the earlier reference to a small cell in the monastery of the Theotocus, 81. 31. The church of the Theotocus and the church and monastery of St Michael are said to have been adorned later by the emperor Heraclius (Michael Psellos, Oration on the Archangel Michael, ed. E. Kurt and F. Drexl, Michael Pselli opera minora, i (1936), 120–41 at 126. 29–127. 5; 132. 8 mentions the hospice); see Elizabeth Fisher, 'Nicomedia or Galatia? Where Was Psellos' Church of the Archangel Michael?', Gonimos: Neoplatonic and Byzantine Studies presented to L. G. Westerink (1988), 175–87.

[32] See the note in French, Pilgrim's Road, 42, and on RECAM ii no. 333.

[33] French, Pilgrim's Road, table 13.

[34] 3. 1–3. If Anastasiopolis is correctly identified with Dikmen Hüyük (French, Pilgrim's Road, 44), then it actually lay 12. 84 m.p. east of the river crossing. Anastasiopolis is assumed to have taken its name from the emperor Anastasius between 491 and 518, having formerly been known as Lagania (Pilgrim's Road, 43; slight doubts in W. Ruge, RE xx (1924), 454 s.v. Lagania). The Life refers to a district called the Λαγαντινή (116. 1; perhaps to be emended to Λαγανεινή), which should be equivalent to the territory of Anastasiopolis. The Synekdemos of Hierocles of AD 528 has an entry Ῥεγεναγαλία, which can be interpreted as ῥεγέων Λαγανία, and should also be a reference to this territory.

[35] 26a. 1–2; 114. 1; 149. 1–2. Note the expression τὰ μέρη νουμερικῶν τῆς Βιθυνίας (152. 38), apparently describing the part of Bithynia adjacent to Galatia, and τῶν μέρων τῆς Ἀγκυρανῶν μητροπόλεως (162. 81).

[36] The word κωμή is used once at 26. 11: ἡ κωμή Μοσσυνέων ἡ ἐπιλεγομένη Ἐνιστράτον (perhaps meaning 'on the highway'). The additional name served to distinguish this Mossyna from several others in Asia Minor, including the Mossyni in the assize district of Pergamum (Pliny, NH 5. 126), the Mossyni of the upper Maeander valley in the Hyrgalean plain (W. Ruge, RE xvi (1933), 376–7), and the Mossyneis who are known from a dedication found in the upper Tembris valley and were presumably different from either of these (pace the editor of the inscription, T. Drew Bear, GRBS 17 (1976), 254 no. 11). Note too ὁ δῆμος ὁ Μοσσυνεανῶν καὶ Συνλαντηνῶν in the territory of Nicaea (I. Iznik, ii. 1. 1206) and the Mossynoeci of Pontus; see Strabo, 11. 14. 5, 528 and 12. 3. 18, 549, where he explains that μόσυνος was an Anatolian word for a tower.

Κωμή also appears fossilized in the place-name Ἀποκουμίς or Ἀπουκομίς (143. 1; 150. 2), which should perhaps be identified with the Galatian Ἀπουκωμή mentioned on an inscription of Rome, Inscriptiones Christianae Urbis Romae, ii. 4439, discussed by D. Feissel, Riv. arch. chr. 58 (1982), 1373–4 fig. 4. For an Ἀποκωμή near Nacolea, see Drew Bear, Nouvelles inscriptions de Phrygie, 35–8 no. 2 with commentary (SEG xxviii (1978), 1200). The word τρικωμία is also used to describe three χωρία which shared a single plain (118. 20–4). For a general discussion of these terms see Patlagéan, Pauvreté, 241–2.

[37] The distances do not exactly harmonize; see Pilgrim's Road, 45 with n. 17.

forty-two in Ayaş (Mnizos),[38] and sixty-five in Nallıhan (Iuliopolis), 179 in all, more than seven times the number of village toponyms preserved in the Byzantine text.

The history of Galatia in the second and third centuries AD, in so far as it can be recovered at all, is largely the history of its cities, and remarkably little can be said about life in the villages as such. In the Life of St Theodore the perspective is completely reversed. This is in part due to the point of view of the writer and his subject, a holy man operating from a rural base in an environment of village communities, but it also reflects the decline in autonomous civic life, which was already evident in the fourth century and was now still more marked.

The metropolis of the province, Ancyra, appears surprisingly rarely in the narrative. Its leading citizens are described as *protectores*, one of whom married Theodore's mother (25. 6) and who, collectively, were responsible for bringing Theodore to their city to help put an end to a plague which was afflicting men and cattle.[39] Some of the leading citizens of Ancyra had vested interests in the area around Sykeon. Megethius who collected imperial taxes from the region would probably have had property there himself (148); another Ancyran *ktetor* sent an agent (ἐπίτροπος) to handle matters concerning his estates there (162. 82); and we get a glimpse of the way in which property might have been transferred to Ancyran citizens, through the marriage of Theodore's mother to a *protector* there (25). In the event the marriage was childless and her dowry would have reverted to Theodore. Had heirs been born, they would presumably have had first claim on her property (33).

The role of the *protectores* at Ancyra seems to have been filled at Pessinus, the metropolis of Galatia Salutaris, by *domestici*, who in the company of the local clergy and many common people also successfully besought Theodore to bring an end to a drought in their city (101. 5–6). The leading men of Anastasiopolis are most commonly described as *ktetores* (= *possessores*), or property owners (58. 1–6; 78. 23; 169. 42–3), although they are also called *oiketores* (75. 7) and there is one mention of a *protector* (76. 3–5). *Ktetor* was the most widespread term used to denote men of substance. One of Theodore's early visitors from beyond the immediate neighbourhood of Sykeon was a distinguished *ktetor*

from Heracleia Pontica (44. 1–2) and *ktetores* are also once mentioned in a rural context, as members of the village communities of south Galatia near Kinna (67. 1–2). Two leading citizens of Amorium are called *illustres* (107. 7, 22), those of Dorylaeum were *oiketores* (130. 13), while the non-clerical population of Germia were simply undistinguished laymen (108. 44) or citizens (71. 47). Comparable terms are found in fifth- and sixth-century inscriptions from central Asia Minor. There were *domestici* at Tavium,[40] and most pertinently *ktetores* at Hadrianopolis and the other cities of Honorias, which were mentioned in the letter sent to the city bishops by the imperial authorities in Constantinople.[41]

Local leadership, on the other hand, lay exclusively with the Church, in the hands of bishops or archbishops. There is no sign that any of the civic magistrates of the earlier empire still existed. The richer inhabitants were not office-holders but landowners pure and simple. Although they as individuals might wield much influence, even in defiance of the imperial government, the cities no longer constituted a significant political force, able to control and exploit their territories. When the term *archon* occurs in the Life it clearly refers to the governor of Galatia Prima, or to imperial officials in general.[42] When Theodore's family suspected that a passing troop of soldiers had abducted him, they troubled the *archon* at Ancyra to arrest the soldiers and enquire after the missing boy (19. 18–19). Governors also occasionally intervened in the affairs of the villages, usually, it seems, to local displeasure. Euphrantas, who must have governed Galatia Prima in about AD 600, twice tried to arrest men suspected of treasure-hunting in their villages. He sent men to arrest a householder of Eukraa, in the territory of Anastasiopolis, on a charge of disturbing old tombs (116. 11–15), and was barely dissuaded by a letter from Theodore from mounting a similar raid (ἐπιδρομή) against the village of Sandos in the upper Siberis valley, where a village householder was suspected of

---

[38] The modern *kaza* of Ayaş includes the region around Güdül, in the upper valley of the Girmir Çay, just as the ancient Mnizene included the upper reaches of the Siberis (36. 1–2).

[39] 45. 1–4; perhaps one of the outbreaks of bubonic plague between 555 and 561. For an inscription of a *protector* at Ancyra, see H. Miltner, *JÖAI* 20 (1937), 43 no. 47 (*AE* (1937), 96).

[40] *RECAM* ii nos. 442, 444, and perhaps 463.

[41] *SEG* xxxv (1985), 1360, see above, Ch. 18 §III n. 93. M. Whittow, 'Ruling the Late Roman and Byzantine City', *Past and Present*, 129 (1990), 3–29 argues for the continued vitality of cities in the 5th and 6th cents., under the leadership of clergy, landowners, and imperial officials with local connections. But the cities themselves retained no powers independent of these powerful groups, for instance in the form of annual magistracies, recognized secular courts, or the ability to raise and disburse public revenue.

[42] For this reason the περιβλ. καὶ μεγαλοπρ. ἄρχων Ἀκύλας, who is mentioned on a building inscription from Holanta near Germia, should be the governor of Galatia Salutaris and not, as suggested in the note to *RECAM* ii no. 142, a local magistrate.

treasure-hunting under the pretext of extending his threshing-floor (114. 15 ff.). The accounts leave it unclear whether the governor was concerned to uphold the law against disturbing graves (τυμβωρυχία), to prevent the escape of evil spirits released by the excavations (the circumstance which attracted Theodore's attention to the two cases), or simply to acquire the supposed treasure for himself or for the authorities. On another occasion Theodore sided with the local peasants against the abusive behaviour of a local overseer (τοποτηρίτης) of a later governor Ioannes, to whom he wrote, apparently asking him to put a stop to his agent's excesses (151). Governors naturally passed through Sykeon travelling to and from the capital (cf. 147. 42–5), and the visit of an *archon* at the monastery (ἀρχοντικὴ παρουσία) on one occasion prevented Theodore from going in person to a local village which had asked for his help, leading him to send a substitute instead (143. 9–10).

No doubt the collection of taxes was the most conspicuous form of imperial intrusion into the lives of local communities, but the traces which it leaves in the Life are few, in notable contrast to the evidence from central Anatolia in the later fourth century.[43] The one revealing episode concerns Megethius, a citizen of Ancyra who held the position of ἀνύτης in the territory of Anastasiopolis, charged with collecting government revenue, and who so oppressed the peasants of Sykeon that they took refuge in Theodore's monastery. Megethius, ignoring its asylum status, simply took the fugitives back, presumably with the help of associates, and had them strung up and flogged. His punishment came in the form of similar beatings inflicted first by Domnitziolus the *curopalates*, for failing to provide fresh horses at the relay station at Sykeon; and when he later reverted to his old ways, from another imperial official the *logothetes* Marcianus, who punished him for renewed oppression of the local villagers. The passage thus implies that the collection of state taxes was still a liturgy imposed on leading men in the provincial cities, and shows that they were also responsible for providing mounts for the official transport system, forms of service which had a pedigree extending back to the early empire.

Ecclesiastical organization and its financing were probably more conspicuous, and perhaps just as oppressive. The hierarchy of Church authority, which had been firmly established in the fourth century, still persisted. Elections to the bishopric were a matter for collaboration between the local clergy, the landowners, and the provincial metropolitan. Theodore was chosen to be bishop of Anastasiopolis by the city's clergy and landowners (κληρικοὶ καὶ κτήτορες) (58. 1–6); he was ordained by the archbishop Paul in Ancyra (58. 22 ff.). Correspondingly, when he left office, he first addressed the clergy and landowners (78. 23 ff.), and then offered his resignation to Paul (79. 1 ff.). The dispute that arose between them was resolved by Cyriacus, patriarch of Constantinople, after he had received petitions stating the case on either side (79. 4 ff.). The appointment of lower clergy was an episcopal prerogative, shown again by Theodore's own rapid promotion through the junior offices of reader, subdeacon, and deacon to the priesthood in two days, at the behest of Theodosius of Anastasiopolis (21. 1–19). Theodosius, or his successor, was also responsible for appointing Philumenus both to the priesthood and to become *hegoumenos* of the monastery of St Michael at Sykeon (41. 5–8). His successor, Ioannes, had to travel to Constantinople to be ordained by the patriarch (130; 133. 3–7) since the decision of Maurice had made Theodore's monastery autonomous, and directly dependent on the patriarch in the capital, not on the local bishop (82. 11–18). Ecclesiastical preferment was as much a matter for patronage as any other form of career, as is well illustrated by the case of Paul, a presbyter from Lycaonia (81. 1–2), who was cured of a crippling affliction in the monastery at Sykeon, and was subsequently promoted, on Theodore's recommendation, to be presbyter of the church of the Holy Virgin at Sykae, in the Galatian district of Constantinople. He ended his career as bishop of an Isaurian city (81. 46–50).

The Church was a wealthy, powerful, and pervasive institution. Physically there were surely churches in almost every village and town, and a great many are named in the Life. The commonest dedication was to St Michael. There were churches of the archangel Michael at Akreina near Pidron in the territory of Iuliopolis,[44] where the modern centre of the district still bears the saint's name and is called Mihaliççik, at Eukraa (116. 45) and at Skoudris, a village close to the Sangarius, either in the valley of the Skopas or of the Siberis (141. 2). The most important shrine of St Michael, however, was at Germia (71. 5; 100. 11, 15). One of Theodore's most conspicuous miracles occurred during a great gathering here, which had attracted visitors not only from the neighbouring village, but also bishops from Claneos, an obscure town in the central plateau near Amorium,[45] another unnamed city, and a high-

---

[43] See above, Ch. 17 § v.

[44] 79. 25–6. The place is to be located at Ikikilisse ('Two Churches', now renamed Ikizafer 'Two Victories') on the strength of a dedication to Zeus Akreinenos which was found there by Anderson, *JHS* 19 (1899), 71–2 no. 22 (*RECAM* ii no. 75).

[45] For which see *MAMA* i. pp. xxvii–xxviii, and vii. p. ix, where it is identified with Durgut.

ranking clergyman sent from Constantinople by the patriarch.[46] An inscription found in the village of Yürme (now renamed Gümüşkonak) commends the body of a certain Stephanos to the archangel Michael,[47] and it is certain that the large, five-aisled fifth-century Byzantine church which can still be seen there was in fact the σεβάσμιος οἶκος of St Michael mentioned by the Life. In this case there can be no doubt that the modern toponym Yürme preserves the ancient name Germia.[48] The fame of the site as a centre of pilgrimage extended far bayond Galatia. Germia was an autocephalous bishopric directly dependent on the patriarch, not subordinate to the local metropolitan of Pessinus. It had been visited by Justinian, and is mentioned by Gregory of Tours.[49] The gatherings there were evidently so important and impressive that some of the later episcopal *notitiae* simply refer to it as Synodium,[50] and in Theodore's day it was so dominated by its famous shrine that it was popularly known locally as τοὺς Ἀρχαγγέλους (167. 34).

Elsewhere in Galatia there were churches of St Theodore (probably the popular soldier saint from Euchaita in Pontus) at Briania (113. 2); of St Eirenicus at Mazamia on the upper Siberis (36. 10–11); of John the Baptist at Trapeza (14. 22–3); a monastery of St Stephen at Vetapa near Kinna (66. 1–2); and a monastery τῶν Δρυινῶν in the same area with a church dedicated to St Paul (64. 2; 27). At Iuliopolis an annual vigil was held for an otherwise unknown St Heuretus (13. 20–1), and there was another famous annual festival of the Virgin at the village of Mousge between Germia and Eudoxias (71. 5–9). Pessinus had a cathedral of St Sophia (the seat of the metropolitan within the city), and a church of the Myriangeloi outside the walls (101). The cathedral at Anastasiopolis was also dedicated to St Sophia (61. 9) and Amorium had an extra-mural church of the Blessed Virgin, while its καθολικὴ καὶ πρώτη ἐκκλησία lay within the walls (107). There were well-known churches of the Virgin also at Heracleia Pontica (43) and at Sozopolis (formerly Apollonia) to which Theodore made a pilgrimage (108). Travelling through Dorylaeum on a journey to Constantinople he stopped at a monastery of St George, called Pegae (130. 15), and the section of the Life which gives a detailed account of his stay in the region of Nicomedia, refers to churches or monasteries of St George, St Anthimus, St Autonomus, St Christopher, the Virgin Mary, St Theodore, and St Michael (156–9).

Churches and monasteries were financed by gifts, and by income, presumably above all from their land. We have already seen how Theodore's aunt and grandmother bequeathed him their wealth, which enabled him in due course to build the large churches of St Michael and St George, and how these foundations in their turn benefited from gifts and endowments made by the emperor Maurice and the *curopalates* Domnitziolus. When the *comes* Bonosus passed

---

[46] τοῦ θεοφιλεστάτου πρωτεκδίκου καὶ πρωτοπρεσβυτέρου τῆς ἁγιωτάτης τοῦ Θεοῦ μεγάλης Κωνσταντινουπόλεως τότε κατελθόντος ἀπὸ τοῦ πατριάρχου (161. 68–70, cf. 103 where we learn that his name was Theodore). His presence is surely to be explained by the fact that Germia was an autocephalous bishopric, and the patriarch had accordingly sent his own representative to the festival.

[47] *RECAM* ii no. 130.

[48] For the topography see M. Waelkens, *Byzantion*, 49 (1979), 447–64, who argues that Germia should be placed at Hamamkarahisar and Eudoxias at Yürme; criticized by K. Belke 'Germia und Eudoxias', *Byzantios: Festschrift H. Hunger* (1984), 1–11, who firmly restates the old case for placing Germia at Yürme. For the church, which is built on a grand scale, see above, Ch. 18 §III at n. 66, and J. W. Crowfoot, *ABSA* 4 (1897), 86–92 with a plan which is reproduced with minimal changes by Ballance, *Reallexicon zur byzantinischen Kunst*, ii (1971), 611 Abb. 2 and by C. Mango, *J.öst.Byz.* 36 (1986), 177–32. The scale of this building, which is highly suitable for a large centre of pilgrimage, and the survival of the ancient toponym in the mordern Yürme are the two chief arguments for placing Germia here. In addition, the Life at 161. 65 and 94 indicates that the village Goeleounta, modern Holanta (see H. Grégoire, *Byzantion*, 11 (1936), 537–9; Waelkens, *Byzantion* (1979), 459), was in the near vicinity (πλησίον, 161. 65). Holanta is 3 km. from Yürme. Waelkens on the other hand relied heavily on a Byzantine inscription found at Holanta, which marked the boundary between the city of Eudoxias and a community called the Ocondiani (*RECAM* ii. no. 137), to place Eudoxias at Yürme. He argued further that the toponym Germia, which is etymologically linked to Therma/Thermia, should be associated with hot springs, which exist not at Yürme but 16 km. NW at Hamamkarahisar. Further, while Theodore was the guest of the bishop of Germia, he stayed at the monastery of Aligete, said to be 15 m.p. (22.5 km.) from Pessinus (101. 3–7). This closely corresponds with the overland distance between Hamamkarahisar and Balıhisar, the site of Pessinus; Yürme, however, lay at least 26 m.p. (40 km.) away. The best solution is to place Germia at Yürme, where the remains correspond perfectly with those of an autocephalous cathedral church, which became an important pilgrimage centre. However, the whole area at least as far as the springs at Hamamkarahisar belonged to Germia's territory, and the monastery of Aligete might well have been located there. This still leaves no site for Eudoxias, which was clearly a separate settlement, not a new name for Germia. The only positive evidence for its position remains the boundary stone, which was found in a cemetery close to the Ilk Okul at Holanta (cf. I. W. Macpherson, *AS* 22 (1972), 219). It could have been carried from elsewhere in the neighbourhood.

[49] E. Honigmann, 'Pour l'atlas byzantin. I. Germia', *Byzantion*, 11 (1936), 542–3. For Justinian's visit, see Theophanes, *Chron.* 1. 240. 12 (de Boor). Gregory of Tours explains why the place became a pilgrimage centre: it contained a fragment of the tunic which Christ had worn (*MGH scrip. rer. Mer.* i (1885), 493; *PL* lxxi. 712c).

[50] See Ramsay, *HGAM* 225 identifying it with Eudoxias, and the table opposite p. 222. The Life calls the church at Germia κοσμοθεωρητόν (161. 2).

through in 610, he distributed a sum of money to all the monks (142. 35 ff.). One nearby village dedicated one of its vineyards to the monastery, as a thank-offering to the saint who had saved their vintage from a hailstorm (144); another, after identical service, made an annual contribution of a fixed quantity of wine and grapes (52. 13–16). The collection of Church dues, however, could lead to trouble. The *oikonomos* of the church at Iuliopolis was responsible for bringing in the revenues from its estates. When the subordinate to whom he had delegated the task absconded with the money (he was eventually tracked down in a place near Nicaea), the *oikonomos* was held responsible, doubtless by his bishop, for making up the lost income (34). At Anastasiopolis the church appears to have collected its dues by contracting the task to a local *protector* called Theodosius. When Theodore intervened on behalf of the peasants of the village of Eukraa to prevent him from extorting money from them, Theodosius demanded two *litra* of gold coin in compensation, presumably equivalent to or more than the amount which he had paid for the privilege of collecting the church's rents. The farming of Church revenues, no less than the liturgy of state taxes, led to abusive exactions.

The conflict with Theodosius seems to have led to an unhappy period for Theodore. Shortly afterwards some men allegedly attempted to poison him (77). He then began to be criticized for wasting the church's livelihood by over-generous gifts to the needy in the city and in his monasteries. He himself received an annnual income of a *nomisma* a day, 365 *per annum*, and defended himself by saying that he kept only forty, giving the rest to the church. However, the charges that he was unfit to govern the see persisted, and he was driven to offer his resignation as bishop (78). It is surely no coincidence that shortly afterwards Theodore obtained autonomous status for his monastery in Constantinople (82). If not, he would have remained subordinate to his successor as bishop of Anastasiopolis, which would not merely have been a serious affront to his pride and self-respect, but a certain source of further dispute and controversy.

These events provide at least one, graphically documented explanation of why a cleric in the late empire might prefer to become a monk, and wield his influence by an assertion of spiritual power, rather than assume the arduous and taxing duties of a bishop, whose role was as much that of a politician as of a priest. There was much to be said at a very practical level for being of the community but not in it, and the unhappy experiences of Theodore as bishop supply another reason why the landscape of late Roman Anatolia began to be dotted with monks, ascetics, hermits, and stylites, each seeking not only personal fulfilment, but a

favoured niche in society, not by becoming ensnared in its intractable toils and conflicts, but by withdrawing into physical isolation. They would not, of course, be completely inaccessible, for that would wipe out all the credit due to conspicuous asceticism. As St Simeon Stylites chose his pillar at Qal 'at Seman, within easy reach of Syrian Antioch, so a follower, the stylite Carinus, established himself close to the main highway between Constantinople and Nicomedia where Theodore sought him out (155. 9 ff.). Around the walls of Nicomedia there was a whole community of hermits, including John the Syrian and the virgin Moschous (159. 89–103). Theodore's own followers were conspicuous among those who sought these well-publicized retreats. Evagrius stayed behind in the Laura of St Sabas after a pilgrimage to the Holy Land to join the famous monastic community there (47. 18–20); Andreas became a hermit at Briania, eight miles (13 km.) from Sykeon (48. 6–10); Arsinus a stylite near the village of Galenoi on the upper Siberis (48. 11–23). Reparatus entered a cell at Colonosos in Lycaonia (49. 5–10), while Elpidius was another who did not return from pilgrimage and led an ascetic life on Mount Sinai (49. 10–15). Galatian monks in the Holy Land recognized and made much of Theodore when he visited them (50. 12–19). Another Theodore led the life of a hermit on Mount Dracon in Bithynia,[51] and later became *hegoumenos* of the monastery of St Autonomus there. Others from Sykeon who went on to head their own monasteries include Stephanus, who became *hegoumenos* of St Theodore Stratelates beside the river Psilis in Bithynia (49. 25–8), and Photius and Kerykos, in charge of the monastery of St George Pegae at Dorylaeum (130. 14–15). Monasticism and asceticism, even when practised in a country whose winter climate was thought too harsh for hermits,[52] offered not only spiritual enrichment, but a form of *otium* which a bishop could never hope to enjoy.

It is evident that much of the unique value of the Life as a contribution to the social history of Asia Minor lies not so much in the areas which have already been discussed, but in its detailed and unselfconscious depiction of life in rural settings. The countryside of north-west Galatia in modern times retains all the characteristics of the central Anatolian steppe: treeless hillsides, notably parched in the summer months, and now largely given over to the growing of cereals; rivers and streams that are virtually dry in summer, but turbulent torrents in early spring after the snows melt in the north, supporting willows or poplars, and sometimes trained to irrigate gardens and orchards. One of the earliest European travellers to note down what he

[51] 49. 23; for the river Dracon see Procopius, *Aed.* 5. 2. 6–13.
[52] Sozomen, *HE* 6. 34.

saw here was Pitton de Tournefort, who observed that most of the countryside around Beypazarı was dry and denuded, providing thin but adequate pasture for the herds of Angora goat. He compared the landscape to Livy's *axylon*, the treeless country where the only fuel was cow dung.[53] In the town itself he saw mills for raising the level of the water for irrigation, and recorded that the place produced excellent pears, the so-called *poires d'Angora*, which were sold in Constantinople. At a rather earlier date the Turkish geographer Haci Halfa described Ayaş as a well-populated town, the most important place in a region that extended to Beypazarı in the west, Yerköy in the south, and Güdül in the north. The last, beside the Girmir Çay, lay in a rice-growing area, as it does today.[54] A century after Tournefort, in the early nineteenth century, another French traveller, Ange de Gardane, briefly described both Beypazarı and Ayaş, the latter lying eleven hours journey further east. Beypazarı, a town of 1,000 houses was set in a fine plain traversed by the Aladağ Çay, where 4,000–5,000 quintals of rice were produced every year. Ayaş was now smaller, with 600 houses, and had lead- and silver-mines nearby. Rice and cotton were grown in the area (surely in the Girmir valley), but it was above all rich in livestock; 1,000 cattle were exported annually (to Constantinople) and there were flocks of up to 45,000 goats, supporting an important wool industry.[55] Georges Perrot in 1862 was less impressed, or less observant. Beypazarı he described as a small town with few resources, cursed with the most disagreeable summer climate that his party had encountered. There were 800 houses, with no greenery except in the torrent below the town that flowed down to the Sakarya. The road from Beypazarı to Ayaş crossed a true desert of scorched hillsides and waterless ravines. But he too noticed the flocks of Angora goats, and also the village women threshing the grain with sleds pulled by oxen, while their men looked on from the shade of a canopy stretched out between two rocks.[56] The English officer Captain Burnaby rode through Nallıhan, then a village of about 400 houses in a corn-growing district, past Çayırhan, where the country was entirely uncultivated, but not, he thought, without promise, to

Beypazarı and Ayaş.[57] Finally Cuinet, in his great survey of geographical information and statistics, compiled at the end of the nineteenth century, listed as principal products, the mohair of Ayaş; the pears, melons, rice, and vines of Beypazarı; and the rice, opium poppies, and silk of Nallıhan.[58]

The scanty evidence for Roman agricultural practice in the area, principally relating to viticulture, has already been discussed.[59] The Life of St Theodore provides a far fuller picture, although it remains significantly different from the one portrayed by modern travellers. Cereal agriculture and viticulture predominated. A passage which describes the exhaustion of grain at Theodore's monastery during Lent, that dangerous period at the end of winter when last year's supplies might be exhausted, but before a fresh harvest or even a spring crop of beans and legumes was available, seems to imply that ἄλευρον, barley, was a more important crop than wheat (104). Galatian barley was, in fact, famous.[60] The land beside the Siberis at Sykeon was given over to cereals (45. 15 ff.); cereals and vines were cultivated at Mazamia, higher up the river (36. 1–6), and also in the village of Kalpinos (35. 15). There were threshing-floors around the village of Sandos, also in the upper Siberis valley (114. 2), haystacks at Eukraa (116. 22–7), and cereal crops growing in the plain which belonged to the *trikomia* of Bouna, Peia, and Hynia (118. 1–5). Bread was naturally a staple food (15. 16; 28. 22; 30. 31) and wooden storage containers were built at the monastery in Sykeon for grain and dried vegetable products (ὄσπρια) (69. 1–10).

Vineyards were apparently equally widespread. Besides being mentioned at Kalpinos and Mazamia, they are noted also at Sandos and Permetaia (115. 45–50), at Reake near Sykeon (52. 2–7), and at Apoukome and its neighbour Halioi (144. 1–6; 150. 10–11). While none of these villages can be precisely located they all appear to lie in the Siberis valley, or at least within easy distance of Sykeon, and this distribution corresponds almost precisely with the indications from the Roman period that vines were an important crop in the valleys close to Iuliopolis (see above, Vol. I, Ch. 10 §1 nn. 36–7). The monastery at Sykeon, like one near Nicomedia (160. 14), contained a wine cellar, and the saint was able to offer a choice vintage to Heraclius when he passed rapidly through in 613 (166. 10).

Other vegetables were certainly grown. The ὄσπρια stored through the winter in the monastery were probably edible pulses, and green vegetables (λάχανα)

[53] Pitton de Tournefort, *Relation d'un voyage du Levant*, iii. 21 (1717), 335. For the use of dry dung (*tezek*) as fuel, see L. Robert, *JSav.* (1961), 115 ff. (*OMS* vii. 19 ff.).

[54] French trans. of the original publication of 1648 by Armain in Vivien de St Martin, *Histoire des descouverts géographiques des nations européennes*, iii, *Asie Mineure* (1846), 703 ff. The village name Çeltikçi found in the Girmir valley reflects local rice production.

[55] Ange de Gardane, *Journal d'un voyage de la Turquie d'Asie et la Perse fait en 1807 et 1808* (1809).

[56] *Revue des deux mondes* 2ᵉ per. 44. (1863), 119 ff., 125; *Exploration archéologique de la Galatie* (1862), 217.

[57] *On Horseback through Asia Minor*, i (1877), 95–106.

[58] *La Turquie d'Asie*, i (1890), 285–6.

[59] Above, Vol. I, Ch. 10 §1 nn. 35–7.

[60] Columella, 2. 9. 16.

are mentioned in several contexts. Theodore saved a crop of young green vegetables from locusts near Pessinus (101. 11 ff.) and they are frequently mentioned as part of the diet: a dish of assorted vegetables and fruit (16. 32; cf. 19. 27); a monk's meal of bread, with meagre vegetables or pulses (μετὰ λεπτολαχάνων ἢ ὀσπρίων), and water not wine (47. 4–5); and the dish of stewed vegetables which was alarmingly contaminated by a lizard (124. 9). When Theodore at the age of 14 withdrew from his home to spend time in the *martyrium* of St George, his concerned family brought him a generous meal of bread, fowl, and various cooked things (15. 1–8); the emperor Heraclius was offered bread made from pure wheat flour (σιλιγνίον), and apples (μῆλα) as well as choice wine (166. 10). At the other extreme, during Lent one might eat no more than a sort of biscuit made from boiled grain (κόλλυβα) (6. 10–13) with water. The saint, during his early retreats between Epiphany and Palm Sunday, ate no more than some fruit or some stewed vegetables, on Saturdays and Sundays alone (16. 31–3; 28. 22–5), or there was the diet of the ascetic Antiochus who had eschewed wine and olive oil for sixty years, and had not even tasted bread for thirty. He subsisted on raw vegetables with salt, a relish, and plain water (73. 8–11).[61] As a rule no meat was eaten in the monastery, except three times a year at festivals (69. 6–7), and pork was explicitly forbidden in the church of St George (70. 7). The story that a whole village suffered food-poisoning after feasting on the meat of one of its oxen which had been slaughtered is told in terms that suggest, as one would expect, that meat-eating was an unusual occurrence (143).

The description of diet has implied that local livestock included cattle, pigs, and domestic fowls, presumably chickens. Of these, cattle were certainly the most important, above all as draught-animals. Ox-drawn wagons were used for bringing lime the eight miles (12 km.) from Arkea to Sykeon (56. 1 ff.) Pestilence was to be feared as much as the slayer of cattle, as it was the scourge of men (45. 1–4). There is no explicit evidence that cattle were used for milk production, or as the basis of a leather industry, and although neither potential was likely to be ignored, both were surely secondary importance. Mules were also used for draught or transport (99. 1), but the term most often used to describe riding-animals is κτῆνος, which is more likely to refer to donkeys than to mules or horses.[62]

The animals belonging to a village community were most commonly simply called ἄλογα, beings without speech or reason, without further specification.[63] No doubt these included sheep and goats, as well as cattle and horses, but by far the most remarkable fact about the references to animals in the Life is the total absence of any specific mention of sheep or goats. In the eighteenth and nineteenth century they were the mainstay of the economy, especially the Angora goat. It seems clear by contrast that the basis of the region's livelihood in the late sixth and seventh century, on the eve of the Persian invasions, was agriculture and viticulture, not pastoralism.

Raw materials for construction and manufacture were not abundant. Theodore's iron cage, in which he passed much of his early manhood, was made not from iron ore, but from re-smelted agricultural tools.[64] In Antiquity, as today, the country east of the wooded mountains of east Bithynia was largely treeless, it is thus no surprise that the adjacent villages of Halioi and Apoukome should have had a violent dispute over access to the products of a wooded area that lay between them.[65]

The context in which the chief elements of the rural economy tend to appear in the Life are the accounts of miracles by the saint where he intervened to avert disaster or ward off pestilence. Throughout central Anatolia rainfall was the key to all prosperity (see above, Vol. I, Ch. 10 §1); Theodore's first recorded miracle, achieved in collaboration with a holy man called Glycerius, brought clouds to a clear sky, and rain to the parched countryside at a place called Trapeza, ten miles (15 km.) from Sykeon (14); much later, one of his most conspicuous feats was to end a drought at Pessinus (101). When his Galatian compatriots talked about him in the Holy Land, they called him the man who could, with a single prayer, fill the whole world with rain (50. 12–19). Rainfall, however, could bring disaster as well as prosperity. The principal rivers of the region, the Scopas and the Siberis, were liable to

---

61 For other evidence on diet from the early Byzantine period, see the material analysed by Patlagéan, *Pauvreté*, 36–53.

62 There are only rare references in the Life to horses (ἵπποι). One belonged to the *topoterites* of the provincial governor (151. 15), another to an *oikodespotes* of the village of Sandos (149.

38; cf. 99. 10). For travel ἐπὶ κτηνοῦς, see 68. 3–4; 81. 2; 115. 11–16. The gentry, such as the bishop of Kadossia from Bithynia (102. 1), two grand ladies of Ephesus (110. 3), or the invalid imperial *a secretis* Phocas (121. 28) might be carried on litters. The term βαδίστης was sometimes used for the pack-animal which Theodore used (157. 30, 33; 160. 56).

63 26a. 21; 38. 2; 43. 15; 99. 11 (contrasted with horses); 107. 23 (where they should be identified with horses, cf. 109. 17–20); 56. 15 and 98. 13 (for oxen); 114. 9; 116. 32; 141. 10; 157. 2; 158. 5; 160. 45 (of a camel); 160. 70 (oxen).

64 27. 5; note that Theodore also wore iron rings on his feet and hands, weighing 15 *litra*, a cross with a collar weighing 18 *litra*, and a belt weighing 33 *litra* (28–34). Then, by chance, he acquired an iron tunic (*lorica*) weighing 50 *litra* (28. 1–4).

65 150. Carpenters, ξυλουργοί, made fittings at the monastery (69. 1–10).

burst their banks and cause serious havoc after heavy downpours or when the snows melted (cf. 141. 21), most commonly, one presumes, in early spring. At Sykeon itself, the arable land was liable to flooding, and men could be drowned trying to cross the river, a point which is precisely confirmed by Procopius.[66] The Scopas was equally dangerous. As we have seen Justinian had had to reinforce the walls of Iuliopolis to prevent their being undermined,[67] and on one occasion its waters almost washed away the village of Karya (53. 1–3). The village of Skoudris was also located in one of these valleys, most probably the Scopas too, and so much rain fell there that the stream simply washed away half its houses, carrying off animals, men, women and children, babies in their cradles, and the chickens from the yards, down into the Sangarius beyond reach of safety (141). The village elders called in Theodore to prevent similar cloudbursts and floods in the future.[68] An unwitting consequence of Theodore's prayers for rain at Pessinus was that the river Gallus, an intermittent torrent flowing down from the slopes of Mount Dindymus, overflowed its banks and flooded the western half of the town, as can still happen in the modern village of Balıhisar.[69]

Violent storms were also a direct hazard to crops, especially to the vines. Theodore protected the grape harvests from devastation by hail at Reake a village close to Sykeon (52. 2–7), at Apoukome (144. 1–6), and at Halioi (150. 1–11). Heavy rain was a more alarming threat to the wagons full of lime being brought to build the church of St George at Sykeon (56). Vines and crops were threatened by other pests, like the grubs at the village of Permetaia (115, 44–50), or the destructive beetles in the harvest at the *trikomia* of Bouna, Peia, and Hynia (118. 21). But the most serious danger was from locusts. In the upper Siberis valley Theodore warded off a June swarm of locusts from the cereal crops and ripening vines at Mazamia (36. 1–6), and later protected the vintage at Sandos from a similar attack (115. 44–50). On the occasion of his visit to Pessinus to relieve the drought there, he made a specific visit to gardens six miles (9 km.) from the city to protect them from locust swarms which were attacking the newly sprouted vegetables (101. 11–32).

It would be an exaggeration to say that the well-being of the region was poised on a knife edge between success and failure, plenty and famine. The overall picture conveyed by the *Life* is of successful, settled rural communities, by no means plunged into abject poverty or destitution. But the many interventions of the saint at crucial moments for the harvest or vintage, or to protect men and livestock from disease, simply underline the fact that in self-sufficient rural communities there was little protective insulation between an adequate living, and no life at all.

These villages themselves contained men and families of genuine substance. The commonest term for a householder is *oikodespotes*, used to describe the leading inhabitants of Alektoria (98. 1), Sandos (114. 1; 115. 43; 149. 1–2), Eukraa (116. 38; 118. 4), and Skoudris (141. 16). At Sandos the *oikodespotai* are equated with the leading men of the village (οἱ πρῶτοι τοῦ χωρίου; 115. 8–9), and the group from the same village who put to flight a party of malcontents, who had violently attacked a proprietor suspected of having disturbed evil demons, are described as οἱ ἐν αὐτοῖς τὰ πρῶτα τελοῦντες πρεσβεῦται, elders who held the leading positions in the community (114. 20–1). Characteristically, no doubt, their part in this episode was to restore and maintain the equilibrium of village life. Elsewhere we find the term *ktetores* in the villages of south Galatia (67. 1–2); the leading men (simply) at Permetaia (115. 3); and heads of households (πρόοικοι) at Aiantioi (124. 1), Alektoria (124. 3–4), and Apoukome (143. 13). The last village apparently contained a formal communal organization called a *koinon*, but central institutions of village government may have been more widespread than this one example suggests. In the village of Buzaia, in the territory of the Bithynian city of Crateia, the inhabitants were able collectively to hire workmen and build a bridge over a dangerous torrent which was liable to flood (43. 1–10), and it is significant that the majority of cases where Theodore intervened in village affairs were prompted by an invitation from the leading men acting as a group (cf. 116. 38; 118. 4).

The repeated appearance of masters of houses, heads of households, property-owners and leading men in the villages of the region surely demonstrates that north-west Galatia was still inhabited by a resilient free peasantry, capable of standing up for themselves whatever their obligations to state and Church. The episodes that show them in conflict with provincial governors or other revenue collectors are better evidence for a tough, stiff-necked peasant autonomy—inevitably breeding minor conflict between local farmers and the representatives of distant and

---

[66] Procopius, *Aed.* 5. 4. 1.

[67] Procopius, *Aed.* 5. 3. 5–6.

[68] Two further miracles were recorded in the *Oration to St Michael* of Michael Psellos (see above, n. 31), at 128. 3–10, and in the *Encomium of Theodore of Sykeon* by Nicephorus Sceuophylax, K. Kirch, *Anal. Boll.* 20 (1901), 249–72 at 261. 9–13. In this case Theodore adjudicated a dispute between two villages about which was the rightful owner of the fruit of a tree which had been washed downstream from one village to the other. The saint miraculously transported the tree back to its original site!

[69] M. Waelkens, 'Pessinonte et le Gallos', *Byzantion*, 41 (1971), 349–73, esp. 352.

sometimes oppressive systems of administration—than they are for a population overwhelmed by oppressive demands and constant harassment to become no more than serfs.

This brings us to the final, and most difficult subject to analyse, the powers of the saint himself, and the nature of his position within the society. There is much that can be readily explained. By his spectacular displays of ascetic heroism in his youth he had clearly earned a moral ascendancy over his immediate community, publicly acknowledged by the local bishop who precipitately elevated him to the priesthood. Family means, and his own enterprise, enabled him to cash in on this reputation, and expand the nucleus of church buildings which already existed at Sykeon, thereby creating a thriving monastery complex, which grew as the years passed and its facilities were improved (55. 1 ff.). The site on the main highway across Asia Minor could hardly have been better chosen. The road east, after all, led to Jerusalem, and not only Theodore's own three visits to the Holy Land, but also the passage of many other pilgrims will have enhanced his own saintly reputation and spread word of his achievements. The road west led to Constantinople, and gave access to sources of power and patronage which he never ignored. Nevertheless Theodore's charisma rested above all on what he had achieved locally. The point is made clear by the three chapters of the Life which are the nearest thing to a summary of his whole achievement. He was called upon when the crops or vines were attacked by beetles, locusts, worms, or mice; when cloudbursts struck, or rivers overflowed their banks; when pestilence broke out among the farm animals, or among men. Within the villages themselves he freed those who were enthralled by evil spirits; reconciled couples at odds with one another; and blessed the childless so that they would have offspring. He ministered to the sick and the unhealthy not so much as a priest but, explicitly, as an experienced doctor, recommending surgery or purges, medicines, or visits to hot springs. He gave counsel to men who were at odds with themselves, and fixed the appropriate measure of repentance for their sins and transgressions by calling for fasting, prayer, and acts of charity. He attempted to bring together disputing parties rather than let them work out their mutual hostility in lawsuits; instead he urged them to complete acts of piety and charity. He protected those who were oppressed by officials, and offered refuge for fugitives from arbitrary injustice (145–7).

Much of this can be intelligibly rationalized. The author of the Life makes no claim for Theodore's cures that they were anything more than might have been achieved by a skilled physician, or for his interventions between disputing parties that they were other than the

actions of a good counsellor or able diplomat. But beyond this there was a miraculous element; Theodore could tap sources of power as other men could not. He could cause the rain to fall or to cease, plague to recede and pests to die; above all he could exorcise demons and evil spirits which dwelt in men, animals, and places, ready to take possession, or to linger undetected until the confrontation with the saint. It is here, in this sharp and manifest conflict between good and evil, that we begin to be confronted with the basic belief system of this rural early Byzantine population.

II. The Making of a Holy Man

At a straightforward level, the Life of St Theodore is clearly an invaluable source of information for the material circumstances and rural social organization of sixth- and seventh-century Galatia. But there is far more to it than this; for to study it simply for what it has to say about villages and crops, roads and travellers, church foundations, and the governors and the governed is like reading Hamlet but ignoring the prince. For the Life was written to provide an inspiring and exemplary account of the doings of a holy man, who, by tapping sources of divine power was able to assume a vitally important role in the community at large. That divine power is not incidental to the account but provides the raison d'être for its composition. It was not something detachable from real life, but a palpable part of it, without which the existence of individuals and communities could not be contemplated. So the society cannot be understood without some attempt to grasp the nature of this power. Moreover the wealth of graphic, or rather precisely ethnographic material which characterizes every page of the Life, provides the means by which to throw light on this divine power in action.

The first object of attention is the holy man, Theodore himself. On the night of his conception his mother Maria claimed to have seen a vision of a great star descending from the heavens into her womb. She reported the dream in turn to Cosmas the father of the child (3. 17–24), to an old man with alleged powers to see the future (4. 1–12), and to the bishop of Anastasiopolis (4. 13–15), all of whom confirmed that the child was destined for greatness in the eyes of God. Stories of similar dreams, their interpretation and fulfilment can be found in almost every culture and at any period; it is fortunate that the Life advances from this banal starting point to show in detail that a holy man was made, not born.

In the narrative chapters that describe Theodore's early years, the key elements in this process are clearly identifiable: the guidance of a divine patron, in this case the warrior Saint George, who appeared repeatedly

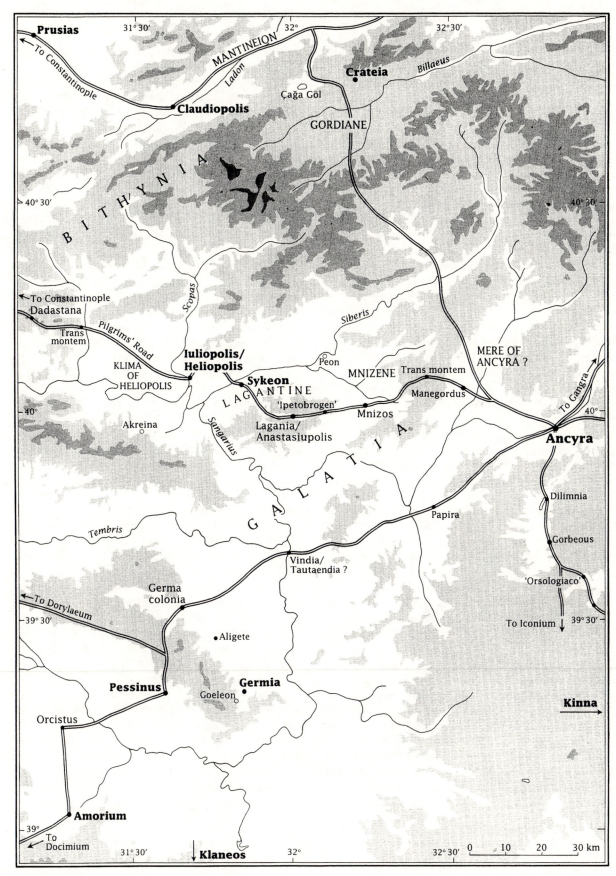

Map 5. The world of Theodore of Sykeon

at crucial moments in visions both to the boy and to those close to him, thus guiding him along the path towards holiness; an increasing devotion to prayer and study of the Bible; an ever more abstemious and ascetic regime of life; progressive withdrawal from the world, and in particular from his family, to isolation; and, crucially, the gradual discovery of an ability to perform miraculous feats. Each of these recurring elements is characterized in some detail.

St George first appeared not to Theodore but to his mother, and stopped her from sending the 6-year-old boy to find a future in Constantinople, presumably with his father there (5. 12–17). Two or three years later the saint appeared to Theodore himself, and led him to his *martyrium* on the hillside, where he would study the holy books after his lessons at school (7. 3–4). Later, when Theodore had recovered from the plague, he again appeared to lead him at night to his rocky chapel (8. 12), and when his mother and other female relatives tried to prevent this, he threatened them with his sword until they released the boy (9. 25–7). He was to protect Theodore from the temptation of the devil (11. 26–9), and later appeared to drive off a black demon which had afflicted him with a serious illness (17).

These early episodes are no more than a prelude to the recurrent presence of St George throughout Theodore's life.[70] They are interesting in that they suggest that the company of the saint, or the presence of the devil and his ministers, was something that became more real and vivid to Theodore after initial unfamiliarity. At first when St George led him by night to the chapel on the mountainside, we are told that he took the form of Theodore's early mentor, Stephanus; only later did he appear in his true form (8. 8–19); likewise the devil who tempted him to destroy himself by leaping from a cliff took the shape of a schoolmate, Gerontius (11. 8 ff.), but the demon which brought on his illness was simply a foul black spirit (17). One learned to recognize the agents of good and evil in one's fellow men, and thereafter those agents became more real than the human form which they took.

These agents were a ubiquitous and indispensable part of man's theological outlook. Of the devil himself—that is of a single source of evil in the world—we hear little; but demons, or evil spirits were present everywhere. God himself was a figure and a power of awesome remoteness, to be reached by prayer, but beyond imagination.[71] Instead one could stretch out

for help to his saints, whose churches and chapels since the fourth century had spread across the face of the countryside and provided communities with a much more intimate form of divine protection.[72] The sense of distance between man and God, and the place of saints in the divine hierarchy, is nowhere better conveyed than by the story of an illness of Theodore, who prayed to the saints Cosmas and Damian for a safe recovery. Cosmas and Damian intervened with the angels, who alone could approach God, the arbiter of life and death. They returned in the company of a tall young man, like themselves but more glorious, the archangel Michael, to tell Cosmas and Damian that Theodore was allowed to live (39).[73]

The interpretation of the visions of saints is fraught with pitfalls, but it is clearly inadequate to regard them simply as the production of an individual and personal mentality. Theodore's own remarkable personality, and the heightened receptivity to divine visions which was implicit in the very fact of being a holy man, may have been responsible for the form which they took, for the occasions when they occurred, for their frequency, and for the significance which he attached to them. But they were reported to others, and recorded by his followers, not as something peculiar to him, but as significant for the whole community. No one disputed the authority of these visions, or questioned them as the channel by which the divine will was transmitted to men. Dreams and apparitions were as real and substantial evidence for the presence of saints as the countless churches which men had dedicated to them.

For all that, the springs of human action did not lie in saintly prompting. Man was responsible for his own actions, at least when he acted for the good, and he therefore had to be trained for the task. The other elements in Theodore's early upbringing are reassuringly concrete in substance, and reinforced one another to create his powerful and inflexible personality. His predilection for solitary prayer and study of the Bible, leading to conflict, defiance, and dissociation from his family, began as soon as he had learned to read, at the age of 8 (5). In one of these early years during Lent, following the example of Stephanus, the pious cook attached to the inn, he refused food after the end of his classes; instead he would accompany Stephanus to the churches on the hillside, and share dry wafers and water with him when they returned home at the end of the day (6. 24–31). This behaviour persisted through his childhood, in defiance of the wishes of his concerned relations, who tried unsuccessfully to make him

---

[70] See Festugière's *index nominum s.v.* Γεώργιος μάρτυς, especially 115. 34: εἶχε γὰρ ἐν ἑαυτῷ ἐν τούτοις συναγωνιζόμενον καὶ τὸν ἅγιον μεγαλομάρτυρα τοῦ Χριστοῦ Γεώργιον, τὸν ἐκ νηπίας ἡλικίας αὐτῷ συνεπόμενον; and 168. 29.

[71] The analogy with *Theos Hypsistos* of later pagan belief is clear, above, Ch. 16 § v.

[72] See above, at nn. 44–50 for Theodore's own world.

[73] The role of angels in the story is typical for Phrygian or Galatian popular Christianity; above, Ch. 16 § v at nn. 264–71.

take at least modest sustenance (6. 35–7; cf. 15). It led in the end to his night visits to the mountainside, the attempts to confine him at home, and the vision of St George which set a seal of approval on all this activity.

The modest asceticism of the child became extreme in his early teens. From the age of 12 he began to observe solitary winters of fasting and contemplation, which began at Theophany, that is 6 January,[74] and lasted until the last Sunday before Easter, including periods of total silence and abstention from company in the first and middle weeks of Lent (10. 12–16). In the first years he conducted his retreat in one of the rooms of the house, and during this period he had learned the Psalms by heart (13). But at 14 the withdrawal was accentuated when he moved to the chapel of St George on the mountainside (15), where he dug himself a cave in which to live (16). Precisely at the same period he began to subject himself to tests of ascetic endurance which were to dominate the next several years of his life. He spent the night of Christmas at the crossing point of the river Siberis, reading the Gospels, the works of the prophets and the Acts of the Apostles. At the end of his vigil he could scarcely remove himself from the ice and the mud to make the climb up to his cave, where he remained until Palm Sunday (16. 21–3).

The apprenticeship was rewarded by the first signs of an ability to effect cures and exorcisms (17–18), and one or two years later he resolved to emulate John the Baptist by withdrawing into the wilderness. Higher up the mountainside he dug a larger cave, walled up the entrance, and hid from the world for two years (18–19. 14). His whereabouts were known only to a single clergyman, who gave him his monk's habit (στιχάριον), and fed him from time to time on stewed vegetables and water (19. 22–8). When his relatives eventually brought him out into the open air he collapsed. His physical condition was appalling: 'His head was covered with sores and suppuration, and was filled with countless worms, so that it stank; his bones stuck out bare through the flesh, and his hair was matted together; no one could stand near him for the stench and the worms that crawled all over him. He looked like a corpse. In a word men looked on him as a new Job, on account of such suffering' (20. 16–22). Even so he refused to return to the house with them, but went back to the chapel of St George, where he was soon visited by the local bishop, who made him a reader, with difficulty cleaned his wounds, and promoted the 18-year-old Theodore to the priesthood on the following day, silencing criticism at this premature ordination (21). Soon afterwards, inspired by reading the Bible, he

undertook his first pilgrimage to the Holy Land, and attracted his first disciples (24–6).

This itself was only a prelude to greater feats of self-inflicted pain. Theodore resolved to spend future winters locked up in a cage; the first, at the request of the villagers of Sykeon, was spent in a wooden structure which they had built within the village itself (27). Then, he moved into an iron cage which they had made for him, and which they carried up in a solemn procession to the mountainside, where it was suspended in mid-air close to the church of St George. Laden with heavy iron chains around wrists and feet, a cross hanging from an iron collar, an iron belt and a coat of armour he passed two further winters in indescribable suffering. Since during daytime he denied himself even the luxury of movement, the water which ran down inside his habit froze to him, and the soles of his feet stuck to the boards on which he stood (29). At first when he moved the skin would be torn from his feet, and left on the ground like sandals, but this became too much even for him to bear and he would have a servant loosen them with warm water. There was no such weakening when he collapsed, weak from fasting, under the hot sunshine of late April; when a follower attempted to throw a drape over the cage to protect him, he was told to remove it (30).

Like most demonstrations of asceticism, Theodore's aim was in part to gain control over his body, to suppress the urgings of the flesh as he grew into manhood, and to gain the will to resist the power of the enemy and the attacks which were mounted on his virtue on every front.[75] But at the same time, like other stylites and hermits, he was bringing the spotlight of local attention on himself. As a direct consequence of his earlier privations he had been joined by his first followers and elevated to the priesthood; during his years in the cage visitors were not only expected, but catered for (31). The wish of the villagers that he spend his first year imprisoned among them underlines that he was already a local celebrity; at the end of his retreat, his grandmother Elpidia, on the verge of death, received a vision of St George who assured her that Theodore had become a saint himself (32).

Progress on the route to spiritual power and mastery was marked by quite specific episodes in which this power was first learned and demonstrated. In later life it was marked by the ability to perform miraculous, or quasi-miraculous actions. It is not difficult to draw up a rough typology of these, which reveals that by far the most important were the curing of the sick, the exorcism of evil spirits, and miracles that appeared to change the course of nature—for instance by bringing rain, causing rivers to subside, or averting pests from

---

[74] See Festugière ii. 179 n.

[75] Peter Brown, *The Body and Society, passim,* esp. 323–38.

crops. Three early incidents in his life show his first efforts in each sphere, and it is important to note that they demonstrate that Theodore's power was not considered to be something innate, but had to be acquired either by heeding the lessons of others, or through personal experience.

The first nature miracle occurred when he was barely 14 years old. Piety had led him to visit a neighbouring holy man, Glycerius, to whom he declared his intention to become a monk. It was a time of drought, and the two went out from the church of John the Baptist, and knelt in prayer in front of the apse. 'If it rains', said Glycerius, 'we shall know that we belong to the ranks of the righteous'; the sky clouded over and as they rose from their prayers the rain began to fall. 'From now on,' he continued, 'whatever you ask of the Lord will be given to you' (14. 20–35). Parallel to this story is the account of Theodore's first exorcism, performed at the same period of his life. A man came to him with his only child, who was possessed by an unclean spirit; Theodore was uncertain what to do, but the father gave him a whip and implored him to go at the child in a fury, ordering the demon to leave the child in God's name. The spirit, we are told, began to disparage him, and treated him as an impostor, mockingly repeating Theodore's words after him, and then fell silent for two days. On the third day the spirit cried out that he was leaving the boy and would contradict Theodore no more. An evil day had arrived for demons that they could be exorcized by so young a boy; full of shame he admitted that he could not bring himself to face his master, the devil. As he said this, Theodore took olive oil from the lamp that permanently lit the church, touched the boy's head, blessed him with the sign of the cross, and ordered the spirit to leave and to cease babbling. The demon cried out, flung the boy to the ground, and left him. Theodore took fright that the child might be dead, but the father told him to raise him to his feet, and he recovered at once. The outlines of this exorcistic procedure are to become familiar from many other cases which the Life records in detail (see below, §III); the significant difference in this instance, is Theodore's need for instruction. The fact that this was given by the child's father—not, for instance by another holy man—is revealing; for it was a common feature of many of Theodore's later exorcisms that they appeared to regulate tensions between kin, and the authority which he exercised was the authority, at one remove, of a parent.

The third episode, placed between these two, is revealing in a different way. Theodore had fallen ill, possessed himself by a demon. As he lay sick he was visited in a dream by St George, who asked him who had brought him to this state. Theodore pointed out the black shape of the demon standing before him.

St George chased the apparition away and brought Theodore to his feet, who at once woke up cured. From this moment, God who gave the holy apostles the power over evil spirits to cure any disease, gave him also power over demons, so that he could expel them from men and cure the sick (17). The phenomenon is familiar in other cultures: a holy man or shaman might only acquire his powers of exorcism after he himself had been cured from possession.[76] If we choose to rationalize the behaviour in psychological terms, we may simply conclude that to master oneself and one's own afflictions by the assertion of will-power is the first step towards a similar mastery of others.

Theodore had followed a programme that was deliberately and spectacularly extreme, but it is worth noting that it was only an exaggeration of a pattern of devotion that others might share. Children aged 6 or 7 were regularly consigned to monasteries to begin a life of service to God.[77] The escalating intensity of Theodore's fasting and asceticism—the observance of Lent at the age of 8, night vigils at the age of 12, the two years of hiding in his middle to late teens, and the two years of harrowing self-torture which must have taken place in his early twenties—no doubt corresponded to what he was capable physically and mentally of enduring. There was method to this regime of preparation, as there was in the training of monastic acolytes.

The goal that Theodore achieved was much more than a mastery of his own bodily desires; a holy man acquired not simply power over himself, but power over others. Fasting, isolation, self-inflicted suffering, and intense study and contemplation channelled entirely in the service of God gave Theodore a reputation for holiness and a moral authority which was simply beyond the reach of other men. Moreover, this power, derived not from men but from God (cf. 17. 12–16), was transcendent, not to be compared with the authority conferred on bishops by election, or provincial governors by appointment. It was power that enabled its holder to speak freely and without fear in any company, even of the emperor.[78] It could be wielded not only in the local community, but wherever there was evil to be faced or exorcized, in Palestine, Nicomedia, or Constantinople.

There are suggestive parallels to be drawn between

[76] See briefly M. Eliade, 'Schamanismus', *Die Religion in Geschichte und Gegenwart. Handwörterbuch für Theologie und Religionswissenschaft*, v (3rd edn. 1961), 1386–8.

[77] Patlagéan, *Pauvreté*, 144–5.

[78] See Festugière's note on ch. 142, where the *parrhesia* of Theodore is shown to master the brutal ferocity of the consul Bonosus, who had suppressed the Jewish uprising at Antioch in 610. Compare Basil's *parrhesia*, Ch. 17 §v at nn. 198 and 215.

Theodore's path to holiness, and the acquisition of power through ascetic self-denial in other societies. In Java, for instance, the orthodox route to power lies through 'yogaistic practices and extreme ascesis... including fasting, going without sleep, meditation, sexual abstinence, ritual purification, and sacrifices of various types'. The aim is to concentrate on a single objective; 'the inward significance of such ascesis is in no sense self-mortification with ethical objectives in mind, but solely and singly the acquisition of power.' 'The conception of concentration which underlies the practice of asceticism is closely correlated with the idea of purity.' 'The essential difference between the heroes and their adversaries... is that the latter eventually permit their Power to be diffused by indulging their passions without restraint, whereas the former maintain that steadfastness, that tense singleness of purpose, which assures the maintenance and continued accumulation of power.'[79] That description cannot be transferred without alteration to fit the case of the seventh-century holy man, for moral and ethical objectives play an explicit part in his asceticism, but it provides a powerful motivation for his behaviour which is surely implicit in the many uses which Theodore was able to make of his position. A decade and a half of training led to the holy man's ability to exercise his power; this was no accident; it was designed to do so. Throughout this same period increasing publicity played a part in reinforcing both his reputation and his abilities. His feats of cure and exorcism, which were increasingly noticed in the later years, brought him so many adherents that it became necessary to build a monastery to house them (40). The apprenticeship was complete; the holy man had come of age.

III. *Exorcism and Cure: The Saint in Action*

At a village called Bouzaia, in the district of the Bithynian town of Creteia, workmen building a bridge removed some gravestones from a hillside. Some said that they intended to use them for construction purposes, but most people believed that they had plundered hidden treasure from the place. At once a crowd of unclean spirits had emerged, to take possession of the leading men and women of the village and make terrible sport with them, or to cast them on their sickbeds; other demons lay in wait on the roads and in the outlying parts of the village territory, where they afflicted farm animals and passing travellers.

By invoking Theodore's name the villagers found that they were able to cow the evil spirits, and they sent

[79] Benedict Anderson, 'The Idea of Power in Javanese Culture', in Claire Holt (ed.), *Culture and Politics in Indonesia* (1972), 1–69, a key article.

for him in person. When he arrived, the demons railed at him: 'Why have you come here, iron-eater? Why have you left Galatia for our district of Gordiane? There is no call for you to leave your territory. We know why you have come, but we will not listen to you, as the spirits in Galatia do. We are made of sterner stuff than they, and cannot easily be mastered.' On the next day Theodore led a procession of the afflicted inhabitants round their village and took them to the hill whence the demons were said to have come. He confronted them with Christ's blessing, made the sign of the cross, beat his breast, and prayed for more than an hour continuously, ordering the demons to leave their victims and go back to the hill. At the end of this treatment they emerged with great shouts, tearing the clothes off the men and women whom they had possessed and throwing them at the holy man's feet.

One particularly obdurate spirit would not leave a woman, and Theodore seized her by the hair, threatening the demon with the sign of the cross and with prayer. The spirit surrendered: 'You are burning me, iron-eater. I am forced to leave and have no reply to you. Only give me one of the things that you are wearing.' Theodore removed a sandal and threw it into the excavation on the hill; at once the spirit threw the woman to the ground and left her.

Theodore then offered further prayers to get rid of the demons in the outlying territory and along the roads. Overwhelmed by God's grace they appeared suddenly, in the form of hares and field-mice, and jumped into the hole. The saint blessed it with a prayer and the sign of the cross, and ordered it to be filled in and restored to its original condition. The procession then returned to the village (43).

This remarkable and vivid description is one of a total of forty-one miraculous exorcisms which Theodore performed. Together with forty-two dramatic cures, and a heterogeneous collection of thirteen other miracles, they offered contemporaries the clearest demonstration of the awesome power that the holy man could command. By contrast with the early chapters in the Life, which showed Theodore acquiring mastery of himself through his solitary trials, these episodes showed Theodore in relationship to individuals or communities, and to the spirits that possessed them. By analysing these relationships one may hope to form a more dynamic impression of society, and of the holy man's role in the community, than the motionless and often blurred snapshot, which is all that most of our evidence from the ancient world will allow.

The pathology of mass exorcism exemplified by the episode at Bouzaia was repeated, broadly speaking, in the other major episodes of mass possession that the Life records. All the cases involved the infection of large numbers of men, women, and animals by spirits that had been released from underground excavations. In one case a man had been extending his threshing floor (114); in another an uprooted gravestone led demons to take possession of six men and eight women (115); and on a third occasion a whole village was afflicted after the cover was removed from an old sarcophagus, which contained the remains of ἀρχαίων ἀνθρώπων Ἑλλήνων, pagans from a bygone age (118). In the first two cases, as at Bouzaia, the saint led a procession to the place whence the spirits had come, where his prayers and ritual actions forced them to return to the hole, which was then refilled.

Two stories were told at greater length, and with significant extra details. At the village of Eukraa, the excavation of a *bounion*, evidently an artificial tumulus, released a whole phalanx of unclean spirits, which attached themselves to men, women, and children. Timotheus, the man who had conducted the excavation, was arrested by the governor of the province, who had become involved in the affair. Suspicions were voiced that both he and Timotheus had an interest in buried treasure that might be found there. The governor had ordered the possessed inhabitants to be flogged, but to no avail, for they were simply seized with uncontrollable mirth and begged for further punishment. They then set fire to Timotheus' haystacks, broke into houses, ate any food they could find, and pillaged everything they could lay their hands on. The spirits even damaged the houses of their possessed victims. Animals suffered too, some dying, others going mad.

Theodore spent a night in prayer at the local church, where the whole community assembled on the following morning. The spirits cried out that they were being violently handled by him. He rebuked them in reply, as though they were miscreant spoiled children, and told them to leave. Lack of sleep led Theodore not to perform the exorcism in person, and he prevailed on Iulianus, one of the clerics from his monastery,[80] to

lead the procession to the tumulus, where the possessed would be cured by a recitation of the Gospels. When this was done the spirits threw their victims to the ground and returned to the hole, which was refilled. After saying mass in the village church, Theodore offered a prayer at the tumulus and erected a cross (116–17).

The last description of a mass exorcism was the most extended of all, and was treated by the biographer as Theodore's greatest miracle. The bishop at Germia had started to excavate a cistern outside the city, where he disturbed many old gravestones, releasing the familiar host of unclean spirits. These took possession both of the wealthier inhabitants and of a great mass of poor townsfolk. Richer people kept children or relatives who had been possessed at home, ashamed that their misfortune might become more widely known, but the great church of St Michael was filled with a throng of humble people, all abusing the bishop roundly for what he had done. Their numbers swelled as time went by.

Theodore was greeted by a defiant crowd of spirits three miles from the town. He entered the church and asked the demons why they had possessed human bodies. They replied that by digging up their place and arousing their anger the bishop had been responsible, not themselves. The bishop and his men, in their insatiable greed, had not even respected the ground provided for their graves. The spirits added that they would not have dared to effect this mass possession without serious provocation, since they knew that the holy man was still alive and they feared his bold and drastic ways.

Theodore ordered them to prepare to leave their victims on the next day, and invoked God and the saints to help him. This provoked a further defiant answer: 'Give in, you eater of demons, son of a harlot, and do not meddle with us, but teach the interferers to act sensibly, and to refrain from stirring us up to do evil deeds. This is the reason why we do not want to leave the bodies which we have possessed, iron-eater.' Theodore rebuked them with the sign of the cross, ordered them to be silent, and told them to restore their victims to their senses. The possessed promptly fell unconscious to the floor.

On the next day Theodore led a great procession to the excavation. The spectators included people from the neighbouring village and other outsiders, for it is clear that Germia's annual gathering of pilgrims was taking place, and all the victims, who had been in the church, were in full view, behaving violently and

[80] Iulianus is the most interesting secondary character in the Life. He was close to Theodore and keenly interested in the nature of his spiritual power. On one occasion he asked him why sometimes his countenance changed as he celebrated the Eucharist, and 'we can see your face shining out in glory, full of grace'. Theodore was at first reluctant to answer, but explained that on these occasions he was elated by a vision of a resplendent cover descending over the host (80). Iulianus revealed this story after Theodore's death, and may, perhaps, have been an imaginative witness. On the occasion when Theodore exorcized a demon from a *silentarius* at Constantinople Iulianus reported that he had dreamed that the holy man was standing by the seashore when the *silentarius* came to him holding a three-headed goose by the feet. As he passed the bird to Theodore it turned into a weasel and jumped into the sea. From that moment the victim was cured

(89). This is a far cry from the routine observation of mice or lizards leaving the body of the possessed (below, n. 99). Of such things are dreams made. The story evidently tells us more about Iulianus' vivid imagination than about common beliefs.

shouting out that they were distressed by the holy man's presence. After a prayer, Theodore told them all to return to the church. The civic elders objected, begging him not to leave the spot before performing the exorcism, but Theodore was reluctant, fearing that he might be accused of vainglory if he deployed his powers, especially in the presence of so many outsiders, who included Jews from the neighbourhood. It is also clear that there were many bishops and representatives of the patriarch of Constantinople present in the crowd, who were suspicious that Theodore lacked confidence in his ability to accomplish the miracle. Associates of the holy man also inferred that he was reluctant to act because of their presence, and on account of the size of the gathering, and Theodore himself acknowledged that he lacked self-confidence and was afraid that he might be accused of glory-seeking: 'I ask you to return to the church, since the huge crowds here include not only the faithful but also Jews and heretics, and I do not wish to be found out here and now, either as a laughing stock at their expense, or as having made a vainglorious parade of power.' Theodore might have added that he was old and debilitated by illness, and acutely conscious of the nervous and physical energy he would have to expend to master the most demanding crisis of his life.

Under pressure he relented, and descended into the trench, where he bowed his head in prayer. His face appeared to radiate with glory and with grace. Still the spirits would not come out but spat on his hair. He refused to move until they left their victims, while they for their part refused to comply until they had been joined by the remainder of the possessed inhabitants of the place, who were still in the houses of the rich or in the town's hospices. Again Theodore stood firm; there was no need for further action since the other spirits would be driven out of their hiding places by an angelic force. As soon as the hidden demons emerged, the other spirits recognized them, greeting them by name and bandying insults at them: 'Skulking away in houses did you no good. It was no use pleading illness and hiding in the hospices. Here you all are. Let us make lament together on account of this iron-eater, or rather this demon-eater, whose birth was a bad day for all of us.' The holy man then ordered the spirits not to tear all the clothes off their victims when they left them, so that they would not be exposed naked, but to allow the men to wear their trousers and the women their undergarments.

Two spirits cried out that they had possessed their victims, both women, before the trench was excavated, and did not want to be incarcerated in a hole where they did not belong. When this claim was confirmed by the company the women were led off to the monastery at Sykeon for later cure.

Once again Theodore returned to the trench and ordered the spirits to form a circle round it, and to prepare to return to their home, where they and their master the Devil would await the everlasting punishment of the Lord. With a great cry the spirits threw off the outer clothing of their victims and leaped down into the hole. Then, one by one, the saint raised them up, as though from a grave. Each one, awakening from possession as though from a drunken stupor, described how he had seen a sign of his cure, a snake, a field-mouse, a lizard, or a mouse emerging from his mouth. After a final prayer Theodore emerged from the trench himself, threw earth in the shape of a cross back into it, and ordered it to be refilled. After this had been done by a team of 350 men, the whole company returned to the church of St Michael, singing hymns, praising God, and braiding garlands in honour of the Lord's servant. At the mass which was then celebrated they all experienced a sense of bodily and spiritual well-being at the display of healing which had taken place before their very eyes (161).

In contrast to the six mass exorcisms, which have many points of similarity with one another, the numerous individual exorcisms, generally described in less detail, do not make up so homogeneous a collection. The main group of twenty-five cases involved the exorcism of individual spirits. The victims came from a wide spectrum of social backgrounds: three married women and one unmarried;[81] nine men ranging in rank from a sailor, who was the victim of sorcery (87), to one of the leading citizens of Nicomedia with the rank of *patēr tēs poleōs*; the man who suffered especially at noon and after dark (159. 38–77);[82] four children, including one living in a monastery;[83] four clerics;[84] one male and four female slaves.[85] With the exception of three of the women and two of the children, the sufferers were not from Theodore's immediate locality, the villages of north-west Galatia, but from larger cities which he visited or where he had connections: two children of Ancyra,[86] a cleric and his wife from Iuliopolis,[87] a paralysed man at Apollonia-Sozopolis in south Phrygia,[88] five persons from Nicomedia and its neighbourhood,[89] and the rest, ten cases in all including all the slaves, from Constantinople.[90] The group thus contrasted with the cases of mass

---

81 35; 60; 71. 14 ff.; 159. 78–88.
82 87; 89; 93 (3 victims); 103. 7–14; 108; 132; 162. 77 ff.; 162. 95 ff.
83 18; 46; 86; 157. 9–17.
84 103 (a priest and his wife); 138; 157. 51 ff.
85 84; 92. 32–6; 94; 140. 11.
86 162. 77 ff. and 95 ff.
87 103.
88 108.
89 132; 157. 9–17; 157. 51 ff.; 159. 38–77; 159. 78–88.
90 84; 86; 87; 89; 92. 1–31; 92. 32–7; 93; 94; 138; 140. 11.

possession which occurred in the rural environment where Theodore himself was at home.

Many of the features of the individual exorcisms can be illustrated from two of the cases. One of Theodore's earliest miracles was to relieve a local woman, who came to him, accompanied by her husband, when terribly afflicted by a spirit. Theodore, as usual, engaged the demon in conversation, and the spirit replied that the holy man should not be angry with him, or condemn him to eternal punishment, for the fault was not his but lay with a local sorcerer, Theodotus Kourappos, who had ordered him to possess the woman. Theodore ordered the spirit to leave the woman alone for a while, and instructed the husband to bring the wife back to him after the harvest. They returned in due course, after the harvest and the vintage, and the spirit again possessed her as they entered the church of St Michael at Sykeon. She remained possessed there for a week until the demon, unable to resist the holy man's powers further, threw its victim down at his feet and left. She returned home, cured and rejoicing (36).

The sorcerer Theodotus then tried to destroy the holy man, first by sending demons, who returned to their master to report that they had been repulsed by a great jet of flame which came from Theodore's mouth, and then by serving him a poisoned fish to eat. When this too failed the sorcerer came in person to beg for mercy. Theodore compelled him to surrender his 'book of supernatural powers' (biblos energetike), and to release from enthralment any house, person, or beast that he had ensnared. This done, Theodotus was pardoned and baptized (37–8). Demons on occasion, therefore, were attributed to the maleficent actions of sorcerers, and these made occasional appearances elsewhere in the Life.[91] However, spirit possession in the majority of cases seems to have been quite independent of sorcery. In any case the exorcistic treatment of the sufferer was the same, whether or not a sorcerer was thought to be involved. Theodore's successful cure of the possessed woman was in no way dependent on his subsequent successful confrontation with the sorcerer himself.

A second case involved a woman called Eirene, who had for long been possessed by spirits which had reduced her to a state of complete apathy. However, her condition was not recognized as the work of demons until, as she sat outside the church watching a procession led by the holy man and the bishop of Germia, they caused her to throw off her cloak and

veils, dash through the crowd, and howl abuse at Theodore. The whole congregation began to chant the Kyrie Eleison, and as it did so, the woman appeared to be suspended above the ground and was transported through the air from the ambon to the chancel screen. The saint offered prayers on the woman's behalf above a great clamour from the demons. At the end of the mass she was lowered to the floor and lay at the entrance to the church. Theodore, as he passed on the way out, seized her by the hair and ordered the demons to leave, thus curing the woman. Shortly thereafter both her husband and her children died and she became a hermit, and lived at Sykeon in a cell close to the church of the Virgin Mary.

Possession, as these two cases show, appeared in two forms. One was complete lassitude and physical collapse on the part of the victim, most commonly described by the word ἀρρωστία.[92] In these cases possession was not usually recognized until the subject came in contact with the holy man, whose presence aroused the demons to violent protest.[93] In extreme cases, like that of Eirene, the victim at such moments is said to have been suspended above the ground by the force of the spirits.[94] The other form was violent and abusive behaviour conspicuous to any observer, akin to the violent symptoms exhibited by the victims of mass possession, and in the possession of animals.[95]

The exorcistic procedure varied little. There was usually a dialogue between the holy man and the spirit or spirits; the former ordered the demons to leave their victim and purge the sufferer, and the latter replied, usually in abusive language, but admitting to his superior powers.[96] These replies tend to be highly stereotyped. The exorcisms have a strong ritualistic character and wide variation would be unexpected. On the other hand the occasional distinctive variations in the answers given to the holy man,[97] readily confirm that these were not fictions, or fictitious dialogues, however much they conformed to a set and repetitive pattern. Theodore's replies likewise varied little. One example will illustrate the pattern. A cleric from a monastery in the territory of Nicomedia was seized by a demon as he emerged from the public bath-house, holding a phial of oil and wrapped in towels. Catching

---

[91] 37–8; 143. 13–16 (a sorcerer's amulet fails to save a man from food-poisoning); 159. 28–37 (a Bithynian cleric who had a reputation for magic potions); 87 (a sailor who had been ensorcelled, περιεργασθείς).

[92] 71. 14 ff.; 84; 86; 89; 92. 32–7; 108; 132; 140. 11; 159. 78–88.

[93] 35; 71. 14 ff.; 132; 140. 11.

[94] 46. 14–16; 71. 27–31; 93. 36–7.

[95] 35. 3; 46. 2; 93. 2; 103. 2, 8–9; 138. 3; 157. 11, 51 ff.; 159. 38–77; 162. 77 ff., 95 ff.

[96] 18; 46; 71. 14 ff.; 84; 86; 92; 93; 108; 157. 51 ff.; 159. 38–77; 159. 78–88; 162. 77 ff.

[97] 35. 4–8; 43. 25–9, 45–7; 84. 10–32; 93. 38–40; and in particular the dialogues in 161 at the miracle of Germia.

sight of the saint in the distance, he threw the towel turban off his head, and ran up in terrible agitation. Theodore struck his chest with his hand and said, 'I am speaking to you, demon; give back sense to this body and do not occupy it, but go straightaway before me to the monastery of St Autonomus.' The man was hurled to the ground, and remained possessed until the next day, continuing to rail at Theodore until the spirit admitted defeat and emerged from his victim with the words, 'I am leaving him, iron-eater.'

Violent language was sometimes reinforced by violent behaviour: on different occasions Theodore whipped a boy (18), seized the sufferer by the hair (71. 14 ff.), struck him on the chest (86), or placed his foot on a possessed girl's neck (140. 11 ff.). Commonly the moment of exorcism itself was marked by the sufferer being thrown unconscious to the ground,[98] and a creature, identified with the demon, was seen to leave the victim's body.[99]

A subsidiary group of exorcisms closely resembled the large number of Theodore's miracles which took the form of a cure from some recognizable physical affliction.[100] In most instances diseases or disabilities were not attributed to spirit possession and were not

treated by exorcistic procedures, but by a combination of manipulation, touching, holding, blowing, or spitting on the afflicted part of the body, the saying of prayers, and by anointing with holy wine, oil, or water. For all that, it is worth noting that in one instance physical affliction was attributed to sorcery (156. 26 ff.), and in two others there was a moral as well as a physical aspect to the treatment and cure. When a crippled monk came to Theodore from a monastery in Lycaonia, he was healed not simply by the holy man's normal procedures, but by heeding the advice that he become reconciled with the abbot of the monastery, since a dispute between them was a partial cause of his condition (81). Again, when Phocas, the imperial *a secretis*, was cured by Theodore of an internal haemorrhage, he at first doubted that the intervention had been successful, fearing that he was too wicked a man to be cured (121). In another case of a dumb child, the narrative makes no specific reference to spirit possession, but a sceptical observer is said to have been convinced of Theodore's powers when he saw a jet of flame issuing from the child's mouth after the holy man's ministrations, a phenomenon that can be readily paralleled in many of the exorcisms.

Conversely there was a group of cases where a physical disease or affliction was directly attributed to the intervention of a spirit, although the cure adopted did not differ significantly from the great majority of cases, in which demons were not invoked to explain the disease.

These examples illustrate the point that there was an uncertain area where disease and cure display some, but not all the characteristic features of possession and exorcism, and show that the two categories were not entirely distinct in contemporary perception. However, it is a relatively simple task to draw up a list of cases where possession by spirits is clearly attested, and claimed as the source of a person's troubles, and to separate these from other cases, usually simply of physical illness, where spirits played no part. This indicates that spirit possession was a discrete, recognizable, and socially important phenomenon in contemporary life, and not merely a convenient metaphor used to describe many forms of affliction or abnormal behaviour.

Two further minor categories of spirit possession require a brief note. The first involved domestic animals, which might be afflicted individually or *en masse*. Theodore performed exorcisms on a bull (98), a mule (99), and most notably on a camel, which defied the efforts of a Nicomedian *camelarius* to control it (160. 20–48). In the first two cases the holy man did no more than utter a prayer or a blessing, and blow into the faces or nostrils of the animals, but the exorcism of the camel involved a dialogue with the demon, and

[98] 18; 35; 43. 49; 71. 31–4; 86. 16–17; 92. 28–9; 132. 14–15; 157. 14–15, 79; 159. 86; 160. 42; 161. 219–24; 162. 89–90, 107.

[99] 43. 53–4; 84. 35 (serpent); 86. 19–21 (the victim saw a vision of a black woman leaving through the window); 132. 24 (mouse); 161. 227–8. Cf. n. 80. Exact parallels for this phenomenon are noted by Michael MacDonald, *Mystical Bedlam: Madness, Anxiety, and Healing in 17th Century England* (1981), 203–4 and 293 n. 150–1: 'The visible spirits that haunted Napier's troubled clients looked like dogs, cats, rats, mice, birds, bees, a weasel, and a colt. These were the same kind of animals that were mentioned as the servant spirits of witches in witchcraft trials, and the common name for such demons, "familiars", suggests a simple psychological reason for the shapes they assumed. Afraid of madness or death, miserable men and women, such as the people Napier treated, personified their feelings in the form of routine pests, the kind of banal vexations that surrounded every villager and seldom caused grave injury, an association that probably provided some reassurance that their maladies were not entirely mysterious.' MacDonald's whole analysis of the cures and exorcisms performed by William Napier, whose papers provide most of the material for the book, provides a rich mine of parallels to throw light on the Life of Theodore.

[100] The cures which did not involve exorcistic procedures included cases involving nine women (three cases of paralysis, one of haemorrhage, one of senility, four of infertility), twenty-one men (two lepers, one case of food-poisoning, eight of paralysis or crippling infirmity, two of arthritis, one of mouth cancer, one of dropsy, one of internal haemorrhaging, one of scalding, one of blindness, one deaf-mute, and two unspecified illnesses, one his own!), twelve children (three dumb, one deaf, one deaf and blind, one blind, two cripples, one lesion on the leg, one case of scalding and one of elephantiasis), and three epidemics (plague at Ancyra, fear of poisoning by a lizard, and food-poisoning).

culminated in the animal being cast sweating to the ground as the spirit left it, two features that were a regular occurrence in the human exorcisms.

The second minor category involved rituals which were designed to purge a place of the evil spirits that infested it. An early chapter of the Life records how Theodore paid repeated visits at midday over a two-month period to a place called Arkea, which could not be approached, especially around noon, on account of Artemis and the other demons that lived there (16. 1–11). Likewise, by spending his customary winter period of solitary meditation at a place called Zumbulios, Theodore managed to rid it of the evil spirits which prevented men from approaching it at midday or after dark (26a). Prayer, and the sign of the cross, also put paid to the spirit which took the form of a black dog and would appear beside a tree on the road between Constantinople and Nicomedia, allowing no one to pass after sundown (155. 9 ff.). Two comments seem appropriate. Firstly, the exorcism at Arkea explicitly involved the mastery of a pagan spirit. Artemis is the only non-Christian deity to be mentioned by name in the whole narrative. The local fear she aroused was obviously akin to the superstitious fear of opening old, pre-Christian graves. Secondly, all three cases imply that noon and darkness were especially favoured by demons, anxieties which can readily be paralleled in other societies and ethnographic traditions. But even universal superstitions help to shape culture and condition personal behaviour, as is nicely confirmed by another episode in which Theodore exorcized evil demons from a man, which only manifested themselves in uncontrollably violent behaviour at noon and at night-time (159. 38–77).

One further unique exorcism of evil spirits from a place occurred at a house in Upper Pylai, south-west of Nicomedia.[101] Men and beasts were possessed by unclean spirits associated with the building, and when the inhabitants sat down to eat, stones were hurled across the tables, causing much injury and smashing the women's looms, and the house itself was plagued with mice and snakes. Theodore spent a night there, saying prayers and singing psalms, before sprinkling the house with holy water, and releasing it from the demons' clutches (131).

IV. Possession and Christian Belief

The case studies of a holy man's miracles collected in the previous section serve a double purpose. They provide material for further analysis of the relationship between the secular world and supernatural forces in seventh-century Byzantine society. They also give an unparalleled sense of the distance which separates the rural Anatolian communities of this period from modern consciousness. Theodore's biographer, the monk George, painted with loving detail ($\lambda\epsilon\pi\tau o\mu\epsilon\rho\tilde{\omega}\varsigma$, 2. 18), a picture not only of the holy man but also of the world to which he belonged, which is as sharp and as attentive as that of a modern ethnographer. Appropriately, this world displays a pattern and contours which are more familiar from ethnographical or anthropological writing than from conventional historical narratives. The fact is all the more remarkable since George wrote as an insider, about his own society and environment. Rather than let the details slip into a background haze, obscured by familiarity, his awareness was sharpened by the need to do justice to Theodore's marvellous actions. There is no better testimony to the compelling powers of the holy man, than the punctilious precision which he inspired in his biographer. Here, as nowhere else in the literature, the archaeology, or the documentary record, it is possible to feel part of the successes and disappointments, the hopes, fears, and faith of the people of the small towns and villages of Anatolia.

Commonplace but fundamental aspects of social conditions and individual behaviour are embedded in the narrative. Hunger, disease and congenital ill-health, drought, storm, and flood help to make up an unchanging backdrop of hardship. Stress and conflict were endemic in personal relations: parents were unable to produce children and maintain the family; family tensions broke out into violence; rivalry and jealousy between peers was sharpened by the recourse to sorcery. Communities rubbed up against one another, with friction breaking out into disputes over land or resources. Outsiders, especially officials and soldiers, were feared for the disruption they caused. Class conflict was etched into the pattern; ordinary villagers, their own resources stretched to the full to maintain a living in harsh conditions, observed richer neighbours, landowners, powerful clergy, or imperial officials with envy and anxiety. When the wealthy reached out too far to take more for themselves, the strained tranquillity of rural life could erupt into violence.

There was little scope for relaxation to relieve the pressure of constant hard work, routine frustrations, inter-personal jealousy, and intermittent hardship. Even in the austere and demanding world of pagan

---

[101] T. Corsten, *I. Apamea*, 101–7 identifies Ano Pylai as the harbour town, located beneath modern Yalova. However, Yalova was surely simply Pylai; Ano Pylai must have been in the hills to the south, doubtless in the pass which ran over Mount Arganthonius to the west end of Lake Ascanius (Iznik Göl); so, naturally, L. Robert, *JSav.* (1979), 275 (OMS vii. 445).

Anatolia, release had come at intervals, during festivals where whole communities thronged together and relieved their tensions with wine, music, and dance, feasts shared with friends, and, for some of the men at least, a breakdown of sexual inhibitions. Theodore's world offered no such options. Communities gathered to share a common toil—or in Christian worship. The Church alone existed to provide a recourse or a refuge from a life which had few earthly pleasures to offer; the promise of Paradise carried a heavy weight of expectation. Christianity, through its ideology, rituals, and preaching had to work with unremitting efforts to persuade ordinary men and women that this promise was a credible one, and that the sacrifices demanded of them by their daily existence would be rewarded in the life to come. Furthermore, until that promise was fulfilled, or until the millennium came, it fell to the Church, to its clergy and above all to its holy men, to unravel the snares that beset everyday life.

Against this background it may be possible to suggest ways of explaining the most remarkable phenomenon of the Life of Theodore, the exorcism of demons.[102] Possession, or more specifically possession by spirits, is familiar in many societies, widely attested in historical contexts from the Palestine of the New Testament to sixteenth- and seventeenth-century Europe, and by an abundant ethnographic and anthropological literature which covers most parts of the undeveloped and indeed much of the developed world.[103] Possession may be defined as the appearance of an altered state of consciousness, in which the subject's own personality is overtaken, or possessed, by another quite separate being, which speaks or acts in ways that are usually uncharacteristic of and dissociable from the behaviour of the possessed person in his or her own right. This is one essential characteristic of possession, which may be empirically verified by observation. However, it is equally essential that at least a segment of the society to which the sufferer belongs believes that this changed state of consciousness should be attributed specifically to possession by spirits, rather than to some other form of psychological or physical disorder.

Possession, therefore, cannot be defined or identified unless it is recognized as such by the society in which it occurs; belief in possession is an integral part of what possession is. This point causes difficulties for commentators who choose to assume that the objective and verifiable 'facts' about possession provide a more reliable foundation on which to base explanations of its significance, than such subjective and intangible entities as mere 'beliefs'. They consequently attempt to explain away, rather than explain, the phenomenon, by accounting for it in terms that do not involve this belief. The most typical product of this approach is the psychological explanation of possession, which seeks to show that it is caused by mental disturbance or malfunction in the sufferer.[104] Victims of possession, on this account, are no more than victims of mental illness.

The approach leaves much unexplained. One flaw is the assumption that mental illness itself is an immutable constant, whose symptoms are determined by recognizable, or potentially recognizable neurophysiological causes, rooted in the physical functions of the body and the brain, and in no way specific to a particular culture or variable between cultures. However, if we accept the persuasive definition of culture and human behaviour, that it is neither something internal to and programmed into human nature, nor is it a purely external product of human activity, but that it is derived from an interaction of the two, then we must conclude that culture is not a particular configuration of brain-cells, nor the material world which man has created for himself, but it is the sense which he makes of this world, its meaningful content. Culture, precisely, is made up of the symbols, whether in language, gesture, productive activity, or metaphysical belief, by which the human race makes sense of and assigns meaning to the world.[105] This line of analysis leads one to see individual psychology, like individual mentality, as a product of this interactive process, not as some immutable disposition in the brain or in the personality of the person concerned.

In fact, even if the symptoms of possession are interpreted and explained in purely neuro-physiological terms, to argue that spirit possession is simply a form of psychological disorder goes nowhere towards interpreting its cultural significance. Whatever its physical origins, possession affected the lives, perceptions, and responses of sufferers, curers, observers, and the

[102] For a survey of Theodore's exorcisms and cures, with an appropriately theological emphasis, see Festugière's introd. pp. xvii–xxiii.

[103] I am very grateful to Gillian Feeley-Harnick and Stuart Clark for discussing the problems raised by spirit possession and guiding me to the immense and absorbing literature on the subject, which has been produced above all by anthropologists and by historians of early modern Europe. I have cited a tiny sample in the notes that follow; my debt to modern discussions is far wider than these titles indicate.

[104] This approach is naturally to be found in Freud, e.g. 'A 17th Century Demonological Neurosis', *Works*, xix (1961), 72–105. It is the pervasive explanation favoured by T. K. Oesterreich, *Possession, Demoniacal and Other, among Primitive Races, in Antiquity, the Middle Ages, and Modern Times* (1966).

[105] Clifford Geertz, 'The Impact of the Concept of Culture on the Concept of Man' and 'The Growth of Culture and the Evolution of Mind', in *The Interpretation of Cultures* (1973), 33–83.

community at large. The physical facts of possession in themselves are of no significance except to the psychiatrist, or to collectors of strange forms of unusual human behaviour. The social and therefore the historical significance of possession derives from the context in which its symptoms occur, and from what society makes of the phenomenon. The most significant thing about spirit possession is precisely that it is treated as such, not as a form of psychological malfunction. To explain possession away, by reducing it to purely medical terms, is to fall into the same trap that ensnares all reductionist explanations of religion and religious phenomena. The fact that both forms of reductionism take no account of belief, which is as integral to the nature of spirit possession as it is to religion, is no coincidence.

Recent studies of trance, possession, and exorcism have tended to explore two separate, but not necessarily contradictory modes of interpretation. The first is, broadly speaking, functionalist, and is most lucidly illustrated in an ethnographical study of Somali society. In this instance a high proportion of cases of spirit possession can be explained as attempts by a relatively deprived section of a community, very commonly women, to call attention to their plight and predicament, thereby attracting sympathy, concern, and very often material compensation for their condition. This theory accounts for several types of possession, including a highly distinctive pattern of behaviour among married women:

Subjected to frequent, sudden and prolonged absences by the husband...to the jealousies and tensions of polygyny, and always menaced by the precariousness of marriage in a society where divorce is frequent, the Somali married woman's lot offers little stability or security. It is scarcely surprising, therefore, that many women's ailments should be interpreted by them as possession by *zar* spirits, which demand luxurious clothes, perfume and delicate foods from their men folk. It is only when these costly demands are met, and all the expenses involved in the mounting of a cathartic dance, directed by an expert female shaman, that the symptoms can be expected to disappear. Even then the relief from their affliction may be only temporary.

This characteristically female affliction operates 'as a limited deterrent against the abuses of neglect and deprivation in a conjugal relationship which is heavily biased in favour of men. Spirit possession is a means of airing this grievance obliquely, and of gaining some satisfaction.'[106]

Possession is here seen as a strategy employed in their own interests by the socially or economically deprived. The procedures of cure, or exorcism, involve an important element of bargaining, whereby grievances are assuaged by material or other forms of compensation.

It is one of the important features of such a system that it enables disadvantaged groups or individuals to make claims of those in positions of power over them, without challenging the existing hierarchy, or the ideological underpinning of the social organization. The spirits, who make the claims on behalf of the victims, are themselves amoral, not subject to the rules by which society normally functions. They can make demands of a husband's generosity, which a wife in her own right could not without challenging the subservient relationship of wife to husband. Their appeasement involves no compromise in society's rules, or any ackowledgement that a particular group is unjustly or unfairly disadvantaged, since it is not the women but the spirits that are being satisfied by the concessions. Possession and cure provide a means by which an unworkably oppressive and slanted ideological system can coexist with an actual state of social relations which is less rigid and pays more attention to the demands and requirements of individual members of the society. It is a strategy which not only serves the interests of the women, or the disadvantaged groups, who can gain some redress for their condition, but also of the dominant groups, who can, quite literally, buy off potentially resistant or subversive elements in their society, without making any substantial concessions that weaken their own position of acknowledged superiority.

This analysis does not completely clarify the question of how far the strategy of spirit possession is consciously contrived to achieve its ends. In some cases possession may have been a deliberate ploy, as is shown by allegations, which were doubtless often true, that possession was not genuine but had been feigned. Self-induced spirit possession, which could only be cured by exorcisms and placation, is not an incoherent notion, but it conflicts with the view that the phenomenon, both in Somali society and generally elsewhere, is generally believed to occur spontaneously, not at the volition of the victim, who indeed often suffers considerable physical discomfort and mental stress as events take their course. Possession in these contexts, therefore, is better interpreted, along classic functionalist lines, as a social fact, which is designed to help society perform as it does, but which is not

[106] I. M. Lewis, 'Spirit Possession and Deprivation Cults', *Man* 1 (1966), 307–26; P. J. Wilson, 'Status Ambiguity and Spirit Possession', *Man*, 2 (1967), 366–78 accepts the essentials of Lewis's analysis but prefers to see 'spirit possession as a means to status or identity definition, which arises in contexts where individual status is jeopardised or rendered ambiguous'. I. M. Lewis, *Ecstatic Religion* (1971) is the clearest and most comprehensive introduction to the phenomena of trance and possession in religious contexts.

recognized or acknowledged as a conscious mechanism by the participants. Although the outcomes of possession and cure are usually implicitly grasped by the victims, curers, and participant spectators, only a conscious exercise of sociological analysis brings the motivation clearly into view.

The weakness of this strictly functional explanation is that it fails to show what meaning possession and exorcism may convey directly to the members of the society where it occurs, or why, indeed, it occurs at all. Without denying the relevance of the functional explanation, it should be possible to interpret such behaviour in terms which make sense within the society itself.

The starting point for this form of interpretation must be the recognition that possession itself is a recognized part of a society's culture. Members of society adopt procedures, broadly similar from one case to the next within any given cultural context, for communicating with the spirits, satisfying their demands, if any, and purging the victims or hosts. The repeated and collective experience of possession creates expectations and patterns of behaviour, which become as familiar as other more conventional forms of activity, behaviour, and communication. Possession and cure in a social context, like any other form of cultural experience, consist of a series of symbolic acts, performed by the participants, by which sense is given to the physical facts of possession. This symbolic system conforms to its own syntactical rules and thereby acquires meaning, just as words, the symbolic signs of which language is formed, only acquire significance when they obey appropriate syntactical rules. Like words, the symbolic acts that together make up the collective experience of possession can be read as a text.[107]

Clearly culture can only be conceived as text in a metaphorical sense, but it is a powerful and fruitful metaphor, if only for the reason that it forces us to look at a culture as a self-contained and self-explanatory entity, analogous to a work of literature, whose meaning cannot lie outside the charmed circle which encloses the text, that is the author's product, and its readers. It does not make sense to say of a text that it has significance beyond the words or symbols that it contains, a significance which would thereby become conceptually inaccessible to its readers. So, cultural behaviour does not hide a further level of meaning, unperceived by and imperceptible to its participants, although detectable by the skilled analysis of an outsider. Just as one cannot look for any reality behind

Hamlet or *King Lear*—for there is no reality that is not contained in the drama—so the explanation of cultural behaviour should not involve analysis in terms that are not integral to, or implicit in the culture itself.

This is not to say that the meaning embodied in cultural activity, be it spirit possession or anything else, need be simple or obvious. On the contrary, the symbolic communication of cultural behaviour will certainly convey a variety of meaning and experience to participants and observers, just as a work of literature does to its readers. In the particular case of trance states, for example, even an observer who is relatively unfamiliar with this form of behaviour, can interpret the sequence of events leading from initial possession to final exorcism at several different levels.

One may adopt overlapping perspectives on the events themselves. The functionalist viewpoint offers a sensible and illuminating, but limited way of reading the text of spirit possession. The mass exorcisms at Bouzaia, Eukraa, and Germia, described in the Life of Theodore (above, § III), respond well to the interpretation that possession here served as a means by which the poorer inhabitants of these communities called attention to grasping and unpopular acts by advantaged individuals or groups, such as Timotheus at Eukraa or the bishop of Germia, which were annulled by the holy man's intervention (see below). However, this is an interpretation which focuses principally on the results that were achieved by the process, at the expense of the preceding stages.[108]

Where the circumstances of possession and exorcism are institutionalized within a religious framework, as they clearly were in seventh-century Byzantine society, the phenomenon should also be interpreted as a ritual. This causes no problems for a society where ritual was at the centre of shared religious experience. Ritual, however, is rarely functional or causative in any conventional sense. Just as no causal sequence leads from prayer to the possible material consequences of prayer,[109] so exorcistic ritual was not designed directly to realize specific material goals.

---

[107] See Geertz, 'Thick Description: Toward an Interpretative Theory of Culture', *The Interpretation of Cultures*, 3–30, and 'Religion as a Cultural System', ibid. 87–125.

[108] I owe the approach directly to Michael Lambek, *Human Spirits: A Cultural Account of Trance in Mayotte* (1982), 9: 'How then are we to describe the interaction of human beings and spirits in Mayotte? If we were to focus, as American culture tends generally to do, on the aspect of intentionality, we could label the activity "curing". Were we to focus on the formal order we could label it "ritual". An emphasis on the inventive aspects suggests "drama", and on the referential, "symbolic activity" or perhaps "myth". The point is, of course, that possession juxtaposes a number of different contextual relations and therefore corresponds to no one of them in particular.' The book's whole analysis of trance and spirit possession in Mayotte is highly relevant to the interpretation of the Life of Theodore.

[109] D. Z. Phillips, *Religion without Explanation* (1978).

Furthermore, the descriptions of exorcism in the Life of Theodore, like those of sixteenth- and seventeenth-century Europe or of recent Malay culture,[110] are usually highly theatrical: the seizing of a personality by a spirit, the dialogue and conflict between the possessed and the curer, and the final dramatic release, usually leaving the victim unconscious as the demons are banished, certainly offer many of the essential elements of a drama with its own meaning to convey.

Arching over all these categories, one can simply see spirit possession as a means of communication, which, by following recognized rules and patterns, enables members of the society to say things to one another which conventional use of language do not. Herein, perhaps, lies the reason why such forms of behaviour often remain difficult or impossible for us, or even for participants, to explain verbally, and why an anthropological attempt to explain them will always take the form of a commentary, never of a definitive exposition.

The events of possession and exorcism also need to be viewed from different angles: that of the victim who claims attention, and is finally cured; that of the exorcist, whose own reputation rests on his ability to master the spirits with reasonable success at regular intervals; that of the spectators or peripheral participants, both for what they may contribute to the process and for what they may learn from it; and finally that of the spirits themselves, whose personalities in many ethnographically attested cases are often very clearly defined, as they appear and reappear in the possessed person over long periods of time.

The material provided by the Life of Theodore does not allow all these approaches to be pursued with equal conviction. The biographer presented all the cases from the viewpoint of the exorcist, whose powers and achievements he chronicled. The condition and predicament of the victims is unevenly characterized, and the spirits themselves are usually presented only as evil demons, agents of the Devil. Despite this reticence, there are cases where the spirits clearly and explicitly sought to achieve a specific goal, and there is a fascinating glimpse behind the mask of anonymity in the great miracle at Germia, when the spirits began to address one another by name, implying that each had personalities that were distinct from one another as well as from the victim whom they possessed (161. 187–90).

The epidemiology of possession also offers material for analysis. It is interesting that in the small towns and villages of central Anatolia possession was regularly a mass phenomenon. Communal solidarity, rather than fierce interpersonal rivalry, provided reassurance to individual villagers, and possession usually occurred, precisely as a communal phenomenon, when the villagers came into conflict with powerful individuals, who may, in some way, have been taking advantage of them. Examples of individual possession occurred mostly in the cities, where alienation may have been more prevalent than in small communities. The regular appearance of slaves, women, and children among the individual sufferers lends some support for the thesis that possession was most common among socially disadvantaged groups, although the case is weakened by several examples of male possession, including victims of high social standing. The phenomenon was evidently more widespread in Byzantine society than in the modern Somali case.

In the villages the triggers of mass possession, and thus of social friction, were identified quite explicitly as the disturbance of pagan graves, and treasure-hunting. The fact that in one case the governor of the province intervened to take action against the leading villager who was known to have opened graves, and that both were rumoured to be digging for treasure, indicates in itself that these activities might disturb the local equilibrium, even if we take no account of the subsequent outbreak of spirit possession.

The history and ethnography of treasure-hunting is not a subject that has claimed much scholarly attention,[111] but investigation would not be fruitless. Today, nothing holds the imagination of a Turkish villager in a firmer grip than the anticipation of the discovery of buried treasure, and hopes are kept alive by sufficient discoveries to persuade the peasant that he too might some day join the lucky few who have crossed the boundary separating dream from reality. Appetites will have been more keenly whetted by windfall finds in the Anatolia of AD 600, whose inhabitants lived their lives among the crumbling ruins of a great civilization, as yet hardly covered by the accumulation of soil and rubble, or despoiled by fifteen centuries of archaeological looting. The graves of the dead were a sure source of booty, and grave-robbing was a commonplace activity.[112] The even balance of

[110] For the latter see R. Firth, 'Ritual and Drama in Malay Spirit Mediumship', Comparative Studies in Society and History, 9 (1969), 190–207. In general J. Beattie, 'Spirit Mediumship as Theatre', Royal Anthropological Institute News, 20 (June 1979).

[111] But see Cécile Morrisson, 'Le Découvert des trésores à l'époque byzantine: Théorique et pratique de l'εὔρεσις θησαυροῦ', Travaux et mémoires, 8 (1981), 321–43, and R. Delmaire, Largesses sacrées et Res Privata: l'aerarium impérial et son administration du IVe au VIe siècle (1989), 409–12.

[112] Scrupulous excavation of a tomb at Sagalassus showed that it had been robbed in the early 7th cent., the date of the lamp used by the intruders and left beside the disturbed pile of human bones, M. Waelkens, XII Kazı Sonuçları Toplantısı (Ankara, 1990, pub. 1991), 122.

village society was surely often seriously upset by men who enriched themselves by plundering the past.

But envy in these cases would only have been a minor spur to social conflict. Christian Anatolia rested on a substratum of pagan beliefs, which had been laid to rest only two centuries before, and which lingered on, quite literally, in sheltered corners such as Arkea, where Theodore had exorcized the midday demon Artemis. The acceptance of Christianity, by now almost universal, did not by any means suppress all pagan superstition (see above, Ch. 18 § 11 at nn. 69–71). Entrusting one's grave to the protection of the gods, with curses and penalties invoked against transgressors, was a central part of pagan belief and practice in Roman Asia Minor and had been inherited by the early Christian communities. It is not a surprise that such prohibitions should be translated, even 300 years later, into the fear that opening graves would release unclean spirits to trouble the living.

In the two best-documented cases, at Germia and Eukraa, the responsibility for the trouble was placed squarely on a disturber of graves. This does not mean that this was his only, or principal sin. The spirits of Germia claimed that the bishop and his associates, in the insatiable pursuit of their own material advantage, did not even leave the dead in peace. The implication is clear that they were oppressing or interfering with the lives and livelihoods of their contemporaries also. Spirit possession was here a means of redress. Its effectiveness was symbolized by the fact that in all six cases of mass possession, release from the spirits came when the disturbed graves were restored to their original condition.

Possession for some, therefore, was a means of voicing a protest or of seeking compensation. But even in the cases where such elements were present, they scarcely made up the dominant theme. They must yield place to the ritual and drama of these occasions. The use of prayer and blessing, anointing with holy oil, and the sign of the cross were the tools of the exorcist; they were wielded in the context of a powerful religious experience: the gathering in the church, the celebration of the Eucharist, the intense, emotional procession winding through the town or village, and the planting of the cross above the old tombs from which the spirits had come. All these features tied possession and cure to the most potent symbols of Christian faith, and were woven together to make a public ritual which was both familiar and awesome. They made possession the property of the Church, and aimed to ensure that the rites of Christian worship, not the trials of a sorcerer, were the first and last resort of those who sought to be healed. By so doing they also focused all eyes on the charismatic figure of the exorcist himself, the holy man.

Theodore invariably occupied centre stage in these convulsive performances. Spirit possession was as important for the curer as for the sufferer. Each exorcism represented a test of his powers, for which he needed all his reserves of physical strength and spiritual concentration; each success was a boost to his self-confidence and reputation.[113] The drama of the event, over and above the sheer compelling need for success, brought pressures that might be hard to withstand. It is hardly fanciful to interpret Theodore's hesitation before performing the miracle at Germia, in the presence of so many critical or sceptical witnesses, as stage fright, or to see the dramatic emotional denouements of the mass exorcisms as *coups de théâtre*.[114]

Thus ritual shaded into a drama played out in front of a mass audience, which was half-participant, half-observer. Drama must have a meaning as well as action if it is to grip its audience, and contemporaries clearly apprehended that these demonstrations of divine power were something more than strange and fantastic events. What the spirits offered was a glimpse of a world which reversed the patterns and ideals by which men were expected to lead their lives. In place of normal behaviour, they showed extremes of listlessness or uncontrollable violence; in place of social living they offered extreme disruption; they did not respect authority but derided it; they had no regard for property but destroyed it; instead of prayers they uttered curses and blasphemy; they served not God, but the Devil. Every manifestation of this spirit world, by providing an unmistakable reversed image of itself, helped society to create its own sense of normality. Each successful intervention by the saint helped to steady the community in its adherence to the order which Christianity dictated.

The Christian faith, following in the wake of centuries of permissive pagan toleration, imposed an uncompromising discipline on its adherents, who were

---

113 Amid the growing rationalism and the religious conflicts of early modern Europe hardly any cases of spirit possession and exorcism escaped the suspicion of fraud, or an accusation that the expulsion of demons had been stage-managed to demonstrate the supremacy of a particular brand of Christianity, or the efficacy of the exorcist as a practitioner. D. P. Walker, *Unclean Spirits: Possession and Exorcism in France and England in the Late 16th and Early 17th Centuries* (1981), disappointingly subscribes to this scepticism. The book accordingly throws virtually no light on the importance of possession as a cultural phenomenon during this period.

114 The essay which best illuminates the role of the charismatic holy man through a modern ethnographic parallel is T. O. Beidelmann, 'Nuer Priests and Prophets: Charisma, Authority and Power among the Nuer', in T. O. Beidelmann (ed.), *The Translation of Culture: Essays in Honour of E. E. Evans-Pritchard* (1971), 375–415, a superb analysis of how power, prophecy, and enthusiastic religion can be interpreted and understood in their cultural context.

no longer volunteers, but conscripts in the army of God. There was no room for dissent; no cosy bargaining with the demons, as with the more familiar domestic spirits that seized the womenfolk of Somaliland. The theatre in which the ritual drama of possession and exorcism was played out offered the community a graphic representation of the struggle between Good and Evil, between God and the Devil. As the last remnants of an ordered Ancient World crumbled into the uncertainty of the Middle Ages, Anatolia's Christians were allowed no room to doubt where their spiritual loyalties lay.

APPENDIX I

Provincial Boundaries in Asia Minor 25 BC–AD 235

The Galatian province has been described as 'a fantastic agglomeration of territories', and any map showing its boundaries between its annexation and the reign of Trajan will amply confirm this observation.[1] At various times it comprised the plain of Pamphylia, the Taurus mountains from Seleuceia in the east to the boundaries of Lycia and Asia in the west, the upland lake district of Pisidia, the great central plateau which comprised Lycaonia, East Phrygia, and Galatia proper, the forested mountains of inland Paphlagonia, and the fertile plains and wooded hills of the basins of the Yeşil and Çekerek Irmak which comprised Pontus Galaticus. Between the time of Nero and the reign of Trajan even this vast area was eclipsed by the addition first of Pontus Polemoniacus, giving the province access to the Black Sea coastline, then of Armenia Minor and the previously procuratorial province of Cappadocia. Under the rule of the Flavians, Nerva, and Trajan a single governor was responsible for this whole heterogeneous territory which stretched from Asia to the Euphrates. Later in the reign of Trajan the frontiers began to contract. Cappadocia, Armenia Minor, Pontus Polemoniacus, and Pontus Galaticus were handed over to a separate governor; under Hadrian or Antoninus Pius a large southern section, comprising Lycaonia, Isauria, and Cilicia was given the status of an independent province known as the *Tres Eparchiae*. This left Galatia in a form which it was to retain at least until the mid-third century and perhaps until the time of Diocletian, stretching from Neoclaudiopolis and Pompeiopolis in northern Paphlagonia, across Galatia itself and most of the central plateau to the borders of Lycaonia and Isauria, and west to include Phrygia Paroreius, the strip of territory sandwiched between Sultan Dağ and the Pisidian lakes, including the cities of Apollonia and Pisidian Antioch.

In the late first and early second centuries AD, when the province reached its greatest extent, the titles of its governors include a detailed register of its various parts: *leg. pro pr. provinciae Galateae Paphlagoniae Pamphyliae Pisidiae;*[2] *leg. Aug. . . . Provinciae Cappadocicae et Galatiae, Ponti, Pisidiae, Paphlagoniae, Armeniae Minoris;*[3] *leg. pro pr. . . . provinciarum Galatiae Cappadociae Ponti Pisidiae Paphlagoniae Lycaoniae Armeniae Minoris;*[4] *leg. Aug. . . . Cappadociae Galatiae Phrygiae Lycaoniae Paphlagoniae Armeniae Mi-*noris;[5] *leg. Aug. pro pr. provinciarum Capp. Galat. Ponti Pisidi. Paph. Arm. min. Lyca;*[6] *leg. Aug. pro pr. Cappadociae Galatiae Armeniae Minoris Ponti Paphlagoniae Isauriae Phrygiae;*[7] *leg. Aug. pro pr. provinc. Gal. Pisid. Phryg. Luc. Isaur. Paphlag. Ponti Gala. Ponti Polemoniani Arm.*[8] It should be noted that there is no consistency observed in choosing which parts of the province to name, or the order in which they were presented. One instance is still more revealing. The many inscribed versions of the career of C. Antius A. Iulius Quadratus, legate under Domitian, do not all preserve the same list, and indeed sometimes omit the key area of Galatia altogether.[9] The same custom of listing the constituent parts of the province persisted for a while after the eastern section was hived off by Trajan: *leg. Aug. pro pr. provinc. Galat. Phryg. Pisid. Lycaon. Paphlag.*[10] and *leg. Aug. pro pr. provinciar. Galatiae Pisid. Paphlagoniae.*[11] Again, however, no consistency is observed. The lesson is clear; these lists must be handled with great care in determining the extent of the province at any one time, since omissions may reflect the true state of affairs or, simply, the caprice of the compiler of the text. Since the problems posed by these inscriptions are not the only ones concerning Galatia's boundaries, a brief statement of the arguments for the development of the province sketched above is required.

The problem of the original extent of the province is indissolubly bound up with the question of the extent of Amyntas' kingdom. Strabo twice states explicitly that the Romans made a province of Amyntas' whole kingdom,[12] and the point is reiterated in the individual cases of the cities of Selge[13] and Sagalassus.[14] This was natural, since Amyntas had allegedly bequeathed his kingdom to Rome, and there is no evidence, or likelihood, that the bequest was divided.[15]

---

[1] R. Syme, *ASBuckler*, 330 = *RP* i. 145.

[2] *AE* (1952), 232, Calpurnius Asprenas governor AD 68–70.

[3] *ILS* 8971, Ti. Iulius Celsus Polemaeanus, AD 78–9.

[4] *ILS* 268, A. Caesennius Gallus, governor AD 80–2.

[5] Many inscriptions cited in *PIR*[2] i no. 507; this list in Rehm, *I. Didyma*, no. 151 cited by Sherk, ii. 1007. C. Antius A. Iulius Quadratus, c.AD 81–3.

[6] *AE* (1925), 161, L. Antistius Rusticus, governor AD 91–4 (?)

[7] *Alt. von Perg.* viii. 3 no. 21, C. Iulius Quadratus Bassus, governor AD 109–12?

[8] *ILS* 1017, L. Caesennius Sospes, governor AD 112–14 (?)

[9] Cf. Sherk, ii. 1009, 1030 n. 200.

[10] *ILS* 1039, acephalous, governor AD 116–17.

[11] *ILS* 1038, L. Cossonius Gallus (?), governor before AD 119; the same formula in *OGIS* no. 535.

[12] 12. 5. 1, 567; 12. 6. 5, 569.

[13] 12. 7. 3, 571.

[14] 12. 6. 5, 569.

[15] 12. 8. 14, 577. For the *kleronomia* of Amyntas, see the discussion in Vol. I, Ch. 5 at nn. 6–16.

The evidence for the extent of Amyntas' kingdom is comparatively straightforward. In 39 BC he had been made 'king of the Pisidians',[16] an area which included the cities of Apollonia and Antioch, and which may be defined as the strip of Phrygia Paroreius south of Sultan Dağ.[17] In 37/6 he was given a larger territory including Galatia, Lycaonia, and parts of Pamphylia.[18] His presence in Pamphylia is confirmed by the coins which he minted at Side.[19] Other territories can be deduced from passing allusions. The Pisidian cities of Selge and Sagalassus have already been cited; in addition he sacked Cremna, where he was to mint a bronze coinage, and was clearly authorized to subdue the rest of Pisidia. Termessus, a free city, naturally remained an independent ally.[20] In the east he defeated Antipater of Derbe, whose territory also included Laranda,[21] and created his own southern capital at Isaura.[22] In the mid-30s Rugged Cilicia, west of Seleuceia on the Calycadnus, had been given to Cleopatra by Mark Antony, but it was transferred to Amyntas, presumably after the battle of Actium. In all probability this gave Amyntas control over the important Tauric pass running from Laranda to Seleuceia, which had been the responsibility of Polemo in the early 30s.[23]

It seems that with one minor alteration this kingdom formed the early Augustan province of Galatia. The exception was Cilicia Tracheia which was given to Archelaus of Cappadocia in 20 BC.[24] The vital port of Seleuceia on the Calycadnus was, however, expressly excluded from Archelaus' possessions, and indeed there is no clear evidence that it had ever been controlled by Amyntas. In the early Augustan period it issued coins with the names of the two philosophers Athenaeus and Xenarchus, both influential with the emperor himself, and it may have been autonomous.[25] On the other hand, since the Augustan province of Galatia certainly extended to include the colony at Ninica on the Calycadnus, which was sited to protect the route over the Taurus from Seleuceia, it is at least possible that Seleuceia itself was also under the governor's jurisdiction.[26]

The only ancient evidence which contradicts the view that the original Augustan province coincided with Amyntas' kingdom is a passage in Dio which states that 'at the death of Amyntas, Augustus did not hand over his kingdom to his sons, but brought it into the empire; and so Galatia and Lycaonia obtained a Roman governor, and the districts of Pamphylia which had formerly been allocated to Amyntas were returned to their own jurisdiction'.[27] As two later passages show, Dio clearly believed that Pamphylia was part of a province separated from Galatia in the Augustan period, as it was in his own day,[28] but in this he appears to have been mistaken. He shows nothing like the same detailed knowledge of early provincial Galatia as Strabo, and mentions only two of its elements, Galatia and Lycaonia, omitting the large and important districts of Pisidia and Phrygia Paroreius. Independent evidence supports the implication of Strabo that Pamphylia was attached to Galatia at this date. In AD 7 Velleius records that M. Plautius Silvanus brought up two legions from the 'provinces beyond the sea' to help crush the Pannonian revolt;[29] an inscription from Attaleia in Pamphylia names M. Plautius Silvanus as leg Aug. pro pr.[30] Moreover, it has been suggested that the troops brought to Pannonia had been used in the previous year to crush an uprising of the Isaurians, which is mentioned by Dio,[31] in which case Plautius Silvanus must have been governor both in Isauria, which was part of the Galatian province and which would normally be approached by a campaigning army from the north,[32] and in Pamphylia, confirming that Pamphylia and Galatia formed a single province at this period.[33]

No alterations to the provincial frontiers are recorded before 6/5 BC, when Deiotarus Philadelphus, the great grandson of the famous Deiotarus, died, and his kingdom Paphlagonia was annexed to Galatia.[34] The date can be calculated from coins and inscriptions of the cities of Gangra/Germanicopolis, Neoclaudiopolis, and Pompeiopolis, which carry era dates referring back to this occasion.[35] The boundaries of Paphlagonia have caused some discussion.[36] It is clear that at least these three cities, which were included in Paphlagonia by Ptolemy, lay in Galatia.[37] The last two were

[16] Appian, BC 5. 319.
[17] Strabo, 12. 6. 4, 569. E. W. Gray suggested emending the text from τὴν γὰρ Ἀντιοχείαν ἔχων τὴν πρὸς τῇ Πισιδίᾳ μέχρι Ἀπολλωνιάδος τῆς πρὸς Ἀπαμείᾳ τῇ Κιβώτῳ καὶ τῆς Παρωρείου τινα ... to τὴν γὰρ Ἀντιοχείαν ἔχων τὴν πρὸς τῇ Πισιδίᾳ καὶ τῆς Παρωρείου τινα μέχρι Ἀπολλωνιάδος τῆς πρὸς Ἀπαμείᾳ τῇ Κιβώτῳ ..., which greatly improves its clarity.
[18] Cassius Dio, 49. 32; see above, Vol. I, Ch. 3 §IV n. 150.
[19] See above, Vol. I, Ch. 3 §IV n. 142.
[20] Strabo, 12. 6. 4, 569; for bronzes of Amyntas minted at Cremna, see Head, HN² 707; Aulock, Lykaonien, 54–5, and Pisidien, ii nos. 911–1047. For Termessus see S. Mitchell, 'Termessus, King Amyntas, and the War with the Sandaliotai', forthcoming.
[21] Strabo, 12. 6. 3, 569, cf. 12. 1. 4, 535 and 14. 5. 24, 679.
[22] Strabo, 12. 6. 3, 569.
[23] Strabo, 14. 6. 6, 671.
[24] Ibid.
[25] Strabo, 14. 5. 4, 670. For the coinage of Seleuceia in the Augustan period, see H. Nicolet, Rev. num. 13 (1971), 26–37.
[26] Cf. S. Mitchell, Historia, 28 (1979), 431.
[27] Dio 52. 26. 3.
[28] 54. 34. 6; 60. 17. 3. The problem was elucidated by R. Syme, Klio, 24 (1934), 122–7, with a change of heart to the view followed here in Klio, 27 (1937), 227 n. 1 = RP i. 42 and ASBuckler 332 = RP i. 145–6. J. G. C. Anderson had already offered the suggestion in Klio (1934), 125 n. 3.
[29] 2. 112. 4.
[30] SEG vi no. 646.
[31] Dio 55. 28. 2–3.
[32] As in the Homonadensian war.
[33] Syme, Klio, 24 (1934), 139–43; Akten VI Epigr. Kongresses (1973), 595–9 = RP iii. 878–81. Jones, CERP² 135 offers another argument in support of this. Pliny, NH 5. 146 probably drawing on an Augustan source, lists the Actalenses among the communities of Galatia. If this is a reference to Pamphylian Attaleia, Pamphylia must have belonged to Augustan Galatia.
[34] Strabo, 12. 3. 41, 562.
[35] Magie, RR ii. 1328; Ruge, RE xviii (1949), 2527–32.
[36] V. Chapot, ASRamsay, 93 ff.; a clear statement by Ruge, RE xviii. 2533 ff.
[37] Ptolemy, 5. 4. 5.

in the north of the region along the northern route to Pontus and the eastern frontier, and milestones from this road confirm that it was still part of the province of Galatia in the third century.[38] The coast, however, was part of Pontus and Bithynia. On the west, Galatian Paphlagonia included Caesareia Hadrianopolis, not only because it may share a common era with the others but since an inscription found there mentions a Iulius Scapula, who is attested as governor of Galatia by three inscriptions of Ancyra.[39]

The annexation of Paphlagonia was followed by the addition of more territory to the east. When Ateporix, dynast of the Caranitis, died, his territory was taken over and a city founded, Sebastopolis, whose era began in 3 BC. In 3/2 BC Amaseia also passed from dynastic rule to direct Roman control, and the two cities, adjoining Trocmian Galatia, became part of Pontus Galaticus.[40] Comana Pontica did not follow until AD 34/5, presumably at the death of its last independent ruler, the Galatian Dyteutus.[41]

Galatia reached its greatest extent in the north-east with the addition of Pontus Polemoniacus. This had been the area ruled by Pythodoris of Tralles, and had passed to her grandson Polemo II in AD 38 during the reign of Gaius.[42] The date is provided by numismatic evidence: the eras of Neocaesareia, Cerasus, and Trapezus can all be shown to have begun in AD 64/5.[43] Ptolemy includes Sebasteia, identified with the modern Sivas, in Polemonian Pontus, and this is confirmed by the coin evidence.[44] The annexation of this area should surely be connected with the military activities of Corbulo and Caesennius Paetus along the Armenian frontier in the years immediately preceding the annexation. Both commanders had experienced difficulties in supplying their forces, and a supply train had been set up from Trapezus through mountainous country to the head-waters of the Euphrates. Trapezus and much of this supply route lay within Polemonian Pontus, and the experience of these years may well have impressed Roman commanders in the area with the need for annexation. Equally important was the fact that annexation gave Rome direct control over the eastern end of the Black Sea coast, and a free hand to contain and curb its notorious privateers.[45]

In the southern half of the province the one major adjustment involved the annexation of Lycia by Claudius in AD 43. Dio states that Lycia was brought under the same jurisdiction as Pamphylia, and this is probably correct.[46] The first governor of the province, Q. Veranius, campaigned between 43 and 48 against the Cietae or Cilices Tracheotae, who will have occupied the mountainous country east of the Pamphylian plain, and to do so he must have controlled Pamphylia itself. Pamphylia, then, and possibly parts of Rugged Cilicia also, will have been taken away from Galatia at this stage.[47]

Pamphylia probably remained united with Lycia for the remainder of the Julio-Claudian period. One governor, Eprius Marcellus in AD 57, is attested in Lycia alone,[48] but a successor Licinius Mucianus certainly controlled both regions.[49] Before the end of Nero's principate Rutilius Gallicus was *legatus provinciae Galaticae* and was honoured in that capacity at Ephesus by two units of the Galatian garrison.[50] The title, not that of the provincial governor, should indicate a subordinate position in the period when either Domitius Corbulo or Caesennius Paetus had overall control of both Galatia and Cappadocia. According to Statius, who wrote a poem in Rutilius' honour some forty years later, his authority extended to Pamphylia and even to the Araxes in Armenia, within the field of Roman campaigning at that time. If Statius' language is pressed, we should suppose that Pamphylia was again joined to Galatia in the later 60s.[51] This may not be sufficient grounds for dating an association that others have preferred to attribute to Galba.[52]

In 68 Galba appointed Calpurnius Asprenas to govern Galatia and Pamphylia.[53] The evidence of Tacitus is

38 CIL iii. 14184[34] (L. Petronius Verus AD 198, 6 mls. NW of Vezirköprü); 14184[27,30] (L. Iulius Apronius Maenius Pius Salmallianus AD 222–4, Vezirköprü); 14184[25] (M. Iunius Valerius Nepotianus c. AD 250, in the Phazemonitis).

39 IGR iii no. 151; Bosch, *Ankara*, nos. 135–7; Sherk, i. 69; iii. 169 no. 7. For the site see G. Mendel, *BCH* 25 (1901), 51 f. and R. Leonhardt, *Paphlagonia* (1915), 244 ff. For the question of the period at which it was attached to Galatia, see above, Vol. I, Ch. 7 § IV n. 132.

40 The evidence is complicated, see Magie *RR* ii. 1285, 1329. The era of both Amaseia and Sebastopolis, beginning in 3/2 BC was established by H. Dessau, *ZfN* 25 (1906), 339 ff. See also Cl. Bosch, *Num. Int. Monatschrift* (1933), 33 f.

41 Strabo, 12. 3. 32–7, 557–60 on dynastic Comana; Kubitschek, *RE* i (1894), 643–4 s.v. *aera* for the date.

42 Dio 59. 12. 2.

43 *RE* i. 644; Head, *HN²* 497–9; Magie, *RR* ii. 1417–18.

44 Ptolemy, 5. 3. 6, 8. For the era see above, Vol. I, Ch. 7 § IV n. 149.

45 See F. Cumont, *ASRamsay*, 104 ff.; for the supply problem see Tacitus, *Ann.* 13. 39 (14. 24; 15. 12).

46 Dio, 60. 17. 3 cf. Suetonius, *Claudius*, 25.

47 A. E. Gordon, *Q. Veranius, Consul 49 A.D.* (1952) published the career inscription of Lycia's first governor (*AE* (1953), 251). Another argument which may support this conclusion is that the family of the first senator from Lycia, M. Arruntius Claudianus of Xanthus, had presumably acquired Roman citizenship through the offices of the procurator M. Arruntius Aquila, who was active in Pamphylia in AD 50; see C. Habicht, *ZPE* 13 (1974), 3 and now, with new evidence, A. Balland *Xanthos*, vii. 6–8, 161–5. Western Rugged Cilicia, however, may have been given to Polemo, see Dio, 60. 8. 2 and Bean and Mitford, *Journeys in Rough Cilicia 1964–8* (1970), 95 no. 71 as interpreted by E. W. Gray, *CR* 22 (1972), 400–1.

48 Tacitus, *Ann.* 13. 33; cf. *IGR* iii no. 553 (Tlos).

49 *ILS* 8816 = *IGR* iii no. 486 (Oenoanda), cf. Pliny, *NH* 12. 9; 13. 88; *AE* (1915), 48 (Attaleia).

50 *ILS* 9499; *AE* (1920), 55 = *I. Eph.* no. 715 on which see M. Speidel, *Armies and Frontiers*, 14, and W. Eck, *AJPhil.* 106 (1985), 475–84.

51 *Silvae*, 1. 4. 76–9. Note, however, that Statius does not record Rutilius Gallicus' career in chronological order, and more than most sources of information he is prone to embellishment. For the many problems of the poem and the career see E. Groag, *RE* iA (1914), 1255–63, and Syme, *RP* v. 514–20.

52 For Galba, see Syme, *RP* i. 42–6; *Historia*, 21 (1982), 466 (= *RP* iv. 121) endorsed by A. Balland in the paper cited below, n. 56.

53 Tacitus, *Hist.* 2. 9.

confirmed by an inscription from Tripolitania, and indeed another inscription from Pisidian Antioch, if correctly restored, shows that he held office at least until AD 70.[54] Lycia at the same period was apparently under Sextus Marcius Priscus, who is attested on inscriptions of Patara, Xanthos, and Lyde.[55] At Patara the emperor's name has been erased, and at Lyde he is described as being the legate of the emperor Vespasian and of all the emperors since Tiberius Caesar. The correct explanation is surely that the erased name is that of Nero, who should also be identified with the Tiberius Caesar of the Lyde text.[56] So, Sex. Marcius Priscus will have governed Lycia on its own from c.68 to 70. The division of Lycia and Pamphylia did not persist. A newly published inscription from Oenoanda in Lycia must be restored to show M. Hirrius Fronto Neratius Pansa governing the two regions, and his term of office should be dated AD 70–2.[57] He was succeeded by Cn. Avidius Celer Fiscillinius Firmus and by L. Luscius Ocrea, the latter unequivocally attested in both Lycia and Pamphylia.[58]

The administrative arrangements for Pisidia in the first century AD are a matter for dispute. Until AD 43 it was attached to Galatia. Then, at an uncertain date central and southern Pisidia were detached from Phrygia Paroreius and joined to the southern province of Lycia and Pamphylia. Ptolemy suggests that the dividing line between the two provinces ran north of the cities of Seleuceia Sidera and Conana, leaving only the strip from Apollonia to Pisidian Antioch in Galatia.[59] Legates of Lycia and Pamphylia are attested at Sagalassus between AD 138 and 141 and at the colony of Comama between 144 and 147.[60] Pisidia south of Burdur Göl may have been detached from Galatia much

earlier than this. The titulature of Galatian governors under the Flavians and Trajan regularly included Pisidia,[61] but this need only denote the northern edge of the region, where it abutted Phrygia Paroreius, and not the whole area as far south as Pamphylia. In fact there is a good case to be made for attaching Pisidia to Lycia and Pamphylia as early as AD 43. Q. Veranius, the first governor of the new province, fought a campaign in the mountains against the Rugged Cilicians (see above, n. 47). Thought had been given to military matters at the outset. But Pamphylia was vulnerable from the north, and the combination of Lycia and Pamphylia without the adjoining part of Pisidia makes no strategic sense. The only evidence that Pisidia south of Burdur Göl belonged to Galatia at this period comes from the boundary stones set up between Sagalassus and Tymbrianassus by Pupius Praesens, a procurator who was also active at Iconium in Galatia, and the imperial legate Q. Petronius Umber, who has always been taken for the legate of Galatia in AD 53/4.[62] However, there is room in the *fasti* of Lycia and Pamphylia for an incumbent at this time between M. Calpurnius Rufus and Eprius Marcellus as there is not in the *fasti* of Galatia between M. Annius Afrinus and the appointment of Domitius Corbulo to his eastern command in AD 54.[63] Petronius Umber accordingly probably governed Lycia, Pamphylia, and its northward Pisidian extension. The procurator is no obstacle, since Pupius Praesens' responsibilities may have extended beyond Galatia to Lycia and Pamphylia, like those of C. Cassius Salmallas and M. Valerius Eudaemon under Trajan and Hadrian respectively (see above, Vol. I, Ch. 5 at nn. 66–71). It should be noticed that Q. Petronius Umbrinus, presumably Petronius Umber's son, also governed Lycia and Pamphylia in AD 76/7 and 77/8, thereby continuing a family tradition.[64]

The Flavian period saw the creation of a vast consular province in central and eastern Anatolia, comprising the territory which had belonged to Galatia (except Pamphylia), Armenia Minor, annexed in 71 or 72,[65] and the previously procuratorial province of Cappadocia. Hints that such a command might develop had already appeared with the appointments of Corbulo and Caesennius Paetus, but the arrangement had not become established. Vespasian and his advisers, with an eye for strategic expediency, saw that it was desirable, if not completely necessary, to bring under a single command, both the frontier area along the Euphrates and the huge hinterland, through which all the troops and supplies had to pass.[66] The first governor of Vespasian's new province

[54] J. M. Reynolds and J. B. Ward Perkins, *Inscriptions of Roman Tripolitania*, no. 346 (*AE* (1952), no. 232); B. Levick, *AS* 17 (1967), 103 and pl. xia (*AE* (1962), 492); W. Eck, *Chiron*, 12 (1982) 284, 285 n. 15.

[55] *TAM* ii. 396, 275, 131.

[56] W. Eck, *ZPE* 6 (1970), 65 ff.; *Chiron*, 12 (1982), 285 n. 16. The evidence of the inscriptions is more compelling than the suggestion of Suetonius, *Vesp.* 8, that Lycia had been free until Vespasian took away its liberty. Perhaps this *libertas* should be understood to mean something other than freedom from direct provincial government. A. Balland, in an unpublished paper shown to me by W. Eck, argues that the liberty of Lycia had amounted to no more than its separation from Pamphylia. In support he cites the phraseology of Cassius Dio, 60. 17. 3, τούς τε Λυκίους . . . ἐδουλώσατό τε καὶ ἐς τὸν τῆς Παμφυλίας νόμον ἐσέγραψεν.

[57] The Oenoanda text was published by A. S. Hall, *Epigr. Anat.* 4 (1984), 27–35, and his interpretation of it has been endorsed by Balland in the study cited in the last note. Hirrius Fronto also appears on inscriptions of Tlos (*TAM* ii. 1. 568) and Xanthos (Balland, *Xanthos*, vii no. 89). For his date of office see W. Eck, *ZPE* 6 (1970), 65 ff.; *Chiron*, 12 (1982), 287; and H. Halfmann, *Asia-Minor-Studien*, 3 (1991), 41–3.

[58] *IGR* iii. 466, and another copy of the same text published by C. Naour, *Anc. Soc.* 9 (1978), 166 (*AE* (1978), 804), both from Balbura; *SEG* vi. 648 from Attaleia.

[59] Ptolemy, 5. 5. 4, and 4. 9.

[60] *CIL* iii. 6885, Ramsay, *JRS* 6 (1916), 132 for Q. Voconius Saxa Fidus at Comama; *IGR* iii. 342 for Cornelius Proculus at Sagalassus; the inscription on the architrave of the temple of

Apollo Clarius is illustrated by M. Waelkens, *AS* 40 (1990), 187 fig. 2. Both texts are adduced by B. Rémy, *L'Évolution administrative de l'Asie Mineure*, 83. C. Sulpicius Iustus Dryantianus, the governor of Lycia and Pamphylia in AD 199, is named on a milestone found in northern Pisidia on the territory of Conana, D. H. French, *AS* 41 (1991), 10.

[61] See above, nn. 3, 4, 6, and 8.

[62] G. E. Bean, *AS* 9 (1959), 15–18 no. 30.

[63] *AE* (1972), 610 and (1956), 186. For Galatia at this time see Sherk, ii. 976–9.

[64] W. Eck, *Chiron*, 12 (1982), 297–8. The idea that Petronius Umber was governor of Lycia and Pamphylia was first put to me by David French.

[65] See Vol. I, Ch. 9 §I nn. 5–6.

[66] See Vol. I, Ch. 9 §II n. 51.

is not known for certain, but an attractive suggestion is M. Ulpius Traianus, the father of the emperor Trajan.[67] One administrative consequence seems to have been the need to appoint a subsidiary praetorian legate, on the model of Rutilius Gallicus, to assist the consular governor,[68] five of whom are attested for the period between Vespasian and Trajan.[69]

The dissolution of this great double province has occasioned some controversy, and the stages in the process are not clear beyond dispute. By 114 there was a separate governor of Cappadocia, Armenia Major (annexed in that year), and Armenia Minor, namely L. Catilius Severus Iulianus Claudius Reginus.[70] The last certain governor of the whole Galatia–Cappadocia complex was C. Iulius Quadratus Bassus, who held the post in 110 and perhaps as late as *c*.112 and 113.[71] Between these two M. Iunius Homullus is attested only in Cappadocia in 113/14.[72] Further, L. Caesennius Sospes, suffect consul in July 114, governed while still a praetorian the whole Galatian province with the apparent exception of Cappadocia which is omitted from the many territories listed on the inscription set up in his honour by a freedman at Pisidian Antioch.[73] Despite difficulties, most notably in finding a plausible explanation for the subtraction of Cappadocia alone, without even Armenia Minor, from the Galatian command at this date, it seems reasonable to date Sospes' term of office to *c*.112–14, contemporary with Homullus in Cappadocia. Both appointments should doubtless be seen in the context of Trajan's plans for his Parthian war, but to attempt to explain the difficulties in this way is an exercise in illuminating *obscurum per obscurius*.[74]

Immediately afterwards, Galatia lost its Pontic extension: an acephalous inscription from Pisidian Antioch dating to 116/17, refers to a *leg. Aug. pro pr. provinc. Galat. Phryg. Pisid. Lycaon, Paphlag*.[75] and another, of a year or two later, to a legate of *Galatiae Pisid. Paphlagoniae*.[76] All the Pontic regions were attached to Cappadocia.

At some date in the second century a large area was subtracted from the south of Galatia, and formed a new province, Cilicia, Isauria, and Lycaonia, or the *Tres Eparchiae*, with its metropolis at Tarsus.[77] The latest date for its creation is provided by an inscription of Isaura from the reign of Antoninus Pius, honouring C. Etrillius Regillus Laberius Priscus as governor of the triple province.[78] The Antiochian inscription from the last year of Trajan or the first of Hadrian mentioning a governor of Galatia, Pisidia, and Paphlagonia might suggest that the *Tres Eparchiae* had already been subtracted from Galatia by that date,[79] but since there were separate governors of Cilicia alone through most of Hadrian's reign,[80] it seems best to defer the event until the early years of Pius, between 138 and 146.[81] The boundary between this new southern province and Galatia is defined by a line which separates those cities known to have formed part of the *koinon* of Lycaonia from those which did not. The former include Laranda (the metropolis), Derbe, Dalisandus, Ilistra, Barata, and Hyde; the latter Iconium, Laodicea Catacecaumene, and Savatra.[82] This line roughly coincides with the ethnic boundary between Lycaonia and Phrygia, since Iconium was reckoned to be a Phrygian city and typically Phrygian remains, such as doorstones and neo-Phrygian inscriptions are found as far south as Savatra and the regions adjoining it.[83] On the south-west the boundary

[67] G. W. Bowersock, *JRS* 63 (1973), 134–5. Doubted by Kreiler, *Statthalter Kleinasiens*, 32–8; regarded as possible by Eck, *Chiron*, 12 (1982), 287–8 n. 20.

[68] Syme, *Tacitus*, 68 n. 5; *JRS* 67 (1977), 40 = *RP* iii. 1046; Eck, *Senatoren*, 3 n. 9; Sherk, ii. 1010–11.

[69] Ti. Iulius Celsus Polemaeanus, L. Iulius Proculeianus, C. Antius A. Iulius Quadratus, C. Valerius Severus (see Sherk, ii. 1001, 1006–11, 1023 for details).

[70] *ILS* 1041 = *ILAfr*. 43; Sherk, ii. 1027; Eck, *Senatoren*, 178.

[71] *Alt. v. Perg*. viii. 3 no. 21, dated by Habicht between 107/8 and 110/11. This is preferable to Sherk, ii. 1020–3 who suggests that his predecessor P. Calvisius Ruso Iulius Frontinus stayed in office until 109, and that Iulius Quadratus Bassus served from 109 to 112 or 113. In fact, as a coin shows (P. R. Franke, *Chiron*, 9 (1979), 379 ff.), Calvisius Ruso was in office by 104/5, evidently the direct successor to Q. Orfitasius Aufidius Umber (*AS* 28 (1978), 93–6), and probably stayed until about 107 (cf. W. Eck, *Chiron*, 12 (1982), 340 no. 242).

[72] Dio 68. 19. 1; *Coll. Wadd*. 6765 (Caesareia); Eck, *Senatoren*, 174.

[73] *ILS* 1017, see n. 8. For the suffect consulship see Syme, *Hermes*, 85 (1957), 493 n. 2 = *RP* i. 351–2 n. 8; Eck, *Senatoren*, 10.

[74] Syme, *JRS* 67 (1977), 38–49 = *RP* iii. 1043–61 (cf. Eck, *Chiron*, 12 (1982), 321 n. 161) argues that Sospes held a temporary legateship in 93, or more probably in 94, after the premature death of L. Antistius Rusticus. His command, however, excluded Cappadocia which might have been taken over by the legionary legate based at Melitene. Armenia Minor, including the fortress at Satala, was also probably excluded from Sospes' command, although it is included in the

list of regions which he governed. Except on this last point, Syme is followed, without acknowledgement, by Timothy Mitford, *ANRW* ii. 7. 2 (1980), 1194–5. R. K. Sherk is certainly right to rebut this suggestion. See his comments in *ANRW* ii. 7. 2. (1980), 1030 n. 200 and *AJPhil*. 100 (1976), 167 n. 1. Moreover, as P. R. Franke points out (*Chiron*, 9 (1979), 381), T. Pomponius Bassus was already governor of Galatia during the 14th year of Domitian (Nov. 93–4), presumably in the autumn of 94. He was suffect consul in September of the same year, an office he will have to have held *in absentia* (cf. Syme, *JRS* 48 (1958), 1–9 = *RP* i. 378–92), an anomaly occasioned in this instance by Antistius Rusticus' death, which will have required him to leave for his province before he originally intended (see also Syme, *RP* iv. 278–94 at 288–90).

[75] *ILS* 1039.

[76] *ILS* 1038; on this text see W. Eck, *Chiron*, 12 (1982), 354 n. 292. The same titles on *OGIS* n. 535 = *IGR* iii no. 316 from Apollonia.

[77] *BCH* 7 (1883), 325 ff.

[78] G. Radet and P. Paris, *BCH* 9 (1885), 433 ff. = Sterrett, *WE* nos. 189 and 190.

[79] See n. 76.

[80] Eck, *Chiron*, 13 (1983), 148 ff. and 217; R. Syme, *Historia*, 18 (1969), 363–6 = *RP* ii. 785–9.

[81] As argued by C. Habicht, *Ist. Mitt*. 9 (1959), 116 ff.

[82] Aulock, *Lykaonien*, 25–32 for the *koinon*; 48–9 for Savatra.

[83] S. Mitchell, *Historia*, 28 (1979), 411–12 for Iconium; for the ethnic boundaries of Phrygia, see M. Waelkens, *Anc. Soc*. 8 (1977), 293. Savatra lies beyond this boundary, but well short of Lycaonia.

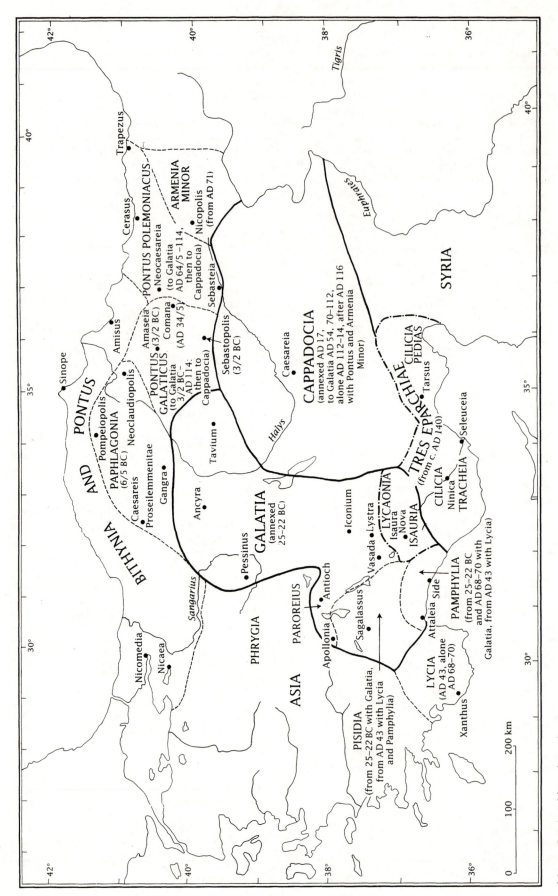

Map 6. Provincial boundaries from 25 BC to AD 235

PONTUS AND BITHYNIA

Sinope
Amisus
Pompeiopolis
PAPHLAGONIA (6/5 BC)
Neoclaudiopolis
Caesareis
Proseilemmenitae
Gangra
Ancyra
Nicomedia
Nicaea
Sangarius
Pessinus
PHRYGIA
PAROREIUS
ASIA
Apollonia
Antioch
Sagalassus
Vasada
PISIDIA (from 25–22 BC with Galatia, from AD 43 with Lycia and Pamphylia)

Trapezus
Cerasus
PONTUS POLEMONIACUS
Neocaesareia
ARMENIA MINOR
Nicopolis (from AD 71)
Amaseia (3/2 BC)
Comana (AD 34/5)
PONTUS GALATICUS (to Galatia 3/2 BC– AD 114, then to Cappadocia)
Sebasteia
Sebastopolis (3/2 BC)
Tavium
Halys
GALATIA (annexed 25–22 BC)
Iconium
Lystra
LYCAONIA
Isaura Nova
ISAURIA
Caesareia
CAPPADOCIA (annexed AD 17, to Galatia AD 54, 70–112, alone AD 112–14, after AD 116 with Pontus and Armenia Minor)

Euphrates
Tigris
SYRIA

TRES EPARCHIAE (from c. AD 140)
CILICIA PEDIAS
Tarsus
CILICIA TRACHEIA
Ninica
Seleuceia

PAMPHYLIA (from 25–22 BC and AD 68–70 with Galatia, from AD 43 with Lycia)
Attaleia Side
LYCIA (AD 43, alone AD 68–70)
Xanthus

200 km
100
0

must have run between the east Pisidian city of Vasada, where a late second- or third-century governor of Galatia is attested,[84] and Isaura, one of the chief cities of the *Tres Eparchiae*. Perhaps the whole of the lake district of Beyşehir and Suğla was Galatian, with the provincial boundary running north-east from Suğla Göl to include Lystra and Iconium.

With these developments under Antoninus Pius the province of Galatia achieved a stable form which it retained until the second quarter of the third century. From a military point of view it had become relatively insignificant, and the new boundaries, dividing Pontus and Cappadocia from east Galatia and separating the Tauric districts of Isauria and Pisidia from Phrygia Paroreius, reflect the fact that it was no longer thought necessary to keep these important areas under the control of a single governor. Not only was the eastern frontier as secure as it ever would be, but the interior of Asia Minor, so often disturbed by tribal uprisings, banditry and brigandage, was now enjoying a longer period of peace and stability than ever before or since. The province of Galatia had lost its old military *raison d'être*, which goes far to explain its apparently haphazard and cumbersome shape in the first and early second centuries, and had reverted to relative unimportance in the Roman scheme of frontier defence and provincial security. When the boundaries were again modified, during the third and fourth centuries, such security could no longer be taken for granted.

---

[84] Swoboda, *Denkmäler*, no. 38; *ILS* 1135. See Sherk, i. 75–6 and *AJPhil.* 100 (1976), 172. Note that Fl. Ulpianus, attested on a milestone of Akkilise, beside Suğla Göl (*JRS* 14 (1924), 76 no. 110 = *AE* (1926), 75, of AD 202) is also known to have been *hegemon* at Seleuceia on the Calycadnus (*Belleten* (1978), 412 no. 38).

APPENDIX 2

Provincial Boundaries in Asia Minor AD 235–535

The provincial boundaries in Anatolia, which had been laid down by the middle of the second century AD, remained essentially stable for over half a century. However, during the third century changes occurred which anticipated the fundamental and well-attested reorganization of Diocletian, and it is likely that the imperfect documentation of this period gives only an inadequate indication of developments which occurred then. A province of Phrygia and Caria, governed by senatorial *legati Augusti*, was carved out of the great proconsular province of Asia by AD 250.[1] In eastern Anatolia the most conspicuous alterations occurred in Pontus. From the Julio-Claudian until the Severan period the old kingdom of Mithridates VI had been divided between several Roman provinces. A coastal strip in the west, including the important cities of Sinope and Amisus, was attached to Bithynia; most of the hinterland south of this area, including the cities of Pompeiopolis and Neoclaudiopolis, belonged to the Paphlagonian section of the province of Galatia; the rest of Pontus, including the real heartland of Mithridates' kingdom in the valleys of the rivers Lycus and Iris, at first formed part of Pompey's original province of Pontus. It was then handed over to client rulers for much of the triumviral and early Julio-Claudian period, before it was reannexed to the empire between 3/2 BC and AD 64 to form Pontus Galaticus and Pontus Polemoniacus, both parts of the province of Galatia. Between the reigns of Vespasian and Trajan these regions belonged to the huge Galatia–Cappadocia complex, and thereafter passed to Cappadocia.[2] These arrangements remained undisturbed until the end of the Severan period. During the principate of Severus Alexander (222–35) the names of the governor Q. Iulius Proculeianus appear on milestones found on the Caesareia–Melitene road in Cappadocia and also on the territory of Zela in Pontus, proving that the two areas were still under the same administration.[3] It also seems that the Trocmian territory of eastern Galatia

around Tavium was attached to this Pontic–Cappadocian complex. Aurelius Basileus appears as provincial governor between AD 226 and 229 on milestones found both on the territory of Tavium and on the territory of Caesareia; a successor under Maximinus (235–8), Licinius Serenianus, was also active around Tavium and on the Caesareia–Melitene road; further, M. Antonius Memmius Hiero, who was certainly governor in Cappadocia between 244 and 249, was also honoured with a statue at Tavium.[4]

Between about 230 and 249 equestrian governors took the place of senatorial *legati Augusti* in Pontus. The names of these *praesides provinciae Ponti* have been noted on milestones of Amaseia, Sebastopolis, and Zela.[5] In AD 250 under Trajan Decius, M. Iunius Valerius Nepotianus, who may have been either of senatorial or of equestrian status, erected a milestone in the territory of Neoclaudiopolis. Although the stone does not preserve his titles intact, he was certainly *praeses* of Galatia and Pontus, and apparently of a third region also. Cappadocia, however, had a separate governor in 251/2.[6] This indication that Galatia was reunited with Pontus in the mid-third century is supported by the inscriptions set up for C. Iulius Senecio at Ancyra, which describe him in a Greek text, as τὸν κράτιστον ἐπίτροπον τῶν Σεββ., πράξαντα καὶ τὰ τῆς ἡγεμονίας μέρη, and in a Latin version as *proc. prov. Galatiae, item vice praesidis eiusd. prov. et Ponti*.[7] The letter forms of the Greek inscription are virtually identical with

---

1 C. Roueché, *JRS* 71 (1981), 103–20, and *Aphrodisias in Late Antiquity*, 12–14, 17–19; Roueché and D. H. French, *ZPE* 49 (1982), 159 ff.; M. Christol and T. Drew Bear, *Travaux et recherches en Turquie* (1982), 34 ff.; S. Frei-Korsunsky, *Epigr. Anat.* 8 (1986), 91–5 for the date.

2 See above, App. 1 at nn. 40–5 and 66, and X. Loriot, *Bull. soc. nat. des antiquaires de France* (1976), 44 ff.

3 See D. H. French, 'Milestones of Cappadocia' (unpub. MS). The text from the Caesareia–Melitene road gives the name of the governor as C. Iul[–6/7–]anus, which French reasonably corrects and restores as Q. Iul(ius) [Proculi]anus, to concur with the milestone from Zela, *AE* (1961), 25.

4 D. H. French, in *Labor Omnibus Unus: Festschrift G. Walser* (1989), 38–44: Aur. Basileus, *CIL* iii. 14184[42] and a newly published milestone from near Caesareia; Licinius Serenianus: K. Bittel, *Beobachtungen an und bei einer römischen Straße im östlichen Galatien* (Heidenheim, 1985), 24 and fig. 33; M. Antonius Memmius Hiero, *RECAM* ii no. 414.

5 Q. Faltonius Restitutianus (? 230/235), French, *Epigr. Anat.* 8 (1986), 75–7; Claudianus (235), ibid. 80; P. Aelius Vibianus (236/8), French, *ZPE* 43 (1981), 152–3; Claudius Marcellus (238/44), *CIL* iii. 14184[16]; Cl. Aur. Tiberius (244/9), French, *ZPE* 43 (1981), 153 no. 5.

6 J. A. R. Munro, *JHS* 20 (1900), 161–2 no. 3; *CIL* iii. 14184[25]. The traces on the stone do not support the idea that *Paphlagoniae* (Munro, loc. cit.; Sherk, i. 86) or *Cappadociae* (Barbieri, *L'albo senatorio da Settimio Severo a Carino* (1952), 288) was inscribed at the end of the text, but Munro's readings are not infallible, and clearly something was added after *Ponti*. Cappadocia under Gallus and Volusianus was governed by Vergilius Maximus; see French, *Festschrift Walser*, 38–44.

7 Bosch, *Ankara*, nos. 64–5. The Greek inscription is *AE* (1930), 144 = (1931), 128. The reading τῶν Σεββ. was reported by the first editor, G. de Jerphanion, *Mél. de l'univ. St Joseph*, 13

those on the inscription set up for the mid-third century Galatian procurator C. Claudius Firmus,[8] and Iulius Senecio should be dated to the same period.[9] Procurators acting *vice praesidis* are a feature of the reign of Gallienus, who may have used the device to disguise the fact that he was systematically transferring senatorial commands to equestrians, or at least to lessen senatorial offence at this policy.[10] The reunification of Galatia and Pontus in the middle of the century was only temporary. Between AD 279 and 293/305 a further four equestrian *praesides prov. Ponti* erected milestones in the territories of Sinope, Neoclaudiopolis, Zela, and Amaseia.[11] It should be noted that the Pontic governors at this period clearly controlled the eastern part of the old province of Pontus and Bithynia, around Sinope and, *a fortiori*, Amisus, as well as part of Galatian Paphlagonia around Neoclaudiopolis. It is difficult to decide whether this marks a new development of the late third century, or whether their predecessors between 236 and 249 had done the same. After the Severan period there is no indication at all of the province to which Paphlagonia was attached, while the last recorded governor of the joint province of Pontus and Bithynia is L. Egnatius Victor Lollianus under Severus Alexander.[12] It is perhaps most economical to assume that the new separate province of Pontus had included the eastern section of Pontus and Bithynia, and parts of Galatian Paphlagonia, since its creation in the 230s. Third-century Pontus was apparently identical with fourth-century Diospontus, later renamed Helenopontus. The variations in the titles of Pontic governors from the time of Diocletian and through the fourth century are more plausibly to be seen as changes of name rather than of substance. In AD 305/6 a milestone found near Sinope names a governor, Aur Hierax, *v.p. praeses Ponti Paflag(oniae)*.[13] The title is without precedent or sequel, and should be seen as no more than a temporary alternative designation of a province that certainly included Paphlagonian

territory. Thereafter the evolution is straightforward. The province was soon called Diospontus, and *praesides* are attested in 308,[14] and between 317 and 323.[15] The provincial name occurs both in the Verona list,[16] and in the list of bishops who attended the Council of Nicaea in 325,[17] a source which also indicates that the province contained the cities of Amaseia, Zela, and Comana. Around 328 it was renamed Helenopontus, after the mother of the emperor Constantine,[18] and *praesides prov. Helenoponti* are recorded between 333 and 335,[19] 340/50,[20] and 361/3.[21] The composition of the province remained unchanged until AD 535, and the lists of bishops attending the Council of Chalcedon in 451,[22] the Synecdemos of Hierocles of 528,[23] and Justinian's *novella* 27 of 535[24] consistently indicate that its main cities were Amaseia, Ibora, Zela, Andrapa (the old Neoclaudiopolis), Amisus, and Sinope.

To the east lay Pontus Polemonianus, originally annexed to the empire in AD 64, which contained the inland cities of Megalopolis-Sebasteia, Neocaesareia, and Comana, and the Pontic coast east of Amisus, from Cerasus to Trapezus.[25] The Verona list identifies a separate province of Pontus Polemonianus in the early fourth century, which was virtually identical with this region, and its continued existence is confirmed by the lists of bishops attending the Councils of Nicaea in 325 and Chalcedon in 451, and by the Synecdemos of Hierocles. According to the last two sources its chief cities were Neocaesareia, Cerasus, Comana, Polemonium, and Trapezus. Since the Nicaea list included Comana in Diospontus, there may have been some minor boundary alterations between the two Pontic provinces in the later fourth or early fifth centuries.[26] In 535 Justinian united the two Pontic provinces under a single *moderator*, abolishing the name of Polemonian Pontus as being too reminiscent of the pagan past, and called the whole province Helenopontus.[27] However, both Neocaesareia and Amaseia, the chief cities of the

---

(1928), 246 and has been repeated in all subsequent editions. A squeeze housed in the *schedae* of the Kleinasiatische Kommission in Vienna shows that the stone in fact has τῶν Σεββ. (leaf), which harmonizes with the *proc. Augg.* on the Latin inscription (= *ILS* 1373).

[8] *AS* 27 (1977), 66 ff. no. 4 with pl. *1b*.

[9] These texts have usually been dated to the period 198–211 on account of the false reading of the Greek inscription cited in n. 7. See e.g. *PIR²* iv. 275: I no. 564; Pflaum, *CP* iii. 1076.

[10] M. Christol, *ZPE* 22 (1976), 173–4 for a list of examples; cf. H.-G. Pflaum, *Historia*, 25 (1976), 109–17. But note the precedent of Q. Faltonius Restitutianus, *proc. et praeses prov. Ponti* in 230/1, *Epigr. Anat.* 8 (1986), 75.

[11] Aelius Quintianus (279–282/3), French, *ZPE* 43 (1981), 161; Cl. Longinus (282/3), French, *Epigr. Anat.* 8 (1986), 71–4; Aur. Priscianus (293/305), *ZPE* 43 (1981), 162–3; Aur. Valentinianus (293/305), *ZPE* 43 (1981), 158 no. 9.

[12] *IGR* iii. 93; *PIR²* iii. 73: E no. 36. Eusebius, *HE* 7. 5. 2, cited by Loriot, *Bull. soc. nat. des antiquaires de France* (1976), speaks of Πόντος τε καὶ Βιθυνία in connection with events that took place in AD 253, but he could be referring to them either as a joint or as separate provinces. Loriot cites other cases of procurators in the mid-third century who held office in *Pontus et Bithynia*, but procuratorial spheres of activity did not always coincide with provincial boundaries, especially in Asia Minor.

[13] French, *ZPE* 43 (1981), 159 no. 10.

[14] Fl. Severus, a milestone from the territory of Amaseia, *ZPE* 43 (1981), 151 no. 4.

[15] Val. Chrysaorius, on a milestone from the territory of Neoclaudiopolis, *ZPE* 43 (1981), 158 no. 9.

[16] See T. D. Barnes, *The New Empire of Diocletian and Constantine* (1982), 201–8.

[17] Ed. H. Gelzer, H. Hilgenfeld, and O. Cuntz, *Patrum Nicaenorum Nomina* (Leipzig, 1908).

[18] See A. H. M. Jones, *The Roman Economy*, 263 (from *JRS* 44 (1954), 21).

[19] Fl. Iulius Leontius, on milestones of Amaseia, Zela, and Sinope, *ZPE* 43 (1981), 158 no. 9.

[20] Fl. Achillius, on a milestone at Sinope, *CIL* iii. 14184¹⁵.

[21] Fl. Domitius Hilarius, on a milestone at Sinope, *ZPE* 43 (1981), 159 no. 11.

[22] Ed. E. Schwartz, *Acta Conciliorum Oecumenicorum*, ii. 6. 105–11.

[23] E. Honigmann, *Le Synekdémos d'Hiéroklès* (1939), who dates the compilation to this year.

[24] Ed. R. Schoell, *Corpus Iuris Civilis*, iii (1954).

[25] See above, App. 1 nn. 43–4.

[26] Comana had also been an anomaly in the 1st cent. AD, when it was annexed not in 3/2 BC, like the other cities of Pontus Galaticus, nor in AD 64/5 with Pontus Polemoniacus, but in AD 34/5. See above, App. 1 n. 41.

[27] *Novella*, 29.

two halves of the new province, were allowed to retain the title metropolis.

The Verona list also identifies a new province of Paphlagonia, whose chief cities, according to the list of bishops at Nicaea, included Pompeiopolis, Ionopolis, and Amastris. This may have been a consequence of Diocletian's provincial reforms, although the possibility that Paphlagonia had been detached from its adjacent provinces earlier in the third century cannot be completely ruled out. Paphlagonia now consisted of a section of the Amnias river valley, west of Neoclaudiopolis, and of the Pontic coastline, west of Sinope. It probably also included the old capital at Gangra, south of Mount Olgassys. On the west, Diocletianic Paphlagonia abutted Bithynia, but between 384 and 387 Theodosius I created a new province called Honorias.[28] The acts of the Council of Chalcedon and the Synecdemos list the cities of Paphlagonia as Gangra, Amastris, Dadybra, Ionopolis, Pompeiopolis, and Sura; while Claudiopolis, Prusias, Heraclea, Tius, Crateia, and Hadrianopolis belonged to Honorias. This shows that with the one exception of Hadrianopolis, which in the second century had belonged to Galatia,[29] Honorias was made up of territory from the old province of Bithynia, to which Prusias still belonged at the time of the Council of Nicaea. In 535 Justinian followed the same course with Honorias as he had with Polemonian Pontus, and attached it to Paphlagonia, which thus comprised the territories of twelve cities. However, at an unknown date, probably still under Justinian, the old division between Paphlagonia and Honorias may have been restored.[30]

Galatia itself, according to the Verona list, was a single province under Diocletian. Surprisingly, however, the Galatian bishops who attended the Council of Nicaea represented only the eastern cities of Ancyra, Tavium, Gdanmaa, Kinna, and Iuliopolis, which all belonged to the later province of Galatia Prima, so there is no early fourth-century evidence for the extent of the province in the west and south-west. The presence of a bishop from Gdanmaa shows that the southern boundary extended far into the central plateau, to the region of Çeşmeli Sebil or Azak, where the site may be located.[31] Iuliopolis had been part of Bithynia in the first two centuries AD, but the transfer to Galatia is indicated not only by the Verona list, but also by the early fourth-century Itinerarium Burdigalense,[32] which places the fines Bithyniae et Galatiae between the stations of Ceratae and Dadastana, that is at the boundary of the city territories of Nicaea and Iuliopolis, not,

as in the earlier Itinerarium Antonini, between the territories of Iuliopolis and Ancyra.[33] The absence of bishoprics from the later province of Galatia Salutaris in the Nicaea list does not indicate that the province had already been divided under Diocletian, for one of them, Trocnades, appears among the bishoprics of undivided Galatia which sent representatives to the Council of Serdica in 343/4.[34]

The earliest information concerning the creation of Galatia Salutaris comes from the Notitia Dignitatum, which probably reached its existing form in the first decade of the fifth century AD;[35] a passage from Claudian's poem in Eutropium may allude to the division of Galatia in 399.[36] According to the list of bishops attending the Council of Chalcedon the cities of Galatia Prima were Ancyra, Aspona, Iuliopolis, Kinna, Lagania, Mnizon, and Tabia; while those of Secunda, or Salutaris, were Pessinus, Amorium, Eudoxias, Therma, Orcistus, Petenissus, and Trocnades. The geographical area of Prima had thus remained almost identical to that of Galatia implied by the Nicaea list. Galatia Salutaris included not only the western parts of the second- and third-century province, around Pessinus, Therma, and Eudoxias,[37] but also sections of the former proconsular province of Asia, including Orcistus,[38] Amorium,[39] Petenissus,[40] and Trocnades.[41] A fragmentary boundary stone, which has been plausibly dated to the sixth century AD, found south and a little to the west of Amorium at Çoğu, implies that Galatia extended this far. It is puzzling, however, that the anonymous governor in the inscription is styled ὑπατικὸς Γαλατίας. Galatia Prima, according to the Synecdemos was governed by a consularis, Salutaris merely by a hegemon.[42] West of Galatia Salutaris

[28] Libanius, Or. 19. 62; Jones, LRE iii. 347.

[29] See App. 1 n. 39.

[30] Novella, 29. 1 (16 July 535). The restoration of an independent Honorias is suggested by the important inscription published by D. Feissel and I. Kaygusuz, Travaux et mémoires, 9 (1985), 397–419, with discussion at 405–7, and the suggestion of a post-550 date on p. 419. It must be said, however, that none of their arguments is completely decisive against a date before 535 for the text.

[31] W. M. Calder, MAMA i. p. xvi and n. on no. 339; vii. p. xxvi and no. 589; AJA 36 (1932), 457; Honigmann, Synekdémos, 28.

[32] Most recently edited in the Corpus Scriptorum Christianorum Latinorum, 175 (1965), 1–26.

[33] French, Pilgrim's Road, 106–7; RECAM ii. 20; Mitchell, in Armies and Frontiers, 149 n. 31. See also Ammianus Marcellinus, 25. 10.

[34] See A. Feder, Corpus Scriptorum Ecclesiasticorum Latinorum, 65 (1916), 74–8 (Arian bishops), 132–9 (Orthodox bishops); from Hilarius of Poitiers.

[35] Jones, LRE 381 (c. AD 408); E. Demougeot, Latomus, 34 (1975), 1079 ff.

[36] In Eutropium, 2. 585 ff., interpreted by T. D. Barnes, Phoenix, 32 (1978), 81–2. Malalas, 348 (ed. Dindorf) indicates that Galatia was divided under Theodosius I.

[37] For the last two see Ch. 19 §1 n. 48.

[38] MAMA vii. 305. ii. 26, dated to the later 320s, describes Orcistus as lying 'in medio confinio Galatiae Phrygiae'.

[39] An Asian border city, as is shown by the portorium document cited above, Vol. I, Ch. 5 n. 65. The Latin Acts of the Council of Constantinople (C. H. Turner, JTS 15 (1914), 161–78) placed Amorium in Pisidia, but this was probably a simple error, not the only one in these records.

[40] W. Ruge, RE xix (1937), 1127–8.

[41] Located at Kaymaz, west of Pessinus, CIL iii. 6997; Ruge, RE viiA (1939), 152.

[42] W. M. Calder, JRS 2 (1912), 255 no. 13 with commentary, dating the stone, perhaps rightly, to the time of Justinian (republished as MAMA i. 499; see now RECAM ii nos. 207–8 for comparable texts). Calder conjectures that Galatia Salutaris had been promoted to receive a consularis, for which see C. Roueché, GRBS 20 (1979), 174–5. Foss, 'Ankara', 33 n. 17 dates the stone either to the 4th cent., before the division of Galatia, or to a time later than Hierocles' Synecdemos, when the governor of Salutaris might have been upgraded from a praeses to a consularis.

lay Phrygia Salutaris, which certainly existed by AD 361,[43] and may date back to Diocletian's reorganization. Phrygia is divided in the Verona list, and in the list of bishops represented at Serdica in 343/4, but not, curiously, in the list of bishops at Nicaea. The anomaly is best explained by assuming that the sources for Nicaea are defective in this respect.

The southern part of the old imperial province of Galatia was incorporated into a new province of Pisidia, whose metropolis was Pisidian Antioch. This certainly existed by the time of Diocletian, since it is recorded by the Verona list as one of the provinces of the Diocese of Asia, and an equestrian *praeses*, Valerius Diogenes, is known to have held office between 311 and 313.[44] It is not impossible that the province, like Pontus and Isauria, was created at an earlier date. A further *praeses*, Flavius Proculus Macedo, described as a *vir clarissimus*, appears on an inscription of Pisidian Antioch set up between AD 367 and 375.[45] In 325, according to the Nicaea list, Pisidia included several cities which had previously been part of Galatia, including Iconium, Neapolis, Amblada, and Pappa; others from the adjoining parts of Asia, namely Hadrianopolis, Metropolis, and Apamea—as well as Baris and Seleuceia Sidera, which had been part of the Pisidian section of Lycia–Pamphylia. This is confirmed for Apamea, at least, by an inscription set up there by Valerius Diogenes to honour the wife of Galerius, Galeria Valeria Augusta.[46]

Adjoining Pisidia to the south was Isauria, a large and difficult stretch of the Taurus which extended from Seleuceia, near the mouth of the Calycadnus, to the territory of the Homonadeis and perhaps even to Vasada. The origin of a separate province of Isauria can be traced back to the first half of the third century on the strength of an inscription set up for Gordian III by *provincie (sic) Isaur.*, found at Zosta (Losta) in the valley of the Çarşamba.[47]

In AD 371 a new province of Lycaonia was formed, which took territory not only from Pisidia, but also from Isauria and Galatia.[48] The metropolis was Iconium, whose bishop claimed control over both Mistea and Vasada to the west,[49] and who also exercised a somewhat uncertain authority over the clergy of parts of Isauria, including Isaura itself.[50] The

lists of the Council of Constantinople in 381,[51] of Chalcedon in 451, and the Synecdemos show that it included Gdanmaa, the outlying bishopric of Galatia Prima, in the north; Perta, Savatra, and Kana in the north-east; Laranda, Derbe, and Hyde in the south-east; as well as Homonadensian territory, Lystra, Vasada, Mistea, and Isaura itself in the south-west.[52] In AD 535 Justinian ruled that the province should henceforth be governed by officials with the rank of *praetor*, on a par with Pisidia.[53]

On the east Lycaonia adjoined Cappadocia, which formed a single province in the early fourth century. The cities of Tyana, Coloneia (Archelais), Cybistra, and Comana sent bishops to the Council of Nicaea, under the leadership of the metropolitan of Caesareia, but the rural nature of the province is well indicated by the fact that they were accompanied by as many as four *chorepiscopi*. The *itinerarium Burdigalense* marked the boundary between Galatia and Cappadocia at Andrapa, on the Pilgrim's Road, making the small town of Parnassus the first Cappadocian city in the north-west of the province, a point confirmed by the list of bishops at Constantinople in 381.[54] The single province of Cappadocia was divided by the emperor Valens in 371/2 into two, Prima and Secunda.[55] The later sources reflect this division, which placed most of the major Cappadocian cities, apart from Caesareia, in Secunda. The three bishoprics of Cappadocia Prima represented at the Council of Chalcedon were Caesareia, Therma, and Nyssa, in contrast to Tyana (the metropolis), Doara, Coloneia, Cybistra, Nazianzus, Parnassus, Sasima, and Faustinopolis belonging to Cappadocia Secunda. The same division can be observed in the Synecdemos, which indicates that Prima had a senior governor, a *consularis*, while Secunda was under a *hegemon*. Justinian in 535 promoted the latter also to consular status, and further indicated that the most important official in Prima was not the governor but the *comes* in charge of the revenues from imperial estates, which were very extensive in the province.[56]

North-east of Cappadocia lay Armenia Minor. Two cities, Satala and Sebasteia, were represented at the Council of Nicaea, but Basil's correspondence of the 370s indicates that it was made up of a tetrapolis, these two with Nicopolis and Colonia.[57] By AD 386 a second province called Armenia

[43] *CTh.* 1. 6. 1 = *CJust.* 7. 62. 23.

[44] Barnes, *The New Empire of Diocletian and Constantine*, 156.

[45] B. M. Levick, *AS* 15 (1965), 53–62, esp. 59–62; for another governor at Antioch, Saturninus Secundus, see Calder, *JRS* 2 (1912), 86 no. 5 and Sterrett, *EJ* no. 96, and for a *commentariensis* there, *JRS* 2 (1912), 88 no. 7. An anonymous governor, *SEG* vi. 561.

[46] *CIL* iii. 13661; for the boundary between Pisidia and Phrygia Pacatiana, between the cities of Sanaos and Apamea, see T. Drew Bear, *Nouvelles inscriptions de Phrygie* (1978), 27.

[47] The lists of the Nicaea council included the bishop of Vasada both in Pisidia and in Isauria. For the province under Gordian see *CIL* iii. 6783.

[48] Basil, *Ep.* 138. 2: Ἰκόνιον πόλις ἐστι τῆς Πισιδίας, τὸ μὲν παλαιὸν μετὰ τὴν μεγίστην ἢ πρώτη, νῦν δὲ καὶ αὐτὴ προκάθηται μέρους, ὃ ἐκ διαφόρων τιμημάτων συναχθὲν ἐπαρχίας ἰδίας οἰκονομίαν ἐδέξατο.

[49] Basil, *Ep.* 188 canon 10.

[50] Basil, *Ep.* 190.

[51] C. H. Turner, *JTS* 15 (1914), 161–78.

[52] W. M. Ramsay, *JRS* 16 (1926), 212–13, argued that an *officialis* attested on a gravestone from Karasenir in Isaurian country south of the river Çarşamba (*MAMA* viii. 170) would have been on the staff of the *praeses* of Lycaonia between *c.*372 and 400, but the dating evidence is precarious.

[53] *Novella*, 25.

[54] See French, *Pilgrim's Road*, 116–17, and *TIB* ii. 252–3 on Parnassus.

[55] Gregory Naz. *Or.* 43. 58 (*PG* 36. 569–71); Basil, *Epp.* 74–6; cf. *CTh.* 13. 11. 2 (27 Mar. 386).

[56] *Novella*, 30. Jones, *CERP*² 182–90, in a detailed discussion of the division of Cappadocia, argues that the conciliar lists and Hierocles reflected ecclesiastical divisions but not necessarily provincial boundaries, and that Caesareia was the only city in Cappadocia Prima, which otherwise consisted of imperial estates. There are no good grounds for this.

[57] Basil, *Ep.* 68, cf. *Epp.* 99, 102–3, 122, and 163 for Sebasteia in Armenia Minor.

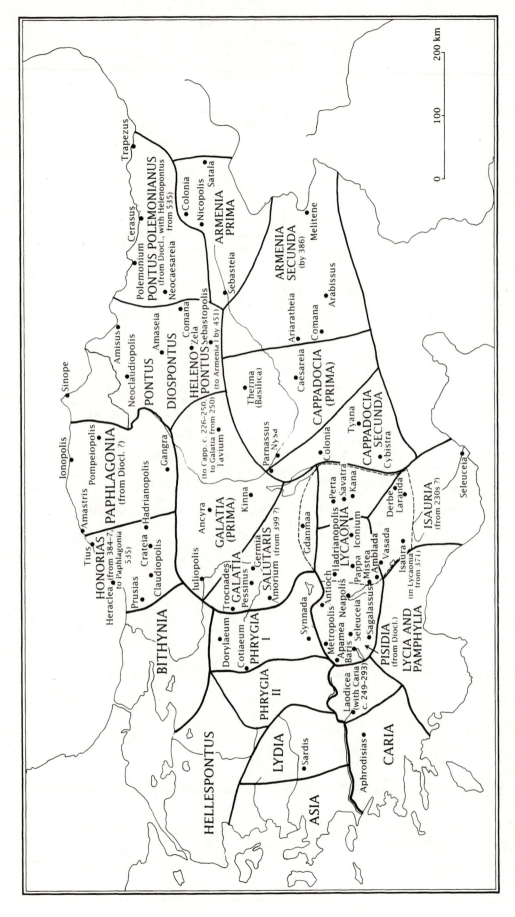

Map 7. Provincial boundaries in Anatolia in late Antiquity

Secunda had been created,[58] whose territory was mainly taken from the eastern parts of Cappadocia.[59] According to the list of bishops at the Council of Chalcedon, the cities of Armenia Prima in the mid-fifth century were Sebasteia, Nicopolis, Satala, and Sebastopolis, closely corresponding to

the Armenia Minor of the fourth century, while those of Armenia Secunda were Melitene, Ariaratheia, Comana, Arca, and Arabissus, that is the eastern part of the earlier Cappadocia.

[58] *CTh.* 13. 11. 2 = *CJust.* 11. 48. 10; cf. *CJust.* 8. 10. 10 (AD 420).

[59] Note that Comana was transferred from Cappadocia to Armenia Secunda before the middle of the 5th cent.; Theodoret, *HE* 2. 5. There are no grounds for thinking that Melitene belonged to Armenia Minor at the beginning of the 4th cent., as is suggested by Jones, *CERP*² 432 n. 17. It, like Cocusus, should have been part of Cappadocia or of

Cappadocia Prima. T. A. Kopeček, *Historia*, 23 (1974), 320–1 cites Basil, *Ep.* 74, which says of Cappadocia διαιροῦσι γὰρ αὐτὴν καὶ ἐπιδιαιροῦσιν, and *Ep.* 75, which implies that councillors had been displaced from Caesareia not once but twice, as arguments for the view that Armenia Secunda had been separated from Cappadocia before its division into Cappadocia Prima and Cappadocia Secunda in 371/2. This is probably correct.

General Index

This index includes the names of Roman provinces and the major cultural regions of Asia Minor. Other geographical designations are listed in the Index of Place Names.

acclamations I, 114 fig. 18g, 201
  at Perge I, 238
Acts of Paul and Thecla II, 60 n. 51, 116
administrative staff (of Roman governors) I, 69, 135
adventus I, 221, 224–5 II, 53
  of Constantius in Ancyra II, 84
ager publicus I, 90, 157, 249
agones, see games
agricultural productivity (under principate) I, 4
ala:
  Antiochiensium I, 74
  Augusta Germaniciana I, 74
  Claudia Nova I, 136
  Moesiaca I, 136
  I Augusta Colonorum I, 74
  I Flavia Augusta Britannica Miliaria C. R. I, 136
  II Lucensium I, 232 n. 28
  VI equitata I, 129
amphoras I, 241–2
angel(s):
  connected with worship of *Theos Hypsistos* II, 45–6
  Jesus Christ as II, 46, 102
  in *Life of St Theodore* II, 136
  pagan II, 46
  in Phrygian epitaph II, 106 n. 439
  of Rubes II, 41
  St Paul hailed as II, 24
  worshipped in S. Phrygia II, 35, 46
Angora goat II, 131, 132
apographe:
  in 4th century Cappadocia II, 76
Apostolic Council II, 4, 5
arbitration:
  by Basil II, 72
  by Gregory the Wonder-Worker II, 54
  in village life I, 183
archiereis (rural) I, 156, 159; II, 23 n. 96
archigalli II, 18 n. 53
Argonauts, voyage of I, 207
Armenia:
  Christian community II, 57
  monasteries in II, 111
  Nero plans invasion I, 40
  Roman claims abandoned I, 237
  under Vespasian I, 118
Armenia Major:
  boundaries II, 155
Armenia Minor I, 93
  annexed to Empire I, 118
  boundaries of II, 151, 154, 155, 161, 162
  controversy in Church II, 78

koinon of I, 116
  part of Galatia/Cappadocia I, 63
  roads in II, 74
  under Vespasian I, 63
Armenia Secunda:
  boundaries II, 101–2
Armeniarch I, 116
armour:
  Celtic I, 16, 21
  of couriers I, 132
  of *diogmitai* I, 196
  imperial factory for at Caesareia II, 76, 79
  on Pisidian relief II, 28
ascetics/asceticism II, 72, 111
  appeal of II, 112, 114
  female groups of II, 116
  impact of II, 119–20
  at Laodicea Catacecaumene II, 102–3
  in *Life of St Theodore* II, 130, 134
  as means to self-mastery II, 138–9
  among Novatian clergy II, 96
  among Novatian laity II, 97
  in works of Palladius II, 109–10
  in Pontus II, 113 n. 32
  power of II, 121
  stronger in country than city II, 99
  in upper Tembris valley II, 106
  see also monasticism/monks
Asia (province):
  cities in 1st century I, 80
  early Christian community II, 41
  extent of I, 72; II, 158
  famine in I, 146
  governors in 3rd century AD I, 228
  imperial cult in I, 100
  inter-city rivalry I, 206
  koinon of I, 109
  Mithridates VI in I, 30
  roads in I, 129
  Roman military I, 121
Asia Minor:
  Antiochus I's precarious hold I, 18
  Celtic raids and extortion I, 23–4, 29–31
  Gothic invasion I, 235
  interior free of brigands II, 157
  Roman control develops I, 29–31 and *passim*
assemblies:
  in cities I, 201, 203 n. 40
  at Ephesus and Magnesia on the Maeander I, 202
  in villages I, 181–2
asses and donkeys I, 143; *II, 20 fig. 6*, 132
assizes I, 200, 206

in Asia I, 62; II, 33 n. 187, 37 n. 215
in Bithynia I, 64 n. 31
in Cilicia I, 64
and coin circulation I, 242 n. 4
economic importance of I, 248
in Galatia I, 65
at Iconium II, 60
in Pamphylia I, 238
at Synnada II, 60
atheism I, 194; II, 37
Attalid kingdom I, 21–2, 24–6, 29, 161
  influence in western Asia Minor I, 85
  see also Pergamum, in Index of Places and Peoples and Attalids I-III in Index of Persons
Attis (priest):
  at Pessinus I, 26, 48
augury:
  of Deiotarus I, 34, 37

Bar-Kochva revolt I, 137
Basileias/Basileion (at Caesareia) II, 66, 83, 116
basilicas (Christian):
  at Germia II, 117, 129
  at shrine of St Thecla II, 117
  in 3rd century AD II, 56, 67
  not widespread before later 4th century AD II, 66
bath houses:
  at Aezani I, 214 n. 112
  at Apamea I, 202, 217
  at Apateira I, 182, 183
  in Bithynia I, 212–13
  in Caesareia (4th century) II, 73
  and civic life I, 216–17
  in Galatia I, 214
  linked with aqueducts I, 213
  in Nicomedia (Byzantine) II, 142
  at Sebaste in Pontus II, 74
  at Sidamaria I, 214
battle:
  Actium (31 BC) I, 34, 90; II, 152
  Ancyra I, 20
  Aphrodisium (Pergamum) I, 21
  Barbalissus (AD 252) I, 237
  of the elephants I, 45–6
  Granicus I, 232
  Issus I, 232
  Kurupedion (281 BC) I, 13
  Lysimacheia (277 BC) I, 13, 15, 45, 48
  Magnesia (190 BC) I, 19
  Meshike (AD 244) I, 237
  Mt. Magaba (189 BC) I, 24, 45, 48, 51, 54

battle: (*cont.*):
  Mt. Olympus (189 BC) I, 24, 45, 51, 58
  Nicopolis (47 BC) I, 34, 36
  Nisibis (AD 242) I, 227
  Pharsalus (46 BC) I, 34, 36
  Philippi (42 BC) I, 34, 37
  Resaina (AD 243) I, 237
  Singara I, 197
  Zela (47 BC) I, 36
beans II, 131
benefactions/benefactors I, 117
  absent from 4th-century cities II, 75
  collapse of II, 90
  distinguished from patronage I, 184
  ideology of II, 81–2
  Jewish, at Aphrodisias II, 32
  in Maeonia I, 183
  of priests at Ancyra I, 107–12
  sparse in central Asia Minor I, 225
  underwrite tax liability I, 256
  of village festival I, 187
  in villages I, 182
beneficiarii I, 69, 122, 133, 135
  cults of II, 22 n. 78
bequests:
  of territory to Rome I, 61–2
bishops:
  administer exemptions II, 79
  at Anastasiopolis II, 123, 130
  in Ancyra II, 91–3
  and ascetics at Ancyra II, 110
  authority over clergy II, 78
  of Constantinople II, 115
  control rural clergy II, 71–2
  at Cotiaeum II, 104
  country II, 98
  decline of power II, 121
  elections of II, 53, 54, 57–8, 128
  Eustathius elected at Sebaste II, 112
  and imperial politics II, 80–1
  at Laodicea Catacaeaumene II, 102, 107
  in Lycaonia and Isauria II, 58, 71–2, 107,
    128
  Novatian II, 96, 97, 99
  outspokenness of II, 77, 78–9
  in Paphlagonia II, 97, 121
  petition imperial authorities II, 80, 81
  political role II, 54, 55, 56, 71, 72, 77–8,
    130
  replace secular authorities II, 127
  in upper Tembris valley II, 105, 107
  see also *chorepiscopi*
Bithynia:
  boundaries II, 153, 158, 159, 160
  Celts in I, 23, 55, 57
  city constitutions I, 88–9
  civic turmoil in I, 203, 204, 206
  country bishops II, 71
  cults in II, 19, 24
  estates I, 160–1, 162
  grain production I, 253
  imperial cult I, 102
  Julian claims pagans persecuted II, 94
  key military area in 3rd century AD I, 232
  koinon of I, 109
  language I, 175
  left to Rome by Nicomedes IV I, 62
  lex Pompeia I, 162
  Novatians in II, 93, 97, 99
  place of exile II, 95
  public building I, 253
  recruits from I, 140
  society in 4th century AD II, 107–8
  wine festivals I, 187

boule:
  of Ancyra in 4th century AD II, 86, 90
  Christian member at Cotiaeum II, 104
  Christian members at Sebaste, Eumeneia,
    and Apollonia II, 41
  as criterion for city status I, 180, 181, 182,
    201
  Jewish members at Aphrodisias and
    Sardis II, 32–3
  meetings of I, 204
  prominent in Roman period I, 201
  role in 4th-century Cappadocia II, 77
boundaries:
  between cities I, 94 n. 150
  ethnic, of Phrygia II, 155 n. 83
  natural I, 5–6
  of Roman provinces I, 5; II, 151–62
brabeutai I, 182–3
brigands I, 77 n. 74, 197, 234–5
  in Honorias II, 121
  in Mysia I, 165, 166

camels II, 124 n. 14, 132 n. 63, 143–4
Cappadocia:
  annexed by Tiberius I, 63
  boundaries II, 151, 154, 155, 157, 161, 162
  breeding mares taxed II, 76
  cereals in I, 168
  Christian community II, 63, 66–73
  Christianity militant II, 94
  cities in 1st century BC I, 81, 82
  cults II, 29, 30
  decline of city councils II, 77
  disputes in Church II, 78
  early evangelization II, 38
  forts and castles in I, 84
  Galatians embroiled with I, 19
  Gothic invasion I, 235
  governors petitioned by Basil II, 80–1
  Hellenization promoted by kings I, 83–4
  lack of cities I, 97–8
  landlords' power II, 121
  language I, 173–4
  legions stationed in I, 139–41
  monasteries II, 116
  pre-Roman epigraphy and coinage I, 86
  roads I, 129; II, 74
  Sassanian invasion I, 237, 238
  split into C. Prima and C. Secunda II, 161
  temple states in 1st century BC I, 81–2
  Vespasian joins to Galatia I, 63
Cappadocia Prima:
  boundary with Cappadocia Secunda II, 161
Caria:
  boundaries II, 158
  Gothic attack feared I, 235
  Hellenization I, 85
  language I, 172
  no early Christian inscriptions II, 38
  prize games I, 225
  province of Phrygia and Caria I, 228; II, 158
  residual pagans II, 118–19
  village base of Carian polity I, 181
castellum I, 121
  of Homonadeis I, 77
cattle:
  in *Life of St Theodore* II, 132
cemeteries:
  of Corycus II, 120
  as focus of Christian worship II, 65–6, 120
  see also tombs
cereals:
  for Alexandria I, 254
  Anatolian grain for Syrian armies I, 253

  annual gift of grain to monastery II, 124
  more barley than wheat in N.W. Galatia II,
    131
  best grain taken by cities I, 224–5, 253
  charitable distributions by Julian II, 84, 91
  civic funds for grain purchase I, 89
  distribution schemes I, 111, 159, 245
  edict of Antistius Rusticus I, 66, 145, 150
  Egyptian for Anatolia I, 254
  experimental cultivation I, 167–8
  farming in central Anatolia I, 144, 245
  in Galatia I, 145, 148 n. 49; II, 131
  harvest linked with goddess of Justice II, 18
  hoarding raises prices II, 83
  imports by sea to Constantinople II, 98
  panis divinus (Ancyra) II, 93 n. 363
  peasant consumption levels I, 255
  price differentials I, 247
  Ptolemy II sends corn to Pontic cities I, 20
  sitonai I, 250, 253; II, 35
  state purchases I, 251, 253
  storage I, 168, 242; II, 131
  for Tarsus I, 208 *fig. 36 f*, 254
  as tax in kind I, 248–9
  transport costs I, 246
  wheat and barley for Cyzicus I, 16
  wheaten bread a luxury II, 109, 132
  Zeus as protector of II, 23
chickens II, 132, 133
chorepiscopi II, 70–1, 72
  under Basil of Caesareia II, 69
  in Isauria II, 59, 161
  and philanthropy II, 71, 83
Christians II, *passim*
  in central Anatolia I, 239
  at Docimeium I, 170 *fig. 30*
'Christians for Christians' inscriptions II, 40,
  104
church building II, 65, 71 n. 127
  not attempted at Claros II, 118
  before AD 300 II, 66
  of bishop Arcadius II, 69
  at Caesareia II, 66
  in Christian cemeteries II, 65
  at Cyzicus by Novatians II, 96
  of Eugenius at Laodicea Catacaeaumene II,
    82, 102
  first at Nazianzus by AD 374 II, 68
  Gregory of Nysa on quantity in
    Cappadocia II, 70
  by Gregory the Wonder-Worker II, 54, 56
  in Isauria II, 117 n. 65
  by John of Ephesus II, 118
  at martyrium of St Thecla II, 116–17
  at Sykai by Novatians II, 96
  by Theodore of Sykeon II, 122, 125–6
  at Tyre after persecutions II, 82 n. 254
Church justice II, 56, 72, 79
  at Laodicea Catacaeaumene II, 107
  in upper Tembris valley II, 106
Church organization I, 4; II, 73
Cilicia I, 7
  boundaries II, 151, 155
  coinage I, 255
  country bishops II, 71
  cult of Astarte II, 29
  in kingdom of Polemo II, 38
  military area in 3rd century AD I, 232
  recruits from I, 140
Cilicia Pedias:
  cities taken by Sassanians I, 238
Cilicia Tracheia (Rugged Cilicia):
  boundaries II, 152, 153

Celtic material culture in I, 54
cities taken by Sassanians I, 238
kingdom of M. Antonius Polemo I, 94
native opposition to Roman rule I, 234
prize games I, 225
recruitment from I, 136, 139
Roman military presence I, 122
circumcision II, 5, 36
citizenship, Roman I, 109, 113, 179, 208 fig. 36c, 256; II, 8
city administration I, 199–206
see also magistrates
city foundations:
in Cappadocia I, 97–8
in central Anatolia I, 96–7
Claudian policy I, 96
in Hellenistic Anatolia I, 81
imperial policy I, 98
in North Galatia I, 86–7
in Paphlagonia I, 92
in Pontus I, 91, 178 n. 120
in Rugged Cilicia I, 94–5
in South Galatia I, 95
supplant tribal groupings I, 176
city planning:
at Ancyra and Pessinus I, 105
at Pisidian Antioch I, 104, 105–6
city territories I, 149, 179
in Galatia I, 87–8
in Paphlagonia I, 93
in Pontus I, 31–2, 91–2, 162
classis Pontica I, 124
transferred to Cyzicus I, 235
climate I, 144
April sunshine II, 137
severity discourages hermits II, 111
winter: in Bithynia I, 168; in Cappadocia II, 74; in Thrace I, 166
see also rainfall
cochineal I, 50 n. 85, 146
cohors:
Apula I, 73
I Augusta Cyrenaica in Galatia I, 121, 122 fig. 20; II, 28 n. 149
I Claudia Sygambrorum veterana equitata I, 121
I Raetorum at Eumeneia I, 121
I T... I, 139 n. 179
II Hispanorum I, 121
II... at Dascusa I, 119
colletiones I, 229, 233
coinage/coins:
and agonistic festivals I, 198, 222 fig. 39
of Amyntas as army pay I, 38 n. 142
of Ancyra I, 145 n. 17
bronze, distributed by troops I, 242, 250
depict fortifications I, 213
economic importance I, 241, 255, 257
in Galatian cities I, 87 nn. 80–2
of Galatian koinon I, 112
of Galatian tribes I, 113
of Iconium II, 23
latest bronze civic (Perge) I, 224
linked to military presence I, 255–6
of Pessinus I, 103–4
in pre-Roman Anatolia I, 86
of Soatra I, 96
widely used in 3rd century AD I, 20, 255
coloni I, 185, 249 n. 44
colonies (Roman and Italian):
at Apameia I, 160
at Attaleia I, 102, 152
constitutions I, 89
date of Pisidian I, 76

foundation coin type at Lystra I, 114 fig. 18a
in Galatia I, 77, 90
at Heliopolis I, 153
land for I, 90–1
at Mallos I, 208 fig. 36c
military responsibilities of I, 76
at Nicopolis I, 32
at Ninica I, 38 n. 138, 77, 114 fig. 18b
in Phrygia Paroreius I, 38
around Pisidia I, 71
in Pontus I, 36–7, 40, 41
Commagene I, 177, 250; II, 30
confession texts I, 191–5
conscription I, 140–1
clergy avoid II, 71, 75, 76
see also recruitment
conversion to Christianity:
of Cappadocia I, 10
before Constantine II, 57–64
role of Gregory the Wonder-Worker II, 53–7
Pauline strategy for II, 7–8
of Sergius Paulus II, 6, 7
Sozomen on II, 63
speed of II, 62–3
corvée labour I, 127, 163, 194
Council of Chalcedon (AD 451) II, 159, 160, 161, 162
rules for monks II, 115
see also monasticism/monks
Council of Constantinople (AD 381) II, 161
Council of Gangra (AD 343?) II, 112
Council of Nicaea (AD 325) II, 51, 68, 91
bishops attending II, 159, 160, 161
Isaurian representatives II, 59, 71, 116
and Novatians II, 96
Council of Serdica (AD 343/4) II, 160, 161
couriers I, 129, 164, 166; II, 23, 103
in 4th century AD Cappadocia II, 74
in Life of St Theodore II, 124 n. 15
creed:
Arian II, 77, 97
of Gregory the Wonder-Worker II, 54 n. 20
Nicene II, 77, 91; endorsed by Novatians II, 96, 97
Crusaders:
cross Anatolia I, 143
culture:
Anatolian regional I, 7
in Cappadocia II, 86
Celtic spreads to Anatolian population I, 19 n. 80
in central Anatolia II, 85–6
of cities I, 207
classical I, 4; in Christian Phrygia II, 106
gap between town and country I, 197
and Greek language I, 174
inscriptions and Greek I, 86
Libanius and Ancyran II, 87
material, of cities I, 198
mixed in Anatolia I, 86; at Hanisa I, 83
pagan, resists Christianity II, 62, 72
in Phrygia II, 105
theory of II, 145, 147
cures:
of Theodore of Sykeon II, 125, 128, 139–44, 143 n. 100
curial class (city councillors):
of Caesareia transferred to Podandus II, 77
decline of II, 120
economic power of I, 244–5
powerlessness in later 4th century AD II, 76–7

see also boule
curses and imprecations (on tombstones):
Christian I, 189
in Phrygia and Lydia I, 188
Phrygian, on a Christian gravestone II, 61 fig. 20
typical of Anatolian population I, 174; II, 149

darnel (toxicity) I, 168
dead, reverence for I, 189
demons (evil spirits) II, 136, 138, 139, 140, 142, 144, 148
Deuteronomy, Book of:
cited by Gregory the Wonder-Worker II, 56
curses invoked I, 189 n. 217; II, 35–6
Didascalia Apostolorum II, 55
diet:
during Lent II, 132, 136, 137
in Life of St Theodore II, 131–2
rural I, 168–70
Diospontus I, 159
Dis Manibus:
use of formula I, 135, 160
domestici II, 127
doreai I, 224
Druids I, 48, 49, 51 n. 93
Drynemetos (Galatian meeting place) I, 27, 49
dux I, 228, 234
dynasts I, 94
reasons for I, 33, 34, 40
succession and marriages among Galatians I, 28, 36
under M. Antonius I, 38–9

Easter:
causes schism among Novatians II, 98, 99
date of II, 91, 96
Edict of Milan (AD 313) II, 64, 91
elephants:
on coin of Caesareia I, 204 fig. 35 f
used against Galatians I, 8
emporium:
at Apamea I, 258 n. 91
in Bithynia I, 187
at Gordium I, 54
at Hanisa I, 83
at Pessinus I, 83
in Propontis II, 125
at Sinope I, 82
at Tavium I, 51, 83
enoria II, 126
epanorthotes (diorthotes) I, 227 n. 5, 228, 229
eparchia (hyparchia) I, 91, 92
estates I, 9
administration of (N. Africa) I, 162–3
of Aelius Aristides I, 165 n. 4
of Ancyran councillors II, 87
Bithynian I, 160–1
of Dio Chrysostom I, 160
of family of Basil of Caesareia II, 65, 82
Galatian I, 111, 149–58
imperial: in Cappadocia I, 98; at Lagina II, 23; at Tymbrianassus I, 67
Lydian I, 161–2
among Ormeleis I, 163–4, 240
at Phocaea I, 166
Phrygian I, 158–60; II, 40 n. 241
power bases of aristocracy II, 121
rents exacted in kind I, 245
of Themistius in Paphlagonia II, 84 n. 270

eucharistic symbols I, *170 fig. 30*; II, 38, 39,
    61 *fig. 18*
Eumeneian formula II, 40 n. 243, 58
eunuchs:
    among Christians II, 107
    at Pessinus I, 48
euporia I, 227
exisotai II, 76, 80
exorcisms II, 60, 93
    in 16th-century Europe II, 148
    of St Theodore II, 139–44; of animals II,
        143–4, explanation for II, 145–50,
        first II, 138, ritual nature II, 149
Expositio Totius Mundi I, 145, 146; II, 88

family:
    changing Christian attitudes to II, 119–20
famine:
    in Asia I, 146
    at Caesareia II, 83
    causes 4th-century migration to
        Constantinople II, 98
    Galen on I, 169
    in 5th-century Galatia II, 109
    at Pisidian Antioch I, 66
    at Prusa I, 203
    as subject for sermons II, 83
    of 1873 I, 145
feasts/feasting:
    demothoiniai I, 110
    among eastern Celts I, 44
    among Gauls I, 43
    in *Life of St Theodore* I, 44
    at Neocaesareia I, 116
    in sanctuary of Men Askaenos II, 24
festivals I, 182
    for Christian saints II, 66, 68–9
    deplored by Eustathians II, 112, 113
    near Nicomedia I, 187
    pagan, as psychological release II, 144
    at pilgrimage centres II, 116, 117
    at Thiounta I, 187
    see also games
fines for grave violation I, 122, 187
fire (divine) II, 43, 44, 50, 51, 143
    worshipped by Magusaioi II, 73
fire beacons I, 129
Flavian frontier policy I, 250; II, 154
flood(s) I, 105
    of Bithynian rivers II, 125 n. 28, 132
    of Iris II, 112
    legend of II, 33, 36
    of Lycus II, 54
foundation legends I, 208
    see also myths
fortifications:
    built in mid-3rd century AD I, 235–6, 238
    Hellenistic, in central Anatolia I, 85
    in Iberia I, 119
    at Isaura I, 72 n. 32, 85
    at Nicaea and Prusias I, 213
    in Pamphylia and Cilicia I, 196
    in Pisidia I, 72 n. 27
frumentarii I, 229, 233
funerals (Celtic) I, 57

Galatia I, 1, 7, 9; II, 151
    asses in I, 143
    Augustan city foundations I, 77
    Augustan province I, 61; II, 152
    boundaries II, 151–62
    cereal farming I, 144–6, 147–8, 248, 253
    Christian community II, 62, 63, 71

Christian inscription before Constantine II,
    38
city foundations in S. I, 94–7
divided religious loyalties II, 95
during civil wars I, 34–41
climate, landscape, and crops I, 143–4; II,
    130–3
cults II, 19, 23–4, 29
estates I, 149–58, 164
    extends to N.E. II, 153
funerary monuments I, 146–7, 148
Galatia as name for whole province II, 4
garrisons in I, 74, 78, 121
Gothic invasions I, 235
heretics numerous II, 109
hospices established by Julian II, 90
imperial administration in I, 63–9
Jewish communities II, 31, 35–6
koinon I, 109, 110, 112, 113, 116
monasteries II, 116, 117
Montanists in II, 39
Novatians II, 97, 98
occupied by Celts I, 19, 51–8
pagan tradition in 4th century II, 92, 94
and Pamphylia in AD 68 II, 153
Paphlagonia attached to I, 92–3
places of exile II, 95
pottery of E. Galatia I, 83
pre-Roman epigraphy and coinage I, 86
public buildings I, 212, 213–14
recruitment from I, 136–42
roads I, 124, 126–9
and St Paul's epistle II, 3–4
St Paul's journeys in II, 3–10
source of slaves I, 30–1, 74
tribes I, 27–9, 42–3 *see also* Index of
    Places and Peoples: Tectosages;
    Tolistobogii; Trocmi; Trocnades
urbanization under Roman rule I, 86–8, 89
varying extent of province II, 151
Vespasian joins to Cappadocia I, 63
villages I, 178–9; in N.W. in 6th
    century II, 126–7
weaving I, 146
wine I, 146–7
wool I, 146, 147–8
    see also Index of Places and Peoples: Celts;
        Galatians
Galatia Prima II, 127, 160
Galatia Salutaris (Secunda) II, 127, 160–1
games (*agones*) I, 111, 198–9, 217–25; II,
    222 *fig. 39*
    Actia I, 222; (Syrian Antioch) I, 218
    Aelia Cornuteia (Apollonia) I, 220
    at Aezani I, 219 n. 146
    agon mystikos I, 218, 219–20
    Antoneineia Olympia Epinicia (Adana) I,
        221
    Asclepieia Sotereia I, 221
    of Asian *koinon* I, 218
    of Athena Promachos (Rome) I, 222, 227
    Attaleia Capetolia (Aphrodisias) I, 222
    Augusteia Actia I, 224
    Augusteia Actia (Tarsus) I 11 n. 71
    Augusti Actia (Nicomedia) I, 111 n. 71
    Augusteios Isopythios (Thyateira) I, 221
    Balbilleia (Ephesus) I, 219
    of Bithynian *koinon* I, 218
    in Bithynian village I, 187
    Caesareia (Attaleia) I, 152
    Capitolina (Olbasa) II, 29
    Capitoneia (Miletus) I, 219
    in Cappadocia I, 82 n. 13
    Commodeia I, 220–1

Commodeion (Caesareia) I, 218
    at Cremna under Aurelian I, 224, 225
Decius Oecumenicus I, 224
Demetria Antoneia (Nicomedia) I, 221
Demostheneia (Oenoanda) I, 210, 220
Didymeia (Miletus) I, 220
Diiphileia Traianeia (Pergamum) I, 219
Elagabalia (Sardis) I, 221
Eusebeia: (Mopsuhestia) I, 224;
    (Puteoli) I, 220
    of Galatian *koinon* I, 112, 116, 219
Galliena Capetolia (Antioch on the
    Maeander) I, 224
Isopythia Asclepieia Sotereia (Ancyra) I,
    218, 221
Marcus Aurelius and I, 220
Megala Severeia (Nicomedia) I, 221
Meleagreia (Balbura) I, 220
    at Neocaesareia as evidence for
        paganism II, 55
    in Nile Delta I, 224
Olympia (Side) I, 224
Philadelphia (Eumeneia and
    Philadelphia) I, 221 n. 166
Philadelphia Severeia I, 221
    in Phrygia and Lydia I, 225 n. 197
    at Pisidian Antioch II, 10
Pythia (Side) I, 222
Romaia (Lycia) I, 218
Romaia Sebasta (Pergamum) I, 219
Severeia Olympia Epinicia (Anazarbus) I, 222
Severeius I, 221
Taciteia (Perge) I, 225
    themides at Termessus I, 225
Valerian promotes I, 237
Valeriana (Nicaea) I, 224
Valeriana Pythia (Aphrodisias) I, 224
    see also festivals
gerusia I, 212
gladiatorial shows/*venationes* I, 110
    at Ancyra I, 111
    Galen and I, 169
    at Neocaesareia I, 116
    at Pessinus I, 105

hecatomb I, 109–10
hegoumenos/hegoumene II, 130
    at Sykeon II, 122 n. 5, 123
Helenopontus II, 159
Hellenization:
    of Cappadocia I, 35 n. 103, 82
    of Celts in Greek cities I, 58
    of Galatian aristocracy I, 35
    of Galatian cults I, 49
    of native cults II, 28
    in Phrygia I, 174
    of Phrygia Paroreius I, 85
    of Pisidia I, 7
    of Pontus I, 82
    of western Anatolia I, 85
heretics:
    in Ancyra II, 93–4
    in 3rd-century Phrygia and Lycaonia II, 59,
        60
    ubiquitous in Asia II, 107
    see also religious groups
hippeis I, 132
    see also couriers
Historia Augusta I, 145
Hittite empire I, 175
Homoioousion II, 92
Homoousion (consubstantiality) II, 92
Honorias II, 121, 127
    created by Theodosius I II, 160

horses:
    breeding I, 132; II, 76, 80
    in *Life of St Theodore* II, 132 n. 62
    racing not practised by Phrygians I, 189
    for transport relays II, 124, 128
hospitality and billeting I, 65
    Basil on II, 75
    Cicero avoids I, 250 n. 47
    at Prusias ad Hypium I, 232
    senators protected from I, 230, 234 n. 108
human sacrifice I, 48
hys (holm-oak) I, 50

imperial freedmen and slaves:
    born of servile mother I, 230 *fig. 41*
    Christian at Nicomedia II, 64
    endow native sanctuary II, 23
    at Laodicea Catacecaumene I, 153, 156
    in Lydia I, 161-2
    among Orondians I, 157
    supervise official transport I, 247
inns:
    on highways in 6th century II, 124
    near lake Manyas I, 167
    rare in Thrace I, 166
    at Sykeon II, 122, 125
Ionia:
    Anatolia viewed from I, 5
    early Christian communities II, 38
    Gothic invasion I, 235
Iranian population in Anatolia I, 47
    see also Index of Places and Peoples:
        Persians
iron:
    mined in Taurus II, 76
    re-smelted II, 132
Isauria:
    boundaries II, 151, 155, 157, 161
    conquests of P. Servilius I, 72
    and Council of Nicaea II, 116
    deities II, 26, 28
    early Christian community II, 38, 58, 59,
        62, 71
    imperial dedication symbolizes Roman
        control I, 66-7, 79
    new province in 3rd century AD I, 228
    nomenclature I, 75
    Novatian centre II, 99
    opposes Roman rule I, 234
    recruits from I, 136, 139, 140
    Roman military presence I, 122
    in time of Alexander I, 85
    tombstones of 3rd and 4th centuries II, 100
    war of AD 6 I, 73, 78, 116; II, 152
    see also Index of Places and Peoples: Isaura;
        Isaurians

Jesus Christ:
    fragment of tunic at Germia II, 117
    letter to Abgar V of Edessa II, 57
Jewish communities I, 172; II, 8, 31-7
    in Acmonia and Eumeneia II, 41
    affinities with Phrygian paganism II, 36-7,
        43, 48
    at Antioch and Iconium II, 5, 8, 9
    belief in angels II, 46
    influence on Phrygian Christians II, 98
    and name of God II, 45
    revolt in Syrian Antioch (AD 610) II, 123
    sympathizers II, 8; see also *theosebeis*
Justinianic Code I, 124

klima II, 126
koinon (commune):
    of Asia I, 100
    of Cappadocia I, 102
    of Galatia I, 103, 109, 110, 112-13, 116
    of Lycaonians I, 176; II, 155
    of Milyadeis I, 176 n. 104
    of Pontus I, 116
    priesthoods of (Galatia) I, 112, 114
    village, in Byzantine Galatia II, 133
ktetores (possessores) II, 127
    in villages II, 133

La Tène pottery I, 51
landscape II, 151
    in central Anatolia I, 1, 2 *figs. 1 and 2*, 6
        figs. 3 and 4, 143
    in the Milyas I, 8 *fig. 6*
    of N. W. Galatia II, 130-1
    in Pontus I, 8 *fig. 5*
languages:
    Aramaic I, 86, 172
    Armenian I, 173 n. 79
    Bessian I, 173 n. 79
    Carian I, 172, 173 n. 72
    Celtic (Galatian) I, 50-1, 173, 175; II, 90
    Coptic I, 173 n. 79
    Gothic I, 174
    Graeco-Aramaic bilingual text I, 86
    Greek: I, 50, 172, 173; rural dialects I,
        174, 193
    Hebrew I, 172; II, 34 *fig. 17*, 35
    Isaurian I, 173
    Latin: I, 135, 160, 172, 173; at Ancyra I,
        135; as language of Roman law II, 53
    Luwian I, 175
    Lycaonian I, 173; II, 11
    Lycian I, 172
    Lydian I, 172, 173
    Mysian I, 173
    Pamphylian I, 172
    Phoenician I, 172
    Phrygian I, 174, 188; II, 93
    Pisidian I, 173
    Sidetan I, 172 n. 67
    Solymian I, 173
    Syriac I, 173 n. 79
legio:
    I Adiutrix I, 133; Anatolian recruitment I,
        138
    I Italica I, 122 *fig. 19*, 133 n. 92, 252;
        Anatolian recruitment I, 138; at
        Apamea I, 121
    I Parthica I, 180 n. 134; Anatolian
        recruitment I, 139
    I Pontica I, 124
    II Adiutrix: Anatolian recruitment I, 138
    III Augusta I, 136
    III Cyrenaica I, 73, 136; Anatolian
        recruitment I, 136-7
    III Gallica: builds hydraulic device I, 119;
        in Cappadocia with Corbulo I, 140
    III Parthica: Anatolian recruitment I, 139
    IV Flavia: Anatolian recruitment I, 138;
        soldiers in Phrygia I, 121, 139
    IV Scythica I, 133 n. 92, 160, 252;
        Anatolian recruitment I, 140; at
        Zeugma I, 119
    V Macedonica I, 133 n. 92, 139, 252;
        Anatolian recruitment I, 136, 138; not in
        Augustan Galatia I, 73 n. 42; in
        Pontus I, 135-6
    VI Ferrata II, 6; Anatolian recruitment I,
        140; campaigns at Samosata I, 119
    VII Claudia I, 121 n. 28, 133, 133 and
        n. 92, 137, 252
    VII (Macedonica) I, 136, 139; Anatolian

recruitment I, 137-8; under Augustus in
    S. Asia Minor I, 73
    X Fretensis: Anatolian recruitment I, 140
    X Gemina I, 133; veterans perhaps at
        Iconium I, 74 n. 55
    XI Claudia: Anatolian recruitment I, 138;
        soldiers at Apamea I, 121, 122 *fig. 19*
    XII Fulminata I, 34; Anatolian
        recruitment I, 139; centurion at Caspian
        Sea I, 121; centurions at Comana and
        Neoclaudiopolis I, 136; at Melitene I,
        118; officers at Ancyra I, 134, 135; road-
        building in Phrygia I, 121; vexillation at
        Trapezus I, 124
    XIV Gemina 133; Anatolian recruitment I,
        139
    XV Apollinaris I, 122 *fig. 21*; Anatolian
        recruitment I, 139; officers at Ancyra I,
        134; vexillation at Trapezus I, 124
    XVI Flavia Firma I, 34; Anatolian
        recruitment I, 139; centurions at
        Ancyra I, 134; recruited in AD 70 I, 118
    XXII Deiotariana I, 74 n. 56; also known
        as *Cyrenaica* I, 136; Anatolian
        recruitment I, 136-7
    XXII Primigeneia I, 133
    XXX Ulpia Victrix I, 132 n. 89, 136
limes I, 34, 118, 119
literacy:
    in Anatolia I, 238; II, 29
    and book copying II, 109
    in Phrygia I, 174; II, 105
locusts II, 133
Lycaonia I, 7, 9; II, 151
    boundaries II, 151, 152, 155, 161
    ceded to Ariarathes I, 29
    cults II, 15, 19, 28
    early Christian community II, 38, 58, 59,
        60, 62
    foundation legend I, 208
    gravestones of 3rd-4th centuries II, 100
    imperial cult I, 116
    language I, 173, 175
    monasteries II, 116
    Novatian centre II, 99
    in Polemo's kingdom I, 38
    recruitment from I, 136
    Sassanians in I, 238
    society in 4th century II, 107-8
    soldiers stationed in II, 75
Lycia I, 7
    boundaries II, 153-4
    dice oracles II, 13
    grain distribution schemes I, 111
    Hellenization I, 85
    language I, 172
    no early Christian inscriptions II, 38
    opposition to Roman rule I, 234
    prize games I, 225
    recruitment from I, 139, 140
Lycia and Pamphylia, province of I, 79; II,
    153, 154
Lydia I, 7, 9; II, 26
    confession steles I, 191-3
    cults II, 19, 22, 29
    early Christianity II, 38, 62
    estates I, 161, 162
    Gothic invasion I, 235
    Jewish communities II, 32, 36-7
    language I, 172
    Montanists II, 39
    residual paganism II, 118-19
    soldiers in 3rd century AD I, 230, 233
    villages I, 180-3

magistrates (civic) I, 88, 89, 97, 199–200
  diminishing role in tax-collection I, 232–3
  dwindling prestige in 3rd century II, 55–6
  none in 6th century AD II, 127
Malay culture:
  role of exorcism II, 248
markets I, 242, 247
  at Church festivals II, 69–70
  rural II, 28
  for slaves I, 257
marriage (Christian):
  abhorred by Encratites II, 100
  denounced by Eustathians II, 112
  among Novatians II, 97
  remarriage eschewed II, 106, 107
  unwanted II, 109
martyrs II, 65, 68–9, 70
mere (regional divisions) II, 126
migration (Celtic) I, 13, 14, 42
military abuses I, 180, 229, 230; II, 92 n. 356
  in 6th and 7th centuries II, 124
military presence I, 9
  and agonistic festivals I, 224
  in an Asian sanctuary I, 194
  becomes ubiquitous in 3rd century AD I, 228, 230
  and bronze coinage I, 255–6
  economic impact I, 134
  widespread in 4th century AD II, 75
military supplies I, 250–3
  for imperial guard at Constantinople II, 88
  for Lucullus I, 31, 248
  organized by curial class II, 76
  through the Pontus II, 153
  from southern Asia Minor I, 238
  for Valerian I, 237
miracles:
  bring rain II, 132
  of Gregory the Wonder-Worker II, 54
  prevent floods II, 133
  role in conversion II, 55
  of St Theodore: first II, 138; at Germia II, 128, 140–1, 147
  typology of II, 137–8
misthotes I, 153, 155, 156, 164
monasteries:
  at Aligete II, 129 n. 48
  at Ancyra II, 110
  of Autonomus at Soreoi II, 99, 130, 143
  in Cappadocia II, 116
  of Cathari near Yalova II, 98 n. 390, 99, 116
  children enter aged 6 or 7 II, 138, 141
  Eustathian II, 113
  evidence for, unreliable II, 115
  geographical distribution of II, 115–16
  gifts to II, 124, 129–30
  growth in numbers II, 115
  juxtaposed wih secular settlements II, 113
  near Kinna II, 129
  at Nicomedia II, 129
  offer hospitality to travellers II, 124
  at Sykeon: acquires asylum status II, 123, 124, 128; of St Christopher (female) II, 122 n. 5, 125; of St Michael II, 122 n. 5; of Virgin II, 125
  Theodore's followers become hegoumenoi of II, 130
monasticism/monks:
  as agents of conversion II, 63, 114, 118–19
  Anatolian, founded by Eustathius II, 111–12
  attractions of II, 130
  Basil's rules for II, 113

in conflict with established Church II, 110, 114–15
  Encratite at Ancyra II, 103 n. 412
  habit adopted by St Theodore II, 137
  at Mantineion II, 97, 115
  on Mysian Olympus I, 165; II, 115
  not liable to taxation II, 80, 121 n. 94
  numbers of II, 114
  origins of II, 110–11; in Constantinople II, 98, 111, 114
  Palladius on II, 109–10
  role anticipated by Apotactites II, 93 n. 359, 111
  Saccophori as II, 102
  of St Macrina II, 112–13
monotheism II, 43–51
Mysia I, 7
  Aelius Aristides in I, 167–8
  brigands I, 165, 166
  Celtic names in I, 57
  cereals and other products I, 169–70
  cults II, 19
  language I, 173
  tribes I, 176
Mysia Abbaeitis I, 181
myths:
  and civic culture I, 207–8

name change:
  of St Gregory the Wonder-Worker II, 53
  of St Paul II, 7
name types:
  Celtic I, 50, 57, 175
  Iranian I, 47; II, 29, 73
  Jewish II, 35
  Macedonian I, 85
  Phrygian I, 175; II, 38 n. 223
  Semitic I, 9 n. 60
  Thracian I, 175
negotiatores I, 154 n. 99, 162
  in Bithynia I, 160
  in central Anatolia I, 35
  in Milyas I, 103
  in Phrygia I, 158
  in Pontus I, 32
neo-Pythagorean ideas I, 188
Noah's Ark II, 33
Notitia Dignitatum II, 160
nudity (in warfare) I, 45

oaths I, 194
  abhorred by Phrygians I, 189, 193 n. 30
  Cappadocian Christians not to swear oaths concerning tax arrears II, 80 n. 235
obaeratio I, 233
oikodespotai II, 133
oikonomos/oikonomissa (vilici) I, 151, 155, 156, 160, 162, 164
  of church at Iuliopolis II, 130
  as village patrons I, 184
olives/olive oil I, 169, 187
  at Bithynian Apamea I, 244
  civic purchase I, 89
  for gymnasium I, 109, 217
  for lamps II, 138
  major import to inland regions I, 257
  not in diet of ascetic II, 132
  not grown in central Anatolia I, 109 n. 57
  in Pamphylia I, 247
oracle(s) II, 12–13, 47
  at Çavdarlı (Phrygia) II, 13, 28
  of Claros: in Christian times II, 118; at Iconium II, 11–12; universal message

of II, 30; in upper Tembris valley II, 11
collected by Porphyry II, 43
of Didyma: against Christians II, 64; concerning altars in sanctuary II, 14; consulted by Ulpius Carpus II, 49; forge pagan theology II, 43; at Miletus concerning divine presence II, 12; praises law of Jews II, 36; on supreme god II, 48
of Glycon I, 173; II, 13
at Oenoanda II, 44, 48
of Phaenno I, 15
reassures Carian Stratonicaea I, 235
Sibylline I, 237
in Theosophy of Tübingen II, 43–4
oral culture:
  in Church I, 236; II, 55
  in Galatia I, 51
  among Magusaioi II, 73

pagan beliefs:
  survival of II, 118–19, 144, 149
pagarch II, 72, 80
Pamphylia:
  boundaries II, 151, 152, 153–4
  dialects I, 172
  diorthotes in I, 228
  Gothic raids I, 235
  importance in 3rd century AD I, 238
  nomenclature I, 125
  plain of I, 151
  public buildings I, 216
  St Paul in II, 6
panegyris I, 105
Paphlagonia I, 7; II, 151
  becomes Roman province I, 91–2
  boundaries II, 151, 152–3, 155, 158, 159–60
  Celt in I, 23
  Christian churches II, 69
  Julian claims pagans persecuted II, 95
  landlords' power in 6th century II, 121
  monasteries II, 111, 115
  Novatians II, 97
  Paphlagoniarch I, 116
  part of Galatian province I, 92–3
  place of exile II, 95
  recruitment from I, 136, 139
  roads I, 127
  sacred mountain Olgassys II, 22–3
Paraclete II, 100
parapompe/prosecutio ('escort duty') I, 132, 134, 232 n. 27; II, 53 n. 7
Parthian Wars I, 236
  of Lucius Verus I, 132, 252
  of Septimius Severus I, 133, 222, 232 n. 26
  of Trajan I, 132, 136, 251 n. 54, 252; II, 155
Parthians:
  inform Chinese about Rome II, 73
pastoralism I, 148, 157
pater tes poleos II, 120, 141
patriotism I, 206–10
  in Christian Phrygia II, 106
patronage:
  exercized by bishops II, 80
  of rural communities I, 184
peace-keeping I, 195–7, II, 22
  diogmitai I, 122, 196, 234
  eirenarchs I, 89 n. 102, 156, 166, 192, 196, 200, 229, 234; II, 35
  eirenophylax I, 158, 196
  paraphylakes I, 195, 196, 200; II, 35
persecution of Christians I, 196; II, 63
  consequences of II, 64–6

and grandparents of Basil of Caesareia II, 68
at Laodicea Catacecaumene II, 41
of Maximinus II, 12, 57, 64–5, 82, *101 fig. 22*
monuments of Great Persecution II, 59
Novatians and II, 96
Perusine War I, 73
Peutinger Map II, 126
philanthropy II, 20, 81, 82
at Ancyra II, 109–10
at Archelais II, 123 n. 5
arguments about II, 113
of Basil II, 73 n. 152
of *chorepiscopi* II, 71, 83
Christian, aped by Julian II, 90–1
at Cotiaeum II, 104
in 4th-century sermons II, 83
introduction of II, 82–3
at Laodicea Catacecaumene II, 107
of monks II, 113–14
Themistius on II, 84
phrouria:
in eastern and central Anatolia I, 84–5
of Homonadeis I, 77
as typical Galatian settlements I, 54, 58
see also *castellum*
Phrygia I, 1, 7, 9
boundaries II, 155, 158
and Caria II, 158; first governor I, 228
Christian community II, 38, 57, 58, 59, 60, 62, 63, 71
Christianity in 3rd century II, 38, 40, 41, 43, 46–7, 48, 49
cities in 1st century AD I, 81
collapse of old kingdom I, 1, 58
confession steles I, 191, 192
Epictetus I, 20
gods and goddesses of justice II, 18–19, 20, 26, 45
Gothic invasion I, 235
gravestones of 3rd–4th centuries II, 100, 105
Great I, 29, 30
heartland of Anatolian cults II, 19
imperial estates I, 158–61, 211
Jewish community II, 32–3, 35, 36–7
language and names I, 174, 175
marble quarries I, 121, 211
Men in II, 25
militarization I, 230
Montanist stronghold II, 9–40, 46
morality and standards of justice II, 43
mother of gods II, 22
Novatians II, 97, 98, 99, 100–2
pagans cohabit with Christians and Jews II, 49
pantheon and cosmology II, 16, 46–7, 48, 49, 50
'Phrygian heresy' II, 39
pulses grown in I, 169
residual paganism II, 118–19
society in 4th century II, 107–8
tribes I, 126
villages and cities scarcely distinguishable I, 181
Phrygia Paroreius I, 144, 175, 176
boundaries II, 151, 152, 154, 157
cities Hellenized I, 85
fertile soil I, 144, 145
part of kingdom of Amyntas I, 38
Roman military presence I, 122
rural prosperity I, 239–40
St Paul and II, 3

Seleucid settlements I, 20
pigs and pork I, 192; II, 132
favoured meat in cities I, 169–70
forbidden in Church of St George at Sykeon II, 132
at Sasima II, 77 n. 199
pilgrimage:
to Apollonia (Sozopolis) II, 129
to Germia II, 129, 140–1
to Holy Land II, 108, 123, 130, 134, 137; denounced by Gregory of Nysa II, 70
of monk Philoromus II, 109
places of, in Anatolia II, 116–17
pirates I, 29
in eastern Black Sea I, 34, 235; II, 153
Pisidia I, 7; II, 23, 150
boundaries II, 151, 152, 154
Celtic presence I, 55
colonies I, 76, 77
cults in II, 19, 25, 26
dice oracles II, 13
Hellenization I, 85
imperial cult I, 104, 105–6
landscape I, 71
language I, 173, 175
no early Christian inscriptions II, 38
opposition to Rome I, 234
part of kingdom of Amyntas I, 38
prize games I, 225
Roman military presence I, 78, 122
rural shrines II, 16
St Paul in II, 6–10
plague:
among cattle II, 132
under Justinian II, 122
under Marcus Aurelius I, 133
plebs frumentaria I, 111
politics (civic and provincial) I, 65, 112, 117, 203, 210
collapse of, in cities II, 56, 75–6, 120–1
inter-city rivalry I, 204–6
politics (ecclesiastical) II, 71–2, 77, 78
at Ancyra II, 91–4
Pollia (Roman tribe) I, 137
Pontus I, 7, 9
boundaries II, 151, 153, 157, 158, 159
city constitutions under Roman rule I, 88–9
coinage I, 255
cults II, 30
Darius appointed king by M. Antonius I, 38–9
early evangelization II, 38
forts and castles I, 84
and Galatians I, 19, 20, 23
Goths in II, 56
Greek colonies on coast I, 81
Hellenization I, 82, 83–4
koinon I, 116
languages I, 172
main routes I, 32
monasteries II, 111
part of Roman province I, 31–4, 91, 93, 228
Polemo becomes king I, 39
pre-Roman epigraphy and coinage I, 86
recruitment from I, 136
roads I, 124, 127–8; II, 74
Roman military presence I, 136
sanctuaries of Zeus II, 22
Sassanians in I, 238
temple states I, 82
Pontus and Bithynia (province):
creation of I, 81, 160

early Christian communities II, 37–8
Pontus Galaticus:
boundaries II, 151, 158
origin I, 94
part of Galatian province II, 151
part of Pontus I, 63
Pontus Polemoniacus:
boundaries II, 151, 153, 158, 159, 160
origin I, 94
part of Galatian province I, 39, 63; II, 151
population:
of cities I, 200
estimate for Roman Anatolia I, 243–4
growth I, 149
portoria (customs dues) I, 68, 248, 249, 256
in Asia I, 256–7
at Derbe I, 96 n. 170
pottery:
production centres I, 242 n. 3
power (divine) I, 192; II, 12, 45, 54
pilgrimage centres as loci of II, 116
of St Theodore II, 134–9, 149
Themistius on II, 88–9
Praetorian Guard I, 136
soldier from II, 28
pragmateutes I, 150, 151, 155, 160, 161, 162, 164
prehistory (of Anatolia) I, 1
continuity from I, 83; II, 19
private armies I, 234; II, 121
procurators, domanial and other I, 149 n. 56
in Africa I, 162, 164
in Asia I, 164, 249 n. 43
in Galatia I, 156
in Lydia I, 161
in Paphlagonia I, 252
in Phrygia: regulates transport dispute I, 230
procurators, provincial:
acting *vice praesidis* II, 159
duties of I, 67, 68, 97, 98
governs Cappadocia I, 97
responsibilities extend across provincial boundaries II, 154
proistamenoi (church leaders) II, 71, 107
property disputes I, 161, 192
prophecy/prophet/prophetess (Christian) II, 50
in Cappadocia II, 60
Montanist II, 39, 47, 100, 104, 105
in Pontus II, 60 n. 49
prophets (pagan) II, 46–7
at Mysian Hadriani II, 13
Propontis I, 15
Hellenized I, 175
Novatians in II, 97, 98, 99
ports of I, 245
Thracians in I, 175
proselytes II, 8, 31
proseuche (place of prayer) II, 31, 36, 46, 51
protector II, 122
at Anastasiupolis II, 130
at Ancyra II, 122, 127
provincia, meanings of I, 61
public buildings I, 117, 211–17
and Graeco-Roman culture I, 80–1; II, 120
in 4th-century Ancyra II, 90
and Hellenism I, 207
Julian legislates on II, 89–90
supervisor at Oenoanda I, 199

quarries (marble) I, 242; II, 20, 28
of Aezanoi I, 240
Jewish labourers in II, 35

quarries (marble) (*cont.*):
  Phrygian I, 159, *170 fig. 30*
  transport from I, 246

rainfall:
  in Anatolia I, 144
  in *Life of St Theodore* II, 132–3
rape:
  during Gothic invasion I, 236; II, 56
recruitment to legions I, 136–41
  abusive I, 229
  of *diogmitai* I, 196
  press-gang methods II, 75
  see also conscription; *legio*
religious groups (mostly Christian):
  Acacian schism II, 114
  Ancyro-Galatians II, 92
  Apotactites (Apotactici) II, 93, 100, 103,
    111
  Arians II, 107; dispute with Orthodox II,
    92–3; and Novatians II, 96–7
  Ascodrobi II, 93
  Athinganoi II, 98 n. 393
  Borboritae II, 93
  Cataphrygians II, 59, 93, 98; *see also*
    Montanists *below*
  Cathari II, 99, 100; *see also* Novatians
    below
  Encratites I, 147 n. 33; II, 93, 100, 102–3,
    111
  Euphemitai: worship Pantokrator II, 50
  Eustathians II, 112–13
  Hydroparastatai II, 100, 102, 103
  Hypsistarians II, 50–1, 68
  Hypsistiani II, 50
  Ioudaioi (full Jews) II, 31
  Israelitai (full Jews) II, 31
  Manichees II, 93, 100
  Marcionites II, 100
  Massaliani: worship Pantokrator II, 50
  Messalians (monks) II, 114
  Montanists II, 39–40, 46, 111; named
    Cataphrygae II, 98; clergy II, 104; in
    Constantinople II, 98; as first Christian
    community in Ancyra II, 93; as heretics,
    not schismatics II, 100; and Pepuza II,
    92; in rural Phrygia II, 71, 105; of
    Thyatira II, 104
  Novatians II, 96–100, *100 figs. 23–4*;
    Ammia, lament for II, 106; of Ancyra II,
    110; discipline of II, 102; in Phrygia II,
    71, 93, 102–4, 111, 116
  Ophitae II, 93
  Orthodox: Arian treatment of their
    bishops II, 78; Basil of Ancyra mediates
    with Arians II, 92; Basil of Caesarea
    defends before Modestus II, 77; in
    Cappadocia II, 107; clergy and laity
    distinguished II, 102; congregation of
    Gregory of Nazianzus II, 68; dispute
    with Arians II, 92–3; endorse
    Homoousian doctrine II, 92; Modestus
    drowns clergy II, 98; and Novatians II,
    96–7, 98; origin of II, 77; rare at
    Laodicea Catacecaumene II, 103;
    Trinitarian doctrine II, 107; views of
    Eusebius of Samosata II, 81
  Passalorhyncitae II, 93
  Pepuzeni (Montanists) II, 100
  Quartodecimani II, 98
  Sabellians II, 92
  Saccophori II, 100, 102, 103, 111
  Tascodrungitai II, 93
  Valentinians II, 100

Zoroastrians: affiliated to Magusaioi II,
  30
Res Gestae I, 73; II, 10
Res Gestae Divi Saporis I, 237
Revelation, Book of I, 146; II, 37
rituals, in civic cult I, 113
roads:
  Amaseia – Zela – Comana Pontica I, 129
  Ancyra – Caesareia I, 129
  Ancyra – Gangra I, *122 fig. 22*
  Ancyra – Sebasteia – Nicopolis I, 129
  Apamea – Lycaonian plain I, 70; see also
    via Sebaste below
  Bosporus to Dorylaeum – Ancyra I, 129
  bridges Maeander at Antioch I, *104 fig. 35d*
  building costs I, 126
  building from Flavians to Hadrian I, 124
  Byzantium – Satala ('Northern
    Highway') I, 127; II, 74, 97
  Byzantium – Seleuceia on the Calycadnus
    (courier route) I, 129; II, 103 n. 416
  Caesareia – Melitene I, 124, 129; II, 74
  Caesareia – Sebasteia I, 129
  Caesareia – Tavium I, 129
  Cilician Gates – Syria I, 129
  at Cremna I, *128 fig. 26*
  Eumeneia – Apamea I, 121
  Eumeneia – Sebaste I, 121
  in 4th-century Asia Minor II, 74
  Iconium – Isaura I, 122
  koine hodos I, 1
  Laertes – Syedra I, 122
  late Roman compared to imperial I, 246
  leophoroi hodoi I, 229 n. 16, 232
  Lydia – Aezani I, 229 n. 18
  Maeander Valley – Phrygia Paroreius I,
    121
  Melitene – Satala I, 124
  military building I, 121
  and military supplies I, 251
  Nicaea – Dorylaeum I, 126 n. 62
  Nicopolis – Satala I, 124
  Olympus – Rhodiapolis – Limyra I, 122
  Ottoman I, 127
  Perge – Magydus I, *128 fig. 25*
  Persian royal (Sardis to Susa) I, 129
  Pessinus – Ancyra – Tavium I, 126
  in Phrygian Pentapolis I, *125 fig. 23*
  'Pilgrim's Road' I, 129, 132; II, 122,
    123–4, 126, 161
  republican, in Asia Minor I, *58 map 4*
  and routes in Taurus I, 70–1
  Samosata – Melitene I, 124
  Satala – Trapezus I, 124
  Sebasteia – Melitene I, 129
  Smyrna – Cyzicus I, 166
  via Appia I, 126, 166
  via Egnatia I, 166
  via Nova Traiana I, 124
  via Sebaste I, 7, 70, 76, 77, 78, *125 fig. 24*,
    247; II, 11
Roman policy in Asia:
  after 188 BC I, 26
  after 133 BC I, 9
  after 63 BC I, 31
rural inhabitants:
  status of I, 162, 176–8
rural shrines (Christian) II, 68–9

sacred grove (*alsos*) II, 16, 26 *fig. 11*
  see also *Drynemetos*
saints:
  among Montanists II, 111
  see also Index of Personal Names *for*

individual saints
salt I, 147, 246 n. 37
sanctuaries:
  at Aezani II, 19
  on mountain peaks I, 82 n. 11; II, 22, 30
  rock-cut II, 16, 28
Sassanians I, 7, 232
  Gordian III and I, 222, 227, 237
  Philip and I, 227, 237
  raids into Asia Minor I, 238
  rise of I, 236–7
  threat from I, 236–8
Seleucids I, 7, 20, 22, 23, 24, 91, 161
  influence in western Asia Minor I, 85
  resurgence under Antiochus III I, 22
Seljuks I, 1
serfs I, 176
settlement:
  patterns in central Anatolia I, 148–9
  types (rural) I, 177
sheep I, 146, 192
  not mentioned in *Life of St Theodore* II,
    132
  in pastoral economy I, 148
  stealing I, 194
shepherds:
  monuments of I, 146 n. 29; II, 20 *fig. 10*
slave trade I, 257; II, 76
  in Bithynia I, 30
  in Galatia I, 47
soils I, 144, 145
sorcerers II, 142, 143
soter:
  title recognizes victory over Galatians I, 18,
    25
spirit possession II, 145–50
  defined II, 145
  interpretations of II, 146
staff (symbol of divine authority) I, 192
state formation:
  contrast between Galatia and Gaul I, 58
  in Galatia I, 27
stationarii/stationes I, 141
  collect fines I, 122
  at Dacibyza I, 129 n. 81
  in E. Pisidia and Isauria I, 77 n. 78; 122
  perhaps collect taxes I, 233
  as protectors of local population I, 233 n.
    33
  responsible for abuses I, 229, 233 n. 33
symmoria II, 71
synagogues II, 31
  at Acmonia II, 9, *34 fig. 15*, 35
  at Pisidian Antioch II, 8
  at Sardis II, 32
  at Stobi II, 31 n. 176

tabellarii I, 129, 164 n. 209
  see also couriers
taxation/taxes:
  Asian after 123 BC I, 30
  assessment and collection in 4th-century
    Cappadocia II, 76
  from Cappadocia under Tiberius I, 63
  change from money taxes to material
    requisitions doubted I, 232
  collection methods militarized I, 253
  confines cities' freedom of action I, 210
  conscription as form of I, 140, 229
  demands lead to land acquisitions I, 30,
    154
  and ecclesiastical politics II, 77, 95
  evasion: by landowners II, 83 n. 267; by
    Sanni II, 57

exactor and I, 159
exemptions for *chorepiscopi* II, 69
impact and forms of I, 68
in kind I, 247–50
Julian makes Christians liable to poll tax II, 95
and land registration I, 256
no major change in methods in 3rd century AD I, 252–3
Maximinus exempts pagans from urban poll tax II, 64, 95
organized by cities I, 98
petitions for exemption II, 80
Roman concern for I, 211
in 6th- and 7th-century Galatia II, 128
temple:
 architecture: Hermogenian I, 103; Roman I, 104
 states I, 81–2; and sacred slaves I, 176–7, 192; II, 10, 30
temples (rural) I, 189
 of Apollo Lairbenos I, 193
 of imperial cult I, 153
 of Men I, 151, 152; II, 25
 relatively unusual II, 16
temples (urban) II, 13–14
tetrarchs (Galatian) I, 27, 29, 107, 154; II, 85
theosebeis (god-fearers) II, 31–2, 36, 43
 in Acts II, 5 n. 28, 8
Theodosian Code II, 89–90
Theophany (6 January) II, 39
Theosophy of Tübingen II, 43, 44, 48, 49
Thesmophoria I, 17
timber and forests I, 7
 absent from N. Galatia II, 131, 132
 on Mysian Olympus I, 166
 at Prusa I, 244
 at Prusias ad Hypium I, 243

time, organization of I, 113; II, 9, 10, 54 n. 17, 65, 70
tombs, disturbed II, 127, 128, 139, 140, 148
 see also cemeteries
topoterites II, 128, 132 n. 62
trade:
 archaeological evidence for I, 241–2
 associations I, 202
 see also emporium; markets
transhumance I, 145
transport:
 clerics and II, 89 n. 336
 economic constraints and costs I, 245–7
 Julian legislates for II, 89
 of marble I, 159, 170 *fig. 30*
 official, for Basil II, 74 n. 167
 for officials I, 65, 67, 132, 230; II, 53
 organized in relays I, 251; II, 124, 128
 on Pilgrim's Road II, 123–4
 see also couriers
treasure-hunting II, 127, 128, 140, 148
Treaty of Apamea I, 23 n. 121, 24
Tres Eparchiae II, 151, 155, 156
tribute (*stipendium*), paid to Galatians I, 16, 19, 20, 22
trimarkisia I, 44

vegetables II, 131–2, 137
Verona List II, 159, 160, 161
villages I, 9
 administration in larger villages I, 181–2, 190–1
 as bedrock of communal life I, 170
 Caesareia reduced to II, 94
 concord of I, 185
 disputes II, 132, 133 n. 68
 in groups I, 178, 185; II, 133
 of Hierapolis I, 187

in Isauria II, 71
in *Life of St Theodore* II, 126–7
leading men in 7th century AD II, 133
living standards compared to those of cities I, 255
magistrates I, 182–3; in 4th century II, 72
names for I, 178
Novatian priest in II, 102
organization I, 5
resilience in 3rd century AD I, 240
revenues I, 185
ruled by gods I, 187–95
safe haven for Christians II, 64
self-government in II, 72
subscriptions to *Xenoi Tekmoreioi* I, 239
vines/wine:
 in Anatolia I, 146–7
 avoided by ascetics in Eucharist II, 100, 102, 103
 in Bithynia I, 187
 evidence of amphoras I, 242 n. 3
 gifts to Galatian monasteries II, 130
 in Lydia I, 192
 in N. W. Galatia II, 131, 133

warfare:
 Galatian I, 22, 43, 44–6
 Pisidian I, 72
water mills I, 245
winter quarters:
 of Caracalla in Bithynia I, 133
 in Cilicia I, 238
 of legions I, 252
wool and textiles I, 146, 257; II, 25
 in Ancyra region II, 131
 looms at Pylai II, 144
 at Saittai I, 180, 202 n. 27
 weaving mill at Caesareia II, 79–80

Index of Personal Names

Entries for Roman emperors and ancient authors are listed in familiar modern forms in capital letters.

Abercius, bishop of Hieropolis II, 38–9, 41
Abgar V of Edessa II, 57
Abgar VIII of Edessa II, 57
Ablabius, Novatian bishop of Nicaea II, 98 n. 388
Ablabius, praetorian prefect I, 179
Abras, Novatian priest I, 100 and fig. 23
Aburgius, praetorian prefect II, 80
Acacius, from upper Tembris valley II, 60 fig. 21, 106
Acesius, Novatian leader II, 96
Achaeus, Seleucid regent I, 17, 22; II, 32
Acilius Diodotus, M., sophist of Caesareia II, 86
Acilius Glabrio, M., 'the sophist' II, 86
Adiatorix, Galatian tetrarch I, 35, 40, 40–1
Adobogiona, sister of Brogitarus I, 28, 35
Adobogiona, wife of Castor I, 28
Aebutius, M. f. Ulp. Victorinus, M. (Ancyra) I, 122 fig. 21
Aelia Corinthia (Galatia) I, 153 n. 95
Aelia Maximina (Nacolea) I, 159 n. 155
Aelia Tecusa (near Ancyra) I, 150
Aelia Terpsis, imperial slave I, 156
Aelii I, 10, 151, 156, 157
Aelii, P., freedmen of choria Considiana I, 153
AELIUS ARISTIDES:
    on Acilius Glabrio II, 84
    attitude to villagers I, 195
    on C. Iulius Severus II, 84
    encomium to Rome I, 80, 141, 165
    on festivals under Hadrian I, 219
    on peace in provinces I, 141, 142, 230
    on powers of Asclepius II, 43
    on proconsuls and legates I, 65
    Sacred Tales I, 166–7
    speeches of reconciliation I, 204
    taught by Alexander of Cotiaeum I, 174
    on travel I, 165, 166–7
Aelius Aug. lib. Fortunatus, P. (Galatia) I, 153 n. 95
Aelius Aug. lib. Onesimus, P. (Nacolea) I, 159
Aelius Eugenius (Laodicea Catacecaumene) II, 107
Aelius Faustus, landowner I, 164
Aelius Faustus, P. (Laodicea Catacecaumene) I, 155
Aelius Macedo, Q., high priest in Ancyra I, 112 n. 78, 114, 116 n. 112
Aelius Menas, P. (Galatia) I, 153 n. 95
Aelius Natalis, P., soldier I, 122
Aelius Nicon, father of Galen I, 167
Aelius Paezon, freedman I, 155
Aelius Procillianus Menodorus (Kinna) I, 96 n. 175
Aelius Quintianus, governor of Pontus II, 158 n. 11
Aelius Sempronius Lycinus, P. (Ancyra) II, 85
Aelius Sempronius Metrophanes, P. (Ancyra) II, 85

Aelius Tryphon, asiarch of Apamea II, 40 n. 243
Aelius Vibianus, governor of Pontus II, 158 n. 5
Aelius Voconius Stratonicus, Q., benefactor of Dorylaeum I, 236
Aemilius Iuncus, proconsul of Asia I, 229
Aerius, ascetic II, 113
Aetius, Arian exile II, 85 n. 289
Agathius, philosopher of Ancyra II, 87
Agathopous, courier I, 132
Agelius, Novatian bishop of Constantinople II, 96 n. 376, 97, 98
Agesilaus, councillor of Ancyra II, 87
Agrippa II, named after M. Agrippa II, 7
Agrippa, M. II, 7
Akichorios, Celtic leader I, 13, 15
Albianus, hermit II, 110
Albiorix, priest at Ancyra I, 107–8
Albucius Firmus, C., magistrate at Pisidian Antioch II, 10 n. 71
Alexander, bishop of Caesareia II, 66
Alexander, Novatian in Constantinople II, 98
Alexander, Novatian from Phrygian Highlands II, 103
Alexander, sophist of Cotiaeum I, 174
Alexander of Abonuteichus I, 188; II, 13, 37
Alexander the Great I, 13
    art of war I, 45
    victories in Asia Minor I, 232
Ambrose, bishop of Milan II, 69, 73
Ammia, Novatian from upper Tembris valley II, 104, 106
AMMIANUS MARCELLINUS II, 82
    account of Julian's stay in Ancyra II, 89
Amphilochius, bishop of Iconium II, 71–2, 73, 81
    Basil's letters to II, 99–100, 107
Amyntas, son of Brigatus, Galatian tetrarch I, 38
Amyntas, son of Dyitalus, Galatian tetrarch I, 85, 86, 87, 90, 91
    accedes to power I, 28
    made king I, 39
    murdered I, 41, 73
    obtains Cilica Tracheia I, 40
    obtains Pisidia and Phrygia Paroreius I, 38, 72
    possessions annexed by Rome I, 61, 62; II, 151–2
    son of Dyitalus I, 38, 154
    in Strabo I, 27
Amyntas, son of Gaezatodiastes, priest at Ancyra I, 108, 109, 111
Amyntiani, freedmen I, 62
Ancharene, daughter of Sacerdos (Savatra) I, 96
Andreas, hermit of Briania II, 130
Anicetus, Apotactite priest II, 103
Anicetus, priest at Laodicea Catacecaumene II, 107

Annia Astilla, landowner (Nicaea) I, 160
Annia Cornificia Faustina, landowner I, 163
Annius Afrinus, M., governor of Galatia I, 66, 79, 96, 104 n. 30, 112 n. 86, 114 fig. 18c; II, 154
Anthimos, rival of Basil II, 78
Antigonus Gonatas:
    defeats Celts (278/7 BC) I, 13, 47–8
    hires Celts I, 15
    treaty with Antiochus I, 18
Antiochus I I, 16, 17, 18, 19, 20, 21
Antiochus I of Commagene, sanctuary on Nemrud Dağ I, 177
Antiochus II I, 20
    land sale I, 176
Antiochus III I, 22, 23
    settles Jews in Lydia and Phrygia II, 32, 35
Antiochus IV Epiphanes I, 110
Antiochus, African hermit II, 125, 132
Antiochus Hierax I, 20, 21
Antipater of Derbe I, 32, 38, 95
    evicted by Amyntas I, 72; II, 152
    son of Perilaus I, 85
Antipater Etesias I, 15
ANTIPATER of Thessalonica I, 107
Antistius Rusticus, L., governor of Galatia I, 66, 145; II, 151 n. 6, 155 n. 74
    grain edict I, 244
Antius A. Iulius Quadratus, C. I, 219; II, 151, 155 n. 69
Antonia Stratonice, high priestess in Neocaesareia I, 116
ANTONINUS PIUS, emperor I, 216, 220
    creates Tres Eparchiae II, 157
    cult of I, 107
Antonius, L., proquaestor of Asia II, 32
Antonius, M. (Mark Antony) I, 35, 81, 90
    appoints Darius king of Pontus I, 38–9
    and Asian taxes I, 248
    and civil war I, 37
    gives Rugged Cilicia to Cleopatra II, 152
    reverses Pompey's policy for Pontus I, 40
    secures invasion route of Parthians I, 38
Antonius Dio, M., (Lydian Philadelphia) I, 184
Antonius Memmius Hiero, M.:
    diorthotes of Galatia I, 228
    governor of Cappadocia II, 158
Antonius Polemo, M., king in Rugged Cilicia I, 94
Antonius Rufus, M., pontarch and high priest in Neocaesareia I, 116
Apollonius, son of Abbas (Hanisa) I, 83
Apollonius, son of Olympichus (Phrygian Apollonia) I, 104
Apollonius, son of Synesis (Nacolea) I, 160
Apollonius of Aphrodisias I, 19
Apollonius of Tyana II, 86
    remonstrates with merchants I, 247
Aponii I, 74, 151
APPIAN I, 39, 62

on Celtic occupation of Galatia I, 19
on Colchis I, 33
Appuleia Concordia, landowner in Galatia I, 155, 164
Appuleii, 155
Appuleius Quartus, L. (Germa) I, 155
Aquila, Galatian sophist II, 85
Aquila, governor of Galatia Salutaris II, 127 n. 42
Aquila, priest from upper Tembris valley II, 106
Aquila (upper Tembris valley) II, 46
Aquila of Pontus (in Acts) I, 109 n. 54
Aquila Romanus, rhetor of Ancyra II, 85
Aquilina, daughter of Archedemus, Christian of Ancyra II, 38 n. 223
Aquillius, M'. (I) I, 30
builds road I, 77
creates province of Asia I, 72
Aquillius, M'. (II), commands Roman troops in 89 BC I, 30
Arcadius, Anatolian bishop II, 69
ARCADIUS, emperor II, 93
Archelaus II of Cappadocia I, 83 n. 23, 93, 94; II, 152
death in AD 17 I, 63, 81 n. 6
Archelaus, general of Mithridates VI I, 30
Archelaus of Comana I, 32
Ardashir, Sassanian king I, 237
Ariamnes, Celtic chieftain I, 44
Ariarathes III of Cappadcoia I, 25
Ariarathes IV of Cappadocia I, 24
Ariarathes V of Cappadocia:
founds cities I, 81, 82
Hellenism I, 35
under pressure from Trocmi I, 26
Ariobarzanes I of Cappadocia I, 118
given control of S.E. Anatolia by Pompey I, 32
Ariobarzanes III I, 86
in debt to Brutus I, 35
gains half of Armenia Minor I, 36
Ariobarzanes of Pontus I, 19, 20
Arion, son of Agathius (Ancyra) II, 87
Aristarchus, ruler of Colchis I, 33
Aristobulus, ruler of Armenia Minor I, 118, 119
Aristocles, priest at Ancyra I, 107–8
ARISTODEMUS of Nysa I, 17
Aristonicus, revolt of I, 29, 195, 206 n. 52
Aristoxenus (Tyana) II, 95
ARRIAN:
biography of brigand Tillirobus I, 166
Ektaxis I, 119
on Roman forces in east I, 119
Arruntius Aquila, Cornutus, governor of Galatia I, 76
Arruntius Aquila, M., procurator I, 140, 141; II, 153 n. 47
Arruntius Claudianus, M., first Lycian senator II, 153 n. 47
Arsaces, king of Parthia, meets Sulla on the Euphrates I, 118
Arsacius, high priest of Galatia II, 20, 90, 91
Arsinus, stylite II, 130
Artavasdes V of Armenia I, 36
Artemas, imperial slave I, 230 *fig. 41*
ARTEMIDORUS of Daldis I, 206
Artiknos, father of Musanus, priest at Ancyra I, 108, 109
Asclepiades, Novatian bishop of Nicaea II, 98 n. 388
Asclepiakos, *mantis* I, 188
Asterius, bishop of Amaseia II, 70, 73

Ateporix, Galatian dynast I, 39, 91, 93, 94, 107–9; II, 153
Athanasius, bishop of Alexandria II, 70 n. 115, 79, 81 n. 249
Athanasius, Encratite (Laodicea Catacecaumene) II, 103
Athanatos ('Immortal'), name taken by family of Epitynchanus II, 47
ATHENAEUS, quotes Posidonius on Celtic feasts I, 43
Athenaeus, philosopher from Seleuceia on the Calycadnus II, 152
Attalus I I, 15, 19, 21–2
victories celebrated in Pergamene reliefs I, 45
Attalus II, brother of Eumenes II I, 25, 26
Attalus III:
bequeathes kingdom to Rome I, 62
grants citizenship to country dwellers I, 177
Attalus, descendant of Pylaemenes, Paphlagonian ruler I, 33, 37
Attalus, son of Apollonius ((N)akokome) I, 184
AUGUSTUS, emperor I, 4
annexes central Anatolia I, 81, 98
authorizes games at Pergamum I, 219
on coin of Lystra I, 114 *fig. 18a*
founds colonies in Asia Minor I, 76–7, 90
introduces provincial procrators I, 67
legions under I, 136–7
makes Dyteutus priest–ruler of Comana Pontica I, 49
'New Deal' (*novus status*) I, 61
oath of allegiance to I, 92
policy in Pisidia I, 73
and status of provincial governors I, 63
takes name Augustus I, 100
territorial arrangements in Galatia I, 88
AURELIAN, emperor:
in Ancyra I, 133
on coin of Cremna I, 222 *fig. 39f*
and sacred games I, 224
Aurelii I, 150, 156, 157, 239
Aurelius Appius Sabinus, *epanorthotes* in Asia I, 228
Aurelius Aristeas (Acmonia) II, 35
Aurelius Athenodotus, sculptor of Docimeium II, 60 *fig. 21*
Aurelius Basileus, governor of Cappadocia II, 158
Aurelius Chrysenius Damatrius, M. (Prusias ad Hypium) I, 213
Aurelius Diodotus, freedman I, 161
Aurelius Dionysius, centurion I, 234
Aurelius Epagathus, freedman I, 156
Aurelius Epitynchanus, high priest in upper Tembris valley II, 64
Aurelius Eucleides, M., freedman I, 156
Aurelius Firminus, T., *librarius* I, 133
Aurelius Frugianus (Acmonia) II, 35
Aurelius Gaius, centurion, praised for decency at Aphrodisias I, 233, 234
Aurelius Helix, wrestler from Eumeneia II, 41
Aurelius Hierax, governor of Pontus and Paphlagonia I, 159
Aurelius Marcianus, L., *dux* at Termessus I, 34
Aurelius Menandrus (upper Tembris valley) II, 106
Aurelius Philippianus Iason, M. (Prusias ad Hypium) I, 213
Aurelius Philokyrios, M., freedman procurator I, 230

Aurelius Plutarchus (Oxyrhynchus) II, 55 n. 25
Aurelius Priscianus, governor of Pontus II, 158 n. 11
Aurelius Stephanus, priest (upper Tembris valley) II, 107 n. 451
Aurelius Trophimus, in verse epitaph of upper Tembris valley II, 104
Aurelius Valens, shoemaker (Apamea) II, 41 n. 244
Aurelius Valentinianus, governor of Pontus II, 158 n. 11
Auxanon, makes dedication to Hecate II, 20 *fig. 10*
Auxanon, Novatian in Constantinople II, 98
Avidius Celer Fiscillinus Firmus, Cn., governor of Lycia and Pamphylia II, 154
Axius, T., governor of Galatia I, 66

BALBINUS, emperor I, 237
BARDESANES OF EDESSA, account of Magusaioi II, 73
Barnabas, apostle:
hailed as Zeus II, 11, 24, 29
at Lystra II, 11
with Paul at Antioch II, 6
returns from Galatia to Jerusalem II, 4–5
Basil, bishop of Ancyra II, 91, 92–3, 112
attacked by Marcellus II, 92
Basil, father of St Basil II, 68, 74
BASIL of Caesareia (St Basil) I, 236; II, 56, 59, 65, 66, 68, 69, 71–3, 74
arrested and beaten II, 79–80
becomes bishop II, 78
on billeting II, 75
and Church controversy II, 78
confronts emperor Valens II, 77, 78–9
funerary oration for II, 82
on grain shortage I, 144
letter to Athanasius II, 79
letters to Amphilochius II, 99–100
on Luke on the best use of wealth II, 83
monastic experiment II, 102, 107
on monks and female ascetics II, 116
on Musonius II, 84
patron of community II, 80
personal letters II, 80
petitions for tax exemptions II, 79
pupil of Himerius II, 86
report on thief at fair II, 79
Rules of II, 113–14
sets up hospices II, 83
on tax and tax officials (*exisotai*) II, 76
Battakes, priest of Pessinus I, 48
Bendidianus (Mysia) I, 173
Berenice, wife of Deiotarus I, 28
Bituitus, Celtic leader I, 31
Bolgios, Celtic leader I, 13, 15
Bonosus, *comes* (at Sykeon) II, 123, 129, 138 n. 78
Bosporia (Ancyra) II, 109–10
Bosporius (Ancyra) II, 87, 110
Boudicca, British rebel leader I, 62, 102
Brennos, Celtic chieftain I, 13, 15, 43
his army I, 44
campaign in Greece I, 47
Brigatus, Galatian king I, 93, 107
Brikkon, Galatian leader I, 57
Brogitarus, tetrarch of Trocmi I, 28, 33, 34, 35, 37
Brutus:
in civil war I, 37
and Deiotarus I, 34, 35, 36
Bryonianus Lollianus (Side) II, 55 n. 25

Busiris, Encratite at Ancyra II, 93, 103 n. 412

Caecilia Tertulla, priestess at Attaleia I, 102–3, 153
Caecilius Hermianus, high priest at Ancyra I, 114
Caesarius, brother of Gregory of Nazianzus II, 80
Caesennius Gallus, A., governor of Galatia–Cappadocia I, 64 n. 24, 124, 126 n. 56, 127 n. 69; II, 151 n. 4
Caesennius Paetus, P.:
    governor of Galatia–Cappadocia I, 63, 135, 138; II, 153, 154
    governor of Syria I, 119
Caesennius Sospes, L., governor of Galatia I, 66 n. 46; II, 151 n. 8, 155
Caesius Verus, M., centurion at Comana Pontica I, 136
Calchas, seer I, 207
Calidii (Nacolea) I, 160
CALLIMACHUS, on Celts I, 21 n. 95; II, 4
Callixeine, high priestess at Pessinus II, 20, 89, 90
Calpurnia Eirene (Galatia) I, 156 n. 122
Calpurnii (Attaleia) I, 153, 154, 155
Calpurnius, M., landowner in Lycaonia I, 153
Calpurnius Asprenas, L., governor of Galatia and Pamphylia II, 4, 151 n. 2, 153
Calpurnius Collega Macedon, C., intellectual and doctor of Pisidian Antioch II, 87 n. 312
Calpurnius Epinicianus, M., freedman I, 153
Calpurnius Epinicius, M., freedman I, 153, 164
Calpurnius L. f. Serg. Frugi, L. (Pisidian Antioch) I, 74
Calpurnius Longus, L. (Pisidian Antioch) I, 153 n. 91
Calpurnius Longus, M., landowner I, 164
Calpurnius Orestes, L. (Iconium) I, 153 n. 91
Calpurnius Piso, L., governor of Galatia I, 78, 107, 137
    perhaps on inscriptions of Oenoanda and Hierapolis-Castabala I, 78 n. 81
Calpurnius Proculus, L. (Ancyra) I, 153
Calpurnius Proculus Candidianus, P. (Ancyra) I, 153
Calpurnius Rufus, L. (Ancyra) I, 153
Calpurnius Rufus, M. (Alastos) I, 153
Calpurnius Rufus, M., legate I, 103; II, 153
Calvisius Ruso Iulius Frontinus, P., governor of Galatia I, 66 n. 43, 97; II, 155 n. 71
CARACALLA, emperor I, 133
    in Ancyra II, 85
    in Dia I, 213
    festivals under I, 221
    grant of citizenship I, 150
    against Parthians I, 236
    portrait on coins I, 204 fig. 35b, 221 figs. 36e–g
CARINUS, emperor I, 92
Carinus, stylite near Nicomedia II, 130
Caristanii (Pisidian Antioch) I, 152, 154
    freedmen I, 75 fig. 12
Caristanius C. f. Serg. Caesianus Iulius, C. I, 75 fig. 10
Caristanius Fronto, C., suffect consul I, 152; II, 6
Cassia Ulpia Fulvia Longina (Charmideanoi, Bithynia) I, 161
Cassignatus, Galatian leader I, 25
Cassius, P., Roman commander 89 BC I, 30
Cassius, the tyrannicide I, 37

Cassius Chrestus, C. (Nicaea) I, 160
CASSIUS DIO I, 36, 39, 88, 213, 220
    on annexation of Lycia II, 153
    on Augustus' 'New Deal' I, 61
    on 'escort duty' I, 134
    on extent of Galatia II, 152
    on games in Rome 28 BC I, 111
    on imperial cult in Asia and Bithynia I, 102
    on Isaurian uprising I, 78
    on Sadalas II I, 62
Cassius Hortensius Paulinus, M. (Ancyra) I, 133
Cassius Salmallas, C., procurator I, 68; II, 154
Castor, grandson of Deiotarus I, 28, 36, 37
Castor, son of Brigatus I, 107
Castor Tarcondarius I, 28, 37, 54, 107
Castrius Constans, governor of Phrygia and Caria II, 40 n. 243
Catilii (Apamea) I, 160
Catilius Atticus (Bithynian Apamea) I, 160
Catilius Longus (Bithynian Apamea) I, 160
Catilius Severus Iulianus Claudius Reginus, cos. II ord. AD 120 I, 160; II, 155
Cato the younger, and Deiotarus I, 34
Cattius Cornelianus, L., soldier at Savatra II, 28
Chaeremon of Nysa, supports Roman troops at Phrygian Apamea I, 252 n. 60
Charmides, landowner in Bithynia I, 161
Charondas, law code of I, 83
Chiomara, wife of Ortiagon I, 24, 43
Chosroes, king of Persia I, 5
Chrestus of Byzantium, sophist I, 85
Chrysanthus, bishop of Constantinople II, 99
CICERO I, 60, 90–1
    De Officiis discussed by Lactantius II, 82
    defends L. Valerius Flaccus II, 33
    on Deiotarus I, 31, 37, 47
    on differential grain prices I, 247
    on fair grain distribution I, 145
    holds assizes in Synnada II, 59
    on income from Asia Minor I, 248
    letters from Cilicia I, 64
    on Narbo I, 76
    as provincial governor I, 34, 37
    on security of Asia I, 165–6
    on Sestullii of Fundi I, 158
Cillius T. f. Fab., T., soldier from Laranda I, 138
Claudia Aquillia, wife of C. Iulius Severus (Ancyra) I, 116 n. 113
Claudia Eias, landowner (Nicaea) I, 160
Claudia Gallitte, landowner (Nicaea) I, 160
CLAUDIAN, In Eutropium on division of Galatia I, 160
Claudianus, governor of Pontus II, 158 n. 5
Claudii, C. (near Ancyra) I, 150–1
Claudii Severi I, 116, 155, 163
CLAUDIUS, emperor I, 93, 94, 95, 96, 98, 99
    annexes Lycia II, 153
    city foundations I, 67, 78
    on coin of Pessinus I, 114 fig. 18c
    dedication in Isauria I, 66, 79
    dedication at Xanthus I, 102
    gives name to agonistic festivals I, 219
    statue put up by Goloenoi I, 181
    temple in Prusa I, 212
    as Ti. Claudius Caesar I, 140
Claudius Antipater, C. (Germa) I, 151
Claudius Aristio, Ti. (Ephesus) I, 203
Claudius Aurelius Tiberius, governor of Pontus II, 158 n. 5
Claudius Balbillus, Ti., founds festival at

Ephesus I, 219
Claudius Bocchus, Ti., high priest at Ancyra I, 112, 114, 116; II, 85 n. 287
Claudius Calpurnianus, C., landowner near Nicaea I, 160
Claudius Candidus, Ti., legionary tribune (Ancyra) I, 135
Claudius Celsinus, first governor of Phrygia and Caria I, 228
Claudius Deiotarus, Ti., high priest at Pessinus I, 48, 112 n. 78
Claudius Diogenianus, L. (near Ancyra) I, 150
Claudius Firmus, C., procurator II, 159
Claudius Gentianus, Ti., philologist of Ancyra II, 84 n. 275
Claudius Gordianus, Ti., first Cappadocian senator II, 85 n. 280
CLAUDIUS GOTHICUS, emperor:
    inscriptions on gates of Nicaea I, 235
Claudius Heras, Ti., high priest at Pessinus I, 48, 116
Claudius Longinus, governor of Pontus II, 158 n. 11
Claudius Marcellus, governor of Pontus II, 158 n. 11
Claudius Nestor, Ti. (Prusias ad Hypium) I, 212
Claudius Pacorianus Eupator, L. (Nicaea) I, 160
Claudius Pardalas (Pergamum) I, 155 n. 112
Claudius Procillianus, Ti., galatarch I, 116
Claudius Pulcher, Ap., governor of Cilicia I, 109 n. 52
Claudius Rutilius Varus, M. (Perge) I, 74
Claudius Severus, C., governor of Arabia I, 155
Claudius Thallus, oikonomos (Nicaea) I, 160
Claudius Theodotus, Ti., high priest at Pessinus I, 116
CLEMENT of Alexandria II, 48
Cleon of Gordiucome I, 38, 41, 49
Cleopatra, her territory given to Amyntas I, 40; II, 152
Clodius Pulcher, P. I, 34, 109
Cocceianus Dio of Prusa I, 160
    see also DIO CHRYSOSTOM
Cocceius Seleucus, M., high priest at Pessinus I, 116
Comboiomarus, Celtic chieftain I, 24
Comentiolus, brother of emperor Phocas II, 123
COMMODUS, emperor I, 153
    on coin of Pergamum I, 208 fig. 36d
    commends citizens of Bubon I, 234
    and festivals I, 220–1
    neocory in Nicomedia I, 213
Considii I, 153
Considius Aequus, Roman knight I, 153
Considius Proculus, praetorian senator I, 153
CONSTANS, emperor II, 92
CONSTANTINE, emperor:
    Ancyra original choice for Council of 325 II, 91
    espouses Christianity II, 63, 64, 77
    father of Constantius II, 94
    Orcistus' petition and rescript I, 179; II, 58, 60, 62
    outlaws pagan practices II, 117
    three sons honoured with statues I, 181
Constantine, infant son of emperor Heraclius II, 123
CONSTANTIUS, emperor II, 84, 86, 89, 92, 93
    affronted by Basil of Ancyra II, 92–3

at Ancyra II, 92
anti-pagan pronouncements II, 95
Cornas(?) (upper Tembris valley) II, 106
Cornelius, host of St Autonomus at Soreoi II, 99
Cornelius, L., consul 190 BC I, 23
Cornelius Dolabella, governor of Syria I, 37
Cornelius Proculus, governor of Lycia and Pamphylia I, 154 n. 60
Cornelius Severinus, Cn.(?) I, 151
Cornelius Sulla, L.:
Asian settlement of 85 BC I, 65; II, 33 n. 187
governor of Cilicia I, 118
offensive against Mithridates VI I, 29, 30, 31
Cornutus Tertullus (Perge) I, 203
Cosconius Fronto, Q., procurator I, 68 n. 63
Cosmas, alleged father of St Theodore of Sykeon II, 122, 134
Cosmion, imperial slave and eirenarch I, 156
Cossonius Gallus, L., governor of Galatia II, 151 n. 11
Crasicius Rufus P. (Galatia) I, 153
Craterus, imperial slave at Nacolea I, 159
Curtia Iulia Valentilla, landowner in Lydia I, 161
Cuspius Pactumeius Rufinus, L., consul (Pergamum) I, 202
CYPRIAN of Carthage II, 53–4, 59
Cyriacus, patriarch of Constantinople II, 123, 128
Cyrillus, son of Domnus (upper Tembris valley) II, 106

Dalmatius, founder of monastery at Constantinople II, 114
Damasius, Pope I, 236
Darius III I, 232
Darius of Pontus, son of Pharnaces I, 38, 39
David, stepfather of St Theodore of Sykeon II, 122
Debbora (Phrygian Apollonia) II, 8 n. 60
Deiotarus I, 84, 86, 87, 154; II, 152
and augury I, 47
education I, 50
king I, 34–7
possessions in and beyond Galatia I, 33
receives work of Mago on agriculture I, 148
services to Rome I, 31
in Strabo I, 27
treasury and palace I, 56 figs. 8 and 9
troops in 51 BC I, 34
Deiotarus, son of Deiotarus I, 28, 35
tomb I, 57
Deiotarus Philadelphus I, 92, 93
becomes king of Paphlagonia II, 152
Demetrianus, M. (Ephesus) II, 38
Demetrius, Christian persecuted at Dorla II, 59
Demetrius (Phrygian Apollonia) I, 104
Demosthenes, *vicarius* of Pontica II, 78, 79
Despoinia, aunt of St Theodore of Sykeon II, 122, 129
DIADUMENIAN, emperor, on coin of Hierapolis-Castabala I, 222 fig. 39a
DIO CHRYSOSTOM (Dio of Prusa) I, 198
advice to local politicians I, 65, 204
on Apamea in Phrygia I, 258
estates I, 160
on levy of produce from Nicaea I, 249
on patriotism I, 207
on political turmoil I, 203
and Prusa I, 202, 207, 212

on status of country dwellers I, 178
and Tarsus I, 203
DIOCLETIAN, emperor II, 158, 160, 161
and bath house at Nicomedia II, 213
persecutions of Christians II, 63, 64, 66, 69
price edict I, 246
Diodorus Pasparos, benefactor of Pergamum I, 202
DIODORUS SICULUS I, 15
on Brennos I, 47
Diogenes, associate of Cicero I, 35
Diognetos, father of priest at Ancyra I, 108
Diomedes (Laodicea Catacecaumene) II, 107
Diomedes, Novatian of Laodicea Catacecaumene II, 100
Dionysius I of Syracuse I, 13
Dionysius, bishop of Caesareia I, 236
Dionysius of Alexandria II, 59
Diophanes, friend of Deiotarus I, 35
Diophantus, Apotactite priest II, 103
Dives and Lazarus:
story in Luke's Gospel II, 82
Docimus, founder of Docimium I, 32 n. 64, 85, 174
DOMITIAN, emperor:
Dacian wars I, 138
vine edict I, 146
Dometianus, bishop of Melitene II, 125
Domitius (Prusias ad Hypium), restores bath house I, 213
Domitius Calvinus, Cn. I, 35, 36
Domitius Corbulo, Cn., consular legate I, 63; II, 153, 154
campaigns in Armenia I, 140; in Syria I, 74, 118, 124
logistics of campaigns I, 252
Domitius Iulianus, P. (Prusias ad Hypium), builds aqueduct I, 213
Domitius L. f. Ani. Aquila, L., soldier I, 138 n. 150
Domitius Valerianus, M., *diorthotes* of Pamphylian cities I, 228
Domnecleius (perhaps identical with Domnilaus) I, 40
Domnilaus, leader of Tectosages I, 36, 40
Domnitziolus, nephew of emperor Phocas II, 123, 124, 128, 129
Domnus, Novatian(?) of north Phrygia II, 104, 108
Dorotheus, priest of Cappadocia II, 80
Doryphorus, village benefactor in Bithynia I, 184
Doudousa, Novatian at Laodicea Catacecaumene II, 100
Drusus, brother of emperor Tiberius:
cult of I, 103
honorary magistrate at Pisidian Antioch I, 75 fig. 11
Dyteutus, elder son of Adiatorix I, 41, 49, 93, 94
ruler of Comana Pontica II, 152

Egnatius Nero (Galatia) I, 156 n. 122
Egnatius Rufus, L., associate of Cicero I, 35
Egnatius Victor Lollianus, L., provincial governor I, 66 n. 49; II, 159
Eirene, woman exorcized by St Theodore II, 142
ELAGABALUS, emperor I, 221
on coin of Sardis I, 222
against Parthians I, 236
Eleusis, bishop of Cyzicus II, 98
Elpidia, grandmother of St Theodore of Sykeon II, 122, 127, 129

Elpidius, ascetic on Mt. Sinai II, 130
Elymas bar-Jesus, sorcerer at Paphos II, 6
Emmelia, mother of·St Macrina II, 112
Epaminondas of Acraephiai I, 110
Epaphroditus, slave of Pardalas I, 155
Epigonus, Pergamene sculptor I, 21
Epikrates (Lydia), curse of I, 189
EPIPHANIUS, bishop of Salamis II, 39, 51, 98
on Aerius II, 113
on folly of Encratites II, 103
on heretics II, 93
on Massaliani or Euphemitai II, 50
on Montanists of Thyatira II, 104
receives letter from Basil about Magusaioi II, 73
Epitynchanos, pagan theologian (upper Tembris valley) II, 47
Epitynchanos, sculptor (upper Tembris valley) II, 14 fig. 3
Eposognatus, Celtic chieftain I, 23–4
Eprius Marcellus, governor of Lycia II, 153, 154
Erastus, L., Ephesian ship's captain I, 204 n. 51
Esther, Galatian Jewess I, 36
Etrillius Regillus Laberius Priscus, C., governor of *Tres Eparchiae* II, 155
Eugenius, Novatian priest of Laodicea Catacecaumene II, 100 and fig. 24, 102, 103
Eugraphius, Apotactite priest II, 103
Eumachus, satrap of Galatia I, 31
Eumelus, protector of the Pylitai I, 184
Eumenes I I, 21
gains Lycaonia I, 55
Eumenes II I, 24–5, 26
Euphrantas, governor of Galatia II, 127
Euphrosynos, associate of Gregory the Wonder-Worker II, 56
EUSEBIUS:
on Attalus' defeat of Antiochus Hierax I, 22
on education of Cappadocians II, 64, 88
on importance of the Great Persecution II, 64
on Magusaioi II, 73
on Marcellus of Ancyra II, 93
on rebaptizing heretics II, 59
on strength of Anatolian Christianity II, 57
Eusebius, anti-Christian governor of Lycia II, 65
Eusebius, bishop of Caesareia before Basil II, 78
Eusebius, bishop of Nicomedia II, 112
Eusebius, bishop of Samosata II, 74, 81
Eustathius, bishop of Sebaste II, 72, 111–12, 113, 114
Eutyches, Christian buried AD 179/80 (Cadi) II, 38, 60 fig. 18
Eutyches, ecclesiastical dissident II, 114
Eutyches, *oikonomos* (Galatia) I, 153
Eutychianus, founder of Lycaonian monastery in Constantinople I, 173
Eutychianus, Novatian hermit II, 98, 111
Evagrius, hermit I, 130

Fabius Cilo, L., governor of Galatia I, 66
Fabricius, C. f. Ani. Tuscus, C., magistrate at Alexandria Troas I, 73
Faltonius Restitutianus, Q., governor of Pontus, II, 158 n. 5, 159 n. 10
Faustus, bishop in Armenia II, 78
Firmilian, bishop of Caesareia II, 59, 67

FIRMUS of Caesareia II, 69 n. 104, 82 n. 256, 83.n. 267
Flavia Menogenis, landowner in Lydia I, 161
Flavia Pollitta, landowner in Lydia I, 161
Flavius Achillius, governor of Helenopontus II, 159 n. 20
Flavius Alcibiades, cavalryman I, 122
Flavius Alexander, T. (Acmonia) II, 35
Flavius Aper, governor of Lycia and Pamphylia I, 210
Flavius Arinthaeus, *magister peditum* II, 81
Flavius Arrianus, governor of Cappadocia I, 64
    see also ARRIAN
Flavius Damianus, T., sophist of Ephesus I, 252
Flavius Diomedianus Diomedes, T., imperial freedman I, 157
Flavius Domitius Hilarius, governor of Helenopontus II, 159 n. 21
Flavius Gaianus, T., *agonothetes* at Ancyra I, 112 n. 85, 116 n. 112
Flavius Iulius Leontius, governor of Helenopontus II, 159 n. 19
Flavius Marcellus, high priest at Savatra I, 96
Flavius Metrophanes, *pragmateutes* near Ancyra I, 150
Flavius Proculus Macedo, governor of Pisidia II, 161
Flavius Severus, governor of Diospontus II, 159 n. 14
Flavius Titianus, T., procurator I, 67
Flavius Ulpianus, governor of Isauria(?) II, 157
Flavius Valentio, T. (Kinna) I, 96 n. 176
Fulvia, wife of M. Antonius I, 37, 40
Fulvius Rusticus Aemilianus, L., governor of Galatia I, 66 n. 43
Furius Victorinus, T., procurator I, 67, 96

Gaezatorix, Galatian chieftain I, 23, 25, 57, 91
GAIUS (CALIGULA), emperor I, 94
Gaius of Eumeneia II, 41, 105 n. 436
Gaizatodiastes, father of Amyntas, priest at Ancyra I, 108, 109
GALBA, emperor II, 153
GALEN of Pergamum:
    on brigands I, 166
    on cereal-growing I, 167
    Concerning the Powers of Foods I, 169
    on diet I, 167–70, 244
    On Digestible and Indigestible Foods I, 168–9
    on grain transported in jars I, 242
    on neologisms I, 173
    on population of Pergamum I, 243–4
    on travel I, 167
    on wine *skylites* I, 147
Galeria Valeria Augusta, wife of Galerius II, 161
GALERIUS, emperor II, 161
GALLIENUS, emperor:
    on coins I, 114 fig. 35d, 204 fig. 35d, 222 fig. 39g
    and fortifications of Nicaea I, 235
    procurators serve as provincial governors under II, 159
    and sacred games I, 224
Gallius, Q., governor of Cilicia I, 35, 109
Gallius Pulcher, Q., priest at Ancyra I, 35, 108, 109
Gallus, brother of emperor Julian II, 89
Gaudotus, Celtic chieftain I, 24

Gauros of Taurea, poet (Hadriani) II, 39
Gavius Balbus, P., census official I, 68 n. 62
Gennadius, martyr at Laodicea Catacecaumene II, 65
GEORGE, biographer of St Theodore of Sykeon II, 123, 144
George, bishop of Alexandria II, 65 n. 78
Germanicus I, 93
    in AD 17–18 I, 93, 104
    slave of at Nacolea I, 159
Gerontius, schoolmate of St Theodore of Sykeon II, 136
GETA, emperor, son of Septimius Severus I, 133
    at Adanda I, 238
    hailed as 'new Ares' II, 28
Glycerinus, freedman procurator (Laodicea Catacecaumene) I, 156
Glycerius, deacon of Venasa II, 72, 113
Glycerius, holy man at Trapeza II, 132, 138
GORDIAN I or II, emperor II, 85
GORDIAN III, emperor:
    on coin at Perinthus I, 204 fig. 35c
    inscription for in Isauria II, 161
    Kinna honours I, 96
    and sacred games I, 222
    victories and death in East I, 227, 237
Gourdos (Iconium) II, 50
Gracchus, C. I, 29
    lex Sempronia I, 248
GREGORY of Nazianzus I, 97; II, 51, 68, 71, 73, 74
    attacks heresies II, 93
    on avarice of tax officials (*exisotai*) I, 76
    and Basil of Caesarea II, 82, 113
    on election of bishops II, 78
    fellow-student of Julian II, 91
    funerary oration for Basil II, 82
    letters to Glycerius II, 113
    and monasteries II, 116
    pupil of Himerius II, 86
    sent to Sasima II, 77, 78
    on wealth of Caesareia II, 83
GREGORY of Nyssa:
    on Basil's confrontation with Valens II, 78
    on election of bishops II, 78
    family II, 68, 69
    on Hypsistiani II, 50
    Life of Gregory the Wonder-Worker II, 54, 55, 57, 62
    Life of Macrina II, 112
    on martyrs II, 70
    on wealth and poverty II, 82
Gregory Thaumaturgus, bishop of Neocaesareia I, 236
    see also St Gregory Thaumaturgus
GREGORY of Tours II, 117, 129

HADRIAN, emperor:
    in Ancyra I, 132
    building in Bithynia I, 213
    and civic development I, 214
    and Lucius Erastus of Ephesus I, 204 n. 41
    milestone of I, 88 n. 90
    and Oenoanda festival I, 210, 220
    promotes new festivals I, 219–20
    temple of at Termessus II, 13
HEGESIANAX, on Galatians I, 16
Helen, mother of emperor Constantine II, 159
Helias, governor of Cappadocia II, 81
Helladius, *curialis* of Caesareia II, 80
Helvius, C., soldier from Gangra I, 137 n. 141
Helvius Basila, T., governor of Galatia I, 103

Heortasius, bishop (upper Tembris valley) II, 105
Hephaistion of Sardis, local leader against Aristonicus I, 195 n. 244
HERACLITUS, philosopher II, 43
HERACLIUS, emperor II, 122, 123, 131, 132
HERENNIUS DEXIPPUS, Athenian historian I, 235
Herod Agrippa I II, 5
Herod the Great II, 7
Herodes, eirenarch arrests Polycarp I, 197
Herodes Atticus, sophist I, 189 n. 217; II, 85, 86
HERODOTUS, on Susa-Sardis couriers I, 129
HESIOD, *Works and Days* I, 181
Hesychius, priest of Holy Trinity II, 107
HIEROCLES, Synecdemus of II, 159, 160, 161
HIMERIUS, orator II, 86, 88
Hirrius Fronto Neratius Pansa, M.:
    commander in Armenia and Iberia I, 119
    governor of Galatia I, 64 n. 24, 66 n. 43
    governor of Lycia and Pamphylia II, 154
HOMER I, 207
Hostilii (Nicaea) I, 160
HYGINUS, on crops paid in lieu of tax I, 249
Hypatius, founder of monastery at Constantinople II, 114
    Life of II, 118
Hyperechius, 'half-way soldier' of Ancyra II, 87–8

IGNATIUS of Antioch, on early Christian communities II, 37
Ioannes, governor of Galatia Prima II, 128
Isaac, founder of monastery at Constantinople II, 114
Italus, *vilicus* at Nicaea I, 160
Iulia Herennia Pansemnion (Laodicea Catacecaumene) I, 107
Iulia Mamaea, mother of emperor Severus Alexander I, 156
Iulia Paula (Laodicea Catacecaumene) I, 154
Iulia Polla (Galatia) I, 156 n. 122
Iulia Severa of Acmonia, endows synagogue II, 9, 31 n. 176, 34 fig. 15, 35
Iulia Tyche (Lydia) I, 161
Iulianus, associate of St Theodore II, 140 n. 80
Iulianus, slave (Kuyulu Sebil) I, 156
Iulii (Sarıkaya) I, 155
Iulii Quadrati (Pergamum) I, 161
Iulius Anicetus, C., freedman (Lydia) I, 161
Iulius Apronius Maenius Salmallianus, governor of Galatia II, 153 n. 38
Iulius Aquila, priest at Ancyra I, 108, 109, 110
Iulius Aquila, C., procurator I, 109 n. 54
Iulius Bassus, governor of Bithynia I, 65, 203
Iulius C. f. Serg. Proculus, C., procurator I, 74 n. 47
Iulius Caesar, see Julius Caesar
Iulius Candidus Marius Celsus, Ti. I, 66 n. 46
Iulius Celsus Polemaeanus, Ti., legate of Galatia II, 151 n. 3, 155 n. 69
Iulius Demosthenes, C. (Oenoanda) I, 210, 220
Iulius Eugenius, M., bishop of Laodicea Catacecaumene II, 65
    builds church II, 82
    probable predecessor of bishop Severus II, 102
Iulius Gavinius Sacerdos, M. (Prusias ad Hypium) I, 213

Iulius Iustus Iunianus, Ti., high priest at
    Ancyra I, 114, 116, 214
Iulius Ligys, *primipilaris* at Phrygian
    Apamea I, 121 n. 27
Iulius Mochus, C. (Galatia) I, 154
Iulius Moschion, C. (Galatia) I, 154
Iulius Nestor, C. (Galatia) I, 154
Iulius Onesiphorus, A., freedman at Laodicea
    Catacecaumene I, 155 n. 109
Iulius Pardalas (Sardis) I, 155 n. 112
Iulius Patricius, Encratite of Laodicea
    Catacecaumene II, 103
Iulius Patroeinus, 'first of Hellenes'
    (Nicopolis) I, 116
Iulius Paullus, senator from Pisidian
    Antioch I, 154 n. 106
Iulius Paulus, C. (Galatia) I, 154
Iulius Paulus, C. (Laodicea Catacecaumene) I,
    154
Iulius Ponticus, priest at Ancyra I, 108, 109
Iulius Ponticus, soldier from Pontus I, 138 n.
    154
Iulius Proculeianus, L., legate of Galatia–
    Cappadocia II, 155 n. 69
Iulius Proculeianus, Q., governor of
    Cappadocia II, 158
Iulius Proculus Quintillianus, proconsul of
    Asia II, 48, 88 n. 326
Iulius Pudens, C., legionary tribune
    (Ancyra) I, 135
Iulius Q. f., Q. (Ancyra) I, 113
Iulius Quadratus Bassus, C.:
    governor of Galatia–Cappadocia II, 151 n.
        8, 155
    praedia Quadratiana I, 154
    slaves in Lydia I, 161
    Trajan's general I, 154, 156
Iulius Saturninus, governor of Galatia I, 66 n.
    43
    medallions at Ancyra I, 208 n. 68
Iulius Scapula, C., governor of Galatia I, 66 n.
    153, 93 n. 132
Iulius Senecio, C., procurator and governor of
    Galatia and Pontus I, 67; II, 158
Iulius Severus, C. (Ancyra) I, 38
    high priest I, 112, 114, 116 n. 113
    hosts troops I, 132, 252
    as member of local aristocracy I, 154–5
    praised by Aelius Aristides II, 84
Iulius Valerius, soldier in Pisidia I, 122
Iulius Valerius Nepotianus, M., governor of
    Galatia II, 153 n. 38
Iulius Vercondaridubnus, C., priest of
    Augustus in Gaul I, 107
Iunius, M., delegate from Rome I, 26
Iunius Gallio, proconsul of Achaea II, 5, 31
Iunius Homullus, M., governor of
    Cappadocia II, 155
Iunius Rusticus, M., cavalryman (Olbasa) I,
    74
Iunius Soranus, *dux* of Scythia II, 69 n. 96
Iunius Valerius Nepotianus, M., governor of
    Galatia and Pontus II, 158
Iustus, name translates Hebrew Zadok II, 31
    n. 176
Izois, Encratite bishop II, 100

Jacob, Galatian Jew II, 36
James the apostle II, 5
JEROME:
    on Celtic language I, 50
    comm. in ep. ad Galatas II, 93
    de viris illustribus II, 92
John, bishop of Ephesus II, 116, 118–19

John, member of Jerusalem apostolic group
    II, 5
JOHN CHRYSOSTOM II, 69, 96, 111,
    114, 115 n. 45
JOHN MALALAS, on heretics in
    Cotiaeum II, 104
John Mark, companion of Paul II, 6
John the Syrian, hermit at Nicomedia II, 130
JOSEPHUS, on Jews of Sardis II, 32
JOVIAN, emperor II, 93
JULIAN (the Apostate), emperor II, 64 n. 68,
    66, 88–91, 96
    establishes pagan organizations II, 118
    and poll tax II, 95
Julius, bishop of Rome II, 92
JULIUS CAESAR:
    at Blucium and Peium I, 33
    on Celts and Gaul I, 48, 49
    cult of I, 100
    victory at Pharsalus I, 36
JUSTIN:
    on Celtic arrival in Asia Minor I, 15
    on Celtic occupation of Galatia I, 19
JUSTINIAN, emperor I, 5; II, 129
    and governors of Lycaonia II, 161
    joins Pontus Polemonianus and
        Helenopontus II, 159
    novella 27 (AD 535) II, 159

Kambaules, Celtic leader I, 15
Kamma, Galatian priestess of Artemis I, 49
Kerethrios, Celtic leader I, 13, 15
Kerykos, at monastery of St George Pegai
    (Dorylaeum) II, 130
Kiderios, Celtic leader I, 15
Kommontorios, Celtic leader I, 14, 15
Konnakorix, Celtic leader I, 31

Labienus, Q. I, 37
LACTANTIUS:
    on Cicero's *De Officiis* II, 82
    on Clarian oracle II, 44
    on importance of decade AD 303–13 II, 64
    as possible source for Jerome on
        Galatians I, 50 n. 84
Lalla, benefactress of Tlos I, 201 n. 22
Lampadius, prefect of Rome II, 82
Laodice, wife of Antiochus II I, 176
Larcius Macedo, A., Galatian road-building I,
    122 fig. 22, 124
Latinius Alexander, high priest at Ancyra I,
    112, 114; II, 85 n. 288
    entertains troops I, 232, 252
Leocritus, Pontic general I, 25
Leonnorius, Celtic leader I, 15, 16, 17, 43
Leontius, bishop of Ancyra II, 93, 110
Lepidus, M., triumvir I, 90
LIBANIUS:
    and Ancyra II, 89
    correspondence with Bosporius II, 110
    and Julian II, 89
    on Julian's attack on the Christians of
        Caesareia II, 94
    on Maximus' transformation of Ancyra II,
        90
    on Nicomedia I, 213
    on Syrian monks in the *pro Templis* II, 114
    on urban temples and rural sanctuaries II,
        16
Licinius, C., soldier from Sebastopolis I, 137
    n. 141
LICINIUS, emperor, 'edict of Milan' II, 64
Licinius, P., consul I, 25, 26

Licinius Mucianus, T., governor of Galatia I,
    66
Licinius Mucianus, T., governor of Lycia and
    Pamphylia II, 153
    supports Vespasian I, 140
Licinius Murena, Roman commander I, 31,
    81 n. 9
Licinius Serenianus, governor of
    Cappadocia II, 60, 159
Livia, wife of emperor Augustus I, 161–2
LIVY I, 83
    on Celts crossing to Asia Minor I, 15
    on Celts settling in Anatolia I, 16, 19
    on Cn. Manlius in Galatia I, 23, 24, 51
    on Galatian landscape I, 143; II, 131
    on Galatians I, 43
    on gladiatorial games at Syrian Antioch I,
        110
    on Gordium I, 54
Lollius, M., first governor of Galatia I, 61, 63,
    73
Lollius M., priest at Ancyra I, 103, 110
M. Lollius, M. f., veteran at Iconium I, 73
LUCIAN I, 213
    on Battle of the Elephants in *Zeuxis* I, 45
    on Celtic language I, 50
    on Christians and atheists in Pontus II, 37
    on Severianus as foolish Celt II, 4 n. 16
LUCIUS VERUS, emperor:
    on coin of Syedra I, 204 fig. 35g
    Parthian war I, 133, 252
Lucretius, Sp., delegate from Rome I, 26
Lucterius Leo, C., of Cardurci in Gaul I, 107
Lucullus, Roman commander I, 31, 179
    commandeers grain in campaign against
        Mithridates VI I, 248
Lucullus, son of Hedys:
    in charge of stable at Dacibyza I, 129
LUKE, author of Gospel and Acts:
    on St Paul's conflict with Judaizing
        Christians II, 8
    on St Paul at Ephesus II, 37
    on St Paul's first journey II, 3, 4
    on St Paul's missions II, 31–2
    to be reconciled with Galatians II, 4
    story of Dives and Lazarus II, 82
    on synagogues at Antioch and Iconium II,
        35
    on wealth, discussed by Basil II, 83
Luscius Ocrea, L., governor of Lycia and
    Pamphylia II, 154
Luturios, Celtic leader I, 15, 16, 43
Lycomedes, ruler of Comana Pontica I, 39
Lydia, Christian convert from Thyateira II, 31
Lydianus. . . . Claudius, M., high priest at
    Pessinus I, 112 n. 78, 116 n. 111
Lydius, leads uprising at Cremna I, 234–5
Lykaon, legendary founder of Lykaonia I, 208
Lysias, Macedonian dynast I, 21, 32 n. 64
Lysimachus, defeated by Seleucus I (281
    BC) I, 13

Ma, daughter of Pappas, Isaurian priestess II,
    48
Macedonius, bishop of Constantinople II, 96,
    97
MACRINUS, emperor I, 221
    campaign in Parthia I, 232
MAGO, the Carthaginian I, 35, 148
Magna, leader of community of virgins
    (Ancyra) II, 109, 110
Mammas, Lycaonian bishop II, 59
Manlius Vulso, Cn., Roman commander:
    campaign in Anatolia I, 19, 22, 23–4, 25

Manlius (*cont*.):
  exacts indemnities I, 71 n. 19
  and Galatians I, 45, 46, 51, 54, 55
Maras, Novatian clergyman of Nicomedia II,
    98 n. 388
Marcellus, bishop of Ancyra II, 91–3
Marcianus, *logothetes* II, 128
Marcion, bishop of Constantinople II, 97
Marcius Priscus, Sex., governor of Lycia II,
    154
Marcus, Novatian priest from Laodicea
    Catacecaumene II, 100
Marcus, son of Mathias (Acmonia) II, 35
MARCUS AURELIUS, emperor I, 114
  sister owns land in Asia Minor I, 163
Maria, deaconess of Archelais II, 123 n. 5
Maria, mother of St Theodore of Sykeon II,
    122, 126, 134, 136
Marius, C.:
  visits Galatia I, 30
  war with Teutones I, 48
Marius Celsus, A., governor of Syria I, 119
Marius Priscus, C. (Galatia) I, 153
Martinianus, prefect of Rome II, 80, 81
MATTHEW, author of Gospel, on motives for
    charity II, 82
MAURICE, emperor II, 123, 124, 128, 129
MAXIMINUS, emperor (Galerius Valerius
    Maximinus Daia):
  attempts pagan revival II, 47, 90
  persecutes Christians II, 47 n. 274, 57, 64–
    5, 82, 95, 118
  rescript outlawing Christians II, 100 fig. 22
MAXIMINUS THRAX, emperor I, 222
Maximus, Caesar of Maximinus Thrax, on
    coin of Ninica I, 114 fig. 18b
Maximus, freedman procurator I, 252, 253
Maximus, governor of Cappadocia II, 81
Maximus, governor of Galatia II, 90, 91
  erects fountains and nymphaea II, 90
Maximus, wealthy citizen of Ancyra II, 87, 91
Megethius (Ancyra) II, 127
  oppresses peasants of Sykeon II, 128
Meirus, son of Aentius (Laodicea
    Catacecaumene) II, 103
Melanippe, Novatian nun (Laodicea
    Catacecaumene) II, 100
Meleager, commander of Antiochus I I, 17
MEMNON of Heracleia I, 16, 23
  on Amaseia I, 31
  on chieftains I, 43
Menas, directs council in AD 536 II, 114
Menas, father of Pylaemenes, priest at
    Ancyra I, 108
Menemachus, estate owner at Sardis I, 176
Menemachus, father of Metrodorus, priest at
    Ancyra I, 108, 109
Menodotus of Pergamum I, 28, 35
Metrodorus, priest at Ancyra I, 108, 109
Midas, legendary king of Phrygia I, 208
Mithridates I Ktistes I, 20
Mithridates II, kingdom plundered by Gauls I,
    20
Mithridates II of Armenia I, 25
Mithridates V Ktistes of Pontus I, 84
  obtains Great Phrygia I, 29
Mithridates VI Eupator of Pontus I, 82, 84,
    86
  aggressive policy I, 25
  Gauls fight alongside I, 19
  growing power I, 29
  kills leading Galatians I, 29, 31
  linguistic mastery I, 172
  protectorate over Galatia I, 30

Roman concern about I, 62
  at sanctuary of Zeus Stratios (Amaseia) II,
    22
Mithridates of Pergamum I, 28, 35
  gains tetrarchy of Trocmi I, 36
  killed I, 37
MODESTINUS, jurist I, 248
Modestus, founder of Lycaonian monastery in
    Constantinople I, 173
Modestus, praetorian prefect of emperor
    Valens II, 77
  drowns Orthodox clergy II, 98
  petitioned by Basil II, 79
  petitions II, 80, 88
Montanus, Phrygian heretic II, 39–40, 59,
    100
  New Prophecy of II, 105
Mopsus, in the cities of Pamphylia I, 207
Morzius of Gangra I, 24
Moschous, hermit at Nicomedia II, 130
Mucius Scaevola, governor of Asia I, 30
Musanus, priest at Ancyra I, 108, 109
Musonius, bishop of Neocaesareia II, 84

Nanas, Christian priestess (Phrygian
    Highlands) II, 47, 105
Naucratius, brother of Basil of Caesareia II,
    68, 112
Nectarius, bishop of Constantinople II, 100 n.
    402
Neikatoris, son of Xenophon (Hadriani) II,
    50
Neoptolemus, Ptolemaic general in Lycia I, 17
NERO, emperor:
  consular legates in Cappadocia I, 63
  plans invasion of Armenia I, 41
  proposes abolition of 'indirect' taxes I, 256
  tax collection in Asia I, 249
NERVA, emperor I, 64
Nestorius, priest of Laodicea
    Catacecaumene II, 107
Nicadas, emporiarch in Bithynia I, 187
Nicephorus (Laodicea Catacecaumene) II,
    107
Nicetas, *comes* at Constantinople II, 124 n.
    19
NICOLAUS of Damascus:
  on morality of Phrygians I, 189
  on spread of imperial cult I, 100
Nicomedes I of Bithynia I, 15, 15–16, 19
Nicomedes IV of Bithynia I, 30, 62
Nilus of Ancyra II, 109, 110
Nonius Calpurnius Asprenas, L.(?), governor
    of Galatia I, 66 n. 49
Nonius Felix, garrison commander (Phrygian
    Apamea) I, 121
NONNUS I, 207
Norbanus Flaccus, C., proconsul of Asia II,
    33
Novatianus, founder of Novatians II, 96, 97
NUMENIUS, of Apamea II, 45
NYMPHIS, historian of Heracleia I, 16
  heads embassy to Galatians I, 20

Octavian:
  civil war I, 37
  makes adjustments in Anatolia I, 40
  takes name Augustus I, 100
  see also AUGUSTUS
Octavius, Cn., delegate from Rome I, 26
Odenathus, dynast of Palmyra I, 237
Ofellius Iullus, C., Ephesian Christian at
    Bithynian Claudiopolis II, 38
Oppius, L., associate of Cicero I, 35

Oppius, Q., Roman commander I, 30
Oppius Aelianus Asclepiodotus, T.,
    epanorthotes in Asia I, 228
Opramoas, makes benefactions at Xanthos I,
    111
Orfitasius Aufidius Umber, Q., governor of
    Galatia I, 64 n. 24; II, 155 n. 71
ORIGEN II, 48, 60
  teacher of Gregory the Wonder-Worker II,
    53
Orobazus, Parthian ambassador I, 118
Orodes, Parthian king I, 37
Ortiagon, Celtic leader I, 24, 43
Otacilia Severa, wife of emperor Philip:
  on coin of Diocaesareia I, 204 fig. 35c

Paccii I, 152, 154
Paccius Niger, Sex., freedman I, 152
Paccius Niger, T., freedman I, 152
Paccius Valerianus Flaccus, Sex. (Attaleia) I,
    152
  and imperial cult I, 103
Pachomius, founder of monasticism II, 114
Pacorus, Parthian prince I, 37
Paenius Numisius, C., cavalryman I, 73 n. 38
Paidopolites, son of Ortiagon and
    Chiomara I, 43
PALLADIUS, author of *Lausiac History*:
  on ascetics II, 109, 110
  on monasteries II, 114
PANTOLEON, *Miracles of St Michael* II, 117
Papas, Lycaonian bishop II, 59
Papirius Alexander, L., high priest at
    Ancyra I, 112 n. 78, 114
Pardalas, owns Anatolian estate I, 155
PARTHENIUS I, 17
Patrocles (Nicaea) I, 213
Paul, archbishop in Ancyra II, 128
Paul, martyr in Lycaonia II, 59, 65
Paul, Novatian bishop of Constantinople II,
    97 n. 376
Paul, priest in Lycaonia II, 128
Paulinus, bishop of Tyre II, 82 n. 254
Paulus, deacon at Laodicea Catacecaumene II,
    107
PAUSANIAS:
  brands Brennos for impiety I, 47
  on Celtic language I, 50
  on Celtic warfare I, 44
  on Celts' arrival in Asia Minor I, 15
  on Celts' occupation of Galatia I, 19
  on Panopeus I, 80, 81, 226
  stories of divine intervention I, 17
Pausanias, sophist of Caesareia II, 86
Perilaus, father of Antipater of Derbe I, 32
PERTINAX, emperor, letter on military
    abuses I, 229
Pescennius L. f. Serg., St. (Pisidian Antioch) I,
    75 fig. 11
Pescennius Niger, civil war and defeat by
    Septimius Severus I, 133, 179, 221, 232
Peter, brother of Basil of Caesareia II, 68, 112
Petronius Umber, Q., governor of Lycia and
    Pamphylia I, 67, 157; II, 154
Petronius Umbrinus, Q., governor of Lycia
    and Pamphylia II, 154
Petronius Verus, L., governor of Galatia I, 66
    n. 46, 127 n. 69; II, 151 n. 38
PHAENNO of Epirus I, 15
Pharnaces I of Pontus, aggressive policy in
    183/2 BC I, 25
Pharnaces II of Pontus, invades Armenia
    Minor and Pontus in 47 BC I, 32, 36
Phellinas, sculptor of Temenothyrae II, 39

Philetaerus, alternative name of Paccius Niger, Sex. I, 152
Philetaerus of Pergamum I, 16, 21
Philetus (on Bithynian estate) I, 161
Philip II of Macedon, art of war I, 45
PHILIP the Arab, emperor:
　on coin of Laranda I, *208 fig. 36b*
　creates no sacred games I, 222
　peace treaty with Sassanians I, 227
　petitioned by Aragua I, 230, *231 fig. 41*
　petitioned by Lydian community I, 229
Philo, freedman of M. Caelius I, 35
Philodamus, father of Seleucus, priest at Ancyra I, 108, 109
Philomelos, Macedonian dynast I, 32 n. 64
Philon, father of priest at Ancyra I, 108, 109
Philopatra (upper Tembris valley) II, 106 n. 449
Philoromus, ascetic at Ancyra II, 109, 110
PHILOSTORGIUS, on Phrygian origin of Novatians II, 97
PHILOSTRATUS:
　on Apollonius of Tyana I, 247
　Lives of the Sophists II, 85
Philumenus, *hegoumenos* of the monastery at Sykeon II, 123, 128
Phocas, emperor II, 24 n. 19, 123
Phocas, *a secretis* II, 143
Phoenix, hipparch at Cyzicus I, 16
Photius, exarch of Rome II, 125
Photius, at monastery of St George Pegae II, 130
Photinus, benefactor of Laodicea Catacecaumene II, 107
PHYLARCHUS, on Celtic feasting I, 44
Pinarius, in care of Deiotarus I, 35
Pinarius Cornelius Severus, Cn., *cos. suff.* AD 112 I, 151
Pionius, martyr at Smyrna II, 36, 48
Plancii (Perge) I, 152, 153, 154
Plancius Varus, M., senator from Perge I, 74, 152, 160, 212
Plautius Silvanus, M., governor of Galatia I, 66 n. 43, 78; II, 151
PLINY the elder, I, 64
　on Cappadocian towns I, 97
　on Galatian tribes I, 43
　on *Proseilemmene* I, 55
　on *tractus Oronticus* I, 90
　on *skylites* wine I, 147
PLINY the younger I, 43, 88, 202
　on buildings in Bithynia I, 212
　on Christians at Amastris II, 38
　on governors of Bithynia I, 65
　panegyric of Trajan I, 231
　requests centurion for Iuliopolis I, 134, 252
　on status of rural Bithynians I, 178
PLOTINUS II, 45
PLUTARCH I, 203
　advice to local politicians I, 63
　on cult of Artemis in Galatia I, 49
　on strife at Sardis I, 203
　on Tosiopae I, 43
Polemo I, son of Zeno:
　in Cilicia and Lycaonia I, 38; II, 152
　defence of Laodicea I, 38
　in Pontus I, 38, 39, 93, 94
　takes over Armenia Minor I, 40
Polemo II of Pontus I, 94; II, 153
　freedman leads revolt against Rome I, 206
Polemocratia, wife of Sadalas II I, 62
POLYBIUS:
　on Attalus' title 'king' I, 21

on Manlius Vulso in Galatia I, 23
on Ortiagon I, 24, 43
on warfare I, 45
Polycarp, bishop of Smyrna I, 196–7
　martyred II, 41
Polycritus, proposes decree at Erythrae I, 17
Pompeius Collega, Cn., governor of Galatia–Cappadocia I, 64 n. 24, 66 n. 43, 124
Pompeius Magnus, Cn. (Pompey):
　cities founded I, 98–9
　defeated at Pharsalus I, 36
　and Deiotarus I, 31
　divides Pontus I, 88, 91–2
　eastern settlement of 63 BC I, 31–4, 40
　lex provinciae of 63 BC I, 88, 89, 162, 178, 210
POMPEIUS TROGUS I, 19, 24
Pomponius Bassus, T., governor of Galatia I, 124, 126 n. 56; II, 155 n. 74
Pomponius Secundianus, P., governor of Galatia I, 66 n. 46
PORPHYRY, *Philosophy to be learned from Oracles* II, 43, 44
POSIDONIUS, on Celtic feasting I, 44
Postumius Severianus Apollothemis, P., landowner (Nicaea) I, 160
Prasutagus, Icenian king I, 62
Primus (Pribeis), Novatian priest at Laodicea Catacecaumene II, 103
Priscilla, Montanist prophetess II, 100
Proclus, soldier from Iconium I, 121
PROCOPIUS:
　Justinian's bridge at Sykeon II, 125, 133
　on road damage I, 126
Procopius, rebel II, 88
Proculus, son of Aur. Menandrus (upper Tembris valley) II, 100
Prohaeresius, rhetor (Athens) II, 86
Prusias I I, 2, 24
Prusias II I, 25, 26
Ptolemy II:
　assists Pontic cities I, 20
　cult with Arsinoe at Limyra I, 18
　Galatian settlement at Alexandria I, 137
Ptolemy III I, 20
Ptolemy VIII Euergetes I, 62
Ptolemy Keraunos I, 13
PUPIENUS, emperor with Balbinus, I, 237
Pupius Praesens, L., procurator I, 67, 157; II, 154
Pylaemenes, ruler in Paphlagonia I, 33
Pylaemenes, son of Amyntas:
　benefactions to Ancyra I, 105, 107, 110, 111, 112
　offers banquets to Galatian tribes I, 110
　presents helmet to L. Calpurnius Piso I, 107
　too young to succeed his father I, 41, 62
Pylaemenes, son of Menas, priest at Ancyra I, 108, 110
Pythodoris of Tralles, queen of Pontus I, 93–4; II, 153
　in Armenia Minor I, 94

Quinctius Flamininus, T., Roman commander I, 25
Quintus, putative brother of L. Sergius Paullus II, 7

Reparatus, Lycaonian hermit II, 130
Rubes of Eumeneia II, 41
Rubrius C. f. Pop., C. (Laodicea Catacecaumene) I, 154

Rubrius C. l. Hilario Rubella, C., *negotiator* I, 154 n. 99
Rubrius Optatus, C. (Laodicea Catacecaumene) I, 154
RUFINUS, *Historia Monachorum* II, 114
Rufus, priest at Ancyra I, 107
Rutilius Gallicus, L., legate in Galatia II, 153, 155

Sabas, martyr in Scythia II, 69
Sabbatios, head of Novatian church in Ancyra II, 98–9
Sadalas II of Thrace I, 62
Saevinius Proculus, L., governor of Galatia I, 66 n. 46
St Anthimus, church or monastery at Nicomedia II, 129
St Antiochus, chapel in Sykeon II, 122, 125
St Antony, founder of eremitic tradition II, 110
St Augustine II, 73
St Autonomus:
　Life of II, 99
　monastery on Mt. Dracon II, 130
　monastery or church near Nicomedia II, 129, 143
St Auxentius I, 173
St Basil, *see* Basil of Caesareia
St Christopher:
　church or monastery at Nicomedia II, 129
　female monastery in Sykeon II, 126
St Cosmas II, 136
St Damas of Caesareia II, 66
St Damian II, 136
St Dionysius of Milan II, 69
St Eirenicus, church at Mazamia II, 129
St Euphemia II, 69 n. 115
St Eupsychius of Caesareia II, 66
　festival with St Damas II, 69
St Euthymius, miracle of I, 50
St Gemellus, church in Sykeon II, 125
St George:
　basilica at Sykeon II, 122, 126, 132, 137
　chapel at Sykeon II, 125, 137
　monastery of St George Pegae at Dorylaeum II, 129
　monastery or church at Nicomedia II, 129
　patron of St Theodore of Sykeon II, 134, 136, 137
St Gordius of Caesareia II, 67
St Gregory, *see* Gregory of Nazianzus; Gregory of Nyssa
St Gregory Thaumaturgus (the Wonder-Worker) II, 38, 60, 65, 66, 69
　canonical letter II, 56–7, 79
　career and life II, 53–5
　cites Old Testament II, 56
　creed of II, 54
　on Gothic invasions I, 236
　leadership of II, 55–6
St Heuretus, at Iuliopolis II, 129
St Hyacinthus of Amastris I, 172
St Ignatius II, 37
St Ioannicius II, 115
St John the Baptist:
　chapel in Sykeon II, 122, 125
　church at Trapeza II, 129
　emulated by St Theodore of Sykeon II, 137
St John Studius, church in Constantinople II, 117
St Kerykos, church in Sykeon II, 126
St Lucian of Antioch II, 65, 68
St Macrina, sister of Basil of Caesareia II, 68, 112–13

St Mamas of Caesareia II, 66
St Martha of Antioch I, 173
St Michael II, 46, 117
    assimilation with Attis doubted II, 22 n. 70
    chapel at Soreoi II, 99
    churches at Akreina, Eukraa, and
        Skoudris II, 128
    churches at Germia and Nacolea II, 117
    church or monastery at Nicomedia II, 129
    church at Sykeon II, 122, 125, 126, 128,
        141
    dead commended to II, 129
    monastery at Sykeon II, 128
    saves St Theodore of Sykeon from illness II,
        136
St Paul:
    against angel worship II, 35, 46
    and Asian communities II, 37, 41
    brings Christianity to Anatolia I, 4
    Colossians, epistle to II, 35
    conversion II, 4
    Corinthians, second epistle to II, 6
    at Derbe I, 96
    Ephesians, epistle to II, 56
    first missionary journey II, 3–4
    Galatians, epistle to II, 3–5, 9, 93
    at Iconium II, 11, 31
    Jewish hostility to II, 31
    and Judaizing 'God-fearers' II, 43
    at Lystra II, 11, 24, 29, 31
    Romans, epistle to II, 8
    route from Perge to Antioch I, 70
    and St Thecla II, 116
    and Sergius Paulus II, 7
    visits to Jerusalem II, 4–5
    on 'witless Galatians' II, 84
St Peter:
    first epistle to Jews in Anatolia II, 3
    member of Jerusalem apostolic group II, 5
    shrine in Rome II, 109
St Peter of Atroa II, 115
St Phocas II, 69, 70 n. 115
St Plato, chapel in Sykeon II, 122, 125
St Sabas, Laura of II, 130
St Sergius and St Bacchus, chapel in Sykeon II,
    125
St Simeon Stylites II, 130
St Sophia:
    cathedral at Anastasiopolis II, 129
    cathedral at Pessinus II, 129
St Stephen, monastery at Vetapa II, 129
St Thecla, Life of II, 112, 115, 116–17
St Theodore of Euchaita II, 69
    church or monastery at Nicomedia II, 129
    as St Theodore Stratelates (Bithynia) II, 130
St Theodore of Sykeon II, 116, 117
    asceticism II, 136–9
    becomes bishop of Anastasiopolis II, 123,
        128
    birth II, 134
    chronology II, 122–3
    environment II, 123–34
    exorcisms II, 138–44
    family II, 122, 129, 134, 136
    founder of monasteries and churches II,
        124, 125
    and Gospels II, 137, 140
    iron cage II, 132
    Life of I, 179; II, 36, 122 ff.
    miracle at Germia II, 128
    miracle types II, 137–8, 139
    miracles II, 132–3
    miracles assessed II, 134
    monastery becomes autonomous II, 130

pilgrimage to Sozopolis II, 129
    visits Constantinople II, 123, 124
    visits Holy Land II, 130, 134
St Theodotus of Ancyra II, 36, 62, 65, 68, 69
    Life of II, 93
Salvidienus Asprenas, L., proconsul of
    Bithynia I, 212
Salvius L. f. Serg., L., soldier at Side I, 73
Saoterus, obtains privileges for Nicomedia
    from Commodus I, 220
Saturninus, Encratite bishop II, 100
Saturninus Secundus, governor of Pisidia II,
    161 n. 45
Sossius, C., soldier I, 136
Saul, previous name of St Paul II, 7
Scipio Africanus I, 23
Scopelian of Clazomenae I, 146
Scribonianus, revolt in Dalmatia I, 137
Scribonii (Vetissus) I, 133, 135
Sedatius Severianus, M., senator from Gallia
    Comata II, 4 n. 16
Seleucus I, defeats Lysimachus (181 BC) I, 13
Seleucus II:
    and Antiochus Hierax I, 20
    battle with Gauls I, 19
Seleucus III, generals defeated by Attalus I I,
    21
Seleucus, son of Philodamus, priest at
    Ancyra I, 108, 109
Selinos, bishop of Cotiaeum I, 174
Sempronia Romana (Ancyra) II, 85
Sempronius Albanus, M. (Attaleia) I, 74
Sempronius Aquila (Ancyra) II, 85
Sempronius Arruncius, high priest at Carian
    Stratonicaea II, 64
Septimius Severus, emperor:
    accession I, 229
    and annona militaris I, 252
    on coin of Caesareia I, 204 fig. 35f
    creates provinces of Osrhoene and
        Mesopotamia I, 236
    defeats Pescennius Niger I, 179, 232
    founds new festivals I, 221
    Parthian expedition I, 222
Sergia L. f. Paulla (Pisidian Antioch) I, 151
    wife of C. Caristanius Fronto II, 6
Sergia Paullina, landowner I, 152, 164
Sergianus Longus, soldier at Ancyra I, 121
Sergii (Vetissus) I, 151–2
Sergii Paulli, senatorial family from Pisidian
    Antioch I, 151, 154, 157; II, 6–7
Sergius, patriarch of Constantinople II, 123,
    124 n. 19
Sergius Carpus, freedman I, 151
Sergius Corinthus, L., freedman, builds temple
    of Men I, 151
Sergius L. f. Paullus, L., proconsul of
    Cyprus I, 152
    convert of Paul II, 6–7, 8
Sergius L. f. Paullus L., the younger II, 6
Servaeus, T. (Savatra) II, 28 n. 149
Servaeus Sabinus, L. (Savatra) II, 28 n. 149
Servenius Cornutus, L., senator from
    Acmonia II, 9
Servilius Caepio, Q., commands army during
    revolt of Aristonicus I, 195
Servilius Isauricus, P.:
    acquires ager publicus I, 90, 91, 95, 157,
        249
    campaigns of 70s BC I, 70, 72, 73
    devotio at Isaura II, 29
Sestullii:
    at Fundi (Latium) I, 158
    in Phrygia I, 154 n. 101; II, 40 n. 241

Sestullius Severus, M., high priest I, 158
Sestullius Severus Flavianus, M., high priest I,
    158
Severus, bishop at Laodicea
    Catacecaumene II, 107
    member of Saccophori II, 102, 103
Severus Alexander, emperor II, 158
    on coins I, 114 fig. 18f, 222 fig. 39c
    festivals celebrate victories I, 221–2
    and Sassanians I, 236
    triumphal arches I, 216
Shapur I, Sassanian king I, 227, 237
Sicinius Clarus, Q., governor of Thrace I, 245
Siculus Flaccus:
    on ager publicus I, 91
    on Roman colonies I, 76
Simonides, epic poet of Magnesia ad
    Sipylum I, 18
Sinatos, Galatian tetrarch I, 49
Sinorix, father of Deiotarus I, 28, 49
Sisinnius, Novatian bishop of
    Constantinople II, 96, 99
Socrates, church historian:
    Ecclesiastical History I, 174, 189; II, 96
    on Novatians II, 96, 97, 98, 99
    on Phrygians II, 189
Solovettius, Galatian commander I, 26 n. 155
Sophronie, virgin of Laodicea
    Catacecaumene II, 107
Sophronius, magister officiorum II, 80
Sotas of Priene I, 17
Soterus, sophist (Ephesus) II, 85
Sotidius Strabo Libuscidianus, Sex., governor
    of Galatia I, 65, 67
Sozomen, church historian:
    on Christianity in Syria and Asia Minor II,
        63–4, 71, 88
    draws on Socrates' Ecclesiastical History II,
        96
    on Eustathius as author of Basil's Rules II,
        113
    on Julian and the Christians of Caesareia II,
        95
    on Leontius II, 110
    on monasticism II, 111, 113, 114
    on Novatians II, 96, 97, 98, 110
Spatale, high priestess (upper Tembris
    valley) II, 47
Statius, poem in honour of Rutilius II, 153
Statius Quadratus, proconsul of Asia I,
    196–7
Stephanos, cook at the inn of St Theodore's
    mother II, 136
Stephanos (Germia) II, 129
Stephanous, hegoumenos of St Theodore
    Stratelates by the Psilis II, 130
Stephanus of Byzantium I, 17
Strabo I, 83, 97
    on Armenia Minor I, 33
    on Ateporix I, 109
    on Augustus' 'New Deal' I, 61
    on Caria I, 178
    on Carian language I, 172
    on Celtic occupation of Galatia I, 19
    on Celtic warfare I, 45
    on extent of Galatian province II, 151–2
    on forests of Mount Olympus I, 166
    on Galatian constitution I, 17, 35
    on Galatian tetrarchs I, 29
    on kings at Amaseia I, 39
    on Lycaonia I, 143
    on Maryandeni I, 177
    on phrouria in E. Anatolia I, 84
    on Phrygian cities I, 85

on Pontus I, 92, 93, 94, 97
on Rhea, worshipped under many names II, 19
on Roman governors I, 63
on Savatra I, 96
on Selge I, 71 n. 13
on *skylites* wine at Amblada I, 147
on Tavium I, 51
on Tectosages I, 54
on temple at Pessinus I, 88; II, 20
on temple states I, 82
on temples of Men at Pisidian Antioch II, 24
on urbanization I, 81
on Zela I, 91
Strato, tyrant of Amisus I, 40
Studius, consul AD 454 II, 117
SUETONIUS, *Life of Vespasian* I, 118
Sulpicius Iustus Dryantianus, C., governor of Lycia and Pamphylia II, 154 n. 60
Sulpicius Quirinius, P.:
and Homonadeis I, 77–8
honorary magistrate at Pisidian Antioch I, 75 fig. 10
Symeon Thaumastorites I, 173
Sympheron, slave of M. Calpurnius I, 153
SYNCELLUS I, 235
Synesis, slave of Cocceianus (Nacolea) I, 160

Ta . . . Achaicus, P., landowner (Nicaea) I, 160
Tabeis, Lycaonian deacon II, 59
TACITUS:
on Corbulo's Armenian campaigns I, 140
on emperor worship in Britain I, 107
on legionary recruitment I, 139
on rising in Pontus I, 206 n. 52
TACITUS, emperor I, 224
acclamations at Perge I, 238
Tarcondimotids of Hierapolis I, 40, 94
Tatis, from Hellenized Phrygian family I, 174
Telephus, founder of Pergamum I, 208 fig. 36d
Terentius, military commander in Armenia Minor II, 78
TERTULLIAN:
convert to Montanism II, 40
on dreams II, 12
Tertullus Varus, high priest at Ancyra I, 112 n. 78, 114, 116 n. 112
Teuthras, legendary founder of Pergamum I, 177 n. 113
Thaddaeus, mission to Abgar V II, 57
Thecla, secret name of St Macrina II, 112
THEMISTIUS II, 87
addresses Constantius on philanthropy II, 84–5
and Julian II, 88
professor of rhetoric at Constantinople II, 86
urges Valens to preserve pagan temples II, 89
Themistocles, general of Achaeus I, 22
Theodora (Phrygia) II, 106
Theodore, burns down temple at Amaseia II, 74
Theodore, churchman of Constantinople II, 129 n. 46
Theodore, hermit on Mt. Dracon II, 130
Theodore of Neocaesareia, *see* St Gregory Thaumaturgus
THEODORET:
on angel worship II, 46
on heresies II, 93

Theodorus, high priest of Asia II, 91
Theodorus, *strator* from Pylai II, 125
THEODOSIUS I:
and Arian debate II, 97
creates new province of Honorias II, 160
decisions on heretics II, 100
outlaws pagan worship II, 117
THEODOSIUS II II, 119
Theodosius, bishop of Anastasiopolis II, 128, 130
Theodotus Kourappos, sorcerer II, 142
Theotecnus, governor of Galatia II, 62, 65
Thomas, patriarch of Constantinople II, 123
THUCYDIDES:
on barbarian warfare I, 44 n. 29
law of nature I, 197
TIBERIUS, emperor I, 81 n. 6, 94
annexes Cappadocia I, 63
city foundations I, 78, 98–9
cult of I, 104, 105, 115
dedication to I, 140
Tieos, Novatian deacon from Laodicea Catacecaumene II, 100
Tillius Cimber, L., tyrannicide I, 37
Timotheus at Eukraa II, 140, 147
Timothy of Derbe II, 5, 35
TIMOTHY the presbyter:
on heretical sects II, 93 n. 363, 102
Titius Iustus (Corinth) II, 31
Titus, companion of St Paul II, 5
TRAJAN, emperor:
agonistic festival I, 219
and building at Prusa I, 212
eastern campaigns, logistics of I, 252
on Greeks and gymnasia I, 216
letters from Pliny I, 88
panegyric of I, 251
Parthian war I, 132, 133
on political turmoil in Greek East I, 203
on trade associations I, 202
statue and temple for in Kana I, 97
TRAJAN DECIUS, emperor:
on coin of Mallos I, 208 fig. 36c
festival at Anazarbus I, 224
offensive in East I, 237
persecutes Christians II, 48, 54, 96
Tranquillina, wife of Gordian III I, 227
TREBONIANUS GALLUS, emperor:
on coin at Side I, 222 fig. 39b
offensive in East I, 237
Trokondas (Iconium) II, 50
Trollius C., Isaurian soldier I, 140
Trophimus, son of Anteros (upper Tembris valley) II, 106
Tryphon, son of Apollonides, benefactor of Takina I, 180
Tuccius L. f. Pom. Secundus, L., *comes* of governor I, 69 n. 73
Turronii, Italian immigrant family in Asia II, 9
Turronius Clado, P., *archisynagogus* II, 9
Turronius Rapo, priest of imperial cult at Acmonia II, 9

Ulfilas, first bishop of Goths I, 236
Ulpii (Sarıkaya) I, 155
Ulpius Appuleius Eurycles, M. (Aezani) I, 214 n. 112
Ulpius Carpus (Miletus) II, 49
Ulpius Maximus, soldier at Ancyra I, 133
Ulpius Traianus, M., father of emperor Trajan II, 155
Ummidii, Italian senatorial family I, 158

VALENS, emperor:
challenged by rebel Procopius II, 88
confronts Basil of Caesareia II, 77–9
divides Cappadocia II, 161
and Themistius II, 88
VALERIAN, emperor:
on coin of Anazarbus I, 222 fig. 39e
and sacred games I, 224
Valerian the younger, promoted to Caesar I, 234
Valerii Paeti, senatorial family I, 155
Valerius, P., protected by Deiotarus I, 35
Valerius Antoninus(?), governor of Galatia I, 66 n. 49
Valerius Chrysaorius, governor of Diospontus II, 159 n. 15
Valerius Diogenes, governor of Pisidia II, 65, 161
Valerius Eudaemon, M., procurator I, 68; II, 154
Valerius Flaccus, L., proconsul of Asia II, 33
Valerius Italus, M., governor of Galatia I, 69 n. 73
Valerius Patruinus, P., governor of Galatia(?) I, 64 n. 24
Valerius Proculus, L., procurator I, 68
Valerius Severus, C., legate of Galatia II, 155 n. 69
Valerius Statilius Castus (Oenoanda) I, 234
Valerius Valens, L. and Q., soldiers from Savatra I, 121, 122 fig. 20
Varenus Rufus, proconsul of Bithynia I, 65, 203
Vedius Antoninus, benefactor of Ephesus I, 220
Velii of Heliopolis I, 153
Velius Rufus Valerianus, D., executed by Commodus I, 153
VELLEIUS PATERCULUS I, 63
Ventidius, P., defeats Parthians I, 38
Veranius, Q., deputy of Germanicus I, 93
Veranius, Q., governor of Lycia and Pamphylia II, 153, 154
Veranius Philagrus, Q. (Cibyra) I, 203
Vercingetorix, Gallic chieftain I, 107
Vergilius Capito, Cn. (Miletus):
baths I, 216
games I, 219
Verres, quaestor in Asia I, 247
Verus, Christian benefactor of Ancyra II, 109–10
VESPASIAN, emperor I, 98–9
and agonistic festivals I, 219
bid for power I, 140; II, 7
creation of eastern *limes* I, 118
cult of I, 107
joins Cappadocia and Galatia I, 63; II, 154
Vibius Gallus, Q., governor of Galatia I, 66 n. 43
Victor, *magister equitum* II, 81
Victor, martyr near river Halys II, 68
Virgin Mary:
chapel in Sykeon II, 122, 125
church at Amorium II, 129
church at Heracleia Pontica II, 129
church at Sozopolis II, 129
church at Sykae II, 128
church and monastery in Sykeon II, 125–6, 142
church or monastery at Nicomedia II, 129
festival at Mousge II, 129
Voconius Saxa Fidus, Q., governor of Lycia and Pamphylia II, 154 n. 60
Voconius Zeno, governor of Cilicia I, 238

VOLUSIANUS, emperor, offensive in East I, 137

Xenarchus, philosopher at Seleuceia on the Calycadnus II, 152
XENOPHON:
    on Iconium I, 84
    on komarchs I, 183
    on Mysian brigandage I, 165

XENOPHON of Ephesus, on eirenarch I, 196

Zarnuas, reputed founder of Magusaioi II, 73
Zeno, father of Polemo (Laodicea) I, 38
ZENO the Isaurian, emperor II, 117
Zenobia of Palmyra I, 224, 237
Zenon, son of Pythodoris I, 81 n. 6
Zeuxis, regent of Antiochus III II, 31
Ziaelas, Bithynian pretender I, 19

Zipoetas I of Bithynia I, 18
Zipoetas, brother of Nicomedes I I, 16
Zipoetas, son of Nicomedes I I, 19
Zmertorix, son of Philonides (Eumeneia) I, 40
ZOSIMUS I, 15; II, 114
    on Gothic raids I, 235
    on siege of Cremna I, 234
Zosimus, Christian or hypsistarian in Phrygia II, 50, 105

Index of Non-Christian Cults

Aether II, 44, 48
Agathe Tyche I, 196
Ahura-Mazda II, 73
Air II, 48
Ambrosia, nurse of Dionysus I, 146–7, 147
Amphilochus, legendary founder of Mallos I, 208 fig. 36c
Anaeitis I, 192
  Barzochara (of mountain peak) II, 30
  cult established by Persians II, 73
  invoked on Lydian tombstone I, 188
  linked with Men II, 24
  sanctuaries in Pontus and Armenia II, 30
Angdistis II, 16, 18, 19, 20
Aphrodite:
  at Ancyra II, 14
  at Pessinus II, 14
  temple near Pergamum I, 21
Apollo I, 191
  at Adada II, 13
  at Ancyra II, 14
  Archegetes II, 47
  associated with Holy and Just II, 25, 26, 36, 47
  at Caesareia, temple demolished II, 66, 95
  at Çavdarlı (Phrygia) II, 13, 28–9
  Clarios at Sagalassus I, 78, 216; II, 13
  at Delphi I, 13
  at Gryneion I, 167
  at Iconium II, 20
  invoked in tombstone curse I, 188
  in Isauria I, 140
  Lairbenos I, 187, 191, 192, 193–4, 197, 204 fig. 35a
  member of Phrygian pantheon II, 16
  among Motelleis II, 14
  at Oenoanda I, 211
  oracle at Claros II, 11, 12, 13, 14, 30, 31, 43, 118
  oracle at Didyma II, 12, 36, 43, 64
  oracle on Mysian Olympus II, 13
  Pandemos, sanctuary at Magnesia ad Sipylum I, 195 n. 237
  Patroos I, 196
  at Pessinus II, 14
  Propylaios at Eumeneia II, 12 n. 14
  Smintheus, temple on coin of Alexandria Troas I, 204 fig. 35h
  Sozon II, 18, 26
  at Thyateira I, 17
  Toumoundos I, 180 n. 139
  near Tymandus I, 11
  worship in Greek cities I, 102
  see also General Index: oracles
Ares II, 12, 26
  and Areioi (Savatra) II, 28
  Enyalios II, 28
  in Isauria, Lycaonia, and Pisidia II, 28

Kiddeudas II, 28
  at Syedra, on coin I, 204 fig. 35g
  rock reliefs at Zekeriye II, 28
Artemis II, 14
  Agrotera I, 196
  Anaeitis, linked with Men II, 24
  in Anatolia I, 49
  chief deity of Xenoi Tekmoreioi II, 16
  with Dioscuri II, 28
  of Ephesus I, 202; on coin of Perinthus I, 204 fig. 35c; in Phrygia II, 26 fig. 13
  Galatian priestess I, 49
  at Iconium II, 20
  among Motelleis II, 14
  name of demon in 6th-century Galatia II, 144, 149
  at Panamara II, 14
  Perasia (Hierapolis-Castabala) I, 222 fig. 39a; II, 30
  at Perge I, 206
  at Pessinus II, 14
  statue in temple of Apollo at Claros II, 118
Asclepius:
  at Aezani I, 133
  at Ancyra I, 114
  Aristides: on his powers II, 43; visits shrines I, 166
  at Pergamum on coin I, 204 fig. 35b
  at Pessinus I, 133; II, 14
  at Pisidian Antioch II, 10 n. 74
  Soter, at Pergamum II, 138
  temple at Aegeae I, 188, 224
  Zeus Asclepius at Pergamum II, 43
Astarte:
  at Hanisa I, 83
  imported to Cilicia and Cappadocia II, 29
Athena II, 18
  at Ancyra II, 14
  of the Mouriseis I, 153
  at Pessinus II, 14
  Polias I, 207
  Promachos, games at Rome I, 222, 227
  temple of A. Polias at Priene I, 103
  temple at Pergamum I, 21
Attabokaoi, priests at Pessinus I, 48
Attis II, 14, 22 n. 70
Augustus, cult of I, 100, 102–5
  at Ancyra and Antioch: benefactions, games and festivals I, 108–12; functions of I, 117; part in civic life I, 112–14; priests I, 114, 116–17; priests at Ancyra I, 107–14; temples I, 101 figs. 13 and 14, 104–5, 106 fig. 16, 107

Castor, temple at Rome I, 34
Chrysea Parthenos II, 26
Concord of the village (near Nacolea) I, 185
Corybantes and birth of Zeus (Aezani) II, 18

Cronos II, 18
Cybebe, synonym of Rhea II, 19
Cybele:
  and Attis II, 14
  on coin of Smyrna I, 204 fig. 35d
  cult at Pessinus I, 48, 49; II, 20–2, 62, 89
  priests meet army of Manlius Vulso I, 48
  sacred stone of II, 89
  shrine at Pessinus I, 26, 82, 89, 105
  synonym of Rhea II, 19

Demeter:
  at Nicomedia I, 221
  at Pessinus II, 14, 89
  priesthood with Men Askaenos at Pisidian Antioch II, 10
  Thesmophorus at Miletus II, 12
  at Thiounta I, 187
  votive to I, 161
Dikaion, Phrygian god of justice II, 16, 18, 36
  see also Hosion Kai Dikaion
Dikaiosyne, at Prymnessus II, 18, 26
Dike, on coin of Syedra I, 204 fig. 35g
Dindymus, mother of Mount II, 20–2
Dionysus I, 191
  at Ancyra II, 14
  less prominent in rural areas II, 16
  Marcus Antonius as new Dionysus I, 37
  at Nicaea I, 207, 208, and fig. 36a
  nursed by Ambrosia I, 146–7
  patron of artistic competitors I, 218
  at Pessinus II, 14
  at Pisidian Antioch II, 10 n. 74
  at Smyrna II, 36
  source of inspiration to Himerius II, 86
Dioscuri II, 14
  with Artemis in Pisidia II, 28
  relief at Fassiler II, 12

Earth II, 24
Elagabalus (sun god), at Nicomedia and Sardis I, 221
Eleusis, mysteries of II, 88
Eleuthera I, 196
Eros II, 14

Fortune:
  in sanctuary of Apollo at Didyma II, 14
  temple at Caesareia demolished II, 66, 95
  see also Tyche

Gallus (river god at Pessinus) II, 14
Ge (Earth goddess) II, 24
Glycon, the new Asclepius I, 207, 213
  oracle of I, 173; II, 13

Hagia Kataphyge (Sacred Refuge) II, 34 fig. 16

Harpocrates II, 14
Hecate:
    at Ancyra II, 14
    invoked on tombstones I, 188
    in Phrygia II, 20 fig. 10, 36, 47
Helios I, 191
    at Ancyra I, 14
    with Apollo, and Holy and Just II, 26, 36,
        47
    at Appia II, 14 fig. 3
    linked with Zeus II, 24
    at Pessinus II, 14
    in Phrygian pantheon II, 16
    at Thiounta I, 187
Hera:
    at Nicaea II, 29
    at Panamara II, 14
Heracles II, 12
    at Ancyra II, 14
    Commodus identified with I, 221
    at Cyzicus I, 16
    at Eusebeia/Tyana I, 86
    festival at Hanisa I, 83
    founder of Cius and Nicaea I, 207
    at Laranda I, 208 fig. 35b
    at Pessinus II, 14
    in Phrygian pantheon II, 16
    at Tarsus I, 208 fig. 36e, 221
    at Tyre I, 221
Hermes:
    at Ancyra II, 4
    on coin of Syedra I, 204 fig. 35g
    escorts dead to underworld II, 26
    at Eusebeia/Tyana I, 86
    linked with Zeus II, 24, 26 fig. 11
    megistos near lake Suğla II, 24
    at Pessinus II, 14
    in Phrygian pantheon II, 16, 26 fig. 11
Highest God, see Theos Hypsistos
Hosia II, 16, 26
Hosion kai Dikaion (Holy and Just) I,
    191; II, 16, 25–6, 26 fig. 14, 45, 46, 47,
    62
    statue of I, 161
Hygieia I, 191; II, 14
    statue at Aezani I, 216 n. 112

imperial cult I, 100, 102–5, 183, 184
    at Acmonia II, 9
    of Antonius Pius I, 107
    economic importance of I, 258
    in Pisidian Antioch II, 9, 10
    of Tiberius I, 106, 107
    of Vespasian I, 107
    see also Augustus, cult of
Isis II, 16
    at Ancyra and Pessinus II, 14
    at Nicomedia I, 212
Iuppiter Optimus Maximus:
    dedications to I, 122 fig. 19, 136
    at Iconium II, 18, 29
    at Olbasa II, 29
    at Pisidian Antioch II, 10, 29

Janus, temple at Rome I, 227
Juno, dedication to I, 122 fig. 19

Kakasbos II, 26
    perhaps at Sagalassus II, 13
'King and Queen' II, 14
Kore:
    at Didyma II, 14
    in Pisidia II, 30

Leto I, 192, 194; II, 13
    at Xanthos I, 102
Lord of Hosts (Theos Dynameon) II, 45
Luna II, 10 n. 71, 25

Ma I, 16
    at Comana Pontica I, 49, 82; II, 30
Magna Mater, temple in Nicomedia I, 212
Maron II, 14
Marsyas, statuette on coin of Mallos I, 208
    fig. 36c
Mazda, Mazdaean ceremony for Mithras at
    Ariamneia II, 29
    see also Ahura-Mazda
Medusa, at Iconium I, 208
Meis/Mis I, 191
    see also Men
Men II, 1, 24–5, 46
    at Ancyra I, 114; II, 14
    Andronenos II, 25
    Askaenos I, 61, 75 fig. 12, 76, 90, 150, 151,
        152; II, 9–10, 14 fig. 1, 24–5, 30
    Axiottenos I, 161, 188, 191
    in central Anatolia I, 151, 152; II, 25
    Dikaios (in Phrygia) I, 191
    dominant cult in Anatolia II, 19, 29
    Gaineanos II, 25
    in Lydia I, 191
    Masphaltenos I, 191
    among Motelleis II, 14
    mother of I, 161 n. 180
    in N. Phrygia II, 62
    Ouranios II, 29 n. 288; at Saittai II, 45
    at Pessinus II, 14
    of Petra I, 191
    Pharnakou I, 82; II, 24, 30
    Selmeanos II, 25
    Tiamou I, 192, 193
    'tyrant' I, 191
    of underworld II, 25
Meter (mother of the gods) I, 147; II, 18,
    19–20, 22
    Aliene II, 20
    Andeirene II, 20
    Atimis I, 193
    Boethene II, 20
    Dindymene I, 22
    Phileis I, 191 n. 225
    Phrygian I, 191; II, 14, 19, 20
    Plastene II, 16 n. 46, 20
    Plitandene II, 20
    Quadratene II, 20
    Silandene II, 20
    Sipylene II, 20
    Tarsene II, 20
    Theon Zizimmene II, 19–20
    Tymene, statuette of II, 20 fig. 8
    Zizimmene identified with Athena II, 18, 23
Midas II, 14, 90
Minerva II, 18
    Zizimmene II, 29
    see also Athena
Mithras I, 86; II, 29–30, 73
Moon II, 46
    in Phrygian pantheon II, 16
    see also Luna; Men
mother goddess II, 14, 19–20, 22, 25
    see also Meter, Mother of the Gods
Mother of the Gods II, 18, 19, 20–1, 22
    sanctuary at Pessinus II, 89
    temple at Amaseia II, 74
    see also Meter; mother goddess
Mother of Zeus:

    at Aezani II, 19
    Julian's hymn to II, 89
Mountain Mother I, 196
Muses II, 14, 29
    and council of Ancyra II, 87
    and Himerius II, 86

Nemesis I, 191
    Adrasteia I, 196
    at Ancyra II, 14
    goddess of Phrygians II, 36–7
    invoked on tombstones I, 188
    at Pessinus II, 14
Nike II, 14
Nymphs II, 25

Pantokrator, linked to cult of Theos
    Hypsistos II, 50, 51
Papas:
    at Nacolea II, 16
    in N. Phrygia II, 62
Perseus:
    at Aegeae I, 207
    at Iconium I, 208
    at Tarsus I, 208 and fig. 36e
Phoebus I, 191
    statue at Çavdarlı II, 13
    see also Apollo
Pluto II, 27
    in Pisidia II, 30
    as warrior god II, 26
Poseidon:
    the earthshaker II, 26, 28, 106
    at Iconium II, 26
    at Pessinus II, 14
Pylon (god of gates) II, 22 n. 78

Rhea, worshipped under various names II, 19
Roma I, 100
    archegetis I, 102–3
    see also Rome and Augustus, cult of
Rome and Augustus, cult of I, 100
    temple at Ancyra I, 101 fig. 13, 103
    temple at Pergamum I, 115 fig. 18e, 219

Sabazios II, 16
    see also Zeus Sabazios
Sagaris (river god at Pessinus) II, 14
Sarapis II, 16, 49
    at Ancyra I, 66; II, 14
    among Motelleis II, 14
    at Pessinus II, 14
Selene II, 28
    see also Luna; Moon
Sophrosyne (Moderation), Phrygian deity I,
    191; II, 36
Sozon II, 18, 26
    epekoos at Laodicea Catacecaumene II, 26
    see also Apollo
Sun:
    invoked with Holy and Just II, 25
    member of Phrygian Pantheon II, 16
    see also Helios

Tantalus, fall located on Mount Olgassys II,
    22
Theos Dynameon II, 45
Theos Hypsistos (Highest God):
    at Aezani II, 62
    altar at Andeda II, 34 fig. 16
    Jewish influence in cult II, 36
    nature of cult II, 44, 49, 50, 51
    and Zeus II, 50

Theos Pereudenos I, 191 n. 225
Thesmos II, 12
Tiberius, *see* imperial cult
Tyche:
  at Ancyra and Pessinus II, 14
  of Iconium II, 16
  at Perinthus, on coin I, 204 *fig. 35c*

Xenoi Tekmoreioi I, 178, 179, 183, 185
  centre at Sağır II, 9–10, 24
  important regional cult II, 16–18
  subscriptions II, 14 *fig. 2*
  in 3rd century AD I, 239

Zeus I, 97, 161, 191
  Abozenos II, 20 *fig. 7*
  Akoueos II, 23 n. 93
  Akreinenos II, 128 n. 44
  Alsenos I, 146 n. 29; II, 20 *fig. 9*
  Ampeleites I, 187, 230 *fig. 41*; II, 18
  at Ancyra II, 14
  Andreas I, 187; II, 14 *fig. 3*
  and Artemis, at Termessus II, 13
  Asclepius, temple at Pergamum II, 43
  Bennios I, 187 n. 205
  Bennios near Appia I, 158; II, 62

birthplace in Steunos cave, Aezani II,
  18–19
Bronton I, 189; II, 23, 62
Bussurigios, Bussumaros I, 187; II, 18, 18
  n. 53
Chrysaoreus I, 178
  at Cihanbeyli I, 155–6
  at Eldes I, 156
  at Emirdağ I, 146 n. 29
Enaulios II, 23
Epekoos II, 24
Epi-/Eukarpios II, 23
Heptakometes I, 153 n. 94
'highest god' II, 44, 45
Hypsistos (Stratonicaea) II, 49
  at Iconium II, 23
Karios, temple at Panamara II, 14
Keraunios II, 64
Manes Daos Heliodromos II, 47
Megistos, sanctuaries at Iconium and
  Perta II, 23
most widely worshipped god in Asia
  Minor II, 19, 22–4
  among Motelleis II, 14
  mother of II, 19, 89
Narenos II, 23

Olympius, near Aelius Aristides' estate I,
  167
at Panamara I, 110; II, 14, 64
in Paphlagonia I, 92 n. 121
at Pergamum on coin I, 114 *fig. 18e*
at Pessinus II, 14
Petarenos I, 146 n. 29; II, 20 *fig. 9*
Phatnios II, 23
in Phrygian pantheon II, 16
remoteness of II, 44, 45, 49
Sabazios I, 240
Sarnendenos II, 23
of the sky I, 147
Soter, at Hanisa I, 83
Souolibrogenos I, 57
Stratios II, 22; at Amaseia I, 92; II, 24 n.
  110
at Tavium I, 83; II, 14, 23
temple at Aezani I, 181, 198, 214; II, 62
temple at Ancyra I, 208
temple at Caesareia, demolished II, 66, 95
temple at Lystra II, 11
and *Theos Hypsistos* II, 50
at Thiounta I, 187
Touitenos I, 179 n. 128
'of the twin oak trees' I, 191 n. 225
at Venasa II, 30

Index of Places and Peoples

(*a*) WITHIN ASIA MINOR

Abbaeiteni I, 176, 181
Abbassium I, 23
Abbrettenoi I, 176
Abonuteichus:
  cult of Glycon I, 50, 88, 173, 207, 213; II,
    13, 30
  home of Themistius II, 84 n. 270
  see also Ionopolis
Abya, *see* Appia
Acmonia:
  inscription of Galatian *koinon* I, 113
  Jewish community I, 172; II, 33, 34 *figs. 15
    and 17*, 35, 36, 39
  legionary recruit I, 137
  Sestullii at I, 158
  slave market I, 257
  synagogue II, 9
Acrasus I, 20, 180 n. 142
Adada:
  members of *Xenoi Tekmoreioi* from II, 16
  temples at I, 114; II, 13
Adana I, 206, 221, 238
Adapazarı I, 140
Adramyttium II, 33
Adrouta I, 180 n. 142
Aegeae:
  coinage I, 208 *fig. 36g*, 232
  games I, 224
  Perseus, Argos, association with I, 207
  Sassanians, capture by I, 238
  Tarsus, rivalry with I, 206
Aegosages I, 22
Aesepus, river I, 167, 175
Aezani:
  administration I, 199–200, 211
  Asclepius, dedication to I, 133 n. 95
  assize centre I, 258
  cult of Holy and Just II, 25
  decline in 3rd century I, 240
  development of I, 214
  festival, agonistic I, 219 n. 146, 225 n. 197
  inscription for 'one god' II, 45
  Mysian inscription I, 123
  paganism, strength of II, 62
  ruins I, 211
  sacred slaves II, 30
  Sestullii at I, 158
  Steunos cave, birthplace of Zeus II, 18–19
  view of I, 215 *fig. 37*
Afyonkarahisar I, 143
Ağabeyköy I, 229, 230
Agatheira I, 180
Agrianians I, 17–18
Aianioi II, 133
Akça Köy II, 20 *fig. 6*
Akkisse I, 122
  priest of Zeus II, 24 n. 101

Akoluk II, 47
Akören I, 153
Akreina II, 128
Aksaray I, 144; II, 118
  see also Archelais
Akşehir I, 129
  see also Philomelium
Aksu, river I, 70; II, 12
  see also Cestrus
Alabanda I, 102
Alastos I, 153, 164
Alektoria II, 133
Alexandria Troas I, 73, 200
  coinage I, 204 *fig. 35h*
  supervision of Celts I, 22
Algizia I, 179
Algouina I, 179
Almassun I, 155
Altıntaş I, 179, 181
  Sestullii at I, 158
Altınyayla:
  walls at I, 94 n. 150
Amanus gates I, 38, 64
Amaseia I, 88, 92, 178
  Brigatus probably ruler I, 93, 107
  in 4th century II, 74
  Galatian province, part of I, 31, 94; II, 153
  Hellenistic territory I, 82, 84, 86
  roads I, 132
  Roman military I, 136 n. 127
  Strabo's birthplace I, 39
Amastris I, 31, 64 n. 31, 88
  building I, 212
  Christians I, 38
Ambitouti I, 43
Amblada:
  Ares, cult of II, 28
  and Celts I, 26, 55
  land, public I, 90
  legionary recruits I, 138 n. 151
  medicinal wine of I, 146
  philosophers II, 85
Amisus I, 64 n. 31, 81, 88
  beleaguered by Celts I, 20
  pre-Constantinian Christianity II, 38
  resists Pharnaces I, 36
  Roman colonists at I, 37
  Strato tyrant of I, 39–40, 41
  temple built by Mithridates I, 82 n. 20
Amnias, river II, 160
Amorium I, 148; II, 98, 128
  Blessed Virgin, church of II, 129
  illustres (leading citizens) II, 127
  Mithras, cult of II, 29
  Roman military at I, 121, 135, 141

Anaboura II, 25
Anastasiopolis II, 126
  cathedral dues II, 130
  church of St Sophia II, 129
  ktetores II, 127
  St Theodore bishop II, 123
Anazarbus:
  coinage I, 232, 237
  games I, 219 n. 221, 222 *fig. 39e*, 224
  Sassanians, captured by I, 238
  Tarsus, rival of I, 206
Ancyra:
  asceticism II, 109, 110, 111
  battle of (243 BC) I, 19–20
  bishopric disputed II, 91–3
  buildings I, 116, 214
  and Caracalla II, 89
  and Celts I, 19, 20, 93
  centurions at I, 118 n. 8, 122 *fig. 21*, 232
  Christians before Constantine I, 62 n. 56
  in 4th century II, 64, 91–4
  Christians, persecution of II, 12, 90–1
  Church disputes II, 78
  cohors I Augusta Cyrenaica at I, 121
  constitution I, 89, 200
  creation of city I, 86–7, 88, 89
  cultural life II, 85
  euergetism I, 225
  foundation myths I, 208
  games and festivals I, 111, 218, 219,
    219–20, 221, 224
  heretical centre II, 92–4
  in 5th–6th centuries II, 120
  in 4th century, prominence II, 74
  imperial cult I, 39, 100, 101, 102, 112, 114
  imperial priests I, 107–12
  imperial temple I, 101 *fig. 13*, 103, 104–5
  and C. Iulius Severus I, 154
  and Julian II, 84–91
  L. Fabius Cilo honoured I, 66
  Libanius and II, 87
  in *Life of St Theodore* II, 127, 141
  monasteries II, 114
  Montanists II, 39, 65
  Novatian church II, 98
  pagan worship I, 66; II, 14
  population size I, 244
  pre-Roman I, 81–4
  provincial administration centre I, 69
  roads I, 122 *fig. 22*, 132
  Roman military I, 133, 134, 135, 141 *170
    fig. 29*, 75
  synod (AD 314) II, 70
  Trajan's troops at I, 252
  walls I, 236
  see also Ankara
Ancyra (Phrygian) = Ancyra Sidera II, 39,
  92–3

Christian community II, 62
Andabilis (Andaval) II, 116
Andeda:
  Judaism II, *34 fig. 16*
  Plancii at I, 152 n. 84
Andrapa–Neoclaudiopolis I, 92 n. 129; II, 161
Andriake I, 249
Anemurium:
  capture by Sassanians I, 238
Angarum:
  site of Novatian synod II, 98, 99
Angdissis, Mount II, 20
Angora, Ottoman:
  corvée labour I, 127
  poor roads of I, 134
  see also Ancyra
Ankara I, 1, 7
  modern city hides Roman city I, 104
  wine industry I, 147
  see also Ancyra
Ankara Çay I, 55
Annesoi II, 72, 112
Anosa I, 183, 185, 230, 246
Antimacheia I, 183, 185, 230, 246
Antioch (Pisidia) I, 90; II, *14 fig. 3*, 151, 152
  acclamation at I, 201
  and Amyntas I, 38
  Antiochus I, founder I, 20
  Antistius Rusticus: grain edict I, 150, 244
  Augustus, colony under I, 76, 77, 90; II, 29
  centurions of the region I, 228, 234
  cohors I Augusta Cyrenaica I, 121
  colonial allotments I, 151
  constitution I, 89
  under Diocletian I, 216
  division into *vici* I, 200
  duumvirs, honorary I, 66
  families, leading I, 74, *75 figs. 10–12*; II, 6–7
  imperial cult I, 104; II, 10
  imperial temple I, *101 fig. 14*, 104, 105–6
    106 figs. 15–16; II, 10
  inhabitants, status of I, 178
  Iuppiter Optimus Maximus, cult of II, 10, 39
  Jews II, 9, 35
  Men Askaenos, cult of I, 90; II, 9–10, *14 fig. 1*, 30
  public building programme I, 78, 216; II, 10
  Roman military I, 73, 74, 141
  St Paul II, 3–10, 37
  senatus consultum (AD 204) I, 230
  via Sebaste I, 70
  Xenoi Tekmoreioi from II, 16
Antioch on the Maeander:
  bridge I, *204 fig. 35d*
  sacred games I, 224
Anyl I, 119
Apamea (A. Cibotus) I, 64 n. 88, 202
  Antiochus I founder I, 20
  assize centre I, 258
  Celtic names at I, 57
  Celts, saved from I, 17
  Christian community II, 40, 41, 58
  euergetism I, 225
  in Galatian wars I, 26
  games I, 226 n. 197
  gymnasium, expenditure on oil at I, 217
  inscription I, 139
  Jewish community I, 33–4, 36
  in Mithradatic War I, 25
  primipilaris, honours I, 121

roads I, *125 fig. 23*
Roman military I, 141
slave market I, 257
treaty of (189/8 BC) I, 23, 24, 25
Apamea (Bithynia) I, 166, 244
  bath house I, 212
  Catilii at I, 160
  Prusa, rival of I, 204
Apateira I, 181, 182, 183, 184
Aphrodisias I, 81; II, 24
  Aurelius Gaius praised I, 233, 234
  defences of I, 195
  epanorthōtes I, 228
  games I, 222, 225
  Jewish community II, 32, 36
  paganism in 5th–6th centuries II, 118
  privileges I, 177
  Sebasteion I, 159; II, 118
Apollonia I, 90, 91, 95; II, 25, 151, 152
  Amyntas, given to I, 38
  Antiochus I, founder I, 20
  Augustan colonists I, 77
  customs' post I, 68
  festival at I, 220
  imperial cult I, 104
  Roman soldiers at I, 73
  Xenoi Tekmoreioi from II, 16
  see also Sozopolis
Apollonia-Sozopolis II, 141
Apollonis (Lycia):
  stationarius at I, 122
Apollonis (Lydia) I, 161
Apoukome II, 131, 133, 134
Appia (upper Tembris valley) I, 158; II, 104
  Christian community II, 40, 59, 60
  city territory I, 181
  texts from I, 196
  tombstone I, *170 fig. 28*
  village names in territory I, 179
  Zeus, cults of I, 187; II, *14 fig. 3*, 18
Appola II, 25
Arabissus II, 162
Aragua II, 18
  petition to the two Philips I, 159, 229, 230,
    230 figs. 40 and 41, 233
Aralleion I, 155, 164
Arania II, 126
Arca II, 162
Archelais I, 84, 95, 96, 97
  Christian gravestone II, 123 n. 5
  colonial magistrates I, 89
  Sassanians near I, 236; II, 161
'Ardabau' (Mysia) II, 39
Argaeus, Mount:
  cult image I, *204 fig. 35f*
  dominates Caesareia II, 86
Ariadne, Cappadocian mountain I, 82 n. 11
Ariandos I, 181
Ariaramneia II, 29
Ariaratheia I, 81 n. 7, 82, 98; II, 80, 162
Ariassus I, 196; II, 22
  prize games (*themides*) I, 218 n. 139, 225
  triumphal arch for Severus Alexander I, 216
Arisbe I, 22
Arkea II, 132, 144, 149
Artanada I, 77 n. 78, 122
Arycanda II, 64
Ascanias, Lake I, 160, 161
Aslanlı Köy II, *20 fig. 7*
Aspendos:
  games I, 218
  grain exports I, 247
  Pamphylian dialect I, 172

Sassanians, safe from I, 238
Aspona II, 160
  Mithras, cult of II, 29
  Palladius as bishop II, 110
Assarlıkaya Hissar I, 54
Assus, poll tax I, 256 n. 82
Astacus, gulf of II, 98
Atkafası I, 148 n. 49, 155
Atlandı I, 155
Attagaina II, 69
Attaleia I, 74 n. 49, 90, 91; II, 152 n. 33
  Augustan foundation I, 77
  Calpurnii I, 152
  freedmen I, 161
  harbour I, 247
  Paccii I, 152
  Rome archegetis, cult for I, 102
  Sassanians, safe from I, 238
Attuda I, 225
Aulutrene:
  dedication I, *122 fig. 19*
  fort I, 121
Axiotta I, 188, 191
Ayaş II, 127, 131
Azak II, 160
Azamora I, 84
Azitta I, 191

Babanomitis I, 92
Bademli I, 157
Bagis I, 176, 180, 181; II, 39
Bağlıca I, 88 n. 90
Bahtıllı I, 181
Balat I, 140
Balbura I, 71, 77 n. 69, 180, 220
Balıhisar I, 54; II, 133
  see also Pessinus
Balıkesir, plain I, 167
Barata II, 116, 155
Barbalissus, battle of I, 237
Bargylia I, 18, 89 n. 97
Baris I, 218, 225; II, 161
Baş Dağ I, 84
Basgoedariza I, 84
Basrı I, 54
Berecyntians II, 19
Beşkavak I, 148 n. 49, 149 n. 54, 152
Beyköy I, 152
Beypazarı II, 125, 126, 131
Beyşehir, Lake I, 95, 157; II, 12, 73
Binbir Kilise ('1001 churches') II, 116
Bithynium-Claudiopolis I, 207
Black Sea:
  coast cities I, 32–4
  Galatians obtain access to II, 151
  Goths reach S. shores II, 56
  Greek colonies on Pontic coast I, 81
  a 'Roman lake' I, 235
  sends wheat sent to Constantinople II, 98
  Sinope best harbour I, 82
Blaene I, 91
Blaundus I, 20, 180, 187, 193
Blucium I, 33, 36, 55, *56 fig. 9*, 84, 86
Boğazköy I, 1, 51, 54
Böğrüdelik I, 149
Bolgatia II, 126
Bolu I, 57; II, 97
  see also Bithynium-Claudiopolis
Boradi:
  invade Pontus II, 56
Bosporus I, 15; II, 115
  monasteries II, 115
Bostandere II, 25
Bouna II, 131, 133

Bouzaia II, 133, 139, 140, 147
Boz Dağ I, 96–7, 145
Bozkır I, 122; II, 28
    see also Isaura Palaea
Bozova I, 71, 152; II, 49
Briania II, 129, 130
Bubon I, 234
Buğdüz I, 150
Burdur, Lake I, 71, 157; II, 154
Büyük Evliya Dağ II, 22
Büyük Nefes Köy:
    site of Tavium I, 51
Byzantium I, 13 n. 24, 64 n. 31
    Bithynian city I, 16
    Celts at I, 15
    demoted to village I, 179
    sacred games I, 221
    soldiers and civilians I, 134, 255
    see also Constantinople

Cabalitis, Lake I, 179
Cabeira I, 82, 94
    cult of Men Pharnakon I, 82; II, 24, 30
    Diospolis founded at I, 32
    fighting at (71 BC) I, 31
    polis developed I, 32
    sacred slaves II, 30
Cadena I, 82
Cadi I, 181, 219, 225 n. 197
    Christian community II, 62
    Christian inscriptions I, 38, 39, 60 fig. 18
    Ummidii at I, 158
Caesarea Trocetta I, 183
Caesareia (Cappadocia) I, 97, 98
    arms factory II, 76
    and Basil in I, 144; II, 79–80, 83, 116
    bishops in 3rd century II, 60
    Christian community II, 38, 67
    Christian epitaph, early II, 38
    coinage I, 204 fig. 35f, 250
    4th-century prominence II, 73–4
    Hellenized centre II, 86
    and Julian II, 67, 89, 94, 179
    Mithras, cult of II, 29
    Persians confronted by Heraclius at II, 123
    poverty and wealth II, 83
    roads I, 132
    Roman military I, 134 n. 114
    sacred games I, 218, 219, 220, 221
    saints, local II, 67
    Sassanians, capture by I, 238
    temples demolished II, 67, 95
    Valens transfers bouleutai II, 77
Caesareia Germanice I, 212 n. 84
    population size I, 224
Caesareia Hadrianopolis I, 92; II, 153
    see also Caesareis Proseilemmenitae
Caesareis Proseilemmenitae I, 92, 93
Caicus, plain of I, 167
Caicus, river I, 7
    Attalus I's battle with Tolistoagii I, 21
    Seleucid settlements I, 20
Calles, river I, 19
Calycadnus, river I, 94; II, 116
Camisa I, 84
Camisene I, 9, 25
Çamlıbel pass, wall in I, 94 n. 150
Çanakçı I, 54
Çankırı I, 246
    see also Gangra
Capralis (Cappadocia) II, 80
Carana I, 94
Caranitis II, 39, 91, 93; II, 153
    ruled by Ateporix I, 109

Çarıksaray, estate I, 157
Çarşamba valley I, 239
    Christian community II, 41, 58, 60, 65
    domainal land-ownership I, 155, 157
    gravestones of 3rd–4th centuries II, 100,
        107
Casae I, 79
Castabala I, 97
Castollus:
    assembly of elders I, 182
Castolupedion:
    market I, 242 n. 5
Catacecaumene, Lydian I, 229
Çatal Hüyük I, 1
Caunos:
    Carian spoken at I, 172
Çavdarlı:
    shrine of Apollo II, 13, 28–9
Çayırhan II, 131
Cayster valley I, 7; II, 38
    paraphylax of I, 196
    pentakoma I, 185
    tombstone curses I, 189, 191
Çekerek Irmak (river) II, 151
Celts I, 3, 4
    Asia Minor, invasion of I, 13–19
    feasts, I, 43–4
    Galatia, settlement in I, 19–20, 51–8
    land tenure I, 42
    language I, 50–1, 175; II, 93
    leader, choice of I, 42, 43
    levies in Roman armies I, 30–1
    military prowess I, 136
    Pontus, in armies of I, 32
    relations with Pergamon and Rome I,
        20–6
    religion I, 47–50
    'simple minded' II, 4
    slaves I, 46–7
    tribal organization I, 27–9
    tribes I, 42–3
    vagrant habits I, 42
    warfare, method of I, 44–6
    weapons I, 45, 46 fig. 7
Cennatae I, 94, 95, 98
Çepni Köy (Phrygian Pentapolis):
    inscription I, 60 fig. 20
Ceramos I, 178
Cerasus I, 94
Ceratae II, 180
Çeşmeli Sebil II, 160
Cestrus, river I, 70, 71, 73
    legionary recruit from I, 138 n. 151
Chalcedon I, 16
    centurions' gravestones I, 232
    Council of (451) II, 115, 159
    monasteries II, 115
Characipolis:
    city territory I, 180
Charmideanoi I, 161
Chiliokomon I, 136, 178
Chrysopolis I, 137
Cibyra I, 71, 203
    harvest tax paid to Rome I, 249
Cibyratis I, 71
    cults II, 28
    languages I, 172–3
Cidyessus:
    Sestullii in I, 158
Cietae Tracheotae I, 176; II, 153
Çifteler I, 87 n. 84
Cihanbeyli I, 144, 148, 155, 164
Cilbiani I, 176
Cilices Tracheotae II, 153

Cilician Gates I, 129, 164, 246
Cilicians I, 70
    see also General Index: Cilicia
Cillanian plain I, 90, 157, 162
Cimiata I, 84
Cimiatene I, 91
Circassians I, 149
Cius I, 16, 88; II, 13 n. 24
    Heracles and I, 207
    Nicaea, rivalry with I, 204
    Pescennius Niger and I, 232
Claneos II, 128
Claros:
    oracle quoted by Lactantius II, 44
    oracle and shrine of Apollo II, 11, 12, 13,
        30, 31, 43
    temple left unconverted by Christians II,
        118
Claudiconium I, 78, 95
    see also Iconium
Claudiocaesareia Mistea I, 78, 95
    see also Mistea
Claudioderbe I, 78, 95
    see also Derbe
Claudiolaodicea I, 78, 95
    see also Laodicea Catacecaumene
Claudiopolis (Bithynia) I, 64 n. 31, 78, 88,
        90; II, 13 n. 24
    bath-house I, 216
    building at I, 212
    Christian gravestones II, 38
    Christian tradition II, 97
    Novatians at II, 99
    winters cold I, 168
Claudioseleuceia I, 78, 95
    see also Seleuceia Sidera
Clistinna I, 138 n. 151
Çoğu II, 20 fig. 9, 160
Colbasa II, 64, 100 fig. 22
Collyda:
    city territory I, 180
    confession texts I, 194
Coloe:
    Attalus' victory at I, 21, 22
Colonia (Armenia Minor) II, 74, 161
Colonosos II, 130
Colossae I, 37
    angel-worship II, 46
Colybrassus I, 140
Comama I, 90; II, 154
Comana (Cappadocia):
    entrusted to Archelaus I, 32
    becomes city I, 98
    capture by Sassanians I, 238
    inscription for centurion I, 136
    priests' high rank I, 81
    temple of Ma I, 82
Comana (Pontus) I, 82
    boundaries II, 153
    Dyteutus ruler I, 41, 93, 94
    Galatia, in AD 34/5 added to I, 63, 94
    inscription for centurion I, 136
    Lycomedes ruler I, 39
    Ma, cult of I, 30
    sacred slaves I, 176–7
    St Gregory the Wonder-Worker at II, 54
    soldiers stationed in II, 75
Conana I, 138 n. 151
Considiana, choria I, 153, 164
    tombstone I, 170 fig. 27
Constantinople:
    Basil and II, 76
    imperial centre I, 4
    imperial guard II, 88

intellectual centre in Greek world II, 84, 85, 112
  John Chrysostom in II, 69
  monasteries of Lycaonians I, 173
  Novatians II, 96, 97, 98, 102
  St John Studius, church II, 117
  St Theodore, visits of II, 123, 141
  synod of 336 II, 92
  synod of 360 II, 92
  synod of 373 II, 81
  synod of 381 II, 161
  Themistius' school of rhetoric II, 85
  see also Byzantium
Cormasa I, 73, 138 n. 151
Coropassus I, 84
Çorum, Trocmian site I, 54
Corycus I, 218
  cemeteries of 3rd–5th centuries II, 120
  trades I, 257
Cossacks:
  19th-century immigration of I, 149
Cotiaeum:
  Arian bishop I, 174
  Christian community II, 46, 59
  Montanists I, 39
  Novatians II, 97, 104
  villages in territory I, 179, 180
  see also Kütahya
Crateia (Bithynia) I, 168; II, 133, 139, 160
Cremna I, 90; II, 152
  Augustus, founded by I, 76, 77
  coinage I, 38
  games I, 224, 225
  gens Rutilia at I, 74
  landscape I, 71
  and Roman rule I, 72
  siege of I, 234–5
  temples II, 13
  walls rebuilt I, 238
Crentius, fort at I, 55
Cromna I, 207
Cuballum, fortress I, 45, 54
Çubuk Bogazı I, 70
Çubuk Ova I, 150
Culupene I, 91, 94 n. 149
Cybistra I, 32; II, 161
Cyme:
  public feasts I, 110, 167, 169
Cyzicus I, 221; II, 95
  Aristides visits I, 167
  dedications I, 187 n. 202; of imperial temple I, 165
  monasteries II, 115
  Novatian bishop II, 97
  Pescennius Niger, defeat of I, 232
  Pontic fleet, base of I, 235
  population size I, 244
  relief depicting Galatian I, 16
  siege of (73 BC) I, 31
  tombstone curses I, 188

Dablenoi and Pronnoetai I, 185
Dacibyza I, 129, 132
Dadastana II, 88, 160
Daeira, cult centre near Tralles II, 118
Dagouta I, 184
Daldis I, 180, 206
Dalisandus II, 155
Dallopoze II, 18
Daoukome I, 179
Dascusa:
  fort at I, 119
Dasmenda I, 84
Dastarcan I, 84

Dasteira I, 84
Demirci:
  magistrate's order to prevent exactions I, 229
Demirözü Çay I, 2 fig. 2
Derbe I, 85, 96
  Amyntas evicts Antipater II, 52, 72
  under Ariobarzanes I I, 32
  Lycaonia, in *koinon* of II, 155
  St Paul, visit of II, 5
  see also Claudioderbe
Dia:
  building at I, 213
Didyma:
  Apollo, oracle and shrine of II, 12, 14, 36, 43, 48, 49, 64
  Celtic attack (277/8 BC) I, 16
  Gothic attack I, 235
Dikmen:
  fort I, 55
Dindymus, Mount I, 87
  and Gallus, river II, 133
  Jewish presence II, 36
  mother goddess II, 19
  Persian settlers II, 73
Diocaesarea (Cappadocia) I, 97
Diocaesareia (Cilicia Tracheia) I, 94
  coinage I, 204 fig. 35e
Dionysopolis I, 187, 193
  early Christian community II, 40, 58
  Montanists II, 39
Diospolis (Pontus) I, 82, 94
  building under Pompey I, 32
Doara II, 78, 161
Docimeium I, 85
  Celtic names I, 57
  estates I, 159
  Jewish presence II, 35
  quarries I, 159, 246; II, 20
  tombstone I, 170 fig. 30
Doidye:
  military colony I, 180
Doksan Dokuz Merdivenli han:
  Aponii at I, 151
Domanitis I, 91
Domitiopolis:
  capture by Sassanians I, 238
Dorla I, 155; II, 59
Doroukome:
  divinities of I, 191
Dorylaeum II, 13 n. 24
  courier's gravestone I, 132
  inscriptions I, 148
  Montanists II, 39, 104
  oiketores (leading citizens) II, 127
  paganism, vitality of II, 60 n. 52
  Phrygian gods at II, 16, 25
  roads I, 129, 132
  St George Pagae, monastery of II, 129, 130
  Sestullii at I, 158
  soldiers stationed in II, 75
  villages in territory I, 179
  walls I, 236
  Zeus Bronton, dedications on tombstones I, 189
Döşemealtı I, 70, 246
Dracon, Mount II, 30
Drymos I, 196
Düğer:
  epitaph to Orthodox priest II, 103
Dura Europos I, 234 n. 36, 237, 250

Eğridir, Lake I, 70, 71
Ekecek Dağ II, 30

Eldes I, 156
Elmadağ I, 151
Emirdağ I, 23
Emirler:
  Sergii at I, 151
Engere, *see* Angarum
Ephesus I, 89 n. 97; II, 45
  Artemis, priesthood of held by Persians II, 29
  Augustus, cult of I, 100
  baths I, 217
  Celtic names I, 57
  cereal prices I, 247
  citizenship decree I, 177
  Claudius Aristio I, 203
  Egyptian grain I, 254
  games I, 219
  Gordian and Tranquillina honoured I, 127
  Goths attack I, 235
  headquarters of courier network I, 129
  Hierapolis, concord with I, 204 fig. 35a
  Pergamon, rivalry with I, 206
  Perinthus, concord with I, 204 fig. 35c
  population size I, 244 n. 12
  St Paul I, 202; II, 31, 34
  Smyrna: concord with I, 80; rivalry with I, 206
  sophistic centre II, 85
  text stressing name of god II, 45
  Verus' Parthian campaign I, 252
Epicteteis (Phrygia) I, 176
Ermenek I, 78
  see also Germanicopolis
Erten:
  Novatian epitaph II, 103
Erythrae:
  Antiochus' letter to I, 18
  Celts purchase protection from I, 17
  Rome and Augustus, cults of I, 100
Erzerum:
  Ottoman corvée labour I, 127
Eski Çalış I, 154
Eskişehir I, 1, 129
  see also Dorylaeum
Etenna I, 87 n. 75, 136
Etenneis I, 71
Euchaita II, 69, 129
Eudoxias II, 160
Euhippe I, 180
  military oppression I, 229–30
Eukraa:
  cereal crops II, 131
  church dues, collection of II, 130
  householder arrested II, 127
  oikodespotes II, 133
  St Theodore, exorcism by II, 140, 147, 149
Eumeneia I, 221 n. 166, 225 n. 197; II, 25
  Apollo Propylaios, cult II, 12
  Celtic name, magistrate with I, 40, 57
  early Christian centre II, 40, 41, 57, 58, 62
  Jewish–Christian overlap II, 48
  Jewish community II, 33, 35
  military at I, 121, 141
Eupatoria I, 94
  polis, beginnings of I, 32
  see also Magnopolis
Eurymedon, river I, 71
Eusebeia by Mount Argaeus I, 81, 83, 84, 86
  see also Caesareia; Kayseri; Mazaca
Eusebeia next to the Taurus (Tyana) I, 81, 86
Euxine I, 235; II, 98
  see also Black Sea
Eyüpler II, 20 fig. 8

Fassiler II, 12
Faustinopolis I, 114; II, 161

Galatians (Gauls) I, 4, 7
    Alexandria, in Egyptian I, 57
    Anatolian cults, adopt II, 29
    Ancyra, founders of I, 208
    Asia Minor, appearance in I, 4
    Delphi, slaves at I, 34
    'witless' II, 85
    see also Celts; General Index: Galatia
Galenoi II, 130
Gallus, river II, 133
Gangra II, 13 n. 24
    capital of Deiotarus Philadelphus I, 39
    council of (340s) II, 112, 113, 114, 115
    foundation legend II, 22–3
    oath I, 84, 91 n. 120, 92; II, 152
    renamed Germanicopolis I, 93
    Tantalus, location of fall II, 22
    see also Germanicopolis
Garsaoura I, 84, 96
    see also Archelais
Garsauritis I, 237
Gauls, see Celts; Galatians
Gazelonitis I, 33
Gdanmaa I, 153; II, 160
Gebren:
    relief of Poseidon II, 26
Gebze I, 129
    see also Dacibyza
Gene I, 97
    see also Kana
Germa I, 152
    Appuleii I, 155
    Augustan colony I, 87, 88, 89, 90
    Christian community, late II, 62 n. 56
    C. Claudii I, 150–1
    military presence, late II, 75 n. 173
    pruning hook on gravestones I, 147
Germanicopolis I, 78, 93, 95; II, 152
    see also Gangra
Germia:
    Gregory of Tours mentions II, 129
    Justinian, visit of II, 129
    location II, 129 n. 48
    St Michael, church II, 117, 128–9, 140–1
    St Theodore, exorcism by II, 36, 140–1,
        147, 148, 149
Geyve I, 160
Girmir Çay I, 55, 88; II, 131
    and Sykeon II, 125
    see also Siberis
Giymir (Perta) I, 96
    see also Perta
Göce Köy:
    tombstone I, 170 fig. 27
Goeleon (modern Holanta):
    Jews at II, 36
Gölbazar, territory of Nicaea I, 187
Goloenoi I, 181
Gönen I, 187
Gorbeous I, 37, 54, 84
Gordasun II, 116
Gordiane, district of I, 139
Gordiucome:
    resists Parthians I, 38
    see also Iuliopolis
Gordium I, 1, 54, 81, 83, 245
    march of Manlius to I, 23–4
    old Phrygian capital I, 54–5
    road at I, 26
    see also Vinda
Gordus II, 18

Göreme II, 116
Gorgoromeis I, 77, 117
Goths I, 9, 235–6
    invade Pontus II, 56
    raids of 250s–60s II, 69
Göynük I, 100, 160; II, 24 n. 99
Göynükören:
    quarries I, 240
Granicus, battle of I, 232
Güdül II, 131
Güllüköy I, 229
Gümüşkonak (Germia) II, 129
Güngörmez I, 88
Günüsü Dağ I, 145

Hacılar I, 1
Hadriani (Mysia) I, 65, 165, 166, 184, 195 n.
    237; II, 13 n. 24, 115
Hadrianopolis (Paphlagonia) I, 92
    imperial edict II, 121, 127
Halala:
    transformed into Faustinopolis I, 114
Halioi II, 131, 132, 133
Halys, river I, 7, 24, 51, 65, 88
Hanisa I, 81 n. 7, 83, 86, 97
Hanisenoi I, 83, 86
Harmozica I, 119
Harpasus, river I, 21
Haymana I, 54, 146, 154
Helenopolis II, 98, 110
Heliopolis (Iuliopolis) II, 126
Hellespont I, 15, 16
Heniochi, tribe of Black Sea I, 33–4
Heraclea ad Latmum I, 89 n. 97
    monasteries II, 115
Heracleia Pontica I, 16, 87 n. 83, 88
    Adiatorix ruler of I, 35, 40
    clerics banished to II, 93
    colony founded I, 81
    exedra built at I, 213
    Galatian troops at I, 31
    games I, 212
    Gauls, attacked by I, 20, 23
    Homer's birthplace, claim to be I, 207
    ktetor II, 127
    Roman colonists I, 37
    Virgin, church of II, 129
    Ziaelas, mediator between Zipoetas and I,
        19
Hermokome I, 179
Hermus valley I, 7, 229 n. 18
    Aelius Aristides, journey of I, 167
    Christian inscriptions II, 38
    community II, 41
    confession texts I, 194
    Seleucid settlements I, 20
    tombstone curses I, 188
Hierakome:
    katoikia I, 183
Hierapolis (Phrygia) I, 98
    Antiochus I, founder I, 20
    Apollo Lairbenos, hieron of I, 187, 193
    church community II, 37
    coinage I, 204 fig. 35a
    Ephesus, concord with I, 204 fig. 35a
    euergetism I, 225
    gendarmes, decree to regulate I, 195
    Jewish population I, 33
    textile products I, 257
Hierapolis (Phrygian Pentapolis):
    bishop Abercius II, 38
Hierapolis-Castabala:
    Artemis Perasia, fire-walking priests of II,
        30

L. Calpurnius Piso at I, 78 n. 81
    coinage I, 22 fig. 39a
    dynasts I, 40
    games I, 221, 226 n. 197
    Sassanians capture I, 238
Hisar Dağ I, 196
Homonadeis I, 72, 73, 95, 176; II, 161
    P. Sulpicius Quirinius' war against I, 77,
        78; II, 24, 161
Hosrev Paşa Han I, 129
Hydara I, 84
Hyde II, 155
Hynia II, 131, 133
Hypaepa I, 181
    temple of Persian cult II, 29
Hyrcanian plain I, 182
Hyrcanis:
    adiutor procuratoris at I, 161
    military settlement I, 180
Hyrgaleis (Phrygia) I, 176

Ibora II, 76
Iconium I, 64, 67, 99, 148
    Aponii I, 151
    Augustan colony I, 77, 89, 90
    a Calpurnius at I, 153
    Christian community II, 59, 60, 72
    Clarian Apollo, oracle of II, 11–12
    Claudian impact I, 95
    cohors I Augusta Cyrenaica and I, 121
    coinage I, 79
    cults II, 20, 23, 26, 28, 29
    fortifications I, 238
    Jews II, 35–6
    legendary origins of I, 208
    Lycaonia, not in koinon of II, 155
    Meter Zizimmene patron goddess II, 18
    mystikoi agones I, 219
    Polemo, capital of I, 38
    pre-Roman centre I, 84, 86
    Roman soldiers at I, 73, 74; II, 75
    St Paul II, 3, 4, 8, 11
    Sassanians, capture by I, 238
    synod at II, 59–60
    theatre I, 214
    Tiberius, high priest of I, 79, 104, 116
    see also Claudiconium
İhsaniye, village festival I, 187
Ikizari(?) I, 84
Ikotarion II, 18
Ilgaz Dağ I, 246; II, 22–3
    see also Olgassys, Mount
Ilgın I, 156; II, 23
Ilistra II, 155
Ilium:
    Antiochus I honoured by I, 18
    Celts besiege I, 22
    Celts consider as base I, 16
İnönü II, 24 n. 105
Insuyu I, 148 n. 49, 156
Ionians, view of Anatolia I, 5
Ionopolis (Abonuteichus) I, 207
Iranians:
    in Cappadocia II, 29, 73 n. 149
Iris, river I, 32; II, 158
Isaura (Isaura Nea) I, 90, 95
    Amyntas, capital of I, 72 n. 32, 85 n.
        49; II, 152
    Augustan colonial foundation I, 77, 157
    Christian community II, 59
    fortifications I, 72, 85
    triumphal arch for Severus Alexander I, 216
Isaura Palaea (Old Isaura) (Bozkır):
    Ares, cult of II, 28

location I, 72 n. 32
Publius Servilius, inscription of II, 29
soldiers at I, 85 n. 49
Isaurians:
strength I, 71
subjugation incomplete I, 70
see also General Index: Isauria
Işıklar Köy:
grave stele I, *186 fig. 33*
Isinda I, 136, 138 n. 151; II, 28
Ismil I, 151
Isparta I, 247
Issus:
defeat of Pescennius Niger I, 232
Istanos I, 150
Iulia Gordus I, 162, 180
Iuliopolis I, 64, 179
church dues II, 130
exorcism II, 141
imperial passage I, 132 n. 91; II, 124
and location of Sykeon II, 126
Pliny and I, 134, 252
St Heuretus, vigil for II, 129
soldiers stationed in II, 75
vine crop II, 131
winters cold I, 168
see also Gordiucome
Izmit, Gulf of II, 98, 99
Iznebolu:
site of Neapolis I, 90
Iznik I, 129
see also Nicaea
Iznik Göl I, 160

Kadınhan I, 245; II, *100 fig. 23*
Kainon Chorion I, 84
Kalecik I, 147
Kalleon II, 125
Kalmizene I, 92; II, 18
Kalpinos I, 131
Kana (Gene) I, 96, 97, 244
soldiers stationed in II, 75
temple, imperial I, 113, 214
Kandrukome I, 179
Kanes, *see* Hanisa
Karacadağ II, 116
view of I, *2 fig. 2*
Karadağ, Lycaonia:
fortresses I, 84, 148 n. 44
monastic settlements II, 116
Karahamzılı:
site of Kinna I, 96
Karahüyük:
Aponii at I, 151
Karakuyu I, 76
Karalar:
site of Blucium I, 55, 57
Karaman I, 129
see also Laranda
Karya II, 133
Karzene I, 92, 236
Kastamonu I, 246
Kavak:
relief II, 24
Kayseri (Caesareia):
Celtic find I, 54
see also Caesareia; Eusebeia by Mount
Argaeus; Mazaca
Kelenderis:
capture by Sassanians I, 238
Kelhasan I, 148 n. 49, 149 n. 54
Keramet, on Lake Ascanias I, 160
Kerkenes Kale:
site of Mithridateion I, 33 n. 74

Kerpiç I, 148 n. 49
Kimistene I, 92
Kinna I, 67, 96; II, 123 n. 12, 126, 129
Kios I, 160
Kireli I, 95
imperial estate I, 157
stationarius I, 122
Kırşehir II, 68
Kızıl Irmak I, 92, 143
see also Halys, river
Kızılbölüklü I, 153 n. 95
Kızılcaağaç:
shrine of Apollo II, 11
Kızılcahaman I, 57
Klossamenoi II, 18
Kobedyle:
military settlement I, 180
Koca (Göce) Köy:
tombstone I, *170 fig. 27*
Konya I, 129, 144; II, 25
see also Iconium
Koresa:
Men of I, 191
Köşe Abdulla I, 155
estates I, 164
Kötü Delik han:
Aponii at I, 151
Kötü Uşak I, 155
Kozanlı:
military presence at I, 122
Kroula, in territory of Hierapolis I, 187
Kula I, 161
Kültepe I, 83
Kumalettos I, 179
Kumdamlı:
records of *Xenoi Tekmoreioi* I, 239
Kurd Köy II, 104
Kurds I, 148 n. 49, 149
Kurupedion, battle of (281 BC) I, 13
Kuşcalı I, 148 n. 49
Kütahya:
site of Cotiaeum I, 181
see also Cotiaeum
Kütükusağı I, 148 n. 49
Küyücek:
tomb I, 57
Kuyulu Sebil I, 148 n. 49, 153, 156
Kybistra:
capture by Sassanians I, 238

Ladik I, 129
see also Laodicea Catacecaumene
Ladon, river I, 208
Laertes I, 122, 139
Lagania I, 173; II, 160
Lagantine I, 92
Lagina (Ilgın):
Zeus Megistos at I, 23
Lalasseis I, 95
Lampsacus:
Manlius meets Celts I, 24
poll tax I, 256 n. 82
supervises Celts I, 22
Laneium:
Aristides' estate I, 167
Laodicea Catacecaumene I, 85, 88, 95, 245;
II, 25, 26
administration I, 164
Apotactites II, 103
buildings I, 214
Celtic names I, 55
Christian community II, 41, 59, 62, 65, 71
couriers I, 132
cursus of freedman I, 153

dams I, 257 n. 88
heretic centre II, 95
Italian settlers I, 154
C. Iulii I, 154
landownership I, 156
Lycaonia, not part of *koinon* of II, 155
monasticism, early evidence of II, 111
Novatians II, 100, 102, 105
Persian settlers II, 73
soldiers stationed in II, 75
tombstones of 3rd–4th centuries II, 100,
102, 103, 107
vines and wines I, 147
Zeus Phatnios, dedication to II, 23
Laodiceia (on the Lycus):
and Achaeus I, 22
Antiochus I founds I, 20
assizes at I, 64; II, 33 n. 187
church community II, 37
euergetism I, 225
festival I, 219 n. 145, 221
and Galatians I, 17
Jewish community II, 33, 35
Parthians, resists I, 36
sacred games I, 220, 221, 226 n. 197
status, dispute over I, 206
textile products I, 257
Laranda I, 84
under Ariobarzanes I I, 32
Christian community II, 60
Heracles at I, *208 fig. 36b*
legionary recruit from I, 138 n. 151
Lycaonia, part of *Koinon* of II, 155
Sassanians, capture by I, 238
see also Karaman
Latmos, Mount:
monasteries II, 115
see also Heraclea ad Latmum
Licineia I, 81 n. 9
Limnai II, 99
Limyra:
Galatians at(?) I, 18
games I, 219
roads I, 122
Losta II, 161
Lycus, river I, 7; II, 158
course reversed II, 54
Lyde II, 154
Lydians I, 7, 161
see also General Index: Lydia
Lyendos I, 181
Lyrbe I, 172
Lyrboton Kômê I, 122, 182, 196
Lysias I, 85
Xenoi Tekmoreioi from II, 16
Lysimacheia, battle of I, 13, 15, 45, 48
Lystra I, 90; II, 24
Augustus, dedication to I, 78
Pluto, cult of I, 28
Roman colony I, 76, 77, *114 fig. 81a*
St Paul at II, 3, 4, 11, 31
stationarius I, 122

Macedones:
military colony I, 180
Macedonians (in Asia Minor) I, 32, 85, 161,
177, 180 n. 142
Macellum II, 89
Macestus, river I, 175
Madenşehir II, 116
Maeander, river I, 6, 228
Christianity, spread of II, 41
sarcophagi, export route of Docimian I,
246

Maeander, river (cont.):
　Seleucid settlements along I, 20
Maeonia I, 181; II, 26
　Jewish influence II, 37
　komarchoi I, 183
　stelae, confession I, 161, 194
Magaba, Mount:
　Celtic defeat at I, 24, 45, 51, 54, 58
Magnesia on the Maeander:
　games I, 219 n. 146
　market on territory I, 184, 210
Magnesia ad Sipylum I, 184
　Antiochus I takes refuge I, 20
　battle of I, 19
　Christian community II, 37
　games I, 219 n. 153
　prophet in territory I, 195 n. 237
　Simonides, birthplace of poet I, 18
　slave, imperial I, 161
Magnopolis I, 82, 93, 94
　built under Pompey I, 32
Magusaioi I, 173–4; II, 30, 73
Mallos:
　coinage, foundation I, 208 fig. 36c
　Sassanians, capture by I, 238
　Tarsus, rival of I, 206
Malos (Galatia) II, 65
　Jewish dedication II, 36, 49
　as Malos of the Kalmizene II, 18
　Montanist church II, 93
　and Theodotus of Ancyra II, 68
　wines I, 147
　see also Kalecik
Malos (Pisidia)
　Xenoi Tekmoreioi from II, 16
Mamakome, in territory of Hierapolis I, 187
Mandragora:
　petition for right to hold market I, 183–4
Mandre I, 179
Mantinea (Bithynium-Claudiopolis) I, 207
　see also Mantineion
Mantineion:
　monasteries II, 115
　Novatians II, 97
Manyas, Lake I, 167
Maraş I, 54
Marmara, Sea of:
　monasteries II, 115, 116
Marmolitis I, 91
Maryandeni I, 177
Masdyenoi I, 177 n. 113
Mazaca I, 237
　see also Eusebeia by Mount Argaeus
Mazamia II, 129, 131
Megalopolis I, 91, 93, 94
　building by Pompey I, 32
　see also Sebasteia
Megistus, river:
　Celtic mutiny at (218 BC) I, 22
　see also Macestus, river
Meiros:
　estates I, 159
Melas, river I, 71
Melita I, 97
Melitene I, 97
　olives grown at I, 109
　position, strategic I, 118, 119
　roads I, 124
　Roman military I, 135; II, 155 n. 74
Mendechora (ancient Pentechora) I, 185
　extortion by frumentarii I, 229
Mersin I, 54
Merzifon Ovası I, 178
Meshike, battle of (AD 244) I, 237

Metropolis (Phrygia):
　extortion at I, 230
　games I, 226 n. 197
　Xenoi Tekmoreioi from II, 16
Metropolis (Phrygian highlands):
　estates I, 159
Midaeion (Phrygia) I, 55; II, 92
Mihaliççik II, 128
Miletupolis I, 166
Miletus I, 89 n. 97
　baths of Faustina I, 216
　Celts at I, 17
　festivals I, 219, 220
　food supply I, 146
　Goths at I, 235
Milyadeis I, 176
Milyas:
　altar to Augustus I, 102
Mistea I, 95, 96, 176; II, 72
　see also Claudiocaesareia Mistea
Mithridateion I, 84
　Trocmian stronghold I, 33, 51
Mnizene I, 92
Mnizus I, 179; II, 126, 160
Mocadeni I, 161, 176, 180
Mopsuhestia:
　coin type, agonistic I, 222 fig. 39g
　games I, 224
　military activity I, 232
　Sassanians, capture by I, 238
Mordiacus, see Magaba, Mount
Morimene I, 86
Moschakome, honours benefactor I, 184
Mossyna, Mossyneis, Mossyni II, 18, 126 n.
　36
Mostene I, 183
Motella I, 187, 193
　gods of II, 14
Mousge II, 129
Moxeanoi I, 176
Murtad Ova I, 147, 150, 162
Mut I, 129
Mylasa:
　games I, 218 n. 139
　imperial cult I, 100
　money dealings, illegal I, 201, 211
Myra, games I, 219
Myriangeloi, church at Pessinus II, 129
Myrina:
　figurines I, 18, 167
Mysians I, 7
　in Lydia I, 161
　see also General Index: Mysia
Mysomacedones:
　military settlers I, 180
Mytilene:
　imperial cult I, 100

Nacolea I, 148
　Concord of the Villages, sanctuary of I, 179
　dikomia near I, 185
　estates I, 159–60
　Holy and Just, cult of I, 25
　Orcistus, dispute with I, 245; II, 60, 62
　politographos I, 89 n. 97
　St Michael, church II, 117
　soldiers stationed in II, 75
　villages I, 179
　Zeus Bronton, dedications to I, 189
Nacrasus:
　Antiochus I founds I, 20
　military settlement I, 180
(N)akokome I, 184
Nallıhan II, 127, 131

Neapolis (= Andrapa Neoclaudiopolis) I, 92
　n. 129, 93
　Pompey founds I, 32
　see also Phazimonitai
Neapolis (Phrygia) I, 85, 90, 95, 151
　Augustan veterans I, 77, 157
　Servilius Isauricus, conquest of I, 72
　stationarii I, 122
　temple at I, 214
Nemrud Dağ I, 177; II, 30
Neocaesareia in Pontus:
　M. Antonius Rufus pontarch, home of I,
　116
　church councils II, 70, 71; disputes II, 78
　coin type, agonistic I, 222 fig. 39c
　festival, agonistic I, 222
　formerly Cabeira/Diospolis/Sebaste I, 94
　Gregory the Wonder-Worker II, 38, 53, 54,
　55, 62, 67
　temples, imperial I, 114 fig. 18f
　see also Niksar
Neoclaudiopolis I, 92, 93, 94; II, 151, 152
　centurion I, 136
　milestone near I, 129
　Roman inhabitants I, 151
　see also Neapolis/Andrapa
Neroassus I, 84
Nicaea I, 64 n. 31, 88, 89, 182
　buildings, public I, 212, 213
　Celtic names at I, 57
　Christian epitaphs, pre-Constantinian II, 37
　Council of (325) II, 51, 59, 68, 71, 78, 79,
　91, 96, 97, 100, 116
　Dionysus on coin I, 208 fig. 36g
　festivals and games I, 219, 220, 221, 224
　fortification I, 235
　gate, north I, 215 fig. 38
　Gölbazar wine festival I, 187
　gymnasium I, 216
　Heracles and Dionysus, association with I,
　207
　lex Pompeia at I, 162
　monasteries II, 115
　Nicomedia, rivalry with I, 204
　Novatian bishopric II, 97
　Pescennius Niger, defeat of I, 232
　under Roman empire I, 160
　villages on territory I, 181
　winters cold I, 168
　see also General Index: creed, Nicene
Nicomedia I, 64 n. 31, 88, 203; II, 13, 24
　buildings, public I, 212, 213
　centurions I, 185
　Christian community II, 57, 64, 65, 68
　churches II, 129
　Diocletian's capital I, 214
　epitaph, pre-Constantinian Christian II, 37
　exorcism II, 141
　games I, 111, 219, 221
　hermits II, 130
　Libanius and II, 89
　market trade I, 159 n. 151
　monasteries II, 115, 131
　Nicaea, rivalry with I, 204
　Novatian bishopric II, 97
　Octavian, cult of I, 100
　roads II, 124
　sack by Goths I, 235
　size I, 244
　villages on territory I, 181, 185
Nicopolis I, 94
　Armeniarch at I, 116
　battle at (47 BC) I, 34, 36
　under Pompey I, 32

Niksar (Neocaesareia) I, 94
Ninica (Claudiopolis) I, 90, 95, 96
    Augustan foundation I, 77; II, 152
    new Claudian city I, 78
    Roman coin type I, 114 *fig. 18b*
Nisibis:
    Roman victory (AD 242) I, 227
    seized by Ardashir (AD 236) I, 237
Nora I, 84
Nysa (Maeander valley) I, 206
Nyssa II, 78

Obora I, 179
Octapolis I, 185
Oenoanda:
    constitution I, 199–200
    festivals I, 210–11, 219 n. 221
    Galatia, part of I, 71, 78
    oracle II, 44, 46
    rural militia I, 195
    rural settlements I, 178
    size I, 244
    Termessus Minor, identifiable with I, 234
    Theos Hypsistos, cult of II, 50
    village organization I, 182, 183, 185
Oinan:
    courier's gravestone I, 132
Okaenoi I, 184
Olba (of the Cennatae) I, 94
Olbasa I, 90
    Augustan colony I, 77
    Augustus, Claudius, dedications to I, 78–9
    games I, 221; II, 29
    gravestone of cavalryman I, 74
    Iuppiter Optimus Maximus, cult of II, 29
Olgassys, Mount I, 91, 93; II, 22–3
    see also Ilgaz Dağ
Olympeni I, 176
Olympus (Lycia):
    guard post I, 122
    public land at I, 91
    road I, 122
Olympus, Mount (Galatia)
    Celtic defeat I, 45, 51, 58
Olympus, Mount (Mysia):
    Apollo, shrine of II, 13
    hermit on II, 98, 111
    monasteries II, 115
    tribes of I, 165, 166
    see also Olympeni
Omana I, 77
Orcaorci I, 54
Orcistus
    Constantine and city status I, 179, 245; II, 58, 60
    doorstone I, 186 *fig. 34*
    foundation of (AD 237) I, 237, 182
    Nacolea, dispute with II, 60, 62
    people's assembly I, 183
    road junction I, 246
    watermills I, 245 n. 19, 258
Ormeleis I, 155, 158, 163–4, 240
Orondeis/Orondians I, 95, 176
    Servilius Isauricus, conquests of I, 72
    territory of I, 90, 157
Ova Çay I, 55
Özgüney I, 75 *fig. 12*

Paeonians I, 17
Palaiopolis:
    prize games I, 218 n. 139
Panamara:
    public feasts I, 110

sanctuary of Zeus II, 14, 64
Pappa/Pappa Tiberiopolis I, 78, 95, 117, 176; II, 25, 161
    eques singularis from I, 133 n. 98
    via Sebaste near I, 125 *fig. 24*
Parlais I, 77, 90
Parnassus (Cappadocia) II, 78, 161
Paros I, 236
Pasa:
    monastery II, 116
Passita (Tembris valley) II, 18
Patara:
    games I, 219 n. 144; II, 154
Pazon:
    site of first Novatian synod II, 98
Pedaieis I, 77
Pegae, monastery near Dorylaeum II, 129, 130
Peia II, 131, 133
Peium I, 84, 85
    Deiotarus' treasury I, 56 *fig. 8*
    visited by J. Caesar I, 33, 36
Peliganos I, 179
Peltai:
    Antiochus I founds I, 20
Penkalas, river II, 18–19
Pentapolis, Phrygian, road I, 1, 125 *fig. 23*
Pentechora I, 185
    see also Mendechora
Pepuza, 'new Jerusalem' of Montanists II, 39, 92
Pergamum:
    Asclepius, cult of I, 138; II, 43
    Athena, sculptures in sanctuary of I, 21, 45, 46 *fig. 9*
    Athena and Aphrodite, temples of I, 21
    Attalus I's victory nearby I, 21
    Celtic names at I, 57
    Celts, victories over I, 21, 23–5, 26
    church community II, 37
    citizenship gained by rural inhabitants I, 177
    Ephesus and Smyrna, rivalry with I, 208
    festivals, agonistic I, 219
    foundation myth I, 208 *fig. 36d*
    imperial cult I, 100
    Iulii Quadrati, home of I, 161
    Jews II, 33
    lex de astynomis I, 201
    pottery production I, 242 n. 3
    Rome, bequeathed to I, 29, 62
    size I, 243–4
    Smyrna, concord with I, 81, 204 *fig. 35b*
    rivalry with I, 206
    temples, imperial I, 114 *fig. 18e*
    walls I, 235
Perge I, 203
    acclamations at I, 238
    games, prize I, 218 n. 139
    games, sacred I, 224
    harbour I, 247
    legendary history of I, 207
    Pamphylian dialect I, 172
    Plancii of I, 152
    Roman soldiers at I, 74, 122
    St Paul and II, 6
    Tacitus, headquarters of emperor I, 238
Perinthus:
    festivals and games I, 221
    grain sent to Apamea I, 244
    Pergamum, concord with (coin) I, 204 *fig. 35c*
    size I, 244
Peristremma, river II, 116

Permetaia II, 131, 133
Perminundeis (Pisidia) II, 11
Persians:
    invasion of Anatolia II, 123
    settlers in Asia Minor II, 73
    see also Iranians
Perta I, 96, 97
    Hadrianic temple I, 113, 214
    philologists II, 85
    Pluto, cult of II, 28
    size I, 244
    Zeus Megistos, temple of II, 23
Pessinus I, 82, 83, 86–7, 88, 89, 93
    Asclepius, dedication to I, 133 n. 95
    buildings at I, 214
    coinage I, 79
    cult, imperial I, 103–4, 105, 114 *fig. 18c*, 116
    cults, pagan II, 14
    Cybele, cult of I, 48, 49; II, 20–2, 62, 89
    Goths, ravaged by I, 235
    Julian at II, 89
    local goddess II, 19
    metropolis of Galatia Salutaris II, 127
    Mithras, cult of II, 29
    Myriangelos, church of II, 129
    mystikoi agones I, 219–20
    shrine and high priests I, 34, 48, 49, 112, 114
    slaves, sacred II, 30
    St Sophia, cathedral of II, 129
    and St Theodore II, 132
    supports Pergamum I, 26
    temple state I, 54
    theatre I, 111
    Trajan, gifts for I, 146
Pessongi I, 26
Petenissus II, 160
Petra (Hellespont) I, 16
Petra (Lydia) I, 191
Phanaroea I, 93
Pharmagoun (Armenia Minor) II, 69
Pharnaceia I, 33, 94
Phaselis I, 91
Phazimon:
    legionary recruit from I, 138 n. 151
Phazimonitai I, 32, 92, 93
Phazimonitis I, 39, 84
Philadelphia (Lydia) I, 221 n. 166
    centre of estates I, 161
    Christian community II, 38
    confession texts I, 194
    festival I, 221 n. 166
    Montanists II, 39
    neocory status I, 258
    Rome and Augustus, early priest of I, 100
    Seleucus I founds I, 180
    workers kidnapped on imperial estate I, 229
Philomelium I, 64, 85, 148; II, 25
    Celtic names at I, 57
    cereal prices I, 247
    Christian community II, 37, 41
    doorstone early I, 239 n. 79
    no oath-taking I, 193 n. 230
    soldiers stationed in II, 75
    Xenoi Tekmoreioi from II, 16
Phocaea I, 81, 166
    synagogue II, 31 n. 176
Phreata ('The Wells') I, 237
Phrygia Cecaumene (Laodicea Catacecaumene) II, 100
Phrygians I, 7, 47
    origins traced back to Trojans I, 208

Phrygians (*cont.*):
  religion I, 187–9
  reverence for gods and the dead I, 188–91
  as slaves I, 47
  see also General Index: Phrygia
Pidron II, 128
Pillitokome I, 156
  dedication to Zeus Megistos II, 23
Pimolisa I, 84
Pimolisene I, 91, 92
Pisidians I, 17
  character I, 71, 72
  relationship with Sparta I, 207
  subjugation incomplete I, 70
  see also General Index: Pisidia
Pityous:
  Gothic raid on I, 235
Plarasa I, 177
Plommeis I, 155
Podandus II, 77
Pogla:
  sends grain to Alexandria I, 253
Polatlı I, 245
Polemonium II, 159
Pompeiopolis (Paphlagonia) I, 88, 91, 93; II, 151, 152
  Claudii Severi, home of I, 116, 163
  Pompey founds I, 32
  see also Taşköprü
Posdala(?) I, 84
  fortress of Trocmi I, 31, 51
Potamia I, 91
Priene:
  Athena Polias, temple of I, 103
  Celtic names at I, 57
  Celts resisted I, 17
  Rome and Augustus, cult of I, 102
Pronnoetai I, 185
Proseilemmene I, 55, 148
Prostanna I, 72, 218 n. 139
Protomeria, (Galatia) II, 26
Protopyleitai (Acmonia) II, 5
Prusa I, 64 n. 31, 88
  Apamea, rivalry with I, 204
  building at I, 202, 212
  and Dio Chrysostom I, 207
  grain riot I, 203
  graves of centurions I, 232
  Himerius, birthplace of II, 86
  monasteries II, 115
  timber from I, 244
  winters cold I, 168
Prusias ad Hypium I, 87 n. 83, 88, 89
  buildings, public I, 213
  Celtic names I, 57
  citizens and country-dwellers I, 178
  civic careers in I, 200
  games, sacred I, 224
  military at I, 122, 232
  timber, prosperity based on I, 243
  walls and Goths I, 235–6
Prusias ad Mare I, 57
  see also Cius
Prymnessus II, 13
  estates I, 159
  Justice, principal deity I, 191; II, 18
  Sestullii in I, 158
  Xenoi Tekmoreioi from II, 16
Psekaleis I, 77
Psilis, river II, 130
Pylai:
  exorcism II, 144
  monasteries II, 115
Pylitai:

market at I, 184

Reake II, 131, 133
Rhodiapolis I, 122
Rhyndacus, river I, 175, 235
Rigosages I, 43 n. 13
Rufinianae, monastery I, 173

Sadagolthina I, 236
Sagalassus;
  Amyntas, part of kingdom of II, 151
  Antoninus Pius, sanctuary of II, 13
  Apollo Clarius, sanctuaries of I, 78; II, 13
  boundary I, 157
  Dionysus, sanctuary of II, 13
  Pisidia, chief city of I, 71, 72, 78, 214–16
  pottery production I, 242 n. 3
  requisitioning edict I, 65, 67, 247 n. 31
  transport I, 247
Sagarausene I, 82
Sağır:
  Men Askaenos temple II, 9–10, 14, *fig. 2*, 24
  Xenoi Tekmoreioi records found I, 239; II, 14 *fig. 2*, 16
Sagylium I, 84
Saittae I, 180, 202, 258
  confession texts I, 194
  Men Ouranios at II, 45
  textiles I, 202 n. 27
  trade associations I, 202
Saklea I, 191
Salt Lake, south of Ankara I, 55, 147; II, 116
  see also Tuz Göl
Samos I, 82, 100
Samosata I, 118 n. 8
  fortress built I, 119; II, 95
  legionary recruits I, 140
  roads I, 124
Samsun I, 246
  see also Amisus
Sandalium I, 72
Sandıklı Ova I, 230
  road at I, 125 *fig. 23*
Sandos, river I, 127, 131, 133
Sangarius, river I, 54, 87, 88, 175
  floods II, 133
  source of II, 98
Sanisene I, 91
Sannabolae II, 116
Sapanca göl I, 64
Sarayönü:
  Novatian epitaph II, 100 *fig. 24*
Sardis I, 81 n. 203
  Antiochus I in I, 18
  bath gymnasium complex I, 216–17
  church community II, 37, 38
  confession texts I, 194
  conventus centre I, 180
  couriers to Susa I, 129
  Elagabalia festival I, 221
  Eumenes at I, 25, 26
  games, four sacred I, 222 *fig. 39d*
  Goths and I, 235
  Hebrew, inscriptions in II, 35
  Jewish community II, 32–3, 36, 37, 49
  Lydian graffiti I, 172
  Maximinus, anti-Christian edict of II, 64
  Menemachus, estate of I, 176
  Persian cult II, 29
  senatus consultum of AD 177 I, 110
  size I, 244
  temples, four imperial I, 114 *fig. 18d*
Sarıkaya I, 149, 155

Sarıyar I, 153 n. 95
Sasima:
  Gregory of Nazianzus and II, 77, 78, 161
  road station II, 74
Satala (Armenia Minor):
  bishop II, 38
  legionary fortress I, 118, 139, 233; II, 74
  roads I, 124
  Sassanians, taken by I, 137
Satala (Lydia) I, 180
  extortion from I, 229
  on territory of Saittae I, 202 n. 27
Savatra (Soatra) I, 67, 84, 96, 87; II, 155
  Ares and Areioi, cult of II, 28
  high priesthood I, 116–17
  and Iulius Severus I, 154
  philologists II, 85
  soldiers from I, 122 *fig. 20*
  see also Soatra
Scamander, river I, 208
Scopas, river (Aladağ Çay) I, 173; II, 125, 128, 132, 133
Sebaste (Phrygia) II, 25
  early Christian community II, 40, 41, 47
  Jews at II, 33
Sebaste (Pontus), *see* Sebasteia
Sebasteia I, 94, 98
  40 martyrs, cult of II, 69
  in 4th century II, 74
  garrison II, 75
  Sassanians, captured by I, 238
  see also Megalopolis; Sivas
Sebasteni Tectosages Ancyrani I, 87
Sebasteni Tolistobogii Pessinuntii I, 87
Sebasteni Trocmi Taviani I, 87
Sebastopolis (Caria) I, 228
Sebastopolis (Pontus) I, 94, 116, 138 n. 151
  foundation I, 153
  garrison II, 75
Sedaseis I, 77
Seleuceia on the Calycadnus I, 77; II, 152
  capture by Sassanians I, 238
  St Thecla, martyrium of II, 116
Seleuceia Sidera I, 94, 195
  Antiochus I founds I, 20
  dedications to Augustus, Claudius I, 78–9
  games I, 218 n. 139
  see also Claudioseleuceia
Seleuceia Zeugma:
  legio IV Scythica at I, 140
Selge:
  and Amyntas II, 151
  games I, 225
  Pisidia, leading city of I, 71
  Pisidian texts I, 173
  Plancii I, 152 n. 84
  roads I, 71 n. 6
  and Roman rule I, 72
  Syrian usurper in I, 237
  wars with Attalids I, 72
Selinus I, 238
Sengen I, 154
Sevdiğin:
  tombstone from I, 186 *fig. 31*
Siberis (Girmir Çay):
  cereal and vine crops II, 131
  crossing point II, 137; II, 127
  floods and pests II, 133
  location of Sykeon II, 125, 126, 127, 128, 129, 130, 132
Sibidunda (Bozova) II, 49
Sidamaria, bath-house I, 214
Side:
  Amyntas at II, 152

aqueduct I, 216
coinage I, 38, 222 *fig. 39b*
festivals and games I, 219, 222, 224; II, 152
and Goths I, 235
harbour I, 247
importance in 3rd century I, 238
Pamphylian dialect I, 172
rivalry with other cities of Pamphylia I, 222
 fig. 39b
Roman soldiers at I, 73–4
slave market I, 257
Silandus I, 176, 180
Sillyon I, 203 n. 40
Pamphylian dialect I, 172
status of inhabitants I, 178
Şimşit I, 150
Sinanlı I, 148 n. 49, 149, 151
Sinope I, 31, 64 n. 31, 81, 82, 91
aqueduct I, 212
capture by Pharnaces I, 25, 36
fleet at I, 235
Sinoria I, 84
Sipylus, Mount II, 19
Sivas (Sebasteia) I, 94 n. 149, 246
corvée labour, Ottoman I, 127
site of Sebasteia/Megalopolis I, 94 n. 149;
 II, 153
Sizma II, 18
Skorpioi I, 43 n. 13
Skoudris II, 128, 133
Smyrna I, 65, 166
Celtic names at I, 57
Christian community II, 37
defences I, 195
games I, 219, 221
Pergamum, concord with I, 81, 204 *fig. 35b*
Pergamum, rivalry with I, 206
Pionius, martyrdom II, 36
and Sestullii I, 158
size I, 244 n. 12
Soa I, 181
 see also Altıntaş
Soatra (later Savatra) I, 84, 86
Sofular I, 173
Söğüt Göl I, 179
Soloi, rival of Tarsus I, 206
Soman Hisar:
fortification I, 55
Sophene:
controlled by Ariobarzanes I I, 32
Soreoi II, 99
Sozopolis II, 141
Virgin, church of II, 129
 see also Apollonia
Stectorium:
Sestullii in I, 158
size I, 244
Steunos cave II, 18–19
Stiphani, Lake I, 84
Stratonicaea:
Goths at I, 235
Maximinus' anti-Christian policy II, 64
and Panamara I, 110
 Theos Hypsistos, inscriptions to II, 49, 50
Zeus and divine angel, dedications II, 45,
 46
Suğla Göl I, 66, 67, 146; II, 57
 see also Trogitis, Lake
Sülmenli:
transport dispute (inscription) I, 170 *fig. 30*
Sultan Dağ I, 71, 157; II, 16, 73
cities on I, 85
vineyards I, 147
Sülüklü I, 149

Sura II, 12
Syedra:
Clarian oracle I, 204 *fig. 35g*
games, prize I, 218 n. 139
road, garrisoned I, 122
Sykai:
Novatian church II, 96
Virgin, church of II, 128
Sykeai:
bridge built by Justinian II, 125
Sykeon II, 116
birthplace of Theodore II, 122
cereals II, 131
churches erected by St Theodore II, 122,
 125, 126
description II, 123–4
flooding II, 133
Heraclius, visit of II, 123
location II, 125, 134
monasteries of Theodore II, 123, 124, 125,
 126, 134, 141
peasants II, 128
St George, chapel II, 125, 137
St George, church II, 122, 126, 132
St Michael, church II, 122, 125, 126, 142
staging posts at II, 124
Virgin Mary, chapel II, 122, 125
Virgin Mary, church II, 126, 142
wine II, 131
Synaus I, 181
Christian gravestone II, 39
cult of Mithras II, 29
Synnada I, 85
assizes I, 64
Christian community II, 59, 60
courier from I, 132
estates I, 159
euergetism I, 225
games I, 219
Gauls at I, 25, 55
Hygieia and Sophrosyne, priest of I, 191
 legio IV Flavia and I, 121
men of in nearby villages I, 179
olives I, 109
procurators at I, 185
site I, 211
soldier I, 139
 Xenoi Tekmoreioi from II, 16
Synodium, name given to Germia II, 129

Tabala I, 180
letter of Pertinax I, 141, 228–9
Tabanlıoğlu Kale:
site of Peium I, 55
Tabia II, 160
 see also Tavium
Taburoğlu Kale I, 2 *fig. 2*
Tahirler, fort I, 55
Takina:
 coloni dominici in inscription I, 249 n. 44
soldiers, complaints against I, 230, 233
status and wealth I, 180
Tamasis I, 202 n. 27
Tarsus I, 203
acclamation, imperial I, 114 *fig. 18g*
Arian bishop appointed II, 78
and Caracalla I, 208 *fig. 36e*
coinage I, 232
divinities I, 191
festivals and games I, 220, 224, 219 n. 153
imports Egyptian grain I, 208 *fig. 36f*, 254
metropolis of *Tres Eparchiae* II, 155
Perseus, claims foundation by I, 207
rivalry with neighbours I, 206

Sassanians, capture by I, 238
Tartars I, 149
Taşköprü, site of Pompeiopolis I, 93
Tatta, Lake I, 147
 see also Salt Lake; Tuz Göl
Taurus mountains I, 151
iron from, tax on II, 76, 80
map I, 52–3
pacification of I, 71–9
protection from Sassanian attack I, 238
Tavium I, 82, 84, 86–7, 88, 89
 domestici II, 127
epitaphs, Christian II, 119–20
foundation date I, 76
frieze, carved I, 106 *fig. 19*
games, *koinon* I, 112, 219
garrison II, 75
graves, Jewish and Christian II, 36
imperial cult, provincial I, 116
philosophers II, 85
poor-house II, 116
roads I, 132, 133 n. 96
 Theos Hypsistos, cult of II, 49
Trocmi, strongpoint of I, 51
vineyards I, 147
Zeus, shrine of II, 23
Tavşanlı, dedication for Zeus Abozenus II, 20
 fig. 7
Taza I, 191
Tectosages, Galatian tribe I, 87, 88
Ancyra banquet at I, 110
battles I, 21
castles I, 84
cavalry I, 45
first mentioned I, 16, 17, 24, 43
organization I, 27
settlement in Galatia I, 54–5
Tefenni II, 26
Teirenōn katoikia I, 181
Telmessus I, 24
games I, 219 n. 144
Tembris valley, upper I, 87, 179; II, 24 and
 n. 105
early Christian community II, 35, 40, 41,
 46, 59, 60
Christian epitaphs II, 60 *figs. 19 and 21*,
 100, 104–6, 107
Clarian Apollo, shrine of II, 11
estates I, 158
Holy and Just, cult of II, 25
Jewish names II, 35
prosperity in 3rd and 4th centuries I, 240
quarries I, 159
stele showing Zeus and Hermes II, 26 *fig. 11*
texts, pagan or Jewish II, 49
tombstone curses I, 188
tombstones I, 170 *figs. 27–9*, 186 *figs.
 31–2*
 trikomia I, 185
Zeus, sanctuaries of I, 187
Zeus Ampelites, dedications to II, 18
Tembrogius (Tembris) II, 106
Temenothyrae (Flaviopolis) I, 139, 176, 180,
 188
Christian epitaph II, 39
Montanists II, 104
soldier I, 139
Temnos:
bandits I, 166
Mount I, 229
Teos:
home guard I, 195
recruitment I, 141
Tepeköy II, 99

Termessus Minor I, 234
see also Oenoanda
Termessus:
and Amyntas II, 152
chief city of Pisidia I, 71
dux appointed I, 228, 234
eirenarch I, 196
fortifications I, 72
games I, 225
lex Antonia de Termessis I, 248
under Roman law I, 72
status of inhabitants I, 178
Theos Hypsistos, dedication for II, 50
Zeus and Artemis, temple of II, 13
Tetrapyrgia I, 184
Themisonium I, 17
Therma II, 160
Thermai Theseos I, 161
Thiounta I, 187
Thracians I, 13, 18
name types I, 175
Thyateira I, 133, 252
Antiochus I founds (false) I, 20
Apollo, dedication to I, 17
brabeutes (benefactor) I, 183
early Christian community I, 37, 38, 62
festivals and games I, 219 n. 153, 221
Livia at I, 161
Montanists II, 39, 104
Rome and Augustus, cult of I, 102
Seleucus I founds I, 180
size I, 244
slave market I, 257
Tiberiopolis (Phrygia):
city territory I, 181
festival, agonistic I, 219 n. 146
Holy and Just, cult of II, 25
law student II, 85
Novatian bishop II, 97
Sestullii in I, 158
Tigranocerta:
Galatian cavalry at I, 31
reduction to kōmē I, 179
Timonitis I, 91
Tium I, 16, 20
stationarius I, 122
Tlos:
benefactress I, 201 n. 22
defence of against Celts I, 17–18
Tmolus I, 181
Tolgeri Hüyük I, 55
Tolistobogii, Galatian tribe I, 87, 88
banquet at Ancyra I, 116
battles I, 21
first mentioned I, 16, 19, 23, 24, 43
and Lampsacus I, 22
organization I, 27, 28
settlement in Galatia I, 55–8
= Tolistoagii I, 21
Tomisa I, 84, 118
Tosiopae I, 43
Toutobodiaci I, 43
Tralles:
acclamation at I, 201 n. 22
early Christian community I, 37
grain, Egyptian I, 254
Trapeza II, 129, 132
Trapezus I, 33, 34, 93, 94
fleet based at I, 135
garrison I, 124
Gothic raid I, 235; II, 56
monasteries II, 115
polis Hellenis I, 81
see also Trebizond

Trebenna I, 77 n. 69
Trebizond, Ottoman corvée labour I, 127
see also Trapezus
Trikomia II, 18
Tripolis (Lydia):
Christian community II, 62
confession texts I, 194
games I, 226
Troad I, 22; II, 33
Trocmi:
boundaries II, 153
cavalry I, 45
Galatian tribal emporium at Tavium I, 83,
84, 87, 88
first mentioned I, 16, 17, 24, 26, 43
fortifications I, 84
Posdala a fortress of I, 31
settlement in Galatia I, 51–4
territory II, 158
Trocnades II, 176; II, 160
Trogitis, Lake I, 77; II, 24 n. 106
see also Suğla Göl
Trojans II, 19
Troy:
and Goths I, 235
Turgut I, 145
Türkmen I, 148 n. 49, 149
Turks:
from Balkans I, 149
Tuz Göl:
salt from I, 147
see also Salt Lake
Tyana I, 97
Apollonius of I, 247
capture by Sassanians I, 238
cult of Mithras II, 29
Hellenized centre II, 86
Syrian usurper in I, 237
temple to Astarte II, 29
see also Eusebeia next to the Taurus
Tyannollus:
benefactor I, 184
brabeutai I, 183
village gathering I, 182
Tymandus:
shrine to Apollo II, 11 n. 6
Tymbriada I, 91; II, 22, 25
Eurymedon, sanctuary of II, 12
Pisidian language I, 173
Tymbrianassus I, 67, 157
Tyriaeum (Lycia):
pentakomia at I, 179, 185
recruits I, 140
Tyriaeum, Tyraion (Phrygia Paroreius) I, 85,
122, 156

Uşak I, 161

Valcaton II, 126
Vasada I, 117, 122; II, 25, 72, 157, 161
Venasa:
festival in Christian era II, 69
Zeus, sanctuary of I, 81; II, 30
Vetapa II, 129
Vetissus:
courier I, 164 n. 209
domains at I, 151, 153
Sarıkaya, identifiable with I, 155
Vezirköprü:
Gangra oath I, 92, 93
see also Neoclaudiopolis
Vinda, Vindia II, 25
Celtic name displaces Gordium I, 50, 55

Xanthos:
festival, agonistic I, 219
grain distribution I, 111
Leto, sanctuary of I, 102
Xerolophus (Constantinople) II, 99

Yağcı Oğlu I, 151
Yalı Hüyük:
dedication for Claudius I, 66, 79
Yalova II, 99, 115
Yapıldak II, 49
Yassıhüyük:
site of Gordium I, 54
Yayla Baba Köy:
sanctuary II, 26 fig. 14
Yaylacık Köy:
site of Caesareia Germanice I, 212 n. 84
Yenice köy II, 49
Yerköy II, 131
Yeşil, river II, 151
Yılanlı Ova I, 71
Yozgat I, 51
Yukarı İğde Ağaç I, 153
Yürme (Germia) II, 129
Yurtbeyci I, 155
Yürüks I, 145, 149

Zeitene I, 92
Zekeriye:
rock reliefs dedicated to Ares II, 28
Zela I, 82, 91, 93, 94
Caesar, victory of I, 36
and Caranitis I, 39
military tombstones I, 136
under Pompey I, 32
Zeleia I, 176
Zengibar Kalesi I, 85
see also Isaura
Zeugma:
legio IV Scythica at I, 119, 140
see also Seleuceia Zeugma
Zir I, 150
Zosta II, 161
Zumbulios II, 144

(b) OUTSIDE ASIA MINOR

Acilisene (Armenia):
shrine of Anaeitis II, 30
Acraephia (Boeotia) I, 110
Actium (Greece) I, 34, 90; II, 152
Africa:
basilicas II, 66
dedication to Clarian Apollo II, 30
heretics II, 59
hermits II, 109 110, 125
imperial estates I, 162–3, 249
Roman military I, 139
Ain-el-Djamala (Africa):
estates I, 162 n. 192
Ain-Ouassel (Africa):
estates I, 162 n. 192
Alani:
threats from I, 118, 119
Aleppo (Syria) I, 129
Alexandria (Egypt):
food supply I, 253
Galatian colony I, 57, 137
intellectual centre II, 84
link with Aphrodisias II, 118
monasteries II, 114
Museum and medical school II, 85
political debate II, 77

Roman military I, 136, 137
St Mark, tomb of II, 109
travel to II, 74
Anchialus (Thrace) I, 221
Antinoopolis (Egypt) II, 114
Antioch (Syria) I, 76; II, 63
capture by Sassanians I, 238
city council's decline II, 76–7
demoted to village I, 179
intellectual centre II, 84, 86
Jewish rising (AD 610) II, 123
Maximinus moves against Christians II, 64
monasteries II, 114
pagan beliefs II, 73
Paul and Barnabas at II, 5
and St Simeon Stylites II, 130
Apamea (Syria) I, 76, 237
Apsaros (Colchis) I, 119
Apulia (Italy):
cohort recruited I, 73
Aquincum (Pannonia) I, 138
Arabia:
Bostra, letter from Julian to II, 94
monastic and ascetic tradition II, 110
Rome's last major acquisition I, 63
via Nova Traiana I, 124, 126 n. 55
Arados (Phoenicia) II, 37
Araxes, river II, 153
Arcadians I, 169
Argos I, 84, 110
Arsinoite nome (Egypt):
monasteries II, 114
Athens II, 13 n. 24
games promoted by Ariarathes V I, 82
intellectual centre II, 84, 86, 112
kinship with Pamphylian cities I, 207
reliefs of Attalus I on acropolis I, 21

Babylon:
Celtic embassy I, 13
Baetica (Spain) I, 110
Balkans I, 9, 42, 124, 227, 232
army of I, 137, 138–9
grain from Anatolia I, 250
settlers in Anatolia from I, 149
Beroea (Macedonia) I, 140; II, 31
Berytus (Beirut) I, 136, 137
Bessians (Thrace) I, 173
Bizye (Thrace) I, 62
Bosporus, Cimmerian I, 84
Bostra (Arabia) II, 94
Britain I, 139; II, 84
dedication for Clarian Apollo II, 30
imperial cult I, 102, 107
Brundisium (Apulia) I, 166

Cadurci (Gaul) I, 107
Callatis (Moesia Inferior) I, 110
Camulodunum (Britain):
imperial temple I, 102
Carrhae (Syria) II, 57
Roman victory I, 227, 242
Romans defeated by Shapur near I, 237
seized by Ardashir I, 236, 237
Carthage I, 163
Caspian Sea I, 121
Chersonese, Thracian I, 13, 18
China:
ambassador to Roman empire II, 73
Chytri (Cyprus) II, 7
Cimmerian Bosporus (Kerch Strait) I, 84
Coele (Syria) I, 63
Colchis I, 84
ruled by Aristobulus I, 33–4

Coptus (Egypt) I, 136
Corinth:
Paul arraigned II, 31
Cyprus I, 228
St Paul in I, 152; II, 6
Sergius Paullus, proconsul II, 6, 7, 8
Cyrene:
legionary recruits from I, 136, 137

Dacia I, 138; II, 23, 24
Dalmatia I, 137; II, 30
legio VII in I, 138
Danube:
Celtic embassies to Alexander I, 13
Celtic tribes I, 23
military disaster under Augustus I, 78
Roman military presence I, 133, 138, 139, 250, 251
Delos I, 16 n. 40
Delphi I, 13, 47
Dyrrhachium (Durres, Albania) I, 166

Edessa (Macedonia) I, 166
Edessa (Syria) II, 57, 74
Egypt:
Apotactites I, 103
conversion to Christianity II, 62–3
imperial estates I, 249
lawsuit before prefect I, 227
legionary recruits from I, 136, 137
monasticism II, 109, 110, 111, 113, 114
Oxyrhynchus basilicas II, 66
sacred games I, 224
Egyptians I, 173
Emmaus (Palestine) I, 138
Emesa:
Black Stone of I, 133 n. 91
resists Sassanians I, 237
Emesenes:
mounted unit of I, 121
Euphrates I, 7, 9
frontier fortifications I, 119
frontier region I, 131 map 9
garrisons set up by Flavians I, 250
region receives Galatian grain I, 250
Sophene, crossing into I, 84
and Vespasian's policy II, 154

Fundi (Latium) I, 158

Gallia Comata:
imperial cult I, 107, 137
Gallia Narbonensis I, 139
Gaul:
contacts with Phrygian Christians II, 41
Druids I, 48
imperial cult at Lugdunum I, 107
inhabitants 'stupid' II, 84
supports Rhine garrisons I, 251
see also Gallia Comata; Gallia Narbonensis
Greece I, 42
invasion by Celts I, 13–15

Harran, *see* Carrhae
Hatra, taken in 240 by Sassanians I, 237
Hebrus, river I, 166
Heliopolis (Syria) I, 153; II, 25
Helvetii (Gaul) I, 27
Henchir Mettich (Africa):
estates I, 162 n. 192

Iberia I, 119
Iceni, kingdom of (Britain) I, 62
Ida, Mount (Crete) II, 18–19

Illyria I, 13
Illyrians I, 13
Iran, *see* Persia
Italians, settlers in Galatia I, 138, 154, 157, 158, 245
Italica (Baetica) I, 110

Jerusalem I, 118, 217
Paul and II, 4–5, 31
place of pilgrimage II, 109
Judaea II, 4

Larisa (Thessaly) I, 89 n. 97
Latium I, 158
Libya II, 79, 110
Lugdunum (Gallia Comata) I, 107, 137

Macedonia I, 13, 138
Celtic invasion I, 13–15
Christian missionaries imprisoned II, 31
cult of Augustus I, 102
rye bread I, 168
Malaya:
exorcism in II, 148
Massalia I, 17, 22–3, 27, 68; II, 4 n. 16
Mesopotamia:
Gordian's expedition I, 227, 237
monasteries II, 114
province created I, 236
Sassanians in I, 237
Mevania (Etruria) I, 154 n. 99
Moesia I, 77, 138
Inferior I, 138
Superior I, 138
Monte Testaccio (Rome) I, 241
Mutina (Italy) I, 73

Naqs-i-Rushtam (Iran) I, 237
Narbo Martius (Gaul) I, 76
Nicopolis (Egypt):
laterculus militum I, 137
Nisibis (Mesopotamia) II, 39
Nitria (Egypt):
hermits II, 114
Novae (Moesia Inferior) I, 138

Oescus (Moesia) I, 138
Osrhoene (Mesopotamia):
province created I, 236
Oxyrhynchus (Egypt) II, 66, 114

Paeonia I, 13
Palestine:
monastic tradition II, 36, 109, 110, 111, 114
Palmyra I, 222 n. 237
Pannonia:
disturbances I, 78
revolt II, 152
Superior I, 138
Panopeus (Achaia):
portrayed by Pausanias I, 81, 82, 226
Panopolis (Egypt) I, 133
Paphos (Cyprus) II, 7
Paraetonium (Egypt) I, 137
Paros I, 230
Parthia I, 118
campaigns of Trajan and Lucius Verus I, 64, 118, 132, 133
Parthians:
alleged conspiracy of I, 119
and Mesopotamia II, 73
Roman offensive action against I, 236–7
threat to Galatia in 1st century BC I, 37–8

Persia I, 1, 3, 91
    couriers I, 129
    cults in Asia Minor II, 29–30
    influence in eastern Asia Minor I, 86
    and Rome in 3rd century AD I, 253
    see also Gentral Index: Sassanians
Persis I, 237
Pharsalus:
    battle at I, 34, 36
Philippi:
    battle at I, 34, 37
    Christian missionaries imprisoned II, 31
    seventh legion at I, 73
Pizus (Thrace) I, 245
Poetovio (Pannonia):
    centurion from I, 122 *fig. 21*
Prausi, Celtic tribe I, 42
Puteoli (Italy) I, 220

Qal 'at Seman (Syria) II, 130

Raphaneae (Syria) I, 118
Red Sea:
    road from Coptus I, 136
Resaina (Mesopotamia) I, 237
Rhegium (Italy) I, 83
Rhine I, 13, 78
    grain sent from Gaul I, 251
    Roman military I, 133, 139
Rhodes I, 24

Rome:
    destination of Paul II, 8
    Docimeium marble imported I, 159
    encomium by Aelius Aristides I, 80
    games for Athena Promachus I, 227
    Monte Testaccio waste dump I, 241
    paganism and Christianity II, 77, 82
    St Peter, shrine of II, 109
    trial of Paul II, 31

Salamis (Cyprus) II, 6
Samos I, 100
Sardinia:
    dedication for Clarian Apollo II, 30
Scaptopara (Thrace):
    petition I, 233
Scetis (Egypt):
    hermits II, 114
Scythia II, 69
Seleuceia (Syria) I, 76
Serdica (Thrace), Council of II, 92, 160
Sinai, Mount II, 130
Singara (Mesopotamia) I, 197
Singidunum (Moesia) I, 138
Somalia:
    spirit possession II, 146, 148
Sophene (Armenia) I, 40, 84
Souk-el-Khanis (Africa):
    estates I, 162 n. 192
Susa I, 129

Syria I, 9
    Christian conversion slower than Asia
        Minor's II, 63
    monastic and ascetic tradition II, 109,
        110–11, 113, 114, 117
    Roman military I, 118, 119, 139–41, 253
    Rome and I, 227, 237
    Sassanians in I, 237
Syros (Greece) I, 110

Tanais (Crimean Bosporus) II, 50
Teutones I, 48
Thasos II, 45
Thessalonica II, 31
Thrace:
    invaded by Celts I, 13–15, 166, 168
    see also Thracians
Thracians I, 138
Tiber, river II, 6
Tomis (Moesia Inferior) II, 13 n. 24
Triballi I, 13
Troesmis (Moesia) I, 138
Tylis, kingdom of (Bulgaria) I, 14
Tyre (Phoenicia) I, 220

Urso (Spain) I, 76

Viminacium (Moesia) I, 138
Voturi (Gaul) I, 43

Zancle (Italy) I, 83